NO MISSION IS IMPOSSIBLE

ALSO BY NISSIM MISHAL

These Are the Years: The State of Israel at 50 (Hebrew)
The History of 2000 Years of Judaism (Hebrew)
Israel at 60: The History of the State (Hebrew)
Cleared for Publication: Behind the Scenes of Israeli Television (Hebrew)
Mossad: The Greatest Missions of the Israeli Secret Service
(with Michael Bar-Zohar)

ALSO BY MICHAEL BAR-ZOHAR

FICTION

The Third Truth
The Man Who Died Twice
The Secret List
Enigma
The Deadly Document
The Phantom Conspiracy
Double Cross
The Unknown Soldier
The Devil's Spy
A Spy in Winter
Brothers

NONFICTION

Suez, Top Secret (French and Hebrew)
Ben-Gurion: The Armed Prophet
The Hunt for German Scientists
Embassies in Crisis
The Avengers
The Paratroopers' Book (with Eitan Haber, Hebrew)
Spies in the Promised Land: Isser Harel and the Israeli Secret Service
Arrows of the Almighty
Ben-Gurion: A Biography (3 Volumes, Hebrew)
Ben-Gurion: A Biography
The Quest for the Red Prince
(with Eitan Haber, reprinted in 2005 as Massacre in Munich)
Facing a Cruel Mirror: Israel's Moment of Truth
Lionhearts: Heroes of Israel (editor)
Bitter Scent: The case of L'Oreal, Nazis, and the Arab Boycott
The Book of Valor (editor, Hebrew)
Beyond Hitler's Grasp: The Heroic Rescue of Bulgaria's Jews
To Be a Free People: The Saga of Israel (editor)
Yaacov Herzog: A Biography
Shimon Peres: The Biography
Mossad: The Greatest Missions of the Israeli Secret Service
(with Nissim Mishal)

NO MISSION IS IMPOSSIBLE

THE DEATH-DEFYING MISSIONS OF THE ISRAELI SPECIAL FORCES

MICHAEL BAR-ZOHAR AND NISSIM MISHAL

Translated from the Hebrew by Michael Bar-Zohar and Nathan K. Burstein

ecco

An Imprint of HarperCollinsPublishers

HarperCollins books may be purchased for educational, business, or sales promotional use. For information please e-mail the Special Markets Department at SPsales@harpercollins.com.

FIRST EDITION

Designed by Shannon Nicole Plunkett

Library of Congress Cataloging-in-Publication Data has been applied for.

ISBN 978-0-06-237899-6

15 16 17 18 19 OV/RRD 10 9 8 7 6 5 4 3 2 1

For my comrades who fought at my side
The living and the dead
Conquerors of Sinai in the "Six Days"
Bravehearts across the Suez in "Yom Kippur"
Defenders of the North in "Peace for Galilee,"
Carrying the dream of peace in their hearts.

—Michael Bar-Zohar

For my grandchildren
Idan, Yoav, Or, Guri, Noam and Noa
I am praying that you'll see, one day,
The dove of peace with an olive branch.

—Nissim Mishal

CONTENTS

Preface: Two Combats   xi

1. **Entebbe, 1976**   1

PART ONE: HOW IT ALL STARTED

2. **To Save Jerusalem, 1948**   29

3. **Black Arrow, 1955**   38

PART TWO: THE SINAI CAMPAIGN

4. **"Bring Down This Plane!" 1956**   51

5. **Kadesh, 1956**   61

PART THREE: THE SIX DAY WAR

6. **"Life or Death," Operation Focus, 1967**   77

7. **"The Temple Mount Is in Our Hands!" 1967**   89

PART FOUR: THE WAR OF ATTRITION

8. **"I Felt I Was Suffocating":**
   The Raid on Green Island, 1969   103

9. **The French Defense Minister:**
   "Bomb the Israelis!" 1969   113

10. **"Why Bomb If We Can Take?" 1969**   123

11. **"The Enemy Speaks Russian!" 1970**   132

12. **White Angels on Jacob's Ladder, 1972**   140

13. **"Stop! Halt! Hands Up!" 1972**   155

14. **That Lady Means Trouble, 1973**   163

PART FIVE: THE YOM KIPPUR WAR

15. The Bravehearts Land in Africa, 1973   179

16. "Commander Killed . . .
Deputy Commander Killed . . .
Second Deputy Commander . . . " 1973   192

17. "I See the Lake of Tiberias!" 1973   203

18. The Eyes of the Nation, 1973   215

PART SIX: THE NUCLEAR DANGER

19. "Opera" in Baghdad and "Arizona"
in Syria, 1981 and 2007   225

PART SEVEN: THE LEBANON WAR

20. "Did They Have Machine Guns?" 1982   239

21. "It Was a Great Concert with Many
Instruments," 1982   248

PART EIGHT: FIGHTING TERRORISM

22. "Abu Jihad Sent Us," 1988   257

23. "Where Is the Ship?" 2002   267

24. Holocaust Remembrance Day
in the Nablus Qasbah, 2002   278

25. The Never-ending Story in Gaza:
2008, 2012, 2014   287

EPILOGUE: THE LOST TRIBE RETURNS

26. From the Heart of Africa to Jerusalem:
Operation Moses (1984) and
Operation Solomon (1991)   309

Aftermath   319

Source Notes   325

Acknowledgments   343

Index   345

PREFACE

TWO COMBATS

Since Israel's Independence War, its army has been involved in two
never-ending combats. A combat on the front lines with Israel's
enemies, who never give in, and an inner combat—the effort to
conceive and apply strict moral and humane principles, unequaled by
any other army.

The combat with Israel's enemies has been and will remain uneven. In 1948, the year the Jewish State was created, its population
numbered 650,000 people, who had to face an invasion by five Arab
nations numbering more than 30 million. In 2015, when the Israeli
population had risen to 8 million, made up of 80 percent Jews and 20
percent Israeli Arabs who don't serve in the army, the population of
the states surrounding it had reached 140 million, and the gap continues to grow. Egypt and Jordan, who have signed peace treaties with
Israel, should be taken out of this equation, but a new, redoubtable
power has joined the enemy camp: the 75 million–strong Iran, whose
fanatic Islamist leaders have sworn to wipe Israel off the map, with
conventional or unconventional weapons.

The IDF (Israel Defense Forces), therefore, has had to develop military techniques to compensate for the alarming gap between it and the Arab armies. This has been accomplished by equipping the army with the most modern and sophisticated weapons, many of them conceived and produced in Israel; by basing its war strategy on containment of the enemy on two fronts while concentrating the main effort on a third; by building a formidable air force and excellent intelligence services; and, especially, by forming several units of special forces, composed of deeply motivated volunteers, centered on physical and mental excellence, rigorous training, and, most of all, inspired by creative, inventive planning to surprise the enemy and to hit them at the most unexpected and vulnerable points, allowing a small number of soldiers—sometimes just a few—to carry out a mission normally requiring companies and battalions. This is how Unit 101, the paratroopers; the special commandos such as Sayeret Matkal, Shayetet 13, Kingfisher, Duvdevan, Shimshon, Maglan; the commando units in every IDF brigade; and others were created. The experience and the tactics of these select units would later be shared with the main bodies of the army. "We could not resist you," a captured Egyptian general admitted after the Six Day War. "You are an army of commandos!"

The battle for moral conduct in times of peace or war is based on an ethical code originating in the Haganah underground, which operated before Israel was even created. The concept of "purity of arms" was forged by the Haganah, meaning that combatants' weapons shouldn't be soiled by hurting civilians, women, children or unarmed enemy soldiers. Several trials of IDF soldiers, in the past and present, have been based on that commandment. A famous court ruling speaks of a "black flag" flowing over any military order that counters the law; the soldiers should oppose it rather than execute it. This concept is enforced by the IDF, and any infractions, including some during the last confrontation with the Palestinians in Gaza, are brought before the courts.

As it tries to protect enemy noncombatants, the IDF strives to protect its own. A principle conceived under fire in the Independence War was never to abandon a wounded or stranded soldier in enemy territory but to rescue him at all costs. Rescuing endangered Jews and Israelis abroad has also become a major commandment, be they terrorist hostages, as in Entebbe (1976), or a community at risk, as the Ethiopian Jews in 1981 to 1991.

Another distinctive term is "Follow me!" The officers in the combat units should not only instruct and train their men and women; they should always be the first to engage the enemy, charging ahead of their soldiers, giving them a personal example of courage and devotion. "Follow me!" has become the battle cry of the Israeli Army and explains the large proportion of officers among IDF war casualties.

The moral values, the strong motivation, the special training, and the unorthodox strategy of the Israel Defense Forces have come together to produce a soldier for whom no mission is impossible.

NO MISSION IS IMPOSSIBLE

On October 6, 1973, on Yom Kippur
(the Jewish Day of Atonement), Syria and Egypt
launched a surprise attack on Israel, simultaneously
invading the Golan Heights in the north and the Sinai
Peninsula in the south. After several painful losses, Israel
defeated her enemies, but at a heavy cost. Three years after the
Yom Kippur War, Israel is still licking her wounds, having lost
2,700 soldiers and much of her deterrent protective power.
Golda Meir has resigned as prime minister and been replaced
by Yitzhak Rabin; Moshe Dayan has been replaced by Shimon
Peres as defense minister. Rabin and Peres distrust and dislike
each other, but they have to work together to deal with the
unending attacks of terrorist groups on Israel.

CHAPTER 1
ENTEBBE, 1976

A German couple boarded an Air France plane in Athens on June 27, 1976, quietly took their seats in first class and placed their bulky carry-on bags beneath the seats in front of them. The man was of slight build, his brown hair and beard framing an oval face, a mustache drooping over a pointed chin and blue beady eyes. Apparently tired, he leaned back in his seat and closed his eyes. His companion, wearing a summer pantsuit, was a tall, blond woman with a pretty face, slightly marred by a prominent jaw.

The Airbus A300 Flight 139 from Tel Aviv to Paris, with a short stopover in Athens, carried 246 passengers—105 of them Jewish and Israeli—and twelve crew members. During the Athens stopover, more people boarded. The passengers from Tel Aviv cast indifferent eyes on two Middle Eastern–looking men in dark suits who were shown to their economy-class seats by a smiling blond hostess.

At 12:35 P.M., fifteen minutes after the aircraft took off from Athens, the two Germans opened their handbags. The man took out a large gaily painted candy box and removed its tin cover. The woman produced a champagne bottle and started spinning it in her hands. Suddenly the man drew a miniature submachine gun out of the candy box and leapt to his feet. He darted to the cockpit and pointed his weapon at the pilots. At the same time, the woman unscrewed the bottom of the champagne bottle and pulled out a handgun and two grenades.

"Hands up!" she yelled at the first-class passengers. "Don't move from your seats!"

Similar shouts could be heard in Economy, where the two Middle Eastern men had jumped from their seats, brandished small submachine guns, and easily subdued the other passengers. The excited voice of the male German hijacker boomed from the loudspeakers. He announced in accented English that he was the new captain of the aircraft and identified himself as Basil Kubaissi, commander of "the Che Guevara Commando of the Gaza Strip,", belonging to the Popular Front for the Liberation of Palestine.

Panic swept the passenger compartments—shouts of fear and anger, and weeping, erupted from almost every seat. The horrified passengers realized that they had been hijacked and were the prisoners of terrorists. The "new captain" and his companions ordered the passengers to throw all weapons in their possession down in the aisles. Some set down pocket knives. Immediately afterward the hijackers submitted the male passengers to thorough body searches. And meanwhile the plane turned and headed south.

In the midst of a cabinet meeting in Jerusalem, a note was quietly handed to Shimon Peres. The fifty-three-year-old defense minister had been David Ben-Gurion's devoted assistant; Peres was credited with establishing Israel's alliance with France in 1956 and with carrying out a "mission impossible"—the building of a secret nuclear reactor close to the southern town of Dimona.

Peres passed the note to Prime Minister Yitzhak Rabin, who put on his glasses and read it. A year older than Peres, with graying blond hair and a pinkish complexion, Rabin had been a fighter in the Palmach, Israel's elite troops during the War of Independence. He had assumed office in 1974, after serving as the IDF (Israel Defense Forces) chief of staff and as Israel's ambassador to the U.S. He had run in the Labor Party primary for prime minister against Peres, but in spite of the support of the party apparatus he had won by only a few votes. The two men loathed each other and Rabin had been forced to accept Peres as defense minister against his own judgment.

These two, in spite of their sour relations, had to cooperate in dealing with Israel's security. Both Rabin and Peres knew the Popular Front well—a terrorist organization led by Dr. Wadie Haddad, a Safed-born physician who had abandoned his profession and devoted himself to the struggle against the Jewish State. He had carried out several bloody hijackings and also used the services of foreign recruits, including the notorious Carlos, an Venezuelan-born terrorist with a chilling record of bombings, kidnappings, and assassinations, that had made him the most wanted man in Europe. Haddad had been the first to organize the hijacking of an Israeli plane, in 1968, and was known to be a devious, cruel fanatic.

The 1967 Six Day War had radically changed the character of the relations between Israel and its enemies. In June 1967, threatened with annihilation by Egypt's president Gamal Abdel Nasser and his allies, Israel had launched a preventive war that had crushed the armies of Egypt, Syria and Jordan; Israel had emerged from the war controlling huge chunks of territory—the Sinai Peninsula, the Golan Heights and the West Bank of Palestine, After Israel's astounding victory, the Arab armies had been largely replaced by newly born terrorist organizations, which claimed that they were continuing the struggle of the Arab world against Israel. They replaced confrontation in the battlefield with hijackings, bombings and assassinations, directed mostly against Israeli civilians. Wadie Haddad's Popular Front was among the most ruthless groups Israel had to face.

After receiving the news about the hijacking, Rabin and Peres called an urgent council of ministers and senior officials. As the group convened, more information about the hijacking arrived. Among the fifty-six passengers who boarded in Athens, four were transit passengers who had arrived in Greece with a Singapore Airlines flight from Kuwait. They were believed to be carrying forged passports. The Mossad,

Israel's national intelligence agency, quickly identified the Germans as Wilfried Böse, a founder of the German Revolutionary Cells terrorist group, formerly associated with Carlos and now of the Popular Front; and Bose's female companion, Brigitte Kuhlmann, as a known member of the Baader-Meinhof terrorist gang. The two others were recognized as Palestinians, Abu Haled el Halaili and Ali el Miari.

The intelligence reports also pointed out that the security personnel at Athens airport had carried out only a perfunctory search of the passengers' bags, and they had missed the four Scorpion miniature submachine guns and the hand grenades that had been concealed in tin candy boxes and a champagne bottle. Additionally, several packages of explosives had been hidden in the hijackers' hand luggage.

At midnight, while the plane still appeared to be heading toward the Middle East, Peres met with Yekutiel "Kuti" Adam, the forty-nine-year-old IDF chief of operations, a brilliant general whose huge, bushy mustache betrayed his family's origins in the Caucasus. They set about to make sure that the IDF would be prepared to storm the aircraft if it landed at Ben Gurion Airport. They took an army jeep and set off for the base of Sayeret Matkal, the IDF's elite commando unit, which had already begun rehearsing an attack on a large Airbus, in case the hijacked plane landed in Israel.

The newly appointed commander of the Sayeret was thirty-year-old Yoni Netanyahu, one of the three Netanyahu brothers, who, according to Peres, "had already become a legend—three brothers, fighting like lions, excelling both in their deeds and in their learning." The brothers, Yonatan "Yoni," Binyamin "Bibi" and Ido, sons of renowned scholar Ben-Zion Netanyahu, were all current or former members of Sayeret Matkal. New York–born Yoni, a handsome, tousle-haired lieutenant colonel, combined his military skills with a deep love for literature, mostly poetry. After the Six Day War, Yoni had spent a year at Harvard and six months at Hebrew University before returning to military service. Tonight Peres and Adam hoped to find him at the Sayeret base; he was away, though, off leading an operation in the Sinai, so the rehearsal was supervised by his deputy Muki Betzer, one of the Sayeret's best fighters.

They did not stay long as Peres, shortly after arriving, was informed that the hijacked plane had made a refueling stop in Benghazi, in Libya, and then was continuing to its destination in the heart of Africa: Entebbe airport, outside Kampala, the capital of Uganda. The first news to come from Entebbe revealed that Uganda's dictator, General Idi Amin, had warmly received the terrorists and had declared them "welcomed guests." It now appeared that the landing in Entebbe had previously been coordinated with Amin.

Amin was a cruel and fearsome ruler who governed his country with an iron fist. A huge man, his uniform covered with scores of medals, he had been called the "wild man of Africa" by *Time* magazine. Once a lowly private, he had climbed the army hierarchy until he became chief of staff, then seized power in a bloody coup and pronounced himself "His Excellency President for Life, Field Marshall Alhaji Dr. Idi Amin Dada, Master of all the animals on land and all the fish of the seas, Conqueror of the British Empire in all of Africa, and especially in Uganda." Until recently, Amin had been Israel's ally and had gone through paratrooper training in the IDF parachuting academy, as the guest of former defense minister Moshe Dayan. Peres had met him at a dinner in Dayan's house and remembered that he was both attractive and scary, "like a jungle landscape, like an indecipherable secret of Nature."

Amin later broke off diplomatic relations with Israel when Prime Minister Golda Meir refused to sell him Phantom jets. He also expelled all Israelis from his country and befriended Israel's worst enemies—hostile Arab nations and terrorist organizations. During the 1973 Yom Kippur War, he even claimed to have sent a Ugandan Army unit to fight against the IDF. And this unscrupulous despot now held in his hands the lives of 250 hostages in Entebbe airport, 2,500 miles from Israel.

When news of this broke in Israel, a storm erupted. Israelis were swept up by feelings of fury and helplessness. Heated debates over the appropriate reaction raged in the media. Many of the hostages' families teamed up to exert pressure on the government. They all made the same demand: free our loved ones.

In the days that followed the situation became clearer. At Entebbe, more terrorists had been waiting for the plane. Amin had sent his private plane to Somalia, to bring over Wadie Haddad and a few of his henchmen. The hostages were being held in the old terminal at the airport, guarded by terrorists and Ugandan soldiers. The terrorists then separated the Jewish passengers from the others, reviving atrocious memories of the Holocaust "selection" by the Nazis in World War II. One of the German terrorists, Brigitte Kuhlmann, was especially cruel. She verbally abused the Jewish passengers with foul anti-Semitic remarks.

Upon arrival, Wadie Haddad gave Amin a list of jailed terrorists in Israel and in other countries whom he demanded be exchanged for the hostages. And the list came with an ultimatum: if Israel did not agree to Haddad's demands before the deadline he set, his men would start executing the hostages. Amin sent the list to Israel.

Prime Minister Rabin appointed a ministerial committee to deal with the crisis. At the committee's meeting on June 29, Rabin asked his chief of staff, General Mordechai ("Motta") Gur, if he thought there could be "a military option."

Gur was something of a legend. After fighting in the War of Independence, he had joined the paratrooper corps and participated in many combat situations beside Ariel Sharon. He had been wounded in a battle against Egyptian troops in 1955. In 1967 he had led the 55th Paratroopers Brigade in conquering East Jerusalem and had been the first Israeli soldier to reach the Temple Mount. "The Temple Mount is in our hands!" he had shouted in his radio as his armored half-track had emerged at the Jewish people's holiest place. After the Yom Kippur War, Gur had been appointed Israel's tenth chief of staff; Rabin held him in high esteem but thought Gur had no solution for the Entebbe affair.

"Yes, there is a military option," Gur responded to everyone's surprise. He proposed parachuting a unit of the IDF somewhere close to Entebbe airport, perhaps over nearby Victoria Lake. His soldiers would attack the terrorists and protect the hostages until it became possible to bring them all home. But the committee rejected the plan. First, it became clear that, after landing, the paratroopers would have great difficulty reaching the airport. Second, the plan did not include any solution as to how the hostages would be brought back to Israel. Rabin would later call this plan a "Bay of Pigs," like the botched U.S. invasion of Cuba in 1961.

Rabin and Peres fought bitterly with each other from the outset. Rabin believed that he had no choice but to negotiate with the hijackers and to agree to release the Palestinian terrorists. But Peres was determined not to free the terrorists because of the negative impact such a deal would have both on Israel's international image and on its ongoing anti-terrorist struggle. The rift between the two men was amplified by their strained personal relations, which had been creating a foul atmosphere at the cabinet meetings.

After the meeting Peres left his office on the second floor of the Ministry of Defense, and through a nearby door entered the western part of the building, which housed the offices of the IDF general staff. Peres urgently summoned the chief of staff and some of his generals.

"I want to hear what plans you have," he said to the group of generals in their olive-colored summer uniforms.

"We have no plans," Kuti Adam answered.

"Then I want to hear what you don't have," Peres said.

It was quickly revealed that while no formal plans had been drafted, some of the men had ideas. Kuti Adam suggested a joint operation with the French army—after all, he argued, Air France was a French company, and the French government should be involved. Benny Peled, the forty-eight-year-old IAF (Israeli Air Force) commander, had an "insane" but original idea. A founder of the IAF, this heavy-set, courageous and cool-headed fighter pilot was gifted with a fertile imagination. He proposed they fly a large number of elite troops to Uganda, conquer Uganda, free the hostages and bring them back home. He suggested employing the squadron of fourteen large Hercules ("Rhino") aircraft for this. They could fly from Israel to Entebbe and then back.

Peres had bought the Rhinos during a visit to Georgia in the United States, a few years before; he had at the time presented Governor Jimmy Carter with his book *David's Sling*. Carter had said to Peres, "All that David needed was a sling but today's David needs more than a sling, he needs a Hercules!"; he had talked Peres into buying several Georgia-made Rhinos.

Peres was intrigued by Peled. At first look, his plan seemed to him and to others like lunacy, but after weighing all other options, he deemed it "quite realistic." His colleagues, though, did not share Peres's assessment. Motta Gur, in particular, was negative; the plan, he declared, "was unrealistic, nothing but a fantasy," and ought to be scrapped.

Peres, however, set aside these doubts and pursued discussions with a small group of senior officers. Among them were the chief of staff; generals Kuti Adam, Benny Peled and his deputy, Rafi Harlev; Dan Shomron (chief infantry and paratroopers officer); Shlomo Gazit (head of military intelligence); Yanosh Ben-Gal (IDF assistant head of operations); and a few colonels, including Ehud Barak, a brilliant officer and former head of Sayeret Matkal(and a future prime minister of Israel). Their discussions were held in utmost secrecy.

The very morning of these discussions, Peres received the list of jailed terrorists whose release the hijackers had demanded. It was most complicated. Forty of the prisoners were held in Israel, among them the notorious Kozo Okamoto, a Japanese terrorist whose group had massacred twenty-four people and wounded seventy-eight in Lod airport in May 1972. Also included were six terrorists jailed in Kenya, where the local authorities denied having them. Another five were in Germany, including the leaders of the ferocious Baader-Meinhof Gang. One was in France and another in Switzerland. A quick glance and Peres realized it was an impossible demand. How could he possibly organize the release of terrorists held in so many countries, subject to different laws and for different crimes? And what if some or all those countries refused?

Rabin, however, continued to insist that Israel negotiate immediately, fearing that when the terrorists' ultimatum expired, they would start killing innocent people. But Peres stood his ground—he contended that Israel could push back the ultimatum, which had been set for Thursday, July 1, at 11:00 A.M. At the same time, he agreed with the decision to negotiate, but stressed he would be doing so only as a "tactical maneuver" to gain time.

On Wednesday, June 30, Peres decided to explore another angle. He summoned three IDF officers who had served in Uganda and had worked with Idi Amin. He asked them to describe Amin's character, behavior and attitude toward foreigners. These men thought Amin would not dare massacre the hostages, but they also felt certain Amin would not confront the terrorists. Peres asked Colonel "Borka" Bar-Lev, who had been friendly with Idi Amin, to telephone the Ugandan ruler. Bar-Lev was unable to reach him despite repeated efforts.

In the meantime, Peres again summoned his top officers. Beni Peled's plan was discussed once more but now with a narrowed focus. Its goal now became not to conquer Uganda but simply to win control over Entebbe airport, release the hostages and fly them back. Peled laid out a revised plan calling for a thousand paratroopers to be dropped from ten Rhino aircraft. Shomron and Ben-Gal estimated that such an operation could be successfully carried out with two hundred men and three Rhinos.

Kibbutz-born Dan Shomron, a paratrooper and a hero of the Six Day War, was opposed to any parachuting. He told Peled that "by the time your first paratrooper hits the ground, you won't have anybody left to rescue anymore." Soft-spoken, but sharp and cool, this future chief of staff was certain that as soon as the terrorists saw paratroopers descending, they would massacre the hostages. So Shomron, who now became the key coordinator, started drafting a plan to land planes carrying his soldiers directly onto the Entebbe runways. Kuti Adam pointed out the need for a stopover base close to Uganda, in case of an emergency. They all agreed it would have to be in Kenya, whose government maintained friendly relations with Israel while loathing Idi Amin. Peres asked the Mossad head, General Yitzhak ("Haka") Hofi, to check discreetly with his Kenyan contacts to ascertain if their country would authorize such a stopover at Nairobi airport. Peres, however, felt dubious about this approach, as Haka seemed to him reserved and skeptical.

Additionally, the emerging mission continued to have an important and stubborn antagonist: Chief of Staff Motta Gur, who strongly believed it could not succeed and insisted that Israel had no military option. He stressed the complete lack of intelligence about what was happening in Entebbe. He called the group working with Peres "the Fantasy Council."

Meanwhile, one far-fetched aspect of the plan did progress—Borka Bar-Lev at long last established a telephone connection with Idi Amin. The talk was discouraging, though. Uganda's ruler bluntly advised him that Israel should accept the hijackers' demands without delay.

This was also the opinion of Rabin, who now had the cabinet's backing to start negotiations right away. He further informed his ministers that the opposition leader, Menachem Begin, agreed with his decision to negotiate. Rabin criticized Peres for using "demagogical lightnings . . . and ornate phrases that sounded totally ridiculous." Indeed, Rabin regarded Peres's responses throughout the crisis as pure demagogy. He did not believe that Peres even meant what he was saying. Most of the ministers agreed that Israel had no military option. Rabin also kept nervously demanding that France immediately be informed of Israel's acceptance of the terrorists' conditions, so that the French foreign ministry could immediately establish contact with Entebbe.

Amid all the angry politicking, some good news came on July 1: the terrorists had by themselves postponed their deadline for capitulation to Sunday, July 4. This stemmed from Idi Amin's departure to an African nations' conference in Mauritius. He was supposed to return in a couple of days. The terrorists wanted Amin to be present when the negotiations took place. So Peres and his "Fantasy Council" now suddenly had a little more time.

Kuti Adam and Dan Shomron thus were able to present the plan they had drafted: The mission would sortie at night, under cover of darkness. The Rhinos would land at Entebbe, and the IDF would acquire control of the airport, kill the terrorists and rescue the hostages.

The whole operation, Dan Shomron emphasized, would not last more than an hour, making all possible use of surprise and speed. First to land would be a Rhino, not asking permission from the control tower. It would arrive at 11:00 P.M., right after a British airliner that was scheduled to come in at the same time. With the Rhino landing in the shadow of the British aircraft, the airport radar would not detect it. Two armored cars laden with commandos would emerge from the Rhino and race toward the Old Terminal, where the hostages were being kept. Five or ten minutes later another Rhino would land and disgorge two more cars, with soldiers who would gain control over the New Terminal, the main runway and the fuel reservoirs. After these men in the first two planes had fulfilled their assignments, two more Rhinos would land, load up the hostages and return home.

Peres now asked the head of the Mossad for his input, but Hofi kept stressing the risks—what if the Ugandan soldiers fired an RPG (rocket-propelled grenade) or a machine-gun burst into the Rhino fuel tank and set off an explosion? In that event, one or more planes might have to be abandoned, ruining the delicate interdependencies of the plan. And then there were the potential human costs—what if soldiers and hostages were killed or wounded? What if the terrorists simply blew up the Old Terminal with all the hostages? Hofi was—to say the least—unenthusiastic.

Peres's council then tore apart every detail of the mission—what snags might occur; whether, if the first Rhino was hit or damaged, the other planes would be able to return; what to do if the airport had antiaircraft guns; whether there were Ugandan MiG jet fighters stationed there, and would there be enough fuel left for the takeoff from Entebbe? . . .

Peres then asked the military for their opinions. Dan Shomron said, "If we start in Entebbe at midnight, we can take off for the flight back at one A.M." He estimated the chances of success were close to 100 percent. Benny Peled thought 80 percent and Kuti Adam, between 50 and 80 percent.

Peres finally approved the plan and set the deadline for carrying it out at Saturday night, July 3, the night before the terrorists' deadline. The generals all agreed, except for Motta Gur, who still stubbornly objected.

"Such an operation without adequate intelligence," he said, "is charlatanism!"

"Motta," Peres asked, "will you reconsider?"

"Without intelligence there is no chance that I'd recommend such an operation. Some of the things I have heard here aren't worthy of an army's general staff. If you want Goldfinger, that's a different story. If you want James Bond—not with me!"

Peres then pulled Gur into an in-depth discussion that lasted all through the night, but Gur still would not budge. And without the chief of staff's support, Peres could not bring the go-ahead to the cabinet for its approval.

Gur, despite his opposition, did agree to assemble the task force—Sayeret Matkal, paratroopers and other units—in a training facility to prepare for the assault, but it would move forward only if the situation were to change. The facility was sealed, and to prevent any leaks, no one was allowed to leave. Shomron was appointed mission commander. An advance command post was to be established in a big air force Boeing that would accompany the Rhinos to Ugandan airspace and control the operation from the sky. Models of the old and new Entebbe terminals were built in the facility, and the soldiers repeatedly rehearsed for an attack and for the rescue.

Peres now set out to freeze the efforts to reach a compromise with the hijackers. Israel's former ambassador to France, Arthur Ben-Natan, had just arrived in Paris to talk with the French about a joint initiative to deal with the terrorists. He was Peres's longtime friend and a former director general of the defense Ministry. Peres telephoned him and conveyed a veiled hint, using "typical" Parisian banter, to delay his talks with the French. "If you meet the French girl tonight," Peres advised, "please don't get too excited. At most, content yourself with a vague flirtation. As a friend, and not only as a friend, I am telling you: don't take your clothes off." Ben-Natan laughed but clearly understood the message and let nothing come out of his "flirtation" with the French.

Two encouraging reports then arrived the following morning, Friday, July 2. The first, from Hofi, the head of the Mossad, informed Peres that Kenya, Uganda's neighbor, had agreed to authorize a stopover for the Israeli planes. The second came from an unexpected source—Paris. The Sayeret operation planner, Major Amiram Levin, had been sent to France to debrief the non-Israeli hostages who had just been released. But most, still terrified, confused and unfocused, could supply no useful information. Suddenly an older Frenchman approached Levin, introducing himself as a former French Army colonel. "I know what you need," he said. He sat down beside Levin and gave him a succinct description of the Old Terminal, where the hostages were being kept, the layout of the various halls and the positioning of the terrorists. He also drew for Levin detailed sketches of the building.

Various sources reported that the total number of terrorists was thirteen, including two Germans and a South American who was apparently the hijackers' commander. The other terrorists were Palestinians. Four had participated in the hijacking while the others had been waiting for the plane in Entebbe. Their rapport with the Ugandans was cordial. The captors were armed with small submachine guns, revolvers and hand grenades. The hostages were being held in the main hall of the Old Terminal, and the French crew of the Air France plane (which had refused the opportunity to be released out of loyalty to their passengers) were confined to the women's restrooms.

Additionally, the Ugandan military unit said to be watching over the prisoners was sixty men strong—but less than a battalion, as earlier reports had stated. In the Old Terminal a wall of crates had been erected, which the terrorists claimed were full of explosives. But intelligence sources indicated that these crates were not connected to any wires and no preparation for blowing them up appeared to have been made.

The Mossad, in preparation for the mission, should it be given a green light, had sent to Entebbe a foreign aircraft that allegedly had mechanical problems. The plane circled over the airport while radioing calls for help and secretly photographing the buildings, runways and equipment, as well as the military aircraft stationed there—two helicopters and eight MiG-21 jet fighters.

Armed with all this new information, Peres hurried to Motta Gur's office and presented him with these new reports. He noticed that on hearing the news, "Gur's eyes shone." The chief of staff reacted with enthusiasm and completely reversed his position. Gur, reassured that he now had enough information, became a staunch supporter of the Entebbe rescue.

Peres hurried to the prime minister's office. Rabin's headquarters was located in a picturesque small house a stone's throw from the Ministry of Defense, in the modest, book-filled room where David Ben-Gurion had planned major moves in the War of Independence. Peres described the plan to Rabin. The prime minister's reaction was lukewarm. He lit a cigarette and asked, "What would happen if the Ugandans identified the plane as it landed and fired at it?"

Peres told him that the IAF commander was certain that the plane could be landed without any response from the ground. Hofi, who had joined the meeting, for the first time expressed cautious support for the operation.

At the next Fantasy Council meeting, one of the officers suggested preparing a "double" of Idi Amin. When the Rhinos started landing in Entebbe, Amin would still be at the African nations' conference. So it might work to have a black Mercedes, similar to Idi Amin's, drive at the head of the Israeli troops. Inside would be an Israeli soldier with his face painted black. At midnight the Ugandans wouldn't clearly notice the figures inside the "presidential" car, and they'd clear a path out of respect for their leader. On the spot, Gur ordered his people to find a large black Mercedes that could be used.

The black Mercedes on its way to Entebbe. *(IDF Spokesman)*

Gur ensured that the elite units chosen for the mission were kept exercising without respite. Their commanders were measuring every yard and counting out every minute in the operational plan, every soldier's assignment and every vehicle's course. The critical moment, of course, would be the first Rhino's landing. Gur detailed the timetable: "From the turning on of the plane's landing lights and until it stops—two minutes. Two more minutes to get the men out of the plane. Five minutes to reach the target. Five more to complete the operation . . . "

Peres, Gur and Hofi hurried to Rabin's office. Gur presented the plan in detail and received guarded approval from Rabin, who ruled that the final decision would be made by an extraordinary cabinet meeting on Saturday, shortly before the planes were set to leave for Entebbe. The code name was to be "Thunderball."

During the meeting, Peres wrote a note and slipped it to Rabin:

Yitzhak—here is the last refinement in the planning: instead of a military ground service vehicle—a large Mercedes with flags will descend. Idi Amin will appear to be coming home from Mauritius. I don't know if it is possible, but it is interesting. —

The IDF planners couldn't find a black Mercedes similar to Idi Amin's, but they did find a white one of the same size in Gaza. It was immediately brought into the departure area and painted black. Amin's double was at hand, and the Sayeret mixed black dye to paint his face.

Then, just as all the pieces seemed to be coming tenuously together, an unexpected problem arose. Peres was scheduled to host a distinguished foreign visitor for dinner at his home: Polish-American professor Zbigniew Brzezinski, the future U.S. national security adviser during the Carter administration. Gur was also invited, but he had to cancel when his father-in-law suddenly died.

Brzezinski was cordially received, and Sonia, Peres's wife, cooked her specialty for him: honey chicken. Mid-dinner, Brzezinki surprised his hosts by throwing a direct question at Peres:

"Why don't you send the IDF to rescue the hostages at Entebbe?"

For a moment, the defense minister was speechless. But then, determined to preserve the secrecy, he explained why the mission was impossible: Entebbe was too far, Israel didn't have enough intelligence and MiG fighters and Ugandan battalions were stationed at the airport.

Brzezinski was not convinced.

At the Fantasy Council's last meeting, the participants felt confident that the mission would succeed. The officers asked Peres a few-last minute questions:

"If the control tower asks our aircraft to identify themselves, should we answer?"

Peres and Gur decided that the pilots shouldn't answer.

"And what about the Air France crew?"

"Bring them home," Peres said. "We should treat them as Israelis in every way."

With the final cabinet meeting approaching to decide if the mission would occur, Peres asked Gur, "When should the planes take off?"

After considering this, the chief of staff answered, "From Ben-Gurion Airport to Sharm el Sheikh in Sinai—at one P.M.; then from Sharm el Sheikh—between four and five P.M."

This meant the planes should leave before the decisive cabinet meeting even took place. Peres then authorized the planes to take off before getting approval from the top. He reasoned that if the cabinet decided against the mission, the planes could still be turned around and brought back.

On Saturday, at 2:30 P.M., the cabinet met; having a meeting on the Sabbath was unusual and it had happened only a few times in Israel's history. Rabin expressed his full support of the operation, so now all three main players—the prime minister, the minister of defense and the chief of staff—were united. After a brief discussion, the cabinet voted and unanimously approved Thunderball.

At 3:30 P.M. the good news was radioed to Sharm el Sheikh, and fourteen minutes later four Rhinos took off. They carried 180 elite soldiers and their arms and vehicles, and the black Mercedes. The soldiers spread swiftly over the large bellies of the Rhinos, curled on the metal floor and tried to get some sleep. A bit later, the flying command post, an Oryx (IAF Boeing), took off, and yet another Oryx, one carrying medical teams and equipment, flew toward Nairobi. The four-thousand-kilometer journey had begun.

At 11:00 P.M., the pinpoint lights of Entebbe began to emerge from the darkness. The Rhinos had flown at an extremely high altitude, so as to elude all radar stations along their way. A minute later, the first Hercules landed on the illuminated runway, hiding from Ugandan radar behind the British airliner that had landed just before it. It rolled forward on the tarmac, miraculously unnoticed by the control tower.

Soldiers of the Doron and Tali units leapt from the plane and placed lit torches by the runway lights. Their assumption was that in a few minutes the built-in runway lights would be turned off by the Ugandans as a defensive measure, and so only their torches would illuminate the runway for the planes yet to come. The soldiers ran ahead of the Rhino and placed their torches intermittently along 540 yards. The aircraft then stopped, and out of it drove the black Mercedes and two Land Rover jeeps; they sped toward the Old Terminal. In the Mercedes, beside the black-painted "Idi Amin," crouched Yoni Netanyahu, Muki Betzer, Giora Zussman and their men.

They were barely one hundred meters from the old control tower when two Ugandan soldiers appeared in front of them. One ran away but the second pointed his weapon at the Mercedes and tried to stop it. Yoni and Giora drew their silenced handguns. "Don't shoot," Muki grunted, certain that the Ugandan was only going through the motions and probably wouldn't open fire; but when the Ugandan did not lower his weapon the two men shot him, first with their handguns and then with a Kalashnikov. Their shots echoed loudly in the night and cost the Israelis their element of surprise. Instead of reaching the Old Terminal gates the cars were forced to stop fifty yards from the old control tower, where the commandos jumped out of their vehicles and sprinted toward the building, killing another Ugandan soldier who tried to block their path.

Muki and his men broke into the Old Terminal through a side door.

The former departure hall was illuminated, and the hostages were lying on the floor inside, most of them asleep. With bursts from their guns Muki and his men killed the four terrorists who were guarding the hall's corners. Only one of the terrorists managed to fire back; the others were all killed before drawing their weapons. Using portable megaphones, the soldiers warned the hostages, in Hebrew, to stay down where they were. Some unfortunately got up and were shot at once. Six were wounded and three killed. Despite this tragic loss, the first stage of the mission was a success, with only fifteen or so seconds having passed between the shooting of the first Ugandan and the takeover of the departure hall. Phase one was now completed, and four terrorists lay dead.

While Muki Betzer was scanning the departure hall, he received a call over his radio; it was Captain Tamir Pardo, the twenty-three-year-old Sayeret communications officer (and a future head of the Mossad), who informed him that Yoni had been shot in the garden adjacent to the hall entrance. "Muki, assume command!" Pardo urgently said. He had just killed the Ugandan soldier who had shot Yoni. Some later claimed Yoni had been shot by Ugandans firing from the old control tower; others believed he had been shot by a terrorist.

An IDF doctor soon arrived and got Yoni to the Rhino. Muki picked up his radio transceiver and announced that he was assuming command.

Other commandos systematically mopped up the remaining passages and halls in the building. In the "small hall" behind the departure hall they found no one, but when Giora's detail moved into the VIP lounge they clashed with two Ugandan soldiers and killed them. Suddenly, two European-looking men appeared before the Israelis, ignoring their calls to identify themselves. At first the commandos thought they were hostages, but when they didn't answer the Israelis' calls, the commandos realized they were terrorists and opened fire. One of the terrorists was carrying a grenade, which exploded, and both were killed.

During the mopping up of the VIP lounge, the customs hall and the second floor, more Ugandan soldiers were killed, but nearly all of the sixty Ugandans stationed at the airport escaped and fled. In total, twelve Ugandans were killed in various firefights.

Suddenly, the lights in the entire airport were cut off, and Entebbe was plunged in darkness. Luckily, the runway where the first aircraft had landed was illuminated by the commandos' torches, and the remaining Rhinos landed easily and discharged more soldiers and armored vehicles.

Back in Israel, Rabin, Peres and Gur anxiously listened to the direct reports radioed from Entebbe. At 11:10 P.M. Dan Shomron's slightly hoarse voice came on, saying, "Everything is fine. I'll report later." Eight minutes passed, and Shomron again radioed: "Low tide." That was the code phrase that all the planes had landed safely. He followed this up with the code word "Palestine," announcing the assault on the Old Terminal. Shomron himself drove his jeep to that building and continued commanding from there.

As gunfire was still blasting in and around the Old Terminal, the just-arrived units had set off on their assignments. The half-tracks of Major Shaul Mofaz silenced the old control tower with a lethal burst. Another Mofaz paratrooper squad killed eight Ugandan soldiers in two clashes. They then joined the forces still mopping up the Old Terminal.

Colonel Matan Vilnai led his forces to the New Terminal. After their breaking in, the brightly illuminated building suddenly went completely dark, and the operation had to be continued with no lights. In accordance with the plan, Vilnai's men did not open fire on the Ugandan soldiers they encountered, allowing them to escape, and in two cases arrested Ugandans and locked them up in the terminal offices. It was then that Vilnai heard two shots from the north of the terminal. On the stairs he found one of his soldiers, Sergeant Surin Hershko, lying wounded, probably shot by a Ugandan security officer. Hershko was quickly evacuated, and his comrades kept advancing, but because of the darkness they couldn't find the entrance to the new control tower.

Yet, even as Vilnai and his men struggled in this confusion, the battle had already reached its finale. The IDF had conquered the airport. Its commanders had located the fuel dumps but decided not to refuel the Rhinos in Entebbe, as that would have delayed their departure by two hours. Matan Vilnai and the captain of the first Rhino, Colonel Shani, advised Shomron now not to delay their departure unless absolutely necessary, so Shomron agreed that they would refuel in Nairobi. There an IDF unit was already waiting, commanded by Ehud Barak, along with an airborne field hospital with twelve doctors and two operating rooms, which had arrived from Israel.

In the Entebbe Old Terminal the liberated hostages were stunned. The arrival of the Israelis and the lightning speed of the encounter, which had left their captors dead, seemed to them a miracle. When they came to their senses they clustered around the soldiers, hugging and embracing them in an explosion of joy and gratitude. Some wept, others joined in prayer. But the troops swiftly put an end to the euphoria. They told the hostages and the Air France crew to gather their belongings and in orderly fashion led them out of the building. They escorted them in the dark and kept counting them, to ensure that all the hostages were accounted for.

At 11:32 P.M. the code word "Jefferson" echoed in radio receivers in Tel Aviv. It meant the evacuation of the hostages had begun. And a minute later: "Move everything to Galila," meaning the hostages were boarding the Rhinos.

The soldiers carried the wounded and the bodies of the hostages killed in the crossfire into an aircraft. One woman was missing: an elderly Israeli, Dora Bloch, who had taken ill earlier and been transferred to a Kampala hospital. Soon she would be murdered by the Ugandans.

Everything else proceeded according to plan, but at 11:50 P.M. the powerful antennae at the Ministry of Defense in Tel Aviv intercepted a worrying message radioed from "Almond Grove," the Sayeret of Yoni Netanyahu, to the unit's medical officer in Entebbe. It was a laconic call for medics, mentioning "Two Ekaterina"—code for "two wounded." But nothing was said about the identity of the wounded.

The military vehicles and units drove back into the Rhinos. The soldiers of Lieutenant Omer Bar-Lev, son of a former chief of staff, blew up the eight MiG jets stationed at the airport to prevent them from chasing and attacking the much slower Rhinos on their way home.

At 11:51 P.M. the radio message everyone in Tel Aviv was praying for finally came—"Mount Carmel." It meant the end of the evacuation. The operation was completed and all the planes had taken off.

"The heart jumps with joy," Shimon Peres wrote jubilantly in his diary.

After the planes took off from Entebbe, Peres instructed Borka Bar-Lev, Idi Amin's former friend, to call Amin from Tel Aviv. Perhaps the Ugandan dictator had now returned from Mauritius, Peres thought. To Borka's surprise, Amin himself picked up the phone. He had returned a bit earlier to Kampala.

Borka spoke to him using a well-rehearsed scenario, one intended to create the impression that Amin had been secretly involved in the rescue; that might ignite a conflict between him and the terrorists he had so eagerly assisted. The phone conversation was recorded by the IDF.

"I called to thank you, Mr. President, for what you did!"

"Yes," Amin said, "I advise you to accept my friends' demands."

Borka was taken aback. "I want to thank you for what you did for the hostages."

"Yes, yes," was Amin's response. "You should negotiate with my friends and make the exchange with them. The hostages will be released, and so would the prisoners."

This dialogue continued for a few minutes, until Borka understood: Amin did not know that the hostages had been liberated! He was sitting in his palace, discussing the ultimatum and upcoming negotiations, completely ignorant of the fact that the Israelis had been to Entebbe, freed the hostages and taken off. None of his officers had dared to inform him that a few miles from his palace a firefight had taken place, the terrorists were dead and the Israeli hostages were on their way back home!

"Thank you, sir," Borka mumbled and hung up, dismayed.

All the aircraft landed safely in Nairobi. The IDF medical team treated the wounded as the Rhinos refueled. Shortly afterward, the planes took off and headed for Israel.

Very few of the liberated hostages slept during the long journey. They were too excited by this extraordinary experience. When the IDF spokesman published a short communiqué about the mission, "IDF forces tonight rescued the hostages from Entebbe airport, including the Air France crew," an unprecedented wave of enthusiasm and rejoicing swept the country.

An elated outburst shook the IDF general staff when Motta Gur informed his officers of the mission's success. He also made a speech, saying, "I cannot sum up the operation even in this early stage without stressing the drive and the influence on its execution that were centered in one man . . . who pressed on and pushed in every direction, both up and down, for the operation. And this is the defense minister, who deserves all the credit."

In the prime minister's office, Rabin and Peres exchanged excited greetings with Knesset members Begin and Elimelech Rimalt and Yitzhak Navon, chairman of the Defense and Foreign Affairs Committee. Rabin briefed the president and Golda Meir, while Peres woke up his wife, Sonia. The fantastic news spread throughout the world, and messages of amazement and admiration poured in from all over.

But then, in the wee hours all this joy was painfully interrupted. Gur came to the defense minister's office. Shimon Peres was lying on his narrow couch, trying to get some sleep.

"Shimon, Yoni is dead," Gur said. "He was hit by a bullet in the back. Apparently he was shot from the old control tower. The bullet pierced his heart."

Peres, devastated, burst into tears.

The following day, the Fourth of July, 1976 (the two-hundredth anniversary of the United States), the rescue planes landed in Israel and were received by a festive, flag-waving crowd. The operation became legendary in Israel and in the outside world. Flowery articles, books, TV shows and movies hailed the glory of the IDF soldiers. Foreign nations regarded the operation as a symbol of courage, dedication and impressive military capability.

All the terrorists who had participated in the hijacking and the imprisonment in Entebbe had been killed, with the exception of Wadie Haddad, head of the Popular Front, who had left Entebbe before the IDF raid. Knowing he was now in the crosshairs of the Israelis, he found refuge in Baghdad, hoping he would be protected there. It took nearly two years for the Mossad to reach him. Israeli agents discovered Haddad's weakness: he adored fine Belgian chocolate. The Mossad laced a box of mouth-watering Godivas with an untraceable poison and recruited one of Haddad's trusted lieutenants, who brought him the deadly box. Haddad gobbled down the chocolates, all by himself. A few weeks later, the ailing arch-terrorist was urgently flown, in critical condition, to an East German clinic, where he died in March 1978.

That same year, Idi Amin's regime collapsed following a war he instigated against neighboring Tanzania. Amin escaped to Libya and later to Saudi Arabia, where he lived until his death in 2003.

The IDF mission in Entebbe had been an astounding success. And yet, Yoni Netanyahu's death left a dark shadow over the popular rejoicing. The IDF changed the name of Operation Thunderball to Operation Yonatan. Peres eulogized Yoni at his funeral:

"What burdens didn't we load on Yoni and his comrades' shoulders? The most dangerous of the IDF's tasks and the most daring of its operations; the missions that were the farthest from home and the closest to the enemy; the darkness of night and the solitude of the fighter; the taking of risks, over and over again, in times of peace and in times of war. There are times when the nation's fate depends on a handful of volunteers. . . . Yonatan was a commander of valor. He overcame his enemies by his courage. He conquered his friends' hearts by the wisdom of his heart. He didn't fear danger and victories didn't make him vain. By falling he caused an entire nation to raise her head high."

Shimon Peres quoted King David's biblical verses mourning his friend Jonathan: "I am distressed for thee, my brother Jonathan; very pleasant hast thou been unto me; thy love to me was wonderful" (2 Samuel 1:26).

SHIMON PERES, LATER ISRAEL'S NINTH PRESIDENT

"From the first moment I was determined not to yield to the terrorists. We had to find a way to liberate the hostages. I had the support of a fine group of generals—Shomron, Adam, Peled, Gazit and their close colleagues. At the beginning our plans were vague. We perfected and honed the project hour by hour. But I felt I was completely alone in that matter.

"The prime minister was ready to exchange the jailed terrorists for the hostages. Most of the cabinet thought like him. Even Menachem Begin, the bold activist, agreed with him. Motta Gur, the IDF chief of staff, ridiculed my little group, compared our plans to James Bond stories and called us the 'Fantasy Council.' I knew that even if I had a good plan, I couldn't get it approved by the cabinet over the objection of the chief of staff and the reluctance of the prime minister. I decided to try obtaining the support of some cabinet ministers. I went to Hayim Tzadok, the minister of justice, a strong supporter of Prime Minister Rabin, but also a very wise and objective man. In utmost secrecy I revealed the plan to him. 'An excellent plan,' he said, 'I'll support it at the cabinet.'

"I got another encouragement from my friend Moshe Dayan, the former defense minister. I found Moshe in the Tel Aviv Capricio restaurant, in the company of Australian guests. I admired Dayan and valued his opinion. We ordered two glasses of wine and moved to a nearby table. I told Dayan about the plan. I remember how his eye sparkled. 'That's a great plan,' he said, 'and I support it a hundred percent.'

"But Motta Gur kept refusing to endorse the project. Only at the very last moment, on Friday morning, I brought him a new and detailed intelligence report about Entebbe, the hostages and the terrorists guarding them. This report made Motta change his mind. He became a staunch supporter of the mission.

"Now, at last, we could go to Rabin and ask for his support."

TAMIR PARDO, SAYERET MATKAL'S COMMUNICATIONS OFFICER, LATER HEAD OF THE MOSSAD

"There were many heroes in this mission. Everybody who took part in this operation—in every category—deserves a place in the Entebbe pantheon. The mission was well prepared but the guy who planned the air force part deserves special appreciation. To fly four Hercules aircraft to the heart of Africa; to land those without being detected; to discharge the forces without being fired at, even one shot; and to get them back after the rescue of the hostages—this is an act deserving our praise. Ido Ambar, who was a colonel in the IAF and head of the planning team, deserves special honors. True, military orders are always signed by generals and senior commanders, while the men who worked day and night, and brought to the task so much talent and creativity, remain sometimes in the shadows.

"We, the takeover force, had trained well, and each and every one of us knew exactly what his place was and what his role in the operation was. During the long flight all I did was try to sleep and to not throw up because of the violent shaking and jumping of the planes that flew at different altitudes and chose different paths.

"I was a twenty-three-year-old captain. In the assault of the Old Terminal I was in the first Land Rover, the jeep that moved ahead of the Mercedes. When our attack started I was beside Yoni. He was about a yard away from me when he was killed. In front of us stood a Ugandan soldier and he kept firing at us. I killed him. I think he was the one who shot Yoni, but there is another version—that Yoni was killed by a soldier firing from the old control tower or by a terrorist.

"I had a lot of esteem for Yoni as a commander. I saw him in action, and he had a very important part in the success of the Entebbe mission. When he fell, I bent over him and saw that he was seriously wounded. I alerted the doctor at once and radioed Muki Betzer, his deputy, to assume command. Later I joined Giora Zussman's detail, and together we entered the Old Terminal. The operation itself took barely a few minutes.

"The following day we came back to Israel with the hostages. I was sent to Jerusalem, to the home of the Netanyahu family, to tell them about Yoni's last moments. That was a painful task."

PART ONE

How It All Started

On May 14, 1948, the British Army and administration
leave Palestine after thirty years of British rule. That
same afternoon Israel's independence is proclaimed
by David Ben-Gurion in the Tel Aviv Museum of Art.
The United Nations, by a vote taken six months before,
on November 29, 1947, has decided to partition Palestine
into a Jewish and an Arab state, but the Arabs reject partition.
The local Palestinian Arabs and the armies of Egypt, Syria,
Lebanon, Jordan and Iraq, as well as units of Arab volunteers
from all over the Middle East, set out to invade and destroy the
Jewish State. David Ben-Gurion is elected prime minister and
minister of defense. The acting chief of staff is Yigael Yadin,
a future world-renowned archaeologist.

CHAPTER 2

TO SAVE JERUSALEM, 1948

O n May 24, 1948, while Israel's Independence War was raging, David Ben-Gurion summoned Yigael Yadin. He approached the map of Palestine, hanging on the wall in his office, and pointed at a crossroads marked "Latrun."

"Attack! Attack at all costs!" he forcefully said.

Yadin refused.

Ben-Gurion, "the Old Man," was sixty-two years old, a stocky Polish-born man with a defiant face, a jutting chin, piercing brown eyes—all this crowned with two tufts of snow-white hair hovering like wings over his temples. Yigael Yadin was half his age—a thin young man, balding and with a luxuriant mustache. Before the war he had studied at Hebrew University, following in the footsteps of his father, a noted archaeologist.

Ben-Gurion was haunted by the situation in Jerusalem. The Jewish part of the city was under siege, surrounded by the Arab Legion—Jordan's first-rate army. Starved, thirsty, its defenders and weapons insufficient, Jerusalem was in immediate danger of collapsing.

Ben-Gurion believed that if Jerusalem fell, the newborn Jewish State wouldn't survive. The fortress of Latrun, near a Trappist monastery, controlled the road from the coastal plain to Jerusalem; it had been occupied by elite units of the Arab Legion. To break the siege, Latrun had to be conquered.

But Yadin had other priorities. The Arab armies had penetrated deep into Israeli territory. The Syrians had reached the Jordan Valley; the Iraqis were close to the Mediterranean coast, threatening to cut the country in two; and the Egyptian expeditionary force had set up camp on the shore of the Lakhish River, thirty-five kilometers from Tel Aviv. Yadin believed he had to stop the Egyptians first.

Latrun, Ben-Gurion repeated, had to be taken. Nothing else mattered as much. A heated exchange erupted between the two, and Yadin angrily slammed his hands on the glass plate covering Ben-Gurion's desk, breaking it. But the Old Man wouldn't budge. While respecting Yadin and even admiring his fiery character, he stuck to his guns. Yadin finally gave in, and in a telegram to the commander of the Seventh Brigade repeated Ben-Gurion's order: "Attack at all costs!"

Wave after wave of Israeli soldiers stormed the Latrun fortress over the next weeks; time after time their attacks ended in failure. Hundreds of Israelis were killed and wounded, but the Arab Legion repelled all the attacks. In the meantime UN envoys were feverishly trying to broker a temporary cease-fire between Jews and Arabs. Ben-Gurion knew that the cease-fire agreement would "freeze" the situation on the different fronts. This meant that if the cease-fire was achieved while Jerusalem was still under siege, that fact would be finalized in the UN reports, and Israel wouldn't be allowed to supply Jerusalem with reinforcements and weapons. The Holy City would fall, and Israel with it.

While Latrun fortress still blocked the road, Aryeh Tepper, a platoon commander in the Harel Brigade, which was fighting near Jerusalem, reported to the brigade commander, a young officer named Yitzhak Rabin. He asked permission to try to reach—by foot—the coastal plain. His brother had fallen in battle, Tepper said, and he wanted to visit his bereaved mother. Rabin not only approved the request but ordered three more soldiers to join Tepper. At nightfall, the four men made their way down steep slopes and tortuous arroyos, quietly slipped by an enemy patrol and finally reached kibbutz Hulda in the plain.

The kibbutz members were stunned. It turned out that following some recent battles the Israeli forces had gained control over a strip of land between Hulda and the approaches to Jerusalem, west of Latrun and concealed from the enemy's eyes by a mountain ridge. This discovery was almost unbelievable: there might be a chance to develop an alternative road to Jerusalem that would bypass the deadly Latrun fortress.

A few days later, 150 soldiers reached Jerusalem by the new route; they were the first reinforcements to Rabin's Harel Brigade. Yet the IDF did not need a footpath but a real road for the transport of weapons to the besieged city. The front commander, General David Marcus, decided to try reaching Jerusalem from the plain by jeep. Marcus, tall, jovial and smart, was an American colonel, a Brooklyn boy who had graduated from West Point and law school. He had volunteered for the U.S. Army during World War Two and parachuted over occupied Normandy on D Day with the 101st Airborne Division. He became a Zionist after witnessing the horrors of the German death camps. The Jewish people, he thought, while preparing legal briefs for the Nuremberg trials, must have a homeland. As a volunteer again, he had come to fight in Israel's Independence War under the pseudonym Mickey Stone and had been appointed by Ben-Gurion as the first Israeli general. Now a senior officer in the IDF, he shared Ben-Gurion's thoughts about the importance of saving Jerusalem.

One night he set out from the plain on a jeep with two Harel officers, Gavrush Rapoport from kibbutz Beit Alfa and Amos Horev, a future general. The jeep slowly advanced through the gullies and up the hills, and the three officers discovered a route connecting with the Deer Path, a steep, sinuous trail that led to the Jerusalem road, far beyond the reach of Latrun fortress. Horev and Gavrush repeated their trip the following night, and after an exhausting three-hour drive suddenly bumped into another jeep that came from Jerusalem, carrying two other Harel officers. They joyfully hugged their comrades; they had proved that it was possible to reach Jerusalem from the plain by jeep!

After several failures and mishaps, jeeps started moving along the new trail and even brought heavy mortars to Jerusalem. To shorten the process, the jeeps would bring their load to a rendezvous point with trucks coming from Jerusalem and transfer the food and the equipment. On their way back the jeeps brought wounded soldiers and civilians from Jerusalem to the plain. But it soon became clear that the jeeps could not transport enough food to the Jerusalem civilian population, which suffered from acute hunger. The city military governor, Dov (Bernard) Joseph, dispatched desperate requests for food, water and fuel.

The engineering department of the Seventh Brigade, using all the heavy equipment it could find, started to build a real road, where trucks could pass, but the Achilles' heel of that enterprise was the sheer Beth Sussin slope, where a four-hundred-foot abrupt drop separated two road portions.

At Ben-Gurion's order hundreds of porters were mobilized—some of them from Tel Aviv and some—about two hundred—volunteers from Jerusalem, who each carried a load of twenty kilograms of flour, sugar and other vital products; night after night they climbed the steep slopes and brought the food to Jerusalem. The army also tried to use some mules and three camels, but those were not very helpful.

Time was running out, and Ben-Gurion ordered an all-out engineering offensive against the treacherous Beth Sussin slope. Every piece of equipment that could be found in Israel—bulldozers, tractors, compressors—was brought to the site. Israel's major construction company, Solel Boneh, sent over its best engineers and workers. Expert stonecutters from Jerusalem were also mobilized, and the roadwork continued day and night. The feverish road paving was not only a technical endeavor but also a heroic operation: hundreds of soldiers and volunteers carried heavy loads on their backs, climbed the slopes, pushed or towed trucks and equipment. Jerusalem's chief rabbi, Yitzhak HaLevi

Herzog, authorized work on the road on the Sabbath and even called it "a great mitzvah [a good deed]."

Nevertheless, the only way to vanquish the steep hill rising over the heads of the workers was to quarry into the rock a succession of serpentines—snakelike paths that would enable the trucks to reach the top.

Suddenly, one night, explosions rocked the Jerusalem Hills, and a murderous shelling swept the new road site. The Arab Legion had detected the feverish activity close to its positions; it ignored what the Israelis were doing there, but started an intense bombardment of the area. The legion batteries relentlessly shelled the site and fired on the IDF soldiers and volunteers, who suffered heavy losses. Egyptian Spitfire planes also strafed and bombed the area several times.

Yet the work continued in a race against the clock. In a few days the UN would announce a temporary truce that would freeze all activities on the ground. Building or paving roads was forbidden as long as the truce was in effect. If the road to Jerusalem was not open, the city would remain besieged for the duration of the truce and probably would collapse even before the fighting resumed. If Israel wanted to continue supplying Jerusalem during the truce, it had first to prove to the United Nations that there was a road to Jerusalem entirely controlled by the IDF.

Forty-eight hours before the cease-fire, the road workers were stunned to see a group of foreign correspondents visiting their construction site. They had been led to the new road by Israeli press officers. Unwittingly, the journalists became of tremendous help to Israel. Their reports in the world press that Israel had secretly built an alternative road to Jerusalem were proof that the city was not under siege anymore.

The *New York Herald Tribune* star reporter Kenneth Bilby called the new road Burma Road, after the highway built in the years 1937 to 1938 between Burma and China that provided supplies to the Chinese Army in spite of the Japanese blockade.

The Israeli Burma Road was completed on the night before the truce began, on June 11, 1948. The work, however, quietly continued till July

14, when the UN observers visited the site and saw the Israeli trucks climbing all the way to Jerusalem. Later, when the Burma Road was paved and officially inaugurated, it was renamed the Road of Valor.

The Burma Road being built behind the back of the Jordanian Legion.
Hans Pinn, GPO (Israel's Government Press Office)

David Marcus, who had contributed so much to the Road of Valor, did not live to see it completed. Unable to sleep on the night before the truce began, he wrapped himself in a sheet and took a walk beyond the perimeter of his advanced command post. A sentry mistook the white-robed figure for an enemy. He shouted at the man in white, asking for that night's password. Marcus failed to identify himself with the password, and the sentry fired at him, one single shot. Marcus collapsed, fatally wounded. His coffin was flown to the U.S. and buried with full military honors. A little-known IDF officer, his left eye covered with a black patch, escorted Marcus's coffin to New York. He was named Major Moshe Dayan.

Years later, Marcus's story would be made into a film, *Cast a Giant Shadow*.

A few hours before the truce began, the trucks rolled on Burma Road, and Jerusalem was saved.

YITZHAK NAVON, LATER ISRAEL'S FIFTH PRESIDENT

"During the siege of Jerusalem, I was the head of Intelligence's Arabic division. With the outbreak of war, we could no longer use Arab agents and had to rely mainly on monitoring our enemies' phone conversations. Thus, for example, when our fighters—among them future generals Dado Elazar and Raful Eitan—were about to retreat from the San Simon Monastery, in the Katamon neighborhood, we overheard a transmission from the Arab commander announcing that his soldiers were exhausted and he had decided to withdraw. As a result, we took control of Katamon. A similar thing happened to us at Allenby Camp. By contrast, when we picked up a discussion about a plan to set a trap for the Bloc Etzion relief convoy (the Bloc is a cluster of Jewish settlements south of Jerusalem), we passed it on to the military staff; but they didn't take us into account, and the convoy departed. On its way back, it was attacked by the Arabs at Nebi Daniel, with lethal consequences. I then resigned my position—what's the use of intelligence if it isn't exploited?—but they convinced me to stay.

"There was great hardship during the siege. The governor of Jerusalem, Dov Joseph, informed the government that the city's entire stock was five days' margarine, four days' noodles and ten days' dried meat. He introduced rationing—two hundred grams of bread per day for adults (plus an egg for children), fifty grams of margarine per week, one tin of sardines every other week, one hundred grams of legumes, fifty grams of sugar and fifty grams of rice. We also ate mallow (malva), which I would pick in a field, and we made soup from grass. Water was distributed in measuring cups.

"And then they broke through on the Burma Road!

"One day, I went down to Tel Aviv on the Burma Road for an interrogation of prisoners. And, to my surprise, I was able to buy candles and matches and sardines—as much as I wanted. Sardines: what a feast!"

The Independence War is crowned with an
Israeli victory. At the end of 1953, Prime Minister
Ben-Gurion, sixty-seven, has resigned and settled in
kibbutz Sde Boker in the Negev, but in February 1955
he is convinced to return as defense minister under
Prime Minister Moshe Sharett. Ben-Gurion accuses
moderate Sharett of weakness and irresolution.
This is also the opinion of the chief of staff,
forty-year-old Moshe Dayan, who is a close ally
of the director general of the defense ministry,
thirty-two-year-old Shimon Peres. The incursions
of terrorists into Israel and the growing
threats of a new war publicly made by Egypt's
president Gamal Abdel Nasser lead Ben-Gurion to
adopt a tough policy toward Israel's neighbors.
After each terrorist act Israel will now hold responsible
the state from whose soil the terrorists have come—
and launch retaliatory raids against its military bases.

CHAPTER 3

BLACK ARROW, 1955

On February 28, 1955, after nightfall, six IDF paratroopers under the command of Captain Saadia ("Suppapo") Elkayam crossed the border into the Egyptian-occupied Gaza Strip. The border was not fenced—just a deep ditch dug by tractors. Suppapo's small advance team quietly moved between two Egyptian army positions, but a couple of Egyptian soldiers in a concealed ambush farther up the road opened fire on the Israelis. Suppapo and his men killed the Egyptians with hand grenades and submachine-gun fire and continued to advance. Very soon they were joined by a column of paratroopers of the 890th Paratroop Battalion. At their head was an already famous officer: Ariel ("Arik") Sharon.

Sharon was escorted by two staff observers and his deputy, the calm, bearded Aharon Davidi. Born in Tel Aviv, a volunteer in the Palmach (storm units of the IDF during the Independence War) since the age of fourteen, Davidi had been nicknamed "the coolest soldier in the army." His tranquillity under fire was legendary. Even in the heat of battle this former Palmach officer would perform his duties unruffled, as if the bullets and the grenades and the bombs were not of his concern. Nobody knew that Davidi worked out in secret before every battle, doing physical exercises that helped him hide his fear from his soldiers. His pockets were full of bread and he would munch crusts during the battle, drawing calm and composure from the food. His soldiers admired his serenity and tried to emulate him.

While Sharon and Davidi led their column into Gaza, another paratrooper unit, led by the battle-scarred Danny Matt, crossed the border close to kibbutz Be'eri, farther to the south. They bypassed some villages and set an ambush on the Gaza–Rafah highway to prevent any reinforcements from reaching Gaza.

After two hours of strenuous marching, the paratroopers stopped in an orchard that offered a view of the railroad station and a large Egyptian military base.

On Sharon's order, the paratroopers charged.

Operation Black Arrow, also called the Gaza raid, was under way.

The Israeli government made the decision to launch Black Arrow after several incidents on the Gaza border. The most recent had been an incursion into Israel of an Egyptian intelligence-gathering detail that had collected information, carried out several sabotage operations and murdered a civilian close to Rehovot. When the identity of the perpetrators was exposed, the IDF decided to deal a severe blow to the Egyptian Army.

In the last few years scores of incidents had erupted on Israel's borders, and many infiltrators had entered the country, stealing and murdering civilians. The IDF had tried to retaliate with raids in enemy territory—and failed. The names of these Arab villages and military positions had aggregated into a long list of shame that the IDF tried to repress. Out of all those failed operations, the fiasco that stunned IDF Head of Operations General Moshe Dayan was the miserable failure of the Givati Brigade at the Jordanian village Falame. On January 28, 1953, 120 soldiers attacked the village, which was defended only by locals, shelled it with mortars and after four and a half hours retreated without accomplishing their mission. Dayan, furious, published a new order: "In the future, if any unit commander failed to carry out his mission claiming that he could not overcome the enemy force, his explanation would not be accepted unless he had suffered 50 percent casualties."

This was a very tough order. But things did not change until Arik Sharon entered the scene.

Arik, the son of Russian-born farmers in moshav ("cooperative village") Kfar Malal, was different. A born rebel, bold and tempestuous, the handsome officer was twenty years old when he was badly wounded in the battle of Latrun. He lay bleeding in a wheat field, watching the Arabs who descended from the hills rushing to murder the wounded Israelis with guns and knives. Another soldier, also wounded, grabbed Arik's arms and dragged him toward the Israeli lines. The other soldier had been wounded in the jaw and couldn't speak. The two men silently crawled across the battlefield, while the desperate cries of their wounded comrades, left behind, resounded in their ears. That experience had a long-lasting effect on Sharon—in the future he would not leave a wounded soldier in the battlefield.

After he recovered, he went back to fighting, then spent four years in the army before becoming a student at Hebrew University in Jerusalem. But his heart was not in it. One evening he lay in wait by the prime minister's office in Jerusalem, and when Moshe Dayan came out of the building he handed him a short note: *I am a student now, but I exist. If you have operations in mind—I am ready.*

Dayan remembered him from the days when he was commander of the Northern District and Sharon his intelligence officer. One day the Jordanian Legion had captured two IDF soldiers and refused to release them. Dayan, back from a general staff meeting, casually asked Sharon, "Tell me, is it possible to capture two legionnaires around here as hostages?"

"I'll check that out, sir," Arik had replied.

He got into a pickup truck with another officer and drove to the Sheikh Hussein Bridge, on Jordan's border, drew his handgun and came back with two legionnaires. Dayan was very impressed: "I only asked if it were possible," he said, "and he went out and came back with two legionnaires as if he had just gone to pick fruits in the garden."

One evening in Jerusalem, while Arik was reading about Duke Godfrey de Bouillon, who had led the Crusaders into Palestine in the eleventh century, he was summoned to the office of Colonel Mishael Shaham, commander of the Jerusalem District. Shaham asked him to assemble a small team of irregulars, cross the border and blow up the home of the Palestinian gang leader Mustafa Samueli in the village of Nebi Samuel. Arik recruited a small group of comrades from the war— Shlomo Baum from Kfar Yehezkel, Yitzhak ("Gulliver") Ben-Menahem and Yehuda Dayan from the university, Uzi and Yehuda Piamenta from Jerusalem, Yoram Lavi from Kfar Malal, and Saadia, the Palmach sapper. The group crossed the border and reached Nebi Samuel undetected. The mission was not exactly a success—they blew up the wrong house and Samueli survived. The Jordanians opened a murderous fire on Arik's men, but they retreated in an orderly way and returned home unscathed. In spite of the failure the conclusion was clear: the men had done their best to execute their mission. If they had been better trained, they certainly would have succeeded.

Arik suggested to Colonel Shaham that they establish a secret unit for special missions across the border. Moshe Dayan embraced the idea in spite of the angry objection of his colleagues. And so, in August 1953, Unit 101 was born.

Unit 101 was to become a legend, even though it was a tiny unit that existed barely five months. There was no mission its irregulars refused: deep reconnaissance incursions into enemy territory, raids on terrorists in their lairs, risky operations amid hostile crowds. One-oh-one produced a group of warriors that inspired the entire army with a new spirit. "Three men revolutionized the IDF," a 101 veteran told us. "The commander who pushed the change from above and believed in it—Moshe Dayan; the officer who initiated operations, conceived and proposed, and relentlessly sought combat with the enemy—Arik Sharon; and the fighter who invented new methods and was a teacher to all of us in his tactical planning—Meir Har-Zion."

Meir ("Har") Har-Zion was a young, fearless kibbutz member with extraordinary scouting instincts, a creative mind and an apparently limitless knowledge of the geography of Israel and Palestine. At the age of seventeen he had been captured by the Syrian Army while hiking with his sister Shoshana north of the Lake of Tiberias; after his release, he had crossed the Jordanian border with a female friend and visited the magnificent ancient city of Petra, in spite of the Jordanian patrols that shot fourteen other Israeli adventurers in the 1950s.

Meir joined the army and was recruited by Sharon. With his friend Shimon ("Katcha") Kahaner and a few other comrades he carried out several daring incursions into neighboring countries. One of their night missions was to reach Hebron by foot, twenty-one kilometers from the Israeli border, kill three terrorists, blow up their house and retreat—another twenty-one kilometers. The mission was a success, but on their way back the 101 fighters clashed with a large unit of the Jordanian National Guard. Meir attacked the Jordanians, killed their commander and led his friends back to Israel, carrying the slain Jordanian officer's handgun.

Sharon and Har-Zion were considered heroes but they also had their questionable sides. Ben-Gurion considered Sharon one of the greatest warriors of Israel but repeatedly noted in his diary that Sharon "is not telling the truth," an accusation that was shared by many senior officers.

Meir Har-Zion, too, had attracted scathing accusations by civilian and military leaders for an act of personal vengeance carried out in enemy territory. His beloved sister Shoshana was captured and murdered with her boyfriend by Bedouins while trekking across the Jordanian border. Meir and three of his comrades crossed the border, caught the five murderers and killed four of them, sending the fifth to tell his tribe about the vendetta. Ben-Gurion had Meir Har-Zion arrested on his return, and he was expelled from the army for six months.

At the end of 1953, Moshe Dayan was appointed chief of staff of the IDF. Soon after, 101 merged with the paratroopers, and Sharon became their commander.

And that February night in 1955, he led his paratroopers into Gaza.

Sharon distributed the missions to his officers. Force B would secure the route of entry and exit of the soldiers to and from the Gaza Strip. Force C, the 101 veterans commanded by Danny Matt, would ambush any reinforcements coming from Rafah. Force D, led by a young officer named Motta Gur, would attack the railway station. Another unit of twenty paratroopers would serve as Arik's reserve.

Force A, charged with the major task—attack and destroy the Egyptian base—was under Suppapo's command. Suppapo was a brave officer, a younger version of Sharon. He was a warhorse, always volunteering for the most dangerous missions. Battle scars were scattered all over his body, but he kept joking, "The bullet that would kill me has not been made yet." His A company was always charged with the most dangerous missions. A few weeks before, when Arik had decided to send Motta Gur's D Company on a raid to Beth Zurif, in the Hebron hills, instead of A Company, Suppapo burst into tears and didn't speak to Motta for several days.

But that night Suppapo was delighted. Arik had instructed him to capture the Egyptian base and blow up its main structures. That very morning Danny Matt had met Suppapo and his young bride in Tel Aviv. They were on their way to receive the keys to their new apartment, Suppapo revealed proudly.

He now led the charge of his men but made a fatal mistake. He mistook a water-pumping facility, surrounded by army tents and positions, for the enemy base. The Egyptians at the facility opened automatic fire on the attackers. After a short firefight, the paratroopers captured the camp.

Suddenly, shots were heard and bullets rained on the paratroopers from the dark compound across the road. The soldiers heard Davidi's voice: "Suppapo, that's a mistake! The camp is on your right!"

Suppapo realized his mistake and darted toward the gate of the compound, followed by two of his men. The enemy's fire increased.

A bullet hit Suppapo's eye and exited through his forehead. A platoon commander, Lieutenant Uzi Eilam, dragged Suppapo's body to a ditch beside the road, where some of the wounded lay. Uzi himself had been wounded; a bullet had shattered his hand, but he kept fighting.

The heavy machine guns kept firing. Company A was dispersed and confused. A feeling of defeat started spreading among the men.

Suddenly Davidi appeared beside them, calmly walking on the road as if the Egyptian bullets were not flying around him. He stood by a eucalyptus tree, exposed to the enemy's fire. Uzi jumped up and stood by him.

"What's going on, Uzi?" Davidi asked evenly.

"Suppapo was killed and we have quite a few wounded."

"Where are they firing from?" Davidi asked.

Uzi pointed: "From here and from there."

Davidi and Uzi threw hand grenades on the Egyptian positions, and one of the soldiers blew up the closest machine-gun nest. Davidi assembled the company and Uzi shouted loudly, "Those of my men who are unhurt—follow me!" He and four of his men found a hole in the camp fence and entered. A paratrooper was killed, but Uzi surprised the Egyptians from the back, blasting their positions one after the other. Several Egyptians were killed while others escaped. In a matter of minutes the paratroopers conquered the entire compound. The battalion sapper led the "porters," laden with explosives, into the camp, and soon all the buildings were blown up. Davidi had Suppapo's men prepare stretchers for the wounded and the dead. Breaching his legendary calm Davidi called out to the men, "Company A lions! Carry on as you did so far. Go on like tigers!"

South of the compound, four Egyptian military trucks came from Rafah, carrying reinforcements. Danny Matt's men were ready. When the first truck approached, Katcha jumped on it and squeezed his trigger into the driver's cabin. The vehicle stopped and the paratroopers attacked the Egyptians with submachine guns and hand grenades. Another man jumped on the canvas top of the truck and fired long bursts on the Egyptians below. The other trucks stopped, and the Egyptian soldiers ran into the fields, firing at the Israelis from afar but not daring to approach.

One after the other the paratroopers' companies returned toward the border, carrying their eight dead and twenty wounded comrades. Sharon radioed, "We are on our way back, we are very heavy." The staff officers who waited for him didn't understand, but his wife, Margalit

("Gali"), who had come to take care of the wounded, understood that
they were heavy with casualties. Many of the wounded were carried on
improvised stretchers made of rifles and shirts. At the last moment, after
he had crossed a large gully and was approaching the border, Uzi heard
that one of the wounded had been left behind. He ran back, found the
abandoned Major Michael Karten, a staff observer, and carried him on
his shoulders to Israel. He did not know that Karten was already dead.

The Egyptians had thirty-six dead and twenty-eight wounded.
Twenty-two of them had been killed by Danny Matt's men.

Following the battle Moshe Dayan awarded the Medal of Valor to
three of the fighters: Uzi Eilam, Aharon Davidi and the late Suppapo.

A week after the battle Ben-Gurion visited the paratroopers' base,
watched their parade and spoke to them. He called them "trailblazers"—
the volunteers who march ahead of the nation.

Legendary paratroopers and commanders. Standing, from right to left:
Assaf Simhoni, Moshe Efron, Danny Matt, Moshe Dayan, Ariel Sharon, Meir
Har-Zion. Crouching: Rafael Eitan, Yaakov Yaakov, Aharon Davidi.
Abraham Vered, Bamachane, IDF (Israeli Defense Forces) archives

Black Arrow inaugurated the era of night retaliation raids. From then on, the IDF would respond to acts of murder and sabotage carried out by the paramilitary Arab infiltrators—called "fedayeen"—with attacks on the enemy's army bases and military targets. This mission started a vicious cycle of terrorist acts and reprisal raids that continued up to the Sinai campaign of 1956.

Ben-Gurion explained forcefully to a reporter, "These raids also have a moral and educational purpose. These Jews [whose settlements are close to the border] come from Iraq, Kurdistan, North Africa. . . . There their blood was free. . . . Here we have to reassure them that the Jewish people has a state and an army, and their life and property have a price. We have to make them stand tall, instill in them a feeling of independence and pride, for they are citizens of a sovereign nation that is responsible for their lives and safety."

UZI EILAM, LATER DIRECTOR GENERAL OF THE ISRAELI ATOMIC ENERGY COMMISSION

"When Suppapo was killed, I was thirty feet away. Suddenly, Davidi appeared next to me, strolling calmly under heavy fire. I stood next to him—it wasn't pleasant sitting when the deputy battalion commander was standing. I learned from him to stay calm and controlled during every battle. This gives tremendous confidence to people, who believe that you know exactly what you want and where you're going.

"I decided to attack with four soldiers, the only ones from my unit who weren't wounded. We cut through the fence and cleaned out the base from behind. Eventually, with just one other soldier, I reached the command building. There were two platoons of Egyptian soldiers there, and a portion of them fled. Then I informed Davidi that it was possible to blow it up; the battalion's sappers arrived and we blew up the two buildings, and also the water-pumping facility.

"After the operation, I was in the hospital for a series of surgeries on my hand, and I was sent to a rehabilitation center.

I escaped, and during the Husan action [a retaliatory raid] I was in a Piper Cub flying over the troops. I also flew in a Piper during the Qalqilya raid. On the eve of the Sinai campaign I was appointed company commander with Motta, and the doctor finally cut off my cast.

"Two months after the Sinai campaign I was discharged. Three years later, when I got married, I left the kibbutz. They were very angry with me, and 'forgave' me only after I took part in the liberation of Jerusalem during the Six Day War."

PART TWO

The Sinai Campaign

In the fall of 1955, Egypt signs a formidable arms
deal with Czechoslovakia, acting as a proxy for the Soviet
Union. Egypt will receive hundreds of jet fighters and bombers,
tanks, cannons, and other weapons with which it can wipe
Israel off the map. In response, Ben-Gurion wants to launch a
preemptive war against Egypt. In July 1956, Egyptian president
Nasser nationalizes the Suez Canal, and Israel suddenly finds
two major allies for an attack on Egypt—France and Great
Britain—who want to take over the canal and dethrone Nasser.
A secret deal among the three nations is reached in October
1956—they will launch an attack on Egypt.

CHAPTER 4
"BRING DOWN THIS PLANE!" 1956

O n a pitch-black night in October 1956, the Israeli Air Force pilot Yoash ("Chatto") Tzidon took off on the commands of his Meteor 13 night fighter, a sleek British-made jet, its black nose cone carrying a rounded radar device.

Chatto knew that his dangerous mission was crucial for the outcome of Israel's next war. Accompanying him in his Meteor was the navigator Elyashiv ("Shibi") Brosh. The pair knew that their assignment, if it succeeded, would stay top-secret for decades to come. Chatto also already knew that, the next day, October 29, Israel would launch its attack on Egypt. Ironically, his squadron, nicknamed "the Bat," hadn't been assigned a significant role; yet somehow, now, at the last minute, it had been tasked with Operation Rooster.

Chatto Tzidon's Meteor nightfighter.
Air Force Journal (AF Archive)

Chatto was accustomed to dangerous assignments. A fighter in the Palmach from the age of seventeen, he had served in a naval unit, departing for Europe in mid-1945 as a founder of the Gideons, an underground group of wireless operators that ran the communications network among the Aliya Bet (illegal immigration to pre-state Israel) command in Europe, illegal-immigrant camps, ships at sea and the Aliya Bet headquarters. He had escorted illegal immigrant ships, established a secret wireless station at a detention camp in Cyprus and participated in a sabotage mission against the British vessel *Ocean Vigour,* which was involved in expelling illegal Jewish immigrants. In Cyprus he met a nurse from Israel, Raisa Sharira, whom he made his wife. During the War of Independence, Chatto would command a military convoy to Jerusalem and, at the fighting's conclusion, would enroll in the first pilot-training program in Israel.

As a combat pilot, he had made the transition to jet aircraft, and in 1955 was assigned to train a squadron of "night-fighter all-weather" jets. He called the squadron Zero Visibility.

In the last week of October 1956, Chatto was urgently recalled from

England, where he was completing his training for nighttime dog fights. In Israel, his superiors informed him, in total secrecy, of the upcoming Sinai campaign, or Operation Kadesh. "In a couple of days," they said, "we'll be at war."

On October 28, Chatto was transferred to the Tel Nof airbase, closer to the future theater of war. It was there, at 2:00 P.M., that he was urgently summoned to the IAF headquarters in Ramleh. The air force command dispatched a Piper plane to Tel Nof to bring him immediately, even though the trip from Tel Nof to Ramleh lasted barely twenty minutes by car. The head of the Air Department, Colonel Shlomo Lahat, locked the door of his office and explained the assignment to Chatto.

Lahat spoke succinctly, after swearing Chatto to secrecy. "You know," he said, "that a joint command treaty was recently signed by Egypt, Jordan and Syria. We have learned that the Egyptian and Syrian military chiefs of staff are now conducting talks in Damascus. All the senior staff of the Egyptian Army, Navy and Air Force is participating in the discussions, which are run by Marshal Abdel Hakim Amer, chief of staff of the Egyptian Army.

"Trusted intelligence sources," Lahat added, "report that the Egyptian delegation will return to Cairo tonight on a Soviet-made plane, Ilyushin ll-14.

"Your mission," Lahat told Chatto, "is to bring down the plane."

Chatto understood the tremendous significance of the assignment. If he shot down the plane, the Egyptian armed forces would be left without a military staff and a supreme commander on the eve of a war. The outcome of the entire conflict might hinge on his success.

Lahat expected that the Egyptian plane would choose a flight path far from Israel, outside the range of its fighter planes. He proposed that Chatto take off in his own aircraft and circle above Damascus while he waited for the Egyptian Ilyushin to take flight.

Chatto disagreed. "If they discover my presence, I could get in trouble with their interceptors. Or my fuel tanks could run out before they've even taken off."

Lahat asked what he proposed instead.

Chatto knew that the up-to-the-minute information would be reported by the IDF special units listening to the Egyptian-Syrian communication channel. "Call me half an hour after takeoff," Tzidon said, "when the plane is over the Mediterranean, in range of our radar."

Lahat looked at him in surprise. "Do whatever you think is best," he eventually said.

The Piper jet brought Chatto promptly to Ramat David airbase, where he had parked his Meteor. Shibi Brosh, the navigator, was already there. The pair prepped the plane, even conducting a nighttime test flight. Chatto knew that his principal problem was that the Ilyushin Il-14 was a relatively slow piston aircraft, and that his own Meteor was fast. To hit the Ilyushin, he would need to slow his plane down as much as possible—to landing speed or even less; but at such a speed, his aircraft might stall with its nose upward, and then dive and crash. An idea came to him about how to overcome the problem—by partially lowering the landing flaps, which he practiced midair.

Night fell. The call came several hours after dinner. Chatto, with nerves of steel, had even managed to sleep for about thirty minutes, when, at ten-thirty, he was awakened. The Egyptian plane had taken off from Damascus, he was told, and it had turned toward the sea in a wide arc. It was somewhere at the edge of the Meteor's range of action, advancing toward Egypt at a height of ten thousand feet, or thirty-two hundred meters.

At 10:45, Chatto and Shibi took off into the night. All of Israel was dark; there wasn't a trace of moon in the sky. Chatto had never seen such darkness.

The Meteor advanced through the total blackness, with the cockpit faintly illuminated by infrared light so that the pilot's and navigator's night vision wouldn't be diminished. On the two-way radio, Chatto listened to the flight controllers on the ground, identifying among them the serene, restrained voice of Dan Tolkovsky, the IAF commander.

Then the first glitch occurred: Chatto discovered that the fuel in the detachable tanks wasn't transferring into the main tanks. The plane had taken off with two reserve wing tanks, each containing 350 liters of fuel, and Chatto realized, just like that, that he had lost seven hundred liters. With no other choice, he detached the reserve tanks from the wings and dumped them into the sea. A short time later, he heard Shibi's excited voice on the internal two-way radio: "Contact! Contact! Contact!"

"Contact!" Chatto radioed to the ground controller.

Shibi sent him precise instructions: "Boogie [unidentified plane] at two o'clock! Same altitude, three miles away, straight forward, moving to three o'clock, now moving to four o'clock, taking a hard right. Lower your speed! Pay attention, you're closing in fast!"

Chatto couldn't see a thing, but he followed Shibi's instructions to the letter, not cluing him in to the problem that would arise when he needed to bring his own speed into line with that of the slow transport plane.

"Eleven o'clock," Shibi continued. "Descend five hundred. Lower your speed. Distance: seven hundred feet."

Chatto strained to see. At first, it appeared that he could make out the Egyptian plane's silhouette; then he discerned a "faint, hesitant" flame emitting from the pipes of the piston engines.

"Eye contact," he reported to ground control.

Tolkovsky's voice echoed in his earphones. "I want a confirmed ID of the vessel whose outline you've observed. Confirmed beyond a shadow of a doubt. Understood?" The air force commander wanted to avoid any mistake that might unnecessarily cost human lives.

Chatto was now behind the Egyptian plane. Out of the corner of his eye, he spotted its exhaust pipe and maneuvered left, until he could discern the stronger light of the passenger windows. He approached the Egyptian plane, coming to it "nothing less than wing to wing."

Gradually, the silhouette of the entire plane became perceptible. The shape of the windows in the passenger section resembled those of windows on a Dakota aircraft, but the cockpit windows were bigger, a feature unique to the Ilyushin ll-14. Chatto could also identify the shape of the Ilyushin's tail.

As he approached the windows, he could make out people in military uniforms walking in the aisle between the seats. Those in the seats also appeared to be wearing uniforms. Flying in close to the Ilyushin had cost him at least ten minutes of fuel, but it had been necessary to confirm the initial identification.

"I confirm ID," he radioed to ground control.

"You are authorized to open fire only if you have no doubt whatsoever," Tolkovsky instructed.

The moment had arrived to test the maneuver Chatto had attempted earlier. He lowered the landing flaps by a third, thereby preventing a stall.

"Firing," he announced into the two-way radio, and pressed the trigger.

Two malfunctions immediately occurred. Someone had loaded the cannons with munitions that included tracing bullets, which, for a moment, blinded him. The second glitch was a blockage in the cannon on the right, which brought about the same effect as an engine breakdown. The Meteor went into a spin, but Chatto regained control and steadied it. Although the Ilyushin had been darkened, he hadn't lost it, and he could see a flame that flickered from the left-side engine. He reported the hit.

"Finish it off, at any cost," Tolkovsky's voice commanded. "I repeat: at any cost!" Chatto knew that if the plane wasn't brought down right now, Israel would lose the surprise factor during its attack on Egypt the following day.

The Ilyushin was now flying with one engine, much slower than the Meteor's landing speed. Firing again—with unequal kickback from the cannons, now that one was blocked—would surely throw the Meteor into a spin. Chatto again lowered the landing flaps, increased the power of the engines, and lurched at the Ilyushin. Suddenly another danger materialized: a collision with the Egyptian plane.

Chatto put this fear out of his mind and sped toward the Ilyushin. When he came within fifty meters of it, he heard Shibi shout, "Change course! Change course! We're going to hit it. I see it on both sides of the cockpit."

Shibi's command probably saved them both. At the last second, Chatto squeezed the trigger and suddenly found himself "in the midst of hellfire."

His shells exploded into the Ilyushin, barely a few feet from the muzzle of the Meteor's cannon. Fire engulfed the Egyptian plane, shooting across it at the same instant that an explosion transformed it into a fireball. Flaming parts flew past the Meteor. The burning Egyptian plane spun and dived—and, because of uneven kickback from its own blocked cannon, so did the Meteor. Both planes plunged. "A fireball and a darkened plane spun one beside the other, and one above the other," Chatto later wrote, "both out of control, as if performing a sickening, surreal dance."

At the last moment, Chatto was able to exit the spin, at an altitude estimated at between 150 and three hundred meters. Simultaneously, he saw the Ilyushin smash and explode into the waves of the Mediterranean.

Chatto climbed to fifteen thousand feet and reported, "Accomplished!"

Tolkovsky wanted to be sure. "You saw it crash?"

"Affirmative. It crashed." Chatto then looked at the fuel gauge and was horrified. "I'm low on fuel—very low. Give me directions to the closest base."

He had no idea where he was. The sole radar that located the Meteor was an aircraft battery device on the Hatzor airbase. The battery's commander took it upon himself to direct "the Bat" to the landing strip.

"I'll fly in this direction as long as I have fuel," Chatto radioed.

"You think you can make it?" The controller's voice sounded dubious.

Chatto attempted to keep things light. "I poured the fluid from Shibi's cigarette lighter into the fuel tank."

Tolkovsky cut him off: "No names!"

The fuel gauge dropped to zero. One minute, two minutes, three . . . Suddenly, Chatto could make out the lights of the Hatzor runway, which had been illuminated for him despite the blackout. The plane glided toward the landing strip, and Chatto touched down.

As the plane barreled down the runway, the engines shut off, one after the other. The final drops of fuel had run out, but the Meteor was on the ground.

The base's whiz technician reached the plane first. "You did it?" he asked.

"Yes."

"So the war has started."

Ezer Weizman, the base commander and a nephew of Israel's first president, arrived immediately.

"Congrats!" Never one to miss a chance to show off, he went on, "Notice, it was only Hatzor that could bring you in." He added, "They're waiting for you at headquarters. There's a problem."

At headquarters, Lahat, Tolkovsky, and Chief of Staff Moshe Dayan were waiting for Chatto and Shibi. They shook hands.

"What's the problem?" Chatto inquired.

"At the last minute, Amer decided not to fly on the Ilyushin. He's going to take off later, on a Dakota."

The spirit of battle overcame Chatto. "If there's time, we'll refuel and go out on a second run," he offered, and Shibi nodded in agreement.

"It would be too obvious and would expose intelligence sources," Dayan said. "Let's leave him be. The moment you wiped out the general staff, you won half the war. Let's drink to the other half."

Dayan pulled out a bottle of wine, and everyone toasted.

The 1956 War had thus begun, yet only a handful Israelis knew.

Operation Rooster would remain top-secret for thirty-three years, with details reaching the public only in 1989. The Egyptians never reported the downing of the aircraft, probably because they weren't aware that it had been targeted; in Cairo, rumors spread that the plane had crashed close to a desert island, and that the army senior staff was still there, awaiting rescue.

Marshal Amer, the Egyptian chief of staff at the time, would commit suicide after the Six Day War.

YOASH ("CHATTO") TZIDON, COMBAT PILOT

In March 1993, four years after details of Operation Rooster were released, a young Egyptian unexpectedly reached out to Chatto Tzidon. He was Ahmed Jaffar Nassim, the son of an adviser to President Nasser, who had died during Chatto's operation. The dramatic meeting between the son and the man who had killed his father took place at the Tel Aviv Hilton.

The meeting, Chatto later said, was "emotional but without bitterness." Jaffar, a disabled man in a wheelchair, wanted to know if it was true that his father had fallen into Israeli captivity and been tortured to death after his plane made a forced landing. Chatto clarified that there had been no forced landing, that the operation had been one of "door-to-door service."

Two years later, Chatto helped Jaffar Nassim gain admission for surgery at Rambam Hospital, in Haifa. "The desire to aid him came out of a feeling of sharing in his sorrow over his father's death . . . as well as the thought that my own son could have found himself in a similar situation."

This was just one way in which Chatto showed an unusual streak of sensitivity toward others. His spouse, Raisa, recalls how on the eve of the 1956 War, at a dinner at the home of friends in London, Chatto met the sister of the hostess, an Auschwitz survivor. She was on her way to Israel and remarked "how much she would have liked to see Paris."

"Why don't you stop on your way?" Chatto asked. The woman replied, "I have a one-year-old baby. I can't."

Chatto had a solution: "I'll take the baby to Israel."

And, just like that, he took responsibility for the little girl, caring for and feeding her on the plane. When they stopped in Rome for a layover, he selected an excellent hotel, entrusting the baby to the hotel matron. The next day, he flew on with the infant to Israel. His wife was waiting for him at the airfield. and when she saw a man in a tweed suit with a baby in his arms, didn't recognize him.

"How did you end up responsible for a baby?" Raisa asked.

He looked at her in surprise. "Her mother had never seen Paris," he said.

In October 1956, while the Soviet Union is involved
in revolts in Warsaw and Budapest against its dictatorship,
and the U.S. is in the final stage of its presidential campaign—
Dwight Eisenhower is running for a second term—Israel attacks
Egypt and achieves a dramatic victory that makes Moshe Dayan
a legendary hero. The British and the French, however,
fail in their campaign to occupy the Suez Canal.

CHAPTER 5
KADESH, 1956

On Monday, October 29, 1956, at 4:59 P.M., Major Rafael ("Raful") Eitan jumped from a Dakota plane in Western Sinai and kicked off the Kadesh mission.

Three hundred ninety-four paratroopers jumped after him from sixteen aircraft. They had been preceded, two hours earlier, by two Mustang aircraft that had torn surface phone lines over Sinai with their propellers and wings, in order to disrupt the Egyptian communications systems.

In Tel Aviv, Chief of Staff Moshe Dayan dispatched an official communique to Kol Israel radio:

"The IDF spokesman announces that IDF forces entered and attacked Fedayeen units at Ras el Nakeb and Kuntila and took positions in proximity to the Suez Canal."

The paratroopers' drop, close to the Suez Canal, deep in Egyptian territory, was the opening shot of the Sinai campaign and the conclusion of a top-secret political operation with Ben-Gurion, Dayan and Peres as the main players.

In September 1955, Israel had suffered a painful blow when the Soviet Union, using Czechoslovakia as a proxy, concluded a huge arms deal with Egypt. The USSR was going to supply Egypt with about 200 MiG-15 jet fighters and Ilyushin ll-28 bombers, and training and cargo planes; 230 tanks; 200 armored troop carriers; 600 cannons; and various naval vessels—torpedo boats, destroyers and 6 submarines. The weapons Egypt was about to receive were of unprecedented quality and quantity. With them, the balance of power in the Middle East could collapse, and Israel risked losing its deterrent power, the guarantee for its existence. Another reason for worry was the establishment of a joint Egyptian-Syrian military command.

A wave of anxiety swept Israel. She had only thirty jet fighters. The numbers of her tanks, troop carriers and cannons were ridiculous when compared to what Egypt was about to receive. Distraught Israelis spontaneously donated money, jewelry and property deeds to a "defense fund" created for the purchase of weapons. Fiery Ben-Gurion wanted to launch an attack on Egypt immediately. Foreign Minister Moshe Sharett, however, dovish and moderate, defeated his motion in a cabinet vote. A few months later, Ben-Gurion hit back by removing Sharett from the cabinet and appointing a new foreign minister— hawkish Golda Meir.

In the meantime, Shimon Peres invested tremendous effort in establishing an alliance between France and Israel. And in spite of the criticism, even the mockery, in government circles at home, his efforts in France bore fruit: he succeeded in obtaining large quantities of weapons and in establishing relations of trust and friendship with French cabinet ministers, army officers and members of parliament. In June 1956, Israel signed the Ge'ut ("High Tide") deal with France for a massive supply of weapons to Israel.

A month later, in a surprise move, Egyptian president Nasser nationalized the Suez Canal. France and Great Britain, the main holders of Suez Canal stock, immediately started planning a military operation against Egypt, to bring the canal back under their power. French and British generals debated successive invasion plans in a World War

II bunker under the Thames. Soon the French leaders realized that the British wouldn't attack Egypt without a solid pretext. Therefore, they turned to Israel.

The paratroopers were dropped close to the Suez Canal.
(Abraham Vered, GPO)

Shortly before sunset on October 22, 1956, several cars stopped by a secluded villa in Sevres, a Parisian suburb. The passengers furtively slipped into the house gates. These were French Prime Minister Guy Mollet, Foreign Minister Christian Pineau, Defense Minister Maurice Bourgès-Maunoury, the army chief of staff, and several high-ranking generals. Their secret guests, who had arrived by special plane, were Israeli Prime Minister Ben-Gurion, hiding his distinctive shock of white hair under a wide-brimmed hat; General Moshe Dayan, concealing his black eye patch under large sunglasses; and Shimon Peres. The two delegations met in a cordial atmosphere. Later in the evening, though, they were joined by British Foreign Secretary Selwyn Lloyd.

With Lloyd's arrival, a cold wind seemed to penetrate the villa. The British foreign secretary apparently couldn't forget that only eight years before, Britain was still the ruler of Palestine and Ben-Gurion was its most formidable opponent. "Britain's Foreign Secretary may well have been a friendly man, pleasant, charming, amiable," Dayan wrote. "If so, he showed near-genius in concealing these virtues. His whole demeanor expressed distaste—for the place, the company and the topic."

But Lloyd was there—and the most secret summit after World War II was under way.

After a first round of talks that continued into the night, Lloyd left to report to British Prime Minister Anthony Eden. "It seems that Lloyd didn't fall in love with Ben-Gurion," Peres noted that night, "but there is no doubt at all that this feeling was mutual from the moment they met."

The conference continued the following day. Several ideas about an action that could justify an Anglo-French intervention were discussed. The various ploys were rejected, one after the other. The French and the British suggested that Israel attack Egypt, conquer the Sinai Peninsula and create a threat to the Suez Canal; France and Great Britain would then intervene to "protect" the canal from the fighting forces.

But Ben-Gurion refused to launch an all-out war against Egypt, just to provide France and Britain with a pretext; he also feared that Israel would have to carry the brunt of such a war on her frail shoulders for several days, perhaps a week, until the Franco-British invasion started.

The following day, while the French and the Israelis were having lunch, General Maurice Challe, the French deputy chief of staff, asked to speak. He suggested that the Israeli Air Force stage an attack on Be'er Sheva and bomb the city. Egypt would be accused, and the Anglo-French forces would intervene immediately. Ben-Gurion, his face flushed with fury, jumped from his seat. "Israel is strong because she fights for a just cause," he said. "I shall not lie, either to the world public opinion or to anybody else." In the sepulchral silence that settled over the room Challe sat down, his face red with embarrassment. The others buried their noses in their plates. The conference seemed about to collapse.

And then Moshe Dayan conceived the magical formula.

Dayan, born in kibbutz Degania, raised in the cooperative village of Nahalal, was a charismatic Israeli hero. A member of the Haganah—the

Jewish defense organization under the British mandate—he had grown up among Nahalal's Arab neighbors, knew them well and respected them. In War World II he had participated in a British patrol operating against the French Vichy forces in Lebanon. An enemy sniper's bullet shattered his binoculars, driving the eye piece into his left eye socket. The eye was lost but the pirate patch that replaced it made the face of Dayan famous all over Israel and later the world. A gifted orator, a lover of poetry, an amateur archaeologist and a womanizer, he also was a fearless warrior. As chief of staff he transformed the IDF into a lean, tough force and commanded the reprisal raids against Israel's restive enemies. Yet, he soon realized that reprisals could not solve the growing tension between Israel and her neighbors, especially Egypt. He supported the idea of attacking Egypt before it mastered the massive influx of arms from the Soviet bloc and was a willing participant in the Sevres conference.

Ben-Gurion, however, kept refusing to launch an all-out war against Egypt. So how to start a war without starting a war? At that crucial moment, when the entire conference depended on a solution to the pretext dilemma, Dayan came up with a plan.

Let's start the war from the end, Dayan said. He suggested parachuting a small Israeli force into the Sinai, about thirty miles east of the Suez Canal, creating an apparent threat on the waterway. France and Great Britain would declare the canal in danger and dispatch ultimata to Egypt and Israel to retreat to new lines, ten miles on each side of the canal. That meant that Egypt would be asked to evacuate the entire Sinai Peninsula, allowing Israel to conquer it and reach the vicinity of the canal. Israel would accept the ultimatum, while Egypt would certainly reject it. That would be the pretext for the French and the British to launch their military operation against Egypt thirty-six hours after the Israelis.

Ben-Gurion hesitated, but after a sleepless night accepted Dayan's plan. When meeting with Dayan and Peres in the villa garden the following morning, he asked Dayan to draw the projected campaign for him. Nobody had any paper, so Peres tore his cigarette pack, and Dayan sketched on it the Sinai Peninsula; a dotted line represented the flight of the planes that would drop the paratroopers, and three arrows showed the main axes of the subsequent Israeli offensive. Ben-Gurion, Dayan and Peres signed, laughing, the small piece of cardboard, and it became the first map of the Sinai campaign.

Back in the villa, Dayan's plan was unanimously adopted and on October 24 a secret agreement was signed among France, Great Britain and Israel. On his return to Tel Aviv Ben-Gurion called a cabinet meeting. He didn't tell the ministers about his trip to France or the agreement they had made, a copy of which he carried in his breast pocket. Yet, he obtained the cabinet consent for an operation against Egypt. As always when in a state of utter tension, Ben-Gurion fell sick with high fever. But that night Menachem Begin, Ben-Gurion's staunch rival, was invited to Ben-Gurion's home for the first time in his life. While Begin sat on a stool beside Ben-Gurion's cot, the Old Man described the decision to go to war, and Begin congratulated him warmly.

On October 29, Raful Eitan and his paratroopers jumped deep behind enemy lines, reached their destination and dug in for the night. In the wee hours, Israeli aircraft parachuted jeeps, recoilless guns and heavy mortars.

While Raful's men were still in the air, Arik Sharon crossed the Egyptian border with the paratrooper brigade, riding armored troop carriers and reinforced by AMX tanks. The column advanced through Sinai, conquering several Egyptian fortresses in fierce battles and after thirty hours approached Raful's compound.

While waiting for Arik, Raful jokingly prepared a cardboard sign: STOP! FRONTIER AHEAD! Shortly after 10:00 P.M., on October 30, the armored column reached the sign. Davidi and Sharon, covered with fine desert dust, jumped from their jeeps and hugged Raful. The mission was accomplished.

Or so it seemed. Sharon had other thoughts. In the last two years he had turned the paratrooper corps into an elite commando unit that had carried out most of the reprisal raids against Israel's neighbors. The

price had been heavy—many of the best fighters had been killed and
Meir Har-Zion himself had almost died during the al Rahwa raid in
September 1956. A bullet had blasted his throat and he was choking to
death when the unit doctor, Maurice Ankelevitz, drew a pocketknife,
stuck it in his windpipe, performing an improvised tracheotomy under
fire, and saved his life.

Yet, in spite of the wounded and the dead, the paratrooper corps was
submerged by a wave of volunteers, most of them members of kibbutz
and moshav agricultural settlements. The battalion became a brigade.
Sharon, now a lieutenant colonel, had become the best fighter in the
IDF. Dayan liked him and Ben-Gurion admired his fighting skills, even
though he criticized his integrity. On October 30, 1956, Sharon was, as
always, hungry for battle.

He had barely finished hugging Raful when he decided to conquer
the famous Mitla Pass—a winding canyon road in the nearby mountain
ridge—and be the first to reach the canal with his paratroopers.

The pass seemed to be empty of enemy forces. The day before, an armored convoy coming from Egypt had crossed the canal and penetrated
the pass, but Israeli jets had attacked and destroyed it completely. The black
carcasses of the burned vehicles still smoked all along the Mitla road.

Sharon sent a radio message, asking permission to take the Mitla
Pass. But the General Staff radioed him a clear order: "Don't advance,
stay where you are." Sharon, Raful and the other commanders didn't
know that the goal of the paratroopers' drop at the Mitla approaches
was not fighting or conquering, but to serve as a pretext for the Anglo-
French intervention.

In the early morning another message arrived from the staff: "Do
not advance!" But Arik did not give up. At 11:00 A.M. Colonel Rehavam
("Gandhi") Ze'evi, the Southern Command chief of staff, arrived at the
compound in a light Piper Cub plane. Arik again requested permission
to enter Mitla, but Gandhi allowed him only to send a patrol to the pass,
on the condition that he wouldn't get entangled in fighting.

Arik immediately assembled a "patrol team" under the command
of Motta Gur. At the head of the column Arik placed six half-tracks;

behind them the half-track of the tanks force commander Zvi Dahab and Danny Matt; then three tanks; then the brigade deputy commander, Haka Hofi's, half-track; six more half-tracks full of paratroopers; a battery of heavy 120-millimeter mortars; and several equipment-carrying trucks. The paratrooper commando joined the column not as fighters but as tourists who came to enjoy the trip to the canal. Davidi made a funny hat out of a newspaper, to protect himself from the sun.

And Arik called all this battalion-sized convoy a "patrol."

At 12:30 P.M. the convoy entered the pass. They quickly advanced in the narrow canyon, between two towering mounts.

And there the Egyptians were waiting.

H undreds of Egyptian soldiers were entrenched in dugouts, natural caves in the rock and behind low stone fences. On the roadside, camouflaged by bushes and bales of thorns, stood armored cars carrying Bren machine guns. Companies of soldiers were positioned above them, armed with bazookas, recoilless guns, anti-tank guns and mid-sized machine guns. And on a third line above, in positions and cubbyholes in the rock, lay soldiers armed with rifles and automatic weapons.

At twelve-fifty, the half-tracks advancing in the pass were hit by a lethal volley of bullets and shells. A hail of bullets drummed on the half-tracks' armored plates. The first half-track swayed to and fro and stopped, its commander and driver dead; the other soldiers, some of them wounded, jumped off the vehicle and tried to find cover.

Motta Gur's half-track was about 150 yards behind. He ordered his men to advance toward the damaged vehicle. Three half-tracks reached the immobile vehicle and were hit too. Motta got around them and tried to escape the ambush, but he was hit as well. He and his men sought refuge in a shallow ditch beside the road.

Haka, who was in the middle of the column, realized that his men had blundered into a deadly ambush. He ordered Davidi to get back and stop the vehicles that had not entered the pass yet. Davidi unloaded the mortars and opened fire on the hills. Haka himself broke through the enemy lines with a company and two tanks. The armored vehicles bypassed the stuck half-tracks and emerged on the other side of the pass, two kilometers down the road.

Mitla, full of burned, smoldering vehicles from the Egyptian convoy from the day before, now became a killing field for the paratroopers. Four Egyptian Meteor jets dived toward the column, blew up eight trucks carrying fuel and ammunition, and hit several heavy mortars.

Motta sent an urgent message to Haka, asking him to come back into the pass and rescue the trapped soldiers. He also requested from Davidi that Micha Kapusta's commando should attack the Egyptian positions from behind.

Micha's commando—the finest paratrooper unit—climbed to the tops of the hills. His platoon commanders started moving down the northern slope, annihilating the Egyptian positions. But at this point a terrible misunderstanding occurred.

The commando fighters that destroyed the enemy positions on the northern slope clearly saw the road. They didn't notice that the slope turned to a sheer drop almost at their feet, and most of the Egyptians were entrenched there. They also failed to notice other Egyptian positions that were located on the southern slope, across the road.

Suddenly, Micha's men were hit by a hail of bullets and missiles from the southern slope. Micha thought that the trapped paratroopers by the road were firing at him. Furious, he yelled at Davidi on his radio to make Motta's people stop firing, while Motta, who couldn't see the enemy positions on the southern slope that were firing at the commando, did not understand why Micha didn't continue his advance.

These were tragic moments. "Go! Attack!" Davidi yelled at Micha, while Micha saw his men falling. The paratroopers dashed forward under heavy fire. Some reached the edge of the rocky drop without noticing it and rolled down, in full sight of the Egyptians, who shot them.

Facing heavy fire, Micha decided to retreat to a nearby hill. But another Israeli company appeared on top of that hill and mistakenly started firing on Micha's men. Micha's fury and pain echoed in the walkie-talkies. His soldiers were fired at from all sides, by Egyptians and by Israelis.

At last Davidi understood the mix-up that had caused Motta's and Micha's contradictory reports. He made a fateful decision: send a jeep that would attract the enemy fire into the pass. Davidi's observers would then locate the sources of the Egyptian fire.

For that mission he needed a volunteer who would be ready to sacrifice his life.

"Who volunteers to get to Motta?" he asked.

Several men jumped right away. Davidi chose Ken-Dror, his own driver.

Ken-Dror knew he was going to his death. He started the jeep and sped to the pass, immediately becoming the target of heavy fire. The jeep was crushed and Ken-Dror collapsed beside it. His sacrifice was in vain. Motta and Micha didn't succeed in pinpointing the sources of enemy fire.

Davidi sent a half-track with four soldiers and a lieutenant to the pass. The carrier reached Motta, loaded some wounded soldiers and returned, unharmed.

And the sources of the shooting still were not discovered.

Davidi again ordered Micha to storm the Egyptian positions. His soldiers ran again down the slope. Another platoon was hit by crossfire from the southern hill. And Micha suddenly saw the abrupt drop at his feet and understood where the Egyptian positions were.

At that moment he was shot. A bullet pierced his chest, he lost his breath and he felt he was going to die.

"Dovik!" he shouted at his deputy. "Take over!"

A bullet hit Dovik in the head. The two wounded men started crawling up the hill. In front of them they saw other paratroopers. They feared their comrades would shoot them by mistake. "Davidi! Davidi" they shouted hoarsely.

At 5:00 P.M. a rumble of tanks suddenly echoed in the narrow canyon. Haka's two tanks returned from the western exit of the pass and turned the tide. They first set their guns toward the southern hill and blasted many of the enemy positions. Egyptian soldiers started fleeing in a disorderly way but were mown down by the paratroopers' machine guns. Simultaneously, two paratrooper companies reached the crests of the two ridges rising on both sides of the road. They came from the western entrance to the pass and systematically mopped up the Egyptian positions. They agreed that their finishing line would be a burning Egyptian half-track in the center of the canyon. Other fighters would come from the east and destroy the remaining enemy positions on the northern and southern hills.

At nightfall fifty paratroopers scaled the hills—half of them, commanded by a twice-decorated veteran, Oved Ladijanski, turned to the southern ridge; the other half, under the leadership of a slim and soft-spoken kibbutz member, Levi Hofesh, attacked the northern one. Their goal was to reach the burning half-track with no Egyptian soldier left behind.

Oved's unit moved up the hill in silence, holding their fire. They reached a fortified machine gun position, hewn in the rocky slope. They attacked it from below with hand grenades, but some of those bounced off the rock and exploded. Oved threw a grenade toward the machine gun, but the grenade rolled down. "It's coming back," Oved whispered to the soldier beside him, pushed him aside and covered him with his body. The grenade exploded against Oved's chest and killed him. One of his comrades succeeded in dropping a grenade into the position, burst in and killed the Egyptians cowering inside.

The survivors of Oved's unit kept advancing and destroying the enemy positions. Levi Hofesh did the same on the northern hill. He realized that the Egyptians had placed their forces in three tiers, one above the other. He divided his soldiers in three detachments, and each mopped up one of the enemy lines. The fighting was desperate; the trapped Egyptians had nothing to lose. It took the paratroopers two hours to advance three hundred yards. Shortly before 8:00 P.M., Levi completed his operation, leaving behind ninety Egyptian dead.

The paratroopers now were the masters of the Mitla Pass. During the night, cargo planes landed nearby and evacuated the wounded—Dovik and Micha, Danny Matt and another 120 paratroopers. Among the seriously wounded was also Yehuda Ken Dror, hanging to life by a thread. In a few months he would succumb to his wounds.

Thirty-eight paratroopers and two hundred Egyptian soldiers died in the Mitla battle. Four more Israelis would die later of their wounds. Dayan seethed with fury, accusing Sharon of losing so many lives in a totally unnecessary battle. Ben-Gurion, alerted, refused to interfere in a row between two senior officers whom he especially liked. But the Mitla battle actually sent Sharon to an informal exile and delayed his advancement in the IDF by several years.

The Mitla battle was gratuitous, indeed. Yet it was a bravely fought battle, in which Sharon's paratroopers demonstrated his principles that one doesn't abandon comrades on the battlefield, even if it costs human lives, and an IDF team doesn't bend, doesn't give up and doesn't retreat until the mission is achieved.

The Sinai campaign lasted seven days and ended with an Israeli victory. Israel had beaten the Egyptian Army and conquered all of the Sinai Peninsula. The Franco-British invasion, on the other hand, failed miserably. The Israeli triumph marked the beginning of eleven years of de facto peace on the southern border that would abruptly end with the Six Day War.

RAFAEL "RAFUL" EITAN, COMMANDER OF THE 890TH PARATROOP BATTALION AND LATER THE CHIEF OF STAFF

[From an excerpt from his book, A Soldier's Story: The Life and Times of an Israeli War Hero, written with Dov Goldstein, Maariv, 1985]

"I was standing closest to the aircraft door. A bit of excitement always hits you over the parachuting site, even if you've done it many times before. All the more so at the start of a large-scale military campaign, at such a distance from Israel. You're plunging into the unknown, into enemy territory. The cockpit of the next plane in the formation was directly across from me, mere feet away. I waved to the copilot. He held his head in both hands, as if to say, 'What you're about to do . . .'

"Red light. Green light. I'm in the air, floating down, over the Mitla crossroads. It's five in the afternoon, dusk. The sun

is setting. You can hear a few shots. My feet hit the ground. I
release myself from my parachute, get organized quickly. We
take our weapons out of their cases. We hold positions in the
staging territory. The companies spread out. It's already dark.
We put barriers into place. We lay mines. We dig in, hole up.
There are trenches there from the days of the Turks. This makes
our work easier. Our two forces take positions at the Parker
Memorial, to the west, and en route to Bir Hasna, to the north.
We mark the ground intended for receiving the supplies being
parachuted in.

"At night I went to sleep. . . . One must muster his forces
before experiencing the pressure of combat. One must remove
the stress and the emotions to a secluded corner. I dug myself
a foxhole, padded it with the cardboard from the parachuted
supplies, spread down one or two parachutes, and tucked myself
in. Good night by the Mitla."

PART THREE

The Six
Day War

The Suez campaign brings Israel almost eleven years
of peace. In 1963, Ben-Gurion resigns and is replaced by
Levi Eshkol. The chief of staff is Yitzhak Rabin. Ben-Gurion,
Dayan and Peres are the leaders of a small party, Rafi, created
after a violent clash between Ben-Gurion and Eshkol.
On May 15, 1967, Egypt's President Nasser suddenly triggers
a sequence of military moves that threaten Israel with
annihilation: he announces that the end of Israel is near.
Israel's efforts to obtain the support of the Great Powers
end in failure. France switches camps; President De Gaulle,
Israel's great ally, unexpectedly imposes an embargo on
weapons for Israel. Under popular pressure Eshkol
reluctantly appoints Moshe Dayan as defense minister in
a Government of National Unity in which opposition leader
Menachem Begin is minister without portfolio. Israel feels
it has no choice but to attack Egypt before it,
itself, is attacked and invaded.

CHAPTER 6
"LIFE OR DEATH,"
OPERATION FOCUS,
1967

June 5, 1967

At four-thirty in the morning, every pilot in the Israeli Air Force was awakened. Their planes stood ready for takeoff, fueled and armed, at the Ramat David, Hatzor, Tel Nof and Hatzerim airbases, and even at the civilian airport in Lod. In their cockpits, the pilots, barred from operating their communications systems, maintained complete radio silence; the control towers had also gone quiet. It was forbidden that anyone, anywhere, might receive even a hint of the massive takeoff. The ground crews directed the planes using signals from colored lanterns. At seven-fourteen, the first planes, French antiquated Ouragans, took flight, followed two minutes later by another takeoff of Ouragans. After they roared into the morning skies, in accordance with a timetable calculated down to the last minute, Vautours, Mystères, Super Mystères and Mirages took flight. The planes took off at a frenzied pace, from several bases, at a frequency of a plane per minute; at the Hatzor airbase, seventy-seven planes took off between seven-fourteen and eight-fifteen, an average of one every forty-eight seconds. Very quickly, there were 183 planes in the sky—in fact, Israel's entire air force. They entered formations of four and set forth, each on its own flight path. Twelve Mirages were left to guard the skies over Israel.

The planes' takeoff was the opening act of the Six Day War.

T he descent into war had begun three weeks earlier, on Israel's Independence Day, May 15. Divisions of the Egyptian Army had unexpectedly thundered into the Sinai Peninsula, stationing themselves along the Israel border. Egypt's president, Gamal Abdel Nasser, expelled the UN observers from Sinai, closed the Straits of Tiran and signed military agreements with Syria and Jordan. Even Iraq announced it was joining in. The Arab street reacted with tremendous excitement, the masses dancing in the squares, waving flags and posters, and screaming slogans of rage and hatred against Israel. Nasser's image appeared across the media, smiling and confident, surrounded by Egyptian fighter pilots, young eagles clad in their G-suits, at the Bir Gifgafa airbase. Turning to the television cameras, Nasser made his historic statement, "If Israel wants war, *ahlan wa sahlan*—welcome!"

Radio and television across the Arab world reported Israel's imminent demise. Britain and the United States couldn't find a way to solve the crisis and reopen the Straits of Tiran to Israeli shipping. The president of France, Charles de Gaulle, abandoned his alliance with Israel and imposed an embargo on the delivery of arms to the IDF.

The people of Israel sensed the danger of extermination hovering overhead. Prime Minister Levi Eshkol and his government appeared hesitant, afflicted with paralysis and trying to buy time. The public forced the leadership to establish a unity government, in which Moshe Dayan, the celebrated hero of the Sinai campaign, was appointed defense minister.

On June 4, the government decided to go to war. The first step would be the air force's Operation Focus, and victory in the war would depend on its success.

Operation Focus had been designed to wipe out the Egyptian Air Force—or, if needed, all enemy air forces—on the ground. Rafi Sivron, a young captain, had prepared the original plan, which rested on a surprise attack on the enemy's airfields, the bombing of the runways to prevent landings and takeoffs, and the destruction of planes on the ground. In 1965, Sivron had been taken on by Major Yossi Sarig, a former commander of the 110 Squadron's Vautour planes, who had been appointed the head of the Attack Section within the Operations Department. The new role fit Sarig like a glove. He had previously carried out dozens of daring photo-surveillance missions, both during the day and at night, over almost every Arab airfield in Egypt, Jordan, Syria and Lebanon. He knew the fields like the back of his hand. In light of the drastic changes that had occurred in the Middle East and within the region's air forces, Sarig immersed himself in the detailed, constantly changing plan for the operation.The surprise factor would be an essential condition of the plan's success. The attack planes would need to strike the Egyptian airfields suddenly and at precisely the same moment. Consequently, they would need to take off and fly in complete radio silence, at the lowest possible altitude—below the zone covered by radar—and to reach their targets at exactly the same time. Most of the flights would need to be carried out over the Mediterranean Sea in order to reach Egypt from the north. Others, directed at the most remote airfields, would fly over Israel's Negev Desert and the Red Sea. It was necessary to lay out precise flight paths and timetables, and endless drills were conducted involving takeoffs and flights at an altitude of up to one hundred feet above sea level.

To carry out its plan, the air force would need 530 attack planes, even though it possessed just two hundred. The solution, it turned out, was born out of a remark made by David Ben-Gurion during a visit to the Ramat David airbase, when he asked the base commander, "How long does it take you to prepare a plane that has just returned for another mission?"

That vital period of time—for refueling from tankers, bringing in ammunition trucks and more—was between an hour and an hour and a half. Ben-Gurion's remark was a wake-up call for the air force staff, who decided to shorten drastically each plane's prep time before its next flight. Fueling pipelines and hoses were laid to the underground hangars where the planes were parked so that they could be refilled the moment they arrived. In each hangar, a load of munitions and bombs for one or two missions was kept at the ready, and the moment it was placed on the plane, another load was sent to the site for the next flight. Ground crews were trained to perform all the preparations and checks in record time. Their commanders stood next to the planes with stopwatches, assessing ways to cut additional minutes and seconds. Contests began among the squadrons' air crews and even among the different bases.

Each fighter plane's prep time was shortened to between five and seven minutes; as a result, the air force's power increased several times over, as the number of planes was multiplied by the number of additional missions they could now carry out. And, as the Arab Air Forces' planes spent longer periods on the ground between flights, it was possible for Israel's Air Force to launch several offensive waves with a much smaller number of aircraft.

The bombing of the airfields was now planned. At some, the runways had been paved with concrete, and with asphalt at others. Each type of runway required a different weapon. The air force had bombs weighing 110, 154, 551 and 1,102 pounds, and needed to match the types of explosives and attack planes with the airfields. Some airfields had just one runway, but Egypt's MiGs could also take off from the taxiway that ran parallel to it; it would be necessary to hit that strip as well. At other airfields, the runways intersected. Several had runways that were more than 1.85 miles long, even though the MiGs needed only a third of that distance; in those cases, it would be necessary to divide the runway into thirds and hit each part with precision strikes.

The research lab at Israel Military Industries (IMI), under the management of the engineer Avraham Makov, had overseen the development of the anti-runway penetration bomb, which would be dropped from roughly 330 feet overhead. A tiny parachute would immediately eject, directing the nose of the bomb at a sixty-degree angle toward the ground; simultaneously, a retro-rocket in its tail would activate, propelling it with great force toward the runway. The 154-pound bomb would penetrate the concrete runway and explode six seconds later, leaving a crater nearly five feet deep and more than sixteen feet in diameter. IMI had also developed a large anti-runway penetration bomb of even greater strength and, by the start of the war, had supplied the air force with sixty-six of the larger model and 187 of the smaller.

The question was how to bomb the runways. Would a plane carrying two bombs drop both during the same pass or would it need to carry out another pass? What should be done in the event of strong winds? What were the chances of strong winds in the morning? And how much damage would the bombs cause the runways?

In order to check, it was decided that the IAF would bomb Israel's Hatzor airbase. At the time, the runway had been taken out of service for repairs. The crews' families were evacuated, and at night IAF planes dived over Hatzor and bombed the runway. After the results were assessed, the air force also calculated how long it would take the Egyptians to plug the holes in their runways and restore the fields that had been bombed. The estimate was roughly forty minutes, starting from the moment the Egyptian base commander took a jeep, went to check the damage and ordered the holes filled in. But the air force wanted the repairs to last two hours and then for the second wave of planes to bomb the field again.

The solution: bombs with timed fuses that could lodge at a great depth without blowing up. The Egyptian commander would surely order that the craters be covered over, and after a predetermined amount of time, the buried bombs would explode, causing damage that would again paralyze the field. It was agreed that any formation going out on a bombing mission would have a bomb or two with a delay mechanism.

And how could Israel be defended while all its planes were in Egypt? Air Force Commander Mordechai ("Motti") Hod took a tremendous risk by placing Israel in the care of ten to twelve Mirages. The air force also decided that several Mirage formations would attack enemy airfields close to Israel so that they could return immediately and defend the country as needed.

The final question: when to attack? Some commanders preferred last light before sunset, knowing that the Egyptians didn't fly at night. But intelligence reported that Egyptian Air Force preparedness focused on first light: the pilots got up early, went out on reconnaissance missions and landed at their bases around 7:30 A.M. (6:30 A.M. Israeli time). Then they would go to drink coffee and eat breakfast. At the same time, the base commanders and General Staff officers were on their way to their offices. Hod himself explained, "When I go from my house in Tzahala to headquarters at seven forty-five A.M. and they tell me on my Motorola that there's a problem, I can't do anything."

The decision was made: the attack would be at 7:45 in the morning.

The plan was rehearsed endlessly. Everything was prepared, but no war appeared on the horizon—until, on May 15, 1967, everything changed.

Sarig had completed his role and departed for the United States to receive Skyhawk aircraft for a new squadron. But ten days later he received an urgent call telling him to come back to Israel immediately. He was driven straight from Lod airport to the so-called "Pit," the underground operational command post at IDF headquarters in Tel Aviv, where he reclaimed his former position and started receiving updates. Intelligence reported that the Egyptian Air Force was changing alert levels and its Tupolev Tu-16 bombers departed for more distant airfields, such as Luxor and Ras Banas.

Hod, Sarig and Ezer Weizman, the IDF's deputy chief of staff and a former commander of the IAF, appeared at a General Staff forum, and Sarig presented Operation Focus. General Herzel Shafir asked, "And what about Syria and Jordan?"

Sarig replied, "Three hours later, we'll carry out Focus in Syria and Jordan, too."

General Yitzhak Hofi interjected, "Look at these air force guys. Ezer Weizman and Motti Hod are bragging, as usual, but now a major is talking this way, too?"

On the night of June 4, final briefings were conducted with the base commanders. The order issued to the pilots was to maintain complete radio silence: "Even if there's a problem with your engine, if you need to come back or even abandon your plane, don't turn on your communications system." The pilots were permitted only the use of a watch, a compass and a map and could have no other aid on hand to help lead them to their targets in Egypt. They were allocated five to seven minutes to bomb the runways and to carry out three more passes over the airfields, to strafe planes and other targets in the area.

The pilots were sent to bed early so that they would be fresh by morning. Many couldn't get to sleep. At stake was a tremendous operation whose goal was the destruction of the entire Egyptian Air Force. The outcome of the war, and even the existence of Israel, depended on it.

One of the pilots, Yair Neuman, wrote in his squadron's log, "June 5, 1967. A day before the great fall of Egypt and its satellites. My hand is shaking!" (Neuman was killed on the first day of the war.) Another pilot wrote, "We felt as though the fate of the entire people of Israel were placed on our shoulders." Another penned, "The eyes of all the world's Jews are on us, in deep anxiety," and his friend added, "God is with the Jews—the burning bush and the burning tanks are in Sinai."

At seven-fourteen, the first plane rocketed skyward, followed by 182 more.

Radio silence was maintained, but to keep the Egyptians from suspecting that something was afoot, several Fouga training jets took off, their pilots speaking by radio while mimicking Mystère and Mirage squadrons carrying out routine practice drills over Israel. If the Egyptians were listening, they could rest assured that this was just another day in the Israeli Air Force.

As the planes neared the skies of Egypt, the IAF electronic combat systems were activated, silencing or disrupting Egypt's transmission networks and radar systems. At the Pit, a nerve-wracking wait began.

At 7:45 A.M., the planes were over their targets. A hundred and eighty-three aircraft dived toward the Egyptian airfields. The meticulous preparations, planning, calculations and training bore fruit. The radio silence was suddenly broken, and the air force's communications networks filled with excited reports from the skies over Egypt. The Egyptians' surprise was total, and the result was better than expected. One after another, eleven Egyptian airfields were blown up, pillars of smoke and fire rising above them. A hundred and seventy-three planes attacked the airfields of El Arish, El Sir, Bir Gifgafa, Bir Tamada, Kibrit, Fayed, Abu Suwayr, Inshas, Cairo International, West Cairo and Beni Suef. The ten other planes carried out patrol and photo-reconnaissance missions.

Egyptian bombers destroyed on the ground. *(GPO)*

The first anti-runway penetration bombs landed on the Kibrit airfield. The pilots spared the runways at El Arish so that they could serve the IAF when the Armored Corps captured it. At Bir Gifgafa, five MiGs were destroyed, with one managing to get away. At Cairo West, fifteen Tupolev Tu-16 bombers, among others, were destroyed. At Inshas, every MiG was wiped out, even though the morning mist made it hard to see. One of the Israeli formations accidentally arrived at Cairo International Airport, but when it spotted fighter planes among the commercial jets, struck many of them. The Abu Suwayr airfield put up exceptional resistance, and several of its MiGs managed to take off and attack Israel's planes. Twenty-seven passes over the field were carried out, dropping 102 bombs.Captain Ben-Zion Zohar stood out during the battle, his Vautour engaging with MiGs, returning to bomb the field, and, on its way back to Israel, even attacking a surface-to-air missile battery, landing on its final drops of fuel. He would later be decorated.

Immediately after, the second wave took to the air—164 sorties over sixteen airfields, some of them not attacked during the first wave, like Luxor, where some of the Egyptian planes had escaped. Then came the third, fourth and fifth waves, the last reaching even the remote airfields of Ghardaqa and Ras Banas.

During the third wave, it became clear that Syrian MiGs and Jordanian Hawker Hunters were attempting to attack Israel. Hod ordered a group of planes to change direction and carry out Operation Focus in Jordan and Syria too. The air force destroyed the entire Jordanian Air Force and eliminated most of Syria's planes.

A few errors occurred during the operation, the most bitter being the attack on H-3 airfield in Iraq. MiGs, Hunters and even Tupolev bombers had set out from the field to try attacking targets in Israel. The field wasn't well known, and it hadn't occurred to anyone that it might serve as a departure base against Israel. Air force pilots carried out three attacks on the Iraqi field, achieving success during the first two. But the Iraqis recovered, and when Israeli planes appeared for a third time, they fell into an ambush. Two Vautours and a Mirage crashed after getting hit and one of the pilots who ejected was taken captive; the three remaining planes returned to Israel with their tails between their legs.

But that failure couldn't overshadow Operation Focus's enormous success. Within a few hours, the enemy's air forces were wiped out. The operation would be the decisive component of Israel's victory in the Six Day War. "The pride surrounding this story," one air force leader wrote, "was simply inexhaustible. There are those who will claim that this was the crowning achievement of all the IDF missions ever."

During the Six Day War the IDF had destroyed 327 Egyptian planes, 30 Jordanian planes, 65 Syrian planes, 23 Iraqi planes and one Lebanese plane. But the price was heavy: during the war, the air force lost 46 aircraft and mourned 24 of its pilots.

MAJOR GENERAL AVIHU BEN-NUN, A FORMER COMMANDER-IN-CHIEF OF THE AIR FORCE

"Before Operation Focus, the IDF chief of staff Yitzhak Rabin visited the squadron base. He met with the pilots and said to us that this mission was 'life or death.' The existence of Israel depended on it. Rabin and Ezer [Weizman] instilled in us the sense that everything depended on us, that if we didn't succeed at our task, there was no future for this country.

"I led a formation of four Mystères to the Fayeed airfield. Every plane carried two bombs, each weighing seven hundred ninety-four pounds. On the way, over the sea, the number four plane disappeared on me, and I felt a stone in my heart. At Bardawil, on Sinai's shore, clouds appeared at an altitude of one thousand feet, and another stone was added. But when we reached Fayeed, I saw a bit of blue sky—and we attacked. I dropped the bombs on the runway and, on the next pass, strafed two MiGs at the edge of the runway, which went up in flames.

"An Antonov An-12 transport plane suddenly appeared in front of me, turned and started fleeing southward. I had a dilemma. It would take ten seconds to bring it down, but perhaps I'd miss the main objective, which was destroying the planes on the ground. Ultimately, I decided to focus on the MiGs. We destroyed sixteen MiGs and also blew up an SA-2 battery across the canal. We even found our number four eventually—he had gone back because of a problem with his fueling system. When I landed, I was told that the squadron commander, Yonatan Shachar, had been hit and had ejected, and I was appointed squadron commander in his place.

"Years later, Cairo's daily *Al-Ahram* published an article about the most decorated pilot in the Egyptian Air Force, who, on June fifth, 1967, had managed to escape the planes chasing him in his Antonov. The entire Egyptian General Staff had been on that Antonov that I hadn't brought down. That didn't bring me much pleasure.

"On the third day of the war, we flew over Jerusalem, and the radio played 'Jerusalem of Gold.' It was the only time I've cried during a flight."

The conquest of East Jerusalem has not been one of the Six Day War Israeli goals. Its main offensive is in Sinai. But when Jordanian artillery starts firing on Israel, the IDF counterattacks and conquers the West Bank. Two cabinet ministers exert heavy pressure on Prime Minister Eshkol to liberate Jerusalem. At first Eshkol hesitates. So does Moshe Dayan. Finally, on the third day of the war, he gives the IDF its green light.

CHAPTER 7

"THE TEMPLE MOUNT IS IN OUR HANDS!" 1967

R ed Sheet! I repeat, Red Sheet!"

In the early morning of June 5, 1967, shortly after the IAF destroyed most of the Egyptian aircraft on the ground, the order "Red Sheet" echoed in the transceivers of the land forces massed on Egypt's border. Thousands of tanks, troop carriers, self-propelled guns, jeeps and trucks crossed the border and charged the Egyptian positions in Sinai.

The Six Day War had started.

Israel didn't want to be drawn into a war with Jordan as well. Foreign Minister Abba Eban alerted General Odd Bull, chief of staff of the United Nation Truce Supervision Organization in Jerusalem, and asked him to convey an urgent message to King Hussein of Jordan: "Israel will not, repeat, not, attack Jordan if Jordan maintains the quiet. But if Jordan opens hostilities, Israel will respond with all of its might." The message was delivered to the king, but in vain. On May 30, Hussein had signed a military pact with Nasser and was convinced that this time the Arabs would crush the Jews. The Jordanian Army was ordered to attack Israel.

At 10:45 A.M., the Jordanian Legion opened fire all along the armistice lines with Israel; Netanya, Kfar Saba, Jerusalem, Ramat David, were shelled. "Long Tom" cannon positioned close to Qalkiliya and Jenin, on the West Bank, fired on Israel's populated centers. Jordanian jets headed for Israeli targets. The legion threw in the battle land forces as well, and occupied Government House, Odd Bull's headquarters in Jerusalem. The IDF Jerusalem brigade, reinforced by tanks, counterattacked and retook the building; it then tried to establish a connection with the Israeli enclave in Mount Scopus, a hill overlooking Jerusalem, where a small unit was guarding a hospital and the old campus of Hebrew University.

Commander of the Central Military District General Uzi Narkiss decided to send the paratroopers to Jerusalem. Their legendary commander, Arik Sharon, was not at their head anymore. Finally promoted to general by Chief of Staff Yitzhak Rabin, he now commanded a division in Sinai. Narkiss dispatched to Jerusalem the newly created 55th Brigade, composed of reserve paratroopers. Its commander was a veteran warrior, Colonel Motta Gur.

Motta was a strange hybrid of an intellectual and a born fighter. He was eighteen during the Independence War, when his training at the Officers Academy had been interrupted and he had been sent with his comrades to conquer Be'er Sheva and fight the Egyptians in the Negev. He liked to describe his baptism by fire to his soldiers. During his first battle, he said, he was just a scared young man, and while the bullets were buzzing around him he suddenly felt an expanding wetness in his pants. He was overwhelmed with shame. Had he peed in his pants? Was he such a coward? As soon as the battle was over he had run to a secluded corner and checked his clothes, then breathed in relief. An Egyptian bullet had pierced his water canteen, and the water had spilled over his pants. . . . He wasn't a coward after all.

After harsh and bloody combats where he had lost some of his best friends, he left the army and enrolled in Hebrew University. There he met Arik Sharon but was not impressed. He heard about the creation of 101, but chose to continue his studies of Middle East history and culture until the day in 1955 when he met Aharon Davidi, an old comrade in arms from the Negev combats.

"I am with the paratroopers now," Davidi said.

"What do you do there?"

Davidi told him about the unit missions; in his soft, matter-of-fact manner, he described the reprisal raids, the incursions deep into enemy territory and the new spirit motivating "the guys with the red boots." Motta was excited. "I am coming!" he said and joined the paratroopers.

As commander of Company D he fought at most of the reprisal raids. He was wounded at a battle in the Gaza Strip and was decorated for bravery by Dayan. Yet, he became the most outspoken critic of Sharon, delivered scathing accusations of his commander after the Mitla Pass battle, and used to say that "I never saw Sharon's back when we were charging the enemy," meaning that the paratroopers' legendary chief was not a hero at all. Nevertheless, he stayed in the paratrooper corps and performed brilliantly. After the Sinai campaign, where he fought at Mitla, he was sent to high-level studies at the Ecole Militaire in Paris. There, beside his martial studies, he and his wife, Rita, discovered French culture: the theaters, the museums, the books of Camus, Sartre, Giraudoux. After his return, he filled several positions in the army. In the evenings he had to tell stories to his four children, and he preferred to write them. His children's books, about "Azit, the paratrooper dog," were best-sellers in Israel and even became a kids' movie.

And on June 5 he was to lead the brigade of war-hardened veterans at the battle for Jerusalem.

In the afternoon of that day, Cabinet Ministers Yigal Allon and Menachem Begin entered the office of Prime Minister Levi Eshkol. Allon, the legendary former commander of the Palmach, was a leader of the left-wing Ahdut HaAvoda party; Begin was the charismatic head of the right-wing Herut. But both of them were political hawks and they urged Eshkol to liberate the Old City. Yet a formidable obstacle stood in their way: Defense Minister Moshe Dayan, who worried about possible damage to the world's holiest places and the international reaction to the conquest of the Old City. He feared that any fighting inside Jerusalem might result in foreign pressure on Israel that would also influence the campaign against Egypt and prevent Israel from completing its war goals. Dayan knew, however, that the fall of Mount Scopus into the hands of the Jordanians would be considered a severe blow to Israel's prestige. He therefore authorized the IDF only to conquer the road to Scopus, in northeast Jerusalem.

Following Dayan's order, Motta assigned the missions of his three battalions that would attack East Jerusalem: Yossi Yaffe's Battalion 66 would storm the Jordanian Police Academy, conquer it and the nearby Ammunition Hill and Hotel Ambassador. The two other battalions would take the Rockefeller Museum in a pincer attack. Uzi Eilam, the hero of Black Arrow, would lead his Battalion 71 through several Arab neighborhoods and the American Colony and approach the Rockefeller Museum; Yossi Fradkin's Battalion 28 would advance farther up along Salah a-Din Street, a major artery in Arab Jerusalem, conquer the museum and the area adjacent to the Old City Wall. The paratroopers would be supported by tanks and artillery. At the outcome of these attacks the paratroopers would control the road to Mount Scopus. All the objectives of the paratrooper assault were in Arab Jerusalem, but none was inside the Old City.

The last briefing of the company commanders was held in the Cohen Family shelter, in the Beit HaKerem neighborhood. During the briefing the house owner's elderly mother entered the shelter. She handed an old, threadbare Israeli flag to Captain Yoram Zamosh. Her voice was breaking when she told the paratroopers that the flag had been floating over her house in the Old City during the War of Independence. She had taken it when she had been forced to abandon her home. She now asked the officers to raise the flag over the Western Wall. Her plea electrified the soldiers; unwittingly, the elderly lady had determined the goal of their mission, even though it hadn't been formulated in any official document.

At 2:30 A.M., Uzi Eilam led his battalion to Arab Jerusalem, crossed the border fences and after bitter fighting, conquered the American Colony and approached the Rockefeller Museum. But the other operations didn't turn out the way they were planned. The paratroopers were not familiar with Jerusalem, and the intelligence reports about the legion's positions and firepower were far from adequate. Battalion 28, which was to perform the second part of the pincer movement, crossed the no-man's-land, followed by several tanks, and headed for the Rockefeller Museum. But at the crossroads by the wall it missed the turn, and instead of advancing through Salah a-Din Street, the battalion entered the Nablus Road. This turned into a death trap.

The dark Nablus Road and the Old City Wall were fortified with elite Jordanian troops manning heavy-machine-gun nests and riflemen positions, equipped with mortars, bazookas and recoilless guns. The Jordanians opened a murderous crossfire on the approaching paratroopers, inflicting heavy casualties upon them. The medic Shlomo Epstein, who was dressing the wounds of Yossef Hagoel, heard the hiss of an approaching shell and threw himself on Hagoel to protect him. The shell crushed his body. Hagoel survived. Lieutenant Mordechai Friedman raised his hand to throw a hand grenade on a spitting-fire position in a dark alley and was mown down by a machine-gun burst. He collapsed and the grenade exploded in his hand.

The battalion commander called for help and several tanks joined the fighting. Some of them were hit, others got stuck. Only after seven hours of fighting did the paratroopers succeed in clearing the entire road, which was less than a mile long. They reached the hotels Columbia, facing the Nablus Gate, and Rivoli, by Herod's Gate. The legionnaires, barricaded on top of the wall, focused their heavy fire on Rivoli. Haim Russak tried to rescue a wounded comrade and succumbed to the fire of a Jordanian machine gun. The medic Nathan Shechter tried to save him, in vain. Shechter, himself, would soon be killed at Rockefeller Museum.

While the battle was raging on Nablus Road, Battalion 66 was engaged in terrible combat. The paratroopers broke into the Arab city and stormed the Police Academy. At their head was Giora Ashkenazi's company, which advanced using bangalores—long pipe-shaped explosive charges that blew up both the barbwire fences and blazed paths across the minefields. Giora was followed by the company of Dodik Rotenberg, which invaded the fortified trenches and the academy building. The companies of Gabi Magal and Dedi Yaakobi mopped the building, and paused, seeing the sinister outline of Ammunition Hill.

The hill was a formidable bastion, a fortified compound that used to be the armory of the Police Academy during the British mandate. The Jordanians had transformed it into an impregnable fortress. The hill was surrounded by fences, scarred by narrow, winding, stone-plated trenches that some writers later described as a bundle of tangled bowels. Most positions were covered, and between them rose concrete bunkers, cunningly positioned. Every inch of the hill was covered by crisscross fire from several sources. The hill was defended by crack troops, the best of the legionnaires. They were excellent, indomitable warriors who knew they had no way out of the hill and had to fight to their death.

Dedi Yaakobi led his paratroopers to conquer the hill, but his men soon realized that they were trapped in a deadly inferno, exposed to heavy and murderous fire from all over. The night thundered with machine-gun bursts, bomb and grenade explosions, shouts of the wounded and death rattles. The paratroopers advanced in the narrow trenches but were easy prey for the heavy fire of the bunker positions. The company broke into several units that all encountered a grim fate. Corporal Meir Malmudi's squad was decimated in a crossfire trap in an open stretch. Yoram Eliashiv, quiet and calm, was slain at the head of his platoon. A bullet pierced the forehead of Yirmi Eshkol, Dedi's deputy. Soon after the battle began, most of Dedi's men were killed or wounded. He called Dodik for help but even before reinforcements arrived, his remaining soldiers, some of them severely wounded, kept running forward in the treacherous trenches, often bumping against the bodies of fallen legionnaires.

A similar fate awaited Dodik's soldiers. Platoon commander Yoav Tzuri led his men through the exposed stretch where Malmudi's soldiers had been killed. He was hit on his turn and fell, dead. Dodik's deputy, Nir Nitzan, led another platoon to the western part of the peripheral trench. He called Eitan Nava, a tough moshav boy, to get out of the trench and run ahead of the paratroopers, shooting at the enemy with his mini–machine gun. Nava knew that this was a suicide mission but didn't hesitate. He jumped out of the trench and ran forward, spraying the Jordanians with continuous fire while also attracting fire from all over. His comrades shouted at him, "Jump in the trench, you'll be killed!" but he kept running, hitting thirty legionnaires before he was slain.

Another fighter, Israel Zuriel, immediately leapt out of the trench and took Nava's place. He survived against all odds.

Most of the medics running in the trenches between scores of wounded were injured or killed. Didier Guttal crouched in one of the trenches, his arm torn from his body. Another medic, Yigal Arad, ran like mad between the wounded of the two companies, dressed wounds, tied tourniquets and firmly fixed broken limbs.

From different directions, the surviving soldiers approached the main bunker. Zvi Magen, a platoon deputy commander, charged ahead of his soldiers and tried to throw a hand grenade on the position; he was killed by a burst of machine-gun fire. In the meantime the sun rose in the east and exposed the paratroopers to the accurate fire of snipers and machine gunners. Yet they kept fighting, advancing inch after inch to the monstrous bunker. It was a double bunker, protected with eighteen-inch-thick concrete plates. Three paratroopers approached the bunker from both sides—Yaki Hetz, David Shalom and Yehuda Kendel. All their efforts to destroy it by automatic fire, bazooka shells and hand grenades failed. Their commander ordered them to bring over bags of explosives, which they piled up by the bunker's walls. A formidable explosion blew up the bunker, yet the soldiers had to confront and kill five legionnaires who had miraculously survived.

The battle ended at six-fifteen in the morning. Thirty-six paratroopers and seventy legionnaires died on Ammunition Hill.

Some legionnaires were captured, and their first task was to bury their fallen comrades. A paratrooper stuck an improvised sign by their grave: HERE ARE BURIED 28 LEGIONNAIRES. Another fighter corrected the sign to read, " . . . 28 *brave* legionnaires."

Ammunition Hill was in the paratroopers' hands, but at what price! Only a few survivors remained of the two companies. An Israeli poet, Yoram Taharlev, wrote a chilling poem about the battle:

Seven came back into the city
And smoke was rising from the hill
The sun was high up in the east
On Ammunition Hill.

On all the concrete bunkers there
On all our dear comrades in arms
Left behind, forever young
On Ammunition Hill.

The paratroopers now held the Police Academy, Ammunition Hill and the Rockefeller Museum, which had been captured by Eilam's 71st Battalion and A Company of the 28th. The road to Mount Scopus was open; that very morning Dayan and several senior officers visited the Israeli enclave. The paratroopers and the other units fighting in that sector were now ordered to encircle the Old City from all over till it fell "like a ripe fruit." The Jerusalem brigade completed the conquest of the Abu Tor neighborhood, south of the Old City; Colonel Uri Ben-Ari, commanding an armored brigade, captured the Mivtar Hill and the French Hill, on the northeastern approaches to the city. The Jordanian high command hurriedly dispatched a task force of forty-two superior Patton tanks to Jerusalem, but Israeli jets destroyed them on the road before they even approached.

At nightfall, Motta Gur dispatched a unit of tanks and Micha Kapusta's paratrooper commando to the last hill rising in the north of Jerusalem—the Mount of Olives and the Augusta Victoria compound. Once again, the Israelis took the wrong turn; the tanks got stuck on a bridge over the Kidron creek, facing the legion's positions. They were met by a stunning volley of shells and machine-gun fire. The commando fighters were hit: some were killed, some fell into the creek and a few of their jeeps overturned or caught fire. Micha Kapusta ran down to the dried-up creek to try to save some of his men. He was joined by the legendary Meir Har-Zion, who was not on active duty but had rushed to Jerusalem to be with his comrades. The slaughter in the Kidron creek was very hard on Motta Gur, who followed it from his new command post at the Rockefeller Museum; beside his troubles with the Kidron creek, he was now subjected to a fierce shelling by the Jordanians. He almost lost his voice shouting at his men to take cover. He sat on the ground among them, dejected and pained by the thought of all these fine soldiers who had died. But he soon regained his composure; on the evening of June 6, it seemed that the Jordanians were breaking down.

At 4:00 A.M., Menachem Begin heard a news broadcast on BBC radio, claiming that the combats in Sinai were coming to an end, and the UN Security Council was about to declare a cease-fire. Begin conveyed the news item to Eshkol and Dayan. They took it very seriously; if they didn't act immediately, the Old City might remain as a Jordanian enclave in Israeli-occupied territory. They therefore overcame their hesitations and gave the order to conquer the Old City.

Motta Gur and his officers watch the Old City from the Mount of Olives, minutes before the final attack. *(GPO)*

At dawn, Motta's paratroopers and several tanks conquered Augusta Victoria and the Mount of Olives. One of the casualties at Augusta Victoria was Giora Ashkenazi, the company commander who had led his men in the storming of the Police Academy the previous night. The advanced command post of Motta settled on the Mount of Olives, close to the InterContinental Hotel. Before them lay, in all its beauty, the fairy-tale scenery of the Old City.

"Jerusalem" was like a magic word that reignited the fighting spirit in the mutilated brigade's soldiers. The 71st Battalion reorganized on the Mount of Olives; the 66th on Scopus, and the 28th by the Old City Wall, also reported they were ready for battle.

The moment had come. Motta radioed an order to his men and the tanks supporting them: "Storm the Old City!"

Motta jumped into his half-track and darted toward the Lions' Gate in the Old City Wall. On the way he bypassed the tanks and emerged at the head of the column. His driver, a huge soldier named Bentzur, accelerated like mad, yet Motta kept shouting at him, words that would become famous in Israeli lore: "Go, Bentzur, go!"

The half-track broke into the Lions' Gate. Perhaps the gate was booby-trapped; perhaps the legionnaires were waiting in the narrow, crooked alleys; perhaps a mine was concealed in the motorcycle lying in the middle of the street, blocking Motta's way. He didn't think of all that. He ordered his driver to run over the motorcycle and head for the Temple Mount, where Solomon's temple had stood thousands of years ago. "Go, Bentzur, go!" he repeated, his mind obsessed by a single thought: what will his little daughter Ruthy say when she hears that he conquered the Temple Mount? The half-truck climbed the narrow streets and suddenly emerged in the large concourse on top of the mount. The golden dome of Omar Mosque glistened in front of him.

Motta's voice echoed hoarsely in the radios and walkie-talkies of the army, soon to be repeated over the Israelis' and the world's radios: "The Temple Mount is in our hands!"

Motta's deputy and close friend Moshe ("Stempa'le") Stempel ran with Yoram Zamosh and a few other paratroopers to the Western Wall, the last vestige of Solomon's Temple. Zamosh drew a folded flag from his pouch. It was the flag old Mrs. Cohen had brought over in 1948 from the Jewish Quarter in Old Jerusalem and given to him a few hours before the battle of Jerusalem began. Zamosh and his comrades raised it over the wall.

The Jewish people in Israel and the Diaspora felt like they were dreaming. The prayer of thousands of years had come true.

One hundred and eighty-two soldiers, ninety-eight of them paratroopers, fell in the battle of Jerusalem.

Three days later, the Six Day War ended. Israel had conquered Jerusalem, the West Bank, the Sinai Peninsula and the Golan Heights.

Was peace any nearer?

GENERAL MORDECHAI ("MOTTA") GUR—FORMER 55TH BRIGADE COMMANDER

[Translated from his speech at the paratroopers' victory ceremony on the Temple Mount, December 6, 1967]

"To the paratroopers, conquerors of Jerusalem:

"When the Temple Mount was occupied by the Greeks, the Maccabees liberated it; Bar-Kochva and the zealots fought the Second Temple's destroyers. For two thousand years, the Temple Mount was barred to the Jews.

"Until you came—you, the paratroopers—and brought it back into the heart of the nation. The Western Wall, every heart beating toward it, is again in our hands.

"Many Jews put their lives in danger, throughout our long history, to reach Jerusalem and live there. Countless songs of yearning expressed the profound longing for Jerusalem beating in the Jewish heart.

"During the War of Independence, tremendous efforts were made to restore the nation's heart—the Old City and the Western Wall.

"The great privilege of closing the circle, of returning to our people our capital and center of holiness, fell to you.

"Many paratroopers, among our best and most experienced comrades, fell during the cruel combat. It was an intense, hard-fought battle, and you acted as one body, storming forward, crushing all the obstacles without paying attention to its wounds.

"You didn't argue. You didn't complain. You didn't file claims. You simply pressed onward—and you conquered.

"Jerusalem is yours—forever."

PART FOUR

The War of Attrition

The conquest of Sinai, the West Bank, Jerusalem and the Golan Heights have put an end to the Six Day War. Israel now expects her Arab neighbors to engage in peace talks in order to recover their lost territories, but the Arab leaders stubbornly stick to their former positions: no to negotiations, no to reconnaissance and no to peace with Israel. Egypt starts a "war of attrition" against Israel.

Some of the main players on the Israeli side have changed. Eshkol has died, in February 1969, and been replaced by Golda Meir. Yitzhak Rabin is now ambassador to Washington and been succeeded as chief of staff by General Haim Bar-Lev, whose cool, soft-spoken behavior hides nerves of steel and an inclination for bold commando operations. He is supported by Defense Minister Moshe Dayan.

CHAPTER 8
"I FELT I WAS SUFFOCATING": THE RAID ON GREEN ISLAND, 1969

"I heard members of Sayeret Matkal getting closer, and I called out for them to get into position. Suddenly a grenade exploded beside me. I stopped feeling my right side. My arm was fine, but a warm object had pierced my neck, and I felt I was suffocating. It was an impossible thing to endure. Suddenly, I heard a death rattle coming out of my throat, a terrible sound I remembered hearing from Egyptian soldiers who'd been hit moments earlier," recalled Ami Ayalon, a naval commando who took part in the battle for Green Island, was severely wounded and later received a Medal of Valor.

It was the summer of 1969, during the war of attrition with Egypt. In an attempt to exhaust Israel, the Egyptians had been attacking IDF forces in Sinai, causing heavy losses. A week before the raid on Green Island, the Egyptians had assaulted an Israeli position facing Port Tewfik. Seven IDF soldiers had been killed, with five wounded, one taken captive and three tanks destroyed. A gloomy atmosphere reigned within the General Staff. In order to recover the IDF's confidence, they decided to launch an effective deterrence operation.

The commander of Shayetet 13 naval commando unit, Ze'ev Almog, devised a plan for a raid on Green Island, submitting it to the General Staff's chief operations officer, David ("Dado") Elazar. Green Island was a formidable fortress located in the northern Gulf of Suez and was originally intended to defend the southern entrance to the Suez Canal. There were roughly a hundred Egyptian soldiers stationed on the island, with six dual-purpose guns on the roof of the fortress, antiaircraft fire-control radar, and twenty positions for heavy and medium machine guns and light artillery. It was also within the range of Egyptian 130-millimeter cannon batteries located on the coast.

Green Island, a fortress in the Red Sea. *(IDF Spokesman)*

The goal of the operation was to undermine Egyptian confidence with a strike deep in the country's territory, where its soldiers felt safe and secure. Moreover, the mission was simultaneously intended to raise IDF soldiers' morale, which was at a nadir because of the growing number of casualties at the canal. The attack could persuade the Egyptians to respect the cease-fire with Israel. The destruction of the Green Island radar would also disrupt the early-warning system of the Egyptian Air Force and facilitate the task of the IAF aircraft on their frequent sorties over Egyptian territory.

The task of seizing the island was assigned to Shayetet 13 and Sayeret Matkal under the command of Menachem Digli. The chief paratroopers' officer, Raful Eitan, was in command of the operation. Raful, who had led his paratroopers on the jump in Sinai in 1956, as a major, had distinguished himself during the Six Day War and was now a general. He realized that forty soldiers would be needed, as it was clear that a raid on the fortified island would require an amphibious landing, face-to-face combat and a high risk of the loss of life.

According to the plan, the raid force would sail in twelve rubber boats. Twenty Shayetet commandos, constituting the penetration force and the first to land, would be in the first five, and the rest of the boats would carry the twenty soldiers of Sayeret Matkal. The Shayetet fighters were instructed to get within just under three thousand feet of the island, and from there to move forward by swimming and diving toward it. The moment they managed to break through the fences and gain a foothold on the island, they would alert the rest of the boats, which would be waiting just under a mile away. The Shayetet soldiers were to swim and dive while equipped with personal weapons and other combat gear weighing just over eighty-eight pounds, and would be linked by rope to the lead commander—not a simple task, as would become clear.

After a model of Green Island was built and the teams had practiced the raid, it was decided that the operation would be carried out on the night of July 19, between 1:30 and 2:30 A.M.

Shortly before H-Hour, Chief of Staff Haim Bar-Lev arrived at the gathering point. Slight of build, always wearing a black armored-corps beret, Bar-Lev had a slow manner of speaking, and his calm, matter-of-fact elocution inspired confidence in his listeners. In a conversation with the soldiers, Bar-Lev emphasized the subject of losses, commenting that if there were more than ten casualties, the mission would be considered a failure. The remarks were delivered against the backdrop of heavy recent IDF losses at the canal; to the chief of staff, a mission with a high human toll was dangerous to morale and outweighed the benefits of capturing the target.

At 8:00 P.M. on July 19, the rubber boats and a small submersible nicknamed "Pig" were lowered into the water, and the soldiers sailed toward their destination. The Shayetet fighters were ready to dive, clad in wetsuits and in Dacron uniforms, wearing sneakers with flippers attached, combat vests outfitted with significant battle gear, as well as life jackets, oxygen tanks, submachine guns, grenades and magazines. At 11:00 P.M., they reached the dive point, three thousand feet from their objective, and started swimming toward the island. Then the complications began: the twenty Shayetet soldiers were situated along two ropes, led by two officers, each pulling ten men carrying nearly ninety pounds of gear apiece. The equipment was too heavy and the number of soldiers too large; the currents were much stronger than they had thought. They lost stability, some men got bogged down and the force struggled to move forward. Dov Bar, the commander of the first wave, decided to transition to diving earlier than planned—but that, too, turned out to be less than easy. The force was carried off course by the current, and half an hour later, Captain Bar rose to the surface and discovered that they were almost two thousand feet from their objective. It was 12:30 A.M.; Eitan and Almog were waiting for updates and calling on the radio, expecting to hear that the fence had already been breached, allowing the Sayeret soldiers to be brought in for battle—but the force hadn't even reached the island.

Bar made a decision on his own: "I decided that I'm getting to the target, no matter what," he later said. He signaled to everyone else to rise to the surface and to continue forward by swimming, contrary to the accepted plan, and only to submerge again just before reaching the target.

The moonlight threatened to expose them, but Bar remained calm. After another half hour of swimming, they reached the island.

It was 1:38 by the time they stripped off their diving gear, eight minutes past the operation's start last deadline. The penetration team cut the first fence with ease but found two more, which would have taken too much time to get through. From an earlier observation, the planners concluded that there should be another opening in a fence nearby. The soldiers, who had surreptitiously taken cover under a small bridge, could make out three Egyptian guards, one with a lit cigarette in his hand. They could spot the fence in question, but it was directly below the Egyptian position. The head of the penetration team feared that the force would be discovered and decided to surprise the Egyptians by opening fire on the guard, and, in doing so, delivering the opening shot of the operation. The battle had started.

The Egyptians, caught very much off guard, responded immediately with gunfire, which passed over the commandos' heads. In less than a minute, they had sent up flares that illuminated the entire island. The Israeli diversion force began firing bazookas at the target.

Almog, Digli and Eitan were waiting with twenty Sayeret fighters for the agreed-upon signal to enter the target. The signal didn't come. But the moment they heard echoes from the shooting and saw flashes of light, Almog decided not to wait any longer and ordered the boats to advance toward the island.

All the same, for ten long minutes the Shayetet commandos fought alone on the island, even though the Sayeret fighters were already supposed to be battling at their side. After crossing through the fence, the Shayetet members had begun advancing while throwing grenades and shooting Egyptian soldiers who crossed their path. This was how they reached the central building. One team went up in the direction of the roof and another turned toward the rooms, with the objective of mopping them. A tall, broad, strong soldier named Jacob Pundik stood under the roof and served as a ladder, earning the nickname "Jacob's Ladder."

First Lieutenant Ami Ayalon climbed onto his shoulders and reached the roof. His team had been assigned to destroy the cannon and machine-gun positions on the fortress roof; he had studied the positions of the different weapons during the rehearsals for the mission. The moment he got on the roof, he was wounded by shrapnel to his forehead. "I threw a smoke grenade to get a little cover," he recounted, "and I shouted to Zali [Zalman Rot], who had gone up, too, to charge the enemy with me, but the grenade didn't explode. I threw an explosive grenade toward the position the shooting was coming from, but it didn't blow up either. Zali threw a grenade at the position from the left side and then, with a long burst of gunfire, I rushed into the Egyptian Position Two. Gunfire came again from Position Ten, which had shot at me earlier. We fired back. The Egyptian, who was shooting with an automatic weapon, fell, and the position started to burn."

As Ayalon and Rot charged the cannon position, the Egyptians opened machine-gun fire. Rot shouted that his fingers had been cut off but went on fighting anyway. Yedidya ("Didi") Ya'ari joined the commandos on the roof to hit the third cannon but was immediately wounded: "I took a bullet in the leg and was laid out like a rabbit. . . . They carried me to the side and I was hit again, in the face and body, by grenade shrapnel that made me deaf and blind. . . . My face was burning and I was half-conscious, and I didn't understand what was happening."

In the meantime the Sayeret fighters landed on the island and joined the fighting. The Shayetet's ammunition started to run out; nevertheless, Bar pressed on with the charge, sending two fighters to Position 5. They were hit by a grenade and killed on the spot. A grenade was thrown at Ayalon, too, badly injuring his neck. He heard himself gurgling like the dying Egyptians and thought that perhaps now was his turn. He crawled back and evacuated to the boats under his own steam.

A detail of Sayeret soldiers joined the fighting on the roof. A team commander, Captain Ehud Ram, advanced, crouching, along the roof; as he was receiving a report from one of his men, a bullet pierced his forehead, and he was killed. After Ram was hit, two teams came down to clear out the internal courtyard; one of the men was hit and later died from his injuries.

It was already 2:15 A.M.. Almog reported to the command post that the Egyptian gunfire was dying down, and that his forces had suffered deaths and injuries. The fighters now set off 176 pounds of explosives in the northern section of the fortress. A tremendous explosion shook the small island, and its cannons and machine guns were destroyed. Minutes later, Eitan ordered the start of the evacuation. Now that the outcome of the battle was becoming clear, Egyptian cannon, positioned on the mainland, opened heavy fire on the island and blasted one of the Shayetet boats.

"When the evacuation began, I already knew the whole truth," said Dani Avinun, one of the wounded. "The dead and injured came past by me. We threw Yedidya Ya'ari—later the commander-in-chief of the navy—into a boat because we were convinced he was dead, and we told headquarters as much on the radio. Later it turned out that he was only wounded."

Close to 3:00 A.M., at the end of the battle, the boats headed back, carrying the exhausted fighters, six dead and eleven wounded. The Egyptian death toll was more than thirty.

Debriefings conducted after the operation revealed more than a few failures. The intelligence data had not been sufficient in regard to the water currents; the identity of the Egyptian soldiers on the island, who proved to be commandos prepared for a raid; or the radar, which turned out to be a dummy; and the cannons, revealed as heavy, outdated machine guns.

Yet, despite it all, the raid on Green Island is considered one of the IDF's shining successes. Some regard it as a historic turning point in terms of planning, preparation and implementation in the field. Eitan later commented, "The execution of the Green Island raid was exceptional in its inordinate success. The achievement was the operation itself, in which we paved the way for a new method of fighting that strengthened our security. The Egyptians, in their worst nightmares, had never dreamed of such a daring operation. During the action, we demonstrated a capability and performance level that served as a milestone for many years to come."

The day after the operation, the newspapers went out of their way to sing its praises: "An event that will be remembered for generations . . . A story that will become a legend . . . A raid on a steep-walled fortress built on stone and coral . . . An event comparable to the story about the British raid on the island of Navarone in the Aegean Sea, during World War Two. 'The Guns of Navarone' is a myth invented in the writer's imagination, but the guns of Green Island are a real-life legend whose story will one day be told."

The Egyptians also treated the operation with gravity. Dr. Mustafa Kabha, in his study "The War of Attrition as Reflected in Egyptian Sources," wrote that "this operation constituted a turning point in the war of attrition. It symbolized the start of a new phase in the war that most Egyptian researchers called 'the counter-attrition stage,' in which the military initiative passed from Egyptian hands to Israel's."

ADMIRAL AMI AYALON, LATER COMMANDER IN CHIEF OF THE NAVY

"I get to the roof and it becomes clear that, in contrast to what we prepared for, there's no cover, and I'm completely exposed to continuous Egyptian gunfire. I raise my head and the bullets are whistling over me, the ricochets are grazing my forehead, and I realize that I'm in a life-or-death situation. . . . I decide to charge, my friend Zali charges after me, and both of us burst into the position. I eliminate two Egyptian soldiers and Zali another two, . . . From there we continued fighting toward the other positions. . . .

"In today's terms, there's a big question mark about whether this operation should have been carried out. I don't think it brought about a reversal in the war of attrition, nor did it demonstrate a professional capacity or special level of performance, as was said after the mission.

"But, in those days, the operation had a dramatic impact on the IDF, on our faith in ourselves, on the morale of Israeli society and also on the Egyptian forces along the canal.

"I have to admit that, from the Shayetet's point of view, this exposed our professional shortcomings, because it was the first operation of its type in the world, the first time in the history of war that a force of divers used the cloak of diving to reach an enemy target underwater, and to start a gun battle the moment it pulled its head out of the water."

Israel's relations with the United States dramatically improved after the Six Day War. Under Presidents Johnson and Nixon the U.S. has become the main supplier of weapons to Israel after De Gaulle's embargo. That embargo is tightened further by De Gaulle's successor, Georges Pompidou.

CHAPTER 9

THE FRENCH
DEFENSE MINISTER:
"BOMB THE
ISRAELIS!" 1969

December 24, 1969

The owner of the Café de Paris in the French port city of Cherbourg
was tossing anxious glances at the entrance. The numerous clients
visiting the restaurant this evening had eaten, drunk and sung,
but fourteen guests who reserved a table for the Christmas meal had
lagged in coming, and now it was after midnight. Foie gras, roasted
turkey and champagne had been left orphaned. The unhappy restau-
rateur didn't know that these same fourteen men, along with 106 of
their friends, were spending the evening in the belly of five state-of-
the-art missile boats in the city's civil port, attuned to the howls of
the raging storm outside and praying to the God of Israel that it would
pass quickly. The tremendous storm threatened to sink one of the Israeli Navy's most important missions, officially called Operation Noa
but later seared into the public lore as the "Boats of Cherbourg."

The affair had begun two and a half years earlier, in June 1967. On the eve of the SixDay War, the president of France, Charles de Gaulle, had abandoned his pro-Israel policy and imposed an embargo—a total ban—on the sale of weapons to Israel. Emissaries of Israel's defense ministry, along with their allies in the French Army, were laboring night and day to smuggle vital arms from France to Israel. But several orders at French factories remained incomplete, including an order of fifty Mirage fighter jets and one of twelve fast missile boats at the Cherbourg shipyards. The shipyards were managed by a friend of Israel, Felix Amiot. About two hundred Israelis had settled in Cherbourg, including naval personnel and their families; they had been received with affection, unsurprising given that the boats' construction provided a livelihood to a thousand French families.

There were still a few cracks in the French embargo, and through them, Israel had received five of the twelve boats immediately after their construction was completed. But on December 28, 1968, the situation changed completely. Following an attempted attack on an El Al plane in Athens by terrorists coming from Lebanon, Raful Eitan and his paratroopers landed at Beirut airport and blew up thirteen planes belonging to Middle East Airlines, stoking de Gaulle's fury because the paratroopers used French-made Super Frelon helicopters. Telegrams were immediately wired to all the French factories building weapons ordered by Israel, principally in Cherbourg. French friends of Admiral Mordechai ("Moka") Limon, the head of the Israeli Defense Ministry delegation in Paris, informed him of the telegram to Cherbourg, and he ordered the officer responsible for the missile boat project, Colonel Hadar Kimchi, to immediately send a recently completed boat, the *Akko*, to Israel. Another boat, the *Tempest* (*"Sa'ar"*), was still in the final stages of construction, but Limon, a former commander in chief of the Israeli Navy, ordered that it be loaded with fifty tons of fuel. Lieutenant Colonel Moshe Tabak outfitted the ship with everything required and "went out for drills in the ocean." A few days later, the *Akko* and the *Tempest* arrived in Israel.

The missile boats had a special status: they had been paid for almost in full (except for the five vessels which had not yet been completed), and they effectively belonged to Israel; nevertheless, their departure despite the embargo enraged de Gaulle. Cherbourg's French officers decided to punish the Israeli Navy by banishing it from the port's military section to the civilian area. It also became clear beyond any doubt that the embargo would be applied to the five remaining boats, which were in advanced stages of construction. This policy would continue even into the days of de Gaulle's successor, President Pompidou.

The missile boats in Haifa Port. *(Moshe Milner, GPO)*

Israel's war of attrition with Egypt, then at its peak, had increased the urgency of supplying the navy with state-of-the-art weaponry, and pressure grew for the acquisition of the five missile boats. Limon, a calm, composed man, flew to Israel and presented the heads of the defense establishment with three ways to bring them over. The first: to wait patiently, perhaps for years, for the embargo to be lifted. The second: to smuggle the boats out of Cherbourg illegally. And the third: to formulate a legal plan to deceive the French government and get the boats to Israel, namely through Israel's theoretical surrender of the boats and their sale to a third party—who would then send them to Israel.

Defense Minister Moshe Dayan and his deputy, Tzvi Tzur, were inclined to take the third route, to avoid breaking the law. The commander in chief of the Navy, General Avraham ("Cheetah") Botzer, and his deputy, Brigadier General Benjamin ("Bini") Telem, dealt with the planning. It would be necessary to wait until all the boats were ready before bringing them out. Zim, the Israeli shipping company, put two boats, the *Dan* and the *Leah*, at the operation's disposal. Large fuel tanks were installed in the belly of both ships, and they performed fueling drills at sea with the navy's missile boats. The refueling ships would meet the flotilla of missile boats during its voyage from Cherbourg to Israel; one boat would wait next to Gibraltar, and the other south of Malta. Zim made two more ships, the *Netanya* and the *Tiberias*, available for the operation in case of a serious accident at sea: one had been outfitted to tow a damaged missile boat, and the second, to aid in the getaway of naval crews.

By the end of August 1969, construction on four of the five boats was complete: the *Storm* ("*Sufa*"), the *Spear* ("*Hanit*"), the *Volcano* ("*Ga'ash*"), and the *Sword* ("*Herev*"). The fifth boat, the *Arrow* ("*Hetz*"), was going to be delivered in November.

In September, Limon met with his friend Mordechai Friedman, the CEO of Netivei Neft, an Israeli state company that pumped oil in Abu Rudeis, in Sinai. Limon and Friedman were looking for an intermediary who would buy the boats from France and focused their attention on Akers, a Norwegian firm that searched for oil. At its head stood Martin Siem, an engineer and World War II hero who had led the anti-Nazi underground in Norway and was a good friend of Friedman's.

Limon had reached the conclusion that the best date for taking the boats would be Christmas Eve, 1969. That night, the French would be celebrating, and their level of vigilance would be low. By then, the *Arrow* would be ready to sail.

In October, Limon and Friedman met with Siem in Copenhagen, where the Norwegian gave his approval to the fictional purchase of the missile boats. However, he wouldn't be able to conduct the acquisition via Akers but through a subsidiary under his control, Starboat, which was registered in Panama.

Operation Noa was under way. Starboat contacted Amiot and expressed interest in acquiring between four and six fast boats that could be used in the search for oil in the North Sea. "Purely by chance," Limon later told us with a wink, "Starboat's requirements matched the specifications and performance capacities of the boats of Cherbourg."

Amiot replied that he had a customer for whom he was building such boats, but if the customer relinquished the vessels, Amiot would sell them to Starboat. The French Defense Ministry was enthusiastic. If Israel would agree to give up the boats and they were sold to a third party, the bothersome issue would be solved. Limon, for his part, pretended to be dubious about the desirability of the deal, and only three weeks later did he accede to the French request. The deal was completed and the papers signed. Wood signs bearing the name STARBOAT were placed next to the missile boats, and with considerable generosity, Limon agreed that Israeli crews would man the boats for the time being. In secret, Limon and Siem had signed an agreement that voided the entire deal with the French.

According to Kimchi, the operation's commander, the contract was long and detailed but noted that the boats' final destination was "a company that dealt with the search for oil in the Gulf of Suez"—in point of fact, Israel. Consequently, before the contract could be investigated in depth by the French bureaucracy, it would be necessary to speed things along and get the boats out of France.

In total secrecy, eighty of the Israeli Navy's best officers and sailors were brought to Cherbourg, flying to Paris in civilian attire and arriving in the port city, in pairs, by train. Barred from speaking Hebrew or attracting attention, they lodged in Cherbourg in private apartments and in the boats themselves. Each crew numbered twenty-four, so the total would be 120 sailors for the five missile boats. Forty additional sailors, beside the eighty who came from Israel, were selected among the IDF Navy personnel already in Cherbourg. As their D Day approached, the sailors discreetly purchased great quantities of food at various locations—1,200 days' worth, based on an expectation of 120 sailors at sea for 10 days. Because the boats' communications systems hadn't been completed, the Israelis spread in the city, trying to acquire walkie-talkies with a three-quarter-mile range. They finally found them in toy stores. The sailors also began turning on the boats' engines each night, claiming that there was a power shortage in the shipyard, and the city grew accustomed to hearing the constantly booming engines. Meanwhile, the Zim ships set sail, placing themselves at predetermined positions at sea.

By Christmas Eve, everything was ready. The teams had settled onto the boats. Admiral Limon, Hadar Kimchi, his deputy, Ezra ("Shark") Kedem, and the commanders of the five boats sat in the *Sword*'s commander's quarters. The French were fulfilling the role that had been "assigned" to them, sitting down for the holiday meal at exactly the appointed hour.

Only one variable wasn't playing its part: the weather.

A terrible storm was raging in the open sea, with huge waves rising from the west; naval personnel rated the water as "sea 7 to 9," fraught with lethal danger to anyone who struggled against it.

The hours passed and the officers collected any bits of information they could about the storm's location and movement. Limon was determined to set sail that night; otherwise, the entire plan might collapse. But the final decision belonged, of course, to Kimchi. Ten P.M., 11:00 P.M., midnight. . . . The storm raged on, and the tension grew. Kimchi decided to delay his final decision until 2:00 A.M. After one o'clock, an updated forecast arrived that inspired hope among the sailors. The direction of the wind was going to change; the storm was turning toward Scotland and Scandinavia. Ten minutes later, another forecast: the wind had indeed shifted course.

The crews feverishly prepared the boats for departure. The boats' engines broke out in a tremendous roar and, at two-thirty, the order was given to sail. First the *Sword*, then the four remaining ships set out toward the open sea. As they disappeared into the darkness, the Israeli defense delegation's vehicles blocked the entrance to the port, in order to frustrate any sudden check by the police. At the Hotel Atlantique, overlooking the sea, lights in the windows turned on and off intermittently, as the families of some of the crew members that had been living there bade farewell to their loved ones.

The docks remained empty. Limon was the last to leave the port. At three-thirty, he awakened Amiot and informed him that the boats had sailed for Israel. Amiot embraced him and burst out crying. Limon handed him a check for $5 million, the final payment for the boats' construction.

The five boats sailed into a stormy sea, fighting hard against the waves. Their connection to naval headquarters in Israel was lost again and again, and the engines didn't function properly. Nevertheless, the original plan was executed; the rendezvous with the *Leah* took place on the night of December 26, and the boats were refueled, if terribly slowly because of unexpected complications. The second refueling took place south of Malta. The most severe difficulty cropped up when water seeped into the *Arrow*'s engine; in the absence of appropriate gauges, the sailors were forced to taste the fuel to see whether it had been contaminated with seawater, which could have damaged the engines. After several rounds of tasting, the problem was fixed and the boat continued on its way.

The storm in the Mediterranean subsided, but it erupted in a new location: the international press. Nearly two days had passed between Christmas Eve and the world's discovery that the boats had vanished from Cherbourg. "Where are they?" reporters asked the staff at the Israeli embassy in Paris; the diplomats nonchalantly answered, "The boats are no longer ours, presumably they're sailing to Norway." But a Spanish helicopter and later a light BBC aircraft discovered the boats at sea, and the global media reported that the "Boats of Cherbourg" had escaped out from under the noses of the French. Front-page headlines and huge articles with aerial photos filled papers around the world. France was ridiculed, while Israel gained fame for the sophisticated operation. When the press revealed that the boats were sailing through the Mediterranean toward Israel, a massive uproar broke out in Oslo, where Siem was forced to respond to difficult, embarrassing questions, and in Paris, where the French government saw itself tricked and humiliated. The French defense minister, Michel Debré, a former staunch supporter of Israel, now demanded that the army chief of staff use any means necessary to stop the boats, even by bombing them from the air. Prime Minister Jacques Chaban-Delmas rejected the idea.

The boats, two limping behind because of glitches and three leading the flotilla, sailed toward Israel, where the entire country awaited their arrival. In the end, they docked in Haifa, where they were received by the defense minister, the chief of staff, and the navy's commander in chief.

Operation Noa had worked out according to plan. Several French generals paid the price by losing their jobs, Siem was exiled to a secondary post in the United States and Limon was forced to leave France.

Despite sharp condemnations in France, the operation generated a wave of admiration for Israel, although Paris's official policy remained chilly and distant for many more years.

HADAR KIMCHI, DEPUTY COMMANDER IN CHIEF OF THE NAVY

"The most difficult moment, for me, was making the decision to get under way. Initially, I had determined that the departure would be at eight P.M., but the terrible storm was raging, and I delayed setting sail. The boats were new, the crews were young and inexperienced with these boats, and there was a lack of standard communications equipment and radar on most of the vessels. I couldn't take the risk. I delayed until ten o'clock, then to midnight, and later to two A.M.

"At one A.M., reports came in by radio that the storm was turning northward. I informed everyone: We're leaving at two-thirty. This was a difficult decision. We struggled with the waves for more than twelve hours. The boats were shuddering; everyone got seasick. At a certain moment, planes appeared above us, taking pictures. I announced on the radio, 'Everyone, comb your hair! They're snapping photos!' Several engines were inoperative during the trip, and when we reached the Aegean Sea I requested over the radio that Israeli ships in the area be ready to tow us. The first captain who answered told me, 'I'm willing—this is for our country, and I'll do it for free.'

I was elated. I asked him, 'Where are you?' He replied, 'Near Copenhagen . . . '

"After him, similar offers came in from six more boats.

"In the end, we arrived safely at the Kishon port. Five years later, I visited Cherbourg again, and I received a warm welcome. The French said, 'You fled, but you got us amazing publicity. Because of you, the Greeks and the Iranians bought missile boats from us, and the engine company got lots of orders too.' "

The war of attrition along the Suez Canal claims
many casualties on both sides. The Soviet Union,
determined to regain her lost prestige in the Arab world,
supplies Egypt with state-of-the-art military equipment—
tanks, aircraft, missiles and electronic installations.

CHAPTER 10
"WHY BOMB IF WE CAN TAKE?" 1969

O n the night of December 26, 1969, three IAF Super Frelon helicopters crossed the Gulf of Suez into Egypt and landed on the sands of Ras Gharib. After setting down behind enemy lines, a company of paratroopers set out, in total silence, for its destination, launching one of the most imaginative operations ever conceived by the IDF.

These were the days of the war of attrition, which had broken out following the Six Day War. Israel controlled Sinai, and the core of the conflict was an endless duel between the IDF and the Egyptian Army along the length of the Suez Canal: artillery bombardments, commando raids, operations deep in Egypt, aerial battles, ambushes and planting of mines. The number of Israeli losses constantly grew. The Egyptians had replaced the military equipment destroyed in the war with a massive supply of sophisticated Soviet weaponry. New tanks and troop carriers, MiG aircraft, ground-to-air missiles and sophisticated radar stations had all arrived from the USSR. Over and over again, the Israeli Air Force attacked the radar stations, which disrupted its planes' freedom of action in the skies over Egypt.

In particular, the air force was troubled by a P-12 radar station that was among the most sophisticated ever built by the Soviet Union, capable of detecting aircraft flying at very low altitudes. The station was spotted in Ras Gharib, at a secure, protected site, and was attacked by the IAF in mid-October. The attack was successful, and the station was completely destroyed. But a few days later, to the Israelis' surprise, it turned out that the station continued to operate; air force experts realized that they had blown up a dummy station built to deceive them, and that the real station was in fact operating at another site hidden in the desert.

On December 22, the IAF conducted a photo-reconnaissance mission in the area. Two sergeants from the Technical Services Unit of the intelligence department were charged with deciphering the images. Sergeant Rami Shalev, who reviewed the photo sequences, recounted, "Suddenly, as I was going through them, I found it! I locked in on the real Ras Gharib radar station. I said to myself, You have a radar station here." The facility was very well camouflaged, resembling two Bedouin tents in the heart of the desert. They were, in fact, two huge containers installed on Russian ZiL trucks. The station was neither defended nor secured; an Egyptian military installation containing a mortar battery was located just a few kilometers to the north. Antiaircraft guns had not been placed in the area around the station, apparently in order not to draw attention. By contrast, a force of roughly fifty Egyptian soldiers was positioned around the decoy station that had been bombed, equipped with machine guns and antiaircraft artillery.

First Lieutenant Yechiel Haleor, from the Technical Services Unit, brought the images to Colonel Yeshayahu Barkat, the head of the aerial-intelligence department. The head of IAF operations, Colonel David Ivry, was also present at the meeting. Barkat instructed Haleor to prepare an "objectives sheet," including the geographical coordinates for bombing the station.

Haleor asked, "Why bomb if we can take?"

Haleor's remark fired up his commanders' imaginations. "To take"—to swipe an entire radar station from under the nose of the Egyptians and bring it to Israel! But would it be possible to transport an entire station over the Gulf of Suez—two heavy containers and a tall antenna? The station was a fifteen-minute helicopter ride from Sinai, then under Israeli control. Ivry called for an assessment of whether helicopters could carry out the task. On December 24, Major Nehemiah Dagan, the commander of the Sikorsky ("Yassour") wing in the helicopter squadron, informed him that it was feasible. At the time, there were only three Yassours that could carry out the operation—new Sikorsky helicopters that had just arrived in Israel. Dagan estimated that if the radar station's two containers were separated, it would be possible to lift them with the helicopters and bring them to Israeli territory. According to early estimates, the weight of the main container, the "heart" of the station, was approximately four tons. Going by the book, the Yassour was capable of lifting roughly three. The weight of the second container was lower, about two and a half tons.

Air Force Commander Motti Hod transmitted the proposal to Chief of Staff Haim Bar-Lev, who assigned the ground operation to the paratroopers. A computer spit out its name: Operation Rooster 53. The head of the 50th Battalion, Lieutenant Colonel Arieh ("Tzidon") Tzimmel, was appointed the operation's commander.

Tzimmel assembled the raid force using two types of fighters: those with battle experience, the majority of them officers, and soldiers with technical skills who would be able to detach the radar station's two containers from the truck platforms on which they were placed, break the connections between them and take down the antenna.

Eliezer ("Cheetah") Cohen, one of the air force's most senior helicopter pilots, turned to First Sergeant Ezra, a radar expert, and told him that he was looking for a model that the helicopter pilots could use for training.

"Why do you need a model when you have a Russian radar at the ready?" Ezra asked. Located at the Tzrifin base among Israel's captured enemy equipment was a Russian radar container taken during the Six Day War; although its parts were out of date, its size and shape were identical to those of a P-12. Cohen, Ezra and the paratroopers' deputy commander, Levi Hofesh, hurried to Tzrifin. Instead of turning to the quartermaster general of the IDF and getting tangled up in bureaucracy, as well as the potential leak of the secret, the three called a tow truck and "stole" the container. It was transported to an air force base, and two Yassour pilots, Nehemiah Dagan and Ze'ev Matas, along with their crews, trained at tethering it to the helicopters and lifting it up.

At the same time, the paratroopers were practicing the capture and dismantling of the radar station. They received wrenches that fit the Russian standards, technical scissors for cutting the cables and connections, oxygen tanks and welding devices in the event that the scissors didn't work. Martin Leibovich, a company sergeant major for the 50th Battalion, was called by his company commander, who blindfolded him and drove him by jeep to one of the airfield's most distant runways. When the blindfold was removed, Leibovich saw before him a soldier from the Ordnance Corps standing next to large oxygen tanks. The soldier kept loudly declaring that he wouldn't be going on the mission because he was a *jobnik*, or pencil pusher. Leibovich took on the role. "I became the locksmith of the operation," he said later. In addition to Ezra and Leibovich, several technical experts were also attached to the mission, as well as a young man who knew how to drive a Russian ZiL truck, in case it was decided to move the trucks with the containers to the canal shore. All these preparations were completed in twenty-four hours.

The following night, three Super Frelons crossed the Gulf of Suez and unloaded their cargo—sixty-six commandos—close to the radar station. There was a full moon out, and so the paratroopers wore light-colored clothes and wrapped their weapons in light-colored fabric, in order to blend into the sand. They spotted the station site close to an oil rig nearby and reached it at a brisk walk, and later by crawling. They split into a blocking force and an attacking force, and charged at the station. An Egyptian guard opened automatic gunfire on them, and a second joined in. After a brief battle, the paratroopers took control of the installation, killing two soldiers and capturing four; three other Egyptians got away. In the bunker and tent next to the station, the paratroopers found detailed files and guidebooks about how to operate the electronic equipment.

They then began dismantling the installation, but the work stretched on. The wrenches didn't fit; the scissors proved completely useless. Eventually, the welding devices were used, but the cables connecting the two caravans needed to be taken apart one at a time. The antenna, held in place on a sturdy steel base, reached a height of almost seventy feet, and it refused to move from its place until several paratroopers climbed on top and used the weight of their bodies to bring it down. The dismantling process, which was supposed to take thirty minutes, lasted more than an hour. At the same time, IAF Skyhawks were attacking Egyptian targets in the Gulf of Suez as a diversionary tactic. The work finally ended, and, at 2:45 A.M., the first Yassour appeared, flown by Dagan. The main container was then tied on with a "hammock," a special sling, and Dagan slowly rose up above the site. At that moment, he realized that the precise weight of the container was beyond expectations: 4.1 tons. The Yassour was built to carry a weight of up to just three tons. But the helicopter lifted off anyway, and the soldiers on the ground cheered with excitement.

The battle is over; the radar is in the paratroopers' hands.
(Zvi Malik, IDF Archive)

The enthusiasm spread to the senior commanders waiting on the other side of the gulf, but that feeling faded away quickly and was replaced by deep anxiety. Inside the helicopter's cockpit, red lights started blinking and sirens wailing. Dagan reported that one of the two hydraulic systems installed on the helicopter had become completely inoperable. It appeared that the cables harnessing the load had become too tightly strung because of the excess weight and had crushed the oil tube, which had spilled oil that damaged the helicopter's hydraulic drive system. According to the operating manual, Dagan had to dump the cargo immediately; otherwise he was risking a fatal accident. But Dagan decided to carry on. From the command post on the Israeli beach in Sinai, the commanders followed him with bated breath. They understood the risk he was taking on, continuing to fly with a load much heavier than the Yassour was capable of carrying, and with just one functioning hydraulic system. "The aircraft was shaking," Dagan recounted. "But we crossed the Gulf of Suez, and we immediately landed on the sand."

Simultaneously, Matas was reaching his destination, loading the second container which was lighter—and the antenna, and starting on his way. Over the Gulf, the Yassour bounced around violently, but Matas kept control and he, too, arrived safely. The three Super Frelons landed next to the defunct radar station and returned the commandos to Israeli territory.

Upon their return, the paratroopers were received by Raful Eitan, who told them about a similar mission carried out by British commandos during the Second World War. The soldiers had landed on a German base in France but brought back only a few components of a radar station, and many were killed. Israel's air force and paratroopers had obtained an intact radar station, without losses—the only operation of its kind in the world. Defense Minister Moshe Dayan sent two bottles of champagne to the commander of the helicopter squadron, a gift to the team.

The secret surrounding the mission was kept for a few days, until it was published by London's *Daily Express*. In the Israeli newspapers, which were submitted to strict military censorship, cartoons appeared showing Israeli helicopters transporting the pyramids and the Sphinx.

IAF experts analyzed the radar systems and learned the principles of the Soviet methods. On the basis of their findings, they then developed new methods of electronic combat. The radar secrets were also revealed to the Americans.

Dagan was honored with a Medal of Distinguished Service, and Chief of Staff Bar-Lev told the paratroopers who had participated in the missions, "You performed one of the most complicated, daring, impressive actions the IDF has ever carried out."

NEHEMIAH DAGAN, COMBAT PILOT

"The first two Yassours arrived from America in September, and within a month we were deeply immersed in the war of attrition. We trained there—four pilots and fifty mechanics. I was appointed commander of the Yassour wing within the Frelon squadron.

"They called me from headquarters and talked to me about lifting a radar container. Officially, I could have lifted two-point-nine tons with a Yassour. We trained only for one day, Ze'evik Matas and me, at lifting a radar container. They told me, 'A radar container weighs three-point-two tons.' I said, 'Look, guys, this is heavier.' They replied, 'Nehemiah, don't wear us out with your problems.'

"We didn't have night-vision devices, so we needed moonlight, and we came in flying low. I feared that there would be problems with tying up the container, that it would be installed too high on the truck bed. But we discovered that the truck had been dug into the ground, and I could hover practically at surface level.

"I lifted the container and saw that it weighed four-point-one tons—one-point-two more than the permitted load. The instant I lifted off, a row of warning lights came on. I said,

'The hydraulic system has gone out on me.' Typically in such a situation, you land and turn everything off immediately.

"I decided that I'd keep going. I told the copilot, Tron, a top expert in the aircraft's mechanics, 'Let's shorten the flight path.' I reached the Red Sea and ordered the aircraft mechanic to look out the window to see whether a fire had broken out in the engines. I landed on the other side of the gulf. The moment that Ze'evik Matas unloaded the second container on our side, they immediately sent him to take my container, which had shaken so hard during the passage. I received a medal, but believe me, I've been in much more dangerous operations."

In 1970 the Soviets heavily increase their involvement in the Middle East conflict, to the point where it may degenerate into an armed confrontation with the United States.

CHAPTER 11
"THE ENEMY SPEAKS RUSSIAN!" 1970

O n April 18, 1970, at the height of the war of attrition, two Israeli Phantom pilots, Eitan Ben Eliyahu and Rami Harpaz, were on their way back from a photo-reconnaissance mission over Egypt. The war of attrition had broken out a short time after the Six Day War. Initially, the fighting had focused mostly on the area around the Suez Canal, but it spread incrementally, and the IAF had been carrying out audacious sorties deep in Egyptian territory.

That morning, as Ben Eliyahu and Harpaz flew toward Israel, several Egyptian MiG-21s appeared at high altitude. There was nothing special about this encounter, but this time, listening devices belonging to the IDF's 515th Intelligence Service Unit (later Unit 8200) recorded strange voices speaking an unfamiliar language. The person who understood the language was a young man named David, who was serving at the Umm Hashiba base, in Sinai. He immediately called his commander, Major Tuvia Feinman, and excitedly reported, "We've recorded transmissions between Soviet fighter pilots."

Feinman responded with a colorful curse. He knew that Russian technicians, trainers and advisers—not pilots—were working in Egypt, and he surmised that the soldier and his friends had recorded a conversation between them.

"No, Tuvia," David responded. "This is something else."

Feinman immediately sent a Bell helicopter to Umm Hashiba, which returned with the recording reels containing the conversations. Feinman, who knew Russian fluently, listened to the tapes and rushed to the head of military intelligence, General Aharon Yariv. At 8.00 P.M., Yariv held a crash meeting with Minister Golda Meir, and that night she passed along the recordings to U.S. president Richard Nixon.

The recordings were definitive proof: not only were the Soviets supplying weapons to the Egyptians, they were secretly sending military troops and fighter squadrons. The planes were adorned with the logos of the Egyptian Air Force, but they were being flown by Soviet pilots!

This marked a dangerous turn of events. Israel didn't want to get entangled in a conflict with a superior power. The Soviet Union had been the main weapons supplier to Egypt and Syria (and later to Iraq) from the mid-fifties onward, and again after the Egyptian Army was defeated by the IDF in 1967. Moscow responded to the Egyptian president's request by sending military experts, advisors, air controllers and pilots. These facts had been kept secret until Israel's discovery.

Thirty-four Israeli soldiers of Russian background reported the Soviet presence. They were serving in the top-secret Masrega ("Knitting Needle") unit, commanded by Major Feinman. In addition to training in intelligence, the soldiers had received a refresher course in Russian. They had formed a special subculture for themselves, with Russian underground songs and Pushkin poems, vodka drinking and stories in Russian, and were nicknamed the "Grechkos," after the Soviet defense minister. As the reports of Soviet involvement in Egypt grew, they were dispatched to the 515th, in Sinai. Bit by bit, they gained mastery of the military terms used by the Russians; however, until April 18, they had only recorded conversations between technical crews. Suddenly, that day, the voices emerging from their radio devices belonged to Soviet pilots.

This raised the latent conflict between Israel and the Soviet Union to a dangerous level. Israel tried not to escalate it. Defense Minister Moshe Dayan instructed the head of the air force, Motti Hod, to halt the attacks deep in Egypt. The United States also advised caution; after all, they said, Israel wouldn't want a confrontation with a superpower. But the Soviets's self-confidence only grew; they moved their missile batteries to the shores of the Suez Canal, and their planes pursued Israeli jets on photo-reconnaissance and bombing missions, trying to engage them in combat. On one occasion, they even hit the tail of a Skyhawk with an air-to-air missile; the pilot managed to land at the Refidim airbase, in Sinai.

Meir and Dayan still hesitated. But on July 25, when Israeli Skyhawks attacked Egyptian positions on the Suez Canal, Soviet MiGs appeared in the sky and chased them into Sinai. "Superpower or not," Meir grumbled to herself, and ordered that Israel strike back at the Russians, as they deserved.

Hod decided to devise an operation against the Russians: an aerial ambush of the sort his pilots had pulled off more than once in the region. David Porat, who had designed ambushes in the past, was chosen to put together something special.

But how does one lay an ambush in the clear blue sky?

Hod established an elite team of the air force's best pilots and on July 30, 1970, ordered it to spring the trap. The area chosen as the site of battle was a third of the way between Cairo and the city of Suez, close to the Katameya airbase, where the Russian squadrons kept their planes. Israel's opening shot in the operation—code-named Rimon 20—was the takeoff of four Phantoms guided by Ben Eliyahu from the Ramat David airbase. The planes crossed the Gulf of Suez and started attacking the Egyptian positions next to Adabiya. The Phantoms mimicked Skyhawks fighter jets with bombing capacities but inferior to the Soviet MiGs. The Phantoms kept flying in an "Indian circle" over their targets—imitating American Indians circling cowboys on horseback—with one pilot at a time diving toward his objective, dropping his bombs and returning to the formation. This was a classic Skyhawk tactic. At their radar stations, the Egyptians and the Russians saw four dots circling above Adabiya, and it seemed clear to the ground controllers that they were Skyhawks.

Simultaneously, a dot of light appeared on their screens, passing from north to south at an altitude of twenty thousand feet. The controllers identified the dot as a lone Mirage jet, apparently on a reconnaissance mission. The Israelis were misleading them here as well. The "lone" dot was in fact comprised of four Mirages, which were flying in a tightly compact formation that was made to look like a single plane. The Mirage pilots even reported via radio on the progress of a reconnaissance mission. Together, they were the bait—what appeared to be an unarmed reconnaissance plane and four antiquated Skyhawks. The commander of the Russian squadrons fell for it and decided to unleash his pilots on the easy prey.

The Russians didn't know that an additional quartet of Mirages had taken off from Ramat David and was flying at low altitude in Sinai, below the mountain ridges, so that their radar stations wouldn't see them. Meanwhile, four more Mirages, engines thundering, were ready on the runways of the Bir Gifgafa airfield, in Sinai. As Ehud Yonay wrote in his book *No Margin for Error: The Making of the Israeli Air Force*, Porat succeeded, through this trickery, in "hiding four Mirages and four Phantoms in the blue summer sky, and another eight Mirages not far away."

The Russians dispatched four quartets of MiGs from the Beni Sueif and Kom Osheim airfields. The first, lead by Captain Kamenev, flew northward, in the direction of the "solo" reconnaissance Mirage, in order to confront it on its journey. The second, led by the squadron commander, Captain Nikolai Yurchenko, was meant to close in on the Mirage with a forceps maneuver from the south. A third quartet, under the command of Captain Saranin, had been directed to strike it from the west. Another formation of four MiGs turned toward the "Skyhawks"; four more MiGs took off a few minutes later. At the air force Pit, Hod pressed a button on his stopwatch and ordered his pilots to attack.

The Soviets were stunned. The "lone" Mirage suddenly became four, which dropped their detachable fuel tanks and turned toward the MiGs. The four Skyhawks suddenly climbed skyward and revealed themselves to be state-of-the-art Phantoms swooping down on the Soviets from on high. Then the four Mirages that had been flying below the Sinai mountaintops burst out, with the quartet that had been waiting on the runways at Bir Gifgafa following in their wake. The voices of the Soviet ground controllers suddenly went silent, as the electronic wizards of the Israeli Air Force blocked their radio channels. The Soviet pilots, accustomed to a constant flow of instructions from their ground controllers, were left disoriented, at a loss for what to do.

An ambush in the clear blue sky. *(AF Journal)*

The Mirage pilot Asher Snir brought down the first MiG. Its pilot ejected, and the canopy of his parachute fanned out amid the aerial battlefield, where thirty-six planes were clashing. Avihu Bin-Nun and Aviem Sella also shot down two planes, and Avraham Salmon and Iftach Spector brought down two more.

The Russian pilots weren't used to wild aerial battles in which their customary formations came apart, and there was no ground controller to guide them. Initially, their voices on the radio stayed calm, but as the battle went on, they sounded increasingly frightened, and some shouted, "Abort!" The Russian ground controllers also lost their cool, trying to contact their pilots and calling them by their names. A number of the pilots broke away and escaped toward their bases; others also tried to get away from the Israelis, however, the Israeli planes pursued them. Two and a half minutes into the battle, Hod glanced at his stopwatch and ordered a halt. The Israeli ground controller's voice emerged from the radio, instructing, "Everyone, cut off contact. Disconnect at once and get out of there!"

The skies indeed cleared at once, and the Israeli jets turned toward their bases. They left behind five burning MiGs in the Egyptian desert; three of the Soviet pilots had managed to parachute, and two were killed.

Moscow was in shock. The next day, Marshal Pavel Stepanovich Kutakhov, the Soviet Air Force commander, arrived in Egypt to ascertain the reasons for his pilots' failure. While grim inquiries were held in Egypt, modest parties were held on airbases in Israel. Air force commanders didn't forget the Grechkos and sent them bottles of champagne. The celebrations' secret participants, of all people, were the Egyptian Air Force pilots, who had been the butt of numerous insults from the Soviet pilots; the Russians had mocked their inability to take on the Israeli Air Force. This was, for the humiliated Egyptians, a moment of sweet revenge on their Soviet allies.

Within days, the news was leaked to the foreign press, and the story of Operation Rimon 20 exploded in dramatic headlines around the world.

GENERAL AMIR ESHEL, COMMANDER IN CHIEF OF THE AIR FORCE

"Bringing down the Soviet jets calls to mind one of the events of the War of Independence, when the first members of the air force took down five British planes that had infiltrated southern Israel. There are those who tell us that the Israeli Air Force is good, but only against other air forces in the region, which aren't at its level. And suddenly we're battling a superpower—a rival from an entirely different league—and we can handle it. And you achieve a result that is exceptional both in absolute terms and against the backdrop of that time. During that same period, the Americans were fighting the Vietnam War and in other conflicts, and weren't managing to achieve results like these. Meanwhile, here we are, in one battle—boom!

"Cynics will say, 'You ambushed mediocre pilots.' That isn't true. The Russians flying in Egypt knew what they were doing. They weren't suckers and knew that failure was forbidden. But our action brought out the Israeli air force's professional ability, acuity and determination.

"The state of Israel puts the best of its resources into the air force. We're able to get to places that no one else can—and to get the job done there. An air force plane knows how to attack in Tehran and to do so in Gaza, and it's in the hands of excellent people.

"Operation Rimon brought together our best attributes, talents and abilities—and is a sort of milestone, a sort of beacon."

After the debacle of the Arab armies in 1967,
several terrorist organizations have stepped into the
vacuum and try to harm Israel by a succession of hijackings,
bombings and assassinations. The major terrorist group is
Yasser Arafat's Palestine Liberation Organization, and
its secret striking force is named Black September.

CHAPTER 12
WHITE ANGELS ON JACOB'S LADDER, 1972

R eginald Levy, the pilot of Sabena Airlines' Boeing 707 flying from Brussels to Tel Aviv, felt a surge of pleasant anticipation. Today was May 8, 1972, his fiftieth birthday, and he was going to celebrate it with his wife, Deborah, presently sitting in first class behind him. Levy, a former RAF pilot, born in Blackpool to a Jewish father, felt a special bond to the land of Israel, and Jerusalem was undoubtedly the best setting for marking this significant milestone in his life.

The Boeing was flying high over Yugoslavia when he suddenly felt the brutal thrust of a gun barrel against his neck. He couldn't see his aggressor, but glancing sideways, he noticed his copilot, Jean-Pierre Arins, slumped in his seat, a mustached man pointing a gun at his head. They were being hijacked.

As he soon realized, his plane had been taken over by four Palestinian terrorists who had boarded in Brussels with forged Israeli passports. The other passengers couldn't guess that "Zeharia Greid" was actually Abd Aziz el Atrash, "Sara Bitton" was Rima Tannous, and "Miriam Hasson" was Theresa Halsa. Their commander, who would soon introduce himself as "Captain Rif'at," was Ali Taha Abu-Sneina. The four hijackers were members of Black September, the new, deadly terrorist organization secretly created by Yasser Arafat. This was their first operation against Israel.

Before taking over the plane, the four hijackers had successively used the plane's bathrooms to take out the weapons they had concealed on their bodies: two handguns, two hand grenades, two explosive belts weighing two kilograms each, detonators and batteries.

Now Rif'at and Atrash were standing in the cockpit, their guns pointed at the pilots. "You will fly to Tel Aviv," Rif'at ordered Levy, his voice clipped, heavy with emotion. "No tricks! We've got explosives and hand grenades."

"But I am flying to Tel Aviv," Levy stammered.

"Yes, you are. But now you'll be following my orders."

In tourist class, a pretty black-haired girl in a flower-patterned mini-dress gracefully slipped into an aisle seat beside the elderly Hershel and Ida Norbert, who were on their way to meet their relatives in Israel after twenty years of separation. They gaped in bafflement at the young woman, who held a round black box tied to her wrist by a length of wire.

In the cockpit, Rif'at grabbed the microphone. "Attention! Attention, all passengers! Stay in your places and don't move. I am Captain Kamal Rif'at, of Black September. We represent the Palestinian people. The plane is now in our command. You must obey orders!"

Shouts and crying echoed throughout the plane. Hershel Norbert stared in horror at the girl in the flowered dress, who jumped from her seat, brandishing her box over her head. "God, a disaster!" Ida moaned. Behind her, a middle-aged Israeli woman fainted in her seat. Another woman, Breindel Friedman from Jerusalem, shrieked in fear as she saw two figures emerge from the cockpit. One of them, wearing a nylon stocking over his head, looked to her like a monster. He held a handgun and a grenade in his hands. The other hijacker was shorter, narrow-shouldered, with sallow skin and a black mop of hair that Breindel decided was definitely a wig.

Another female hijacker appeared in the aisle, wearing a light-colored pantsuit; she collected the passengers' passports in a large bag. She suddenly picked up the flight attendant's microphone and shouted, "If the Israelis don't give us what we demand—we shall blow up the plane. Everybody will die—everybody!" Some of the passengers burst into tears. "Help us, God!" a woman shouted in Hebrew. "This is the end!"

The news of the hijacking reached Defense Minister Moshe Dayan while he was on a helicopter tour of Israeli positions along the Suez Canal. "Fly straight to Lod!" he said to the pilot. But the first one to reach Lod airport (later named Ben-Gurion) was the commander of the Central Military District, General Rehavam ("Gandhi") Ze'evi.

Like Yitzhak Rabin, Haim Bar-Lev and many other senior officers, Ze'evi was a former member of the Palmach, the paramilitary underground during the British Mandate that became the elite corps of the IDF during the Independence War. Skinny to the point of looking like a skeleton, he appeared one Friday night in the dining room of his kibbutz, head shaved, torso naked and a towel wrapped around his waist; the resemblance to the Mahatma was striking, and he won the nickname "Gandhi" for the rest of his life. He had an odd sense of greatness; on becoming commander of the Central Military District, whose emblem was a lion, he brought to his compound two lion cubs that he kept in a cage at the entrance to his office.

And yet, he was an excellent soldier, daring, smart and resourceful. Two years before, several terrorists had hijacked four American airliners, landed them in Jordan and Egypt and blown them up. Gandhi had gathered his staff officers, and amid their smirks and ironical grins had asked them for a response to the hypothetical landing of terrorists in Lod aboard a plane and the taking of hostages. Undeterred by his officers' attitude he had devised a plan, Isotope, to stop the plane and later overpower the hijackers. When Moshe Dayan and Transport Minister Shimon Peres reached the airport, Isotope was already partly implemented. Commando units were in place and orders had been given to direct the plane to Runway 26, "the silent runway," which was situated far from the main terminal.

Several senior IDF officers arrived in haste and crowded the tiny third-floor room that had turned into an improvised command head-quarters. Beside the new chief of staff Dado Elazar stood the Head of Operations Israel Tal, IAF Commander Motti Hod, Head of Intelligence Aharon Yariv and a few members of Shabak, the Internal Security Service, in civilian clothes. Dayan maintained permanent contact with Prime Minister Golda Meir and kept her informed of the developments.

The plane landed at 7:05 P.M. The hijackers' scheme was a daring gamble. The very landing in Lod, in the lion's mouth, was a challenge to Israel's formidable might. By threatening to blow up the plane with its innocent passengers, the terrorists were placing a gun at Israel's head that should force her to accede to their demands. But their smart and daring plan had one flaw: they did not realize that Moshe Dayan and his colleagues could not afford to be defeated by terrorists who challenged Israel on its very soil, with the whole world watching.

Using the plane radio, Captain Rif'at stated his demands: Israel would release 317 Palestinian terrorists held in its jails; they would be flown to Cairo immediately. The Sabena plane would wait in Lod airport until the Palestinians landed in Cairo. Then it would fly to Cairo, and there the hijackers would free the hostages.

Dayan, cold and cynical, assumed control of the operation. His main goal was to draw out the negotiations and wear down the terrorists; a military operation should be planned, but only as a last resort. General Yariv was charged with the negotiation with Rif'at. Soon he was joined by Victor Cohen, the head of the Shabak Investigation Department, who spoke fluent Arabic. Yariv politely asked Rif'at, "How much time do you give us to satisfy your demands?"

"Two hours," Rif'at snapped. "If you don't comply in two hours—we shall blow up the plane."

"But in two hours I could barely get fifteen people over here," Yariv protested.

Actually, the IDF had gotten more than fifteen people over, but they were not the people Rif'at had in mind. The newcomers were the members of the legendary Sayeret Matkal (Unit 269)—the best commando team of the IDF, a unit where only the most qualified and the most daring soldiers could serve. The Sayeret had been created in 1957. Its members and commanders were never identified, its missions never disclosed, and its very existence was protected by rigid censorship. The soldiers serving in the Sayeret were discreetly handpicked, subjected to a variety of tests, then trained at a secret base. The Sayeret was a rumor, a mirage. At its head, in 1972, was a daredevil, Colonel Ehud Barak.

Raised in kibbutz Mishmar HaSharon, the young soldier had soon been noticed for his creative mind and his bravery. He was a gifted piano player, known for his passion for taking apart and assembling clocks and watches. He had soon become the most decorated soldier in the IDF, for his courage and military feats, some of which remain secret to this very day. He left the army to study physics and mathematics at Hebrew University, earned another degree at Stanford University, in the U.S., worked for a while at the Weizmann Institute and finally reenlisted. In 1971, he was appointed commander of the Sayeret.

On the night of May 8, while Yariv and Cohen were negotiating with Rif'at, the Sayeret was at a remote area of the airport rehearsing a surprise attack on a Boeing 707, placed at their disposal by Israel Aircraft Industries. Under the dazzling light of powerful arc lamps, the commandos were rehearsing a simultaneous penetration into the plane through the pilot's cockpit and the emergency exits. In the shootout that would ensue, the terrorists would be neutralized before they had time to trigger their explosive charges.

As night fell, Dayan's major concern was to immobilize the hijacked aircraft on the ground and prevent it from taking off. Benyamin Toledo, an El Al veteran mechanic, escorted by Barak and another soldier, sneaked to the back of the plane. Toledo crawled to the aircraft's belly and expertly removed the valve controlling the hydraulic system of the landing gear. The oil immediately started to spill on the runway. A few moments later Toledo quietly laid the valve in front of Dayan.

Still, Dayan was not fully satisfied. Five minutes later, Toledo and another mechanic, Arieli, were crawling under the Boeing again. This time their objective was the plane tires. As the compressed air started hissing its way out, the plane sank down a few inches without anybody noticing. Only Captain Levy saw the hydraulic oil warning light engage. He called the control tower and reported the problem. A moment later he reported trouble with the tires.

"Tell those guys," Dayan told Levy, "that they can't take off."

"I already have," Levy said, and asked that somebody come to repair the hydraulic gear. Dayan answered that this would take time, as the airport authorities would have to bring over an expert from Tel Aviv. Captain Rif'at tacitly agreed to wait, but now he demanded to talk immediately with the Red Cross representatives in Israel. Their arrival was also delayed. At 1:30 A.M., Rif'at lost patience and threatened the Israelis that if the plane was not repaired in one hour, he would blow it up; to which Cohen calmly answered that the aircraft could not be repaired during the night. Finally, Rif'at agreed to wait until 8:00 A.M.

Under the cover of darkness, the Sayeret fighters surreptitiously approached the plane. They felt they were ready to attack it right then, but Dayan chose to wait a little longer. Yet, he told General Elazar, "Starting from now, you must be ready for action."

At about 3:00 A.M., a momentary lull descended upon the airport, and several of the Israeli officers fell asleep in their chairs. Dayan had found refuge in the air controllers' room, but was soon driven out by the flushing and gurgling of a nearby toilet. He finally stretched out on a sofa in the children's playroom, flanked by a plastic-foam giraffe and a rubber effigy of Popeye.

With sunrise the Red Cross officials arrived and were allowed to visit the plane. At 9:00 A.M., they were back at the terminal and told Moshe Dayan that the situation in the plane was unbearable. The food and water had run out, the air-conditioning didn't work, the passengers were exhausted and the hijackers were tense and nervous. "Will you release the prisoners?" the Red Cross envoys asked Dayan, but he stuck to his delaying tactics. "We agreed to negotiate," he said.

There was something absurd in the situation. It was a glorious sunny day, and Lod airport was carrying on its routine activity: planes were taking off and landing, crowds of passengers filled the terminal halls, arriving and departing. And in full sight of all, at the distant end of a runway, a hundred hostages were held in an explosive-rigged plane that could blow up any moment.

Captain Levy was alone in the cockpit when one of the hijackers, Atrash, walked in. Levy felt it was now or never. He threw himself on the Palestinian, grabbed his gun, aimed it at him and pulled the trigger.

Nothing happened.

He pulled the trigger again. Nothing.

Only now did he realize that the safety catch was on.

Atrash jumped him and wrung the gun out of his hand. He then released the safety catch and aimed the weapon at Levy's head.

Levy begged for his life. "Don't shoot!" he managed. "Don't! If you kill me, that would be the end of everything!"

To his great surprise, a lopsided grin spread on Atrash's face. "I should have killed you," he slowly said, "but you might be right, and we'll still need you to get out of here."

Captain Rif'at entered the cockpit. He suspected that the Israelis were delaying the negotiation because they didn't believe he could blow up the plane. He stuck a small plastic bag in Levy's hands that contained some of the explosive he had brought on board. He ordered him to get off the plane and meet "the people in the control tower." He didn't mince words. "Tell them that the plane is rigged with this stuff, and that we have enough of it to blow up not one but five planes. If you return with a negative answer or do not return at all, we'll blow up the plane."

A Red Cross car took Levy to Dayan. The pilot carried out his mission calmly. A quick examination by two officers proved that the contents of the plastic bag were indeed a powerful explosive. In the meantime word came from Shabak analysts who had discovered Rif'at's true identity. The man was a serial plane hijacker. He had hijacked an El Al plane to Algeria in 1968 and a Lufthansa plane to Aden in February 1972.

When facing Dayan and the generals, Levy gave them a clear and succinct report about the situation aboard the plane, the terrorists and their positions. The two female hijackers had placed their explosive belts in the front and the rear of the plane cabin, and carried hand grenades. The pilot's report was to be of great help to the Sayeret fighters later. While he was speaking, an observer positioned on the terminal's roof reported that he had identified one of the female hijackers and she could be easily recognized by her dress's color.

Dayan was cheered when Levy described to him his confrontation with Atrash in the cockpit and the Palestinian's decision not to kill him. That confirmed Dayan's motive in delaying the negotiation and wearing down the terrorists. Dayan had been right: the terrorists did not want to commit suicide; they wanted to live, that was why they had spared Levy's life.

Dayan reached his decision. "Go back," he told Levy, "and tell those guys that we agree to release the prisoners. We'll bring them to the airport so they can see them with their own eyes. We'll repair the plane and you will fly it to Cairo."

Levy seemed relieved, but he took Dayan aside. "I have a last wish," he said. "If we don't get out of this alive, will you make sure that Israel takes care of the education of my daughters?"

Dayan promised. Before Levy left, Dayan asked him, "Are there any sick people aboard?"

"No."

"Any pregnant women?"

Levy chuckled. "Not yet." Even in those fateful moments, the guy's sense of humor had not evaporated.

Dayan was deeply moved by the pilot's courage. But when he turned to Dado Elazar, he was his old cynical self. "Dado," he quipped, "you have until four P.M. to free the passengers. I must be back at the office by five. I have an appointment."

Levy returned to the hijacked plane. Shortly before four, the terrorists saw a magnificent sight: a TWA Boeing was being towed by a small tractor to the vicinity of their plane. That was the plane that would take the released terrorists to Cairo! Rif'at and his comrades also saw buses carrying handcuffed prisoners dressed in sweatsuits; it was clear that these were the terrorists, soon to be released. Rif'at and his three friends burst into wild shouting, "The Zionists have surrendered!" They jumped with joy, hugging and embracing each other.

They were wrong. The "prisoners" in the buses were Colonel Yitzhak Mordechai's paratrooper recruits, who had been dressed and cuffed and brought over as a deception. As for the Boeing, it was a wreck, recently purchased by the Israel Aircraft Industries; it even had been stripped of its engines.

The operational plan was ready. According to an agreement with the terrorists, a convoy of small service vehicles was to approach the Sabena plane, carrying the mechanics who were about to repair the aircraft. But actually the "mechanics" were sixteen Sayeret fighters. Barak had divided his men into attack details. Among their commanders were Uzi Dayan, Moshe Dayan's nephew and a future commander of the Sayeret, who had been home sick with rubella, but hurried to volunteer for the mission; Dany Yatom, a future head of the Mossad; Mordechai Rahamim and Benyamin ("Bibi") Netanyahu.

At the last moment an argument had set the two Netanyahu brothers, Yoni and Bibi, against each other. They were members of the Sayeret (and their third brother, Iddo, who was studying in the U.S., would join the Sayeret the following year). Sons of a famous Israeli scholar of right-wing convictions, Professor Benzion Netanyahu, the two young men, raised in Israel and America, were known for their courage. Both of them wanted to participate in the Sabena mission. Barak was willing to take only one of them. Yoni pulled rank and seniority on his younger brother, but Barak finally opted for Bibi.

In order to make the deception work, the commandos donned white overalls, urgently brought from the nearby Tel Hashomer hospital. They got on their service vehicles but were intercepted by Gandhi, who had noticed that their overalls were too white, too immaculate. That was not the way mechanics were supposed to look. The terrorists might see through the ruse, Gandhi said, and the entire plan would be doomed. Gandhi ordered the soldiers to crumple and soil their overalls and roll about on the runways, so they would look as mechanics should after a long day's work. He also added some older, real mechanics to the team, lest the youthful faces of the commandos arouse suspicion.

An important challenge facing the Sayeret was the use of handguns. The attack should be carried out with handguns, but the fighters had trained in the use of all sorts of firearms except handguns. "That was the first time in my life that I held a gun," Netanyahu later admitted. In order to overcome that obstacle it was decided to bring over several reserve fighters of the Sayeret who were employed as security guards in the El Al planes. Those men had been extensively trained in the use of handguns and were considered experts. One of them, Mordechai Rahamim, even had become a hero when he'd single-handedly pounced on four terrorists armed with Kalashnikov submachine guns and hand grenades who had attacked an El Al plane in Zurich. Athletic, Kurdistan-born Rahamim had jumped out of the plane, killed one of the terrorists and kept firing at the other three, until the Swiss security forces arrived. The world press sang the praise of this young man who'd held at bay three Kalashnikov-armed terrorists with nothing but his handgun. Rahamim was covered with glory, and his gun, a Beretta 0.22, became very popular in Israel.

Rahamim was called at the last moment to join the Sabena commando. Some Sayeret members lay in wait by the terminal, and as soon as an El Al plane landed, they would snatch the security guards and embed them in the team.

The major concern was the explosives. The mission commanders knew that if the charges exploded, the aircraft would turn into a death trap. The first task of the rescue team, therefore, was to neutralize the explosive belts. A minute before the mission was launched, Chief of Staff Elazar pulled Rahamim aside. "Morduch," he said emotionally, using Rahamim's nickname, "break into the plane and find the charges!"

Finally, the small convoy got on its way and slowly approached the plane. The terrorists ordered the "mechanics" to pass, each one in his turn, before the cockpit, where Captain Rif'at stood with a gun in his hand and watched them. On the ground, beside the "mechanics," stood the Red Cross representatives. Every fighter had to open his overalls when passing in front of the plane to show he was not armed. Actually, all of them had stuck their handguns in the backs of their belts. The Red Cross men noticed the soldiers' guns but didn't do or say anything.

The soldiers started moving around the plane, equipped with tool-boxes and other instruments. They secretly assembled the ladders they would use to climb into the plane. "I was certain I was not going to come out of this plane alive," Rahamim recalled. He whispered to his friends what to tell his family after his death.

And then, suddenly—a new problem. One of the security guards, Yaakov Tzur, who had just arrived with a long El Al flight from abroad, declared that he could not function. "I must relieve myself," he said. "I held back all the way to Israel, and you kidnapped me right from the plane. I have to bend down and do my thing." The incident was both embarrassing and comic, but nobody was in the mood for laughing. Every minute counted. Tzur's comrades tried to convince him that the mission would be very short, and later he would have as much time as he wanted. Netanyahu, the head of his detail, asked him, "Yaakov, you need a small one or a big one?" But Tzur didn't wait, pulled down his trousers and crouched under the plane. And all the Sayeret, and all the generals and all the people of Israel had to wait patiently until Tzur got up and buttoned his pants.

Now, finally, the commandos positioned their ladders. At 4:24 P.M., they heard Barak's shrill whistle. That was the signal. In seconds they climbed to the exit doors and the cockpit entrance. The first to break into the plane from the front left exit door were Mordechai Rahamim and Danny Arditi. Mordechai found himself face-to-face with Atrash, who fired at him. Mordechai fired back but missed. At the same moment Bibi and Arik broke in by the front right exit door, while Omer Eran and Danny Brunner got in by the back left exit door. Omer saw Atrash and shot him.

Danny Yatom failed to enter by the front door, which got stuck after Captain Rif'at fired at the commandos. Meanwhile Uzi and his detail broke in by the back door. Uzi saw in front of him a swarthy man and fired, thinking he was one of the terrorists. The man was actually a di-amond merchant from Belgium, who was severely wounded but sur-vived. Less lucky was an Israeli passenger, Mary Holtzberg-Anderson, who was caught in the crossfire and fatally wounded. Uzi's task was to find Rima Tannous, the female hijacker who was somewhere in the back of the cabin with her explosive belt. He moved from the back toward the center of the cabin and suddenly a passenger, Marcelle Eini, pointed at a woman crouching in the aisle, holding an armed hand grenade. "Don't shoot!" Rima begged. "Don't shoot!"

Uzi grabbed her hand and very cautiously pulled the live grenade from her stiff fingers, "finger after finger." He threw the explosive charges out of the plane and had Rima taken outside.

In the meantime, Mordechai Rahamim was slowly moving forward. Rif'at fired at him from the cockpit door. Rahamim fired back till he emptied his magazine, then crouched behind a seat to reload. While doing so, he tried to calm down a frightened woman sitting next to him: "Don't worry," he mumbled in English, "it will be all right." He did not know that the lady was Reginald Levy's wife. During the exchange of fire, Rif'at escaped to the toilet and Rahamim pursued him there and shot him dead.

On the plane wing, after the rescue. Ehud Barak is in white overalls. *(Ron Ilan, GPO)*

Bibi and Marko Eshkenazi also moved toward the front, looking for Theresa Halsa. Bibi caught her at the left side of the cabin. Marko found in her clothes a battery for the activation of her explosive charge. She violently objected to being taken out of the plane and Marko slapped her; his gun went off and the bullet wounded both her and Bibi.

And then it was over.

The takeover had lasted ninety seconds. The two male hijackers were dead. The women were captured. The passengers were jumping with joy, kissing each other.

Dayan and his staff joined the rejoicing. He congratulated his men and got into his car. When he arrived at his office in Tel Aviv, he glanced at his watch. It was 5:05 P.M. He was on time for his appointment.

Hershel and Ida Norbert were almost smothered with love by their family. But Norbert couldn't forget the sight he had glimpsed by the plane window when the Sayeret attack started. He had seen white figures climbing up and down ladders on the wing of the plane. That reminded him of the book of Genesis in the Bible, describing Jacob's ladder and the angels ascending and descending upon it.

For him and a hundred other passengers, they were angels indeed.

BENYAMIN NETANYAHU, SAYERET MATKAL FIGHTER AND LATER PRIME MINISTER

"What is seared deep into my memory is the moment before the raid, as we stood in white mechanics' overalls on the plane's wing and waited to receive permission to break in. Everyone who has gone through the experience of waiting before a raid involving opposition gunfire knows that, in these moments, every fighter withdraws into himself.

"I had reached the unit before dawn, and there was no one there. We realized that something was happening at the airport, went there and quickly organized in teams. My brother Yoni came and told me, 'I need to be there.' He explained that he was the most experienced fighter in the unit, a claim that was hard to argue with because it was true. I told him that I had to lead my soldiers, and he persisted in taking over my command. I refused. He said, 'Then the two of us will take part in the mission.' I asked him, 'What will we tell our parents if something happens to one of us?' Eventually we turned to Ehud Barak to decide, and Ehud determined that I should go with my soldiers.

"When the signal was given to break in, we pounded on the emergency door over the wing; it let loose, and we threw it onto the runway. Terrorist bullets were whistling around us and hit the hostage Miriam Holtzberg-Anderson. This, too, was a moment seared into my memory until today.

"As we were looking for the terrorists, one of the passengers pointed at a woman crouching between the seats and shouted, 'She's a terrorist.' I pulled her hair, and it turned out that she was wearing a wig. I pulled again and asked her where the explosives are. Marko Ashkenazi ran toward us and said, 'Bibi, I'll deal with her.' I saw that the pistol in his hand was cocked. Because the terrorist wasn't armed, I called at him, 'Marko, no!' But it was too late. The pistol had already discharged the bullet, which hit her and, in a two-for-one, me, too.

"The great significance of Operation Sabena was strengthening the principle that when there is a military option, we execute! Operation Sabena was a groundbreaking operation from the standpoint of resisting hijackings and fighting terror without compromise. Since then, the terrorists' methods have changed, and with them the painful price of hits by suicide bombers, missiles and more. But terror won't stop unless we fight it, and the danger won't disappear if we don't address it."

The IDF code of ethics states that no Israeli soldier
can ever be left behind enemy lines and abandoned,
be it on the battlefield or in captivity.

CHAPTER 13

"STOP! HALT! HANDS UP!" 1972

O n June 21, 1972, Sayeret Matkal embarked on Operation Crate 3, whose objective was the abduction of senior Syrian Army officers from Lebanese territory, in order to trade them for three Israeli pilots held captive over the previous two years in Syria.

"The Crate operations were born after we submitted several crazy plans to the General Staff about how it might be possible to free the pilots, and all were rejected," recounted General (Res.) Uzi Dayan, the operation's deputy commander and later the head of Sayeret Matkal. "One day, I got angry and went to the defense minister and told him, 'Maybe you're too old to understand this, but the captives are our friends. We're hoping that if the situation were reversed, they would also be doing everything to free us.'"

The defense minister was Moshe Dayan, Uzi Dayan's uncle. Chief of Staff David Elazar was also troubled by the plight of the pilots— Gideon Magen, Pinchas Nachmani and Boaz Eitan—who had undergone severe torture in Syrian prisons. The chief of staff had been looking for a way to speed up negotiations over the prisoner exchange and ordered the submission of operational proposals for the abduction of Syrian officers. The Sayeret's idea had fallen on receptive ears and would also be approved by Prime Minister Golda Meir.

The thinking was that, in exchange for such a valuable bargaining chip, senior members of the Syrian intelligence establishment would agree to free the Israeli pilots, as well as influence their Egyptian allies to release ten captives jailed in Egypt.

Operation Crate 1 got under way after several observation missions conducted by Sayeret commanders from the Mount Dov sector, next to the Lebanese border. The location selected as suitable for the abduction was a dirt road in Lebanon, ascending the mountain from the north, at a point where vehicles had to slow down. The Sayeret commandos penetrated into Lebanon in the dead of night and reached the target area. The mountain slopes were covered with dense vegetation. The Sayeret set an ambush with Ehud Barak serving as commander of the raid team and Benyamin Netanyahu as head of the blocking team. They lay in wait for hours, but the Syrians never came, and the mission was called off.

A second attempted abduction, Operation Crate 2, was scheduled for June 19 in the Rosh Hanikra sector, in upper Galilee. This time, the ambush was set on a different route within Lebanese territory. Again, Barak commanded the operation and Netanyahu headed the blocking team. Both of Bibi Netanyahu's brothers, Yoni and Iddo, also took part in the mission. "This was the only operation that Bibi, Yoni and I all participated in together," said Iddo Netanyahu. "Actually, we did something which was not allowed in the IDF." Indeed, the IDF did not allow several brothers to participate in the same mission for fear that they could be all killed or wounded.

The role of the blocking team was to prevent reinforcements from reaching the zone of action and to trap anyone attempting to flee the encounter with Barak's unit. As they lay in wait, a Lebanese shepherd appeared and spotted the border fence barbwire that had been flattened down by one of the teams. He and his flock nearly stumbled onto the hiding men; Bibi Netanyahu radioed Barak, and he instructed his men to capture the shepherd immediately. The commandos grabbed him and laid him down next to them. The shepherd was scared to death, certain he was going to die. "To shut him up, I told him, *'Uskut!'*- 'Shut up!' in Arabic—and signaled with my hand that we would slit his throat if he didn't keep quiet," Iddo Netanyahu said. The shepherd got the message.

But then a new issue arose: a Lebanese armored car armed with a cannon, as well as an additional vehicle, were following the officers' convoy at a distance of roughly 1.25 miles. The two vehicles positioned themselves next to Bibi Netanyahu's concealed detail, and the convoy continued toward the mountain ridge. Netanyahu whispered the news into his radio, informing Barak, who instructed him to keep hiding. Barak reported to General Motta Gur, now commander of the Northern District, and to the chief of staff, who instructed him to halt the operation immediately and withdraw back to Israel.

Barak tried to argue, attempting to persuade the senior command that it would be possible to carry out the assignment without risk, but the response was total refusal. A disappointed Bibi Netanyahu instructed his men to prepare to go. This was his last mission before his discharge from the army, and he had so much wanted it to succeed.

"In the end, the convoy passed mere meters from us," Uzi Dayan said, "and we looked at them longingly." Later they found out that among the Syrian and Lebanese senior officers in the convoy was no other than the chief of staff of the Lebanese Army.

When the Israeli troops returned to the assembly area next to kibbutz Hanita, the debate continued. "Why did you stop us?" Barak asked the chief of staff and the senior officers who were with him. "We were so close to them, we could have carried out the assignment without any trouble. They were in our hands, and we let them go."

Elazar tried to calm him down. "I didn't want to endanger the troops at the ambush—the Lebanese armored car would have discovered them."

Barak countered, "You're forcing us not to tell the truth. If I had known that the mission would be called off, I wouldn't have reported the Lebanese vehicle to you. You could have trusted my opinion. I'm telling you that we could have carried out the assignment successfully. In the future, I'm not going to tell you about any armored cars!"

Two days later, on June 21, authorization was given for Operation Crate 3. Bibi Netanyahu had already been a civilian for twenty-four hours; Yoni Netanyahu was appointed the operation commander, and Uzi Dayan, his deputy.

This time, to avoid yet another aborted mission and retreat, Barak decided to stay at the forward command post, together with General Gur and his later successor, Yitzhak Hofi, so that the operation would be completed.

The group this time was much larger. The Sayeret Matkal force was accompanied by a covering team of paratroopers, an armored unit and members of the Egoz commando unit. In addition, tanks and anti-tank cannons were allocated to provide cover as well. It appeared that nobody wanted to take any chances this time.

"In the lead-up to the mission," Iddo Netanyahu recounted, "we trained a lot for the abduction under Yoni's command—how to grab them, how to pull someone out of a moving vehicle and more. Yoni decided to demonstrate how to do it and chose one of the team members, the poor guy! During the demo, Yoni sprinted unexpectedly at the soldier, who was sitting in a vehicle, grabbed his hair and pulled him out. The guy was thrown from the vehicle onto the ground, and the maneuver was deemed a success—except that the boy was still suffering from scalp pain days later."

At daybreak, the forces breached the border fence and penetrated into Lebanon. Yoni Netanyahu went forth and checked that the path leading to the road was clear of mines. At 11:00 A.M., the Syrian officers' convoy came into view, accompanied by two armored cars and two Land Rovers. The convoy moved in the direction of the village of Rameish and stopped less than a mile to the north.

At 11:25, the Sayeret commandos left their hideout in two vehicles, approaching the breach and stopping next to it. The soldiers pretended to fix a broken-down vehicle; meanwhile, the Syrian convoy started to move forward.

At noon, the convoy passed the village of Ramia. Yoni Netanyahu received the order to enter the ambush site on the road. Uzi Dayan's team took up positions by the vehicle, and the rest of the unit spread out along the road in the direction from which the Syrian officers would arrive.

Then something unexpected happened: some Lebanese villagers had seen the Israelis. They stopped a Volkswagen that was driving ahead of the convoy, warning the driver of the Israeli soldiers waiting in the area. The surprised driver continued a few feet, quickly turned around and started fleeing eastward. The soldiers lying ready at the front of the ambush position, awaiting the convoy, saw the Volkswagen turning around, swiftly getting away. One of the commandos ran to Netanyahu and reported what he had seen, just as Netanyahu was receiving word from the command post that the convoy was also starting to turn and head back.

"We realized that they were starting to turn around," Dayan said. "We immediately started running toward them. Yoni's jeep also got there, half a minute later. Initially, they didn't really understand what was happening—they might have thought we were a different Lebanese unit. I shouted at them in Arabic, 'Stop! Halt! Hands up!'"

This was the critical moment: who would pull the trigger first? Dayan fired warning shots at the feet of the Syrians and Lebanese. They were in shock but, after a moment, opened fire as well. The exchange was short but left four Lebanese escort troops dead, among them an officer. A Syrian officer and an Israeli commando were wounded.

Amid the tumult, two officers, one Syrian and one Lebanese, fled north and vanished into the vegetation. The rest of the officers were captured: an intelligence officer at the rank of brigadier general; two armored corps colonels, who served in the operations wing of the Syrian Army; and two pilots with the rank of lieutenant colonel who belonged to the Syrian Air Force intelligence. The Syrian officer who managed to escape was the head of Syrian field intelligence.

The teams of Yoni Netanyahu, Dayan and Muki Betzer conducted wide sweeps in search of the escaped Syrian and Lebanese, but without success. In addition to the officers, a green Mercedes had also gotten away. The blocking team to the east was alerted by radio and gave chase to the Mercedes. The car was later found abandoned, riddled with bullets, next to Ramia. It turned out that the Volkswagen and the Mercedes had happened upon the combat zone by chance, without any connection to the officers' convoy.

The battle scene, minutes after the shooting was over.
(Courtesy of Aviram Halevi & "Israel Defense")

The mission concluded shortly before 1:00 P.M. The soldiers, who had spent just ninety-three minutes in Lebanon, returned to Israel in euphoria. Dayan later remembered, "On the way back to Israel, we already heard the newscast on the radio that there had been an operation in Lebanon. I was driving back in a Chevrolet Impala, and I remember that we worried about filling the holes that the bullets had left in the Land Rovers and the Impala, the latter of which stayed in the service of the intelligence wing for years to come."

The next morning, the Jordanian newspaper *Al Ra'i* commented, "This was the greatest victory for Israeli intelligence in the history of the Arab-Israeli conflict. Israel landed a heavy intelligence blow to the Syrian Army."

Following the abduction, Syria demanded that Israel return its officers without conditions because they weren't prisoners of war. A year later, the two sides agreed to an exchange of captives, and on June 3, 1973, the three members of the air crew returned to Israel. In return, Israel released the abducted officers, as well as forty-one additional Syrian and Lebanese captives. Israel agreed to grant clemency to Kamal Kanji, a Druze leader from Majdal Shams, in the northern Golan Heights, who the previous month had been sentenced to twenty-three years in prison for spying for Syria.

UZI DAYAN, LATER THE DEPUTY CHIEF OF STAFF

"I personally knew the captive pilots, whom we wanted to free following the abduction of the Syrian officers. "Pini" Nachmani had grown up on the moshava of Yokneam, and his mother knew mine. He had also trained in the air force academy with my cousin. He had been a leading navigator in the Sikorsky helicopters of the 114 Squadron, and had participated in many of the operations that his unit had carried out. Through him, I knew Gideon Magen, a Phantom squadron commander, who had also fallen captive.

"When the pilots were released, we met them at the Ramat David airbase, and Nachmani's first words were 'I knew you'd eventually get us out.' It turned out that he had been updated by his wife, Rochaleh, who had written him a letter that had reached him via the Red Cross, and in it she had told him, 'We went fishing in the Kfar Baruch lake and came back with five particularly fat fish.' Nachmani, who knew his wife didn't like fishing, asked the Red Cross representative about operations conducted recently, and he brought him a newspaper clipping about the operation. . . ."

"The greatness of this mission was in our devotion to the task, that we didn't give up. We went back three times before the operation succeeded. Its uniqueness was that it wasn't a mission to bring back intelligence or to strike the enemy—it was intended to save our pilots jailed in a Syrian prison."

After the massacre of the Israeli athletes at the
Munich Olympics, Golda Meir's anti-terrorism adviser,
Aharon Yariv, and the head of the Mossad, Zvi Zamir,
have told the prime minister that if Israel assassinates the
Black September leaders, their organization will cease to exist.
Several Mossad operations in Europe have resulted in the
deaths of Black September commanders. But the major figures
still live with total impunity in the Lebanese capital, Beirut.

CHAPTER 14
THAT LADY MEANS
TROUBLE, 1973

The night of April 9, 1973, the moon was full in Beirut, capital of Lebanon.

It was long after midnight when a couple of lovers appeared, walking along Verdun Street. The man was tall, athletic, clad in a fashionable suit. The woman, small, black-haired, wore a black dress clinging to her slight frame and large breasts. As two gendarmes approached on the same sidewalk, the couple tenderly embraced, their sweet hug lasting until the gendarmes disappeared from sight. The couple then continued walking till they reached a posh apartment building; at this point the two separated. The man, together with some other guys and a blond girl who had emerged from the dark, swiftly entered the building; the woman in the black dress stayed in the street, where she was joined by another, auburn-haired girl.

Across the street was parked a red Dauphine. A huge sentry got out of the car, suspiciously watching the two ladies. He drew his gun and started across the street. But he was in for his life's surprise. The two women suddenly flung off their vests, drew Uzi submachine guns from between their curves and sprayed him with fire. The sentry jumped for cover and dived behind a low fence. A bullet hit the Dauphine's steering wheel and the shrill wail of the car horn tore the stillness of the night.

Operation Spring of Youth was on its way.

The couple the gendarmes had crossed on the street were not a couple of lovers. The tall man was Muki Betzer, one of the best Sayeret fighters. His girlfriend was none other than Ehud Barak, the Sayeret commander. Barak was wearing a black wig, his face was heavily made up and his brassiere was stuffed with hand grenades and old socks. Under his vest he carried weapons and a walkie-talkie. The "other girl" was Amiram Levin, a future Sayeret commander and IDF general. They both had chosen female disguises because they were short and slight; so was "the blond girl," Loni Rafaeli, who got in the building with the men, all of them Sayeret fighters.

Operation Spring of Youth was born at the height of the secret war that Israel waged against the terrorist group Black September. The group had been created by Palestine Liberation Organization leader Yasser Arafat after King Hussein of Jordan had massacred many thousands of PLO members in Jordan, in September 1970; hence "Black September."

At first, the new terrorist organization attacked Jordanian targets, leaders and secret agents; but soon it turned against Israel, hijacked the Sabena Boeing 707 (see Chapter 12) and slaughtered eleven Israeli athletes at the 1972 Munich Olympics. Following the advice of Mossad head Zvi Zamir and the prime minister's adviser on terrorism Aharon Yariv, Golda Meir unleashed the operational team of the Mossad against Black September's leaders, operating undercover in Europe. Zamir and Yariv believed that the elimination of the organization leaders would cause the demise of the entire group and put an end to its terrorist actions. In quick, ruthless Mossad operations in Rome, Paris, Athens and Cyprus, several Black September leaders were killed. But the Mossad and the IDF believed this was not enough, that it was necessary to hit the organization leaders in their very bastion—Beirut. The Lebanese capital had become the base of myriad terrorist groups and organizations that carried out their activities with total impunity. It was time to prove to the terrorist leaders that there was no place under the sun where Israel's long arm wouldn't reach them.

The goal of the operation was to kill three major leaders of Black September and the PLO: Kamal Nasser, the main PLO spokesman; Kamal Adwan, the PLO operations commander, in charge of the activities in the territories occupied by Israel; and the chief commander of Black September himself, Muhammad al-Najar (Abu Yussuf). All three of them lived in a tall apartment building on Verdun Street—Nasser on the third floor, Adwan on the second and Abu Yussuf on the sixth floor at the northern wing of the house. The original idea was to launch a large-scale IDF operation, with the landing of big elite units in Beirut, blockage of the streets around the building, an elaborate attack on the house—but Ehud Barak cancelled that plan. Such a plan, he said to his superiors, means losing the most important factor on which its success depends—surprise. The Sayeret could carry out the mission with fourteen fighters, who would quietly penetrate into Beirut, sneak into the house and break into the terrorists' apartments like a bolt from the blue sky.

Spring of Youth commanders, from right: Amnon Lipkin-Shahak, Shaul Ziv, Emanuel Shaked, Ehud Barak. *(GPO)*

Moshe Dayan accepted the plan but decided to enlarge it. We don't land in Beirut every day, he said; this mission will be quite unique—so let's get the best out of it and hit several enemy targets simultaneously. Chief of Staff Dado Elazar and Chief Paratroop Officer Colonel Mano Shaked decided that while the Sayeret dealt with the three PLO leaders, another team of paratroopers from Airborne Battalion 50 would attack the headquarters of Nayef Hawatmeh's Popular Democratic Front for the Liberation of Palestine (PDFLP), a Maoist, left-leaning terrorist organization. The Battalion 50 team would be led by lieutenant-colonel Amnon Lipkin-Shahak, a lanky, cool-headed officer decorated for "leadership and courage under fire" in a 1968 attack on a PLO base, codenamed Operation Inferno.

The plan was that Lipkin's paratroopers would kill the guards at the entrance of the terrorist headquarters on Khartoum Street and blow up the building with two hundred kilos of explosives (about 440 pounds), killing everybody inside. At the same time other paratrooper units would land outside Beirut and carry out smaller diversion operations.

The Sayeret and the Battalion 50 team would approach the Lebanese coast in navy missile boats and land on Beirut's beach in Zodiac rubber dinghies. A small team of Mossad agents, who would fly to Beirut from several European cities, would be waiting for them on the beach. The agents would arrive a few days before the operation with false passports; they would rent cars, tour the city and get familiar with its streets and avenues. On the night of the mission they would drive the soldiers to their targets and back to the beach after the operation was over. Barak asked for three American cars into which he could squeeze his fourteen men.

The IDF computer supplied the mission's code name: Spring of Youth.

The intensive training of the units started right away. Mano Shaked and Chief of Staff Elazar spent a lot of time with the fighters. Shaked personally wanted to make sure that his paratroopers were becoming familiar with Beirut's streets. He would show one of them air photographs and maps, then place the man with his back to the maps and ask him, "What is on your right? What is on your left?" He believed that his boys should achieve a sense of orientation "with eyes closed" in the neighborhoods where they would operate.

The paratroopers and the Sayeret trained for landing from the sea, moving to their targets by foot or civilian cars, then retreating to the beach and departing aboard their Zodiacs. A model of the house that the Sayeret would attack was built of wood and fabric in a remote army base, and the commandos stormed the apartments using live ammo; they also trained in an abandoned police barracks in Samaria. The Battalion 50 team used the Lamed neighborhood in Tel Aviv as a "model" of Beirut. Some of the houses in that area were still in the building stage and could be used for training purposes without raising the neighbors' suspicion.

Or so their commanders thought.

One night in March 1973, a Lamed resident, sitting by his window, saw some suspect characters sneak between the houses, and heard heavy footsteps and short calls. He alerted the police, who arrived promptly, and Mano Shaked had a lot of trouble convincing them to go. Another doubt was voiced by the owner of a men's store on Disengoff Street. One after the other, young guys came to his store and each asked to buy a suit, one size larger than what he needed. The store owner did not know that these were paratroopers who were supposed to set out for Beirut wearing civilian suits and needed the extra size in order to conceal their weapons under their jackets. The merchant started asking questions, and the paratroopers persuaded him to forget what he heard, what he sold and who bought it.

But the civilians were not the only ones asking questions. One night, after hours of rehearsing the landing in the north of Tel Aviv, the weary paratroopers crouched on the beach, awaiting the rubber boats. One of them, Lieutenant Avida Shor, approached the chief of staff. "May I talk to you, sir?" In no other army in the world would a junior officer dare to approach the chief of staff, but Israel was different.

"Shoot!" Elazar said to the young man.

Avida, member of kibbutz Shoval, was one of the finest paratroop fighters. He had proven his courage in the Tripoli raid, when his unit had landed on a desert beach 133 miles beyond the Israeli border, at- tacked and blown up four terrorist bases and returned practically un- scathed. Avida was also known for his high moral principles. He now drew a small notebook out of his pocket and said to Elazar, "We plan to blow up the PDFLP headquarters with two hundred kilos of explosives. But I made my own calculations and found out that we can bring down the house with only one hundred and twenty kilos."

"What difference does this make?" General Elazar asked.

"The difference is," Avida said forcefully, "that there is another build- ing next to the PDFLP headquarters. It is a seven-story house, inhabited by scores of civilian families. I believe that we should use fewer explo- sives and avoid casualties among the civilians." Then he added, "The ter- rorists should know that we were there and could carry out the mission, but that we would not harm women and children."

There was a moment of silence. Finally Elazar nodded. "I'll buy that," he said. "One hundred and twenty kilos it will be."

From April 1 to April 6, several tourists arrived in Beirut: Gilbert Rimbaud, Dieter Altnuder, Andrew Whichelaw, Charles Boussard, George Elder and Andrew Macy. Most of them carried British or Bel- gian passports and were later identified by foreign sources as Mossad agents. They checked into various hotels and rented cars from Avis and Lena Car. At least three of the cars were American-made, as Barak had requested: a Buick Skylark, a Plymouth and a Valiant.

On April 5, nine missile boats and "Dabur" fast patrol boats took to sea from Haifa port, carrying the Sayeret, the Battalion 50 team and Flotilla 13—the IDF Navy SEALs. Before departing, the soldiers were shown the latest aerial photographs of Beirut, the landing beach and the targeted buildings. The Sayeret fighters received photographs of the three terrorist leaders they had to kill. Some of the men were given si- lenced Beretta handguns. The targets were designated with women's names: Aviva, Gila, Varda, Tzila and Judith.

After nightfall the boats approached Beirut; the city was bathed in light, its nightclubs and restaurants bustling with activity. At the same time, on the Israeli boats, navy soldiers covered the fighters with large, transparent plastic sleeves to prevent their civilian clothes and the makeup some of them were wearing from getting wet. They boarded twelve rubber boats, and shortly before midnight reached the two landing areas—Ramlet Al-Baida and Dove beaches. The beaches were deserted, and the last couple of lovers had left the sandy stretches. In total silence, like ghostly apparitions, the dinghies emerged from the black sea.

Barak's Sayeret and Lipkin-Shahak's team quietly disembarked. Simultaneously, other paratrooper teams prepared to land at some secondary targets. A Flotilla 13 team would land at the Al-Uzai neighborhood, and head for a sea-mines plant and a terrorist base. Another paratrooper team would attack and blow up a warehouse in Beirut port, while the paratrooper commando unit targeted a weapons workshop north of Sidon. The floating headquarters of the mission, headed by Mano Shaked, and a paratrooper rescue unit approached Beirut's beach in two missile boats. Everything was in place.

On the beach, the rented cars and their Mossad drivers were waiting. The soldiers jumped from the Zodiacs and ran to the cars. One of the fighters in Barak's team was Yoni Netanyahu. Barak felt he owed Yoni compensation, after having preferred his younger brother, Bibi, for the Sabena hostage mission. The Sayeret soldiers piled up in the American cars, which drove to Verdun Street and parked in the neighboring Ibn el Walid Street, close to the target building. The men got out and walked in small groups to the big house. The other three cars carried Lipkin-Shahak's paratroopers to Ghana Street, and they surreptitiously moved toward the PDFLP headquarters at the neighboring Khartoum Street. By 1:29 A.M., both teams were in place.

When the odd couple—Ehud Barak and Muki Betzer—reached the house on Verdun Street, they found out that the building's gate was not locked and the guard wasn't there; there would be no problem entering the building. The intelligence reports they had received specified that some security guards would be sitting in a gray Mercedes parked across the street, but there was no Mercedes in sight. The Sayeret teams entered the building and climbed the stairs to the terrorists' apartments. Only

Barak and Levin, who had remained outside, suddenly discovered that the security guards were sitting in the red Dauphine and engaged in a shooting fight with the man who got out of the car. The strident blare of the Dauphine's horn, whichwas hit by a bullet, echoed in the sleeping neighborhood, and the surprise effect was lost.

Muki Betzer, Yoni Netanyahu and two other soldiers reached Abu Yussuf's apartment and blew open the door with an explosive charge. For Betzer, the two seconds between the activating of the charge and its explosion seemed an eternity. The door blew off its hinges, and the commandos hurled themselves into the apartment. They stumbled upon Abu Yussuf's sixteen-year-old son. "Where's your father?" one of them asked in Arabic. The teenager stared in horror at the strangers wearing nylon stockings over their heads, then ran to his room and slipped down the drainpipe to a friend's apartment on the fifth floor. Abu Yussuf's remaining four children were in the apartment, but nobody touched them. Suddenly, a bedroom door opened before the soldiers and there was Black September's chief, Abu Yussuf, in his pajamas. He jumped back into the bedroom and slammed the door. His wife, Maha, tried to get her husband's handgun from the wardrobe. The fighters fired at the door, and Muki kicked it open. Several bursts of gunfire hit Abu Yussuf and Maha, who stood behind him. Yoni and another soldier shot him dead. Abu Yussuf, the man responsible for the Munich Massacre, lay dead on the floor.

Muki left the apartment and ran down the stairs, followed by his men.

In the other wing of the house the two other Sayeret teams approached the apartments of Adwan and Nasser. A few fighters, led by Amitai Nahmani, reached Adwan's apartment and one of them kicked the door open. Adwan stood in front of them, a Kalashnikov submachine gun in his hands. He hesitated for a split second before diving behind a curtain, simultaneously firing at the Israelis and wounding one of them. A soldier who had climbed the water pipe outside the building jumped into the room. At that moment Nahmani shot Adwan. The soldiers searched the apartment, refraining from harming Adwan's wife and two children; they stuffed files and documents into two suitcases and rushed out.

At the same moment the third team, led by Zvi Livne, blew up Kamal Nasser's door. The soldiers broke into the bedroom, where two women lay in their beds. Nasser was not there; the men fired under the beds, searched the closet and finally found the PLO spokesman in the kitchen, where they shot him. As they came out, the door of the apartment across the landing suddenly opened. One of the men fired instinctively and mortally wounded an elderly Italian woman who had been awakened by the shooting.

In the meantime a firefight had erupted in the street. A base of the Lebanese gendarmerie was located at a nearby corner; minutes after the exchange of fire with the security guard started, a Land Rover jeep from the gendarmerie arrived at the scene. Barak and Levin fired at the approaching jeep and hit the driver. The jeep crashed into the cars parked in the street. All its passengers were hit by Barak and Levin, soon joined by the fighters who came out of the building. Another gendarmerie jeep rushed up the street. The soldiers opened intense fire and stopped it as well. Barak ordered his men to get into the cars—and then a third jeep appeared. It was also met by heavy fire and a grenade thrown by Betzer. The gendarmes jumped off the burning vehicle and escaped to the entrance of a neighboring house.

The soldiers ran to the cars, and Yoni was the last to jump into the third car. The entire operation had lasted half an hour. The cars sped toward the beach, but as they approached the beach promenade, two gendarmerie jeeps appeared in front of them, moving slowly and inspecting the area. The American cars crawled behind the Land Rovers in perfect order, till the jeeps turned the corner. The Sayeret team safely arrived at the beach.

At the same time, in another part of Beirut, Lipkin-Shahak's paratroopers stealthily approached the headquarters of the PDFLP. They were fourteen, too—four details of two paratroopers each; Lipkin-Shahak; the unit physician; a Flotilla 13 fighter and the three drivers. The attack would start after two paratroopers would approach the building guards and kill them with silenced Berettas. The two paratroopers chosen for that task were Avida Shor—the one who had convinced Elazar to use fewer explosives—and his friend, Hagai Maayan from kibbutz Magen.

They strolled in a leisurely way up Khartoum Street and stopped by the entrance to the terrorists' building to light their cigarettes. The guards stood there. "Excuse me," Shor said to one of them in English. When the guards turned toward the Israelis, Shor and Maayan drew their handguns and shot them. As he fell down, one of the terrorists groaned, "Allah!"

Nobody noticed the two other guards sitting in a Fiat jeep armed with a "Dushka" Russian-made machine gun that was parked across the street. They suddenly opened fire and riddled the two paratroopers with bullets. Avida Shor was killed on the spot; Maayan was to succumb later. Yigal Pressler, another paratrooper who followed the two, was wounded. Lipkin called Shor and Maayan by radio but there was no answer. For Lipkin-Shahak, "this was a moment of real trouble. Shor doesn't answer, Maayan lies wounded in the street, Igal is bleeding— and we still have to blow up the building!"

From porches, windows and even from the street, the terrorists opened heavy fire on the paratroopers with rifles, Kalashnikovs and machine guns. For Lipkin-Shahak this was "real hell." He radioed to Mano Shaked that there was "a complication."

"Do you need help?" Shaked asked.

"Not for the moment," Lipkin-Shahak said. Shaked immediately launched the diversionary operations, in order to pin down the Lebanese Army forces that might try to interfere in the fighting. The rubber boats, laden with soldiers, darted toward the beaches. The attack was advanced by three minutes, but these were precious minutes.

In Khartoum Street, a full-scale battle was raging between the paratroopers and the terrorists. A soldier tried to haul the wounded Igal to safety; one of the terrorists thought that Igal was one of them and tried to drag him to a nearby courtyard. He let go only after a fierce struggle with Avishai, a Flotilla 13 frogman. The explosions and the bursts of gunfire were accompanied by the terrorists' shouts: *"Yahood! Yahood!"* ("Jews!") To the Israelis' amazement, in the heat of the battle, while the street trembled with the fusillade, local civilians calmly kept going in and out of the neighboring buildings or stood on their porches and watched the combat with interest.

Under the heavy fire four paratroopers managed to enter the building lobby. Firing long bursts with their automatic weapons and throwing hand grenades, they repeatedly hit terrorists who came down the stairs. They now controlled the lobby. One of the paratroopers, Aharon Sabbag, suddenly noticed the lights on the elevator screen blinking in quick succession as the elevator descended to street level. He watched the numbers as if hypnotized. Four . . . three . . . two . . . one . . . As the elevator stopped, he emptied his whole magazine into the cabin. Nobody came out alive.

At that moment the car carrying the explosives broke into the lobby, and the sappers rapidly placed the charges by four of the supporting columns. The soldiers set the fuses for a 180-second delay, then retreated, while their comrades covered them by firing RPGs, bazookas, eighty-one-millimeter mortar shells and tear gas grenades on their way out. The paratroopers loaded the body of Avida Shor, and the still breathing Hagai Maayan, into one of the cars. The driver ignored Lipkin-Shahak's order to wait for the others and rushed down to the beach. The fighters tossed iron nails on the street, to delay any pursuing vehicles, then piled up in the two remaining cars and sped madly toward the beach. The entire operation had lasted twenty-four minutes.

Israeli helicopters emerged over Ramlet Al-Baida beach and evacuated the wounded, while the other men boarded the rubber boats and headed toward the missile boats. The six Mossad agents neatly parked the cars on the beach, leaving the keys in the ignitions, then jumped into the Zodiacs. The car rental bills would be paid in a few days through American Express. In the meantime the diversionary operations of the paratroopers and Flotilla 13 were completed as well, and the soldiers returned to the mother ships from other beaches.

Amnon Lipkin-Shahak turned back—and was petrified. He felt "like Lot's wife" from the Bible, as he saw a huge smoke mushroom rise over the PDFLP building.

In Haifa port Dayan and Elazar were waiting for the commandos. The mission was crowned with total success. The PDFLP headquarters had been destroyed and scores of high-ranking terrorists were buried beneath the ruins. Three of the top leaders of Fatah and Black September were dead. The world press described the IDF's amazing feat on its front pages. In the days to come, following the deaths of Black September's top leaders, the organization crumbled and then simply ceased to exist.

Mano Shaked, impressed with Lipkin-Shahak's calm under fire, awarded him his second medal. Ehud Barak and three other fighters were also decorated.

Less than six months after Spring of Youth, the Yom Kippur War exploded on the banks of the Suez Canal and the peaks of the Golan Heights.

EHUD BARAK, SAYERET MATKAL COMMANDER, LATER DEFENSE MINISTER AND PRIME MINISTER

"About four months earlier, Head of Operations General Kuti Adam had told us that several Fatah leaders were living in these buildings in Beirut, and asked if we could act. We said that we might. We passed on questions to the Mossad, received answers, but the issue calmed down. We made other plans—a raid on an officers' club in Syria and freeing pilots from a prison next to Damascus.

"I was with my wife on a weekend in Eilat when I was summoned to the chief of staff's office. Dado showed me some photographs and told me, 'Here, these buildings.' The chief infantry and paratroopers' officer Mano Shaked proposed that we attack with a task force from the Thirty-fifth Brigade. To me, this looked like an assault on a fortified target—you arrive with forty guys, set down roadblocks, raid every house. . . . I said, 'It's impossible with such a large force. We need the element of surprise. We need to do this with fourteen or fifteen people, to come in civilian attire with American cars and kill them.' This was approved.

"I told my people, 'We'll kill them in bed.' But two of the team commanders said to me, 'What do you mean, kill them in bed? We kill people in bed? What have they done that makes killing them justified? Does that square with our principle of "purity of arms"?'

I said, 'They are bad, dangerous people, working with Arafat.' They said, 'That's nice, but you don't have authority. We want to know that the chief of staff thinks this is legitimate.' I said fine, but I brushed it off. They reminded me of what I had said again and again, and eventually I brought in the chief of staff—and he explained it to them.

"They carried out the task very well. Both were killed in the Yom Kippur War."

AMNON LIPKIN-SHAHAK, COMMANDER OF A PARATROOPER BATTALION, LATER THE CHIEF OF STAFF

"During the battle, we loaded Yigal Pressler, who was wounded, and the body of Avida Shor into one of our cars. But suddenly we saw that the car had disappeared, along with the driver, an older man from the Mossad. We all managed to get into two cars, and we sped off toward the beach. We found the driver there with the third car. I asked what had happened. He told me that, during the War of Independence, he had fought at the Koach fortress, in Galilee, and his commanders had told him, 'You don't move from here.' He didn't move, and fought, even when his friends retreated, until the Arabs won. He hid under the corpses, and that was how he survived. He later crawled out of there and managed to get away.

"Now, during the battle against the terrorists, he recalled that during the War of Independence, he had nearly been killed because he had stayed until the end. 'I thought that you wouldn't get out of there,' he told me, 'and I decided to drive to the beach where we landed, hoping that someone would save me.'

"He had simply fled."

PART FIVE

The Yom Kippur War

Since the 1967 Six Day War, Egypt and Syria have been planning their revenge. On October 6, 1973, Yom Kippur, they attack Israel simultaneously. Israel has its same leaders, and the chief of staff is David Elazar. The Arab leaders have changed: Egypt's Nasser has died and been replaced by Anwar Sadat. Syria's Salah el Jadid is in prison, after a coup by his defense minister, Hafez al-Assad. King Hussein is not a member of the Sadat-Assad alliance; on the contrary, he has secretly warned Israel's leaders of the forthcoming attack. Unfortunately, his warnings have not been taken seriously.

CHAPTER 15

THE BRAVEHEARTS LAND IN AFRICA, 1973

A t 4:30 P.M., on October 15, 1973, the paratroopers of the 247th Reserve Brigade climbed into their half-tracks. The last-minute briefing had just ended, and harried staff sergeants ran to the commanders' half-tracks, carrying the operational maps. A soldier pressed an open tin of cold goulash in his comrade's hand, one of the authors of this book. "Eat something," he cracked, "you'll get your next meal only in Africa."

Africa. For nine days thousands of IDF soldiers and officers were expecting that mission: the moment when their battered army would break through the Egyptian lines that had been established in Sinai, would cross the Suez Canal and emerge at the enemy's rear. They knew that this mission would tip the scales of the war. They also believed that they were taking part in a crazy gamble— penetrating through a gap in the Egyptian lines, advancing between two huge Egyptian concentrations and reaching the canal. But exactly because of the mission's daring and tremendous risk taking it had great chances to be crowned with success. The Egyptians certainly wouldn't even imagine that the IDF would take such a risky gamble before it had succeeded in crushing their forces entrenched on the eastern bank of the canal.

The war had started on October 6, 1973, Yom Kippur—the Jewish Day of Atonement. At 2:00 P.M., the armies of Syria and Egypt simultaneously attacked Israel on two fronts—in the Golan Heights and along the Suez Canal. In the Golan Heights, the Syrians were stopped only because of the desperate courage and the resolve of a few. In the south, the Egyptians crossed the Suez Canal to Israeli-occupied Sinai, conquered most of the IDF forts along the canal and entrenched themselves strongly in a five-mile-deep strip of land in Sinai, causing painful losses to Israel. Defense Minister Moshe Dayan seemed to waver, as he expressed fear for the possible collapse of "the Third Temple" symbolizing the state of Israel; the pretentious declaration of Chief of Staff Elazar that "we'll break their bones" turned out to be just a bubble of hot air.

The counteroffensive of Division 162, under the command of General Avraham ("Bren") Adan, was launched on October 8 and ended in failure. He confronted the Egyptian army and tried to cross the canal, but was repelled. The mission was reluctantly handed over to General Arik Sharon, whose Division 143 also included the famous 247th (former 55th), the reserve Paratroopers Brigade that had conquered Jerusalem in the Six Day War.

At forty-five, Sharon was back in the saddle. After several years in minor positions, he finally had been brought back from the cold by Chief of Staff Yitzhak Rabin, who appreciated his military talent. Ben-Gurion himself had asked Rabin to "take care" of Sharon, whom he loved, in spite of the flaws in his character. Sharon had been promoted to general, and had performed brilliantly in the Six Day War; his combined assault on Abu Ageila fortress in Sinai was being taught in military academies around the world. He had left the army in 1973 after serving as commander of the Southern District and had turned to politics, joining the Likud party, but when the Yom Kippur War broke out he returned as commander of Division 143. In the meantime, Sharon had been hit by two tragedies: his wife, Margalit, had been killed in a car crash, and their eleven-year-old son, Gur, died in an accident, playing with an old rifle. Sharon, though, found solace in the arms of Gali's younger sister, Lily, who married him, gave him two sons and became a wonderful support for him for the rest of her life.

Sharon's superiors in the IDF didn't really want him to cross the canal. Sharon was a maverick, undisciplined, arrogant and a lover of publicity. Besides, he had just become a right-wing political leader, while most of his superiors, including Chief of Staff Elazar, were former members of the left-leaning Palmach. But after Adan's failure of October 8, and Dayan's intervention in favor of the 101 founder, they had no choice but to turn to Sharon.

Sharon, determined that it would be him who'd cross the canal, conceived a plan that seemed absolutely insane. On a patrol in enemy territory, the reconnaissance battalion of his division discovered an intriguing fact. The Egyptian forces that had crossed the canal and occupied a five-mile strip along it were divided into two armies—the Second and the Third. The reconnaissance battalion found out that there was no land continuity between the two armies, but a kind of narrow no-man's-land was separating them. This gave Sharon the idea to send a brigade along the "seam" between the two armies. After reaching and crossing the canal, it would establish a bridgehead in the rear of the Egyptians, lay bridges over Suez and bring the war to the Egyptian heartland. The idea was insane indeed—so insane that nobody in a normal state of mind would believe it could be carried out.

Michael Bar-Zohar, one of the authors of this book, accompanied Sharon and Colonel Amnon Reshef, the commander of an armored brigade, on their climb to the top of an arid hill, and Sharon ordered Reshef's artillery to fire phosphorus shells at five-hundred-meter intervals along the "seam" between the two Egyptian armies. When the firing started, Sharon watched through his binoculars the white smoke mushrooms that sprouted along the "seam" to the very canal; the lack of any movement in the no-man's-land between the two armies proved that there were no Egyptian units there. Still, no crossing was possible as long as the bulk of the Egyptian armor was deployed on the African side of the canal; it could easily destroy the bridgehead and eradicate any IDF unit that had crossed the waterway. Sharon had to wait for the elite Egyptian armored units to cross the canal and engage the Israeli armor. And the Israeli armor was ready.

He didn't have to wait long. On October 14, hundreds of Egyptian tanks, including a large part of the crack 4th Armored Division, crossed the canal. A formidable battle ensued, and after a few hours the burning carcasses of 250 Egyptian tanks were strewn in the sands of Sinai. The IDF lost only twenty-five tanks. The time had come to launch Sharon's plan, code name Bravehearts.

And bravehearts they were indeed, all those reserve paratroopers who had fought in most of Israel battles, their feats crowned with the conquest of Jerusalem. Motta Gur wasn't their commander anymore—he had been appointed IDF attaché to the Israeli embassy in Washington. The leader of Brigade 247 was another legendary commander—Danny Matt.

Born in Cologne, Germany, raised in a religious moshav on the coastal plain, Danny—barely sixteen—had joined the British Coast Guard, then enlisted in the British Army and participated in the last stages of World War II. Back in Israel he joined the Palmach and settled in kibbutz Ein Zurim, in a cluster of agricultural villages south of Jerusalem, called Bloc Etzion. On May 12, 1948, two days before Israel was created, a huge mass of Arab irregulars attacked the bloc, massacring scores of its inhabitants. Danny, manning a position close to Ein Zurim, found himself facing thousands of Arabs, who were yelling; waving rifles, axes, and knives; and submerging the area. Feverishly, he attached thirteen grenades to his belt, grabbed a machine gun and started firing at the advancing crowd. The first wave of attackers collapsed, but they were replaced by hundreds of others, all of them screaming and charging his isolated position. He knew that if they reached him they'd tear him to pieces, and so he kept firing, mowing down line after line of attackers. He started pulling hand grenades with his right hand, removing the triggering pin with his teeth, while firing the machine gun with his left. Scores of dead attackers piled in front of him. As he ran out of ammunition he threw away the machine gun, removed the pin of his last grenade, raised the grenade above his head and ran toward kibbutz Revadim. The mass of Arabs parted before that crazy bearded man waving an armed hand grenade. He reached the kibbutz, followed by a fierce crowd of enemies; somebody dragged him into a house, another guy sheared his beard with a pair of scissors, a third shaved his stubble with an old razor, without water or shaving cream, tearing pieces of skin from his face, while outside the Arab crowd kept yelling, "Where is the bearded one? Where is the murderer? Give us the murderer!"

Fortunately, at that moment the Jordanian Legion arrived and took all the kibbutz men prisoner. Danny put on large sunglasses and joined his comrades. He was not recognized. He spent a year as a prisoner of war in Jordan. Upon returning he grew his beard again, joined the paratroopers, commanded an elite company, participated in all the reprisal raids and was severely wounded in the Mitla battle. He spent two years at the War College in Paris, later distinguished himself in the Six Day War—and finally assumed command over the famous 247th Brigade.

O n October 15, at sunset, several units carried a diversionary attack on the Egyptian forces, while Danny's brigade, riding on half-tracks, moved toward the Suez Canal on a narrow asphalt road, code-named Spider. One battalion of the 247th was late arriving to the assembly area, but Danny refused to delay the mission and moved forward with the two remaining battalions. The plan was that at 8:00 P.M., the paratroopers would reach the canal, board rubber boats and cross the waterway in proximity to Deversoir, where the canal flows into the Great Bitter Lake. Sharon, on the commanding half-track, was not far behind them.

The crossing, however, almost failed because of a traffic jam. The paratroopers' half-tracks got stuck in the middle of a nightmarish tangle of hundreds of vehicles. Heavy trucks, jeeps, pickups, and even private cars surrounded by crowds of reserve soldiers were massed along several miles on the narrow road, blocking Danny Matt's convoy. Once in a while, the paratroopers' vehicles would break through and advance a couple of hundred yards, then become immobilized again. The troubled voices of Sharon and his deputy echoed in the brigade commander's radio over and over again. The most crucial mission of the war could end in failure because the IDF could not overcome traffic congestion.

The Israeli tanks cross the Suez Canal on the pontoon bridge.
(Bamachane, IDF Archive)

The road cleared only after midnight. Headlights off, the convoy sped on the Spider route toward the red flashes and the smoke mushrooms hovering over the nearby hills and across the canal. At a road crossing a naval unit loaded a score of rubber boats on the half-tracks. The IDF artillery shelled the crossing areas in order to drive away the Egyptian soldiers that might be positioned there. A tank battalion and a commando on half-tracks from another brigade emerged at the head of the convoy to protect it on its way to the canal.

But the escort was the first to be hit. Darting forward before the paratroopers, the tank battalion fell into an Egyptian ambush. Most of the tanks and the commando half-tracks were hit and burst into flames. The losses were heavy, but Danny Matt's convoy bypassed the burning armor and continued its advance toward the canal. Miraculously, the Egyptians did not notice the advance unit and it easily reached the canal bank. But when the bulk of the convoy approached, with the brigade commander's half-track at its head, it was met with heavy, sustained fire. Egyptian soldiers of the Second and Third armies, stationed in the sandy flatlands by the canal, sighted Matt's half-track, which signaled with its headlights to Sharon, who watched the convoy from a nearby hill. The sheaf of antennae, protruding from the canvas top of the vehicle, was another sign that this was the commander's half-track. The Egyptians attacked the convoy with bazookas, machine guns and other weapons. Missiles whooshed beside the vehicles and the paratroopers returned fire. Yet, the Egyptians were too far away, as Sharon had surmised, and most of their fire was ineffective.

After several turns of the road the enemy fire weakened. The convoy stopped in a kind of courtyard, surrounded by steep sand ramparts. The soldiers climbed up the western rampart and descended on its other side. At their feet glistened a calm, silvery stripe—the Suez Canal. The rubber boats were unloaded and swiftly brought to the water. The paratroopers jumped into them, and one after the other the boats ploughed the Suez waters, heading for the African bank. At 1:25 Danny Matt radioed the word "Aquarium," meaning the boats were in the water. He then boarded one of the first boats. Bar-Zohar crouched beside him. A few shells exploded by the fast moving boats. Most of the fighters were excited, feeling they were experiencing a dramatic moment, a game-changing event that could seal the outcome of the war.

Danny Matt's outward calm concealed tremendous tension. Never in his life had he felt such crushing responsibility. "We were carrying out a mission that could change the war's outcome. I felt that the entire nation of Israel was raising its eyes toward us," he later said.

The boats coasted by a low stone jetty. The paratroopers crossed a sandy strip, covered with low shrubs. Danny, never departing from his cool, radioed the code word for the landing on the African bank of the canal: "Acapulco; repeat, Acapulco!"

While excited senior officers radioed congratulations to Matt, the paratroopers scouted the area. They had landed in the very middle of a fortified Egyptian compound: sand ramparts, stone and concrete walls, reinforced positions, underground bunkers. A terrible fight could have taken place here if the Egyptians had stayed and confronted the paratroopers, but they had escaped from the heavy artillery shelling. In later years historians and writers would express their amazement that the paratrooper force that had established the bridgehead was so small and vulnerable—barely 760 men.

A grove of firs, eucalyptuses and young palms stretched out behind the compound. Small units of paratroopers took position on top of the ramparts.

Arik Achmon, one of Matt's two deputies, stopped by to see a friend. "To be in the first half-track that entered the Old City of Jerusalem," he cracked, smiling, "and in one of the first boats to cross into Africa—that's quite something in a man's life, isn't it?"

Thundering explosions were heard from the eastern bank of the canal. The paratroopers didn't know that a formidable battle was raging between Reshef's armored brigade and large Egyptian forces. The fighting took place around the Tirtur ("Rattle") route that ran parallel to the Spider road that Matt's men had used to reach the canal. The fierce combat spread to the "Chinese Farm." It also delayed the crossing of the canal by large Israeli forces, because the Cylinder Bridge, a prefabricated Israeli invention, dragged by eighteen tanks, wouldn't reach the Canal before October 17.

But Sharon wouldn't give up. Two huge bulldozers arrived at the canal and breached a passage for heavy vehicles. The breaching site (the "Yard") had been prepared by Sharon long before, when he still was commander of the Southern District. He had used red bricks to mark the thinner ramparts, which could be easily breached. Now he dispatched to the breach several pontoons that should together form a floating bridge. But as some of the pontoons lagged behind, the engineers brought over the "Crocodiles," monstrous amphibious tank carriers that had been invented by a French officer and named Gillois after him; a while before, the Israeli defense ministry had bought the old Gillois from the NATO surplus stocks and refurbished them—and as dawn broke on October 16, the Crocodiles started carrying the first tanks of Hayim Erez's armored brigade across the canal.

The Yard and the bridgehead across the waterway bustled with activity. The Egyptians did not realize that an Israeli task force had landed behind their backs. It took more than two days for the Egyptian high command to find out that Israeli units had taken positions on the canal's western bank. On October 16, Egypt's President Sadat made a speech before a special session of the parliament and announced that he had ordered work to start on the Suez Canal, blocked since the Six Day War, in order to reopen it to international shipping. That same afternoon he was surprised to hear the statement of Golda Meir before the Knesset that IDF units were operating on the western bank of the canal. But even then, the Egyptians assumed that this was a limited raid of a commando unit in their territory.

During the heavy fighting against the Egyptians on the eastern bank some of the members of Sharon's advanced command unit were hurt; Sharon himself was lightly scratched, and the white dressing on his forehead became, for the soldiers, the symbol of the canal crossing. From his position in the Yard, Sharon tried to convince his superiors to allow his division to cross the canal and exploit their initial success. He pointed out that Hayim Erez had crossed with twenty-seven tanks on the Crocodiles and had darted westward; Erez had destroyed several bases of ground-to-air missiles and cleared the skies for the Israeli fighter planes. But there was more: Erez almost didn't meet any resistance, and he had the feeling that the road to Cairo was opened before him. He radioed Sharon, "I can get to the Nile!"

Shortly before the crossing of the Suez Canal, a meeting of senior IDF
commanders in Sinai. From left to right: General Ariel Sharon,
Division commander; General Moshe Dayan, Minister of Defense; Colonel Braun.
General Adan; one of the authors of this book, Sergeant Michael Bar-Zohar;
General Tal; General Tamir; General Gonen. (*Uri Dan*)

But Sharon's superiors firmly refused to let Sharon cross. First, they
demanded that he lay another bridge over the water and open the roads
leading to the canal. They feared an Egyptian move to block the road to
the canal and to annihilate the paratrooper bridgehead, as long as the
roads were not secured and the bridges not in place. They also ordered
Sharon to stay in the Yard and let Adan's Division 162 cross the canal in
order to encircle the Third Army. Sharon's repeated pleas to let him cross
were to no avail. Some commentators insisted that Sharon had been
stopped for political reasons.

But in the meantime the Egyptians understood that an Israeli task
force had crossed Suez and established a base on the African side. Now
a new chapter in the fighting started: desperate efforts by the Egyptian
Army to annihilate the bridgehead. From the second day after the crossing
and up to the cease-fire, nine days later, Matt's paratroopers in Africa and
Sharon's other units in the Yard were submitted to nonstop heavy bombardment that caused large numbers of casualties. The Egyptians attacked

Sharon's fighters with artillery and mortars, their jets dived on them with bombs and missiles, their helicopters dropped napalm barrels or fired at them day and night, in the light of parachuted flares. But the crossing continued; the pontoon bridge was completed, the Cylinder Bridge finally reached the canal and was laid between its two banks. Matt's paratroopers watched, from the top of the ramparts, the never-ending convoys that crossed the bridges on their way to the African side. Arik Sharon enjoyed the enthusiastic admiration of the troops, and when he crossed the canal he was received by shouts of "Arik, King of Israel."

On October 24 the fire ceased. The Third Army was surrounded; Matt's paratroopers had occupied the fertile agricultural strip along the canal and advanced northward to Ismailia, a large Egyptian town; the paratroopers also had advanced south, to the city of Suez; the Israeli armor had stopped at the "101st kilometer," sixty-three miles from Cairo.

Time had come for Israel and Egypt to lay down their weapons and start talking. The talks, held at the 101st kilometer, would result in a separation of forces; five years later the two countries would sign the Camp David Accords, and the following year, a peace treaty.

MOSHE ("BOGIE") YA'ALON, LATER CHIEF OF STAFF AND DEFENSE MINISTER

"The Yom Kippur War is part of my DNA.

"The announcement of war hit me like thunder on a clear day. I was a civilian, a reserve sergeant, a newlywed. The commanders of the Fiftieth Airborne Battalion had wanted to send me to an officers' course, but I didn't want to sign on for permanent service, and I was discharged. On Rosh Hashanah [the Jewish New Year] eve, I was elected secretary of Kibbutz Grofit in the Negev.

"When I was told about the outbreak of the war, on October sixth at two P.M., I thought they were pulling my leg, but in the evening I was already at the Sirkin base with my comrades from the 247th Paratrooper Brigade. On October sixteenth, we crossed the canal on the floating bridge. We took shelling, secured the bridgehead and ended the war in the city of Suez. You find yourself at war, planes attacking, shellings, bombings, clashes . . . I thought that I wasn't going to survive all this.

"But, ironically, it was at war that I had time to think. Bad news arrived about the fall of the forts along the canal, about friends who had been killed or wounded. A sense of distrust in the political and military leadership grew in me. I felt powerless. Perhaps the country is going to fall! Where is the leadership? Where is the intelligence? Where are all the people we're supposed to trust?

"I told myself, if I come out of this war alive, the kibbutz will get along fine without me. I'm staying in the army, returning to permanent service as a platoon commander. I can't be at peace with myself if I go back to the kibbutz. My priorities must change.

"At the end of the war, I went looking for the Fiftieth Battalion. They were deployed at the Gidi Pass, in Sinai. Ya Ya [Colonel Yuval Yair] was the battalion commander. I told him, 'Ya Ya, I'm coming back to the army.'"

While the paratroopers are crossing the Suez Canal,
a fierce battle is taking place at the "Chinese Farm," bordering
with the roads leading to the canal. Disappointed with
the commander of the Southern District's performance,
Golda appoints former chief of staff Haim Bar-Lev
as commander of the Southern Front.

CHAPTER 16

"COMMANDER KILLED . . . DEPUTY COMMANDER KILLED . . . SECOND DEPUTY COMMANDER . . ." 1973

I f the Chinese Farm could speak, it would recount the two consecutive nights of bloody battle that took place on its soil in the fall of 1973, recalling the dead, the injured, the moments of despair and the acts of heroism it left recorded in the history of the IDF and the Egyptian Army.

In the mid-fifties, a strip of land covering 5.8 square miles located on the Sinai Peninsula had been converted into an agricultural compound with the help of the Japanese government. Close to the Suez Canal, it had been crisscrossed with deep ditches dug for irrigation. The Israeli soldiers who reached it during the Six Day War in 1967 couldn't tell the difference between Chinese and Japanese characters, and had nicknamed it the "Chinese Farm."

The Chinese Farm was located north of the Great Bitter Lake. It was close to both the Spider and the Rattle routes to the canal, and to the important junction between Rattle and Lexicon—code name for a road that ran parallel to the canal. Israel's plan was to occupy the farm, so that the "corridor" to the canal remained free; that would ensure the success of the crossing (see chapter 15). In many aspects, the conquest of the Chinese Farm would be critical to the survival of the bravehearts' bridgehead.

Arik Sharon, who had been tasked with capturing the Chinese Farm and crossing the canal, said on the mission's eve, "We should not expect any surprises. There's not a living soul there [in the Chinese Farm]. Our force would move without shooting, without [doing] anything, and would enter the area. This entire territory is empty." But the reality turned out to be entirely different. Waiting for the Israelis was a big surprise—bigger than they could have imagined.

On the night of October 15, the 14th Armored Brigade, led by Colonel Amnon Reshef, moved toward the Suez Canal; its goal was to occupy the east bank of the canal, north of the two roads, and thus protect the paratroopers' crossing. Amnon Reshef was a tall, skinny guy sporting a huge mustache; tanks had always been his natural habitat. The Haifa-born officer had distinguished himself during the Six Day War, where he had fought in the Sinai and on the Golan Heights. His brigade, the only tank brigade that faced the Egyptian Army when it attacked Israel on the first day of the Yom Kippur War, had been badly mauled. After the first day of fighting Reshef had only 14 of his 56 tanks left; 90 of his soldiers had been killed.

Reshef had recovered quickly, received fresh reinforcements, reorganized his brigade, participated in a victorious battle against Egyptian armor the previous day, and that night he led his men into battle, hoping to surprise the enemy. Riding on tanks and half- tracks, the armored and infantry forces advanced without knowing what the Egyptians had in store for them. But Lieutenant Colonel Amram Mitzna, leading Battalion 79, had a bad premonition. Before the battle he wrote a farewell letter to his wife and left it with his jeep driver.

At nine-fifteen that evening, Mitzna's spearhead battalion arrived in the area where it was supposed to secure the route for crossing the Suez. But it quickly ran into Egyptian tanks, armored personnel carriers and artillery. Punishing battles unfolded, sometimes within a range of just a few feet. Mitzna later recalled, "The first encounter was on Rattle road. Suddenly hellfire came at us from all sides. There was hysteria all along the communication network. The brigade's order was to shoot anything that moved. Tanks were crashing into tanks. The 184th Tank Battalion was firing at the 79th . . ."

The Israeli battalion destroyed numerous Egyptian targets but also paid a heavy price in its own blood. A shell that struck Mitzna's tank killed the operations officer and gunner, and Mitzna was thrown from the vehicle and badly wounded.

The 184th Battalion, trailing Mitzna, began to take heavy fire, causing severe losses. Barely half of its tanks managed to cross the Lexicon–Rattle junction. The battle spilled over to the neighboring Chinese Farm, where the Egyptians had entrenched themselves with crack troops, tanks and every possible kind of weapon, including the anti-tank Sagger missile freshly arrived from the Soviet Union. The Sagger was an individual guided missile, carried in a small suitcase by a soldier. The Israelis later nicknamed the suitcase carriers "tourists." But these tourists were deadly. When an Israeli tank was in sight, the tourist would open his suitcase, produce his missile and guide it by remote control until it blew up the tank. That weapon destroyed scores of Israeli tanks in the terrible battle than engulfed the entire Chinese Farm.

Bloody battle at the Chinese Farm. *(GPO)*

Very soon, the area looked less like a farm and more like a killing field. "We felt like we were ramming a steel wall,"recalled one of the officers. "Every time we went in with tanks, Egyptian soldiers would pop out of the ditches and shoot at us with missiles. We fired back at them with machine guns and tank cannons. We cut them down, killing them by the dozen, and more always appeared in their place to strike at us. With each charge, we lost people and tanks."

Amnon Reshef fought beside his soldiers, taking hits from enemy shrapnel and shells; in a close encounter with the Egyptians his battered tank shot four out of five enemy tanks, and the fifth escaped. Reshef reported this incident on his radio, not in order to brag, but to reassure his men that their colonel was fighting beside them.

On a large area, tanks were burning and exploding. The desert battlefield was soon covered with charred and gutted vehicles by the hundreds. The carcasses of Israeli and Egyptian tanks lay beside each other. Dead and wounded lay on the sand, their uniforms crumpled and torn, their faces covered with soot from the firing; it was impossible to distinguish between the dead Egyptians and Israelis. One tank gunner tried to find Israeli wounded soldiers in an original way. He moved between the wounded, asking each one in Hebrew, "Are you a Jew?" In the middle of this living hell, surrounded by gunfire, explosions and death rattles, one of the wounded proved he had lost a lot of blood but had kept his sense of humor. Yiftah Yaakov of kibbutz Manara, a nephew of Yitzhak Rabin, blurted, "Yes, but it's hard to be a Jew in the Land of Israel. . . ."

At this stage, Colonel Reshef realized that the battalion's objective wouldn't be achievable because of the Egyptians' forceful resistance, the Israelis' heavy losses and the urgent need to reorganize the brigade, which had come apart during the fighting. "Around us," he recalled, "weapons stockpiles, hundreds of trucks, and artillery batteries abandoned by the Egyptians were blowing up. The Egyptian infantry ran among our tanks, hitting them with bazookas. Every so often, four or five Egyptian tanks would initiate assaults from a range of between six hundred fifty to just a couple feet."

At 4:00 A.M., Reshef launched a force of paratroopers and tanks into action to clear out the junction. Murderous fire suddenly burst out, and the soldiers were caught in a firetrap. The paratroopers attempted to get away, but the Egyptians gave chase, shooting at them from close range. One of the units lost most of its soldiers—twenty-four men—in an attempt to open Rattle road from west to east. The attempt to reopen Rattle failed, but most of the Egyptian tanks that participated in that battle were hit.

That night, as Danny Matt's paratroopers crossed the canal not far away, the battle for the Chinese Farm claimed the lives of 121 of Reshef's fighters; evacuating the wounded under fire lasted until the early hours of the morning. Out of Reshef's ninety-seven tanks, fifty-six had been destroyed. The Egyptians had succeeded in blocking both Rattle and Spider. The IDF's major problem remained opening the blocked routes to bring over the pontoon bridges and enabling the flow of Israeli troops to the other side of Suez. At a certain moment, Minister of Defense Moshe Dayan, shocked by the losses and the failure to reopen the roads to the canal, wanted to bring back Matt's paratroopers, lest they be slaughtered at the bridgehead. The idea was rejected by the IDF superior officers.

It was evident that new forces would be needed to reopen the roads, and the fighters of the 35th Paratroop Brigade were chosen. The 890th

Paratroop Battalion, led by Lieutenant Colonel Itzhak Mordechai, was assigned the task.

On October 16, the 890th was in Abu Rudeis, in southwestern Sinai, preparing to land by sea behind the Egyptian forces. Suddenly, Mordechai received an urgent call from Brigade Commander Uzi Yairi, who announced a change of assignment: the landing had been called off, and the battalion would be dispatched to the crossing zone in order to reinforce the units going across the canal. "The roads are blocked," Yairi said. "Not a single tank has managed to get past the Spider road. The IDF is waiting for it to be opened."

Mordechai, who was smart and confident, had been born in Kurdistan and immigrated to Israel at the age of five. After growing up in a moshav, he had joined the army and participated in many a perilous commando mission deep in Egyptian and Syrian territory. A born fighter, he had been deeply impressed by a former paratroop commander, now a general, Raful Eitan. Idling in Abu Rudeis was not to his liking; he was excited and invigorated when he got Uzi Yairi's call.

The soldiers of the 890th, as well, were excited by the news. They had been waiting for the moment when they would join the fighting, following ten days of standing by. A few hours later they were flown by Hercules aircraft from Abu Rudeis to Refidim, a large IAF base in western Sinai; buses waiting for them headed for Camp Tassa, where Sharon's advanced headquarters were located. The routes were blocked, and the battalion had to force its way through; only that evening did it reach camp. All the while, its assignment remained insufficiently clear. Mordechai was told, "The Rattle and Spider roads are blocked off—there's no way to evacuate the injured, no way to reinforce the troops. Your assignment is to clear out the roads of Egyptian anti-tank detachments."

Mordechai responded, "And what about artillery?'

Yairi told him, "It will take an hour to bring in an artillery-coordination officer, and we're squeezed for time."

This was the reason the paratroopers set out for battle without an artillery-coordination officer—and only in battle would it become clear how damaging his absence would be. Nor did the commanders receive up-to-date intelligence about the array of Egyptian forces on the Chinese Farm, which the previous night had conducted a lethal battle against Sharon's troops. The paratroopers' assignment was to clear out the roads and to prevent the Egyptians from penetrating the "corridor" and hitting Israeli troops. But the situation on the ground was completely different.

The 890th was flown by helicopter from Camp Tassa toward the Spider road. During a briefing in General Avraham Adan's tent, Yairi and Mordechai received their instructions: troops from the battalion would fan out immediately and clear the roads. The request for tanks and armored personnel carriers was rejected, as the division commander preferred a quiet night attack without tank noise. Anyway, he said, the tanks' efficiency was limited at night. Chief of Staff David Elazar, and the front commander, Haim Bar-Lev, pressured Yairi to launch the battalion immediately. "If the routes aren't open by morning," they said, "the force that has already crossed the canal will be in danger, and we'll need to bring them back." Mordechai felt that a tremendous responsibility had been put on his shoulders.

At midnight, the 890th moved in two columns from a point along the Spider road toward Rattle junction. At first, their advance was rapid and easy. But soon, they noticed the twisted and charred remains of the previous night's battle. Along the way, the soldiers passed a half-track full of dead bodies. The brigade's deputy commander, Lieutenant Colonel Amnon Lipkin-Shahak, recounted, "I was sure that these were the bodies of Egyptian soldiers, but, as I got closer, I could see that they were Israeli paratroopers. For me this was an inner earthquake, the first time I realized that there could be a situation in which Israeli soldiers could be laying, one corpse next to another, no one removing them."

At 2:45 in the morning, Yaki Levy, the commander of Company B, which moved at the head of the battalion, reported to Mordechai that he had engaged the enemy. A burst of heavy gunfire had hit the center of the group, "and suddenly everyone was writhing on the ground," remembered a medic. A few minutes later Levy was killed. His deputy, Jackie Hakim, took control and after a few minutes was also hit. The command then passed to the other deputy, Ben-Zion Atzmon.

The paratroopers tried to figure out where the shooting was originating and whom they were fighting against. "I stopped and looked through my binoculars to see the Egyptian force opposite me," recounted Lieutenant Hezi Dabash. "I was expecting to find bands of tank-hunters, but they looked more like an organized army. I ordered my men to shoot, but not a weapon was fired except for my own Uzi."

At this stage, Mordechai sent Aharon Margal's company to outflank and attack the Egyptians assaulting Levy's men. As they moved, they were fired upon, and Margal was badly wounded; he later died from his injuries. First Lieutenant Menachem Gozlan's platoon was then dispatched to outflank the Egyptians from the left. Gozlan began running with eight other soldiers and, after covering fewer than two hundred feet, was hit along with all the rest. Groans of pain and calls for help from the wounded drew more shooting. Two companies were trapped in a firing zone, and the ground seemed to boil from all the shells, smoke and shooting in every direction. It was obvious to the battalion commander that, rather than informal squads of soldiers ("tank hunters"), they were up against a well-entrenched formation, reinforced with tanks, anti-tank missiles, mortars and artillery.

Mordechai then dispatched Company H to rescue the wounded from Company B. Eli Shorek, the company commander, got on the radio and heard, "Commander killed . . . deputy commander killed . . . another deputy commander killed . . ." Soon, he himself was injured, and, for the entire night, the soldiers tried to rescue their comrades, dragging them to a little knoll that became known as Wounded Hill.

By four, the command realized that the battle at the Chinese Farm had gone very wrong. The battalion's state was catastrophic. Every attempt to locate the Egyptian core and outflank it had ended in chaos, causing additional losses. Given the situation, Mordechai gave the order to retreat. "All of us got up," one of the fighters recalled, "and ran wildly toward the canal as bullets flew around us. At the canal, we saw a terrible scene—a defeated paratrooper battalion, licking its wounds. I went into shock, and started to cry." The medevac station for the wounded filled up. Mordechai pressed for tank reinforcements and armored personnel carriers for an evacuation. The attack on the Chinese Farm seemed to have failed. Yet, while the battle raged, the pontoons were advancing on Spider road toward the canal, as the Egyptians were too busy fighting the paratrooper battalion.

A few half-tracks from the reconnaissance unit Bamba arrived and evacuated a group of the wounded. But everyone feared the sunrise, which would make it harder to evacuate. A medic remembered, "I ran four times to evacuate the wounded, and dawn lifted during the final trip. I was drained. I've never been as afraid anywhere as I was there." As the injured were evacuated, the medic spoke with the battalion commander; when he finished, he got up and was hit by a mortar shell. In an instant, he had gone from evacuator to casualty awaiting rescue.

An hour later, several tanks arrived to help the paratroopers. Their commander was Ehud Barak, who had returned from studying in the United States after hearing about the outbreak of war. He had established an improvised armored group, Unit 100. Barak arrived with tanks and armored personnel carriers, but couldn't advance at night, and even when dawn broke, failed to locate the paratroopers. Mordechai informed Barak by radio that he would set off a flare as identification, but then he would need to move fast to a new position, because all the Egyptian fire would be concentrated on the battalion's command post. Barak identified the flare and charged the Egyptian posts but en route drew the fire of Sagger missiles, which rained on his tanks, striking some of them. His Unit 100 retreated, leaving behind burning tanks and tank crews.

The situation in the area continued to worsen. Mordechai ordered all his men to enter the irrigation ditches. Suddenly, two Egyptian jets swooped in to attack. One was brought down and the second dropped altitude before turning back.

At six, the brigade commander, Yairi, asked for authorization to evacuate. But General Shmuel Gonen, the Southern District commander, refused. "We must maintain position at all cost; there is no possibility of reinforcement or replacement." Gonen believed that the paratroopers' presence in the area prevented the Egyptians from advancing toward Spider road. Only after the intervention of front commander Bar-Lev was permission given, and, at 11:00 A.M., the paratroopers' evacuation from the ditches began.

For seventeen hours, from night until the afternoon, the 890th Paratroop Battalion had fought against Egypt's 16th Division, which was reinforced by tanks, anti-tank weaponry and artillery—and against units of Egypt's Second Army. The battalion had lost forty-one dead and 120 wounded.

After more tank battles that lasted the entire day, the Egyptians, who suffered heavy losses, realized they could not continue fighting. In the early evening the Egyptian command ordered its forces to evacuate the Chinese Farm. The evacuation was carried out under cover of night; Rattle and Spider roads remained definitely open.

The heavy price paid for opening the roads was 161 dead and hundreds of wounded. But the roads were open and the crossing tipped the scales of the Yom Kippur War.

YITZHAK MORDECHAI, DECORATED WITH THE MEDAL OF COURAGE

"One of the hardest moments I've had was when dawn broke and I had to face the fact that the battalion's entire chain of command had been hit. During the nighttime battle, I had sent in new commanders to replace the officers who had been killed, to rescue fighters from burned-out tanks and to continue maintaining position, no matter the price, on the exposed dunes.

"Another difficult moment was when mortar and artillery barrages were being fired toward my position, and I say to the soldier standing to my left, 'Why aren't you shooting?' And then I raise my head and see that he has taken a bullet to the head and has been killed.

"These were seventeen of the hardest, most complicated hours of fighting that the paratroopers battalion could have come up against. We were required to stand against large enemy forces and lethal fire, to rescue the wounded, to stabilize our line of combat, and, in this way, to prevent the enemy from reaching the roads and blocking them."

In the north, the Syrians advance on the Golan Heights, and a handful of Israelis are trying to stop them and save northern Israel from an invasion.

CHAPTER 17

"I SEE THE LAKE OF TIBERIAS!" 1973

A t a meeting of the IDF general staff at 4:45 on the morning of the third day of the Yom Kippur War, Defense Minister Moshe Dayan issued an unprecedented directive: "There will be no retreat—not even a centimeter—on the Golan Heights. Even if we lose the entire Armored Corps, we have to come to a decisive conclusion in the north. The Golan Heights is our home, and if the front collapses there, they"—the Syrians—"will be in the Jordan Valley. We need to consider every necessary action, including bombing Damascus."

In September 1973, the Syrians had begun building up their forces on the Golan Heights. By the start of the war, in October, their numbers had grown from 550 tanks to 900, in addition to a concentration of 140 artillery batteries located less than two miles from the border.

These were dark omens. It was obvious that the Syrians were planning to attack, but the scale of the assault was unknown. Syrian documents published after the war revealed that the Syrian chief of staff had planned to seize the Golan within twenty-four hours. It can now be said that they came very close but were halted in battles drenched in blood.

On October 6, General Yitzhak ("Haka") Hofi, the commander of the Northern District, summoned his senior staff and announced that war would erupt that evening. The 7th Armored Brigade had already been deployed as a reserve force. Hofi ordered that Israeli settlements on the Golan be evacuated, but many of the residents of moshav Ramat Magshimim refused to leave until that afternoon. Hofi reviewed the plans for the Golan's defense along with General Rafael Eitan, who had assumed the command of a division in the north. There was speculation that the Syrians would break through the border with an immense force from the north, coming by way of Quneitra, a town that Israel had occupied during the Six Day War. The Syrians would come that way, the IDF experts said, in part because, for the Syrians, Quneitra had become a symbol and a goal for liberation, and because this route led to the strategically valuable Daughters of Jacob Bridge, spanning the Jordan River. A secondary force would probably enter from the south by way of the Rafid Gap.

With the outbreak of war, the 7th Armored Brigade, under the command of Yanosh Ben-Gal, was rushed to the Golan's northern sector and Yitzhak Ben-Shoham's 188th, the Barak ("Lightning") Brigade, was sent south. Syria's 51st Brigade crossed the border and advanced in a three-prong offensive, passing Hushaniya, in the back of the Golan, and progressing in the direction of Camp Nafach and the Oil Road. Yitzhak Ben-Shoham took positions south of Hushaniya, spreading his tanks along a large front. At 9:30 P.M., an officer from the Northern Command's operations department, Uri Simchoni, got on the radio and informed Colonel Ben-Shoham, "This is the operations officer speaking. The Syrians keep reporting that they're behind you, that Hushaniya is in their hands, and that they're already at the junction past Hushaniya."

Ben-Shoham replied, "Negative. They intend to get there, but they seem to have gotten mixed up at the junction. . . . I'm firing at them right now and engaging them from the north."

Ben-Shoham was killed a few hours later, during the battle for Nafach, along with his deputy. The Barak Brigade was almost entirely wiped out and ceased functioning. Contrary to the IDF assessments, the Syrians had actually decided to attack through the Golan's vast, flat southern sector. They realized that, from there, it would be possible to launch a tank assault on a large front, unlike in the mountainous northern area, where the invader would be compelled to advance in a single tank column, thus giving the advantage to the defenders. The Barak Brigade, indeed, paid a dire price for this mistaken assessment.

Ben-Gal, a Holocaust survivor, later analyzed the Barak Brigade disaster: "In a routine defense situation, spreading out your forces is a good thing, but during war, that logic is a disaster. They scattered their tanks and became cannon fodder."

The Barak Brigade had fought for its life to halt the Syrian brigades, which had breached the border, the anti-tank canals and the minefields, and in the darkness were quickly swooping across the Golan. They were stopped only at Camp Nafach, where Eitan and his headquarters had been located and then forced to retreat. The surviving Barak fighters retreated as well.

The situation seemed desperate. On October 7, Israeli antennae intercepted the chilling shouts of a Syrian brigade commander on the radio, as he screamed, ecstatic, "I see the Lake of Tiberias!" His brigade indeed was fewer than ten kilometers from the Sea of Galilee (Kinneret, in Hebrew).

Everything had to be thrown into the battle, to prevent a bloody Syrian invasion of the Galilee and the Jordan Valley. On the second day of the war, Ugda Mussa, a division of reservists led by General Moshe ("Mussa") Peled was dispatched to the Golan. The performance of this combat-scarred, rugged farmer from moshav Nahalal in the battle for the Golan would deeply impress the experts at the American Armor Museum in Fort Knox, Kentucky, and earn Peled the title "One of the five greatest armor commanders in history," alongside mythological figures like General George Patton and Field Marshal Erwin Rommel.

The front commanders faced a fateful choice: should they deploy the division to prevent the Syrians from crossing the Jordan River or launch a counterattack? Under Peled's pressure they finally decided that the division would attack in the direction of the Rafid Gap, despite the large numeric advantage held by Syria's tanks.

General Hofi explained, "We opted to attack even though, during an offensive, you're risking more than during a defensive maneuver. However, you can achieve more . . . On defense, it's possible to cause losses to the enemy, to grind him down, but not to determine the outcome of the battle. . . . If we had left the attack for a later stage, we would have been forced to attack while climbing the mountain, because the Syrians would already have been on the slopes of Lake Kinneret. . . . If the Syrians had advanced a little more, the Jordan Valley and the Kinneret would have been in their hands, and the battle would have become much harder. . . . The speed of the attack was significant because it didn't leave them time to reorganize."

The Golan Heights hero, Avigdor Kahalani, with Yossi Eldar at the height of the battle. (*Uzi Keren, Bamachane, IDF Archive*)

At dawn on October 8, Peled's division entered the battle, determined to repulse the Syrians from the southern Golan. The battle proved slow and grueling, unfolding in a very narrow area with no room for maneuver or flanking actions. En route, the division liberated Ramat Magshimim, the only settlement to have fallen into Syrian hands. At the end of the first day of fighting, Peled's men had managed to split the Syrian formations and repel them ten and a half miles back.

The next day they were battling the Syrians on three fronts: from the west, against retreating forces; from the east, against attacking forces; and from the north, against forces that were under attack. The division wiped out the armored brigade it was fighting, closed the Rafid Gap and, eventually, with the capture of Hushaniya, forced the retreating Syrians out of the gap. The next day, the Syrians were pushed out of the area completely, meaning that in less than three days, Peled's division had repelled five Syrian brigades and destroyed the southern pillar of the network of armor positions established by the Syrians in Israeli territory.

Peled's offensive had been coordinated with a reservist division led by General Dan Laner, which had reached the Golan on Saturday night, within hours of the war's eruption, and had launched its attack by Sunday. A kibbutz member, Austrian-born Laner had been parachuted into Yugoslavia during World War II and had fought the Nazis with Tito's partisans. After a brilliant career in the IDF he had been recalled from retirement to lead a division headed for the Golan Heights. His men aided in halting the advance by the Syrian Army and by an Iraqi expeditionary force that had rushed to its help. Simultaneously, Eitan's division had stopped the Syrians in the Quneitra area.

In the Golan's northern region, the 7th Armored Brigade continued fighting. Avigdor Kahalani, whose fame had preceded him ever since his daring fighting in the Six Day War, led the 77th Battalion to Quneitra and Booster Ridge. Two other units were dispatched to the area, which would later be called the Valley of Tears. With the start of battle, Syria's planes bombed and Israel's air force bled; within hours, Mount Hermon had fallen, becoming an excellent observation point for shooting at Israeli forces. At nightfall, the other units evacuated the Valley of Tears. Kahalani, for his part, discovered that Syrian shooting capabilities also functioned at night; they were using Russian tanks equipped with infrared projectors that could zero in and fire at the Israeli enemy.

"My tank crews are shouting at me that they're unable to stop the

Syrians," Kahalani recounted. "Israeli tanks that had previously been considered top notch are suddenly being exposed for their weaknesses. Within our force, only the commanders and drivers have infrared goggles, but not the gunner, who needs them. I ask myself, how do we stop the Syrians? I'm the battalion commander, everyone's turning to me, and I feel that I'm not fulfilling expectations. I'm responsible for the area, and they'll accuse me of not being up to the task."

Kahalani ordered the lighting of flares, and after three went into the air, he discovered that they had been the last ones. The soldiers in the tanks were anxious, unable to see where to aim their cannons or how to advance. Meanwhile, the Syrian Air Force was flashing into view overhead—certainly not the sort of lighting Kahalani had been looking for.

"Turn off the infrared," he commanded his soldiers. "You can stick your heads slightly out of the tank turrets and navigate forward." Around them, tanks that were hit or on fire illuminated the area, but it wasn't clear whether they belonged to Israel or the enemy. "Stop and silence your engines," Kahalani instructed. "Listen for the noise of their chains and you'll be able to locate them."

The soldiers did as they were told, shutting off their engines, listening for the sound of the enemy's tanks, and shooting. The shells fired into the darkness yielded results; the Syrians were halted. In the dark, it was very difficult to identify enemy tanks until they were within a few meters of Israeli forces. A tank standing sixty-five feet from Kahalani's, with a cannon pointed toward Syria, was revealed to be a Syrian T-55, and only at the last minute did they fire at it, as well as at another Syrian tank to its side. The Syrians had come so close that they had effectively merged with the Israelis, the forces mixing one with the other.

At daybreak, Kahalani's men discovered 130 Syrian tanks one mile from the Israeli positions. The Syrians started advancing, firing two or three shells and then moving forward. Kahalani ordered the fourteen Israeli tanks that remained operable to ascend to their positions. In the following battle, most of the battalion's officers were killed as they stood, exposed, in their tanks' turrets. At the end of combat on Sunday, only seven functioning tanks remained.

On the following morning, Kahalani was ordered to move toward the Valley of Tears. Raful Eitan called him on the radio, "I trust you," he said. "Wage the battle with deliberation and calm. Don't worry—we'll get them."

On October 9, two-thirds of the Golan was in Syrian hands. Ben-Gal, the brigade commander, authorized a company fighting the Syrians to withdraw from the Valley of Tears to a line 2.5 miles away. Kahalani was called from Quneitra; during the retreat, Syrian planes circled overhead, searching for tanks to prey upon. Thousands of artillery shells were landing in the area; the earth was shaking. Eight Syrian helicopters carrying commandos landed from behind, closing off the route to kibbutz Gonen, which was serving as a resupply point and evacuation site for those wounded and killed. Kahalani and his team felt that they were trapped.

At this stage, Ben-Gal reached a new decision: he instructed Kahalani to return to the Valley of Tears and try to halt the Syrians. Kahalani sped off alone, with the seven remaining tanks left behind preparing to join him. When Kahalani arrived to his destination, he discovered a troubling picture: Israeli tanks retreating from the firing ramps. He was furious. He tried to report through the brigade's communications network, but it was overwhelmed with calls for rescue and assistance. The situation was very bleak. Only three tanks still had shells, while the Syrians had large numbers of tanks. Israel's line of defense was shrinking every few minutes. Kahalani realized that if the Syrians crossed the line of IDF positions, Israel's strategic advantage would be lost because, in flat territory, the number of Syrian tanks would prove decisive.

He decided to move forward. As he advanced, he was surprised to encounter a Syrian tank between one hundred and 130 feet to his right. Fortunately, the dust hid him from the enemy tank, and the Syrian soldiers couldn't make out who he was.

Kahalani stopped his tank and shouted at his gunner, "Shoot it fast!" The shell struck the center of the Syrian tank, and it burst into flames. They had barely exhaled in relief when another three Syrian tanks appeared. The gunner fired, setting another tank on fire, while Kahalani

pointed at the second tank, which had managed, in the interim, to identify them and aim its barrel. "Fire! Fire!" Kahalani shouted at the gunner, but the tank didn't fire; the shell casing had gotten stuck. In these
critical moments, two of the tank crewmen acted frantically, attempting
to extract the empty shell casing, pulling at it virtually with their finger-
nails. At the last second, the hollow casing came out; a new shell went
in and was fired straight into the front of the Syrian tank. The third tank
was also destroyed.

"We must make a supreme effort to bring every possible tank to the
area," Kahalani said over the radio to Brigade Commander Ben-Gal,
who responded, "Starting now, you are the area commander. I'm connecting all the forces to your radio network. And Avigdor, take care of
yourself!"

These were the pivotal moments in the battle for the Golan. The
question was who would be first to capture the positions on a hill some
sixteen hundred feet away. A hundred and fifty Syrian tanks entered the
valley, with just Kahalani left to face them. He destroyed ten tanks in a
nearby wadi, while calling for help from the brigade.

The picture before him was frightening, and Kahalani radioed Ben-
Gal again, asking him to send every possible tank to the area to halt
the Syrians. The brigade commander dispatched a battalion that was
fighting a couple of miles to the north. The battalion had just eight
tanks remaining but sped toward Kahalani and stopped behind him.
Kahalani ordered them to close off the approach of the wadi so that he
could move southward, collect the rest of the tanks and charge. While
advancing toward the new positions, five of the battalion tanks were immediately hit, and its commander was killed. Kahalani assigned one of
the tanks that had run out of ammunition to block the wadi entrance.
He headed south with the rest of the battalion's remaining tanks; seven
tanks from another company joined him.

Over the radio, suddenly, Kahalani's voice stopped in midsentence
replaced by the thunder of a terrific explosion. One of the soldiers called
the deputy battalion commander. Kahalani was killed, he announced.
Kahalani was unable to deny the report—he was facing another tank

and was more focused on the gunner than on the radio. Only minutes later did he announce by radio that everything was fine, and that he was still alive.

"A stations," he radioed. "This is Kahalani. A large Syrian force is moving against us. . . . Our goal is to capture the positions on the hill and then take control of the valley from above. . . . Move! Take the positions and destroy the Syrians." However, paralyzed by fear, the soldiers didn't charge. Kahalani grabbed his microphone again. "Watch the Syrians. See how well they're fighting. See their motivation. What do I see in our battalion? Cowards? We're Jews! We're Israelis! What, we're better than those people and not capable of repelling them? Come on, guys, I'm asking you to start moving."

Kahalani charged. A moment later another tank followed, then another, and another and another. . . .

The Syrians were sweeping over the ridge, their tanks crossing the Israeli defense line. Meir ("Tiger") Zamir, a company commander, reported the approach of enemy tanks from his front and from his back; he was left without a single shell, he said. Five Syrian tanks charged Tiger's force but a young major, Avinoam Baruchin, set two alight. "They're crushing us," Baruchin shouted. Syrian tanks approached Kahalani's force unchecked, killing and wounding dozens of Israelis.

"Nobody retreats a single step!" Ben-Gal thundered on the radio. He later recalled this fateful moment. "For twenty or thirty minutes, no one was in control of the soldiers—not the company commanders, not the battalion commander and not the brigade commander. Everyone was fighting his own war. I was planning to give instructions to retreat and had taken my microphone in hand, but told myself that we'd wait a little longer. . . . I called Raful and said that we cannot hold any longer. Raful asked that we hold 'only a little more.' "

As the battle continued, Israeli units kept collapsing under Syrian pressure. Just over thirteen hundred feet separated them from seizing the controlling positions that would determine the battle's outcome. With a tremendous effort they advanced and reached the coveted positions, opening fire on the Syrian tanks. At that very moment, eleven tanks under the command of Lieutenant Colonel Yossi Ben-Hanan arrived and joined Kahalani's forces. Kahalani recalled later that they fired "like crazy" at the Syrians, managing to hit approximately 150 of their tanks.

And all of a sudden the Syrians started pulling back!

Ben-Gal later said, "I was sure we'd lost the battle. If it had gone on another half hour, we would have lost. For whatever reason, the Syrians broke down first and decided to retreat. They apparently assumed they didn't have a chance to win. They didn't know the truth, that our situation was desperate."

The perception on the ground was that the rapport between the two fighting forces had started to reverse.

"Victory is in our hands!" Kahalani shouted excitedly over the radio. "They're retreating and we are wiping them out!"

"You're tremendous," Ben-Gal responded. "You're a hero of Israel. You're all heroes! I love you. Take care of yourself."

"Gentlemen," the voice of Division Commander Raful Eitan broke into the radio receivers, "you saved the people of Israel."

The fighting to stop the Syrians went on without pause for four days and three nights. The remnants of the IDF armor had to fight without backing from the air force, the infantry, the artillery, the engineering corps, anti-aircraft batteries; they badly lacked the necessary equipment for nighttime combat. "We felt as if the nation had abandoned us," Kahalani said, "as if we had been thrown onto the battlefield with a ratio of one Israeli tank against eight Syrian ones. For us, it was a great shock."

And yet, the Syrians were routed.

The Syrian forces retreated in a disorderly way, leaving behind 867 tanks and thousands of other vehicles. Kahalani and his comrades reconquered all of the lost territories and even penetrated into Syrian territory.

By the end of the war, the 7th Armored Brigade had lost seventy-six fighters. For Kahalani, the joy of triumph mixed with great personal sadness. His brother Emanuel had been killed in the tank battles in Sinai; also killed was his wife's brother, Ilan, another tank soldier. For his feats during the war, Kahalani would receive the Medal of Valor.

AVIGDOR KAHALANI, LATER THE DEPUTY COMMANDER OF THE FIELD CORPS

"I had several brushes with death during the war. I remember one such instance in Syrian territory. I was in the tank turret. A Syrian plane passed over my tank, shooting a burst of machine-gun fire over my head. It turned around and came at us from behind, and I didn't see it, focused as I was in running the battle. My operations officer looks back and sees the plane dropping its bombs in our direction, and then he punches me in the face and shouts, 'Get inside, fast.' I didn't understand what was happening. I got inside the tank and clung to the side. The bomb hit my tank. I heard a huge explosion and realized that I was not alive anymore. I was covered in gunpowder and passed my hands over my body to check whether I still had all my limbs. My body was shaking as if it had been jolted by an electric shock.

"I pulled my head out, saw a giant cloud of smoke and a twenty-six-foot-deep hole around me. I looked right and left and saw a terrible sight—all the tank commanders who had been next to me, standing in the turrets with their heads out in the open, had been killed.

"But there was also a happy moment that I remember: they had promised us before the war that, for every Syrian tank that was hit, we would get a crate of champagne. At the end of the fighting, I sat in my tank and tried to count how many burned-out Syrian tanks there were in the valley, but I couldn't calculate the number of champagne crates because there were so many."

As the war nears its end, the Golani Brigade makes a tremendous effort to retake the "eyes of the nation"— the Hermon fort with its array of antennas, watching and listening devices.

CHAPTER 18

THE EYES OF THE NATION, 1973

I don't want to look at the Hermon mountains anymore," the disheveled, sooty Benny Massas said. "My comrades' blood was spilled here like water." Benny was a Tiberias boy, a stocky, tousled Golani fighter wearing a green army cap. He was facing a television reporter on top of Mount Hermon, a couple of hours after the terrible battle was over. He was said to be one of the heroes of the battle, relentlessly charging the Syrians till the Golani flag was raised over the place. "Why did I charge?" he repeated the reporter's question. "Because we were told that the Hermon Mount is the eyes of Israel!"

The Hermon post was a fort on top of Mount Hermon, bristling with antennae, radar sensors, bowl-shaped dishes and listening devices, and manned by Golani Brigade soldiers. Not far from it, across the border, the Syrians had erected their own post. The Israeli fort had been captured by the Syrians at the outbreak of the Yom Kippur War. The battle had been lost within two hours, with thirteen Israeli soldiers killed and thirty-one taken captive. The post, dominating the Syrian plains and laden with electronic equipment, was of crucial importance for Israel. The intelligence gathered by its sensors and antennae was priceless. Two days later, a Golani elite unit had attempted to retake the Hermon but they, too, had been defeated, losing another twenty-five fighters.

Golani's wounded pride had led their commander Amir Drori to request of the Northern District chief of staff: "Save the Hermon for me for next time!"

The next time arrived thirteen days later, on the sixteenth day of the war, October 21. General Hofi, a former deputy of Sharon's at the Mitla battle and now the commander of the Northern District, decided to exploit the window of opportunity before the declaration of cease-fire by embarking on an operation to simultaneously capture both the Israeli and Syrian posts on the Hermon. The plan went as follows: Sayeret Matkal, under the command of Major Yoni Netanyahu, would take position as a barrier between the two posts; a paratrooper brigade would seize the Syrian post and the Hermon peak. The Golani Brigade, commanded by Colonel Drori, would recapture the Israeli post.

The troops were weary after two weeks of fighting, yet the mission had to be carried out. The offensive was set for 6:00 P.M. Starting at two, Sikorsky helicopters transported 626 paratroopers from two reduced battalions, an engineering unit and a heavy mortar detail, to the departure point for the seizure of the Syrian post, located 7,812 feet above sea level. The Syrians noticed the paratroopers' airlift and dispatched 24 MiG-21s and five helicopters with commando troops against them, but IAF planes downed 10 MiGs and 2 helicopters.

The paratroopers' first objective was the capture of the Pitulim post, located at a critical junction between the roads to the mountain peak and the Syrian Hermon post. As they crossed the road to the junction, they took enemy fire and an officer was killed. Despite continuous shooting, the fighters charged the Syrian force, wiping it out. They continued their advance and three hours later reached the Syrian Hermon post. They clashed with the Syrian soldiers; twelve Syrians were killed and the rest retreated. The paratroopers crossed the fences surrounding the post, entered and discovered that it had been abandoned. The Syrian soldiers had opted to flee. Six trucks full of soldiers were immediately sent as reinforcements by the Syrian command and were hit by the paratroopers. At 3:25 A.M., the paratroopers' commander reported to his superiors that the Syrian post on the Hermon was in the IDF's hands.

But the main operation was recapturing the Hermon's Israeli post. It turned out to be much bloodier and more complicated. It would extract a heavy price in Golani blood, with fifty killed and eighty wounded.

Before they left for battle, one of the company commanders, First Lieutenant Yigal Passo, spoke to his soldiers: "Take care of yourselves; I need you whole. Work slowly, and use your heads. I don't want pointless charges and acts of heroism; we'll kill them one by one." Passo himself was killed hours later, during the punishing fight for Hill 16, part of the capture of the Israeli Hermon post.

Golani's soldiers ascended the mountain in three prongs. The main force was from the 51st Battalion, which started climbing on foot and was supposed to reach an elevation of 5,295 feet. The ascent was very difficult, lasting seven hours before they arrived, close to midnight, at a site nicknamed Tanks' Curve. The climb was quiet—so quiet that some believed the seizure would be smooth and easy, that the Syrians had already fled, that everything would soon be over. Just 2,600 feet separated them from the post, and nothing suggested that they were marching toward a firetrap. The IDF artillery blasted every hill on their way before they approached, but as the shells were falling too close to the advancing soldiers, the Golani commander instructed the artillery to skip a couple of hills. So it turned out that Hill 16 was spared by the Israeli cannon.

But on Hill 16, a large Syrian unit was hiding in fourteen trenches, as well as between the surrounding boulders. Golani's fighters knew nothing of what awaited them.

At 2:00 A.M., a fighter marching before the troops at Tanks' Curve heard noises. He crouched down and then, between the boulders, discerned the shape of a soldier who was wrapped in a blanket and wearing a stocking cap. The Syrian soldier, no less surprised, raised his head and asked, in Arabic, "Who are you?" The Israeli didn't hesitate, pulling his weapon out first and killing him. In response, gunfire came in on all sides, and on the radio, shouts of "Encounter!" broke out.

A brutal battle ensued. The Syrians, using MAG-58 machine guns plundered from Israel, shot with great accuracy at the Golani fighters on the mountainside, causing many casualties. Another Golani company also encountered Syrian troops, and during its charge, its fighters and their commanders were wounded.

David Tzarfati, a Golani fighter, later remembered: "From two-thirty, Hill Sixteen became another world. I heard screams of terror, shouting, crying, howling, like at a massacre. I told myself, 'This is it. No one can hear me now. This isn't a joke—it's death.' I disconnected from everyone and got my head down on the ground, hard."

The heroes of the Hermon—"the cannibals, the phalanges, the Indians . . ."
(Zeev Spektor GPO)

The deadly battle continued, with gunfire raining down on the hills from every direction. In the chaos and uncertainty over which positions were occupied by Israeli forces, artillery fire landed very close to IDF soldiers fighting on Hill 16. As shrapnel fell on the battalion commander

and his aides, he radioed for a halt to the gunfire and ordered to use warning shots to ascertain where each unit was positioned, and only then to
start shooting again. After a check, the batteries were ready to resume the
gunfire, but an artillery-coordination officer, liaising between the units,
was shot, along with his radio, and the artillery fire was held up.

Motti Levy, a Golani fighter, recalled, "The hill became a jungle: I
can hear the screams of soldiers who've been wounded. I can hear my
friend Hassan staggering on the mountain like a sleepwalker, yelling,
'Mother! I'm dead! Dead!' Eighty percent of the company is in critical condition; five meters above me I hear battle cries in Arabic. It's an
awful situation."

At three, Brigade Commander Drori arrived at the site of battle with
his staff and said to the soldiers, "Hold your positions. Reinforcements
will be here soon." David Tzarfati shouted back, "We need to pull back!
We need to pull back! There are many dead, many wounded!"

The brigade commander replied, "Quiet, soldier. Backup is coming.
Maintain position."

At four, the brigade's reconnaissance company advanced toward the
Hermon's upper cable-car station. Its members didn't know the size of
the Syrian force opposing them. En route, Company Commander Vinick
wanted to examine the roadway leading to Tanks' Curve, in preparation for joining the battle and assisting the 51st Battalion. While he was
advancing along the road, Syrian soldiers concealed in a trench fired a
continuous salvo at him. He managed to shoot several bullets before
falling, drenched in blood. A signaler and a medic who tried to reach
him were also shot and wounded.

As the battle claimed more and more casualties, the commanders of
the Northern District instructed the paratroopers to prepare to complete
the assignment given to Golani. After several minutes, the operation's
commander instructed the paratroopers to descend from the Hermon
Syrian post and assist Golani. The promise made to Golani that it would
recapture the Israeli Hermon post was thus annulled. But Golani continued fighting.

At four-fifty, A Company found itself in battle on Hill 17. The fighters had prepared to charge but didn't realize they were about to attack a major Syrian formation comprising a considerable force, entrenched in thirty-five positions. The company began moving northward along a secondary incline, falling directly into a Syrian trap. Sixteen fighters were killed, and the company commander was fatally wounded, dying two weeks later in the hospital.

At five-fifteen, Brigade Commander Drori was wounded too; the 51st Battalion commander, Yehuda Peled, replaced him, but he also was wounded a few minutes later. Major Yoav Golan, the brigade operations officer, took over. Golan had been wounded at the Suez Canal, and by the time the Syrians captured the Hermon he had already been recognized as disabled by the IDF. Yet, he was fighting together with his comrades. He sent into battle a mechanized company and decided to activate heavy artillery on the Hermon post and on Hill 17, where Syrian commando forces had entrenched themselves. All that time the Golani fighters did not budge from the positions they had acquired for so much blood; two-thirds of the fighters had been killed or wounded. Benny Massas, one of the battle heroes, felt he and his comrades preferred to die on the mountain than to go back without conquering the post.

But the Syrians were first to break down. The artillery onslaught and the Golani desperately clinging to their positions determined the battle's outcome. At eight-fifteen, the Syrians began fleeing the battle zone. En route to the post, Golani fighters eliminated another ten Syrian commandos, and twenty were taken captive. Israeli soldiers entered the post with great caution, fearing that the site had been booby-trapped.

At ten-fifty, Yoav Golan radioed, "The post is in my hands! The Israeli Hermon post is in our hands! We're up there now, combing the site."

Minutes later, one of Golani's officers announced on the brigade's communication network, "All network stations throughout the world! The flag has been raised!"

Indeed, the flags of Golani and Israel were hoisted, following a bloody battle that had extracted a terrible price. Benny Massas and his comrades had recovered "the eyes of Israel."

A soldier named Alaluf summed up the fighting: "Who recaptured the Hermon? The brigade commander, Amir Drori? During the first wave, he got wounded and was down on the ground. The battalion commander? During the second round of gunfire, he fell, too. I'm not angry at them. They were my officers. But it was Yigal Passo and his ordinary soldiers who captured it. I, Motti Levy, Tzarfati, Eddie Nisim, Dahari, Azout, Blutstein: the so-called Cannibals, the Phalanges, the Indians."

GOLANI FIGHTER DAVID TZARFATI

"It was a hard, blood-soaked battle. I didn't think I'd survive. I had a sense that I belonged to the dead, that I would soon join them. . . . After the massive shelling, I lay down, unable to move or react. I was in a state of waking sleep, not wanting to live. . . . I was cut off from everything surrounding me, as if I were in a bubble.

"There's one moment that follows you your entire life—it's the truest, strongest moment, which gave me the strength to go on living, to continue functioning. . . . It was at eight A.M. as I was still lying down, useless, and my company commander, Yigal Passo, lay dying, after he was hit at four in the morning, and, in a weak voice, he tells me, 'David, you'll be the representative of those who died. You'll tell everyone about this battle.' And then he asked me to cover him, got up and, with his final bit of energy, started running toward the Syrian positions. Even in his final moments, he continued fighting. At the end of the battle, we evacuated those killed, and Yigal Passo's corpse was among them."

PART SIX

The Nuclear Danger

Opera, 1981

In 1977, Menachem Begin, leader of the right-wing
Likud party, wins the elections and dethrones Labor for
the first time. He regards the nuclear reactor Osiraq, which
Saddam Hussein is building in Iraq, as an existential danger
for Israel and decides to destroy it in spite of major objections.
This is Operation Opera.

Arizona, 2007

In 2001, Ariel Sharon is elected prime minister at the head
of the Likud; he then splits the Likud and creates a new party,
Kadima. After suffering a massive stroke, Sharon is replaced by
Ehud Olmert, who will launch Operation Arizona.

CHAPTER 19

"OPERA" IN BAGHDAD AND "ARIZONA" IN SYRIA, 1981 AND 2007

Friday, June 7, 1981, was the eve of the Festival of Shavuoth ("Pentecost"), the celebration of God giving the Torah to the Jewish people on Mount Sinai. Thousands of Israelis assembled in the synagogues, but thousands of others preferred to celebrate on the country's golden beaches. And so it was that at 4:00 P.M., the festive crowds sunning on Eilat's southern beach saw eight F-16s roaring in the blue sky, passing at low altitude over the Gulf of Eilat and continuing into Saudi Arabia. The F-16 had taken off from the Etzion airbase in Sinai. Eight F-15 fighter jets followed close behind. By coincidence, King Hussein of Jordan was, at that moment, sailing in his royal yacht in the Gulf and saw the jets passing overhead. He immediately transmitted a warning to his military, requesting that the armies of the surrounding countries be notified but, for whatever reason, the alert wasn't shared. This was a good thing, because Israel's air force planes were en route to Operation Opera, the destruction of the nuclear reactor being built next to Baghdad by Saddam Hussein.

The planning of the operation had begun years earlier. On August 26, 1976, Iraq had signed a deal with the French government for the construction of a nuclear reactor that the French called Osirak and the Iraqis referred to as Tammuz. The French also committed to supplying Iraq with eighty kilograms of 93-percent-enriched uranium, enough to produce an atomic bomb. When Israel found out, by its intelligence sources, it launched a diplomatic effort to prevent the reactor's delivery to Iraq. A nuclear weapon in the hands of Saddam Hussein could be a terrible danger for our very existence, the Israeli envoys explained to their counterparts in Paris. But all their efforts to convince the French that they were dealing with the devil failed miserably. According to foreign sources, the torch was then passed to the Mossad, which sabotaged several parts of the French reactor before they could be loaded onto ships for Iraq. But the damage was repaired and the construction of the reactor proceeded, to be completed within a short period. After his election as prime minister in 1977, Menachem Begin reached the conclusion that the only remaining option was military intervention. Defense Minister Ezer Weizman recommended a military operation, as did the IDF new chief of staff, Raful Eitan. Laying the groundwork for the mission was assigned to David Ivry, the commander of the air force. A brilliant colonel, Aviem Sella, would take on the meticulous planning of all aspects of the operation at IAF headquarters, along with several young officers. It soon became clear that the reactor would be fully operational by September 1981, and Begin decided to hit it in the spring. The program initially submitted by the air force was called Ammunition Hill.

An unexpected contribution to the planners' efforts came, of all places, from Iran. The Islamic Revolution had taken place in 1979, transforming Iran from a close American ally into a sworn enemy of the United States. Israel had concluded a deal with the U.S. government for the supply of F-16s, but the scheduled delivery was still far away, as other "clients" had a priority. After the Islamic Revolution in Teheran, however, the planned delivery of F-16s to Iran by the United States was canceled, and the White House agreed that the planes be given to Israel instead, ahead of schedule.

The F-16s turned out to be much better suited to the Iraq mission than Israel's other air force planes. According to the plan, eight F-16s would carry out the attack, with eight F-15 fighter jets escorting them while serving as a flying command station. The pilots and flight crews began training in secret, using a model of the reactor built in the Negev Desert. The IDF chief of staff himself participated in one of the simulated attacks, wanting to see from the navigator's seat whether the preparations could meet expectations. At the end of the simulation, General Eitan said nothing, taking off for home in his own light plane. Next to him sat Sella, who badly wanted to hear the senior commander's opinion. But Raful remained silent.

Raful Eitan had a place apart in the Israeli military elite. The tough, close-mouthed soldier was the descendant of a family of Subotniks, a sect of Russian peasants who had converted to Judaism and immigrated to Palestine at the end of the nineteenth century. The Subotniks settled in Galilee and became the best farmers in Israel. Raful, too, was born and raised on a farm at moshav Tel Adashim and remained an olive grower and a carpenter all his life, while emerging as a fearless fighter in the Palmach and the IDF. One of the first officers to join Arik Sharon's paratroopers, he had received the much coveted red ("battle") lining to his silver wings, after jumping with his battalion at Mitla and opening the Sinai campaign. He fought in all of Israel's wars, was severely wounded in the Six Day War, carried out several commando missions with his paratroopers and was among the staunchest defenders of the Golan Heights in the Yom Kippur War. In 1978, the tight-lipped, scarred warrior replaced Motta Gur as IDF chief of staff.

In the flight back north, he didn't speak for a long time, even though he knew what Aviem Sella wanted to hear from him. Finally, after half an hour in the air, he murmured, "The government will authorize this."

Aviem Sella let out a sigh of relief.

Yet, many major figures in the security establishment opposed the mission, including the head of military intelligence, Yehoshua Sagi; the head of the Mossad, Yitzhak Hofi; Ezer Weizman, who by then had left the defense ministry and changed his mind; and Deputy Prime Minister Yigael Yadin, who went so far as to threaten to resign. Patiently and methodically, Begin began convincing his cabinet of the operation's importance, persisting until he had won the ministers' support. Operation Ammunition Hill was set for May 8, 1981. That day, everything was in place. The pilots were sitting in their planes, already prepared for takeoff, when Begin received a letter from opposition leader Shimon Peres, a former minister of defense, pleading that he call off the attack, fearing that the international community would respond harshly and that Israel would be as isolated as, borrowing words from the Book of Jeremiah, "a juniper in the desert." Begin feared that if Peres, the opposition leader, knew about the top-secret mission, others might know as well and the secret would leak, jeopardizing Ammunition Hill. He therefore decided to delay the mission but was far from giving up. The operation was given the new code name Opera, and a new date—June 7.

Placed at the head of the octet of planes that would attack the reactor was Ze'ev Raz, a commander of one of the F-16 squadrons and a native of kibbutz Geva, in northern Israel. Leading the second group was the squadron commander Amir Nachumi. Among the pilots were Amos Yadlin, later the head of military intelligence, and Captain Ilan Ramon, the group's youngest member. Ramon was inexperienced but had served as the squadron's navigation officer, and had particularly impressed Raz when he calculated and then proved that it would be possible to carry out the attack without refueling in midair, despite the trip's 960-kilometer distance.

David Ivry decided that the planes would be gassed up when the engines were already running, an unusual and risky process. He also ordered the pilots to dump the detachable fuel tanks en route, despite the danger that they might hit the two bombs, each weighing a ton, that would be hanging under each plane's wings. The mission carried considerable danger: at that time, Iraq was deeply enmeshed in its brutal war with Iran, and it was reasonable to assume that the reactor would be defended by missile batteries and fighter planes. The pilots had no doubt that their F-15s would be forced to face off against numerous MiGs.

They knew they were taking enormous risks. If they were attacked by the enemy, their chances of survival were almost nil. Even if a pilot, whose plane had been hit, managed to parachute into Iraqi territory, hundreds of miles away from home, he would most probably be captured, cruelly tortured and put to death. Yet every pilot who heard about the mission volunteered to be among the chosen few.

On June 7, they set out, crossing the Gulf of Akaba, flying above the northern Saudi Arabian desert, bypassing Jordan from the south, penetrating Iraq and cutting across the Euphrates River as they neared their target. One of the prominent landmarks on the flight path was supposed to be an island at the center of a lake. Raz saw the lake and looked for the island, but it had disappeared. Doubts arose in his mind—perhaps they were flying over the wrong lake? Only later did the squadrons learn that the flat island had been submerged after heavy rains in the region caused the water level to rise.

The nuclear reactor eventually appeared to them, surrounded by high, thick defensive walls that were the pride of Saddam Hussein. Raz initiated contact with his comrades, urging them to increase altitude lest they run into electrical wires or tall power poles in the area. But one fact astonished everyone: no air defense was in place! Not a single MiG was visible in the sky nor was a single missile fired at them. A few negligible antiaircraft cannons fired some shells, but they missed.

The planes plunged toward the reactor, dropping their bombs at a thirty-five-degree angle. A portion of the explosives obliterated the dome covering the reactor; others carrying timed fuses penetrated deeper and blew up the center of the internal installations, the true core of the core. Most hit their target, and the reactor was completely destroyed. One pilot erred and dropped his bombs on an adjoining structure.

In total, the run over the reactor lasted eighty seconds, with the planes then immediately turning back toward Israel. As procedure required, the commanders called on each of the pilots to identify themselves, one after another, as "Charlie." All did so, except for Ramon. He didn't respond to the repeated calls of his commanders; only during his debriefing did it come out that he had feared a tardy MiG attack and had believed, being the last in the formation, that it was he who would be hit. He was so focused on the "imaginary battle" that he had ignored the calls on the radio. But he eventually opened his mouth, and the mission's lost boy was found. (Ramon was to become the first Israeli astronaut, but died tragically in 2003 in the crash of space shuttle *Columbia*.)

Nevertheless, the pilots felt certain that on their way home, they would encounter Iraqi MiGs scrambled to intercept them: planes that would take off from the H3 airbase, located in western Iraq and close to the Jordanian border, could easily attack them as they returned to Israel. But nothing happened. Not a single Iraqi plane raced to meet them, and all sixteen jets arrived home safely. A foreign attaché who had been staying in Baghdad at the time later said that the reactor's air-defense commander had been sitting in a Baghdad café, and his underlings hadn't managed to reach him. He was hanged in a public square in Baghdad the next day, under Saddam Hussein's orders.

The pilots, back from Baghdad. *(IDF Spokesman)*

In the course of the attack, ten Iraqi soldiers and a French engineer staying in the structure next to the reactor were killed.

Back home, news of the incredible operation was received with immense excitement. Those who had opposed the mission—everyone except Shimon Peres—acknowledged their error and heaped praise on the mission and the pilots. Not so with the foreign nations. Israel was harshly denounced at numerous international forums. U.S. President Ronald Reagan, a friend of Israel, joined the chorus of condemnation, even imposing sanctions on Israel: a temporary freeze on weapons deliveries.

The dark prophecies of the mission's opponents—that Saddam Hussein would build a nuclear weapon within two or three years—would prove completely false. Only in 1991, during the first Gulf War, did Israel's allies come to understand how important its mission had been. Dick Cheney, the Bush administration's defense secretary (and later, the U.S. vice president), thanked Israel during the war for its "daring, dramatic action."

The IDF chief of staff awarded a citation to Ze'ev Raz for the flawless mission. Raz insisted that all the participants deserved a medal, though one air force commander would claim, "What do they deserve medals for? They showed up at the game and the other team never set foot on the field." But the comment ignored the psychological effort, daring and determination of the pilots who had carried out the assignment.

After the mission was over, Israel published the Begin Doctrine, which stated that Israel would prevent any hostile Middle Eastern country from developing nuclear technology, because of the danger that an atomic weapon would be used against Israel.

ZE'EV RAZ, FIGHTER PILOT AND LEADER OF THE IRAQ ASSAULT

"Ironically, I'm proudest of something else. During the Yom Kippur War, I was sent from Ramat David to the Sinai to intercept enemy planes. I was flying a Phantom. Suddenly, a MiG appeared in front of us, and my navigator locked in on it; the missile's infrared radar also started buzzing, because it sensed the plane's heat. But I didn't fire the missile. My navigator shouts, 'Ze'evik, why aren't you taking down the plane? Bring it down already!'

"And I don't fire. Something seems unclear. Why is this MiG flying alone? Why is it here? I came within a distance of four hundred meters, cannon range, and suddenly he breaks off and flies to the side. And then I saw: it's not a MiG. It's our Mirage!

"Several years go by, a short time after we established the Hawk Squadron, and David Ivry, the commander of the IAF, called me. It certainly couldn't have been easy for him because, during my pilot training, I had struggled a bit, and he barely gave me my wings. He asked me, 'Think about the reactor in Baghdad. Long range, low altitude: can we do this?' I went to my navigation officer, Ilan Ramon, and he told me it's possible.

"We did it without refueling in the air, and the Americans truly couldn't believe it. Only afterward, when we returned, did I find out that one of the pilots, Elik Shafir, had discovered a glitch in his fueling system before takeoff. Instead of getting off the runway and handing off his place to someone else, he took off with less fuel and flew, carrying out the bombing and landing on his last drops of fuel. I told him, 'Elik, that was crazy, but in your place, I would have done the same thing.'"

Sixteen years later, Israel acted on the Begin Doctrine a second time.

In mid-2007, according to foreign reports, two Mossad agents sneaked into a Kensington hotel room in London, where they hacked into the laptop of a visiting senior Syrian official and viewed its contents. The laptop contained a trove of top-secret information. The most dramatic discovery of the Mossad was that Syria was secretly building a nuclear reactor.

The documents and photographs obtained by the Mossad confirmed a strange, dubious report by another source, Iran's deputy defense minister, Ali Reza Asgari. Asgari had defected a few months before and been debriefed by the Americans. He had revealed that a nuclear reactor was being built in the Syrian Desert as a joint venture of Iran, North Korea and Syria. Iran had financed the reactor, which was built and equipped by North Korea. Satellite images confirmed the information: in Dir al-Zur, in eastern Syria, a nuclear reactor identical to the one in Yongbyon, in North Korea, was being constructed. The Mossad also obtained photographs from the reactor showing North Koreans at the site. Israeli experts determined that the construction had reached an advanced stage, and that the reactor would be fully operational by September 2008.

The head of the Mossad, Meir Dagan, and Prime Minister Ehud Olmert urgently passed the information on to the United States. Syria was a sworn enemy of Israel, an ally of Iran and the Hezbollah terrorist organization. It could not be allowed to develop a weapon of mass destruction. Yet, when the intelligence was brought to the CIA and the White House, the Americans remained unconvinced and demanded additional evidence. President Bush asked that any operation be delayed until more reliable intelligence could be obtained.

In July 2007, the IAF carried out several high-altitude sorties and programmed its Ofek-7 spy satellite to photograph the reactor. The detailed photographs established clearly that Syria was building a nuclear facility identical to the North Korean reactor at Yongbyon. The Aman (the IDF intelligence department) listening service, Unit 8200, produced transcripts of intensive exchanges between Damascus and Pyongyang. The Mossad supplied photographs and even a video filmed inside the reactor. All these materials were dispatched to Washington but the White House still hesitated. The Americans wanted definite proof that radioactive materials had actually been placed in Dir al-Zur.

The IDF was ordered to obtain that definite proof. According to the international media, members of the Sayeret Matkal then flew in two helicopters to Dir al-Zur. The Sayeret commandos risked their lives, flying into one of the most secret and most heavily guarded areas in the most hostile Arab country. After landing, using special equipment brought over from Israel, the commandos collected radioactive soil samples from around the reactor. The samples were handed over to the Americans, proving that the danger was real. Stephen Hadley, George Bush's national security adviser, dubbed them the "smoking gun." But when Olmert spoke with Bush by phone and asked that the U.S. bomb the reactor, he received a disappointing answer: Bush responded that the U.S. couldn't attack a sovereign nation. Olmert, according to the same reports, replied that he was deeply troubled by such a response, and that he intended to act "in Israel's defense."

Indeed, Israel passed into action.

The Syrian reactor, before and after the visit from the Israeli Air Force.
(US Government)

According to Britain's *Sunday Times*, at 11:00 P.M. on September 4, 2007, fighters from the Air Force Shaldag ("Kingfisher") commando unit were sent on a crucial mission. They secretly penetrated into Syria and took positions around the reactor. Their mission was to "paint" the reactor's walls with laser beams in preparation for the anticipated attack, and in doing so, to signal its location for the air force. They spent the following night and day in hiding, On the evening of September 5 at eleven o'clock, ten F-15 planes took off from the Ramat David airbase, flying northwest to the Mediterranean Sea. On their way, three broke off from the pack and returned to the base. It's reasonable to assume that, at this stage, the IDF had activated electronic efforts to misdirect Syrian radar operators, who would have been left with the impression that all the Israeli planes had returned home. In fact, seven of them continued flying, moving eastward along the length of the Turkish–Syrian border and penetrating Syrian territory from the north. They reached their target and, from a distance, fired air-to-ground Maverick missiles and half-ton smart bombs toward the laser-painted walls of the reactor. The strike was precise, and the reactor was completely demolished. Planes and commandos safely returned to base.

According to reports published later, Israeli leaders following the mission from the Pit—the air force bunker and command post—feared a ferocious Syrian response; Syria was armed with thousands of missiles capable of causing major casualties in Israel. Olmert urgently spoke by phone with Prime Minister Erdoğan of Turkey—during a high point in relations between the two countries—and requested that he inform the Syrians that Israel wasn't interested in war.

The stunned Syrian government initially maintained complete silence about the attack; eventually, the Syrian state news agency released a statement that Israeli fighter planes had penetrated Syrian territory at night and "had dropped munitions above desert territory" without causing any damage; Syrian planes "had driven them away."

In contrast to the bombing of the Iraqi reactor, Israel kept silent this time. To this day, it hasn't admitted to wiping out the Syrian facility. But one of the clues left from the mission was the discovery of a discarded fuel tank from an Israeli plane, bearing a Hebrew inscription, in Turkish territory. Israel denied any violation of Turkish airspace, and Turkey accepted its claims at face value.

Officially, Israel did not admit its forces had carried out the strike at Dir al-Zur. But a confirmation came from then opposition leader Benyamin Netanyahu, who had been fully briefed about the mission by Prime Minister Olmert. Interviewed on a live newscast on the Israeli television, Netanyahu declared: "When the cabinet takes action for Israel's security, I give it my full backing . . . and here, too, I was a partner in this affair from the first moment and I gave it my full support."

The Syrian operation would have a strange epilogue the following year, on the evening of August 2, 2008. That night a festive party was held at a seaside mansion in Rimal al-Zahabiya, in northern Syria, close to the port of Tartus. It was the home of General Muhammad Suleiman, a close advisor to President Assad and a major figure behind the scenes of the Syrian security establishment. His office was in the presidential palace, adjacent to that of Assad, yet he was discreet and a man of the shadows; only a select few in the political and military establishment knew he existed.

Suleiman was among the initiators of the Syrian nuclear project. He had supervised the building of the reactor and managed (apparently not very successfully) its security. The Israelis had good reasons to believe that Suleiman would initiate the construction of a new reactor; he was also responsible for transferring missiles and other weaponry from Iran to Hezbollah, in Lebanon. As a result, Suleiman had placed himself in the IDF's crosshairs.

During the Rimal al-Zahabiya dinner, guests sat around a long table on the house's veranda. In front of them, the waves of the Mediterranean lazily rolled toward the beach. The image was peaceful and relaxing. The merry guests, however, didn't notice the sudden emergence, from the black Mediterranean waves, of two figures in divers' gear pulling out sniper rifles from waterproof cases and, after being given the signal, firing two bullets into Suleiman's head. The general collapsed forward on the food-laden table; only when some partygoers saw blood on his forehead did they realize that he had been shot. In the ensuing chaos, no one saw the shooters, who dived back underwater and returned to their mother ship, which took them—according to foreign media—to the base of Shayetet 13. British newspapers reported that the snipers had arrived at Suleiman's home on the deck of an Israeli-owned yacht, shot Suleiman, and disappeared.

The operation stunned the Syrian government. Was there nowhere in the country where Syria's leaders could feel safe? In their embarrassment, authorities announced that "Syria is conducting an investigation to locate those responsible." Meanwhile, in Israel, several months later, citations were awarded to Shayetet 13 without details, causing some to wonder if, perchance, one of the unnamed operations had happened to take place in the calm waters off Rimal al-Zahabiya.

PART SEVEN

The Lebanon War

In 1982, Begin and Defense Minister Ariel Sharon launch the controversial operation Peace for Galilee against the terrorist organizations in Lebanon. It is carried out by the IDF under Chief of Staff Rafael Eitan. The war ends in an Israeli victory, but it is marred by the massacre of hundreds of Palestinian civilians by the Christian Lebanese Phalanges organization at the refugee camps Sabra and Shatila, in Beirut. An Israeli board of inquiry relieves Sharon of his duties and harshly blames Eitan, even though they were not personally involved.

CHAPTER 20
"DID THEY HAVE MACHINE GUNS?"
1982

"The morning after the night of fighting, when Beaufort was already in our hands and we knew the heavy price we'd paid, I looked from up close at the antenna—the antenna that, from every vantage point on Beaufort, I could see stick sticking out, threatening. I suddenly had a tremendous desire to knock it over, because, in my eyes, it symbolized all the evil possible. I asked Roni to hang a flag off the side. Roni took the flag from my armored personnel carrier and hung it on the tip of the antenna. This, for me, was a moment of enormous satisfaction, excitement, breathlessness . . . seeing the Israeli flag waving on the antenna that I had hated so much," recounted Lieutenant Colonel Zvika Barkai, who commanded the Golani Brigade's engineering company.

The battle for Beaufort took place during the first Lebanon War, which broke out on June 6, 1982. During the battle, Golani soldiers fought PLO terrorists at a fortress that had, over the years, become a symbol of the threat against Israel's northern towns and kibbutzim. Terrorists had fired every weapon at their disposal, including rockets, from the fortress toward the Galilee Panhandle, and especially at Metula, on the Lebanese border. On numerous occasions, Israel's air force had bombed the fortress but had never managed to dislodge the terrorists, who continued to embitter the lives of residents in northern Israel. It was with good reason that the fortress had earned the name "the Monster."

Built in the twelfth century on a mountain next to the Litani River, Beaufort had been a Crusaders fortress. Its strategic importance is tremendous: at just under four hundred feet in length and 2,350 feet above sea level, it overlooks southern Lebanon and the Galilee, as well as the routes leading to the Lebanese city of Sidon and the coastal plain.

Beaufort wasn't just a target to be captured; it was, for both sides, a symbol of power, control and strength. Everyone looked in fear at the fortress, which had taken on the image of a fire-breathing monster or volcano—except that, instead of lava and ash, it spewed smoke from missiles and cannons. As a consequence, the battles there were cruel and bloody, each side understanding that victory meant extending control over the entire region.

The task of capturing Beaufort and the fortified combat trench next to it had been assigned to Sayeret Golani, the brigade's commando unit. For a year and a half, it had trained and rehearsed for various conquest scenarios at different times of day, and using various methods: a raid with helicopters, armored personnel carriers or on foot. Another unit sent to the fortress was the brigade's engineering company, whose role was to seize the antenna post south of Beaufort.

At noon, IDF forces, including Golani troops, crossed the border fence and made their way into Lebanon to carry out the government's decision "to take all northern Israeli towns out of the range of terrorist fire from Lebanon." Menachem Begin and his ministers had made that decision after a prolonged period of restraint by Israel in the face of numerous terrorist attacks and unceasing shooting on northern towns by terrorist organizations, mainly Fatah, which numbered 23,000 terrorists under the leadership of Yasser Arafat. The terrorists were arrayed across the "Fatah Land," which included the western slopes of Mount Hermon, the area south of Mount Lebanon on the Nabatieh plateau, and in the region between Tyre and Beirut.

In 1978, Israel had launched Operation Litani. The IDF had pushed the terrorists to the northern shore of the Litani River; a UN force of peacekeepers had been created but had kept anything but the peace. The terrorists had recovered and reverted to their wicked ways. Their activity had reached its peak in July 1981, when they attacked Israel's northern towns with artillery and missile salvos. A cease-fire had been finally reached, but Israel knew well that this wouldn't last long, and the power of the terrorists in south Lebanon had to be eliminated; that's why the plans for Operation Oranim ("Cedars") were born in the operations centers of the IDF. Israeli agents and officers had secretly visited Lebanon and established close relations with the Christian community and its armed units, the Phalanges. Some Israeli leaders planned to join forces with the Christians, carry out the military operation together and later establish a "new order" in Lebanon.

What had brought about the end of Israeli restraint and the decision to go to war was an attempt on the life of Israel's ambassador to Great Britain, Shlomo Argov, by a gang of terrorists, which had left Argov critically wounded. Prime Minister Menachem Begin chose to ignore the fact that these terrorists belonged to a splinter group and not to Arafat's PLO. Begin and Defense Minister Ariel Sharon were determined to hit the PLO terrorists and to put an end to the terrorist attacks originating in Lebanon. Thus started Israel's military campaign, based on the Oranim blueprints, now dubbed Operation Peace for Galilee.

Long convoys of armored personnel carriers moved along the road to the Litani, creating long traffic jams and a delay in the timetable. Only at five in the afternoon did a Golani force cross the Litani en route to Beaufort. The fighters understood that the battle would take place in darkness. "During the trip, we started preparing the teams for nighttime combat. This fact didn't especially bother us, because our familiarity with the objective was total," Barkai said.

But a Sayeret junior officer, Nadav Palti, remembered it differently. "After a year of preparations and near-attacks on Beaufort, at the moment of truth, we weren't ready. The equipment hadn't come in; the soldiers weren't sufficiently awake following forty-eight hours without sleep. The tanks were causing problems, and Giora ["Goni"] Harnik, who had been the Sayeret commander for a year and a half and was considered 'the Beaufort expert,' had been discharged just a day before the war started."

In the early evening, while the Sayeret approached the Beaufort, its new commander, Moshe Kaplinski, was struck by a bullet in the chest in a sudden outburst of gunfire.

Goni Harnik immediately arrived in the area. Handsome and slim, with tousled hair, the son of a musician and a poetess, he was a charismatic leader, worshiped by his soldiers. He was a close friend of Gabi Eshkenazi, the deputy commander of the Golani Brigade; four years before, when Ashkenazi had been severely wounded during Operation Litani in Lebanon, young Harnik—a company commander in his battalion—had assumed command and successfully carried the mission to its end.

Tonight, hearing that Goni had returned to the battlefield, Ashkenazi urgently called him to take over the Golani Sayeret. As he sped toward his soldiers in an armored personnel carrier, in the dark and without lights, the vehicle hit the low stone fence of a mountain terrace and flipped over. Harnik, injured, ran the rest of the way.

When the soldiers and officers heard his voice on the communications network saying, "The Avenging Officer [Harnik's code name] reporting," they all breathed a sigh of relief. They believed in him and admired him, and felt calmer. He began by imposing order and coordinating the operation's next steps. Harnik and Barkai agreed that Barkai's soldiers would lead and Harnik would follow in their footsteps. Barkai's men set out on foot for their destination. "Going first on the ascent to Beaufort with an advance group of five people was an unpleasant feeling. It was obvious that, if they opened fire, I would be the first to get hit," he said. "I looked through my binoculars and could make out a terrorist lying in the central bunker, his weapon pointed at me. I gave the order to charge; at the same time, a heavy burst of fire came in our direction, the results of which I saw only later—it hit the Sayeret soldiers who were in the rear."

Barkai and his soldiers crossed a minefield and infiltrated the antenna station. In the trenches surrounding it, they fought face-to-face with the terrorists. The company's doctor and the patrol-team commander were wounded. Israel's fighters killed several terrorists at close range, and the engineering company eventually seized the antenna position.

Following the engineering company, Harnik's force advanced toward the fortress. As the soldiers started climbing, they crossed a white gravel path close to the road leading to the fortress. Their dark silhouettes stood out on the white background. "I received an order from Harnik: 'Forward!'" remembered Motti, a Sayeret detachment commander. "We started to run. We needed to pass along a firing zone on the western side of Beaufort. They opened hellfire on us. You see how the bullets are flying straight at you. I look back and see that there are seven or eight people left! When we started out, we were twenty-one. I tell Harnik that I'm missing soldiers, and he answers, 'Motti, go ahead. I'll send them after you.' In hindsight, I know that, during this sprint through the area, they were simply slaughtering us." Three Sayeret commandos were killed in the onslaught.

Nevertheless, the Sayeret continued toward the combat trenches leading to the fortress, moving under unceasing machine-gun fire. A team commander and a fighter were the first to jump into the trenches. The trenches were very narrow, and moving within them with full pack and a weapon was extremely difficult. The two continued without trouble until two bursts of fire mowed them down, and both fell to their deaths. But three other soldiers kept running toward the objective with a bag of grenades that they tossed into the ditches.

Meanwhile, Harnik had reached the entrance to the fortress with five soldiers. All around them, the shooting was fierce. Numerous terrorists were killed, others were seen fleeing the site. One stubborn terrorist, hiding at a small position covered in camouflage netting, fired a burst of bullets at Harnik, and the venerated commander was killed on the spot.

The remaining fighters continued clearing the site, aware that their principal problem was the bunker that spewed intense fire. Two soldiers crawled over to it, hurling a large explosive charge and retreating. The huge thundering explosion that followed left no doubt that the bunker had been destroyed.

By 10:00 P.M., the fighting was over. The soldiers counted the corpses of thirty terrorists. Golani had six dead and nine wounded. The news about Harnik's death left all of Golani and the supreme command in shock. Golan Heights' hero Avigdor Kahalani, now a commander of the Ga'ash Division, was unable to face the news. "I wanted to believe that there was a mistake, that I would receive another message cancelling the first, but it didn't come."

Goni's comrades were amazed to learn that his mother, Raya Harnik, had darkly foreseen her son's future. When he was just four years old, she had written a poem saying:

> I will not
> Sacrifice my first born
> Not me.

And when Goni was six years old, Raya had written these chilling verses:

> That day I'll stand, eyes wide open, facing the calamity
> My whole life freezes before this tomorrow
> A lodestone I am, iron doesn't cry
> I already feel the burning
> The dryness in my throat and the looks and the fury
> And night after night my life is crying the cry of that day. . . .

Ariel Sharon, with the Beaufort conquerors. *(IDF Archive)*

The day after Beaufort's capture, Begin's helicopter landed by the vanquished citadel. The prime minister was accompanied by Defense Minister Sharon. During a TV interview conducted at the fortress, Begin said that not one of Israel's soldiers had been killed during the battle, and that there hadn't even been any injuries. It later came out that no one had bothered to update the prime minister about the outcome of the fighting. This unfortunate comment—along with his question to the soldiers: "Did they have machine guns?"—provoked a harsh response from the public, and particularly among parents whose loved ones had been wounded or killed in the battle.

Meanwhile, during the first three days of the war, battles against the terrorists raged all over Lebanon. The Galilee Division moved on to the coastal plain, going as far as the Litani River. An armored force advanced toward Sidon; the Ga'ash Division progressed toward the town of Nabatieh; and the Sinai Division fought on the western slopes of Mount Hermon, but avoided conflict with the Syrians in the area, even when they opened artillery fire on IDF forces.

But on June 9, Israeli restraint toward the Syrians came to an end. Israel's request that they pull their forces back to their prewar positions went unanswered, and Israel decided to act with all its might. (See Chapter 11.)

GABI ASHKENAZI, DEPUTY COMMANDER OF GOLANI BRIGADE, LATER THE IDF CHIEF OF STAFF

"As a deputy commander of Golani Brigade, I went through several difficult moments during this battle. The first was when I was informed that Sayeret Commander Moshe Kaplinsky had been wounded. I sent Goni Harnik to replace him, and three or four minutes later, they're reporting that his armored personnel carrier has turned over in the village of Arnoun, near the Beaufort, and that he has started running on foot, his back badly hurting, to where his soldiers were located. I said to myself, the spine of the command has been hit, and now Goni has disappeared on me. . . . But within a few minutes, Goni shows up on the radio, we speak, the battle goes on and I have the feeling that the situation is under control.

"The second difficult moment was at the end of the battle, when they told me that Goni had been killed, together with five fighters. That really hurt. Goni and I had gone through a lot together, and I felt that I had lost not only an excellent commander but a good friend, as well as an exceptional fighter.

"Given that the battle had been planned for daytime and took place at night, in a situation in which the commanders had been hit, the Sayeret and the engineers company fought in a manner worthy of commendation, and all because of the quality of the fighters, the commanders and their familiarity with Beaufort.

"At the end of the battles, when I descended from Beaufort, I didn't believe that we would spend two decades there, and that in the year 2000, it would be me, as commander of the northern district, who would evacuate Beaufort and IDF forces from Lebanon."

The Syrian Army and Air Force treat Lebanon as if it were part of Syria. They have established batteries of ground-to-air missiles in the Lebanese Beqaa. During the war with Lebanon, Israel will be confronted by the Syrian missiles and fighter planes.

CHAPTER 21

"IT WAS A GREAT CONCERT WITH MANY INSTRUMENTS," 1982

On June 9, 1982, three days after the start of the first Lebanon War, IAF pilots waited with great tension and suspense for the signal to embark on one of the air force's most complicated missions: attacking Syrian missile batteries in Lebanon's Beqaa Valley. In Jerusalem, the government continued to discuss the operation, struggling over fears of an escalation with the Syrians, who were politically and militarily involved in Lebanon. The debate was tense and stretched on for many hours. The time set for the start of the operation was pushed back, and Air Force Commander David Ivry retired to his office to concentrate on the latest flashes from the battlefield. Colonel Aviem Sella, the head of IAF operations, circulated among the pilots, checking their readiness, providing encouragement and trying to ease the tension.

At 1:30 P.M., IDF Chief of Staff Rafael Eitan called the air force commander from the prime minister's office, telling him, "Time to act. Good luck!" At two, the offensive got under way.

When the green light was given, twenty-four F-4 Phantom jets from IAF Squadron 105 took off, armed with missiles. Soaring alongside them were Skyhawk fighter aircraft, Kfirs—Israeli-made combat jets— and F-15s and F-16s armed with heat-seeking air-to-air missiles. For Israel's electronic-disruption effort, the air force had enlisted Hawkeye early-warning aircraft, Boeing 707s and Zahavan drones. At the peak of the action, approximately one hundred Israeli planes were in the air.

The Syrians likewise threw roughly one hundred aircraft into battle—MiG-21s and -23s. Nineteen surface-to-air-missile batteries had been spread across the Beqaa Valley, where they were ready to launch SA-3, SA-6 and SA-8 surface-to-air missiles, among the most advanced, state-of-the-art engines developed by the Soviet Union.

Surface-to-air missiles were still a source of trauma for Israel's air force. The war of attrition with Egypt, followed by the Yom Kippur War, had left behind bad memories and a sense of powerlessness against Egyptian missiles. The former defense minister, General Ezer Weizman, had coined the famous phrase "the missile that bent the plane's wing," which had motivated IAF commanders to look for a solution to this difficult problem. For five years, the top minds in the air force had labored with members of the military industry to develop a technological response that would protect the planes from the enemy's missiles and bring the plane's wing back to its natural place.

Now the hour of judgment had arrived: Would the Jewish brain again come up with an answer? Would the pilots' nightmare come to an end? Would the IAF reestablish control over the region's skies?

The attack's opening move was the launch of drones over the Beqaa Valley, an act of misdirection. The aircrafts' radar profile had been designed to resemble that of fighter jets, and the Syrians fell into the trap. As Israel's military planners had thought, the Syrians immediately launched surface-to-air missiles at the drones, exposing the precise locations of their batteries, which in turn became targets for Israeli radiation-seeking missiles. Simultaneously, the IDF ground electronic sensors pinpointed the batteries' locations and its artillery began shelling them.

Twenty-four Phantoms then suddenly appeared, each carrying two

"Purple Fists," anti-radiation missiles that zero in on radar installations by detecting the heat from antiaircraft systems. The planes launched the missiles at the batteries from nearly twenty-two miles away; also fired were Ze'ev surface-to-surface missiles, a sophisticated short-to-medium-range weapon that had been developed in Israel. The entire time, drones circled above the area, transmitting the results back to the operation's commanders.

After the attack's first wave, the Syrian batteries went silent for several minutes, and then the second wave arrived. Forty Phantoms, Kfirs and Skyhawks fired various types of bombs, among them cluster bombs that destroyed the batteries and their crews. The third wave took on the few remaining batteries, and within forty-five minutes, the attack had ended as a complete success. Most of the batteries had been wiped out.

During the offensive, the Syrians had fired fifty-seven SA-6 missiles but had managed to hit just one Israeli plane. For several long minutes, the Syrian command had been in complete disarray, and when it realized its battery system had collapsed, scrambled its MiGs. During the aerial battles that ensued, Israel's F-15s and F-16s brought down twenty-seven MiGs using air-to-air missiles.

"From an operational standpoint, in contrast to what was planned, the attack on the missile batteries was one of the simplest missions I ever oversaw," said Colonel Sella, who had been charged with the operation's ground management. "Everything went like clockwork. As a result, even after the first planes successfully attacked the batteries, I ordered their continued bombing. The perception was that any change, any pause or shift, could only create turmoil that would disrupt the progression of matters."

Toward 4:00 P.M., Sella reached a decision that he later described as the most significant of his life: to halt the operation. "At this stage, we had already destroyed fourteen batteries. We were an hour before last light, and we hadn't lost a plane. I believed we couldn't achieve a better outcome. When I leaned back for a minute in my chair, I took in some air and said to myself, 'Let's stop—we've done our work for the day. They're going to bring more batteries tomorrow in any case.'"

Sella went to David Ivry, who was observing the mission with Chief of Staff Eitan. Sella leaned into Ivry's ear so that Eitan wouldn't hear and said, "I'm requesting authorization to stop the operation. We won't accomplish more today. We'll destroy the rest tomorrow."

Ivry thought for a moment and nodded in agreement. The handful of planes then en route to an additional attack returned on Sella's orders to their bases. Defense Minister Ariel Sharon didn't love the decision, to put it mildly, even criticizing it harshly during a meeting with Eitan. But Sella's theory that the Syrians would move additional batteries to the Beqaa Valley overnight proved correct.

Over the next two days, Israeli bombers, escorted by fighter jets, set out to strike the new SA-8 batteries relocated by the Syrians. Because of the paralysis of Syria's defensive batteries, its air force dispatched planes to intercept the Israeli aircraft. In the battles that followed, Israel's pilots again had the upper hand: eighty-two Syrian aircraft were downed over the course of the first Lebanon War. The Israeli Air Force lost two planes to ground fire. During the campaign, what became known as the "biggest battle of the jet age" took place, involving approximately two hundred planes from the two sides.

"This situation, in which our planes were dominant and the Syrians were in a state of panic, gave us a huge psychological advantage," Ivry said. "The aerial picture on the Syrian side was very unclear. We added in electronic means for disrupting their ability to aim and keep control, meaning that the Syrians entered the combat zone more as targets than as interceptors."

When Ivry, who had also been the air force commander during Israel's attack on Iraq's nuclear reactor, was asked what his most exciting moment had been, he answered without hesitation that it was the end of the missile attack during the first Lebanon War. "When it became clear that we had succeeded in destroying the Syrian missile apparatus and that not one of our planes was damaged, it was a moment of true spiritual transcendence. This was a struggle involving the entire air force—a big concert with lots of instruments of various types, and everyone needed to play in perfect harmony."

The missile batteries were wiped out. *(AF Journal)*

The operation's success gave Israel complete control over the skies of Lebanon and made it possible for air force planes to freely assist IDF ground forces. Nevertheless, the air force abstained from striking Syrian ground troops, in keeping with a decision made by the cabinet, which feared sliding into an all-out war with Syria. On June 11, 1982, following mediation by the American emissary Philip Habib, a cease-fire between Israel and Syria took hold.

The mission, Operation Mole Cricket 19, was considered one of the four most important in the history of the air force. (The other three were Operation Focus, the assault on the combined Arab Air Forces during the Six Day War; Operation Opera, the attack on the nuclear reactor in Iraq, in 1981; and Operation Yonatan, the rescue of hostages in Antebbe, in 1976.) Western air forces regarded the mission as an example of the successful use of Western technology against Soviet defense strategy. The results of the attack caused a great deal of astonishment among the military leaders of the Warsaw Pact, overturning their sense of confidence in the USSR, and particularly in the Soviet bloc's surface-to-air-missile apparatus.

AVIEM SELLA, SQUADRON COMMANDER

"For the sake of this operation, we developed, with the help of a great team of scientists from the Weizmann Institute, a computerized control and planning system that would make it possible to prepare and command a multivariable campaign: to manage hundreds of planes with hundreds of weapons facing dozens of missile batteries and dozens of radar installations. It was a dynamic system operating in real time with thousands of variables. The primary and most outstanding programmer was a Haredi [Orthodox Jew] who lived in Bnei Brak, Menachem Kraus, who had no formal education but immense and unique knowledge. He was involved in all of the operational programs and, at the moment of action, sat with us in the Pit, in his civilian clothes.

"At the end of the day, we would conduct a nighttime debriefing and discuss what we had learned. I arrived at one debriefing where all the squadron commanders were participating, as well as all the wing commanders and former air force commanders. And, all of a sudden, everyone is standing and starts to applaud me for the perfect operation. I was very moved, because this sort of thing is quite rare in the middle of a war. I also got a little statuette, which was inscribed, 'To Sella, the thinker behind the fight against missiles, your vision has been fulfilled and we're standing tall once again—the fighters of Air Force Base 8.'"

PART EIGHT

Fighting Terrorism

After the 1982 Lebanon War, the PLO terrorists and
their leaders have been exiled to Tunisia, where they live
with total impunity, protected by the Tunisian government.
But in 1988, Prime Minister Shamir approves a
mission to change that situation.

CHAPTER 22
"ABU JIHAD SENT US," 1988

March 7, 1988. The Mothers' Bus, so called because of the large number of women it carried, was on its daily morning trip from Be'er Sheva to the Dimona nuclear reactor. At a deserted stretch of the highway it was suddenly stopped by three men, standing in the middle of the road beside a military vehicle. Only after the men boarded the bus, waving automatic weapons, did the passengers realize that these were Arab terrorists. Panic broke out on board the bus, yet forty of the passengers, all of them workers at the Dimona reactor, managed to escape. The terrorists seized control of the bus and held hostage the remaining nine women and two men. Israeli Special Forces arrived almost immediately, and surrounded the vehicle. The terrorists began negotiating with them over the release of the hostages in exchange for Palestinian prisoners in the Israeli jails. They threatened to murder a hostage every half hour. First among those killed was Victor Ram.

The first intelligence reports that reached the Israeli unit indicated that the terrorists had crossed the border early that morning, coming from Egypt-controlled Sinai, and had hijacked a military jeep on their way. Order was given to the fighters of the Special Unit of Israel's border guard (Yamam) to raid the bus. Which they did, killing the hostage takers, but not before the terrorists murdered two of the female captives, Rina Pazarkar-Sheratzky and Miriam Ben Yair. During the negotiations, one of the terrorists shouted, "Abu Jihad sent us!"

Abu Jihad. The name was highly familiar to the IDF's intelligence services. Abu Jihad—or "Father of Jihad," whose given name was Khalil al-Wazir—was Yasser Arafat's deputy, and the head of the PLO's military wing. He was born in Ramleh, in then Mandatory Palestine, and grew up in refugee camps in Gaza. Before he was even twenty, he was organizing resistance groups composed of other Palestinian youths and was among the first to join Yasser Arafat's Fatah movement. Abu Jihad had participated in the first Fatah operation in Israeli territory, planting a bomb at a National Water Carrier facility on January 1, 1965. Following the Yom Kippur War, he planned a series of lethal terrorist assaults on Israel, including a 1974 attack in Nahariya that killed four Israelis and wounded six; a raid on the Savoy hotel in Tel Aviv on March 5, 1975, which killed eight hostages and three IDF soldiers, among them Colonel Uzi Yairi; a massive bombing in the crowded Zion Square in Jerusalem by a booby-trapped refrigerator that killed fifteen people on July 4, 1975; the Coastal Road massacre of March 11, 1978, in which thirty-five were murdered; and the killing of three Israeli sailors in Limassol, Cyprus, in September 1985.

By 1988, Abu Jihad was running the first Palestinian armed rebellion—the Intifada—from afar, and in the eyes of many Palestinians, had become a symbol of the struggle against Israel. He had married Intisar al-Wazir—also known as Umm Jihad, or "Mother of Jihad"—an impressive woman who was a leader in her own right. She gave him three sons and one daughter. Expelled from Lebanon with his PLO cronies after Israel's 1982 invasion, he was banished four years later from Jordan and settled in Tunis with the rest of the Fatah leadership.

Abu Jihad had already been marked for assassination a few years earlier; several operations had been planned but were abandoned at the last minute. However, with the Mothers' Bus attack of March 1988, the cup runneth over. Following the attack, the head of the military intelligence department, General Amnon Lipkin-Shahak, reached the conclusion that Abu Jihad should be eliminated. General Lipkin-Shahak knew what he was talking about: he was a decorated hero of Operation Spring of Youth in 1973. (See Chapter 14.)

The IDF new chief of staff, Dan Shomron, (the brain behind the Entebbe mission) approved an operation in principle and assigned its management and preparation to his deputy, Ehud Barak, the former commander of Sayeret Matkal. Outwardly, it appeared to be an incredibly complicated mission, more than 1,550 miles from home. The Mossad was asked to help. Ever since the Fatah leadership had settled in Tunis, the Mossad had been widening its effective intelligence network. Its agents in Tunis surreptitiously visited Abu Jihad's neighborhood, Sidi Bou Said, photographed his home and even succeeded in drawing up precise blueprints of the structure and its internal layout. A Mossad female agent had visited the house under false pretexts and submitted a report on its furnishings and interior: a corridor leading from the entrance to a couch and armchair-filled guest room; a door that led to Abu Jihad's study; another door, to the kitchen; and a staircase to the second floor, where the bedrooms of Abu Jihad, his wife, and daughter, Hanan, were located. The couple's baby, Nidal, a two-year-old, slept in his parents' room, while the family's two older boys studied in the United States.

The operation was planned as follows: the commandos of Sayeret Matkal would approach Tunisia's coast on Israeli naval ships. Members of Shayetet 13, the naval commando unit, would bring them to shore, and from there, they would reach Abu Jihad's home with the aid of the Mossad. The Shayetet and the navy had secretly mapped Tunis's coastline and located beaches for the Israeli landing. Air force jets were eventually dispatched for a surveillance flight, refreshing the IDF's intelligence before the operation.

Even so, the risks remained very high. Any encounter with PLO forces, Tunisian Army units or local police could lead to disaster, and it was clear that a retreat by Israeli forces or an evacuation of wounded participants would be much harder than in countries adjacent to Israel.

Abu Jihad's neighborhood was home to many PLO leaders on Israel's most-wanted list, and it was obvious that there would be a large presence of well-trained Fatah guards. Any misstep could end in battle or the entrapment of IDF soldiers. The operation could also lead to severe political consequences: Tunisia wasn't an active enemy of Israel, and it would be hard to explain an attack on Tunisians. One question kept Defense Minister Yitzhak Rabin particularly restless: how would it be possible to confirm that Abu Jihad was home on the night of the mission?

The Mossad had assured Rabin that it would have up-to-the-minute information about Abu Jihad's whereabouts within his home, which it hoped to secure via intelligence reports and careful surveillance. In the meantime, final preparations were under way. An exact replica of Abu Jihad's home was built in Israel, where Sayeret Matkal trained for the infiltration and assassination. Elite officers were selected for the operation, and each was assigned a precise role.

The team that would go up to the bedrooms and the officer who would shoot Abu Jihad were also chosen. Heading the operation would be Sayeret Matkal's commander, Moshe Ya'alon. Bogie, who had returned to active service as a sergeant after the 1973 Yom Kippur War, was now a colonel and considered one of the best Sayeret commanders. During the preparation for the mission Bogie decided to visit the area. He flew to Rome and from there, with a false passport, to Tunis. Once in Tunis, he was taken by Mossad agents on a tour near Abu Jihad's home. The next day, Ya'alon returned to Israel via Rome and joined his men.

The force set out in four missile boats, accompanied by a submarine, on Wednesday, April 13. Two of the boats transported the Sayeret Matkal and Shayetet 13 commandos, and were protected by the other two. One of the boats, containing a sophisticated electronics center, served as the operation's command post under Barak's command. A fully equipped and staffed medical operation unit had been set up in the other. The flotilla initially sailed northwest, toward the Greek islands, then turned west and later south, until it reached the coast of Tunisia.

That same day, three Mossad agents had appeared at a car-rental company in Tunis bearing false IDs. Calling themselves Ayish a-Saridi,

George Najib and Uataf Allem (the third was a woman), they rented three minibuses—two Volkswagen Transporters and a Peugeot.

The missile boats reached their destination on April 15. That day, Israel intercepted a transmission sent to the PLO by French agents, who warned that "the Israelis are cooking up something." This was a cause for concern, but Barak ordered that the operation move ahead.

That night, two Boeing 707s belonging to the Israeli Air Force arrived in the skies over Tunis, one a receptor for electronic transmissions and the other providing air cover and serving as a refueling plane for the fighter jets circling in the region.

The operation commenced. The submarine drew closer to the appointed beach—A-Rouad, next to Ras Carthage—and reported that it was completely empty. Two pairs of Shayetet fighters, aboard tiny "Hazir" ("Pig") submersibles, reached the shore, and met the trio from the Mossad, which had brought the rented vehicles. The Shayetet divers reported by radio that the beach was secure, and five rubber dinghies were immediately lowered into the sea, delivering twenty sayeret commandos to the shore. The landing point was a short distance from Sidi Bou Said. The commandos had been divided into four teams—A and B to carry out the operation, and C and D to provide protection. The fighters in A and B were armed with twenty-two-milimeter Berettas outfitted with silencers, as well as mini-Uzis. Several members of the C and D teams carried rifles and grenades. The Sayeret members wore coveralls concealing bulletproof vests and supple Palladium boots. Attached to their heads were communications devices with microphones and earphones, and their belts carried tiny pouches with ammunition and first-aid supplies. They were also equipped with surgical masks, to conceal their faces.

That evening, the Shin Bet had detained Fayez Abu Rahma, a relative of Abu Jihad who lived in Gaza. His interrogation had been cursory and unfocused, and he was released a few hours later. Actually, the arrest had a single, secret objective: to cause Abu Rahma to call Abu Jihad in Tunis, which would allow the Mossad and Military-intelligence's listening systems to confirm that the terrorist leader was in fact in the North African city.

But as H-Hour approached, a last-minute hitch occurred. While Sayeret Matkal was getting ready on the Tunisian beach, an urgent message was received from a Mossad agent. Abu Jihad wasn't home! He was in the city, at a meeting with another Palestinian leader, Farouk Kaddoumi. The unit was forced to wait. The risk was great: an elite unit of the IDF sitting tight on an isolated beach in an enemy country, thousands of miles away from home. A nerve-wracking hour and a half passed before Yaalon received word that Abu Jihad had returned home, escorted by two bodyguards—one who remained in the car, outside, and a second who went into the house. The sayeret fighters piled up in their vehicles and immediately departed for Sidi Bou Said, passing the darkened ruins of the ancient port of Carthage, where Hannibal had set sail to Spain, launching his legendary campaign against the Roman Empire.

The soldiers reached their destination shortly before 2:00 A.M. Abu Jihad's car was parked in front of his house, and his bodyguard was dozing off in the driver's seat. Two fighters approached the vehicle, one disguised as a woman. The "lady" was carrying a large box of chocolates that concealed his hand, holding a silenced pistol. When they reached the car, one of them shot the bodyguard through the head. The others moved into the garden surrounding the house, while members of the A team broke through a reinforced wooden door with the help of specialized, noise-reducing equipment. The A and B teams snuck into the house; in the basement, the commandos killed the second bodyguard, as well as an unlucky Tunisian gardener who had chosen to sleep there. Members of the A team ran upstairs, toward Abu Jihad and his wife's bedroom.

Abu Jihad wasn't sleeping. An hour earlier, he had kissed his sixteen-year-old daughter, Hanan, good night, and after leaving her room had sat at his desk to begin writing a letter to leaders of the Intifada back in Israel. A faint noise outside startled him, and he picked up a firearm—his special silver-handled pistol—and turned toward the door. Umm Jihad realized what was going on and called, "Verdun, Verdun," in reference to Verdun Street, in Beirut, the location of the building where terrorist leaders had been killed during Operation Spring of Youth.

Abu Jihad opened the door. Standing before him were masked men, their weapons drawn. He managed to push his wife into an alcove in the wall and raise his revolver, but the officer facing him shot an entire magazine into him, as did the rest of the group afterward. Abu Jihad collapsed in front of his wife. While the attackers still fired at the terrorist leader, Umm Jihad jumped toward her husband and bent over his body, embracing the corpse and eventually shouting at the attackers, "Enough!"

The shooters didn't harm her nor her daughter, Hanan, who had been awakened by the sound of the shooting and burst into the room. One blurted out in Arabic, "Go to your mother!" but she saw the attackers firing at her father on the ground and, for a moment, stood opposite one of the commandos entering the room without a mask. She looked at his face—a face, she said, that she would never forget. He, too, shot her father in the head. Umm Jihad and her daughter saw a woman who had accompanied the Israeli unit; she was videotaping the entire operation. The two-year-old baby, Nidal, woke up and burst into tears. Above him stood a Sayeret commando spraying gunfire into the ceiling, but he didn't harm the child. The PLO later claimed that the attackers had fired seventy bullets, and that fifty-two had struck Abu Jihad.

Retaking the hijacked "Mothers' bus." *(GPO)*

The commandos left the room quickly, descending the stairs, grabbing official documents and other papers they found, and ripping a small safe out of the study wall to take with them. Above them, Umm Jihad heard a woman's voice shouting at them in French to hurry: *"Allez! Allez!"*

The operation had taken less than five minutes. The commandos exited and stood in front of the house, where their commanders counted them, to ensure that everyone was there. From her window, Umm Jihad looked at them and counted twenty-four people. Their vehicles sped toward the beach; inside, the commandos found crates of soft drinks prepared by the Mossad. The boats awaited them at the beach, and they ventured out into the open sea, together with the Mossad agents who had taken part in the operation. Other agents had stayed in Tunis and called the police to report that the attackers' vehicles had been seen traveling toward the city—the opposite direction from the get-away route. Police in Tunis placed roadblocks on the roads leading out of Sidi Bou Said toward the capital, and the country's president scrambled ground forces and helicopters, also ordering the closure of the airport and seaport. But, with the exception of the three rented vehicles abandoned on the beach, not a trace of the Israelis was found.

By the following day, the episode made front-page headlines around the world; there could be no doubt that the operation had been the work of the Israelis. Abu Jihad had been killed, but his name wasn't forgotten. Years later, his talented wife, Umm Jihad, was appointed to serve as a minister in Yasser Arafat's government, after the establishment of the Palestinian Authority. She and her daughter would describe the assassination to Israeli writers and journalists.

THE FAMILY OF MIRIAM BEN YAIR, KILLED IN THE MOTHERS' BUS ATTACK

Miriam Ben Yair's daughter, Rachel, in tears: "When the terrorist turned toward my mother, she begged him, 'My daughter is getting married next month; please have mercy on me.' He shot her to death. She was on her way to the Nuclear Research Center, where she worked as an executive secretary. Invitations to my wedding that she had been planning to distribute to her friends were found in her bag."

Ben Yair's husband, Eliyahu: "Friends met me in the street and asked, 'What, you haven't heard? The Mothers' Bus was attacked!' I raced to Soroka hospital. My wife's sister, Frieda, a nurse there, told me, 'It's over.'"

Her son, Ilan: "My mom was a pretty woman, full of joy. She knew French very well and worked at the Nuclear Research Center from the time the French built the reactor. Her family was her entire world, and she dreamed of leaving one day, to raise her grandchildren. She didn't get to. She was forty-six at her death."

Eliyahu: "It was Major General Yitzhak Mordechai who comforted us. He would visit us often, talk to us. He was like a member of the family."

Rachel: "We knew that Abu Jihad was responsible for the murder. His death gave us a certain relief, but the pain remains deep and sharp, just as it was before."

Iran has become the major supplier of weapons,
mainly missiles, to the terrorist organizations in Gaza.
The weapons usually leave Iran aboard innocent-looking
cargo vessels; then they are either unloaded in Sudan and sent
to Gaza in truck convoys via Egypt and Sinai, or left aboard
the ships that traverse the Suez Canal and dumped in Gaza
waters, where local Arab divers recover them. One of the most
recent cases is the capture in March 2014 by Israeli commandos
of the boat *Klos C*, carrying a concealed load of missiles.
The most famous mission of this kind, however, is the
capture of the weapons on the ship *Karine A*.

CHAPTER 23
"WHERE IS THE SHIP?" 2002

A t 3:58 in the morning on January 3, 2002, two rubber Morena-
type boats pulled next to the hull of the *Karine A*, a freighter making its way in the Suez Gulf. An electronic signal was flashed to
the Shayetet 13 commandos on the Morenas, and they swiftly began
climbing from the boats onto the deck of the ship. Suddenly, helicopters swooped down from overhead, and more fighters dropped out
of them, sliding down on assault ropes. Quickly and without using
weapons, the soldiers spread throughout the ship. They immediately
started searching for a shipment of weapons purportedly sent from
Iran to the Palestinian Authority.

Hovering simultaneously overhead were Israeli Air Force fighter
jets; Sikorsky helicopters carrying members of Unit 669, the IDF's airborne rescue and evacuation team; a plane equipped for intelligence
gathering, surveillance photography, and refueling; and a Boeing 707
serving as the command post for IDF Chief of staff Shaul Mofaz, Navy
Commander Yedidia Ya'ari, Air Force Commander Dan Halutz, and
additional senior officers, who would stay in the air for approximately

two hours until the start of the operation, tracking what was taking place below. "It was a long flight," a senior officer recalled, "three hundred miles from the Israeli coast. The plane was crowded and very cold, and you could cut the tension with a knife. "

Until the last minute, the mission commanders feared that the raid would be called off because of the stormy weather. The waves were rising nearly ten feet, the winds reaching speeds of almost forty miles an hour. It was hard to sail in such conditions, and even harder to rappel down ropes from a helicopter onto the deck of a ship. But the *Karine A,* according to highly reliable intelligence, was in the Red Sea, en route to the Suez Canal, and the IDF needed to do everything in its power to take hold of the ship before it reached its destination.

The operation planner and field commander, Vice Admiral Eli ("Chiney") Marom, was assisted by a superb meteorologist. Marom understood that if they waited for the ship to reach the originally planned interception point, approximately twenty-five miles south of Sharm el-Sheikh, the storm would be at full force. After additional assessments and calculations, he decided that his forces would sail to a point twice as far from Israel as the preselected location, 150 miles south of the Suez Canal. The shayetet officers who heard his suggestion didn't believe it possible, as it carried a much greater risk that something would go wrong; they were also uncertain that the fuel supplies for the helicopters and boats would suffice. But Chiney persisted, suggesting that the fighters take with them barrels of fuel for refilling at sea, and that the helicopters, which couldn't circle for long in the air, would act in full coordination with the naval forces to best use the window of time at their disposal. The chips had fallen, and the mission got under way.

Chiney was forty-seven, a moshav boy, whose father had escaped his native Germany when the Nazis came to power, and landed in China. There he had wed Chai Lee, the daughter of a Russian-born Jewish woman and a Chinese man. The couple had immigrated to Israel and Chai Lee had changed her name to Leah. Young Eli had inherited her slanted eyes and his comrades at the naval officers' academy had nicknamed him Chiney. His Asiatic features made an American paper call

him the "Israeli Chinese Admiral." He was known as an excellent officer. "The fact that Chiney looked different," one former comrade said in
a press interview, "forced him to constantly show that he was better. He
became one of the best very quickly."

The night of the operation had been preceded by a long period of complex surveillance that combined multipronged intelligence gathering and
preparations. It had all begun when some top-secret reports were delivered to the IDF intelligence headquarters. The documents dealt with a
project to smuggle weapons by ship from Iran to the Gaza Strip. This
wasn't the first time the Palestinians had tried to smuggle weapons to
Gaza by sea. In May 2001, the Israeli Navy had captured a small boat, the
Santorini, as it sailed to Gaza from a Hezbollah base in Lebanon. On its
deck, the Israelis had found a small but significant cache of weapons: Russian Strella missiles with which the Palestinians intended to bring down
IAF planes. It was undeniable proof that Yasser Arafat was speaking out
of both sides of his mouth, talking about his people's desire for peace to
leaders in the West and, at home, in Arabic, about jihad.

A seemingly unimportant finding alerted the sensors of the Israeli
intelligence community: the Palestinians had paid too much for an old
ship. The navy head of intelligence recalled, "We realized that the ship
in question had been acquired for a task that wasn't innocent at all; they
had done everything to conceal their activities. They were treating this
like a secret mission, using special technology."

Intelligence operatives immediately began tracking the activities of
the people involved in the purchase and the handling of the ship, and
searching for any tiny piece of information that might lead them to crack
the mystery of the *Karine A*. In early December, they had assembled a
partial picture of the Palestinian operation: the ship had been purchased
in the summer of 2001 by Palestinians using multiple straw companies.
Fearing detection by the Mossad or other intelligence organizations, the
Palestinians changed the ship's name, *Rim K*, to *Karine A*. As eagle-eyed Israeli Mossad agents watched, the ship sailed from Lebanon to Port Sudan,
where it was loaded with large quantities of rice, clothing, toys and household appliances, with plenty of space left over for the weapons awaiting

the ship at its next destination—Kish Island, off the coast of Iran. Under the darkness of night, an Iranian ferry loaded the *Karine A* with eighty-containers, each holding nearly eighteen hundred pounds of weaponry.

The ferry's Farsi-speaking crew provided the *Karine A* captain with a list of the containers' contents, as well as clear instructions for the rest of the trip. The weapons had been loaded into eighty sophisticated, buoyant, hermetically sealed containers built by Iran's military industry. When the *Karine A* approached Gaza, its crew would dump the containers in the water. Each container was equipped with a compartment that could contain water or air. When the compartment filled with water, the container would submerge; a diver would later approach and turn a switch, compressed air would displace the water, and the container would float to the surface. At this stage, small boats would collect the containers and bring them to the beaches of Gaza, where they'd be collected by Palestinian police personnel and brought to the terrorists.

After the ship was loaded, it set sail for the crucial leg of its journey. However, it was forced to dock for eleven days at the port of Hodeidah, in Yemen, because of technical problems. The stop in Yemen gave the IDF the vital time window it needed to plan and prepare for the seizure of the ship.

The ship and its lethal cargo in the port of Eilat.
(Jo Kot, Yedioth Ahronoth Archive)

In Chief of Staff Shaul Mofaz's office feverish discussions started, with the participation of the Shayetet commanders and air force and intelligence personnel. Maps were spread and operational plans submitted; everyone understood that the pivotal moment was growing close.

"What are you calling the operation?" Mofaz asked at one of the meetings.

"Noah's Ark," replied the head of the navy's operations division.

"A nice name," Mofaz smiled.

In the lead-up to the final decision, Chiney explained to the chief of staff, "Everything is based on the discovery of the ship. The moment we found out about it, the rest was simply a matter of scheduling."

Mofaz remained uneasy. "Will you be on one of the patrol boats?" he asked Chiney.

"Yes."

"You'll know how to process all the intelligence about the ship?"

"Yes."

"You'll also be able to positively identify it, what's on it, its dimensions?

"Definitely."

"Were you ever in the Straits of Tiran?"

"Many times."

"Now, then, how would you sail the ship through the Straits of Tiran?"

"It's not too complicated. All we need to know is how to start the ship's engine."

Mofaz summed up his position. "I cannot risk that this mission would fail. If you see that conditions in the sea are such that it can't be done, you must stop and think it over again; or you put this on hold temporarily, and we wait, let's say, for a day; or we let the ship go away."

A few days before the operation, the team went to the home of Prime Minister Ariel Sharon, presenting him with the details of the mission. Sharon listened, asked questions, requested a look at the maps and praised the operation's daring. He then authorized it, aware that its success depended on the precise coordination between the Shayetet commandos and the pilots of the helicopters from which they'd be rappelling down. "This is like jumping onto a truck on a winding road," a member of the Shayetet later said.

There remained some unresolved questions: Was the ship's crew armed? Was the hidden weaponry booby-trapped or loaded with explosive charges programmed to be operated remotely? Were there Palestinian fighters on board? The mission could become a bloodbath, if Palestinian armed terrorists were protecting the ship. To address all the contingencies it was decided that a Shayetet doctor and a medic would be part of the takeover team, and that one of the helicopters would be fully equipped for emergency surgery, if needed.

One night, shortly before the mission, the chief of staff and the operation's commanders watched a simulation during which Shayetet commandos rappelled onto a commercial ship from two helicopters. Mofaz was highly satisfied with the exercise. The commandos then departed to Eilat, where they would wait for the green light. But Mofaz and the intelligence experts were still preoccupied with the ultimate question: Where was the ship? Why couldn't they locate it? They knew without a doubt that it was making its way toward the Suez Canal, but a definitive ID was missing. Only a few days later, on January 1, 2002, the chief of staff received word that the *Karine A* had been conclusively identified, forty miles north of Jedda, Saudi Arabia, at a distance of four hundred miles from the area where the takeover was planned. The last reports noted that the ship's name, *Karine A*, was written clearly and prominently on the ship's hull.

On the morning of D Day, the various units began moving toward their destination. Chiney boarded a "Dvora" patrol boat, while Shayetet commander Ram Rotenberg boarded a helicopter alongside his fighters. About two hours before H-Hour, Mofaz and officers from the navy and Air force climbed onto the special Boeing that would fly them above the Red Sea area where the takeover would unfold.

Even before the operation began, the Boeing's passengers were glued to their monitor screens; they watched Chiney and his command team at sea, trying to identify the *Karine A*, which finally appeared on the radar in the middle of a group of ships twenty miles from the takeover point. Using various indicators they attempted to determine which ship was the *Karine A* but without success. An IAF patrol plane was also unable to identify the target, due to a dense fog covering the waters. The navy's small flotilla drew closer to the group of ships. So as not to be identified, Chiney grouped the vessels in a unique formation, with a patrol boat in front and a patrol boat in the back and the rubber boats in between; from a distance, they looked like a single big ship.

The tension on the boats and in the Boeing kept growing. The window of opportunity was getting shorter—they needed to complete the mission by 4:15 A.M.; the choppers couldn't stay in the area a minute longer.

Chiney continued to calculate the timing and geographical issues, and decided the operation had to begin at 3:45.

"But where is the ship?" wondered a Shayetet officer. "Where the hell did it disappear? Could it have managed to get away?"

Suddenly, about 4.5 miles away, a Shayetet intelligence officer spotted a ship with a prominent smokestack, three loading cranes and a mast at its center, the distinctive characteristics of the *Karine A*. The report quickly climbed up the chain of command, and the excitement grew. The ship had been found.

It was three-forty. Now they began moving closer to the ship, which was growing increasingly visible. The Israeli force raised its speed and came within very close range, almost next to it. Shaul Mofaz asked again for clear confirmation. "That's the ship! That's the ship!" came the answer from below.

The moment of decision was approaching. All the senior officers on the Boeing remained glued to their monitors, where they could follow the takeover from start to finish; the process looked like a Hollywood thriller.

At four the electronic signal flashed through the flotilla receivers. That was the go-ahead for Noah's Ark, which began at once. From above, the officers in the Boeing could see the Shayetet fighters bursting from the sea and air onto the *Karine A* deck, surprising the thirteen-member crew, the majority of whom were asleep. They could make out that no gun battle was taking place on the ship, and could identify the Shayetet commanders conducting a preliminary search for the weapons. Most important of all, and unbelievably, the entire operation lasted just seven minutes.

A sigh of relief could be heard aboard the Boeing, and Chief of Staff Mofaz hurried to call the officers below. He congratulated them without concealing his happiness: "You did wonderful work! From above, it looked amazing. What now? What's the next stage?"

"We've completed the takeover, and our forces are doing a sweep," Shayetet Colonel Ram Rotenberg responded.

"Are you seeing anything yet?" Mofaz persisted, seeking a smoking gun, weaponry that would prove to the world—and to the United States in particular—that Yasser Arafat was engaged in smuggling Iranian arms into the Palestinian territories.

"Not yet—right now we're going down into the holds. We'll report back the moment we find something," the commander replied.

Chiney, who in the meantime had boarded the ship, rushed to the cargo hold with the Shayetet commander. With flashlights, they illuminated the area but couldn't find a thing. A few minutes went by, but the search bore no fruit. They saw nothing but bags of rice, bundles of clothes and children's toys. "We can't see anything, not a weapon and not a mortar," one of the searchers blurted out in despair. For a moment, an appalling doubt stole into their hearts: Had they captured the right ship? Was Noah's Ark a failure? Had they risked their lives for nothing?

And then came the turning point. A quick, rough interrogation of the ship's captain, Omar Akawi, an employee of the Palestinian transportation ministry, yielded results. A commando fighter considered the Shayetet tough guy began shaking him with no excessive gentleness, and the confession wasn't long in coming. "It's in the forward hold," Akawi ultimately blurted.

The commandos hurried to the bow. "We initially thought that we hadn't found anything," Lieutenant Colonel G recalled. "But we discovered the first crate, then the second, and a sense of great pride overwhelmed us. It was the first time we encountered such quantities of weapons. Every Katyusha launcher that was uncovered was accompanied by a round of applause, and the guys greatly rejoiced."

The soldiers took over the vessel commands and the ship was turned toward the Gulf of Eilat. One of the commandos ran to his officer. "We need to raise the Israeli flag," he said.

"But we don't have one," the officer countered.

"We do. I brought it from home," the commando said.

A few hours later, an Israeli flag flowing from its mast, *Karine A* docked in Eilat. The methodical search revealed that the ship had been loaded with sixty-four tons of weaponry, including Katyusha rockets, Sagger anti-tank missiles, Israeli-made mortars (that had been supplied to Iran before Khomeini's takeover), rocket-propelled grenade launchers, Ra'ad missiles, various kinds of rifles and land mines. "All this was an internal Iranian affair," a senior officer joked, "their Iranians were beaten by our Iranians, Mofaz and Halutz [both officers of Iranian origin]."

The day after the operation, Prime Minister Sharon hosted American General Anthony Zinni at his farm. At the end of the meeting, he told him, "You can tell Yasser Arafat, when you see him today, that he needn't worry about his weapons ship, the *Karine A*. We got it, and it's in our hands."

After the story went public, the United States cut its ties with the Palestinian Authority for an extended period. President Bush was furious that Arafat had lied to him, and that was one of the reasons the Americans would soon give their approval to Operation Defensive Shield.

SHAUL MOFAZ, THEN IDF'S CHIEF OF STAFF, LATER MINISTER OF DEFENSE

"The story of the *Karine A*, beyond the smuggling of fifty tons of weapons and terror supplies from Iran to the Palestinians, is about the agreement between them, according to which the Palestinians, in exchange for the weapons they received, would give the Iranians a foothold within the Palestinian Authority. Its significance was the entry of Iran's Revolutionary Guards into the cities of the West Bank.

"When we received the intelligence about this, it was clear

that we needed to take control of the ship in order to capture the weaponry and—no less important—to expose Arafat's true face as a terror leader to the world.

"After the Shayetet and the air force's amazing operation, Prime Minister Arik Sharon decided to send me to the White House to present Condoleezza Rice, the national security adviser, with all the intelligence that we'd acquired and to reveal the deal reached between Arafat and the Iranians. She looked over the material, astonished, and ran with it to President Bush. She asked if I could stay in Washington; I said that I could not because the Intifada was at its worst. This material led to President Bush's famous declaration that the Palestinian Authority is a terror organization.

"The central dilemma during the operation had been conclusively identifying the ship. The fear was that if we couldn't identify it with one hundred percent certainty, we might mistakenly capture another country's ship, something that could cause great trouble. Consequently, when I boarded the Boeing command post, the first thing I asked for was to see the ship's identification on the radar."

In 1993, Israel and the PLO have signed the Oslo Accords, hoping to reach a peace solution soon. Unfortunately, the accords fail and a new wave of terrorism sweeps Israel. After a stunning increase in suicide bombings by Palestinians, Prime Minister Sharon and Defense Minister Benyamin Ben Eliezer launch a large-scale operation in the West Bank, targeting the terrorist organizations. The operation is directed by Chief of Staff Shaul Mofaz.

CHAPTER 24
HOLOCAUST REMEMBRANCE DAY IN THE NABLUS QASBAH, 2002

On the rainy, stormy night of March 29, 2002, an IDF force entered Ramallah, the capital of Yasser Arafat's Palestinian Authority. The troops' raid on his headquarters, the Mukataa, was carried out on foot, and wasn't met by particularly intense Palestinian resistance. Avi Peled, the commander of the Egoz Commando Unit, later remarked, "We knew that, for the Palestinians, the Mukataa was the end of the line, the holy of holies. We were sure that they would fight us till the last bullet. But apparently our entrance into the Mukataa and the Palestinian Preventive Security headquarters in Beitunia had broken them psychologically, and their resistance collapsed everywhere."

That was the start of Operation Defensive Shield, one of the IDF's largest-ever operations in the West Bank, territories also referred to by Israelis as Judea and Samaria. The goal was to strike at the area's terrorist organizations and to stop a wave of terror attacks that had reached unprecedented numbers. During the preceding month, referred to as

Black March, 135 Israelis had been killed by terror attacks, eleven of them suicide bombings within Israel's pre-1967 borders. The low point was a terrorist attack on a Passover seder in the Park Hotel, in Netanya: a suicide bomber entered the hotel undetected and killed thirty guests and wounded 140 others celebrating around the Passover table.

The horrifying images broadcast in Israel and around the world that night melted American objections to an Israeli military response. The next day, the government authorized Operation Defensive Shield and mobilized thirty thousand reservists. Called up for the operation were the Golani, Nahal, Yiftach and paratrooper brigades, as well as both regular soldiers and reservists in the infantry, armored and engineering corps. At the Knesset, Prime Minister Ariel Sharon explained the goals of the operation: "The IDF's soldiers and their commanders will go into cities and villages that have become shelters for terrorists, to capture and detain terrorists and, above all, those who dispatch them, to seize and confiscate weapons and fighting supplies intended to hit Israel, and to uncover and wipe out terror installations, terror laboratories, weapons-creation factories and hideouts."

In Ramallah. the IDF demolished the buildings of the Mukataa compound, except for the structure that housed Arafat himself. Fighters from the Egoz commando took positions in rooms along the corridor leading to Arafat's office, while outside, Israeli tanks encircled the site. Sheltered within the Mukataa's detention center were several fugitive criminals involved in terror activities against Israel. The head of Palestinian intelligence had ordered them clandestinely brought into Arafat's compound, under the assumption that they would be safe there from the IDF. After a lengthy standoff, the Americans had intervened, and the fugitives were transferred to a prison in Jericho under British oversight.

In Ramallah, the IDF had uncovered weapons labs and captured scores of fugitive men and materiel. Toward the end of the fighting, it had seized Marwan Barghouti, the commander of the Fatah armed faction, the Tanzim; Barghouti would be later sentenced to life in prison for his numerous terror attacks.

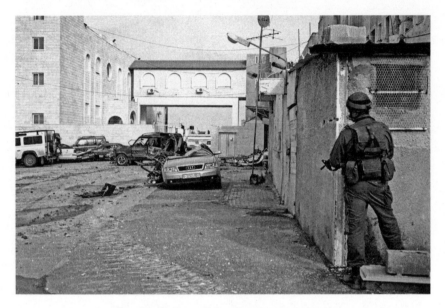

The siege in Ramallah. *(Yoav Guterman, GPO)*

From Ramallah, on to Nablus. Nablus was considered a stronghold of Palestinian resistance, and its Qasbah, a maze of narrow, tortuous streets and convoluted passages had become a source of dread for the IDF's General Staff, which was deeply concerned with the risks of fighting there. Densely populated, the Qasbah contained booby-trapped homes, sniper positions and a great number of terrorists. Hundreds of them hid in the crooked alleys, IEDs were planted everywhere and gas containers were buried in the ground, ready to explode. The IDF elite soldiers braced themselves before approaching the Qasbah, expecting bloody surprises at every street corner.

The assault on Nablus began on April 5, with the operation under the command of Brigadier General Yitzhak ("Jerry") Gershon, chief of the Judea and Samaria Division. He orchestrated the movements of the paratrooper brigade, which came from the west; Golani, which approached from the south, and the armored Yiftach Brigade, which occupied the eastern part of the city, including its hostile refugee camps. The Palestinians had planted dozens of mines within delivery trucks and water tanks lining the roadways, and IDF engineers systematically defused them, one by one.

The paratroopers attacked the Qasbah from all sides simultaneously. Their secret weapon was a revolutionary battle method: passing through walls. The paratroopers had developed various instruments allowing them to break walls with heavy sledgehammers or blow large holes in them and thus move from one house to another without even stepping into the murderous streets. That method had been used for the first time a month and a half earlier, during the seizure of the nearby Balata refugee camp. Aviv Kochavi, the commander of the paratrooper brigade, explained that, "in the crowded Qasbah, where the narrow streets contained numerous mines and obstacles, and where snipers could shoot from every corner, we developed an alternative system of fighting: we moved exclusively through the walls and buildings to surprise the enemy, who alone was left to circulate in the alleyways, becoming an exposed target. The strategy kept the enemy disoriented and vulnerable to our fire, which caught it off guard largely from the sides, from behind or from above."

In the Qasbah, the gangs of terrorists concentrated under a single command. Most of the fugitive Palestinian fighters, the majority of them Tanzim and the minority Hamas, had also holed up there. With great determination, the Palestinians fought with Kalashnikovs and M-16s, prepared to die as "martyrs."

But the soldiers of the IDF were also highly determined. The battle in the Qasbah moved from house to house. The goal was to limit, at all costs, the number of IDF fighters wounded in battle, and as a result, it was decided that a small operational force would be sent every few minutes to the houses where the terrorists were positioned. The terrorists would begin shooting, thereby exposing themselves to the fire of Israeli snipers waiting on the opposite side. The alleyways were left to the fugitive fighters, and the IDF made use of sniper positions in the homes. Israeli gunmen charged out of unexpected places and hit Palestinians who had prepared to fire on troops that were farther away.

By the third day of the war, the IDF was already in control of two-thirds of the Qasbah. Lieutenant Colonel Ofek Buhris, the commander of the 51st Battalion, had been deployed to Nablus with his soldiers after fighting in the Mukataa and Jenin, and was in charge of locating explosives' labs and capturing fugitives. He was assigned to entrap Ali Hadiri, one of Hamas's senior engineers, who had prepared the explosive that blew up at the Park Hotel in Netanya. During the raid on the house where the terrorist was staying, a hail of gunfire burst from within, killing a company commander in the Golani Brigade and badly wounding Buhris. Golani soldiers broke into the house and killed Hadiri and another terrorist.

On April 8 at about 7:00 A.M., all of a sudden, dozens of Palestinians emerged from one of the Qasbah houses, their arms in the air. The surrender of the terrorists had begun. Reports arrived hourly of additional groups turning themselves in; by the afternoon, further surrender deals were being proposed through the Shin Bet and the Civil Administration, Israel's governing body in the West Bank. By six-thirty that evening, the last of the armed men had left the houses of the Nablus Qasbah, their arms raised and waving improvised white flags as a sign of surrender. After seventy-two hours of fighting, seventy terrorists had been killed and hundreds arrested.

But the battle that would become most identified with Operation Defensive Shield would take place in Jenin, remembered because of the number of Israeli casualties—twenty-three dead and seventy-five wounded—and because of Palestinian claims of a massacre carried out by the IDF in the city's refugee camp.

The armed Palestinians, massed at the center of the camp, had laid a trap of thousands of explosive devices and had set up numerous ambushes in the camp's narrow alleyways. Israel's soldiers entered the camp with the assistance of tanks, assault helicopters and D9 bulldozers, which cleared explosives and opened booby-trapped doors. Progress was slow, with Palestinian snipers firing on the troops and making their advance difficult.

On the seventh day of action, a group of reservists from the Nahshon Brigade were caught in an ambush that killed thirteen soldiers. Their comrades charged the terrorists in an effort to rescue the wounded, but that resulted in more injuries. In the raid's aftermath, the IDF decided to change procedure and destroy every house in which terrorists could hide. The policy included a warning to armed Palestinian fighters to surrender before the bulldozers began their work, which convinced many, among them the most senior terrorists, to turn themselves in. A high-ranking member of Islamic Jihad, Mahmoud Tawalbeh, was killed after refusing to surrender, when a D9 bulldozer caused a wall to collapse on him in the house where he was hiding.

During the fighting, rumors were spread of a massacre carried out by the IDF in Jenin's refugee camp; the Palestinians even cited three thousand as the number killed. The international media accepted the Palestinian claims unquestioningly, until a UN investigative committee arrived on the scene and determined that the real figure was just fifty-six. The IDF claimed that the vast majority of the dead Palestinians were armed terrorists. It may be that the camp's complete closure to the media caused the proliferation of the rumors throughout the world.

The city of Bethlehem was seized by the Jerusalem reservist brigade. Immediately after their entry into Bethlehem, the troops detained dozens of fugitives and quickly gained control of the ancient town. But about forty armed terrorists barricaded themselves in the Church of the Nativity. The IDF, aware of the location's great importance for the rest of the world, had sent the Shaldag commando unit to block off the terrorists' entrance into the church. But the air force ran into delays while flying in the soldiers, and dozens of terrorists managed to hole up in the church, certain that the Israeli forces wouldn't enter or arrest them.

Leading the armed men was Colonel Abdallah Daoud, the head of Palestinian intelligence in Nablus, who took as hostages the forty-six priests staying in the church and roughly two hundred other civilians, among them children. The IDF imposed a blockade on the church for thirty-four days, disrupting the supply of food and water in order to break the will of the wanted men. The Vatican cautioned Israel not to damage the church.

On May 10, 2002, the standoff concluded after Israel agreed to the expulsion of 13 of the fugitives to 6 European countries, as well as the transfer of 26 others to Gaza. During the blockade, six Palestinians were killed, and Israel captured documents revealing that the residents of Bethlehem, principally Christians, had suffered from harassment by armed men belonging to the Tanzim and Al Aqsa Martyrs Brigades.

Over the course of Operation Defensive Shield, five of the six Palestinian cities in the West Bank were occupied. Within a short period, and at a cost of thirty-four dead soldiers, Israel succeeded in putting a stop to the vicious wave of terror, severely degrading the military capability of the Palestinian Authority, isolating Arafat, capturing a great number of fugitives and uncovering vast quantities of explosives and other weapons.

AVIV KOCHAVI, COMMANDER OF THE PARATROOPERS BRIGADE AND LATER THE DIRECTOR OF MILITARY INTELLIGENCE

"The battle of the Qasbah ended precisely on Holocaust Remembrance Day. The entire brigade was dispersed throughout the Qasbah and the rest of Nablus, after a series of intense battles and a decisive victory over the armed fighters. I decided that we wouldn't give up on marking this special day. We set up a public address system and high-powered speakers, and turned on the radio at the moment of the memorial siren, which echoed through the entire area. Just hours after the end of the battle, all the soldiers of the paratroopers brigade stood at attention in memory of the victims.

"It was a very emotional moment and has remained engraved in my memory for two reasons: first, because we proved—against the backdrop, fittingly, of Holocaust Remembrance Day—that there's no place we won't go in order to defeat terror and defend the citizens of Israel. And second, by implementing innovative, sophisticated tactics, we proved that it's possible to do battle in a manner that is simultaneously resolute, professional and ethical, despite fighting in a built-up, crowded area against numerous terrorists. More than seventy terrorists were killed by the brigade, and hundreds were wounded or captured.

"The battle ended with the surrender of the terrorists: after they were squeezed and surrounded on all sides, their leader called the representative of District Coordination, who was with me at the command post, and asked to organize his surrender with three hundred of his men. We arranged the terms, and the terrorists marched to a specified location, where they turned over their weapons and were arrested."

YITZHAK ("JERRY") GERSHON, COMMANDER OF THE WEST BANK DIVISION AND LATER OF THE HOME FRONT COMMAND

"An all-out war on terror was being waged in Judea and Samaria when I assumed my functions as commander of the West Bank Division. The IDF had been fighting terrorists for ten months but, for various reasons, hadn't looked its best. I felt that the weighty task of providing security had been placed on my shoulders, and I understood that it was me and the forces under my authority who would make the difference. We changed the operational paradigm and led hundreds of special operations, some in refugee camps.

"The change was felt on the ground and yielded meaningful operational successes. More and more commanders and decision makers at the level of the military staff reached the sensible conclusion that it was our obligation to decide the fate of this war that had been forced upon us.

"When Defensive Shield was authorized, two operations of the most sensitive nature were assigned to us: Ramallah and Nablus. Ramallah was the site and seat of Arafat's power and the center of the Palestinian Authority; Nablus was the terror capital. The character of the operations resembled that of the intensive activity that preceded Defensive Shield, requiring initiative and aggressiveness, determination and creative thinking. The operation highlighted the intelligent integration of all the components of military force, along with tight coordination with Shin Bet, the Internal Security Service.

"Defensive Shield achieved a physical and psychological turning point in the Palestinian terror in Judea and Samaria."

In 2005, Prime Minister Ariel Sharon unilaterally retreats from the Gaza Strip. The Jewish settlements are evacuated and the settlers forced to leave their homes and seek new homes in Israel. The IDF pulls out all its forces from the Strip. Israel's leaders hoped that Gaza, now fully independent, will devote all its efforts to building a thriving economy and a prosperous free society.

The opposite happens. The Hamas terrorist organization seizes power in Gaza and turns it into a base of bloody, incessant attacks on Israel's civilian population.

CHAPTER 25
THE NEVER-ENDING STORY IN GAZA: 2008, 2012, 2014

"Cast Lead," 2008

O n December 27, 2008, at 11:30 A.M., several F-15 jets of the IAF dived over scores of targets all over the Gaza Strip. The lead plane launched its missiles on Arafat City, a large government complex in the center of Gaza. The attack targeted a graduation ceremony for police cadets, most of them members of the "Izz al-Din al-Qassam," Hamas's death squads. The other jets, and a few helicopters, launched massive aerial bombings on roughly one hundred Hamas targets across the Gaza Strip. In a few minutes they pulverized command posts, armories, underground rocket and missile launchers, and the organization's training sites. Operation Cast Lead had begun.

This first round of bombing caught Hamas completely off guard and unprepared. One hundred fifty-five terrorists were killed, eighty-nine of them at the police graduation ceremony.

As the campaign continued, the air force assaulted forty tunnels in the Philadelphi Corridor (a narrow strip along the border of Gaza and

Egypt) with bunker-busting bombs, in order to disrupt the smuggling of arms from Egypt. Strategic targets were also blown up, the objective being to undermine Hamas rule: government offices, television studios, the central prison, the general intelligence building, the city hall in Beit Hanoun, the Islamic University and more.

"We're talking about a great number of aircraft in a very small area with the goal of attacking buildings in very crowded places, where any misfire could hit a school or nursery," former IAF brigadier-general Ran Pecker-Ronen told the journalist Amir Bohbot. "Their accuracy was amazing, the execution perfect. I don't believe there's another air force in the world capable of carrying out these sorts of attacks at such a high level of precision."

The Israeli government, headed by Ehud Olmert, decided to launch Cast Lead after a large-scale, prolonged barrage of thousands of Qassam rockets on the towns and cities near Gaza. For many months, residents of the area had lived in fear, forced to sleep in safety rooms and bomb shelters. It was an absurd situation; no other nation in the world would have accepted being subjected to the daily firing of rockets on its civilian population. The cease-fire that had been reached via Egyptian mediation in June 2008 had collapsed completely, and Israel's southern region was subject to a real war, in which Palestinians fired rockets, Israel responded with bombings by the air force, and the pattern continued. The residents of the south were paying the price.

The objective of Cast Lead would be to end the Palestinian missile fire, destroy Hamas operational abilities and prevent its rearmament.

The IDF received authorization to carry out targeted killings, and eliminated senior members of Hamas and Islamic Jihad one after another, among them Said Siam, the Hamas government's interior minister; his brother Iyad Siam, another Hamas senior official; and Nizar Rayan, number three in Hamas's political wing. Rayan was killed when his home was bombed from the air; he died along with eighteen friends and relatives who had stayed in the house in spite of the IAF warnings. The building in which he lived had served as a command post, communications center, storage facility for weaponry and ammunitions, and a tunnel entrance.

The Southern District commander, General Yoav Galant, told the journalist Shmuel Haddad, "In the past, each Hamas commander built himself a three-story house, in which the basement level served as a storage area for materiel, the middle level as a command post, and the family lived on the third floor. For years, they assumed that the IDF wouldn't strike the building because of the family. We've changed the paradigm, warning the family by a telephone call and by firing a small, harmless 'knock on the roof' warning missile. Later, the building is bombed, and from then on the Hamas terrorist is left to worry about the fact that he has neither a command station nor a home for his family."

On January 3, the IDF launched the operation's second stage with the shelling of Gaza and the entrance of ground forces into the Strip's northern end. The offensive was intended to seize missile-launching areas, to cut off Gaza City from the rest of the Strip and increase the damage that the IDF was inflicting on Hamas, principally at points where the air force had no advantage—like armories, tunnels, bunkers and underground command posts. Ten thousand reservists fought alongside twenty thousand regular soldiers.

The forces fought primarily on built-up territory, facing ambushes, suicide bombers, and booby-trapped houses. It was a house-to-house—and, at times, face-to-face fight—battle. Homes used for terrorist activity or found to be booby-trapped were razed; during the fighting, roughly six hundred houses were destroyed.

Israel's offensive in Gaza began with the Golani, Givati and the paratrooper brigades breaking into the Strip from different and unanticipated directions. Merkava tanks of the armored 188th "Lightning" Brigade, which had defended the Golan Heights in the Yom Kippur War, blocked the passage from Rafiah and Khan Younis to Gaza City, thus disrupting the supply of arms to Hamas. The 401st Brigade, nicknamed "Iron Trails," established a buffer zone in the center of the strip, by the former settlement of Netzarim. IDF engineers, often employing mini-robots, defused explosives and booby-trapped houses. Saving the soldiers' lives was the mission's top priority; consequently, massive efforts were spent preventing unnecessary risks, even at the cost of civilians being hit.

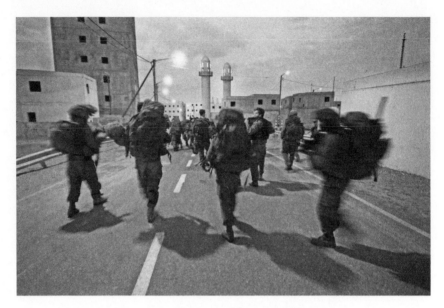

Cast Lead—the fighters at the gates of Gaza.
(Neil Cohen, IDF Spokesman)

"The entry into Gaza was relatively quick," said a senior officer after the battle. "We felt that Hamas was in shock, which in turn significantly undermined the resistance they had prepared. The houses were packed very close together, with a portion of them booby-trapped. There were also motorcycles at the ready for abductions. Almost every other hour, there was an attempt by a male or female suicide bomber to run at us and detonate an explosive belt. In the booby-trapped houses, we found shafts leading to tunnels designated for kidnapping soldiers."

On January 6, the Palestinians claimed that an IDF mortar had killed thirty people sheltered at the al-Fahoura school, a facility run by UNRWA, the United Nations Relief and Works Agency. The shell had targeted the school yard, where a rocket had been launched at Israel; in response, the IDF had fired three mortars. Two hit the school yard, killing two of the terrorists in action, while the third errantly struck the neighboring school, thirty yards away. But an investigation by Canada's *Globe and Mail* revealed that, contrary to Palestinian reports, not thirty people but just three had been killed by shrapnel, when they had gone outside the building.

Hamas's ability to resist the IDF operation was weaker than the Israelis had anticipated. The Palestinians intensified the rocket fire into Israeli territory; over the course of Cast Lead, 730 rockets were launched into Israel, among them long-range Grad weapons that reached Ashdod, Ashkelon, Yavne and Be'er Sheva.

Hamas systematically fired from houses of civilians, whose lives it did not hesitate to put at risk. An IDF officer found a document that contained Hamas's battle plan, including the deployment of terror teams next to a mosque, the placement of large improvised explosive devices (IEDs) in a heavily populated area and even the booby-trapping of schools and the zoo. Yuval Diskin, then the head of the Shin Bet, Israel's domestic intelligence service, told journalists, "A considerable portion of the activists are hiding in hospitals, some at Shifa, some in maternity hospitals. A few are going around in doctors' and nurses' uniforms." The Shifa hospital director categorically denied his statements.

One incident seared into the public consciousness was the death of three daughters of Izzeldin Abuelaish, a Palestinian doctor who had for years worked in hospitals in Israel. Two IDF tank shells had struck his home in Jabalia, killing the three girls and injuring another. At the moment of the attack, Dr. Abuelaish was speaking with TV Channel 10 reporter Shlomi Eldar. Crying out hysterically, he pleaded with the journalist, a friend, to ask the IDF to stop shooting at his home. The IDF subsequently claimed that it had targeted the home because of shooting originating from there.

After twenty-two days of fighting, Prime Minister Olmert stopped the operation, rejecting the third stage proposed by General Galant—to cut off the Gaza Strip from Sinai. Olmert declared a unilateral ceasefire: "Hamas's military capabilities and control infrastructure have been hit hard. The present campaign has once again proven Israel's strength and deterrence capability."

On the Israeli side, thirteen had been killed, among them ten soldiers. According to IDF estimates, 1,166 Palestinians were killed, 709 of them members of Hamas. The Palestinians counted 1,417 dead. Four thousand homes were entirely destroyed, along with 48 public and government buildings.

Operation Cast Lead produced severe damage to Israel's international image. On September 15, 2009, Richard Goldstone, a South African former judge appointed by the UN Human Rights Council, submitted a scathing report to the UN portraying Israel as having committed war crimes and "crimes against humanity."

In April 2011, however, Goldstone made his mea culpa in a *Washington Post* article, admitting that his report hadn't been accurate and contained unjust accusations againt Israel. "If I had known then what I know now," he wrote, "the Goldstone Report would have been a different document."

YOAV GALANT, HEAD OF ISRAEL'S SOUTHERN COMMAND

"We embarked on the operation in order to hit Hamas and create deterrence, and to force it to halt its missile fire for an extended period. No less important, in my eyes, was the need to sear into its consciousness that it would pay a heavy price for targeting Israel's citizens and sovereignty. Hamas was surprised by the timing of the action, the force of the attack and the wide-scale entry of ground forces into its territory, as well as by the timing of the withdrawal and the speed with which it was carried out.

"This was the first time that the IDF struck at Hamas so comprehensively. The attack was carried out in a focused, continuous, intensive way, with thousands of bombs dropped on hundreds of targets, among them command posts, weapons caches, tunnels, bunkers and government offices. The ground maneuvers were performed by strengthened battalion forces, and at any given moment, there were seven thousand fighters within the Strip. The IDF achieved tight coordination between our intelligence and air, sea and land forces.

"Two weeks after the start of the operation, I recommended to the chief of staff that we carry out the third stage of the original plan: to cut the Gaza Strip off from Sinai by encircling and occupying Rafiah. This process would have brought about a disruption of the pipeline used for weapons smuggling, suicide bombers and more. But the plan wasn't authorized because it might have led to great losses."

Four years later...

PILLAR OF DEFENSE, 2012

The electronic signal flashed across the navigation system of the drone, which, according to the London *Sunday Times*, was circling above the mosques and refugee camps of Gaza. The drone dived toward Gaza City center. Its cameras scanned the streets, focusing on a silver Kia carrying a tracking device, which crossed an intersection and turned into Omar Mukhtar Street.

The passenger of the Kia was Ahmed Jabari, Hamas's chief of staff. He had become the commander of Hamas's military wing in 2003, after his predecessor, Mohammed Deif, was severely wounded during an Israeli Air Force attack. Jabari, a member of a Hebron-based clan, had been imprisoned in Israel for thirteen years because of terrorist activities. When he was freed, in 1995, he became a key Hamas figure, managing overseas relations, fund-raising and the planning of terror attacks. As Hamas's military chief of staff, he oversaw weapons production, the use of mortars and rockets, the smuggling of arms, and other military and intelligence activity. Jabari had directed dozens of terror operations against Israeli citizens, as well as the firing of Qassam rockets into Israeli territory; he was responsible for the kidnapping of Gilad Shalit and had signed the agreement for his return.

To the IDF, Jabari, fifty-two, was mortal. He knew it and took meticulous security precautions. Foreign sources claim that he told no one where he spent his nights or which vehicles he would use; he occasionally even disguised himself by wearing women's clothes. In the past twenty-four hours, he had been closely watched with the help of Shabak agents; their reports revealed that Jabari had spent the night in a certain house in Gaza, parking his vehicle outside. Lurking in the skies above was a surveillance aircraft belonging to the air force's Squadron 100. And so, on November 14, at 3:45 in the afternoon, a Shabak operations director in Tel Aviv received a fateful telephone call from Gaza: within three minutes, one of the several cars serving Jabari would depart from a certain address in Gaza. The Shabak agent added that he would provide an additional warning thirty seconds later.

Without wasting a moment, the operative in Tel Aviv informed the head of the Shabak, Yoram Cohen, who in his turn called the IDF chief of staff, Benny Gantz, and Prime Minister Benyamin Netanyahu. When confirmation arrived thirty seconds later from al-Mukhtar Street, Amikam Norkin, head of Air Force Operations, was sitting, ready and waiting, in the command room at military headquarters in Tel Aviv. The air force drone was approaching Jabari's car. At 3:55, Norkin gave the order: "Go!"

The drone's systems zeroed in on the silver Kia. An electronic signal activated the drone's firing system. Two missiles detached from the fuselage, plunging toward the car. An enormous explosion echoed along the two-way street, and the car was obliterated in a cloud of fire. When the smoke dissipated, passersby pulled the corpses of Ahmed Jabari and another passenger, Raed al-Atar, a commander of Hamas's southern division. Thousands of Gaza residents streamed to the site, sounding calls for revenge.

That was how, at 4:00 P.M. on November 14, 2012, Operation Pillar of Defense began. The final unraveling at the Gaza border had begun a week earlier, when a few border skirmishes culminated with a massive barrage of rockets and mortars unleashed by Hamas, its rockets hitting Israeli communities near Gaza, as well as the larger cities of Ashkelon and Ashdod. Israel could no longer tolerate such assaults, which had increased in frequency during the previous months. Hamas had willingly violated the terms of the cease-fire with Israel, reached after Cast Lead.

Once again, the IDF had to deal a stunning blow to Hamas, to restore
deterrence and quiet.

Pillar of Defense—back to Gaza.
(Gil Nehushtan, Yedioth Ahronoth Archive)

Jabari's assassination would be the crushing blow that would launch
the operation, which had been decided upon just the day before by the
Israeli cabinet—the inner circle of political leaders, headed by Netanyahu. Among them were Defense Minister Ehud Barak, Foreign Minister
Avigdor Lieberman and Minister of Homefront Defense Avi Dichter. The
decision had been obscured by a smokescreen of conciliatory declara-
tions about Gaza by the prime minister and the defense minister during
a visit to Israel's northern border. This deception was perhaps the reason
that Jabari, typically so fastidious about his own security, felt such in-
explicable confidence that day—a mistake that would cost him his life.

The task was assigned almost entirely to the air force. Israel had
learned the lessons of Cast Lead, which had set off a surge of criticism
around the world because of harm caused to Palestinian civilians. This
time, Israel envisioned a surgical operation that would hit terrorists and
their installations but would, as much as possible, spare the lives of
civilians. Minutes after Jabari's assassination, the first wave of air force
planes pounced on Gaza, attacking Hamas training camps in the north,
as well as storage facilities and launch sites that housed long-range Fajar

5 missiles, which could travel seventy-five kilometers and hit Tel Aviv and Jerusalem. This was an impressive military and intelligence accomplishment, drastically diminishing Hamas's ability to fire into major population centers and wiping out years of intense, secretive efforts by the organization to smuggle and produce missiles. By the end of the first day, Hamas's long-range strategic capabilities had been almost entirely eliminated. But, after recovering from the initial shock, Hamas responded forcefully, firing more than sixty rockets at Israel's southern towns. In response, Israel immediately activated Iron Dome, its new missile-interception system, bringing down twenty-four rockets.

By evening, it had become clear to Israel's civilian population that the operation wasn't a one-off strike, but that it might last for several days. On the campaign's second day, Hamas and Islamic Jihad renewed the shooting toward towns near Gaza, with missiles also fired at several Negev towns and, for the first time, Tel-Aviv and Jerusalem. In Tel-Aviv, the sound of real sirens was heard for the first time since the first Gulf War, in 1991. But the hardest, most painful strike was on Kiryat Malachi.

At 9:52 A.M., a Grad missile hit a residential building, killing three people and wounding six, among them two children. "At the time of the siren," a neighbor said, "we went to the stairwell. After a few minutes, we heard a huge explosion in the building—we heard screams from the top floor and then saw our neighbor coming down with two wounded girls. . . . The neighbor who was killed had been standing on his balcony and had been trying to photograph the barrage of missiles. He took a direct hit."

Only a handful of the hundreds of missiles launched at Israel would hit their targets, but they caused heavy damage and trauma. Yet the Israeli public responded stoically, without panic, supporting the operation without regard to political outlook or social views.

By November 15, the air force had blown up 450 targets, among them seventy subterranean rocket-launch sites. But in the same period, more than three hundred rockets and mortars were fired at Israel. The leaders of Hamas, Egypt and Turkey boiled and raged against Israel, but the enlightened world took its side. Leaders of the European Union and others expressed unequivocal support for Israel's right to defend itself; the most effusive of all came from the president of the United States, Barack Obama, who took Israel's side while denouncing the terrorists of Hamas and Islamic Jihad. Under Obama's heavy pressure, President Morsi of Egypt changed course, ending his attacks on Israel and beginning feverish work to reach a cease-fire. But in the interim, the fighting continued. Day after day, air force planes and naval ships pounded Hamas nerve centers in Gaza, and day after day, Hamas and Islamic Jihad fired hundreds of rockets on Israel's towns.

Yet, the IDF had imposed strict limitations on its response. "Each day, I needed to struggle with dilemmas that arose during the operation," said General Tal Russo, commander of the Southern District. "For example: we received intelligence that a certain Hamas commander was in his home, and we had to decide whether we would hit him there. I decided not to attack, so as not to hit people who weren't involved. The IDF's sensitivity and caution about not hurting such people saved the lives of many Hamas and Islamic Jihad commanders."

Egypt's Prime minister, Hisham Kandil, arrived in the Strip, and Israel ceased fire during his visit. Upon his departure, terrorists shot two rockets at Tel Aviv and one at Jerusalem, with all three intercepted or falling in open territory. The Israeli air force attacked smuggling tunnels and government buildings, television stations and bridges, the Islamic Bank and pipelines funneling gas and oil to the Strip. IAF aircraft hit the office of Hamas prime minister Ismail Haniyeh. Haniyeh was not in his office, of course; he was hiding underground with his colleagues, while their people were paying with their lives the bloody cost of Israel's incursion.

A fifth Iron Dome battery was placed in Tel Aviv and, within an hour, shot down a missile. The emir of Qatar, Turkey's prime minister, and senior Hamas and Islamic Jihad officials rushed to Cairo for discussions with Egypt about restoring the calm. Secretly, Israel sent over the head of the Mossad, Tamir Pardo.

Nevertheless, Gaza continued shooting. November 20, perhaps the worst day of fighting, saw heavy salvos of rockets fired from the Strip. Despite Iron Dome's successes, rockets and mortars struck a house in Be'er Sheva and killed three soldiers at the Eshkol area. In Rishon Lezion, a rocket destroyed the top three floors of a residential building but only slightly injured three people.

The following morning, after intensive mediation by Egypt, a cease-fire was reached, with the Palestinians pledging to halt all hostile activities and Israel ending its air force attacks.

In total, the Palestinians suffered 120 deaths, most of them armed fighters. Roughly 1,500 rockets had been fired at Israel, with 413 intercepted by Iron Dome.

Operation Pillar of Defense was over, but without a decisive result. Israel had landed a tough blow to Hamas and Islamic Jihad, destroying rockets and launchers and eliminating senior Hamas officials, chief among them the leader of its military wing. But Hamas and Islamic Jihad hadn't been broken and had continued firing barrages of rockets until the cease-fire. In several southern Israeli cities, spontaneous demonstrations demanded that the government continue the operation. The protesters and their supporters insisted that the cease-fire would be fragile and temporary, and that it wouldn't be long before Israel was forced to open a more extensive campaign against the Gaza terrorists.

The protesters were right. Barely twenty months later, Israel was on the warpath again.

Protective Edge, 2014

The police officer who received the call during the night of June 12, 2014, dismissed it as a prank. Only later, when a worried father called, it was established that three teenagers, Eyal Yifrach (nineteen), Gilad Shaar (sixteen) and Naftali Frenkel (sixteen), students in yeshivas in the Etzion Bloc of settlements, had disappeared while trying to hitchhike home. One of them had used his cell phone but his call had been interrupted. Soon the police found a burned-out car by the Dura Arab village, west of Hebron. It was clear that the boys had been abducted and the kidnapping car had been set on fire, while the terrorists and their captives had moved to another vehicle.

An unprecedented search was launched throughout the West Bank. Soon, reliable field agents reported that the boys had been abducted by Hamas terrorists; the IDF started arresting notorious Hamas militants throughout the West Bank. Thousands of Israeli soldiers were dispatched to towns, villages, fields, orchards and other areas where the captives might have been hidden or buried.

The entire nation followed with bated breath the search for the missing. The IDF mission was named Shuvu Achim—"Come back, brothers." The three distraught mothers pleaded on radio and TV with the kidnappers to release their sons. They even traveled to a meeting of the UN Human Rights Council in Geneva, a notorious anti-Israeli body, whose members listened in frosty silence to the mothers' passionate pleas. The nerve-wracking search continued for eighteen days. IDF intelligence experts discovered the identities of the kidnappers, two Hamas militants. Caves were penetrated, wells and septic tanks drained, houses inspected, hundreds of Hamas militants arrested and interrogated.

The boys were finally found in a shallow grave in a rocky, sun-parched field just north of Hebron. Israel was devastated by the cruel, senseless murder of the three innocent boys. Three Israeli right-wingers, motivated by insane lust for revenge, kidnapped and savagely murdered a sixteen-year-old Palestinian boy, Mohammed Abu Khdeir. Even though the police found out and arrested the murderers, the rage in the Palestinian community was immense. Many Palestinians had danced in the streets when they had learned that three Israeli boys had been assassinated, but now they sought revenge for the death of one of their own. The worst—and most unexpected—reaction came from the Gaza Strip. Hamas and the Islamic Jihad started shelling the civilian Israeli settlements and towns with scores of deadly rockets. Prime Minister Netanyahu didn't want to confront Hamas again in a new round of senseless fighting. He publicly declared that "quiet will be answered by quiet." But the nice words didn't work. The attacks from the Gaza Strip only increased. The IDF first reacted by precise bombings of strategic targets in Gaza, while repeating its calls for a cease-fire. But Hamas would not stop. Israel, left with no choice, concentrated large masses of soldiers and armor by the border. Yet the army didn't cross the border fence into Gaza. Netanyahu, Defense Minister Yaalon and Chief of Staff Gantz willingly accepted a cease-fire proposed by Egypt, but Hamas rejected it outright.

Then, on July 17, the ninth day of the conflict, IDF spotters suddenly noticed a group of Hamas fighters, armed to the teeth, virtually sprouting from the ground in Israeli territory, close to kibbutz Sufa. IDF commandos charged at them, probably shooting some, but the intruders collected their dead and wounded and vanished as they had come—in a masterfully camouflaged hole in the ground. The hole, it turned out, was the exit of an underground tunnel, running for more than a mile from a Hamas entry point inside the Gaza Strip, deep under the border fence and almost to the very gates of the kibbutz.

Two other attack tunnels had been discovered and destroyed since October 2013, but the new tunnel posed a deadly threat to both civilians and military in Otef Aza—the area "enveloping" the Gaza Strip. After long and strenuous deliberations the cabinet ordered the IDF to launch a ground offensive in the Gaza Strip, with one main objective—finding and destroying the tunnels.

Thousands of IDF soldiers and scores of tanks crossed the border and entered the outskirts of Gaza City, supported by artillery and the IAF. They warned the civilian population to evacuate certain neighborhoods where they intended to operate; a massive exodus started, but simultaneously Hamas fighters occupied the areas, tended ambushes and planted mines, side charges and other explosive devices, boobytrapping the houses where concealed tunnel shafts were located. This caused heavy street fighting. During the following weeks the IDF discovered 32 attack tunnels that ran for hundreds of yards, sometimes a few kilometers, from Gaza, at 70 to 75 feet under the border fence and ended chillingly close to Israeli kibbutzim and villages. They were reinforced by concrete walls, equipped with electricity and abounded with weapons, ammunition and explosive caches and niches where Israeli Army uniforms and headgear had been stocked. What would have happened to the south of Israel if these tunnels had not been discovered? Hundreds of terrorists, maybe more, might have penetrated into the country and conquered peaceful towns and villages, slaughtering their populations or holding them hostage. The chance discovery of one tunnel had led to an astounding achievement for Israel's security, but it also triggered a wave of anger at the IDF since they hadn't acted earlier against the tunnels.

The price was high—the IDF lost sixty-seven of its best fighters, many of them officers charging ahead of their troops. The Gazan civilian population was painfully hit—over sixteen hundred dead, many of them terrorists, but also a large number of children. The IDF was criticized for destroying numerous blocks of houses, for its artillery shooting into densely populated areas and even firing at several UNRWA schools that had become refugee shelters. The IDF claimed that in several cases fire was opened on its soldiers or missiles fired on Israel from schools and mosques; yet the criticism, from within and without, did not abate.

It became clear that a regular army, trained to fight regular armies on the battlefield, was not prepared for fighting a terrorist organization entrenched in cities and towns. All the Israeli operations against the terrorist organizations—like Operation Litani, the first and the second Lebanon Wars, Operation Grapes of Wrath against Hezballah in South Lebanon (1996) and the three major missions in Gaza—had ended without a conclusive outcome. In the future the IDF had to develop new, creative methods of fighting terror organizations like Hamas, Hezbollah and ISIS, sparing as much as possible the civilian population.

The Protective Edge mission ended with a cease-fire, like other similar missions in the past. Yet all the demands of Hamas had been rejected and its leaders emerged from their underground bunkers to an image of terrible devastation and loss. Israel's victory was clear but not decisive. Hamas still had 20 to 30 percent of its rockets, most of its military units had survived and its leadership was intact. Israel's leaders had to cope with an angry nation, embittered by the feeling that once again, Hamas had been spared a decisive blow.

The real hero of the Protective Edge mission was the Iron Dome system, which during fifty days of fighting had succeeded in shooting down

735 Qassam, Grad and M-75 missiles fired at Israel's populated areas, disregarding the rockets falling in empty fields. Iron Dome had made its debut during the Pillar of Defense operation, but this time the results were even more staggering. During Protective Edge only 224 missiles fell in Israel's cities and villages, killing five people. The relatively light losses enabled the IDF to carry out its mission without any pressure from a battered and bleeding civilian population. By protecting Israel's civilians, Iron Dome had tipped the scales of the conflict.

Iron Dome—the star of operation "Protective Edge."
(Yariv Katz, Yedioth Ahronot Archive)

The Iron Dome was composed of a very sensitive radar that detected the firing of one or more missiles; a sophisticated computer calculated the exact trajectory of the enemy projectile, and a battery of Tamir anti-missile missiles, activated by IDF soldiers, would intercept the enemy rocket before it reached its target and blow it to smithereens in the clear blue sky.

The Iron Dome's father was a curly-haired, mustachioed and warm Moroccan Jew, Amir Peretz. A former paratrooper who had spent a year in a hospital after being severely wounded, he had later served as mayor of Sderot, a town located barely 3.7 kilometers from the Gaza border fence.

Shortly after being appointed defense minister in 2006, Peretz ordered the army—despite fierce opposition of the generals, the defense ministry, the media, learned engineers and scientists and a large part of the body politic—to launch a project for defending Israel from the Qassam and other rockets. The man charged with the project was a brilliant scientist, Dr. Danny Gold.

The objections were based on the then-limited threat of the rockets; the huge funds needed to develop another anti-missile system besides the Israeli-American joint Project Arrow for intercepting long-range missiles; the preference of many experts for the laser-based Nautilus system and the cynical disbelief that something would come out of the minister's project.

A popular newspaper, expressing the feelings of many, published a screaming front-page headline:

Iron dome—a failure known in advance.

Perhaps they were right. The minister of defense had been involved in the partly failed Second Lebanon War; he had been ridiculed by photographs published in the media showing him trying to watch IDF maneuvers through binoculars whose lens covers had not been removed. . . . And after all, he was a trade union leader, a politician, not a general; what did he understand about military matters?

That was 2007. But in 2014, during and after Protective Edge, the Israeli media and political leaders competed in showering kudos, compliments and flowery messages of gratitude on Peretz, who alone had made Iron Dome a reality and turned the small interceptor system into a game changer. The thousands of rockets still in the hands of Hamas had suddenly become obsolete.

During the Protective Edge mission, the Israeli military industries delivered the ninth Iron Dome battery to the army. "With thirteen batteries we'll be able to fully protect all of our cities and inhabited areas; when we put in place twenty-four batteries, all of Israel's territory will be safe," Peretz told the authors of this book. General Gabi Ashkenazi, a former chief of staff,who had been utterly opposed to the project (but had dutifully carried it out), quipped: "Binoculars or no binoculars, Amir Peretz saw farther than all of us."

On September 23, about three weeks after the cease-fire, Israeli commandos located the two Hamas terrorists that had murdered the three teenagers on June 17, starting the vicious circle of violence. Amar Abu Aisha and Marwan Qawasmeh were killed in a firefight in Hebron.

AMIR PERETZ, FORMER DEFENSE MINISTER

"A month after I assumed my position, I summoned the General Staff and asked them, Why don't we have any means to counter the terrorists' most primitive weapon—the Qassams? They said there were two kinds of threats: tactical and strategic. The Qassams were not even a tactical threat: in seven years we had seven people killed. One a year—that doesn't justify spending millions.

"I said: Let me tell you a story I heard from an old man in a Sderot street. 'Long ago,' he said, 'in my native village in Morocco, a rumor reached the village elders. The Angel of Death was coming to the village to take a life sometime during the next two weeks! What to do? The elders decided to inform the population that, one, the Angel of Death was coming; two, he'll arrive during the next two weeks; three, nobody knows whose life he will take.'

" 'And what was the result of that?' the Old Man said. 'All the inhabitants of the village ran away, to the last of them!'

"I told the generals that the same thing happens with the Qassam rockets. We don't know when and where they would hit and who is going to get killed, but that disrupts the normal life of thousands of Israelis. Our duty is to guarantee them a peaceful life. So perhaps it is not a strategic or a tactical threat on our lives—but it is a moral threat.

"They didn't buy that; they were all against me. The army and the industries, civilians and military, media commentators and editorial writers, they all attacked me. I felt completely alone.

"When the matter was brought before Prime Minister Olmert, he washed his hands of it. 'You're minister of defense,' he said to me, 'it's your decision and your budget.' At least he didn't veto the project.

"When I finally made the decision to go ahead with the plan, I was attacked again for choosing the Iron Dome project instead of the Nautilus that was based on the destruction of enemy missiles by laser beams. I rejected that project for two reasons: first—at the time Nautilus was static, and the equipment couldn't be moved from one position to another. And the second reason—laser beams couldn't work properly when the sky was covered with clouds. That meant that for at least three months a year our towns and cities would be exposed and defenseless. Iron Dome, on the contrary, could easily be moved, and guaranteed protection in all weather and all through the year.

"I chose Iron Dome and once again found myself isolated and vilified. The following ten months were a nightmare.

"But today? The entire nation is praising the Iron Dome. It has also become a unique case in the U.S.-Israeli relations. The American president and lawmakers voted extraordinary budgets for the Iron Dome, beyond the annual help of three billion dollars to Israel. That was the first time that the U.S. financially participated in a project in which no American industries were involved, just 'blue and white,' a pure Israeli achievement."

The Lost Tribe Returns

FROM THE HEART OF AFRICA TO JERUSALEM: OPERATION MOSES (1984) AND OPERATION SOLOMON (1991)

On an October night in 1981, two Israeli naval vessels, the missile ships *Reshef* and *Keshet,* arrived secretly to the coast of Sudan. Fighters from Flotilla 13 descended from the ships on rubber rafts, embedding radar echo reflectors into the coral reefs as a way of indicating safe routes to the shore. The task was difficult; the reefs were spread over a wide area, and the fighters acted clandestinely because Sudan was an enemy country. Mapping the approach paths to the beach, they located four inlets that would facilitate their assignment: bringing the Jews of Ethiopia to Israel through Sudan.

The operation had in fact begun in 1977, when Prime Minister Menachem Begin summoned the head of the Mossad, Yitzhak Hofi, and told him, "Bring me the Jews of Ethiopia!" Begin knew about the unstable regime of Ethiopia's dictator, Mengistu Haile Mariam, the deep distress of the country's Jews and the longing of this ancient, legendary community to immigrate to Israel after living and preserving the commandments of Judaism in Africa. The Mossad was recruited for the task; initially, small numbers of Jews were brought to Israel from Addis Ababa, Ethiopia's capital, but Mengistu quickly locked the gates leading out of his country. Thousands of Ethiopian Jews had heard about the stirring idea—literally to "ascend," in the Hebrew, to Jerusalem—and had set out on foot toward neighboring Sudan. The trek would eventually lead to the deaths of thousands, who, for the length of the journey, found themselves at the mercy of thieves, wild animals, disease and hunger. The trip would become a saga of agony and heroism. Upon their arrival in Sudan, the majority would be absorbed into refugee camps, where they were forced to hide their Judaism, fearing the authorities and other refugees. The Mossad dispatched numerous agents to Ethiopia under various covers, and they did their best to get many of the Jews out of Sudan. At Begin's request, the Egyptian ruler, Anwar Sadat, reached out to the Sudanese dictator, Gaafar Nimeiry, to ask that he look the other way as Ethiopian Jews made their escape. Nimeiry agreed—in exchange for large bribes—but only a handful of Jews were able to leave his country with real or fake documents, while the vast majority remained in camps under terrible conditions.

Then an idea arose: to bring them out of Sudan by sea, with assistance from the IDF. Along with several former Flotilla 13 commandos, agents of the Mossad—among them Yonatan Shefa, Emmanuel Alon and others—acquired a resort named Arous on the Sudanese coast, running it as a diving and leisure center for tourists from Europe. The site served as a vacation village with an array of activities; but the visitors weren't aware that, on certain nights, the staff would drive hundreds of miles in antiquated, dilapidated trucks, picking up numerous Jews at secret meeting points and bringing them to the Sudanese shore. The operation—along with every other operation run by the Mossad in

Sudan at that time—was conducted by a young, courageous agent, a yarmulke-wearing blond by the name of Danny Limor.

On November 8, 1981, a civilian ship called the *Bat Galim* ("Daughter of the Waves") departed from the port of Eilat carrying a military commander, Major Ilan Buhris; also on board were medical equipment, field kitchens and roughly four hundred beds. Members of Flotilla 13 embarked with two commando boats known as Swallows, as well as nine Zodiacs, and the *Bat Galim* raised anchor. The Mossad dubbed the mission Operation Brothers—a fitting name, as its organizers indeed viewed the Ethiopian Jews as brothers.

On November 11, the *Bat Galim* reached its destination. That night, numerous Jews arrived on the beach in tarp-covered trucks, which had traveled many hours, risking interception by the Sudanese Army at any moment; they were even forced to break through Sudanese military checkpoints while making the trip. The passengers, exhausted by the long journey, and some of them quite afraid, were lifted onto the rubber boats and then brought to the ship. Many of them had never seen the sea in their lives; a few tried to drink the water. They were received on deck with bread, jam and hot tea. The Israelis subsequently organized a group sing-along as a way to calm them and even screened a movie; many of the passengers had never seen one. Two and a half days later, the ship docked at the Sharm el-Sheikh base in Sinai, where 164 immigrants descended onto the shore.

Preparations immediately got under way for a second voyage, which set sail in January 1982 and brought another 351 immigrants to Israel. The third, in March 1982, almost ended in disaster: one of the boats, transporting four Mossad agents, got stuck among the coral reefs at the same moment that Sudanese soldiers armed with Kalashnikovs suddenly appeared and threatened to shoot them. Fortunately, the mission commander responded with remarkable chutzpah, unleashing a verbal barrage at his Sudanese counterpart: "Are you crazy? You want to shoot at tourists? You can't see that we're here to organize a diving expedition? We're tourism-ministry employees, bringing visitors to the country, and you want to shoot them? Who's the idiot who made you an officer?" The

English-speaking commander was embarrassed, apologized, and took off with his soldiers. In fact, he had been looking for smugglers. *Bat Galim* set sail without further difficulties and delivered 172 additional immigrants to Israel, although the incident made clear that this method was too risky and wouldn't work anymore; it would be necessary to find another way of extracting Ethiopia's Jews.

One morning, tourists at the resort discovered that the entire staff, minus the locals, had disappeared. The "guides"—members of the Mossad—had left letters apologizing for the facility's closure, citing budgetary reasons. The tourists were flown back to their respective countries and received a full refund.

Meanwhile, back in Israel, it had been decided to transport the immigrants by other means, flying them on the air force's Hercules planes, known as Rhinos. Mossad agents found an abandoned British airfield south of Port Sudan, and a special air force team prepped it for landings. Ethiopian Jews would be picked up at a secret meeting place and brought to the airfield, where the landing strip was illuminated with special torches. But when the air force's Hercules landed, the Ethiopians were scared nearly to death. The flying metal colossus, which they were seeing for the first time in their lives, landed with a roar of the engines, moving straight at them. Many fled, returning only after the Israeli organizers won them over with heartfelt explanations. In the end, the plane took off with 213 Israel-bound Jews.

The incident at the airfield taught members of the IAF and Mossad several lessons: on the next trip, the plane would land and lower the ramp from its tail beforehand, and the truckloads of immigrants would go directly into the Hercules' open belly, without seeing the monster thundering toward them across the runway.

But Sudanese authorities discovered the operation, as well as the airfield. The Israelis found another landing area, roughly forty-six kilometers from Port Sudan, deciding then to arrange an airlift that would include seven Rhino flights, with two hundred Jews departing on each. Overseeing the mission would be the head of the Mossad and Brigadier General Amos Yaron, the paratroopers' chief officer. The operation was carried out between 1982 and 1984, during which fifteen hundred immigrants were brought to Israel.

On the eve of each operation, a truck would arrive at the landing area and light up the runway. The plane coming from Israel would touch down, run along the landing strip and turn around, opening its large tail door. Members of the air force's Shaldag commando unit would form two lines leading to the gaping door in the shape of a funnel, and when the trucks arrived, the immigrants would walk through the funnel, directly into the belly of the plane, where they would seat themselves on the floor. Many didn't even realize they were inside a plane.

On one of the flights, an elderly, distinguished Kess—a religious and social leader—got up and asked who the senior officer was. The flight crew accompanied him to Brigadier General Avihu Ben-Nun, of the air force. The Kess stood before him and slowly, ceremonially, pulled out an ancient sword from his belt and extended it toward him. "Until now, I've been responsible for their fate," he said, gesturing with his hand in the direction of his brothers. "From now on, you are," he continued, handing the sword to a visibly moved Ben-Nun.

At the end of 1984, the situation in Sudan destabilized even further; the country needed emergency humanitarian assistance and food. Israel took advantage of the situation, directing a request to the United States to aid Sudan—in exchange for Jewish immigrants. U.S. Vice President George Bush immediately responded, instructing the American embassy staff in Khartoum to initiate negotiations with Nimeiry. The talks proved a success, and Sudan agreed to the Ethiopian Jews' orderly departure by air, on the condition that they not fly directly to Israel but through a third country. The Mossad identified a small, Jewish-owned Belgian airline and launched Operation Moses: over the course of forty-seven days, the Belgian Boeings would complete thirty-six flights, transporting 7,800 Jews to Israel.

Following leaks by Israeli leaders to the world media, Nimeiry halted the operation. But Bush didn't give up, dispatching seven U.S. Air Force Hercules planes to Gadarif, in Sudan, in an operation called Queen of Sheba. The American planes flew five hundred remaining Jews from

Sudan directly to Israel's Ramon airbase. This mission crowned the close cooperation between the Israeli and American air forces in their common purpose—rescuing the Jews of Ethiopia.

Although Operations Moses and Queen of Sheba concluded successfully, thousands of Jews remained in Ethiopia. During the various stages of this exodus, many families were separated or torn apart, with children arriving in Israel without their parents and vice versa. The ruptures caused tremendous difficulties, and even tragedies, during the Ethiopians' absorption into Israel. At the same time, a lethal civil war had broken out in Ethiopia, and immediate danger loomed over the lives of the country's Jews. Emissaries of the Mossad and the Jewish Agency gathered thousands of Jews in makeshift camps in Addis Ababa, where they awaited a miracle that would bring them to Israel.

And the miracle happened.

In May 1991, seven years after Operation Moses, Operation Solomon was launched. It was carried out at the height of the civil war, as rebel forces opposing President Mengistu advanced from every direction on Addis Ababa. Israel was aided once again by George Bush, by then the American president, whose mediation produced an agreement between the Israeli government and the head of the collapsing regime several days before Mengistu's final defeat. Secret, dogged work by Uri Lubrani, of Israel's foreign ministry, acting under orders from Prime Minister Yitzhak Shamir, made it a reality.

As part of the agreement, Israel paid $35 million to Mengistu in exchange for bringing the Jews to Israel, while the Americans promised Mengistu and several senior members of his regime that they would receive diplomatic asylum in the United States. In exchange for an unknown sum, the rebel leaders agreed not to disrupt the operation and to observe a temporary cease-fire. The cease-fire, agreed upon by both government and rebel forces, was short: thirty-four hours. Israel had to fly all the Jews out of the country before the fighting resumed.

The mission was overseen by the IDF's deputy chief of staff, Amnon Lipkin-Shahak, who bore responsibility for flying approximately fifteen thousand Jews to Israel within thirty-four hours. The organization of the mission was exemplary, with Israel sending "anything that could fly" to Addis Ababa. El Al dispatched thirty passenger planes and the air force sent numerous cargo jets; leading them, of course, were the Rhinos. Hundreds of soldiers from various units, including infantry, Shaldag and the paratroopers, were sent to Addis Ababa to organize the immigrants and bring them aboard the planes. Especially prominent were soldiers of Ethiopian background who had arrived in Israel during Operation Moses and were now serving in the IDF. The sight of Ethiopian soldiers in IDF uniforms, many of them proudly wearing the red berets, red boots and silver paratroopers' wings, inspired great excitement among the new immigrants, and even the toughest Ethiopian-Israeli paratroopers couldn't stop their tears. The soldiers spread out to secure the airfield, leading the Jews onto the planes. They were divided into groups and each given a number; numbered labels were initially attached to their clothing, but a different process was subsequently discovered—sticking the labels on their foreheads. Within a few hours, 14,400 Jews were brought aboard the planes. Lipkin-Shahak oversaw the operation with his characteristic calm and composure.

As part of the operation, a Boeing 747 was going to break the world record, with 1,087 passengers on board. During the flight, a baby was born, and 1,088 immigrants deplaned in Israel.

The lost tribe returns on eagle's wings. (*Zvika Israeli, GPO*)

Many Jews remained in Ethiopia, still aspiring to immigrate to Israel. Ethiopian Jewry's fight to "ascend" had left many behind. In Israel, too, Ethiopian Jews were forced to struggle hard to be absorbed into Israeli society, to be recognized as Jews, to achieve true equality and to adapt to a modern society, where the worldview and traditions by which they had lived for thousands of years came apart.

BENNY GANTZ, LATER THE IDF CHIEF OF STAFF

"I took part in numerous assignments during my military career, among them secret operations. My life has been in danger more than once: I've been shot at, crossed paths with terrorists, lost fighters and saw friends die next to me. But the mission of bringing the Jews of Ethiopia to Israel, in which I participated as a Shaldag commander, was the most important, from a national standpoint, of all the operations I've taken part in. This mission, in substance, encompasses the entire concept of a national home for the Jewish people. The idea that you can carry it out—that's Zionism. It wasn't a heroic mission of individuals. It was the heroic mission of a country.

"I'm a son of Holocaust survivors, and during the evacuation, I couldn't not think for a moment about what would have happened if we'd had a country back then; perhaps everything might have been different. How might European Jewry have looked? There, in Ethiopia, I realized that the state of Israel was doing something great and powerful.

"There's a memory that I carry with me to this day: we're landing in the dark, leaving the plane, which looks like a terrible monster, reaching people sitting, folded on the ground, wrapped in blankets, carrying them in our arms into the belly of the plane, the door closing, taking off, the pilots turning on the lights, and then our eyes meeting, so many eyes looking toward you in fright, and it's impossible to communicate with them.

"The thing that most bothered me about the operation was the moment when the first caravan of immigrants came toward us on the airfield, and suddenly I could make out the stickers with numbers on their foreheads. That made me crazy, and I asked that the numbers be removed immediately.

"Since then, there've been moving moments of coming full circle. I met a singer in a military troupe who told me, moments before singing the national anthem, that she had been a baby during Operation Solomon."

AFTERMATH

Yitzhak Navon (1921 to): Ben Gurion's secretary since 1951, Navon became the fifth president of Israel (1978 to 1983) and later was elected minister of education and culture.

Yitzhak Rabin (1922 to 1995): Chief of staff (1964 to 1967). Ambassador to the U.S. Prime minister of Israel (1974 to 1977, 1992 to 1995). Was assassinated in November 1995.

David ("Dado") Elazar (1925 to 1976): Commander of the Northern District in the Six Day War. Chief of staff (1972 to 1974), was forced to resign after the Yom Kippur War by decision of the Agranat Board of Inquiry. Died of a heart attack (1976).

Uzi Eilam (1934 to): Brigadier general in the IDF. Director general of the Israeli Atomic Energy Commission (1976 to 1985) and chief scientist and director (research and development) in the Ministry of Defense (1986 to 1997).

Moshe Dayan (1915 to 1981): Lieutenant general. Chief of staff (1953 to 1958). Minister of Agriculture (1959 to 1964). Minister of defense

(1967 to 1974). As minister of foreign affairs (1977 to 1979) he played a major role in negotiating the peace treaty with Egypt.

Ariel ("Arik") Sharon (1928 to 2014): Major general. Commander of the Paratroopers Corps (1954 to 1957). Discharged from the IDF in 1973, minister of defense (1981 to 1983), removed from his position by the Kahan Board of Inquiry after the War in Lebanon (1982). Served in several ministerial positions, elected prime minister in 2001, and as such carried out Israel's unilateral disengagement from the Gaza Strip. After suffering a stroke in 2006, he remained in a coma until his death in 2014.

Meir Har-Zion (1934 to 2014): Captain. A founder of Unit 101, member of the first paratrooper battalion, was awarded the Medal of Courage, lived on a farm in the Gilboa mountains named after his sister Shoshana; died in 2014.

Aharon Davidi (1920 to 2012): Brigadier general. Commander of the Paratroopers Brigade. Director and founder of Sar-El volunteer program of the IDF.

Shimon ("Katcha") Kahaner (1934 to): Colonel, member of Unit 101. Raises cattle on a farm in northern Israel, across the gully from his late friend Meir Har-Zion.

Mordechai ("Motta") Gur (1930 to 1995): Lieutenant general. Commander of the 55th Paratroopers Reserve Brigade, which captured Jerusalem in the Six Day War (1967). Israel's military attaché in Washington (1972 to 1973). Chief of staff during Operation Entebbe (1976). Minister of health (1984 to 1986). Deputy defense minister (1992 to 1997). Diagnosed with terminal cancer, he committed suicide with his handgun.

Yoash ("Chatto") Zidon (1926 to 2015): Combat pilot and commander in the Israeli Air Force. The head of weapon system and planning in the IAF. Member of Knesset (1988 to 1992).

Ezer Weizman (1924 to 2005): Major general, commander of the IAF (1958 to 1966). Minister of defense (1977 to 1980). Seventh president of Israel (1993 to 2000). Died at home in Caesarea.

Rafael ("Raful") Eitan (1929 to 2005): Lieutenant general. Chief of staff (1978 to 1983). Established the right-wing political party Tzomet. Deputy prime minister (1998 to 1999) then retired. Swept by a wave into the sea from Ashdod's wharf during a severe storm.

Shimon Peres (1923 to): Defense ministry director general and deputy defense minister under Ben-Gurion. Defense minister (1974 to 1977, 1995 to 1996). Minister of foreign affairs (1986 to 1988 ,1992 to 1995, 2001 to 2002). Prime minister (1984 to 1986, 1995 to 1996). Ninth president of Israel (2007 to 2014).

Rehavam ("Gandhi") Ze'evi (1926 to 2001): Major general, commander of the Central Military District. Established the right-wing Moledet party (1988). Minister without portfolio (1999). Minister of tourism (2001). Assassinated in the Hyatt Hotel in Jerusalem in 2001 by four Palestinian gunmen from the Popular Front for the Liberation of Palestine.

Avihu Ben-Nun (1939 to): Major general, Israeli Air Force (1957 to 1992). Combat pilot. Commander of the Israeli Air Force (1987 to 1992).

Mordechai ("Motti") Hod (1926 to 2003): Major general. Combat pilot. Commander of the Israeli Air Force (1966 to 1973).

Amichai ("Ami") Ayalon (1945 to): Admiral, commander of Flotilla 13 (1979), commander of the Israeli Navy (1992 to 1996). Recipient of the Medal of Valor. Head of Israel's Internal Security Service (the Shin-Beth) (1995 to 2000). Minister without portfolio (2007 to 2008). Senior fellow at the Israel Democracy Institute.

Haim Bar-Lev (1924 to 1994): Lieutenant general. Chief of staff (1968 to 1971). Responsible for the Bar-Lev Line, fortifications built along the Suez Canal. Several ministry positions, and ambassador to Russia (1992 to 1994).

Hadar Kimchi (1929 to): Commander of the Cherbourg Operation
(1968). Deputy commander of the Israeli Navy (1971 to 1973).

Mordechai ("Moka") Limon (1924 to 2009): Admiral, commander of the
navy (1950 to 1954). Head of delegation of procurement of the Ministry
of Defense in Paris (1962 to 1970).

Nehemiah Dagan (1940 to): Brigadier general. Combat pilot (helicopters).
Commander of the IDF education department (1985 to 1988).

Eitan Ben Eliyahu (1944 to): Major general. Combat pilot. Commander
of the IAF (1996 to 2000).

Amir Eshel (1959 to): Major general. Commander of the IAF since 2012.

Benyamin Netanyahu (1945 to): Captain, Sayeret Matkal. Israel's
ambassador to the UN (1984 to 1988). Minister of finance (2003 to
2005). Prime minister (1996 to 1999) (2009 to).

Uzi Dayan (1948 to): Major general. Nephew of Moshe Dayan. Fifteen
years in Sayeret Matkal. Deputy chief of staff. Head of the National
Security Council (2003 to 2005).

Ehud Barak (1942 to): Lieutenant general. Commander of Sayeret
Matkal. Chief of staff (1991 to 1995). Prime minister (1999 to 2001).
Minister of defense and deputy prime minister (2009 to 2013).

Amnon Lipkin-Shahak (1944 to 2012): Lieutenant general. Commander
of the Paratroopers Brigade. Head of Military Intelligence (1986 to 1991).
Deputy chief of staff (1991). Chief of staff of the IDF (1995 to 1998).
Member of Knesset and Cabinet Minister.

Moshe ("Muki") Betzer (1945 to): Colonel. Deputy commander of Sayeret
Matkal. First commander of Shaldag (commando of the Israeli Air Force).

Moshe ("Bogi") Ya'alon (1950 to): Lieutenant general. Commander of
Sayeret Matkal. Commander of the Paratroopers Brigade. Chief of Staff
(2002 to 2005). Minister of defense (2013 to).

Danny Matt (1927 to 2013): Major general. Commander of the Paratroopers Regular Brigade. Commander of the Paratroopers Reservist Brigade 247 (55). Chair of the IDF appeal court.

Yitzhak Mordechai (1944 to): Major general. Commander of the Paratroopers and Infantry Corps. Commander of the Northern Command (1993 to 1995). Minister of defense (1996 to 1999). Deputy prime minister (1999 to 2000). Retired from political life in 2001.

Amnon Reshef (1938 to): Major general. Commander of the Armored Corps. Chairman, Association for Peace and Security.

Avigdor Kahalani (1944 to): Brigadier general. Commander of the 7th Brigade of the Armored Corps. Decorated with the Medal of Valor, the Medal of Distinguished Service and the President's Medal. Minister of internal security (1996 to 1999). Chairman, the Association for the Soldiers' Welfare.

Tamir Pardo (1953 to): Communications officer, Sayeret Matkal. Head of the Mossad (2011 to).

Shaul Mofaz (1948 to): Lieutenant general. Commander of the Paratroopers Brigade. Commander of the Judea and Samaria Division. Chief of staff (1998 to 2002). Minister of defense (2002 to 2006). Deputy prime minister and minister of transports (2006 to 2009). Later head of the opposition in the Knesset. Retired from political life in 2015.

Dan Shomron (1937 to 2008): Lieutenant general. Commander of the Paratroopers and Infantry Corps. Chief of staff (1987 to 1991). Chairman of the Israeli Military Industries.

Meir Dagan (1945 to): Major general, various military positions. Medal of Courage. Director of the Mossad (2002 to 2010).

Gavriel ("Gabi") Ashkenazi (1954 to): Lieutenant general. Deputy chief of staff (2002 to 2005). Director general of the defense ministry (2006). Chief of staff (2007 to 2011).

Aviem Sella (1946 to): Colonel. Combat pilot. (Advancement arrested because of his involvement in the Jonathan Pollard affair.)

Eliezer ("Chiney") Marom (1955 to): Admiral. Commander of the Israeli Navy (2007 to 2012).

Aviv Kochavi (1964 to): Major general. Commander of the Paratroopers Brigade. Commander of military intelligence. Commander of the Northern District.

Itzhak ("Jerry") Gershon (1958 to): Major general. Commander of the Paratroopers Brigade. Commander of the Judea and Samaria Division. CEO of Friends of the IDF in the U.S. (2008 to 2015).

Dan Halutz (1948 to): Lieutenant general. Combat pilot. Commander of the IAF (2002 to 2004). Chief of staff (2005 to 2007). Resigned after the second Lebanon War.

Yoav Galant (1958 to):Major general. Commander of the Southern District during Operation Cast Lead. Appointed chief of staff in 2010, but the appointment was cancelled. Minister of Housing (2015 to).

Dr. Izzeldin Abuelaish (1955 to): Palestinian doctor. Since 2009, lives with his family in Toronto. Founder of the trust Daughters for Life, for the education and health of girls and women in Gaza and the Middle East. Active in promoting the peace movement.

SOURCE NOTES

The sources marked with an (h) are in Hebrew

1: Entebbe, 1976

"Operation Yonathan (Thunderball)—The full report," IDF Archives, November 1977. (h)

"The secret notes of Peres," Itamar Eichner, Yedioth Ahronoth, 17.7.2011 (h)

"A rescue operation which shocked the world," Haim Isrovitz, Maariv, 27.6.2006. (h)

Parts from Motta Gur notes (Internet site: The heritage of Gur). (h)

"Exposure: The Mossad photograph, Operation Entebbe on the way," Sharon Rofe-Ofir, Ynet 1.7.2006. (internet site)

Bar-Zohar Michael, "Shimon Peres, the biography," Random House, New York 2007, pp. 313–348.

"Operation Entebbe," Journal of the Defense Minister, 27 June 1976, IDF Archives.

Peres Shimon, "Entebbe Diary," Yedioth Ahronoth, Tel Aviv, 1991. (h)

Rabin Yitzhak, "The Rabin Memoirs," Maariv, Tel Aviv, 1979, p. 527. (h)

Gur Mordechai (Motta), "The Chief of Staff," Maarakhot, Tel Aviv, 1998, pp. 236–288. (h)

Interview of Shimon Peres.

Interview of Tamir Pardo.

2: To Save Jerusalem, 1948

Yitzhaki Arie, "Latrun—the battle for the road to Jerusalem"; "Latrun, road seven is 'Burma Road'—the siege was broken," Kama publishers, Jerusalem 1982, volume 1, pp. 269–282, volume 2, pp. 321–339. (h)

Shamir Shlomo (Gen. res.) "At all costs—to Jerusalem," "Road Seven to Jerusalem," Maarakhot, Ministry of Defense, Tel-Aviv, 1994, pp. 415–454. (h)

Talmi Menachem, "The new route," Cultural service of the IDF, 1949. (h)

Oren Ram, "Latrun, the new hope," Keshet publishers, Tel-Aviv, 2002, pp. 309–332. (h)

Rabin Yitzhak, "The Rabin Memoirs," op.cit. 1979, pp. 52–56. (h)

"The man who discovered the Burma Road," Eli Eshed, E-magoo.co.il, Internet magazine, 28.5.2005. (h)

Interview of Yitzhak Navon.

3: Black Arrow, 1955

Eilam Uzi, "Eilam's Arch," Gaza raid—Black-Arrow Mission, 28.2.1955, Yedioth Books (Miskal) 2009, pp. 32–39. (h)

"Black Arrow—fiftieth anniversary to the unification of the mythological paratrooper unit 101," Kobi Finkler, Channel 7, 23.1.07. (h)

Bar-Zohar Michael and Haber Eitan, "The book of the Paratroopers," Levin Epstein publishers, Tel-Aviv, 1969, pp. 32–39. (h)

"We were here. The IDF attacks in Gaza, 1955," Yanai Israeli, Walla, 7.3.2008. (h)

"Black Arrow, a pierced heart: the paratroopers hero and the Gaza mission," Roi Mendel, Ynet, Yedioth Ahronoth, 7.3.2012. (h)

Interview of Uzi Eilam.

4: "Bring Down this Plane!" 1956

Tzidon Yoash (Chatto), "By day by night, through haze and fog," Maariv publishers,1995, p. 216. (h)

"Hour of the bat," Elazar Ben-Lulu, Internet site of the IDF. (h)

Interview of Yoash (Chatto) Tzidon.

5: Kadesh, 1956

"Myths and facts," a historical research; The Mitla Pass 26th anniversary," Monitin Magazine, October 1981. (h)

"The Independence War was not a war of few against many—The Mitla Myth," Moshe Ronen, Yedioth Ahronoth, 4.8.1999. (h)

"The longest day in Sinai," Uri Dan, Maariv, 28.10.1966. (h)

"Being there—testimony on Sharon, Gur, Eitan, Hofi, Davidi and others," Monitin, November 1966. (h)

Ben-Gurion David, "A letter to the Ninth brigade, 6.11.1956," Ministry of Defense, IDF archives. (h)

Dayan Moshe, "On the Sinai campaign, 6.11.1956," Ministry of Defense, IDF archives. (h)

"Operation Steamroller, operation orders 64/56, 28.10.1956 including annex 4—A paratroop drop," IDF archive. (h)

"On the parachuting at the Mitla," Dr. Arieh Gilai, the Paratroopers' internet site. (h)

"The brigade's reconnaissance unit, a personal story of the Mitla battle," Uri Getz, the Paratroopers' internet site. (h)

"Heavy mortars battalion 332, testimony about the Mitla battle," Yakov Tzur, the Paratroopers' internet site. (h)

"Company A, Battalion 890, the cave mopping at the Mitla battle," Avshalom (Avsha) Adam, the Paratroopers' internet site. (h)

"Nahal squad commanders course 906, fighting route at Kadesh, personal testimonies," Shai Marmur and Rafi Benisti, the Paratroopers' internet site. (h)

"Machine-gunner company E battalion 88: At the Mitla battle I stood exposed on a half-track," Moshe Hassin as told to Dr. Arieh Gilai, the Paratroopers' internet site. (h)

"Fighter and Sergeant-Major, company A, A personal story about the Mitla parachuting and the caves' battle," Moni Meroz, the Paratroopers' internet site. (h)

"The Mitla battle," Shraga Gafni, Maarakhot, Ministry of Defense, number 113, 1960. (h)

Bar-Zohar Michael and Haber Eitan, "The Mitla trap," the book of the Paratroopers, Op. cit. pp. 132–140. (h)

Bar-Zohar Michael, "Ben-Gurion," Volume 3 (out of 3) Am-Oved publishers, Tel-Aviv, 1977, pp. 1207–1286. (h)

Bar-Zohar Michael, "Shimon Peres, the biography," Random House, N.Y. 2007, pp. 144–154.

Dayan Moshe, "Diary of the Sinai Campaign," New York, Harper and Row, 1966.

Eitan Rafael (Raful) "A soldier's Story," Maariv publishers, Tel-Aviv, 1985, p. 65. (h)

6: "Life or Death," Operation Focus, 1967

Cohen (Cheetah) Elazar and Lavi Zvi, "The Six Day War, The Suez is not the limit," Maariv, Tel-Aviv, 1990, pp. 263–291. (h)

"The Focus plan—as a thunderball out of a blue sky," Pirsumei Teufa (Aviation magazine) Rishon Lezion, pp. 55–80. (h)

Yanai Ehud, ed.; General (res.) Yiftach Spector, "Moked, Aerial Supremacy," Keter publishers, Jerusalem, 1995, pp.162–170. (h)

Churchill Randolph and Churchill Winston, "The air strike—the Six Day War," Houghton Mifflin, Boston, 1967, p. 82.

Rabin Yitzhak, "The Rabin Memoirs," Maariv publishers, 1979, pp.186–191. (h)

Weizman Ezer, "On Eagles Wings," Maariv publishers, Tel-Aviv, 1975, pp. 259–273. (h)

"The Focus Plan—how it was planned and how it was carried out," Zeev Shiff, Haaretz, 10.4.1981. (h)

"Our Air Force was annihilated—the picture was black," Yaakov Lamdan, "Laisha" (woman's weekly magazine), 5.6.1989. (h)

"A forced gamble," Meir Amitai, Haaretz, 4.7.1997. (h)

"Like a thunderball from a blue sky," Noam Ophir, the IAF magazine, 1.6.2002. (h)

A 1983 interview with Abd-El-Hamid Helmy, Commander of the Egyptian Air-Force, "Al Ahram" Internet site.

Steven Pressfield, "Lion's Gate," Sentinel HC, New York, 2014.

Interview of Colonel (res.) Yossi Sarig. (h)

Interview of General (res.) Avihu Bin-Nun. (h)

7: "The Temple Mount Is in Our Hands!" 1967

Narkiss Uzi, general (res.) "Jerusalem is one," Am-Oved, Tel- Aviv, 1975, pp. 160–163, 173–175, 200–201, 241–253. (h)

Landau Eli, "Jerusalem Forever," chapters: "The day of Jerusalem"; "Ammunition Hill;" "The temple Mount and the Western Wall are in our hands"; pp. 25–32, 111–147, 161–171, Otpaz, Tel-Aviv, 1967. (h)

Nathan Moshe, "The battle for Jerusalem," Chapters: "Ammunition Hill"; "The Lions` Gate"; "The Victory Gate"; pp. 131–191, 293–333, 334–349, Otpaz, Tel-Aviv, 1968. (h)

Dayan David, "From Hermon to Suez"—History of the Six Day War. Chapter: "Jerusalem of Iron"; "Here is the Western Wall"; pp. 144–154, 155–161. Massada, Ramat-Gan, 1967. (h)

Weizman Ezer, op. cit. pp. 283–297. (h)

Kfir Ilan, "The Fighting IDF- Military and Defense Encyclopaedia," Volume 4, chapter: "Jerusalem of Iron," pp. 89–99, Revivim Publishers, Maariv, Tel-Aviv, 1982–1986. (h)

"Motta made History," Moshe Bar-Yehuda, Military Magazine, 24.5.1968. (h)

"We've got the scoop," Ravit Naor, Maariv, 18.4.1997. (h)

"The hill was acquired by blood," Yoram Shoshani, Yedioth Ahronoth, 8.1.1968. (h)

Oren Michael, "Six Days of War," Presidio Press, 2003.

"Jerusalem of blood, songs and prayers," Yehuda Ezrachi, Maariv, 13.6.1967. (h)

"Jerusalem will be built," Yehuda Haezrachi, Maariv, 16.6.1967. (h)

"Against fortified bunkers and 120 mm. mortars," Amit Navon and Moshe Zonder, Maariv, 18.4.1997. (h)

"The battle for Jerusalem continued because of lack of communication with the IDF forces after the Jordanians broke the ceasefire," A. Gazit, Maariv, 8.6.1972. (h)

"The Battle over the Bridge," Hotam magazine, 18.1.1974. (h)

"The blowing of the Bunker at Ammunition hill," Shimshon Ofer, Davar, 25.8.1967. (h)

"Ammunition hill in retrospect," Haim Fikersh, Hatzophe, 17.5.85. (h)

"Dayan ordered me: Take my picture when I enter the old city," Ilan Bruner, Maariv, 18.4.1997. (h)

"This year in built Jerusalem!," Menachem Barash, Yedioth-Ahronoth, 8.6.1967. (h)

Gur Mordechai (Motta)—"The Temple Mount is in our hands—Victory Parade, 12.6.1967," Defense Office publications, p. 335. (h)

8: "I felt I Was Suffocating": The Raid on Green Island, 1969

"Tens of Egyptians killed on IDF invasion to Green Island," Eitan Haber, Yedioth Ahronoth, 20.7.1969. (h)

"The Canons of Green Island"—Haolam Haze, Magazine, 23.7.1969. (h)

"At Least 25 Egyptians killed on IDF attack on Green Island." Military correspondent, Davar, 21.7.1969. (h)

"On Green Island 25 years ago," Yehuda Ofan, Al-Hamishmar, 21.7.1969. (h)

"The hottest day in Suez," Eitan Haber, Yedioth Ahronoth, 21.7.1969.

"Heroes of Green Island," Zeev Shiff, Haaretz, 13.3.70. (h)

"Green Island: First attack," Uriel Ben-Ami, Bamahane, 27.7.1977.

"In fire and water," Judith Winkler, Haaretz, 27.6.1979. (h)

"Exodus of the naval commando fighters," Bruria-Avidan-Barir, Laisha, 17.4.1989. (h)

"50 critical moments," Meirav Arlozorov, Bamahane, 23.3.1994. (h)

Eldar Michael (Mike), "Flotilla 13—The story of the Naval commandos," Maariv publishers, Tel-Aviv, 1993, pp. 386–414. (h)

Mustafa Kabha, "The Egyptian attrition and the Israeli counter-attrition," Egyptian sources, Yad-Tabenkin, Institute of Research, pp. 79–100.

Interview of Ami Ayalon. (h)

9: The French Defense Minister: "Bomb the Israelis!" 1969

"Suddenly, one morning, 6 boats disappeared," Sigal Buhris, Between the Waves magazine, no. 89, 20 years to the operation.(h)

"The 48th soul," Uri Sharon, Davar, 9.8.1991. (h)

Limon Moka, Tzur Miron, "Jewish Pirates—Boats of Cherbourg," Maariv publishers, Tel-Aviv, 1988, pp. 138–184. (h)

"They had a general rehearsal," Idith Witman, Hadashot, 25.12.1988. (h)

"In memory of the boats on their way," Ilana Baum, Maariv, 26.12.1988. (h)

"The story of A.M. Lea," Joseph Michalsky, Davar, 23.12.1979. (h)

"Five boats are about to arrive today," Lamerhav Daily, 31.12.1969. (h)

"Egyptian spokesman: we are confident that France is not to blame for the smuggling of the five boats," Shmuel Segev, Maariv, 31.12.1969. (h)

Rabinovitz Abraham, edited by Effi Melzer, "The boats of Cherbourg," Effi Melzer Publishing House, Military research, Reut Publishers, 2001. (h)

Interview of Hadar Kimchy.

10: "Why Bomb if We Can Take?" 1969

"The night of the Radar," Eitan Haber, Yedioth Ahronoth, 8.1.1971.

Kfir Ilan, op. cit. Paratroopers, Volume 4, pp. 123–125

Fiksler Yoel, "Rooster 53—Operation for bringing the radar from Egypt, December 26–27, 1969," S.H.R. publishers, Rehovot, 2009. (h)

Cohen Eliezer (Cheeta), Lavi Zvi, "The sky is not the limit," "Imaginary, crazy rooster," Maariv publishers, Tel-Aviv, 1990, pp. 387–392. (h)

"An American request for information about the Egyptian radar is expected," Nissim Kiviti, Eitan Haber, Yedioth Ahronoth, 4.1.1970. (h)

"Remember, you are entering the Lion's lair!" Eitan Haber, Yedioth Ahronot, 28.12.1969. (h)

"Expiatory Rooster," Dani Spector, Yedioth Ahronoth, 30.12.2009. (h)

"Heritage paper 66—The snatching of the Egyptian radar," Oded Marom, IAF friends Magazine, 2012. (h)

"Operation 'Rooster'—Israel Captures Egyptian Radar in War of attrition," Jewish Virtual Library, December 26–27 ,1969.

Interview of Nehemiah Dagan.

11: "The Enemy Speaks Russian!" 1970

Yonai Ehud, "No Margin for Error," op. cit. pp. 231–134.

"The Russians did not believe it's happening," Amir Rappaport, Omri Assenheim, NRG, 13.8.2005. (h)

Cohen Eliezer (Cheeta), Lavi Zvi, op. cit. pp. 411–415. (h)

Amir Amos, "Fire in the sky," Defense ministry, Tel-Aviv, 2000. (h)

"Our pilots overcame the Russian pilots," Arie Avneri, Yedioth Ahronoth, 2.8.1970. (h)

"Commander of the Russian Air Force investigates the interception of the MiGs," Egyptian news agency, Yedioth Ahronoth, 2.8.1970. (h)

"The four MiGs that were shot down yesterday were flown by Russian pilots," Yedioth Ahronoth, 31.7.1970. (h)

"Will the USSR accept her fighters being hurt?" Eitan Haber, Yedioth Ahronoth, 3.8.1970. (h)

Interview of Amir Eshel.

12: White Angels on Jacob's Ladder, 1972

"Brilliant 90 seconds of The Matkal Commandos," Moshe Zonder, Maariv, 25.3.1994. (h)

"23 hours of anxiety ," Yedioth Ahronoth reporters, 12.5.1972. (h)

"We released Sabena," Moshe Zonder and Amit Navon, Maariv,16.5.1997.

"That is how I shot The prime Minister," Yossi Asulin, Southern local paper, 25.4.1997. (h)

"The breaking into Sabena," Yosi Argaman and Zvi Elchayani, Bamahane, 20.5.1992. (h)

"Kidnapping Diary: hour by hour," Zeev Shif, Haaretz, 12.5.1972. (h)

"The hot line between Lod and Jerusalem," Yosef Harif, Maariv, 12.5.1972. (h)

Kaspit Ben, Kfir Ilan, editor: Dani Dor, "Netanyahu—The road to power, the break through into Sabena airplane," Alfa Communication, Tel-Aviv, 1997, pp. 65–70. (h) Birch Lane Press, USA, 1998.

Interview of Benjamin Netanyahu.

13: "Stop! Halt! Hands Up!" 1972

Argaman Yossef, "Intelligence and Israel's security,"—"Kidnapping of the Syrian Generals—Top Secret," 1990, pp. 32–42. (h)

"Trapping the five Syrians—great victory of the Israeli Intelligence," Yedioth Ahronoth, 22.6.1972. (h)

"Syrian Intelligence officers have more influence than other officers," Ilan Kfir, Yedioth Ahronoth, 22.6.1972. (h)

"Frightened and distraught, the five high-rank Syrian officers were taken prisoners," Yehezkel Hameiri and Eitan Haber, Yedioth Ahronoth, 22.6.1972. (h)

Zonder Moshe, "Sayeret Matkal, the Uzi Dayan era," Keter, Jerusalem, 2000, pp.182–183. (h)

Kaspit Ben , Kfir Ilan, Dani Dor ed., "Netanyahu—The road to Power," Alfa communication, Tel-Aviv 1997, pp. 68–70. (h).

"The Kidnapping of the Syrian Generals," Yosef Argaman, Bamahane, 29.7.1987. (h)

"Heroes of operation Crate reveal: that is how we kidnapped the Syrian officers," Shaul Shai, Moria Ben-Yosef, "Israel Defense," Internet site, 25.3.2012. (h)

Interview of Uzi Dayan.

14: That Lady Means Trouble , 1973

Documents of the IDF Archives, file 401 (papers 4,6–16)

Bar-Zohar Michael, ed., "The Book of Valor," Yaakov Hisday on Avida Shor, Ministry of Defense publishers, Magal, Tel-Aviv, 1977, pp. 184–187. (h)

Bar-Zohar Michael, Mishal Nissim, "Mossad—The Greatest Missions of the Israeli Secret Service," The Quest for The Red Prince, Harper Collins, New York, 2012, pp.186–213.

"We heard a huge explosion, the building was cut in two," Tal Zagraba, "Shavuz," Internet site. (h)

"The autumn of 'Spring of Youth'," Onn Levi, Davar, 23.4.1993. (h)

"Bravery does not console," Oded Liphshitz, Al Hamishmar, 24.4.1993. (h)

"Mental strength is our weapon," Ehud Barak, Yedioth Ahronoth, 25.4.1993. (h)

"Barak dressed like a woman entered the terrorist buildings," Dani Sade, Yedioth Ahronoth, 25.4.1993. (h)

"General Barak, dressed like a woman, on a lovers' stroll to the terrorists' homes in Beirut," Gil Keisari, Haaretz 11.4.73. (h)

"The raiding force captured important papers regarding the terrorist organizations in Israel and in the occupied territories," Haaretz reporter on Arab subjects, Haaretz, 11.4.1973. (h)

"Six Israeli Mossad agents arrived in Beirut—a few days before the IDF raid," David Herst, The Guardian, quoted in Maariv, 11.4.1973. (h)

"I heard shootings in the corridor and I said: Certainly the Israelis are attacking," Zvi Lavi, Maariv, 13.4.1973. (h)

"If we would have learned a lesson from this," Uri Milstein, Hadashot, 29.3.1985. (h)

"Western papers on the IDF raid in Beirut, Reuters, AFP, UPI; Daily Express, London: "The Israeli intelligence is the most efficient in the world," as quoted in Hazofe, 12.4.1973. (h)

"I'll never forgive Ehud Barak for taking part in the killing of my husband," D'isi Adwan, in Amman, Zoher Andreous, Maariv, 16.5.2000. (h)

"IDF Raid—Shock treatment," Eitan Haber, Yedioth Ahronoth, 13.4.1973. (h)

"Prime minister of Lebanon demanded to fire senior officers after the raid; He retired after his demand was rejected," News agencies in Beirut, Yedioth Ahronoth, 12.4.1973. (h)

"Israeli Agents arrived in Beirut on Friday to prepare the operation," Arthur Chatsworth, Daily Express, as quoted in Yedioth Ahronoth, 12.4.1973. (h)

"Chief of Staff Elazar confirms important documents were captured in Beirut; 900 terrorists were hit in 1972," Reuven Ben-Zvi, Yedioth Ahronoth, 12.4.1973. (h)

"Mission impossible in the heart of Beirut," Dan Arkin, Maariv, 11.4.1973. (h)

"The Mercedes cars were rented in Beirut seven hours before the raid," News agencies' correspondents in Beirut, Maariv, 11.4.1973. (h)

Interview with Kamal Adwan, a week before he was killed, Robert Stephens, The Observer, as quoted in Maariv, 15.4.1973. (h)

"The Operation in Beirut (the full story as told by the participants)," Benjamin Landau, Bamahane, 6.9.1972. (h)

Interview of Amnon Lipkin-Shahak.

Interview of Ehud Barak.

15: The Bravehearts Land in Africa, 1973

"Bridge over troubled waters," Uri Dan, Haolam Haze, 16.9.1991. (h)

"The Crossing of the Suez Canal," Uri Milshtein, Maariv 7.10.1974. (h)

"Luckily, Erez managed to steal 30 command cars and Nahik found the boats," Ariela Ringel-Hoffman, Yedioth Ahronoth, 2.10.1988. (h)

"A bridge over Suez," Uri Milshtein, Haaretz, 27.10.1978. (h)

"The bridgehead was captured," Ilan Kfir, Yedioth Ahronoth, 16.11.1973. (h)

Oren Elhanan, Lieutenant Colonel (res.), "History of the Yom Kippur War"—The crossing; IDF History Department, December 2004, pp. 205–232. (h)

Kfir Ilan, "My glorious brothers of the Canal"; Chapter 14: "October 15–16: Acapulco"; Chapter 15: "October 16: Africa"; Chapter 21: "October 17: Heroes of the bridges," Yedioth Ahronoth Publishers, Tel-Aviv, 2003, pp. 205–213, 214–222, 270–283. (h)

Bergman Ronen, Melzer Gil, "The Yom Kippur War real time"; Chapter 3: "The Crossing." Yedioth Ahronoth Publishers, Tel-Aviv, 2003, pp. 221–288. (h)

Dan Uri, "Bridgehead," Chapter 23: "The paratroopers are crossing," A.L. Special Edition, Tel-Aviv, April 1975, pp. 157–169. (h)

Herzog, Chaim. "The War of Atonement," Greenhill Books, London, 1988.

Interview of Moshe (Bogi) Yaalon.

16: "Commander Killed ... Deputy Commander Killed ... Second Deputy Commander ..." 1973

Segal Maozia, "Testimonies from the sandy battlefield: the paratroopers' combat in the Chinese Farm," Modan publishers. Ben-Shemen, 2002, pp. 80–230. (h)

Ezov Amiram, "Crossing—60 hours in October 1973," Dvir Publishers, Or Yehuda. 2011, pp. 55–220. (h)

"Bloodshed in the Chinese farm," Ilan Kfir, Yedioth Ahronot,24.4.1974. (h)

"The hell was here," Yael Gvirtz, Yedioth Ahronot, 17.6.1994. (h)

"Slowly, slowly, they tell about the night when they were sent to the slaughter," Batia Gur, Haaretz, 17.9.1999. (h)

"Itzik, here is Ehud, I'm coming to help," Shiri Lev-Ari, Hair, 29.1.1999. (h)

"The Deputy company commander mumbled: It's over, the battalion is gone ... 890 is gone ... everybody was killed," Yael Gvirtz, Yedioth Ahronoth, 17.9.1991. (h)

"Regiment 890 at the Chinese farm," Eitan Haber, Yedioth Ahronoth, October 1985.

"The battle of the Chinese farm, a wound that won't heal," Nava Zuriel, Maariv, 4.2.2006. (h)

"The Armor fighters demand that their part in the Chinese farm battle be recognized," Dana Weiller, Maariv, 7.10.2008. (h)

"History, memory and rating," Zeev Drori, Maariv, 28.4.2004. (h)

"Overlooked but not forgotten," Abraham Rabinovitch, Jerusalem post, 3.10.2007.

Interview of Itzhak Mordechai.

17: "I See the Lake of Tiberias!" 1973

"Back to the Valley of Tears (Emek Habacha)," Yaron London, Yedioth Ahronoth, 6.10.1992. (h)

"The battle in the Valley of Tears," Renen Shor, Bamahane, 19.12.1973. (h)

"Why was Barak's brigade abandoned?" Emanuel Rozen, Maariv, 24.9.1993. (h)

"Syrian Documents captured: The Golan Heights have to be taken within 24 hours," Davar 19.4.1974. (h)

"The fighting of Division Mussa," Amir Oren, Bamahane, 30.1.1974. (h)

"The battle of the Golan," General (res.) Chaim Herzog, Yedioth Ahronoth, 30.9.1974. (h)

"Destroy Damascus," Igal Sarna, Yedioth Ahronoth, 17.9.1991. (h)

"Look at the Syrians, how brave they are," Avigdor Kahalani, Yedioth Ahronoth, 24.9.1993.

"Bravery or death," David Shalit, Haaretz, 7.8.1993. (h)

Milshtein Uri, "The Yom Kippur War"; the Paratrooper Corps; The bloodline; The breaking of the war," Yaron Golan Publishers, Tel-Aviv, June 1992, pp.162–222. (h)

Interview of Avigdor Kahalani

18: The Eyes of the Nation, 1973

"That's how the Hermon fort fell," Eitan Haber, Yedioth Ahronoth, 28.12.1973. (h)

"Here lie our corpses," Igal Sarna, Hadashot, 24.9.1985. (h)

"We captured. We the cannibals," NRG Internet site, 24.9.2004. (h)

"The monster on the mountain," Haolam Haze, 14.11.1973. (h)

"It was very important for them not to walk the way of the paratroopers," Gadi Blum, Hair, 13.9.1991. (h)

"File Operation Dessert is published—that's how the Hermon was taken," Ahikam Moshe David, Maariv, 12.5.2012.

Lieutenant Colonel (res.) Oren Elhanan, op. cit. pp. 276–279. (h)

Asher Dani, ed., "The northern command in the Yom Kippur war, Operation Dessert"; Re-capturing the Hermon, The Syrians on the fences, Maarakhot Publishers, 2008, pp. 261–289. (h)

Shemesh Elyashiv, "Slow and wise with quick success (Paratrooper brigade 317 in the battle for capturing the Syrian Hermon, October 21–22, 1973)"; The hell with you, move forward! (On speed in the battlefield), Modan publishers, Maarakhot, 2011, pp.48–67. (h)

Becker Avihai, "Indians on hill no.16, a company at the Hermon battle," Ministry of Defense publishers, Jerusalem 2003.

Interview of David Zarfati, Golami brigade fighter.

19: "Opera" in Baghdad and "Arizona" in Syria, 1981 and 2007

"Opera," -1981

"IAF Commander, at the time of the nuclear-reactor bombing, David Ivry," from an interview published in the IAF magazine, Aharon Lapidot, Journal 118, 1.12.1997. (h)

Nakdimon Shlomo, "Tamuz in Flames," Yedioth Ahronoth Edition, 1986. (h)

"We made a bet which one of us will stay in Baghdad's central square," Alex Fishman, Amit Meidan, Yedioth Ahronoth, 1.8.1997. (h)

"Comparison: Entebbe, Iraq, Tunis," Hadashot, 3.10.1985.

"The pilot who led the attack on the nuclear reactor, the pilot who planned the operation," Yedioth Ahronoth reporters, 16.6.1981. (h)

"A special interview with an unnamed Colonel—the planner," Yaakov Erez, Maariv 12.6.1981. (h)

"Operation Opera, Lieutenant General Aviem Sella, one of the planners," Ron Ben Ishai, Yedioth Ahronoth, 28.4.1995. (h)

"Opera," Shlomo Nakdimon, Bamahane, 1.6.2001. (h)

"Israeli aircraft attacked the Iraqi nuclear reactor from Iranian territory—claims a British writer," Amos Ben-Vered, Haaretz, 9.8.1991. (h)

"The Government communique," Maariv, 9.6.1981. (h)

Interview of Zeev Raz.

"Arizona," 2007

"Attacking the nuclear reactor in Syria—step by step," Gordon Thomas, Epoch times, 21.11.2008. (h)

"The Story of 'Operation Orchard'—How Israel destroyed Syria's Al Kibar nuclear reactor," Erich Follath and Holger Stark, Der Spiegel, February 11, 2009.

"Israel thwarted Syria's plan to attack," infolive.tv, September 17, 2007.

"Sayeret Matkal collected nuclear material in Syria," Ynet, 23.9.2007. (h)

"Israel forwarded intelligence to the USA prior to the attack," Ynet, 21.9.2009 (h)

"Due to secrecy Syria did not protect the site which was bombed," Arie Egozi, Orly Azulai, Yedioth Ahronoth, 4.11.2007. (h)

"Report: a Commando unit landed in Syria a month before the bombing of the nuclear reactor," Yossi Melman, Haaretz, 19.3.2009. (h)

"The Iranian connection," Alex Fishman, Yedioth Ahronoth, 16.9.2007. (h)

"Sayeret Matkal collected nuclear samples in Syria" Jerry Louis, as quoted by Yossi Yehoshua and Idan Avni, Yedioth Ahronoth, 23.9.2007. (h)

"The night of the bomb," Michael Bar-Zohar and Nissim Mishal, Yedioth Ahronoth, 13.8.2010. (h)

20: "Did They Have Machins Guns?" 1982

"I knew that we had to conquer the Beaufort," Mazal Mualem, Bamahane, 8.6.1988. (h)

"Conquest of the Beaufort," Brigadier General (res.) Avigdor Kahalani, Maarakhot 413, July 2007. (h)

"Revenge Commander calling," Igal Sarna, Yedioth Ahronoth, 6.1.1987.(h)

"Hadad raised his flag over the Beaufort and said: We are here with the help of God and the IDF," Joseph Walter and Shaya Segal, Maariv, 9.6.1982. (h)

"Battle over the Beaufort restarted," Moshe Zonder, Tel-Aviv magazine, 2.7.1993. (h)

"Cannon crews facing the fortress," Igal lev, Maariv, 11.6.1982. (h)

"Battle of the Beaufort—the officers were the first to attack," Shira Ben-Zion, Bamahane, 14.7.1982. (h)

"I started advancing and got scared. Darkness, night, moving shadows," Tal Zagraba, Bamahane, 11.1.2008. (h)

"The battle for the Beaufort, Lebanon war, Arab documents and sources," Collecting materials, editing and analysis: Reuven Avi-Ran, Maarakhot, Tel-Aviv, 1987, pp. 20–25. (h)

Tamir Moshe (Chico), "A war with no medals," Maarakhot, Ministry of Defense publishers, 2006, p. 28. (h)

Interview of Gabi Ashkenazi.

21: "It Was a Great Concert with Many Instruments," 1982

Rosenthal Rubik, "Lebanon: the other war," Sifriat Poalim, Hakibutz Haartzi, Hashomer Hatzair, 1983, pp. 67–75. (h)

Cohen Eliezer (Cheeta) and Lavi Zvi, op cit. pp. 604–620.

Ben David Ofer Colonel (res.), "The Lebanon campaign," Tel-Aviv, pp. 68–72. (h)

Reuven Avi-Ran, op. cit. pp. 91–93.

"Six Days in June," Lior Shlain and Noam Ofir, IAF Magazine, no.145, 1.6.2002. (h)

"David Ivry, the ninth Commander (October 1977–December 1982)," Aharon Lapidot, IAF Magazine, no. 118, 1.12.1997. (h)

"How we destroyed the disposition of land to air rockets in the first Lebanon war—1982,"Major General (res.) David Ivry, Fisher strategic research institute, air and space, 2007. (h)

Interview of Aviem Sella.

22: "Abu Jihad Sent Us," 1988

Zonder Moshe, "Sayeret Matkal, the assassination of Abu Jihad," Keter Publishers, Jerusalem, 2000, pp. 238–248. (h)

"Liquidation of Abu Jihad: a professional work in less than 5 minutes," Uzi Mahanaimi, Dani Sade, Edwin Eitan reporting from Paris; Yohanan Lahav reporting from London, Yedioth Ahronoth, 17.4.1988. (h)

"The Liquidation," Noemi Levitzki, Yedioth Ahronoth, 5.4.1993. (h)

"The Jihad against Abu Jihad," Ronen Bergman, Yedioth Ahronoth, 23.3.2012. (h)

"The Israelis shot my father and mother shouted: Stop!" Semadar Perri, Yedioth Ahronoth, 22.4.1994. (h)

"That is how Abu Jihad was killed," Al Hamishmar, 17.10.1990. (h)

"4000 Israelis took part in the elimination of the terrorist Abu Jihad," according to Robert Fisk, The Independent, as quoted in Maariv, 13.4.2001. (h)

"Um Jihad, his widow, talks . . ." Yassar Muassi, Emza Natania, 29.10.1993. (h)

Interview with family members of Miriam Ben- Yair.

23: "Where Is the ship?" 2002

"Disclosure: That's how the Shayetet captured the weapons-carrying boat Karine A," Hannan Greenberg, Maariv, 13.1.12. (h)

"The old man and the sea," Amir Oren, Haaretz, 11.1.2002.

"Suddenly, out of the dark, the commando fighters appeared," Yoav Limor, NRG Internet site, 6.1.2002. (h)

"Seized arms would have vastly extended Arafat's arsenal," James Bennet, New York Times, January 12 2002

"The weapons-carrying boat Victoria, accompanied by IDF forces, docked in Ashdod port," Amir Buhbut, Maariv, 16.3.2011. (h)

"The Navy captured the weapons-carrying boat that made its way from Turkey to Gaza," Amir Buhbut, Maariv, 15.3.2011. (h)

"The Idf forces captured a weapons-carrying boat from Syria to the Gaza strip," Ron Ben Ishai, Yoav Zeitun, Ynet, 15.3.2011. (h)

"What brought to the capture of the Karine A," Jacky Hugi, Maariv, 22.1.09. (h)

"Broke the waves," Nahum Barnea, Yedioth Ahronoth, 29.9.2004. (h)

"Israel recorded Arafat talking about buying the weapons-carrying boat," Ilan Nachshon, Yedioth Ahronoth, 17.1.2002. (h)

"I have been on many enemy boats," Igal Sarna, Yedioth Ahronoth, 11.1.2002. (h)

Lecture by Admiral Eli (Chiney) Marom at a conference in the Israel Intelligence Heritage and Commemoration Center, 29.2.2012. (h)

Interview of Shaul Mofaz.

24: Holocaust Remembrance Day in the Nablus Qasbah, 2002

Harel Amos, Issasharof Avi, "The seventh war," Yedioth Ahronoth publishers, Tel Aviv, 2005. (h)

The battle over the Qasbah in Nablus: 13 armed Palestinians were killed," Amira Hess, Amos Harel, Aliza Arbeli, Haaretz, 7.4.2002. (h)

"You are alive and fighting like in a movie," Felix Frish, 8.4.2002. (h)

"Two soldiers were killed in Jenin camp," Amos Harel. Amira Hess, Haaretz, 8.4.2002.(h)

"At 6.30 the last wanted terrorists surrendered in the Nablus Qasbah," Amos Harel, Haaretz, 9.4.2002. (h)

"A senior military Fatah commander was killed in the Qasbah," Globe's, 7.4.2002. (h)

"Between the walls" Alex Fishman, Yedioth Ahronoth, 30.3.2012. (h)

"Lieutenant Colonel Ofek Buhris is expected to be the first decorated soldier of operation Defensive Shield," Yoav Limor, NRG, 31.5.2012. (h)

"The terrorists did not notice us, they walked calmly like reserve soldiers on leave," Tal Zagraba, Bamahane, 20.3.2009. (h)

"Adventures of the naval commando in the alleys of Jenin," Yoav Limor, Israel Today, 30.3.2012. (h)

"Ten years to Defensive Shield," Ron Ben-Ishai, Ynet, 30.3.2012. (h)

"Did we defeat Palestinian terror?" Bamahane, 1.4.2012. (h)

Interview of Aviv Kochavi.

25: The Never-Ending Story in Gaza: 2008, 2012, 2014

Cast Lead 2008

"Head of UNRWA: There are members of Hamas in the organization. It's not a problem," Diana-Bachor-Nir, Ynet, 4.10.2004. (h)

"Gaza: 10 killed in IAF attck: Senior Hamas commander killed," Amir Buhbut, NRG, 29.12.2008. (h)

"IAF attacked targets at the strip northern part," Nir Yahav, Yehoshua Breiner, Walla!, 31.12.2008. (h)

"Galant after the liquidation: we pressured Hamas heavily," Shmulik Hadad, NRG, 15.1.2009. (h)

"Mashal offered Quiet for lifting the siege," Reuters, Ynet, 29.12.2009. (h)

The government confirmed recruiting thousands of reserve soldiers," Walla!, 28.12.2008. (h)

"IDF opened artillery fire: hundreds of shells were fired," Ynet, 3.1.2009. (h)

"The ground operation started: IDF hit tens of terrorists," Ynet, 3.1.2009. (h)

"The ground operation started: IDF forces entered the Gaza strip," Hanan Greenberg, Ynet, 3.1.2009.

"Palestinian report: The IDF split the Gaza strip into three parts," Or Heller, Allon Ben David, Nana 10 Internet Site, 4.1.2009. (h)

"The target—attacking Gaza. The result—perfect," Amir Buhbut, NRG, 27.12.2008. (h)

"General Security service: Hamas activists are hiding in hospitals in Gaza," Rony Sofer, Hanan Greenberg, Ynet, 31.12.2008. (h)

"Head of a Gaza hospital: Diskin Lies," Daniel Edelson, Ynet, 31.12.2008. (h)

"Han Yunes: two Hamas senior commanders were liquidated in the attack," Amir Buhbut, NRG, 4.1.2009. (h)

"IDF to the Supreme Court: Rockets were launched from the hospital, that is why it was bombed," Shmuel Mitelman, NRG, 15.1.2009. (h)

"The Chief of staff visited secretly the fighters in Gaza," Yehoshua Breiner, Walla!, 8.1.2009. (h)

"General Galant, Commander of the southern district, returns to the sea of Gaza," Amir Buhbut, NRG, 9.1.2009. (h)

"IDF: Fire was opened from the doctor's house and UNRWA compound," Hanan Greenberg, Ynet, 17.1.2009.

"Commotion in Sheba hospital: The doctor from Gaza is spreading propaganda," Dudi Cohen, Meital Yassur Beit-Or, Ynet, 17.1.2009. (h)

"Olmert declared ceasefire: mission accomplished," Rony Sofer, Ynet, 17.1.2009. (h)

"With bared teeth: Oketz dogs to catch stone throwers," Amir Buhbut, Maariv, February 4 2010.

"Israeli commander: 'We rewrote rules of war for Gaza conflict'," The Belfast Telegraph (Jerusalem), March 6, 2010.

"Rockets hit Israel, breaking Hamas truce," Isabel Kershner, International Herald Tribune, June 25, 2008.

"Israel Rejected Hamas Ceasefire Offer in December," IPS, January 9 2009.

"Gaza-Israel truce in jeopardy," Al Jazeera, December 15, 2009.

"In Gaza, Both Sides Reveal New Gear," Defense News, January 5, 2009.

"Israeli troops, tanks slice deep into Gaza," Ibrahim Barzak and Jason Keyser, Associated Press, January 4 2009, azcentral.com., February 18, 2009.

"Israeli arsenal deployed against Gaza during Operation Cast Lead," Journal of Palestine Studies (Institute for Palestine Studies), XXXVIII (3): 175–191. ISSN 1533–8614. Esposito, Michele K. (Spring 2000). March 6, 2010.

"Israel enters Gaza: Negotiating with extreme prejudice," Klein Aaron, Time, January 3, 2009.

"Palestinians: Mother, 4 children killed in IDF Gaza offensive," Amos Harel, Yanir Yagna and Yoav Stern, Ha'aretz, January 3, 2009.

"Reconsidering the Goldstone report on Israel and war crimes," Richard Goldstone, Washington Post, April 1, 2011.

Interview of Yoav Galant.

Pillar of Defence

The IAF Commander said "Kill the bastard." The missiles were fired at Jabari. The Sunday Times report, Uzi Mahanaimi, as quoted in Maariv, NRG, 18.11.12. (h)

"Hamas Military leader Ahmed Jabari killed on a missile strike by Israeli Defense force," Ted Thornkill, The Huffington Post UK, November 15, 2012.

"IDF refrains from killing civilians, but still has not learned the nature of Hamas," Amira Hess, Haaretz, 16.11.12. (h)

"The assassination and the state of alert," Nahum Barnea, Sima Kadmon, Alex Fishman, Eitan Haber, Yoaz Hendel, Yedioth Ahronoth, 15.11.12. (h)

"The Hamas commander was killed; a large scale operation in the Gaza strip," Amos Harel and Avi Issasharof, Aluf Ben, Amir Oren, Yossi Verter, Haaretz, 15.11.12. (h)

"A smokescreen," Alex Fishman, Yedioth Aharonoth, the Magazine,16.11.2012. (h)

"Efforts to reach a ceasefire," Nahum Barnea, Shimon Shiffer, Alex Fishman, Yedioth Ahronoth, 18.11.2012. (h)

"A defense of iron," Eitan Haber, Yedioth Ahronoth, 18.11.12. (h)

"Netanyahu: I agree to a general ceasefire, but if the [rocket] firing does not stop, we'll invade Gaza," Barak Ravid, Haaretz, 18.11.12. (h)

"In our field," Alex Fishman, Yedioth Ahronoth, 21.11.12. (h)

"Rockets fall in two schools in Ashkelon; A senior Jihad commander killed," Gili Cohen, Yanir Yanga, Haim Levinson, Jacki Hugi, Haaretz, 20.11.12. (h)

"A night meeting of the "Nine"; Obama presses for a ceasefire," Yedioth Ahronoth, 20.11.12. (h)

"'Red Paint' from Beer-Sheba to Tel-Aviv," Yedioth Ahronoth, 16.11.12. (h)

"Israel and Hamas agreed to a ceasefire under Egyptian patronage," Barak Ravid, Jacki Hugi, Haaretz, 22.11.12. (h)

"The Mediator of the agreement: The head of the Mossad," Itamar Eichner, Yedioth Ahronoth, 22.11.12. (h)

"The light behind the cloud," Alex Fishman, Yedioth Ahronoth, 23.11.12. (h)

"Release Order," Eitan Gluckman, Matty Saiber, Zeev Goldshmidt, Yedioth Ahronoth, 23.11.12. (h)

"The Star War," Amir Shuan, Amira Lam, Yedioth Ahronoth, the Magazine, 23.11.12. (h)

Protective Edge

"Eitan's heroism," Yossi Yehoshua, Yedioth Ahronoth, 4.8.2014. (h)

"From depth I thee called," Eitan Glikman, Yedioth Ahronoth, 6.8.2014. (h)

""The hero who chased the terrorists," Yossi Yehoshua, Yedioth Ahronoth, 4.8.2014.

"Hamas tunnel in Gaza," Yossi Yehoshua, Yedioth Ahronoth, 31.7.2014. (h)

"The bombers," Ariela Ringel-Hoffman, Yedioth Ahronoth, 1.8.2014. (h)

"Fighting above and under the houses," Gili Cohen, Haaretz, 31.7.2014. (h)

"Advancing in the pace of the bulldozer," Amos Harel, Haaretz, 31.7.2014. (h)

"Hamas members coming to sting and disappear," Odded Shalom, Yedioth Ahronoth, 25.7.2014. (h)

"The light at the end," Alex Fishman, Yedioth Ahronoth, 12.8.2014. (h)

"Death tunnels," Semadar Perri, Yedioth Ahronoth, 12.8.2014. (h)

"Exposure to the future: new technologies," Haaretz, 1.8.2014. (h)

"I would have jumped into the tunnel—Colonel Ofer Winter," Yossi Yehoshua, Yedioth Ahronoth, 13.8.2014. (h)

"A non-choice war," Sima Kadmon, Yedioth Ahronoth, 15.8.2014. (h)

"An operation getting confused," Alex Fishman, Yedioth Ahronoth, 15.8.2014. (h)

"Bank of targets and reality?" Asaf Hazani, Haaretz , 15.8.2014. (h)

"Sorry we have told you to return home," Yedioth Ahronoth, 14.8.2014. (h)

"IDF has lost its creativity," Michael Bar-Zohar, Ynet, opinions, 11.8.2014.

"ISIS (Dai`sh) in Gaza," Michael Bar-Zohar, Ynet, opinions, 24.8.2014. (h)

Interview of Amir Peretz.

26: From the Heart of Africa to Jerusalem: Operation Moses 1984 and Operation Solomon 1991

Adega Abraham, "The voyage to the dream," self-edition, Tel-Aviv, 2000. (h)

Shimron Gad, "Bring me the Jews of Ethiopia," Maariv publishers, Hed-Arzi, Or-Yehuda, 1988. (h)

Shimron Gad, "The Mossad and the Myth; the best smugglers in the world," Keter, Jerusalem, pp. 207–233. (h)

Toren Yaron (editor) "Operation Solomon: Beita Israel coming back home," The Jewish agency—Department of Immigration and Absorption, Jerusalem, 1994, pp. 28–35. (h)

"The price: 4000 dead," Ronen Bergman, Yedioth Ahronoth, 3.7.1998. (h)

"The one responsible for Operation Solomon: All the Falashmura should be brought to Israel," Bareket Feldman, Haaretz, 28.5.2006. (h)

"The Shayetet and the Mossad in a rare documentation, in Operation Moses," (Hadashot), channel 2, Israeli TV. (h)

"Military Operations behind enemy lines, Shaldag unit," Michal Danieli, PAZAM, Internet site, 1.7.2011. (h)

"Third place: Shaldag," Yoav Limor and Allon Ben David, Ynet, 14.2.2008. (h)

"Operation Solomon," IAF Internet site. (h)

"Flotilla 13 landed in Sudan," Arie Kiezel, Yedioth Ahronoth, 18.3.1994. (h)

"There was no one who was not moved, even me," Ravid Oren, Yedioth Ahronoth, 20.5.2011. (h)

"The IDF rescued the Ethiopian Jewry," Hadashot, 26.5.1991. (h)

"Shai said no," Orit Galili, Haaretz, 3.6.1991. (h)

"Exodus from Ethiopia," Tudor Perfitte, Yedioth Ahronoth, 1.11.1985. (h)

"Following him in the desert," Smadar Shir, Yedioth Ahronoth, 17.7.2009. (h)

Interview of Benyamin (Beni) Ganz.

ACKNOWLEDGMENTS

The story of the perilous missions described in our book is based on a multitude of sources: books and articles; archival documents, some of which had never been published before; Internet sites; interviews with a great number of past and present IDF officers, soldiers and statesmen. We thank the IDF Archives, the authors of the books and articles presented in our bibliography and the fighters themselves—some of them still in uniform, many of them retired or holding major civilian positions. The IDF spokesman, General Yoav ("Poli") Mordechai, together with his devoted staff, gave us very useful assistance from the moment this project was born.

We are also very grateful for the help of Ms. Nily Falic, chairperson of the FIDF—"Friends of the IDF"—association; General (res.) Gershon ("Jerry") Yitzhak, former director of the FIDF in New York, and his successor, General (res.) Meir Khalifi; the Hecht Foundation; and General (res.) Avigdor Kahalani, the ultimate Israeli hero, today chairman of the Association for the Israeli Soldiers' Welfare.

Our project was encouraged and supported by our excellent agent, Al Zuckerman, "Mr. Writers' House"; his foreign rights magician, Ms. Maja Nikolic; and our publishers, Dov Eichenwald of Yedioth Aharonoth Books for the Israeli version, and Dan Halpern at Ecco/Harper-Collins. The English manuscript, translated together with Nathan K. Burstein, took its final shape after additional research and rewriting; once again, the contribution of our home editor, Nilly Ovnat, was invaluable. In New York we got the devoted and efficient assistance of our editor, the excellent Gabriella Doob; and Katherine Beitner was incomparable in spreading the good word. Special thanks to Ecco's associate publisher, Craig Young, for his wise counsels and ideas.

And finally, thanks again to our superb ladies, Galila Bar-Zohar and Amy Korman, who stood by us while this second book—after Mossad—was researched, written and saw the light of day.

INDEX

Abu Aisha, Amar, 304
Abu Jihad (aka Khalil al-Wazir):
    assassination of, 258-64, 265
Abu Khdeir, Mohammed, 299
Abu Rahma, Fayez, 261
Abu-Sneina, Ali Taha, 141
Abuelaish, Izzeldin, 291, 324
Achmon, Arik, 186
Adam, Yekutiel "Kuti," 4, 7, 8, 9, 10,
    11, 24, 174
Adan, Avraham "Bren," 180, 181, 188,
    198
Adwan, Kamal, 165, 170
Ahdut HaAvoda party, 91
Air Force, U.S., 313-14
Air France Flight 139, hijacking of, 1-5.
    See also Entebbe
Akawi, Omar, 274
Akers (Norwegian firm), 116
Al-Ahram newspaper (Cairo), 86
Al Aqsa Martyrs Brigades, 284
Al Ra'i newspaper (Jordan): Crate
    Operation story in, 160
al-Wazir, Hanan, 259, 262, 263, 264
al-Wazir, Intisar. See Umm Jihad
al-Wazir, Khalil. See Abu Jihad
al-Wazir, Nadal, 259, 263

Alaluf (IDF soldier), 220-21
Aliya Bet, 52
Allem, Uataf (pseud.), 261
Allenby Camp: and War of
    Independence, 35
Allon, Yigal, 91
Almog, Ze'ev, 104, 106, 107, 109
Alon, Emmanuel, 310
Altnuder, Dieter, 168
Aman (IDF Intelligence Department),
    233
Ambar, Ido, 25
Amer, Abdel Hakim, 53
Amer, Marshal, 58
American Armor Museum (Fort Knox,
    Kentucky), 205
Amin, Idi, 5, 6, 9, 10, 14, 15, 17, 21, 23
Amiot, Felix, 114, 117, 119
Ammunition Hill (Jerusalem), 92,
    94-96
Ammunition Hill, Operation, 226,
    228-32
Ankelevitz, Maurice, 67
Arab Legion. See Jordanian Legion
Arad, Yigal, 95
Arafat City: Cast Lead Operation and,
    287

Arafat, Yasser
  Abu Jihad and, 258
  and assassination of Black September
    leaders, 175
  Defensive Shield Operation and, 279,
    284, 285
  as Fatah leader, 240, 258
  Mukataa as headquarters for, 278
  Peace for Galilee Operation and, 240
  as PLO leader, 139, 141, 164, 241
  Umm Jihad in government of, 264
  U.S. and, 274, 275
  and weapons supplies for terrorist
    organizations, 269, 274, 275, 276
  See also Palestinian Authority
Arditi, Danny, 150
Argov, Shlomo, 241
Arieli (Israeli aircraft mechanic), 144
Arins, Jean-Pierre, 140
Arizona, Operation, 224, 232-35
Armored Corps (IDF), 84
Army, U.S., 31
Asgari, Ali Reza, 232-33
Ashkenazi, Gavriel "Gabi," 242, 245-
    46, 303-4, 323
Ashkenazi, Giora, 93-94, 98
Ashkenazi, Marko, 152, 153
Assad, Hafez al-, 178, 236
Atar, Raed al-, 294
Atomic Energy Commission, Israeli, 46,
    319
Atrash, Abd Aziz el, 140-41, 146, 147,
    150
Atzmon, Ben-Zion, 198
Augusta Victoria compound: Six Day
    War and, 96, 98
Avinun, Dani, 109
Avishai (Flotilla 13 frogman), 172
Ayalon, Amichai "Ami," 103, 107-8, 110-
    11, 321
Azout (IDF soldier), 221

Baader-Meinhof terrorist gang, 4, 8
Balata refugee camp, 281
Bamba (IDF reconnaissance unit), 200
Bar, Dov, 106-7, 108
Bar-Lev, "Borka": Entebbe and, 9, 10,
    21

Bar-Lev, Haim "Kidoni"
  "Chinese Farm" and, 198, 200-201
  Green Island raid and, 105-6
  and hijacking of Sebana Airlines plane,
    142
  named chief of staff, 102
  professional career of, 321
  Ras Gharib raid and, 125, 129
  War of Attrition and, 105-6, 125, 129
  Yom Kippur War, 191, 198, 200-201
Bar-Lev, Omer, 20
Bar-Zohar, Michael, 181, 185
Barak Brigade. See 188th Brigade (IDF)
Barak, Ehud
  and Abu Jihad assassination, 259, 260,
    261
  and assassination of Black September
    leaders, 164, 165, 166, 168, 169-70,
    171, 174-75
  "Chinese Farm" and, 200
  as commander of Sayeret Matkal, 144
  Crate Operations and, 156, 157, 158
  decorations for, 174
  Entebbe and, 8, 20
  and hijacking of Sabena Airlines
    plane, 148, 150, 153
  personal and professional
    background of, 144, 322
  Pillar of Defense Operation and, 295
  and prisoner exchanges, 156, 157,
    158
  Spring of Youth Operation and, 164,
    165, 166, 168, 169-70, 171, 174-75
  Yom Kippur War and, 200
Barghouti, Marwan, 279
Barkai, Zvika, 239, 241, 242-43
Barkat, Yeshayahu, 124
Baruchin, Avinoam, 211
Bat Galim (Israeli rescue ship), 311,
    312
Baum, Shlomo, 41
"Bay of Pigs" plan, Israeli, 6-7
BBC
  and "Boats of Cherbourg," 119
  Six Day War and, 97
Beaufort, battle for, 239-46
Be'eri (kibbutz), 39
Begin Doctrine, 231, 232

Begin, Menachem
  Entebbe and, 10, 22, 24
  and Government of National Unity, 76
  and Iraq's Osirak nuclear reactor, 226, 228
  and Lebanon, 238, 240, 241, 245
  and Likud party, 224
  as minister without portfolio, 76
  Opera Operation and, 224
  Peace for Galilee Operation and, 238, 240, 241, 245
  and rescue of Jews from Ethiopia, 310
  Sinai Campaign and, 66
  Six Day War and, 91, 97
Beirut, Lebanon
  assassination of Black September leaders in, 162, 163-75
  bombing of airport at, 114
Ben-Ari, Uri, 96
Ben Eliezer, Benyamin, 277
Ben Eliyahu, Eitan, 132
Ben-Gal, Yanosh, 8, 9, 204, 205, 209, 210, 211, 212
Ben-Gurion, David
  Black Arrow Operation and, 37, 45
  and Britain, 64
  Eshkol and, 76
  and Har-Zion arrest, 42
  named defense minister, 37
  proclaims Israeli independence, 28
  and Rafi party, 76
  resignations of, 37, 76
  retaliation/reprisal strategy of, 37, 46
  Sevres summit and, 63-66
  Sharett and, 37
  Sharon and, 42, 67, 180
  Sinai Campaign and, 50, 61, 62, 63-66, 72
  Six Day War and, 79
  War of Independence and, 14, 29-30, 31, 32
Ben-Hanan, Yossi, 212
Ben-Menahem, Yitzhak "Gulliver," 41
Ben-Natan, Arthur, 12
Ben-Nun, Avihu, 86-87, 136, 313, 321
Ben-Shoham, Yitzhak, 204
Ben Yair, Eliyahu, 265

Ben Yair, Frieda, 265
Ben Yair, Ilan, 265
Ben Yair, Miriam, 258, 264-65
Ben Yair, Rachel, 264-65
Bentzur (Israeli soldier), 98
Beth Zurif: raid on, 43
Bethlehem: and Defensive Shield Operation, 283-84
Betzer, Moshi "Muki," 4, 17-18, 26, 159, 164, 169, 170, 171, 322
Bilby, Kenneth, 33
Bin-Nun, Avihu, 136
Black Arrow/Gaza Operation, 38-39, 42, 43-47
Black March (2002), 278-79
Black September (terrorist group)
  assassination of leaders of, 162, 163-75
  hijacking of Sabena Airlines plane by, 140-53, 164
  and Munich Olympics massacre, 164
  as strike force for PLO, 139
Bloc Etzion settlements: and War of Independence, 35, 182
Bloch, Dora, 20
Blutstein (IDF soldier), 221
"Boats of Cherbourg," 113-21, 322
Bohbot, Amir, 288
Boneh, Solel, 32
Böse, Wilfried, 4
Botzer, Avraham "Cheetah," 116
Bou Said, Sidi, 259
Bouillon, Godfrey de, 41
BourgIIs-Maunoury, Maurice, 63
Boussard, Charles, 168
Bravehearts, Operation, 179-90, 193
Britain. See Great Britain
British Army, 28, 182
Britton, Sara. See Tannous, Rima
Brosh, Elyashiv "Shibi," 51, 54, 55, 56, 57, 58
Brothers, Operation, 311
Brunner, Danny, 150
Brzezinski, Zbigniew, 15-16
Buhris, Ilan, 311
Buhris, Ofek, 282
Bull, Odd, 89, 90
Burma Road, Israeli, 33-34, 35, 36

Bush, George H.W., 313, 314
Bush, George W., 233, 234, 275, 276

Camp David Accords, 189
Carlos (terrorist), 3, 4
Carter, Jimmy, 7-8, 15
Cast a Giant Shadow (film), 35
Cast Lead, Operation, 287-93, 294, 295, 324
Central Intelligence Agency (CIA), 233
Chaban-Delmas, Jacques, 120
Challe, Maurice, 64
Cheney, Dick, 231
Cherbourg, Boats of, 113-21, 322
"Chinese Farm": Yom Kippur War and, 186, 191, 192-201
Church of the Nativity (Bethlehem), 283
Coastal Road massacre, 258
Cohen, Eliezer "Cheetah," 125-26
Cohen, Victor, 143, 144
Cohen, Yoram, 294
Cohen Family:, flag of, 92, 99
Columbia (space shuttle), 230
Crate 1, Operation, 156
Crate 2, Operation, 156-57
Crate 3, Operation, 155, 158-61
Czechoslovakia: Egypt's arms deal with, 50, 62

Dabash, Hezi, 199
Dagan, Meir, 233, 323
Dagan, Nehemiah, 125, 126, 127, 128, 129-30, 322
Dahab, Zvi, 68
Dahari (IDF soldier), 221
Daily Express (London): Ras Gharib raid story in, 128
Daoud, Abdallah, 283
Daughters of Jacob Bridge, 204
Daughters for Life, 324
David (Israeli language specialist), 132, 133
Davidi, Aharon
    Black Arrow Operation and, 38-39, 43, 44, 45, 46
    Gur and, 91

professional career of, 320
Sinai Campaign and, 66, 68, 69, 70
David's Sling (Peres), 7-8
Dayan, Moshe
    appointed defense minister, 76, 78, 102
    appointed IDF chief of staff, 42
    and assassination of Black September leaders, 166, 174
    Bar-Lev and, 102
    Black Arrow Operation and, 45
    "Boats of Cherbourg" and, 116
    "Chinese Farm" and, 196
    Crate Operations and, 155
    and downing of Ilyushin ll-14 plane, 58
    Entebbe and, 5, 24
    and failed operations of IDF, 39-40
    Golan Heights and, 203
    Gur and, 91
    and hijacking of Sabena Airlines plane, 142, 143, 144, 145, 146, 147, 152
    Jerusalem and, 88, 91-92, 96, 97
    and Marcus's death, 34
    Peres and, 5, 24, 37
    personality and character of, 65
    professional career of, 64-65, 319
    and Rafi party, 76
    Ras Gharib raid and, 128
    as revolutionizing the IDF, 41
    Sevres summit and, 63-66
    Sharett and, 37
    Sharon and, 40, 67, 181
    Sinai Campaign and, 60, 61, 63-66, 72
    Six Day War and, 78, 88, 91-92, 96, 97
    and Soviet pilots with Egyptian Air Force, 134
    Spring of Youth Operation and, 166, 174
    Unit 101 and, 41
    War of Attrition and, 128, 134
    Yom Kippur War and, 180, 181, 196, 203
Dayan, Uzi
    Crate Operations and, 155, 157, 158-59, 160, 161

and hijacking of Sabena Airlines plane, 148, 150, 151
and prisoner exchanges, 155, 157, 158-59, 160, 161
professional career of, 322
Dayan, Yehuda, 41
de Gaulle, Charles, 76, 78, 112, 114, 115
Debré, Michel, 119-20
Defensive Shield, Operation, 275, 277, 278-85
Deif, Mohammed, 293
Dichter, Avi, 295
Digli, Menachem, 105, 107
Dimona nuclear reactor, 2, 257
Dir al-Zur (Syria) nuclear reactor, 232-35
Diskin, Yuval, 291
Doron Unit (IDF), 17
Dovik (Davidi deputy), 70, 71
Drori, Amir, 216, 219, 220, 221

Eban, Abba, 89
Eden, Anthony, 64
Efron, Moshe, 45
Egoz Commando Unit (IDF), 158, 278, 279
Egypt
Black Arrow Operation and, 38, 39, 43-46
and Camp David Accords, 189
Czechoslovakia arms deal with, 50, 62
and downing of Ilyushin ll-14, 53-58
French relations with, 63
Green Island raid and, 103-11
and Hamas-Israeli mediation, 288, 298
Jordan's military pact with, 89
Pillar of Defense Operation and, 296, 297
and prisoner exchanges, 156
and proposal for cease-fire in Gaza, 300
Ras Gharib raid and, 123-30
and rescue of Jews from Ethiopia, 310
Sinai Campaign and, 50, 53, 60, 61-73

Six Day War and, 3, 77-87, 89, 92
Soviet relations with, 50, 62, 122, 132-38
War of Attrition and, 102, 103-11, 115, 123-30, 132-38
War of Independence and, 28, 30
Yom Kippur War and, 178, 179-90, 192-201
Egyptian Air Force
Green Island raid and, 105
Sinai Campaign and, 53
Six Day War and, 79-87, 89
Soviets pilots and, 132-38
War of Attrition and, 105, 132-38
Egyptian Army
Black Arrow Operation and, 39
"Chinese Farm" and, 192-201
IDF defeat of (1967), 133
Ras Gharib raid and, 123-30
Sinai Campaign and, 53, 72
Six Day War and, 78
Yom Kippur War and, 179-90, 192-201
890th Paratroop Battalion (IDF), 38, 72, 196-201
Eilam, Uzi
Black Arrow Operation and, 43, 44, 45, 46-47
professional career of, 319
Six Day War and, 47, 92, 96
Eini, Marcelle, 151
Eitan, Boaz, 155-56
Eitan, Rafael "Raful"
and Beirut airport bombing, 114
death of, 321
Golan Heights and, 204, 205, 207, 209, 211, 212, 227
Green Island raid and, 105, 106, 107, 109
and Iraq's Osirak nuclear reactor, 226, 227
Jerusalem and, 35
and Lebanon, 238, 248, 251
Peace for Galilee Operation and, 238
personal and professional background of, 227, 321
Ras Gharib raid and, 128
as role model for Mordechai, 197

Sinai Campaign and, 61, 66, 67, 72-73, 105, 227
Six Day War and, 105, 227
War of Attrition and, 105, 106, 107, 109, 128
War of Independence and, 35
Yom Kippur War, 204, 205, 207, 209, 211, 212, 227
El Al planes, 114, 146, 149, 315
Elazar, David "Dado"
and assassination of Black September leaders, 166, 167-68, 172, 174
"Chinese Farm" and, 198
Crate Operations and, 155-56, 157
death of, 319
Green Island raid and, 104
and hijacking of Sebana Airlines plane, 143, 145, 147, 149
Jerusalem and, 35
Palmach and, 181
prisoner exchanges and, 155-56, 157
professional career of, 319
Spring of Youth Operation and, 166, 167-68, 172, 174
War of Attrition and, 104
War of Independence and, 35
Yom Kippur War and, 178, 180, 198
Eldar, Shlomi, 291
Eldar, Yossi, 206
Elder, George, 168
Eliashiv, Yoram, 94
Eliyahu, Eitan Ben, 132, 134, 322
Elkayam, Saadia "Suppapo," 38, 41, 43, 44, 45, 46
Entebbe raid (Uganda, 1976)
Air France crew at, 13, 16, 20, 22
Air France Flight 139 lands at, 5
and Amin's "double," 14, 15, 17
Fantasy Council and, 10, 11, 14, 16, 24
and France, 7, 10, 12-13
heroes at, 25-26
and hijackers demands, 8
hostages at, 5-16, 20, 21-22, 24, 252
importance of, 252
Israeli attack on, 16-22
Israeli plans for attack on, 5-16, 24, 25

Mercedes at, 14, 15, 16, 17, 25
return of Israelis from, 22-23, 26
Epstein, Shlomo, 93
Eran, Omer, 150
Erdogan, Tayyip, 235
Erez, Hayim, 187
Eshel, Amir, 137-38, 294, 322
Eshkol, Levi, 76, 78, 88, 91, 97, 102
Eshkol, Yirmi, 94
Ethiopia
civil war in, 314
rescue of Jews from, 309-17
European Union, 296-97
Ezra, First Sergeant (IDF), 125-26

Falame (Jordan): attack on, 39-40
Fantasy Council: and Entebbe, 10, 11, 14, 16, 24
Fatah terrorists, 174, 240, 258, 259, 260, 279. See also specific person
fedayeen, 46, 61
Feinman, Tuvia, 132-33
50th Battalion (IDF), 125, 126, 166, 167, 168, 169, 189, 190
51st Battalion (IDF), 217, 219, 220, 267, 282
51st Brigade, Syrian, 204
55th Paratroopers Reserve Brigade (IDF), 6, 90, 99, 320
515th Intelligence Service Unit (IDF), 132, 133. See also Unit 8200 (IDF)
Flotilla 13 (IDF Navy Seals), 168, 169, 171, 172, 173, 309, 310, 311, 321
Focus, Operation
importance of, 252
and Six Day War, 77-87, 252
4th Armored Division (Egyptian), 182
14th Armored Brigade (IDF), 193
401st Brigade "Iron Trails" (IDF), 289
Fradkin, Yossi, 92
France
and "Boats of Cherbourg," 113-21
Egypt's relationship with, 63
and embargo on weapons for Israel, 76, 78, 112, 114, 115
and Entebbe, 7, 10, 12-13
and Iraq's Osirak nuclear reactor, 226

Israeli relations with, 62, 63-66, 76, 78, 112, 113-21
Sevres summit and, 63-66
Sinai Campaign and, 50, 60, 62-66, 72
Six Day War and, 76, 78
and Suez Canal, 50, 60, 62-66, 72
warning to PLO from, 261
Frenkel, Naftali, 298-99
Friedman, Breindel, 141
Friedman, Mordechai, 93, 116

Ga'ash Division (IDF), 244, 245
Galant, Yoav, 289, 291, 292-93, 324
Galilee Division (IDF), 245
Gantz, Benny, 294, 300, 316-17
Gaza
Black Arrow Operation in, 38-39, 42, 43-47
Cast Lead Operation in, 287-93, 294, 295, 324
Egyptian proposal for cease-fire in, 300
Hamas in, 286, 287-305
Iran as weapons supplier for terrorists in, 266, 270
Israeli retreat from, 286, 320
kidnapping and murder of three teenagers in, 298-99, 304
Pillar of Defense Operation in, 293-98, 302
Protective Edge Operation in, 298, 299-304
terrorists in, 286, 287-305
underground tunnels in, 287-88, 300-301
Gazit, Shlomo, 8, 24
German Revolutionary Cells, 4
Gershon, Yitzhak "Jerry," 280, 285, 324
Gideons, 52
Givati Brigade (IDF), 39-40, 289
Globe and Mail newspaper (Canada): and Cast Lead Operation, 290-91
Golan Heights
Six Day War and, 3, 99, 102
Syria and, 202, 203-13
Yom Kippur War and, 174, 180, 202, 203-13, 289

Golan, Yoav, 220
Golani Brigade (IDF)
Cast Lead Operation and, 289
Defensive Shield Operation and, 279, 280, 282
Peace for Galilee Operation and, 239, 240, 242, 243-46
Yom Kippur War and, 214, 215-21
Gold, Danny, 303
Goldstein, Dov, 72
Goldstone, Richard, 292
Gonen, Shmuel, 200
Government of National Unity, 76
Gozlan, Menachem, 199
Grapes of Wrath, Operation, 301
Great Britain
and Defensive Shield Operation, 279
Sevres summit and, 63-66
and Sinai Campaign, 50, 60, 62-66, 72
Six Day War and, 78
and Suez Canal, 50, 60, 62-66, 72
and War of Independence, 28, 137
in World War II, 128
"Grechkos" (Russian language specialists), 133, 137
Green Island: raid on, 103-11
Greid, Zeharia. See Atrash, Abd Aziz el
Gulf War, first (1991), 231, 296
Gur, Mordechai "Motta"
and Black Arrow Operation, 43, 47
and Brzezinski visit, 15
Crate Operations and, 157, 158
Davidi and, 90
Dayan and, 91
death of, 320
Eitan as IDF chief of staff successor to, 227
and Entebbe, 6-7, 8, 9-10, 11-12, 13, 14, 15, 16, 19, 22, 24, 320
Jerusalem and, 6, 91, 92, 96, 97, 98-100, 320
Peres and, 12, 13, 24
and prisoner exchanges, 158
professional career of, 6, 90-91, 320
Rabin and, 6
Sharon and, 6, 90, 91
Sinai Campaign and, 67, 68, 69, 70, 91

Six Day War and, 6, 90, 92, 96, 97, 98-100, 320
speech of, 99-100
and Temple Mount, 6, 98-100
War of Independence and, 6, 90
Yom Kippur War and, 182
Gur, Rita, 91
Gur, Ruthy, 98
Guttal, Didier, 95

Habib, Philip, 252
Haddad, Shmuel, 289
Haddad, Wadie, 3, 6, 23
Hadiri, Ali, 282
Hadley, Stephen, 233
Haganah, 64-65
Hagoel, Yossef, 93
Hakim, Jackie, 198
Halaili, Abu Haled el, 4
Haleor, Yechiel, 124
Halsa, Theresa, 140-41, 152
Halutz, Dan, 267, 275, 324
Hamas
  and Cast Lead Operation, 287-93, 294, 295, 324
  cease-fire between Israel and, 288, 298
  and Defensive Shield Operation, 281, 282
  Egyptian mediation between Israel and, 288, 298
  and Egyptian proposal for cease-fire in Gaza, 300
  in Gaza, 286, 287-305
  and kidnapping and murder of three teenagers in Gaza, 299, 304
  and Pillar of Defense Operation, 293-98, 302
  training camps for, 295
  U.S. denunciation of, 297
Haniyeh, Ismail, 297
Har-Zion, Meir "Har," 41-42, 45, 67, 97, 320
Har-Zion, Shoshana, 42, 320
Harel Brigade (IDF), 30-32
Harlev, Rafi, 8
Harnik, Giora "Goni," 242, 243, 244, 245-46

Harnik, Raya, 244
Harpaz, Rami, 132
Hasson, Miriam. See Halsa, Theresa
Hatzor airbase (Israel): bombing of, 81
Hawatmeh, Nayef, 166
Hawk Squadron (IAF), 232
Hebron: Israeli attack on, 42
Hershko, Surin, 19
Herut party, 91
Herzog, Yitzhak HaLevi, 32-33
Hetz, Yaki, 95
Hezbollah, 233, 236, 269, 301
Hod, Mordechai "Motti"
  and hijacking of Sebana Airlines plane, 143
  professional career of, 321
  Ras Gharib raid and, 125
  Six Day War and, 81, 82, 85
  and Soviet pilots with Egyptian Air Force, 134, 135, 137
  War of Attrition and, 125, 134, 135, 137
Hofesh, Levi, 71, 126
Hofi, Yitzhak "Haka"
  Crate Operations and, 158
  Entebbe and, 9, 11, 12, 14, 15
  Golan Heights and, 204, 205-6
  and Iraq's Osirak nuclear reactor, 227
  Mount Hermon and, 216
  and prisoner exchanges, 158
  and rescue of Jews from Ethiopia, 310
  Sinai Campaign and, 68, 69, 70
  Six Day War and, 82
  Yom Kippur War, 204, 205-6, 216
Holocaust Remembrance Day, 284-85
Holtzberg-Anderson, Mary, 150-51
Holtzberg-Anderson, Miriam, 153
Horev, Amos, 31-32
Hulda (kibbutz), 31
Husan reprisal raid, 47
Hussein (king of Jordan), 89, 164, 178, 225
Hussein, Saddam, 224, 225, 226, 229, 230, 231

IAF (Israeli Air Force)
  and Abu Jihad assassination, 259, 261

Cast Lead Operation and, 287-88
"Chinese Farm" and, 197
Entebbe and, 7, 14, 25
Green Island raid and, 105
and Iraq's Osirak nuclear reactor,
226-32
Karine A attack and, 267, 272, 273,
276
Kedesh/Sinai Campaign, 64
Lebanon War and, 248-50, 251-52
Mount Hermon and, 216
Peace for Galilee Operation and, 240
Pillar of Defense Operation and,
293, 294, 295-96, 297, 298
Ras Gharib raid and, 123, 124, 129
and rescue of Jews from Ethiopia,
312, 313-14, 315
and *Santorini* capture, 269
Six Day War and, 77-85, 89
and Soviet pilots in Egyptian Air
Force, 132-38
and Syria's nuclear reactor, 233, 234
and terrorism in Gaza, 300
U.S. cooperation with, 314
War of Attrition and, 105, 123, 124,
129, 132-38
War of Independence and, 137
Yom Kippur War and, 197, 216
See also specific squadron
IDF (Israeli Defense Forces)
and Abu Jihad assassination, 259,
260, 261
and assassination of Black
September leaders, 164, 165, 166
Black Arrow Operation and, 38, 39,
46
and Cast Lead Operation, 288, 289,
290, 291-92
"Chinese Farm" and, 192-201
code of ethics for, 154
Defensive Shield Operation and,
278, 279, 281-82, 283, 285
Entebbe and, 5, 6-7, 9, 10, 15, 19, 20,
21-22, 23
Ethiopian soldiers in, 315
failed operations of, 39-40
and family members on same
mission, 156

Golan Heights and, 203-13
Green Island raid and, 103, 104, 106,
109, 110
and hijacking of Air France Flight
139, 4, 5
and hijacking of Sebana Airlines
plane, 142-43
and Iron Dome system, 303
Karine A attack and, 267, 268
and kidnapping and murder of three
teenagers in Gaza, 299
Litani Operation and, 241
morale in, 105
and no soldier left behind, 154
Oranim ("Cedars") Operation and,
241
Peace for Galilee Operation and, 240
Pillar of Defense Operation and,
293, 295, 297
Ras Gharib raid and, 123-30
and rescue of Jews from Ethiopia,
310
retreat from Gaza of, 286
revolutionizing of, 41
Sinai Campaign and, 61, 72
Six Day War and, 82, 83, 85, 88, 90,
92
Spring of Youth Operation and, 164,
165, 166
and Sulieman assassination, 236
and Syria's nuclear reactor, 233, 235
and terrorism in Gaza, 299-301, 302
War of Attrition and, 103, 104, 106,
109, 110, 123-30
War of Independence and, 33, 142
Yom Kippur War and, 179-90, 192-
201, 203-13
See also specific person or unit
illegal immigrants: to Israel, 52
Ilyushin II-14 plane: downing of,
51-59
Inferno, Operation, 166-75
Intifada, 258, 262, 276
Iran
Islamic Revolution and, 226
and missiles for Hezbollah, 236
and Syria's nuclear reactor, 232-33
U.S. relations with, 226

as weapons supplier for Palestinian
Authority, 267-76
as weapons supplier for terrorists,
266
Iranian Revolutionary Guards, 275
Iraq
French relations with, 226
Golan Heights and, 207
Haddad in, 23
Osiraq nuclear reactor of, 224, 225-
32, 251, 252
Six Day War and, 78, 85
Soviet Union as weapons supplier
to, 133
War of Independence and, 28, 30
Yom Kippur War and, 207
Iron Dome (Israeli air defense
system), 296, 297-98, 301-5
ISIS, 301
Islamic Jihad, 283, 288, 296, 297, 298,
299
Islamic Revolution (1979), 226
Islamic University, 288
Isotope, Operation, 142-53
Israel
Ethiopian Jews in, 314-15
French embargo on weapons to, 76,
78, 112, 114, 115
French relations with, 62, 63-66, 76,
78, 112, 113-21
Independence Day (May 15) in, 78
proclamation of independence of, 28
Soviet relations with, 133-34
U.S. relations with, 112, 133, 134,
226, 231, 305
U.S. as weapons supplier for, 112,
226, 231
Israel Aircraft Industries, 144, 148
Israeli Military Industries (IMI), 80-
81, 303, 323
Ivry, David, 124-25, 226, 228, 232,
248, 251
Izz al-Din al-Qassam (Hamas death
squads), 287

Jabari, Ahmed, 293-94, 295
Jadid, Salah el, 178
Jaffar Nassim, Ahmed, 58-59

Jenin: battle at, 282-83
Jerusalem
Cohen flag for, 92, 99
Six Day War and, 6, 47, 87, 88, 89-
100, 102, 180, 320
War of Independence and, 29-36, 52,
92, 99
Zion Square bombing in, 258
Jerusalem reservist brigade, 283
Jewish Agency, 314
Johnson, Lyndon B., 112
Jordan
Egypt's military pact with, 89
PLO massacre in, 164
Sinai Campaign and, 53
Six Day War and, 3, 78, 79, 82, 85,
88, 89-100
War of Independence and, 28, 29, 183
Jordanian Air Force, 85
Jordanian Army: Six Day War and,
89-100
Jordanian Legion
IDF hostages of, 40-41
Sharon and, 40-41
Six Day War and, 90, 93, 94, 95, 96-
97, 98
War of Independence and, 29, 30,
33, 183
Jordanian National Guard, 42
Jordanian Police Academy
(Jerusalem), 92, 93-94, 96, 98
Joseph, Dov (Bernard), 32, 35

Kabha, Mustafa, 110
Kaddoumi, Farouk, 261, 262
Kadesh, Operation: Sinai Campaign
and, 53, 61-73
Kadima party, 224
Kahalani, Avigdor, 206, 207-11, 212,
213, 244, 323
Kahalani, Emanuel, 212
Kahaner, Shimon "Katcha," 42, 44,
207, 320
Kamenev, Captain (Soviet pilot), 135
Kandil, Hisham, 297
Kanji, Kamal, 161
Kaplinski, Moshe, 242, 245
Kapusta, Micha, 69, 70, 71, 96-97

Karine A (ship), 266, 267-76
Karten, Michael, 45
Kedem, Ezra "Shark," 118
Ken-Dror, Yehuda, 70, 71
Kendel, Yehuda, 95
Keshet (Israeli missile ship), 309
Khdeir, Mohammed Abu, 299
Kidron Creek: battle on, 96-97
Kimchi, Hadar, 114, 117, 118, 120-21, 322
Kiryat Malachi: Israeli strike on, 296
Klos C (ship), 266
Kochavi, Aviv, 281, 284-85, 324
Kol Israel radio, 61
Kraus, Menachem, 253
Kubaissi, Basil, 2
Kuhlmann, Brigitte, 4, 6
Kutakhov, Pavel Stepanovich, 137

Labor party, 224
Ladijanski, Oved, 71
Lahat, Shlomo, 53-54, 58
Laner, Dan, 207
Latrun, fortress of: and War of Independence, 29, 30, 31, 40
Lavi, Yoram, 41
Lebanese Army, 157, 172
Lebanon
  Beqaa Valley in, 247, 248-53
  evacuation of IDF forces from, 246
  Israel's first war with, 238, 239-46, 247, 248-53, 301
  Peace for Galilee Operation and, 238, 239-46
  PLO expelled from, 258
  and prisoner exchanges, 156-57, 158-61
  Six Day War and, 79, 85
  Syria's relations with, 247, 248-53
  U.S. mediation between Israel and, 252
  War of Independence and, 28
  See also Beirut
Lebanon War, first, 238, 239-46, 247, 248-53, 301
Lebanon War, second, 301, 303
Lee, Chai, 268
Leibovich, Martin, 126

Levin, Amiram, 12-13, 164, 170, 171
Levy, Deborah, 140, 151
Levy, Motti, 219, 221
Levy, Reginald, 140, 141, 145, 146-47, 151
Levy, Yaki, 198, 199
Lieberman, Avigdor, 295
Likud party, 180, 181, 224
Limassol (Cyprus): killing of Israeli sailors in, 258
Limon, Mordechai "Moka," 114, 115, 116, 117, 118, 119, 120, 322
Limor, Danny, 311
Lipkin-Shahak, Amnon
  and Abu Jihad assassination, 259
  and assassination of Black September leaders, 165, 166, 169, 171, 172, 173, 174, 175
  "Chinese Farm" and, 198
  decorations for, 174, 259
  professional career of, 322
  and rescue of Jews from Ethiopia, 314, 315
  Yom Kippur War and, 198
Litani, Operation, 241, 242, 301
Livne, Zvi, 171
Lloyd, Selwyn, 63-64
Lod Airport (Israel): Sabena Airlines plane at, 143-53
London *Sunday Times* newspaper, 234, 293
Lubrani, Uri, 314
Lufthansa plane: hijacking of, 146

Maayan, Hagai, 172, 173
Macy, Andrew, 168
Magal, Gabi, 94
Magen, Gideon, 155-56, 161
Magen, Zvi, 95
Makov, Avraham, 80
Malmudi, Meir, 94
Marcus, David, 31-32, 34-35
Margal, Aharon, 199
Marom, Eliezer "Chiney," 268-69, 271, 272, 273, 274, 324
Marom, Leah (Chai Lee), 268
Masrega "Knitting Needle" Unit, IDF, 133

Massas, Benny, 215, 220
Matas, Ze'ev, 126, 128, 129, 130
Matt, Danny
  Black Arrow Operation and, 39, 43,
    44, 45
  "Chinese Farm" and, 196
  personal and professional
    background of, 182-83, 323
  Sinai Campaign and, 68, 71
  Six Day War and, 183
  War of Independence and, 182-83
  Yom Kippur War and, 182, 183, 184,
    185-86, 188, 189, 196
Medal of Courage
  for Dagan, 323
  for Har-Zion, 320
  for Mordechai, 201
Medal of Distinguished Service
  for Dagan, 129
  for Kahalani, 323
Medal of Valor
  for Ayalon, 103, 321
  Black Arrow Operation and, 45
  for Kahalani, 212, 323
media
  and Abu Jihad assassination, 264
  and assassination of Black
    September leaders, 174
  and "Boats of Cherbourg," 119
  Cast Lead Operation and, 290-91,
    292
  Defensive Shield Operation and, 283
  and Iron Dome system, 303
  and kidnapping and murder of three
    teenagers in Gaza, 299
  and Park Hotel suicide bombing, 279
  and Ras Gharib raid, 128-29
  and Soviet pilots with Egyptian Air
    Force, 137
  and Suleiman assassination, 236
  and Syria's nuclear reactor, 233, 234
  See also specific organization
Meir, Golda
  Amin and, 5
  appointment as foreign minister of,
    62
  and assassination of Black
    September leaders, 162, 164

Entebbe and, 22
  as Prime Minister, 102
  and prisoner exchanges, 156
  and Sabena Airlines hijacking, 143
  and Soviet pilots in Egyptian Air
    Force, 133, 134
  Spring of Youth Operation and, 162,
    164
  War of Attrition and, 133, 134
  Yom Kippur War and, 187, 191
Mengistu Haile Mariam, 310, 314
Miari, Ali el, 4
Middle East
  balance of power in, 62
  Soviet involvement in conflict in, 131
  See also specific nation
Middle East Airlines: and Israeli
    attack on Beirut airport, 114
Mitla Pass, battle at, 67-73, 91, 183,
    227
Mitzna, Amram, 194
Mofaz, Shaul, 19, 267, 271, 272, 273,
    274, 275-76, 277, 323
Mole Cricket 19, Operation, 248-52
Moledet party, 321
Mollet, Guy, 63
Mordechai, Yitzhak, 148, 197, 198,
    199-200, 201, 265, 323
Morsi, Mohamed, 297
Moses, Operation, 313-14, 315
Mossad
  and Abu Jihad assassination, 259,
    260-61, 262, 264
  and assassination of Black
    September leaders, 162, 163-75
  Entebbe and, 11, 12, 13
  and Haddad chocolates, 23
  and hijacking of Air France Flight
    139, 3-4
  and Iraq's Osirak nuclear reactor,
    226, 227
  Karine A attack and, 269
  Pillar of Defense Operation and, 297
  and rescue of Jews from Ethiopia,
    310-11, 312, 313, 314
  Spring of Youth Operation and, 162,
    163-75
  and Syria's nuclear reactor, 232, 233

Mothers' Bus: terrorists' seizure of, 257-59, 264-65
Motti (Sayeret commander), 243
Mount Hermon
  Fatah on, 240
  Peace for Galilee Operation and, 245
  Yom Kippur War and, 214, 215-21
Mount of Olives: Six Day War and, 96, 98
Mount Scopus (Israel), 90, 92, 96
Mukataa (Arafat headquarters), 278, 279, 282
Munich Olympics (1972): massacre of Israeli athletes at, 162, 164, 170
Nablus Qasbah, Defensive Shield Operation and, 280-82, 284-85
Nablus Road (Jerusalem), 93
Nachmani, Pinchas "Pini," 155-56, 161
Nachmani, Rochaleh, 161
Nachumi, Amir, 228
Nafach, battle for, 204, 205
Nahaariya: attack on, 258
Nahal Brigade (IDF), 279
Nahmani, Amitai, 170
Nahshon Brigade (IDF), 282-83
Najar, Muhammad al-, 165. See also Yussuf, Abu
Najib, George (pseud.), 261
Narkiss, Uzi, 90
Nasser, Gamal Abdel
  Ben-Gurion's policies and, 37
  death of, 178
  Israeli relations with, 3
  and Jordan-Egypt military pact, 89
  nationalization of Suez Canal by, 50, 62-63
  Sinai Campaign and, 50
  Six Day War and, 3, 76, 78
Nasser, Kamal, 165, 170, 171
National Water Carrier facility: bombing of, 258
Nautilus system, 303, 305
Nava, Eitan, 94-95
Navon, Yitzhak, 22, 35-36, 319
Navy, Egyptian, 53
Navy, Israeli
  and Boats of Cherbourg, 113-21

Karine A attack and, 272, 273
  Pillar of Defense Operation and, 297
  Santorini capture by, 269
  See also Shayetet 13 (naval commando unit)
Nebi Daniel: Arab attack at, 35
Nebi Samuel: Sharon's attack on, 41
Netanyahu, Ben-Zion, 4, 148
Netanyahu, Benyamin "Bibi"
  Crate Operations and, 156, 157, 158
  and hijacking of Sabena Airlines plane, 148, 149, 150, 152-53, 169
  Pillar of Defense Operation and, 294, 295
  and prisoner exchanges, 156, 157, 158
  professional career of, 322
  reputation of, 4
  and Syria's nuclear reactor, 235
  and terrorism in Gaza, 299, 300
  terrorist organizations comment by, 163
Netanyahu, Iddo, 4, 148, 156, 157, 158
Netanyahu, Yonatan "Yoni"
  and assassination of Black September leaders, 169, 170, 171
  Crate Operations and, 156, 158, 159
  death of, 18, 22, 23
  Entebbe and, 4-5, 17, 18, 20, 22, 25-26
  and hijacking of Sabena Airlines plane, 148, 152-53, 169
  Mount Hermon and, 216
  personal and professional background of, 4
  and prisoner exchanges, 156, 158, 159
  reputation of, 4
  Spring of Youth Operation and, 169, 170, 171
  Yom Kippur War and, 216
Netivei Neft Oil Company, 116
Neuman, Yair, 83
New York Herald Tribune: Burma Road story in, 33
Nimeiry, Gaafar, 310, 313
Nisim, Eddie, 221
Nitzan, Nir, 94-95
Nixon, Richard M., 112, 133

*No Margin for Error: The Making of the
  Israeli Air Force* (Yonay), 135
Noa, Operation, 113-21
Noah's Ark, Operation, 271-76
Norbert, Hershel, 141, 152
Norbert, Ida, 141, 152
North Korea, 232-33
nuclear dangers
  Arizona Operation and, 224, 232-35
  Begin Doctrine and, 231, 232
  and Iraq's Osiraq nuclear reactor,
    224, 225-32, 251, 252
  and North Korea, 232-33
  Opera Operation and, 224, 225-32,
    252
  Syria and, 224, 232-35

Obama, Barack, 297
Ocean Vigour (British vessel), 52
Okamoto, Kozo, 8
Old City (Jerusalem), 92, 93, 96, 97-
  100
Olmert, Ehud, 224, 233, 234, 235,
  288, 291, 305
100th Squadron (IAF), 294
101st Airborne Division, U.S., 31
105th Squadron (IAF), 249
110th Squadron (IAF), 79
114th Squadron (IAF), 161
143rd Division (IDF), 180
162nd Division (IDF), 180, 188
184th Tank Battalion (IDF), 194
188th Brigade (IDF) (Barak
  "Lightning" Brigade), 204, 205, 289
Opera, Operation, 224, 225-32, 252
operations. *See specific operation*
Oranim ("Cedars"), Operation, 241
Osiraq nuclear reactor (Iraq), 224,
  225-32, 251, 252
Oslo Accords, 277

Palestine
  British departure from, 28
  partitioning of, 28
  and War of Independence, 28, 29-36
  See also West Bank
Palestine Liberation Organization
  (PLO)

and Abu Jihad assassination, 259,
  260, 261, 263
Arafat as head of, 139, 141, 164, 241
assassination of leaders of, 163-75
exile to Tunisia of, 256, 257-65
French warning about Israelis to, 261
Oslo Accords and, 277
Peace for Galilee Operation and,
  239-46
See also Black September; *specific
  person*
Palestinian Authority
  Bush (George W.) comment about,
    276
  Defensive Shield Operation and,
    278-85
  Iran as supplier of weapons for,
    267-76
  Ramallah as capital of, 278
  Umm Jihad and, 264
Palestinian Preventive Security
  Headquarters (Beitunia), 278
Palmach, 52, 91, 142, 181, 182, 227
Palti, Nadav, 241-42
Pardo, Tamir, 18, 25-26, 297, 323
Park Hotel (Netanya): bombing at,
  279, 282
Passo, Yigal, 217, 221
Patton, George, 205
Pazarkar-Sheratzky, Rina, 258
Peace for Galilee, Operation, 238,
  239-46
Pecker-Ronen, Ran, 288
Peled, Avi, 278
Peled, Benny, 7, 8, 9, 11, 24
Peled, Moshe "Mussa," 205, 206-7
Peled, Yehuda, 220
Peres, Shimon
  accomplishments of, 2
  Brzezinski and, 15-16
  David's Sling by, 7-8
  Dayan and, 5, 24, 37
  and Entebbe, 5, 7-8, 9, 10, 11-12, 13-
    14, 15-16, 19, 21, 22, 24
  and French-Israeli relations, 62
  Gur and, 12, 13, 24
  and hijacking of Air France Flight
    139, 2, 4, 5

and hijacking of Sebana Airlines plane, 142
and Iraq's Osirak nuclear reactor, 228, 231
and Netanyahu (Yoni) eulogy, 23
professional career of, 321
Rabin and, 3, 7, 10
and Rafi party, 76
Sevres summit and, 63-66
Sinai Campaign and, 61, 62, 63-66
Peres, Sonia, 15, 22
Peretz, Amir, 302-3, 304-5
Phalanges, 238, 241
Piamenta, Uzi, 41
Piamenta, Yehuda, 41
Pillar of Defense, Operation, 293-98, 302
Pineau, Christian, 63
Pollard (Jonathan) affair, 324
Pompidou, Georges, 112, 115
Popular Democratic Front for the Liberation of Palestine (PDFLP), 2, 4, 23, 166, 168, 169-70, 171-74, 321
Popular Front for the Liberation of Palestine (PFLP), 2, 3, 4, 23, 321
Porat, David, 134, 135
President's Medal: for Kahalani, 323
Pressler, Yigal, 172, 175
prisoner exchanges
Crate Operations and, 155-61
and Mothers' Bus attack, 257-58
Project Arrow (Israeli-U.S. joint project), 303
Protective Edge, Operation, 298, 299-304
Pundik, Jacob, 107
"purity of arms" principle, 175

Qalqilya reprisal raid, 47
Qatar, 297
Qawasmeh, Marwan, 304
Queen of Sheba, Operation, 313-14
Quneitra (Israeli town), 204, 207, 209

Rabin, Yitzhak
and Abu Jihad assassination, 260
as ambassador to U.S., 102
assassination of, 319

and Entebbe, 6, 7, 8, 10, 13-14, 15, 16, 19, 22, 24
Gur and, 6
and hijacking of Air France Flight 139, 2-3
named chief of staff, 76
Peres and, 3, 7, 10
professional career of, 2-3, 319
Sharon and, 180
and Sharon's promotion to general, 90
Six Day War and, 86
War of Independence and, 30-31
Rafaeli, Loni, 164
Rafi party, 76
Rafid Gap, 204, 205, 207
Rahamim, Mordechai, 148, 149, 150, 151
Rahma, Fayez Abu, 261
Ram, Ehud, 108
Ram, Victor, 257
Ramallah: and Defensive Shield Operation, 278, 279, 285
Ramon, Ilan, 228, 229-30, 232
Rapoport, Gavrush, 31-32
Ras Gharib, Israeli raid on, 123-30
Rayan, Nizar, 288
Raz, Ze'ev, 228, 229, 231-32
Reagan, Ronald, 231
Red Cross
and hijacking of Sabena Airlines plane, 145, 146, 149, 150
and Nachmani exchange, 161
"Red Sheet" order, 89
Reshef, Amnon, 181, 186, 193, 195, 196, 323
Reshef (Israeli missile ship), 309
retaliation/reprisal raids, 37, 46-47
Revolutionary Guards, Iranian, 275
Rice, Condoleezza, 276
Rif'at, Captain (aka Ali Taha Abu Sneina), 141, 143, 144, 145, 146, 147, 149, 150, 151
Rimal al-Zahabiya dinner (Syria): Suleiman assassination at, 236
Rimalt, Elimelech, 22
Rimbaud, Gilbert, 168
Rimon 20, Operation, 134-38

Road of Valor. *See* Burma Road, Israeli
Rockefeller Museum (Jerusalem), 92,
   93, 96, 97
Rommel, Erwin, 205
Roni (IDF soldier), 239
Rooster 53, Operation, 123-30
Rooster, Operation, 51, 52-59
Rot, Zalman "Zali," 108, 110
Rotenberg, Dodik, 94
Rotenberg, Ram, 272, 274
Russak, Haim, 93
Russo, Tal, 297

Sabbag, Aharon, 173
Sabena Airlines plane: hijacking of,
   140-53, 164
Sabena, Operation, 140-53, 164
Sabra refugee camp, 238
Sadat, Anwar, 178, 187, 310
Sagi, Yehoshua, 227
Salmon, Avraham, 136
Samueli, Mustafa, 41
San Simon Monastery (Katamon
   region), 35
Santorini (ship), 269
Saranin, Captain (Soviet pilot), 135
Saridi, Ayish a- (pseud.), 260-61
Sarig, Yossi, 79, 82
Savoy Hotel (Tel Aviv): raid on, 258
Sayeret Matkal (IDF commando unit)
   and Abu Jihad assassination, 259,
      260, 262, 263
   and assassination of Black
      September leaders, 164-71
   Crate Operations and, 155-61
   creation of, 144
   Entebbe and, 12, 15, 20, 25-26
   Green Island raid and, 103, 105, 107,
      108
   and hijacking of Air France Flight
      139, 4
   and hijacking of Sabena Airlines
      plane, 143-44, 145, 147, 148-49,
      150-51, 152
   Mount Hermon and, 216
   Peace for Galilee Operation and,
      241-42, 246
   prisoner exchanges and, 155-61

Spring of Youth Operation and,
   164-71
   and Syria's nuclear reactor, 233
   War of Attrition and, 103, 105, 107,
      108
   Yom Kippur War and, 216
   See also specific person
Second Army, Egyptian, 181, 185, 201
Sella, Aviem, 136, 226, 227, 248, 250-
   51, 253, 324
Seventh Brigade (IDF), 30, 32
7th Armored Brigade (IDF), 204, 207,
   212, 323
71st Battalion (IDF), 92, 96, 98
77th Battalion (IDF), 92, 207
79th Battalion (IDF), 194
Sevres (France) summit, 63-66
Shaar, Gilad, 298-99
Shabak (Internal Security Service),
   Israeli, 143, 146, 294
Shachar, Yonatan, 86
Shafir, Elik, 232
Shafir, Herzel, 82
Shaham, Mishael, 41
Shaked, Emanuel "Mano," 165, 166-
   67, 169, 172, 174
Shaldag "Kingfisher" commando unit
   (IAF), 234, 283, 313, 315, 316, 322
Shalev, Rami, 124
Shalit, Gilad, 293
Shalom, David, 95
Shamir, Yitzhak, 256, 314
Shani, Colonel, 19-20
Sharett, Moshe, 37, 62
Sharira, Raisa, 52
Sharon, Ariel "Arik"
   and Arab Legion hostages, 40-41
   Ben-Gurion and, 42, 67, 180
   Black Arrow Operation and, 38, 39
   "Chinese Farm" and, 193, 197, 198
   Dayan (Moshe) and, 40, 67, 181
   death of, 320
   Defensive Shield Operation and, 279
   election as prime minister of, 224
   Gur and, 6, 90, 91
   Har-Zion and, 42
   as IDF paratrooper commander, 42,
      43-46

and Israeli retreat from Gaza Strip, 286, 320
and Kadima party, 224
Karine A attack and, 271-72, 275, 276
and Lebanon, 238, 241, 245, 251, 320
and Likud party, 180, 181, 224
military promotions for, 90
Nebi Samuel attack and, 41
Peace for Galilee Operation and, 238, 241, 245
personal and professional background of, 40, 180-81, 320
personality and character of, 40, 42, 181
popularity of, 67
principles of, 72
Rabin and, 180
as revolutionizing the IDF, 41
and Sabena Airlines hijacking, 150
Sinai Campaign and, 66-72
Six Day War and, 90, 180
stroke of, 224
and terrorist operations in West Bank, 277
War of Independence and, 40
Yom Kippur War and, 180-82, 183, 184, 185, 186-88, 189, 193, 197, 198
Sharon, Gur, 181
Sharon, Lily, 181
Sharon, Margalit "Gali," 44-45, 181
Sharon, Rita, 91
Shatila refugee camp, 238
Shayetet 13 (naval commando unit)
and Abu Jihad assassination, 259, 260, 261
Green Island raid and, 104, 105, 106, 107, 109, 111
and *Karine A* attack, 267, 268, 271-72, 273-74, 276
and Syrian nuclear reactor, 236
War of Attrition and, 104, 105, 106, 107, 109, 111
Shechter, Nathan, 93
Shefa, Yonatan, 310
Sheikh Hussein Bridge (Jordan): capture of Arab Legion hostages at, 40-41

Shin Bet, 261, 282, 285, 291, 321
Shomron, Dan, 8, 9, 10, 11, 12, 19, 20, 24, 259, 323
Shor, Avida, 167-68, 172, 173, 175
Shorek, Eli, 199
Shuvu Achim mission (IDF), 299
Siam, Iyad, 288
Siam, Said, 288
Siem, Martin, 116, 117, 119, 120
Simchoni, Uri, 204
Simhoni, Assaf, 45
Sinai Campaign
beginning of, 58, 61
Britain and, 50, 60, 62-66, 72
and downing of Ilyushin II-14 plane, 51-59
first map of, 66
France and, 50, 60, 62-66, 72
impact of, 76
Israeli "defense fund" for, 62
Kadesh Operation and, 53, 61-73
and Mitla Pass, 67-73, 91, 183, 227
Rooster Operation and, 51, 52-59
and Sevres summit, 63-66
Soviet Union and, 65
Suez Canal and, 50, 60, 61, 62-66, 72
Sinai Division (IDF), 245
Sinai Peninsula
Israeli control of, 123
and rescue of Jews from Ethiopia, 311
Six Day War and, 3, 78, 88, 89, 97, 99, 102, 180, 193
Soviets and, 134, 135-36
War of Attrition and, 103, 134, 135-36
Yom Kippur War and, 179, 180, 192-201
See also "Chinese Farm"
Sivron, Rafi, 79
Six Day War (1967)
beginning of, 72, 78, 89
cease-fire in, 97
Egypt and, 3, 77-87, 89, 92
end of, 99
Focus Operation during, 77-87, 252
and French-Israeli relations, 114
Golan Heights and, 3, 99, 102

impact of, 3
Iraq and, 78, 85
Jerusalem and, 47, 87, 88, 89-100, 102, 180, 320
Jordan and, 3, 78, 79, 82, 85, 88, 89-100
Lebanon and, 79, 85
Sinai Peninsula and, 3, 78, 88, 89, 97, 99, 102, 180, 193
Soviet equipment in, 125
Syria and, 3, 78, 79, 82, 85
United Nations and, 78, 97
West Bank and, 6, 88, 90, 99, 102
See also specific person
16th Division, Egyptian, 201
66 Battalion (IDF), 92, 93-94, 98
Snir, Asher, 136
A Soldier's Story: The Life and Times of an Israeli War Hero (Eitan and Goldstein), 72
Solel Boneh Construction Company, 32
Solomon, Operation, 314-16, 317
Soviet Air Force, 132-38
Soviet Union
  and Egypt-Czechoslovakia arms deal, 50, 62
  Egyptian relations with, 50, 62, 122, 132-38
  involvement in Middle East conflict of, 131, 132-38
  as Iraqi weapons supplier, 133
  Israeli relations with, 133-34
  and Lebanon War, 252-53
  Sinai Campaign and, 65
  as Syrian weapons supplier, 133
  U.S. relations with, 131
  War of Attrition and, 132-38
Special Forces, Israeli, 257
Spector, Iftach, 136
Spring of Youth, Operation, 163-75, 259, 262
Starboat Corporation, 116, 117
Stempel, Moshe "Stempa'le," 98-99
Stone, Mickey. See Marcus, David
Straits of Tiran
  and Karine A attack, 271
  Six Day War and, 78

Subotniks, 227
Sudan
  Jews of Ethiopia in, 309-17
  U.S. aid for, 313-14
Sudanese Army, 311-12
Suez Canal
  Britain and, 50, 60, 62-66, 72
  Egypt nationalizes the, 50, 62-63
  France and, 50, 60, 62-66, 72
  Ras Gharib raid and, 123-30
  Sinai Campaign and, 50, 60, 61, 62-66, 72
  War of Attrition and, 122, 123-30, 132, 134
  Yom Kippur War and, 174, 179, 180, 181, 182, 183, 185, 187, 188, 190, 191, 199
  See also Green Island
suicide bombings, 277, 279
Suleiman, Muhammad, 236
Syria
  Arizona Operation in, 224, 232-35
  Golan Heights and, 202, 203-13
  Lebanon's relations with, 247, 248-53
  missiles of, 235, 247, 248-53
  Mount Hermon and, 215-21
  and nuclear dangers, 224, 232-35
  Peace for Galilee Operation and, 245
  prisoner exchanges with, 155-61
  Sinai Campaign and, 53, 62
  Six Day War and, 3, 78, 79, 82, 85
  Soviet Union as weapons supplier to, 133
  and Suleiman assassination, 236
  U.S. mediation between Israel and, 252
  War of Independence and, 28, 30
  Yom Kippur War and, 178, 180, 202, 203-13, 215-21
Syrian Air Force, 208, 209, 247
Syrian Army, 42, 160, 207, 247

Tabak, Moshe, 114
Taharlev, Yoram, 96
Tali Unit (IDF), 17
Tannous, Rima, 140-41, 151
Tanzim terrorists, 279, 281, 284
Tawalbeh, Mahmoud, 283

Technical Services Unit, Israeli, 124
teenagers, kidnapping and murder of
three West Bank, 298-99, 304
Telem, Benjamin "Bini," 116
Temple Mount (Jerusalem): Six Day
War and, 6, 98-100
Tepper, Aryeh, 30-31
terrorists/terrorism
and Abu Jihad assassination, 258-64,
265
Cast Lead Operation and, 287-93
Defensive Shield Operation and,
275, 277, 278-85
emergence of, 139
in Gaza, 286, 287-305
and *Karine A* attack, 266, 267-75
and kidnapping and murder of three
teenagers in West Bank, 298-99
and Lebanon, 238, 239-46
Netanyahu's (Bibi) comment about,
163
Peace for Galilee Operation and,
238, 239-46
Pillar of Defense Operation and,
293-98, 302
and PLO-Tunisia mission, 256, 257-65
weapons supplies for, 266, 267-76
in West Bank, 277, 278-85, 298-99
See also specific person or organization
Third Army, Egyptian, 181, 185, 188,
189
35th Brigade (IDF), 174, 196
Thunderball, Operation, 15, 16, 23.
See also Entebbe
Time magazine: Amin comment in, 5
Toledo, Benyamin, 144
Tolkovsky, Dan, 54, 55, 56, 57, 58
Tron (IAF pilot), 130
Tunisia
and Abu Jihad assassination, 258-64,
265
PLO exile to, 256, 257-65
Tunisian Army, 259
Turkey, 235, 296, 297
28th Battalion (IDF), 92, 93, 96, 98
247th Reserve Brigade (IDF), 179,
180, 182, 183, 189-90, 323
Tzadok, Hayim, 24

Tzarfati, David, 218, 219, 221
Tzidon, Raisa Sharira, 52, 59
Tzidon, Yoash "Chatto"
baby story about, 59
and downing of Ilyushin ll-14 plane,
51-59
and Jaffar Nassim, 58-59
professional career of, 320
War of Independence and, 52
Tzimmel, Arieh "Tzidon," 125
Tzomet party, 321
Tzur, Tzvi, 116
Tzur, Yaakov, 150
Tzuri, Yoav, 94

Uganda. *See* Amin, Idi; Entebbe
Ugda Mussa reservists (Israeli), 205
Umm Jihad (aka Intisar al-Wazir),
258, 259, 262, 263, 264
Unit 100 (IDF), 200
Unit 101 (IDF), 41-42, 43, 90, 320, 321
Unit 269 (IDF), 143-44
Unit 669 (IDF), 267
Unit 8200 (IDF), 132, 233. *See also*
515th Intelligence Service Unit
(IDF)
United Nations
and Jenin refugee camp, 283
Litani Operation and, 241
and partitioning of Palestine, 28
Six Day War and, 78, 97
War of Independence and, 30, 33, 34
United Nations Human Rights
Council, 292, 299
United Nations Relief and Works
Agency (UNRWA), 290, 301
United Nations Truce Supervision
Organization, 89
United States
Arafat and, 274, 275, 276
Defensive Shield Operation and,
275, 279
Iran's relations with, 226
and Iraq's Osirak nuclear reactor, 231
and Iron Dome project, 305
and Israeli-Lebanon war, 252
Israeli relations with, 112, 133, 134,
226, 231, 305

and *Karine A* attack, 274, 275
mediation between Syria and Israel
  by, 252
Pillar of Defense Operation and, 297
Project Arrow and, 303
and rescue of Jews from Ethiopia,
  313-14
Six Day War and, 78
and Soviet pilots with Egyptian Air
  Force, 133, 134
Soviet relations with, 131
Sudan aid from, 313
and Syria's nuclear reactor, 233-34
as weapons supplier to Israel, 112,
  226, 231
and weapons supplies for terrorists,
  274, 275, 276

Valley of Tears, 207, 209
Vietnam War, 138
Vilnai, Matan, 19-20
Vinick, Commander (IDF), 219

War of Attrition
  Egypt and, 102, 103-11, 115, 123-30,
    132-38
  Green Island raid and, 103-11
  Ras Gharib raid and, 123-30
  Sinai Peninsula and, 103, 134, 135-36
  Soviet involvement in, 132-38
  Suez Canal and, 122, 123-30, 132,
    134
  turning point in, 110
War of Independence
  Arabs and, 28, 35
  British in, 137
  Jerusalem and, 29-36, 52, 92, 99
  Jordan and, 28, 29, 183
  planning during, 14
Warsaw Pact, 253
Washington Post: and Cast Lead
  Operation, 292
Weizman, Ezer, 58, 82, 86, 226, 227-
  28, 249, 321
Weizmann Institute, 144, 253
West Bank
  Defensive Shield Operation in, 278-
  85

Iranian Revolutionary Guards in,
  275
kidnapping and murder of three
  teenagers in, 298-99, 304
Six Day War and, 6, 88, 90, 99, 102
terrorists in, 277, 278-85, 298-99,
  304
West Bank Division (IDF), 285
Whichelaw, Andrew, 168
World War II, 6, 31, 62-63, 64, 65, 110,
  116, 128

Yaakobi, Dedi, 94
Yaakov, Yaakov, 45
Yaakov, Yiftah, 196
Ya'alon, Moshe "Bogie," 189-90, 260,
  262, 300, 322
Ya'ari, Yedidya "Didi," 108, 109, 267
Yadin, Yigael, 28, 29, 30, 228
Yadlin, Amos, 228
Yaffe, Yossi, 92
Yair, Yuval "Ya Ya," 190
Yairi, Uzi, 197, 198, 200, 258
Yamam (Israeli border guard), 258
Yariv, Aharon, 133, 143, 144, 162,
  164
Yaron, Amos, 312
Yatom, Danny, 148, 150
Yemen: and Iran as weapons supplier
  for terrorists in Gaza, 270
Yifrach, Eyal, 298-99
Yiftach Brigade (IDF), 279, 280
Yom Kippur War (1973)
  Amin and, 5
  beginning of, 174, 178, 180, 193
  Bravehearts Operation during, 179-
    90, 193
  "Chinese Farm" and, 186, 191, 192-
    201
  Egypt and, 178, 179-90, 192-201
  Golan Heights and, 174, 180, 202,
    203-13, 289
  Mount Hermon and, 214, 215-21
  Sinai Peninsula and, 179, 180, 192-
    201
  Suez Canal and, 174, 179, 180, 181,
    182, 183, 185, 187, 188, 190, 191,
    199

Syria and, 178, 180, 202, 203-13, 215-21
traffic congestion during, 184
Yonatan, Operation, 23, 252
Yonay, Ehud, 135
Yurchenko, Nikolai (Soviet pilot), 135
Yussuf, Abu (aka Muhammad al-Najar), 165, 170
Yussuf, Maha, 170

Zamir, Meir "Tiger," 211
Zamir, Zvi, 162, 164

Zamosh, Yoram, 92, 98-99
Ze'evi, Rehavam "Gandhi," 67, 142, 148, 321
Zero Visibility Squadron (IAF), 52
Zidon, Yoash "Chatto". See Tzidon, Yoash "Chatto"
Zim (Israeli shipping company), 116, 118
Zinni, Anthony, 275
Ziv, Shaul, 165
Zohar, Ben-Zion, 84-85
Zuriel, Israel, 95
Zussman, Giora, 17, 18, 26

Bloodtypes
Bodytypes
YOU and

An interactive journey for reaching
your genetic potential

Joseph **Christiano**

Living in Health—Body, Mind and Spirit

BLOODTYPES BODYTYPES AND YOU by Joseph Christiano
Published by Siloam Press
A part of Strang Communications Company
600 Rinehart Road
Lake Mary, Florida 32746
www.creationhouse.com

Scripture quotations marked NLT are from the Holy Bible, New Living Translation, copyright © 1996. Used by permission of Tyndale House Publishers, Inc., Wheaton, IL 60189. All rights reserved.

Scripture quotations marked NAS are from the New American Standard Bible. Copyright © 1960, 1962, 1963, 1968, 1971, 1972, 1973, 1975, 1977 by the Lockman Foundation. Used by permission. (www.Lockman.org)

Cover and interior design: Judith McKittrick

Library of Congress Catalog Card Number: 00-109817
International Standard Book Number: 0-88419-742-5

This book is not intended to provide medical advice or to take the place of medical advice and treatment from your personal physician. Readers are advised to consult their own doctors or other qualified health professionals regarding the treatment of their medical problems. Neither the publisher nor the author takes any responsibility for any possible consequences from any treatment, action or application of medicine, supplement, herb or preparation to any person reading or following the information in this book. If readers are taking prescription medications, they should consult with their physicians and not take themselves off of medicines to start supplementation without the proper supervision of a physician.

0 1 2 3 4 5 6 7 RRD 8 7 6 5 4 3 2 1
Printed in the United States of America

Dedication

As I better understand the role genetics play in my life, I am humbled by the fact that I am only a representative of something much greater. Just as God has seen fit to extend His grace to me for spiritual life, He has also provided me with a genetic foundation for physical life. I am thankful to my parents, Joe and Helen, for passing on to me their genetics and the understanding of who my Creator is. My father has passed on to where the true meaning of life dwells, and my mother is here, still cheering me on. Thanks, folks, for giving to me. I love you.

> Don't let the excitement of youth cause you to forget your Creator. Honor him in your youth before you grow old and no longer enjoy living.
>
> —ECCLESIASTES 12:1, NLT

Acknowledgments

I will be eternally thankful to my wife, Lori. She has continually supported and "pushed" me to see this work completed. You are the truest example of what a man needs most in life. I love you, Kid.

I want to thank the entire staff at Strang Communications Company and Siloam Press for their support and expertise in making this book a success. I am appreciative for the creative minds of all the team members in the design department.

A special thanks goes to Barbara Dycus, managing book editor at Strang Communications Company. Her steady hand, constant input and many hours of expertise have made this work enjoyable.

I am grateful for my nutritionist and team member Maria Gamb, certified holistic health counselor, particularly for her part in the dietary portion of this work. Her expertise in matching and mixing the food groups, menus and recipes for each blood type is greatly appreciated.

I thank the many people who have shown support for this work and who have experienced the positive benefits of lifestyle changes by eating foods compatible to their blood types and exercising according to their body genetics. Some of these people were willing to take the time to share their experiences in the testimonial section of this book. I thank each one of you.

Last, but by no means least, I thank God for the years of opportunity and experience in health and fitness that have allowed me the pleasure of passing on the treasures in this work to my fellow man.

Contents

Introduction *1*

SECTION I Developing a Plan for a Healthy Lifestyle

1 Genetics—Your Foundation for Success........................... 9

2 Bridging the Gap—Setting Goals, Staying Focused......... 25

SECTION II Instinctive Eating— Eating According to Your Blood Type

3 How to Become an Instinctive Eater................................ 43

4 Your Four-Week Test Plan.. 53

5 Diet and Nutrition.. 61

6 Blood Type A... 83

7 Blood Type B... 99

8 Blood Type AB 117

9 Blood Type O 135

10 Family Meal Planning 153

11 28-Day Pick-a-Meal Recipes... 173

SECTION III Body Genetics—Reaching Your Genetic Potential

12 Body Genetics 219

13 A Survival Kit for Your Journey..................................... 233

14 Body Redesigning 90-Day Workout Programs................. 255

SECTION IV Real People, Real Results...................... 265

Epilogue.. 289

Notes 291

Appendix 293

SECTION V Body Type Workout Programs............. 295

TABLE OF CHARTS

2-1 Reasons to Change—Positive Values;
Reasons Not to Change—Negative Fears 32

2-2 Setting Goals—Are You Making Progress?............. 34

2-3 Checklist of Pitfalls 37

3-1 Benefits of the Journey Experience 45

4-1 Determining Your Blood Type 55

4-2 Monitor Your Progress 59

5-1 Glycemic Index of Common Foods 63

5-2 Sample Pick-a-Meal Daily Plan #1 72

5-3 Sample Pick-a-Meal Daily Plan #2 72

5-4 Protein and Exercise 79

5-5 28-Day Pick-a-Meal Planner 81

12-1 Exercise Paradox 221

13-1 Body Fat Test 244

13-2 Rule of Thumb for Healthy Eating 246

13-3 Initial Measurement Sheet 247

13-4 90-Day Master Measurement Recording Sheet 248

13-5 Progress Report Card 249

13-6 Dietary Analysis 250

13-7 Determining Your Body Type 251

13-8 Troubleshooting the Pear Body Type 252

13-9 Troubleshooting the Apple Body Type 253

13-10 Troubleshooting the Banana Body Type 254

14-1 Selecting How Much Weight to Use 258

14-2 Training Heart Rate Expressed
in 10-Second Count 259

14-3 Regulating Your Body Weight 260

14-4 Charting Your Exercise Journey 262

Introduction

Has the new millennium brought advancement into your life? Is progress not just happening "out there" around you—but within you as well? No, I am not referring to the advancements in computer technology or the development in space travel or information technology. I am referring to progress with the things that make the greatest difference in your life, things over which you have control, such as personal relationships, happiness and contentment in your life, vibrant health, functional age, healthy eating, weight management, physical activities and regular exercise. *I am talking about your lifestyle.*

Are you content with your lifestyle in these areas? Are you making continual progress toward better health? Are you getting better with age? Are you advancing with time—or is time advancing and leaving you behind?

One in three, or 58 million, American adults aged twenty through seventy-four are overweight.[1] Being overweight and physically inactive accounts for more than 300,000 premature deaths each year in the United States, second only to tobacco-related deaths.[2]

**Are you
content with
your lifestyle
in these areas?
Are you making
continual
progress
toward better
health? Are
you getting
better with
age? Are you
advancing
with time—
or is time
advancing and
leaving you
behind?**

If for some reason you are not making as much progress as you would like to make, then hold on, because help is right around the corner. Your lack of progress might not be entirely your fault. You may be suffering from the consequences of being a victim of the "Instant Gratification Syndrome" so prevalent in our culture today. This instant gratification mind-set, which most of us are programmed to accept as normal human expectations, has caused many an enthusiastic person to become disillusioned and discouraged.

Since this is the time in which you and I live, then surely there must be a quicker, more direct path to take to get your weight under control, your body in shape and your lifestyle healthier.

Meet Your Personal Trainer

As you and I establish a one-on-one relationship throughout this book, I want you to consider me as your personal fitness trainer and nutritional guide. My role will be to show you how to combine specific selections of exercises that are most compatible for your body type with specific food selections that are most compatible for your blood type. Our one-on-one relationship throughout this book will be the next best thing to your hiring me to be your personal trainer.

So, as your personal trainer and nutrition guide, it is my job to get you to where you want to go just as quickly as possible. This interactive book will help you identify with the various mechanisms that I have designed for you as an individual, like the charts on Determining Your Blood Type or Troubleshooting Your Body Type. If I were your fitness trainer, I would ask you questions about your current level of physical activity, exercise and your involvement in some form of recreational sports. I would ask you a series of background questions related to your medical history, diet experiences and fitness goals. I would want to know as much about you as possible so I could prescribe the most beneficial strategies to reach your goals. Then I would provide you with a dietary program designed specifically to meet your individual nutritional needs.

This book will help you to develop such a dietary program.

You will find that your interactive journey will place you on the exact path to meet your specific bodily needs. I will help you learn to reach and maintain your healthy body weight, reduce your body fat percentage, improve bodily functions, heal your body systems, reduce the likelihood of disease, control low blood sugar and improve metabolic function. I will have you fill out a dietary analysis of the foods and fluids you consume and the dietary supplements that can help you experience optimal health.

We will look at the role exercise plays in maintaining good health. I will help you to determine your body genetics and to develop an exercise program to meet your specific genetic requirements. Your exercise program will be tailored to your current needs—but it will be progressive in nature to allow you to advance as you improve in health and fitness.

I will help you learn to incorporate specific exercises to redesign your current physical appearance by creating a symmetrical balance between your upper and lower body. Your program will consist of cardiovascular conditioning and anaerobic conditioning (strength training for increasing lean muscle mass and strength). Your program will be designed not only for cosmetic results, but also to improve your energy level and your performance in day-to-day tasks and sports. It will aid your health by strengthening your immune system and improving your circulatory system. It will ultimately establish a solid foundation upon which you can build for the rest of your life. I want to help you not only to develop such a plan, but to learn to be consistent in applying it to your daily life. I will show you how to properly execute each exercise. I will provide you with a way to monitor and review your progress, providing tips to keep you focused and motivated. The combination of my expertise and your willingness to commit to the plan will settle the issue of instant gratification forever. The instant gratification syndrome ultimately leads to discouragement at not being able to obtain the results you want immediately—or even close to immediately! It is my observation that there is a more valid reason for not seeing the results you want. My experience over the past thirty-five years has revealed that the primary reason for failure at following a fitness plan is due to the lack of knowledge for applying the proper dietary and exercise methodologies to reach your goal. Success will be possible when your healthy lifestyle strategy is based on your specific genetic requirements and the synergistic effects they produce in concert with one another.

I will help you learn to reach and maintain your healthy body weight, reduce your body fat percentage, improve bodily functions, heal your body systems, reduce the likelihood of disease, control low blood sugar and improve metabolic function.

This book is the closest thing to having a personal fitness trainer—and a whole lot less expensive. The book is designed to work interactively with you by implementing my expertise through charts, programs and information, plus the mechanisms that will lead you in the right sections of the book for your specific needs.

Naturally, our modified version of one-on-one training will depend on your willingness to succeed and how long you will apply the contents of what is in this book. The synergy of our one-on-one relationship through this book will take you to a new level of understanding of the importance of proper application of exercise and diet to benefit you most. Your adherence to your strategies will speed up the time for accomplishing your short- and long-range goals. It will also give you a greater sense of value in making this approach to a healthier you a lifetime of vibrant living.

From Me to You

I often refer to *instinctive eating* and *body genetics* as the fitness twins. Have you ever noticed the increased performance of your car engine when you fill the gas tank with high-octane fuel instead of low-octane fuel? The answer is obvious. The engine runs poorly on low-octane fuel. It interferes with the engine's performance. When you use high-octane fuel, your engine will perform more efficiently and smoothly. The drive will be faster because the higher octane is what your engine requires.

The same principle is true about the fuel you use in your body's "engine." By applying the higher-octane dietary and exercise strategies that are compatible to your genetics, you will enjoy the positive results sooner.

Having been an avid proponent of getting regular exercise,

eating healthily and taking nutritional supplements for most of my life, what I share in this book will come from my own personal and professional experiences over thirty-five years. My own journey for finding better ways of achieving a more healthy, balanced life has caused my innate curiosity and desire to search beyond the mundane for more accurate and direct paths to optimum health.

I travel all over the country speaking and sharing the benefits of physical fitness to people via live television or radio interviews and seminars. I didn't just wake up one morning to discover I was in a tip-top fitness condition—it has been a lifestyle. There are times when I do not feel like exercising or eating correctly for my blood type. Sometimes I think, *Why bother?* But, time is slipping by, and I'm an aging "baby boomer" with the obvious signs to prove it.

But when I look at my daughters and the eight grandchildren they have given me, I think about the positive role I can play in their lives. I value my relationship with my wife, and I know the importance a healthy body and mind have in our relationship. I look at other family members and wonder what it would be like if I were too sick to enjoy the time I spend with them.

No, maintaining my health is not a mechanical function to me. My good health didn't just happen. I have to work hard to get it— and to keep it. So will you. You will need to look beyond the sweat and discipline and focus on the really important things in your life, weighing them against an unhealthy and sickly lifestyle. Hopefully you will see the value in the principles in this book.

These new findings are important to adapt to our lifestyles so that faster results and responses for positive bodily performance can be achieved. Throughout the years I have learned to make it a point to be more open-minded and willing to accept new truths and information that become available to me. This open-mindedness can be applied to diet, exercise, personal relationships, my spiritual life—or to any area of my life. New research and studies are constantly being made available, so it would be foolish not to take the opportunity to become more informed. Such information can enhance your life and provide the impetus for continual progress.

I strongly encourage you to put into practice the strategies, guidelines and new information you read in this book. Just reading about them cannot bring you a healthier lifestyle. Change will require *the will to change.*

So, if you are serious about redesigning your body . . . if you want to know a healthy way of eating . . . if you want to live an energetic and youthful life that is high on performance and low on maintenance . . . then now is the time to make your decision. The journey will never end if you will remember that you are an inspiration in constant transition. Let's take the journey together—one-on-one!

Bloodtypes
Bodytypes
YOU and

Section I

Developing a Plan for a Healthy Lifestyle

Chapter 1

Genetics—Your Foundation for Success

DNA! Genome! Cellular profiling. Stem cells. Cloning! Blood types. Body types. What is it all about? Is the existence and physiological makeup of humankind just a mixture of theories, personal points of view and yet-to-be proven truths? Are we dabbling into mysterious areas that should be left alone, or are we finally beginning to learn more about ourselves?

In man's conquest to survive, questions arise every day: What role do genes play in determining health, disease, longevity, bodily function and performance? What is the origin of man—where did he come from? Do we all come from one main gene pool, or are we descendants of individual generational ancestry? Did we evolve from nothing to crawling on all fours to an eventual upright position, or did God create us? Is man degenerating because of cellular mutation, becoming less than what he started out as, or is he a result of an evolutionary process, making him far superior to what he was at the beginning of time? Why do some people enter life with blue eyes and blond hair and others with brown eyes and brown hair? Are certain body genetics designed for physical and athletic superiority while other body genetics determine the run-of-the-mill hopefuls? Do the ABO blood types react differently to the same foods? Is there a link between red blood cells and your health?

Our genetic makeup is the foundation of all that is life.

Although phenomenal advancements have been made through modern-day discoveries in technology, science and medicine, it will still take light-years to unravel the amazing intricacies of man. The world's best scientific minds have made amazing discoveries, but in the light of all that we still do not know about ourselves, technology seems to move at a snail's pace.

Whether you believe that God created every human being or that our existence is a result of some theoretical development of nothingness into something, the answers to our questions lie far beneath the surface—with our genetic foundation.

Our genetic makeup is the foundation of all that is life. Nothing relating to our ability to survive our environment, to fight off illness, infection or stress, to supply our bodies with nutrition or to make physiological adaptation is a matter of happenstance. It is no coincidence that our body is programmed with the innate ability to defend itself from uninvited invaders such as parasites, viruses and bacteria by creating an army of antibodies.

Our genetic foundation is a mixture of trillions of cells with codes that identify, program and link everything in our existence—from the color of our hair to our bodies' susceptibility to disease to foods that are compatible to our potential life span and capability to survive.

Some people would rather merely swim in shallow water than go below the surface to discover answers to the questions and issues of life. But there is a bottomless sea to dive into for the inquisitive and health-conscious individual who seeks knowledge of the role genetics play in our lives.

For example, did you know that . . .

- Gene therapy is now being researched intensively in most developed countries—for a host of very good reasons. Instead of treating deficiencies by injecting drugs, doctors will be able to prescribe genetic treatments that will induce the body's own protein-making machinery to produce the proteins needed to combat illness.[1]

- Researchers succeeded in making artificial copies of human genes that could be manipulated to produce large amounts of specific proteins. Such genes can be introduced into the human body where, in many cases, they substitute for a defective gene.[2]

- In a study that could lead to new treatments for diabetes and provide guidance on the use of genes in treating disease, scientists show that a common genetic variation increased the risk of contracting Type 2 diabetes.[3]

- Australian scientists have identified a new gene responsible for controlling appetite in humans—a discovery experts say could lead to the first gene-based drug to treat obesity and diabetes.[4]

- In the not-too-distant future, scientists may be able to grow replacement organs and new blood vessels to replace clogged ones, eradicate diseases as diverse as Alzheimer's and cystic fibrosis and tell which medication to prescribe.[5]

Gaining more knowledge and understanding about the complexities of our genetics humbles me—and convinces me of the existence of One much greater than man, with infinite creative wisdom that stretches far beyond the finite knowledge of man. The fact that man has the ability to make scientific advancements and acquire information about the genome of man serves only to prove how much greater his Creator must be.

One of the most common questions that people ask of creation scientists is this: How did such a variety of ethnic groups and diverse races arise from one human pair?

Research is revealing more and more about the origin of blood types. Much of this research points out the possibility of the emergence of all known blood types from our common ancestors, Adam and Eve. In his dissertation titled "Blood Types and Their Origin (Answering the Critics)," Jonathan Sarfati tells us:

There is one gene in humans that controls the ABO blood type. There are three versions of the gene, or alleles: A, B, or O. . . . For a husband and wife to pass on all alleles to their children, they need to, between them, have the A, B, and O alleles. . . . If Adam and Eve were genetically AO and BO, for example, their children could have had AB, AO, BO or OO genetic makeup, giving AB, A, B, or O blood types. Indeed, about 25 percent of their children would have been of each type.[6]

The fact that man has the ability to make scientific advancements and acquire information about the genome of man serves only to prove how much greater his Creator must be.

There is so much more to be discovered about man and our genetic makeup—birthed in us at the moment of conception. Although scientists are discovering new things about our genetic structure daily, there is much more that remains unknown. One scientist has observed:

Data supporting the complexity and design of life at all levels, and especially that of man, loom larger than was previously supposed—as large in fact as the enormous "gaps" in the fossil record . . . The further we look into the complexity to the real world of man and his living companions, the more baffling and unexplainable, at least in standard evolutionary theory, the whole complex becomes . . . To the skeptic, the proposition that the genetic programmes of higher organisms consisting of something close to a thousand million bits of information . . . containing in encoded form countless thousands of intricate algorithms controlling, specifying and ordering the growth and development of billions and billions of cells into the form of a complex organism, were composed by a purely random process is simply an affront to reason.[7]

It has taken gifted scientists years upon years to discover the things they know about man today. But it will take hundreds of more years to understand how to apply the new information.

It is when we are willing to be taught and are open to more knowledge that we continue to grow. I am growing daily in my own knowledge, particularly in my knowledge about the link between blood types and nutrition. Since I coauthored the book *The Answer is in Your Bloodtype,* I have discovered new studies about the origin of blood types. These findings lean more closely to my personal beliefs in creationism.

My purpose for mentioning this is twofold: First, I humbly admit that no one has all the answers. But as long as we are willing to be open to greater learning and understanding, progress can be continual. Second, since I happen to believe that God is the Creator of all creation, it stands to reason that I would embrace studies that line up with my beliefs. As we learn more about the complex design of man, it just makes good sense to me that Someone greater than you or I is in charge of this whole thing.

Regardless of where you stand concerning the origins of blood type, one thing we can agree on is that eating foods compatible to our blood type and avoiding foods that are not compatible is a more accurate and individualized approach to eating than anything man has experienced.

I am not a scientist, biochemist or genealogist, so I'll leave the research and discoveries to the experts. My interest is to help you reach a basic level of understanding about your body so you can take care of it in a way that will contribute to living a healthier and more balanced life.

During my summer vacations from school as a kid, I remember going with my father while he worked a few hours a week for my cousin, who owned an excavation and construction company. I watched the construction workers build the foundations for new buildings, or as they called it, "pour a cellar." It was quite a process. The first thing they did was excavate the land and prepare the ground. Then they measured out the area where the foundation would be laid. After determining the proper elevations and measurements, they began to set up the forms.

Until I saw the entire process completed for the first time, it was hard to understand why they were using all those heavy planks to make a huge square in the dirt. But I learned that those planks played a very important role in the next part of the procedure. When the huge cement trucks were ready to pour the concrete, they poured it into the wood forms, which shaped the foundation of the building.

I learned that each foundation differed in size, shape and materials. Certain job sites required the forms to be dug deeper in the ground, while other forms were extended higher. The deeper or higher the forms were laid, the thicker the concrete base or foundation would be. The design and composition of each poured foundation determined the size and weight of the structure that it could support.

Each building structure, whether a residential home, a high-rise building or a strip mall, required a unique foundation that functioned as its basis for structure, stability and support. Similarly, our ability to survive, support and improve our structure will be determined by the mixture of the material found in our foundation. Our foundation, of course, is our genetics.

Consider yourself as a general contractor who wants to redesign or custom-build a house. In this case, the foundation of the house you want to construct, or reconstruct, is your genetics. Instead of brick, mortar and wood, you are using the materials that comprise your body.

> **The amount of time and effort you put into customizing and building your "house" (your body) will help it to last for many years.**

The amount of time and effort you put into customizing and building your "house" (your body) will help it to last for many years. By understanding the purpose of a strong "foundation" (your genetics) and by using the proper "tools and materials" (the proper nutritional and exercise applications and methodologies), you can assure a healthy, happy future.

You have a specific biological makeup that was given to you at conception. It's the genetic substance that makes up your entire existence.

I have three daughters—Amy, the oldest, and twin daughters, Jenifer and Cara. Amy's genetic foundation has given her facial features that resemble mine, while genetically, Jenifer and Cara have their mother's facial features.

But your genes are not limited to your facial characteristics. Not only do your genes determine if you will look more like Mom or Dad and what color your hair and eyes will be, but also how susceptible you are to certain diseases and illnesses. Your cellular profile and the way your body responds to certain foods, viruses and bacteria are determined by your genes also.

Have you heard of infants who could not tolerate a traditional milk formula but flourished on a formula using soymilk? The infant did not reject the traditional milk formula simply because it was uncooperative—the formula was not compatible to its blood type. How about the little boy who grew up wearing husky-size jeans because of his large buttocks and thighs? It wasn't his fault—he was born with a body type that included large buttocks and thighs. Knowing your children's blood types can help you make healthy food selections for them at an early age.

You are what you eat, but it is also vitally important for you to eat what you are!

Two very important considerations can greatly help you maximize your genetic potential. These are providing your body with the best nutritional program for your specific genetics and applying the best fitness approach for your genetic structure. Let's take a look at each consideration before we go any further.

Blood Types and Nutrition

You are what you eat, but it is also vitally important for you to eat what you are! Each of us should eat a diet that is compatible with our blood type.

We can begin to get an understanding of this important concept by taking a look at the animal kingdom. It is instinct that drives animals to eat. Lions are meat eaters—they won't be happy if you try to feed them a diet rich in fruits and vegetables. Other animals are vegetarian by instinct, and they will not eat meat. This is no accident—instinct is a protective mechanism for all animals, including humans.

Each blood type has different characteristics that allow it to eat, digest and assimilate food best for that group. Type Os are blessed with strong stomach acid and powerful enzymes that can metabolize almost anything—even some food not recommended for them. Types A, B and AB must be more careful in their eating habits or suffer the consequences.

What are these consequences? What happens when we eat food not compatible for our blood types? Agglutination happens, which can be explained as follows:

Your body has antibodies that protect it from foreign invaders. Your immune system produces all kinds of antibodies to protect you and keep you safe from foreign substances. Each antibody is designed to attach itself to a foreign substance or antigen.

When your body recognizes an intruder, it produces more antibodies to attack the invader. The antibody then attaches itself to the intruder and a "gluing" effect (agglutination) takes place. In this way, the body can better dispose of these foreign invaders.[8]

When it comes to eating foods that are not compatible with your blood type, this "gluing" effect can take place in the digestive system, joints, liver, brain or blood. Continual ingesting of foods not compatible to your blood type can cause havoc in your body systems. This agglutination of cells, or clumping, will eventually break down the function of that particular system and lead to health problems.

One main reason why certain foods are identified as "Avoid" foods is because of the protein molecules, or lectins, that they contain. It is when these dietary lectins that are present in certain foods enter the host's body that problems prevail.

In my book *The Answer is in Your Bloodtype*, I included information on the specific characteristics of each blood type in relation to nutrition. Let me give you an overview of some of these characteristics.

BLOOD TYPE O

Individuals with type O blood have the thinnest blood, strongest immune systems (with the exception of some diseases), strongest stomach acid and live the longest of all the blood types at present.

Genetically, stomach acid was designed to break down the high-protein diets on which our original ancestors thrived. As food sources changed, type Os were able to adapt to metabolizing almost any food because of this strong stomach acid.

Since the ancestors of type O were hunters, descendants carrying this gene tend to be larger, stronger individuals. If you were to check the blood types of most competitive bodybuilders and professional athletes, an overwhelming number of them would be blood type O. Most American Indians and Eskimos are also Os.

One of the factors contributing to the longevity of blood type Os is the fact that, at least in the United States, many of the diseases that once killed type Os have been all but eradicated. These diseases include typhoid, cholera, smallpox, plague, malaria and other diseases that exist only in Third World countries today.

Because type Os have the thinnest blood of any type, they are less likely to be affected by blood clots or the buildup of plaque—making them less susceptible to heart disease, at least at an early age. They also seem less susceptible to cancer. [9]

Since the ancestors of type O were hunters, descendants carrying this gene tend to be larger, stronger individuals.

Strengths:
- Thinnest blood
- Strongest stomach acid
- Strong immune system
- Longest life span
- Metabolizes food well
- Neutralizes cholesterol
- Low blood clot risk

Weaknesses:
- Thin blood may not clot well in brain
- Intolerant of newer dietary and environmental conditions
- Greatest threshold for abuse of smoking, alcohol, etc.

Health risks:
- Strokes
- Blood disorders like hemophilia and leukemia
- Arthritis and/or inflammatory diseases
- Ulcers
- Allergies

Nutritional profile:
- Animal protein primary source
- Foods rich in vitamin K
- Eat beef, salmon, mozzarella cheese, pinto beans, artichoke, broccoli, greens, figs, plums

- Avoid pork, wheat, corn, lentils, navy beans, cabbage, Brussels sprouts, potatoes, melons, oranges

BLOOD TYPE A

Many people with blood type A must avoid almost all animal protein in favor of a vegetarian diet.

The first mutation from blood type O is A. As man migrated to locations where meat was not readily available, he adapted to a different diet—specifically vegetarian. These early migrations were to places like Europe, Asia and Australia, regions totally different from the plentiful plains of Africa where animal protein was abundant. These early migrators learned to survive on fruits, vegetables and grains. As a result, many people with blood type A must avoid almost all animal protein in favor of a vegetarian diet.

Individuals with type A blood have the thickest blood of all blood types types. In the United States, meat and potatoes have comprised the traditional staple diet. Type As do not tolerate either meat or potatoes well. When Type As eat these foods that are inconsistent with their blood type, their already thick blood agglutinates, or gets thicker and stickier. The thick blood requires the heart to pump harder, inevitably causing high blood pressure, hypertension, an enlarged heart muscle and an increase in heart disease. This is the major reason why type A individuals have the shortest life span today.

Another downside to type A blood is that in the adaptation/mutation to a vegetarian diet, type As lost the stomach acid necessary to metabolize meat protein. Type As have very low stomach acid by genetic standards; while the low acid accommodates the metabolism of fruits and vegetables, it does a miserable job metabolizing animal protein.

A constant diet of mainly meats and potatoes provides fewer nutrients to the body, lowers immune function and thickens the blood, leading to heart disease, cancer and earlier death. For precisely these reasons, type As are susceptible to heart disease and cancer. Japanese are an exception; they eat a staple diet of fish, rice and green tea—the perfect diet for individuals of type A blood.[10]

Strengths:
- Adapts well to dietary and environmental changes

Weaknesses:
- Thick blood
- Shortest life span
- Affected by stress more than other blood groups
- Sensitive digestive tract
- Vulnerable immune system
- Must avoid almost all animal protein

Health risks:
- Heart disease
- Cancer
- High blood pressure
- Hypertension
- Enlarged heart muscle
- Decreased immune function
- Anemia
- Liver disorders
- Gallbladder disorders
- Diabetes

Nutritional profile:
- Eat soy beans, tofu and green tea for antioxidant qualities; grouper, cod and salmon; soy cheese and soy milk; lentils; broccoli; carrots; romaine lettuce; spinach; blueberries; blackberries; cranberries; prunes; raisins
- Avoid animal fat; meat or dairy products; meat-and-potato diet; kidney, lima and navy beans; wheat; eggplant; peppers; tomatoes; cantaloupe; honeydew melons

BLOOD TYPE B

Type B blood is not as thin as type O blood, nor is it as thick as type A blood. For the most part, type Bs can eat meat in moderation without great fear of developing heart disease. Type B individuals have the ability to eat and metabolize dairy products, which both type O and type A do not tolerate well at all.

It is believed that improper foods, or the improper metabolism of specific foods, lower the immune system of Bs and make them susceptible to autoimmune diseases. Type B individuals average the second longest life span after Os. This is probably due to the fact that animal protein, which contains all those essential amino acids, is good food for Bs. Additionally, since type Bs can eat a large variety of foods, they are able to acquire all or most of their essential vitamins, minerals and amino acids from food more easily than As and ABs.

Type B individuals have the genetics to be the second most muscular, next to type O. While Bs build muscle easily, some gravitate to sports, perhaps as coaches and trainers, but the vast majority tend to pursue careers in medicine, law, science and technology.[11]

Strengths:
- Naturally strong immune system
- Acquires most essential vitamins, minerals and amino acids from food more easily than As or ABs
- Lives longer than As and ABs
- Second most muscular

Weaknesses:
- Some chronic medical problems such as skin disorders or foot problems

Health risks:
- Polio
- Lupus
- Lou Gehrig's disease
- Multiple sclerosis

Nutritional profile:
- Can eat meat in moderation
- Metabolizes dairy foods fairly well
- Eat lamb; venison; cod; grouper; farmer, feta and mozzarella cheese; kidney, lima, navy and soy beans; broccoli; cabbage; collard and mustard greens; pineapple; plums
- Avoid chicken, American cheese, ice cream, wheat, white and yellow corn, pumpkin, tofu, persimmons, rhubarb

BLOOD TYPE AB

It is believed that blood type AB is the result of mixing types A and B. Since both A and B are dominant genes, AB is the only blood type with two dominant traits.

ABs are susceptible to both A and B diseases, making them prone to cancer, heart disease and autoimmune diseases. Research has also noticed a clear trend for women of this blood type to have many menstrual problems—such as excessive bleeding, clotting, cramping, irregular menstrual cycles—either leading to hysterectomies or continued misery. A large number of the women who experienced menstrual problems also experienced migraine and other headaches. There is a clear pattern of hormonal imbalance that plagues this blood group. ABs are slightly more muscular than As, but less muscular than Bs. It is easier for an AB to build muscle than an A, but in some cases, ABs have as difficult a time building muscle as As.

Eating properly for an AB requires guidelines similar to As, but with small amounts of animal protein. ABs should acquire their vitamins, minerals and essential amino acids through plant and vegetable proteins.[12]

> ABs are susceptible to both A and B diseases, making them prone to cancer, heart disease and autoimmune diseases.

Strengths:
- Only blood type with two dominant traits
- Friendliest immune system

Weaknesses:
- Pattern of hormonal imbalance
- Tendency to chemical imbalance disorders

Health risks:
- Cancer
- Heart disease
- Anemia
- Autoimmune disease
- Women tend to have menstrual problems and migraine and other headaches

Nutritional profile:
- Limited to small amounts of animal protein
- Eat turkey; cod; mahi-mahi; navy, pinto and soy beans;

oat and rice flours; collard, dandelion and mustard greens; figs; grapes; plums

- Avoid chicken, duck, all pork and venison, clams, crab, haddock, lobster and shrimp, kidney and lima beans, white and yellow corn, peppers, guava, mangoes, oranges

Blood Types Determine What to Eat

In this book you will learn to eat what you are—to eat according to your blood-type genetics. With proper diet, including nourishment from the food and supplements specific to your needs, the chance of disease is greatly reduced. In fact, proper diet according to blood type, coupled with exercise, enables your immune system to be its strongest. A strong immune system can make the difference between a longer or shorter life span.

Since the body cannot repair itself without protein, protein is the key element in the equation for good health. We must all have protein; the form of that protein determines how long we will live. For individuals with blood types A and AB, animal protein from meat is unacceptable, with a few exceptions. For Bs, while meat is not particularly harmful in the short run, it contributes to heart disease and a host of other assorted ailments in the long run.

The body accesses body fat for fuel when it has burned its sugars and carbohydrates. The goal is to keep the body in an anabolic state for as many hours a day as possible. In this way the body always has the fuel it needs to rebuild and repair. Carbohydrates provide energy, but they don't fulfill the body's need to build strong bones and boost immune function.

Body Types and Exercise

By following your blood-type-specific diet program, maintaining your body in an anabolic state with the use of protein and adding necessary nutrients to your daily program through supplementation, you can reach your genetic potential. But to maintain that genetic potential and enjoy a healthy long life, you will also need to understand your body's genetics regarding your genetic structure and to follow a fitness plan to maximize the positives and minimize the negatives of your body type.

THE PEAR BODY TYPE

The pear body type finds its weight distribution problems in the lower body—the hips, thighs and buttocks. This body type is considered to be bottom heavy. The upper body is generally slender, with a shallow bustline and narrow shoulders.

The challenge for the pear body type is to redesign the body by filling out the chest/bust and adding width to the shoulders while isolating toning and firming exercises to the lower body area.

Characteristics of a Pear:

- Narrow shoulders
- Straight waist
- Lower body weight in hips, thighs and buttocks
- Wide pelvic and hip structure
- Need to reduce lower body
- Need to build muscle mass in upper body

me

without pregnancy Belly

THE APPLE BODY TYPE

When the apple body type gains weight, the weight goes mostly to the upper body. It stores most of its body fat around the waist, upper back and arms. The abdomen often protrudes or bulges forward. Apples usually have thin legs and buttocks, creating an out-of-balance symmetry with the upper body.

The challenge for the apple body type is to build the upper and lower leg muscles while shaping and toning the upper body. The apple will need to concentrate on the abdominal muscles also.

Characteristics of an Apple:

- Upper body stores fat around waist, upper back and arms
- Lower body is undersized
- Thin buttocks and legs
- Abdominal area out of proportion and protrudes
- Need to shape and tone upper body
- Need to build hips, thighs and buttocks

THE BANANA BODY TYPE

Weight gains for the banana body type are distributed equally between the upper and lower body. The banana lacks shapeliness, tending to have a straight-line figure. Often the waist area for a banana is nearly as wide as the upper and lower body.

The challenge of redesigning the banana is to firm and tone muscles to incorporate an hourglass shape. The banana should concentrate on the abdominal muscles, try to elongate the thighs and tone the buttocks.

Characteristics of a Banana:
- Lacks pleasing lines and shapeliness
- Pelvic bone, ribs and shoulders equal width
- Wide waist
- Need to firm and tone muscles
- Need to elongate thighs
- Need to tone buttocks

Positioned for Success

Your genetics have determined what you are and how your body responds, reacts and performs. With the understanding of the principles I have outlined in this chapter, you are positioned for success—just as soon as you get started. By applying the information and strategies set forth in this book, you will discover how to eat foods compatible to your blood type and how to choose exercises compatible to your body type.

Genetically speaking, you and I have been given just so much clay to work with. Why not follow the right path and enjoy the journey reaching your genetic potential?

My desire is to help you reach a new level of improved health, physical appearance and an energetic life as quickly as possible. But please remember, it is your *journey in life* that is most important. Your genetic predisposition is basic to your success. The better you understand the role your genetics play, the greater and faster the results will come.

On your journey, take what you have learned, appropriate the experiences you have applied to your lifestyle and pass them along for the good of others. That will add more worth to your life. *Roads were not built for destinations—they were built for the journey.*

Chapter 2

Bridging the Gap

As a health and fitness professional, I am familiar with getting one-on-one with my students. I find it to be very productive and profitable, while at the same time personal and relational. Whether consulting with a student in my office or taking a student through a workout in the gym, that one-on-one relationship is the most rewarding part of my profession.

I derive great satisfaction as I watch a student accomplish what he or she set out to do with the help of my innate gifts of nurturing and tutoring. My greatest reward for pouring all my expertise into my students is experiencing their success—and knowing that I played a part in it.

Motivation and accountability are the two dynamics that make a one-on-one relationship so powerful and effective, whether it is applied to health and fitness, marriage and family relationships or any other area of your life. Through the years I have had many successful students who took the dare, were willing to go the extra mile and in the end have thanked me for their success because of my guidance and expertise, for which I am very blessed.

But let me also set the record straight—the one-on-one relationship is a two-way street! Due to the many years of working one-on-one with my students, I have benefited from them as well. I have been fortunate to develop my innate abilities and sharpen my instincts when it comes to things like determining specific dietary requirements for someone simply by listening or reading what information was given to me. I have learned to better understand my students' psychological and emotional needs by listening to their comments and the way they answer my questions. In that way, I have been able to see past their general reasons for wanting to get into shape and get in touch with their real reasons.

By observing their athletic abilities, their exercise performance, their body genetics and how they responded to cues and directives, I have been able to make immediate adjustments to the exercise methodology that would better suit them. Yes, I have greatly benefited throughout all these years from the one-on-one relationships.

I took the time to share that with you so you and I can establish a one-on-one relationship also. Even though it will take place as we journey through this book, and not in person, you will be amazed at what progress you can make. How will it work? It will happen as you learn to trust me—and the information and guidelines that I am providing for you in this book.

If you hired me as your personal trainer, you would have to trust me. So your dependency on my guidance in this book is not all that different. Knowing that what I am giving you comes in part from years and years of working in the trenches in those one-on-one relationships should give you a comfort zone. Ultimately those experiences provided me the expertise and ability to prescribe for you the specific dietary guidelines and exercise methodology for your genetics, just as if we were meeting one-on-one. The bottom line for you is to *trust* and then *apply* the information and strategies from this book that come closest to meeting your individual needs.

Perhaps you are afraid that you will never be able to accomplish your personal fitness and diet goals without the continual guidance of a personal fitness trainer. Should you doubt the possibility of succeeding without a personal trainer, please read Lyn's success story on page 282 in Section IV— Real People, Real Results. Keep in mind that her extraordinary results did not come from training sessions in a gym with me as her personal trainer. Before we met she had established the specific goals she wanted to accomplish. She was determined to do her best at attaining her goals. I didn't meet this woman personally—during the process of reaching her goals, she sought me out to help her develop individual prescriptions for diet and exercise. Obviously, her results speak for themselves. You can tell that by looking at her fabulous before and after photos.

No more time for wishing and hoping— now is the time to take action.

Fear Never Wins

It takes trust for you to be able to allow someone to take you by the hand and lead you to where you have never been before. Most people fail to reach their potential, never enjoying the benefits of the other side because they are afraid to take the first step. They become paralyzed by fear.

If you are fearful and untrusting, it may not be me in whom you are afraid to place your confidence. It may be the fear of failure that holds you back. Just remember that fear is an emotion. It breeds doubt, and doubt becomes an attitude issue that can slow down your progress and eventually lead to failure. To find out what kind of end results you are capable of, and to enjoy a healthier and more fulfilling life, you must be willing to leave the place where you are now—regardless of your present physical and mental condition. Stepping out of that place is the only way to experience a better lifestyle.

No more time for wishing and hoping—*now is the time to take action.* It is going to take a leap of faith to reach your full potential. If you are willing to step out and take that leap of faith, bridging the gap between wishful hoping and the joy of victory with the sweet smell of success, then take my hand and let's go, one-on-one.

The Gap

I recently made a business trip to Toronto, Canada. On the drive back to Buffalo, New York, my wife, Lori, my business agent Frank and I decided to stop in Niagara Falls to eat lunch. If you have never been to Niagara Falls on the Canadian side, you must make plans to go sometime—it is totally awesome.

There are many restaurants in the Niagara Falls tour district. Five hundred twenty feet straight up the Skylon Tower there is a revolving restaurant, accessible only by an elevator that travels up the outside of the tower. That elevator ride in and of itself almost took my appetite away. Once we were seated, we were mesmerized by the sight of the falls and of the five-hundred-foot gorges below. You can see for miles and miles, both in America and Canada.

As I sat there, I thought of a story that took place in Niagara Falls many years ago when the Great Blondin walked across the falls on a tightrope while pushing a wheelbarrow. Obviously it was so unbelievable to watch. I could imagine the crowds of people who watched. As I thought about this incredible feat, I could see how it served as a prime example of how fear had paralyzed that crowd of onlookers from stepping out in faith to walk that tightrope also.

I could hardly imagine crossing that spectacular "gap" on a tightrope while pushing a wheelbarrow. Glancing down five hundred feet to the cataracts below, it seemed inconceivable that anyone would take such a step of faith. But the Great Blondin went across the falls and back on nothing more than a cable and a wheelbarrow that he pushed. When he returned to his starting point, the crowds cheered wildly, shouting out their approval of his fearless deed. "Do you think I could do it again?" he yelled to the crowds.

"Yes, we believe you can," they responded instantly. So off he went again, crossing the huge gap of dangerous whirlpools separating the United States and Canada. When he returned, the people cheered and applauded once more, amazed at his lack of fear.

Once more the acrobat asked the crowd, "Do you believe I could do it again?"

"Yes, yes, you can!" they called back in unison. Above the din of the crowd, one person yelled out, "I know you can!"

Hearing the voice, the Great Blondin yelled back these words, "If you know I can, then are you willing to get in the wheelbarrow and go across the falls with me?"

There was no answer—only silence.[1]

I wonder, *What happened to that person?*

Later during an interview, the acrobat was asked how he kept fear from interfering with his performance. How was he able to maintain his balance? He responded by saying that he overcame his fear as long as he stayed focused on the cable in front of him—instead of on the water below. By staying focused on the cable, he never saw anything else. Everything else was out of focus.

> **Decide today to step out, focus on the goal and go for it!**

Has fear been preventing you from making a decision to seek a healthier, fitter lifestyle? What do you have to lose but excess body fat, a body that needs some redesigning and the agony of digestive discomforts? Decide today to step out, focus on the goal and go for it!

Time for a Change

I am sure you have heard that familiar saying, "If a man can't change his mind, he can't change anything." Of course, this theory applies to women as well. So before you and I can go one-on-one, you have to make a commitment to being willing to change. In this book, I will cover all aspects of exercise and diet. You will be able to identify strategies that will work best for you. But you must consider first things first—and that is, *Are you willing to change?*

We tend to be creatures of habit. Change comes very slowly and with reservation—if it comes at all. We tend to cling to our comfort zones and refuse challenges that will cause us to make changes. For example, you may have already, from past experience, found a particular diet plan that allowed you to lose weight. In your mind you think that anytime you need to lose a few pounds, all you have to do is follow that same diet plan again.

Stop for a moment and think that theory through from a different perspective. You will discover that the diet gave you temporary results at best. A plan that cannot keep you from gaining back the fat again obviously does not work. It gave only temporary results. It should be considered the last dietary path on this earth that you should want to travel.

At least I see it that clearly. So, are you willing to change your thinking? Assume that indeed what I am presenting to you in this book is a new, different dietary approach to eating that is more effective than your previous experience and one that can be adaptable for your lifetime. Would you be willing to change? Would it be worth the change?

Rather than returning to your former way of thinking by implementing your original diet plan, the one that only provided a temporary drop in weight, wouldn't it make good logical sense to make a change? Indeed, it does make good sense, particularly if this change can help you maintain your weight forever, avoid certain unnecessary health disorders and give you a sense of mental victory because you were willing to stretch your boundaries to bridge the gap.

Consider that New Year's resolution where you joined with half of all America to start a jogging program—you remember, the one where you tried to get in shape all at one time, the one that nearly killed your knees. Why would you return to something that doesn't provide success as an end product? Worst yet, why would you think that what didn't work previously would eventually become profitable to you if you used it again? That's a sure way to go insane.

But if I can offer you an exercise program concept that is based on your body genetics and specifically designed for your body type, wouldn't it be worth the change to try an exercise program that can deliver the results you want?

On a separate sheet of paper, write down a list of reasons why you *should not* change. If your only reasons are staying out of shape, being tired all the time, aging faster than necessary, allowing the onset of unnecessary diseases and illnesses plus not enjoying a lifestyle of vitality and high energy, then you might as well not bother with the list. My guess is that any valid reasons you could come up with would fit on the head of a pin!

I want you to be willing to open your mind to new things that can be helpful and beneficial. If you are willing to change, then there is hope. Not all changes can be achieved overnight. That's not even necessary. But change must begin for you to be successful.

The outward behavioral changes will take place naturally when you are ready and willing to change on the inside. Take a good look on the inside. Examine your deepest concerns about your health—or lack thereof.

Improving your health—or ignoring it—can affect the more important areas of your life, such as family, relationships, career or anything that means the most to you. On a separate sheet of paper, write down a list of positive values that will occur in the important areas of your life if you choose to embrace change. These may include not being tired and uncomfortable all the time, having the energy and stamina to do more with your family, having more energy for your career or being able to engage in a sport that up to now has been impossible for you to do.

Now compile a list of fears or doubts that can prevent you from what you might accomplish with change. It may be the fear of failure that we talked about earlier. Or it may be the fear of making a commitment to something you have never tried before.

Compare your list of positive values to the list of your fears. Would you rather be paralyzed by fear from experiencing these positive values, or would you rather eliminate your fears so you can enjoy the values? This is a prudent and wise decision to make before you step out in faith, which is the first plan of action. The Holy Scriptures say, "For as he thinks within himself, so he is" (Prov. 23:7, NAS). Behavioral changes will be easier to make after you have reexamined your motives and fears.

Your list of positive values and of your fears may look something like Chart 2-1 on the next page.

To make this transition in your thinking even easier, try focusing on the reasons to change—not on the changes themselves. Remember our tightrope walker—he was able to cross the huge gap between our country and Canada because he stayed focused on the rope, not on anything else. In actuality,

...ns to Change—
...sitive Values

Family relationships—Being there for your loved ones: children, parents, wife, husband

Friends—Enjoying fellowship and socializing

Career/profession—Performance, appearance, image

Future—Preventative measures today for a solid tomorrow

Health—Getting rid of fatigue, excess weight, sickness and disease

Reasons Not to Change—
Negative Fears

Fear of change—Lack of trust, doubts and fear of the unknown

Fear of commitment—Lack of discipline

Fear of failure—Past experiences

Laziness—Negative attitude, lack of motivation, shortsightedness

the biggest gap he had to overcome was not the one that separated the United States and Canada—it was the gap between his fear of falling and the goal he wanted to achieve.

Goal Setting

As your one-on-one coach, I can give you all the information regarding the role your genetics play in your health and fitness plans. I can provide you with easy-to-follow dietary and exercise guidelines that are specific for your genetics and will provide the results you are looking for. I can even call you or e-mail you with words of encouragement. But if you are not equipped with goals, if you are not sure where you want to go on your journey, then it will be very difficult for you and I to get there. Establish your goals first. Set up a schedule for reaching each goal along the journey. Determine how you are going to reach each goal.

Include both short-range and long-range goals. Be sure that they are realistic enough that you can achieve them. When you see—and feel—the immediate results of short-term goals, they become golden nuggets of encouragement to help you continually press on to the long-range goals.

If you have set goals in the past and have not made much progress over the past few months or years, then reset your goals using a more realistic strategy. If this is the first time you are attempting to set fitness goals, making them realistic is vitally important to your success. Setting your goals is like deciding where you are going before you turn on the engine in your RV to begin a cross-country trip.

Before you begin your journey to a healthier lifestyle, decide where you are going—set those goals. Remember that your goals are your goals—and yours alone. Nobody can tell you what your goals should be. Your goals will become your personal destination stops along the path to a healthier lifestyle. Make them clear and distinct.

For example, if there is a particular dress size that you want to get down to, write that dress size down. If you want to get your blood pressure and cholesterol levels down, write down the normal levels you want to reach. If you are a man and want to build your chest and shoulders muscles, then write down the size you want to be

Be specific. Don't just say you would like to weigh "somewhere around" 150 pounds. If your goal is to weigh 150 pounds, write down that amount. If you have a deadline for reaching a specific goal, perhaps a wedding or some other social event to attend, write down the date and set your goals. Your goals have to be clear as a bell, not fuzzy. They must be specific and exact.

When you are through mapping your destiny, then you are prepared to take the next step. The next step is to put a price tag on your goals. What is their value to you? Some might be more valuable than others, but affix a price to each. If you want to be healthier in order to save money that you have been spending on medications and trips to the doctor's office, figure the exact cost and write it beside your goal.

Maybe you are tired all the time, day in and day out, and you want more energy. Write down the exact value of more energy to you. There is a value to each and every goal you desire, so write down each and tag them with their values to you.

We are beginning to make progress, so let's recap. By now you have a better picture of where you are heading. You realize that first of all you have to be willing to make changes. Making a decision to change will give you the mental foundation to step out, progress and see what lies ahead on the other side.

Searching within and identifying your concerns and fears will enable you to make the behavioral changes that will become a part of your lifestyle. Soon all the doubts and fears that once held you hostage to failure and unhappiness will be stored in your trash bin, waiting to be deleted from your thinking. You have also written a map to follow—your specific, exact goals—and determined their values.

Now the next thing is a word of precaution. I want you to remember that once you have your goals in place and begin the journey, *there will come* possible roadblocks, detours and holdups that can subtly blur your vision and interfere with your staying focused on your goals. As a necessary step of preparation, let's look at the importance of staying focused.

Setting Goals—Are You Making Progress?

2-2

Make clear distinct goals—not fuzzy goals.

Be specific—List specifics like size, time, line, weight, outfit or event.

Place a value on it—How important to you is reaching this goal?

Verbalize it—Reinforce your positive thinking by repeating your goal.

Write it down—Place a list of your goals in a convenient location for review.

Staying Focused

A few years ago I was caught off guard by an experience I had while I was reading. As I read an article from a magazine, I realized I was really struggling to see the printed words. It was as if I had lost my vision overnight. I knew that sooner or later all of us begin to lose our nearsighted vision over time. But this was ridiculous. The day before I had been able to read the fine print easily. But on this day I could hardly see the lines on the pages.

I had to make one of two decisions. I could keep on trying to read, ignoring the aging signs and living with the aggravation and frustration of not being able to see up close. But that would only keep me from enjoying the pleasure of reading. I opted not to make that choice.

My other choice was to do something about it, and I did. I realized I needed some help if I were to continue reading—particularly anything up close. I humbly decided to visit the local pharmacy in my neighborhood and pick out a pair of glasses labeled 125 power. I put those idiotic-looking glasses on, and all of a sudden they weren't so idiotic-looking anymore. I was amazed at how clear the words were. I could actually read the fine print. So off I went with my first pair of glasses in forty-seven years.

A couple years passed, and it was time to face reality again. I made an appointment with an optometrist for a thorough eye examination, something I hadn't done in twenty years.

At the doctor's office, he sat me down in a chair facing that familiar wall chart across the room. He directed me to cover first one eye, focus on the chart and read the letters as far down the lines as I could. Then I repeated the procedure with the other eye. I was able to see as far as the bottom line with my left eye, but only half the way down with my right eye.

The optometrist swung that huge machine right up to my face so I could look through the various lenses. As he began making adjustments, he asked me to focus again on the chart and read the lines. We went through the entire eye exam, making adjustments with the lenses to determine what prescription I needed to correct my vision. After twenty minutes of making adjustments and corrections, he asked me to look through the lens on the machine one final time. As I did, I was able to see clearly and could read all the way down to the bottom line with both eyes. It was wonderful to see so clearly. Suddenly the letters didn't have fuzz growing on them!

Then he had me read the chart again, but without the lenses. That really blew me away! "That's how you were seeing things before you came in to see me," he reminded me. It was unbelievable how out of focus my vision had become over the years.

Now I have 20/20 vision—with my contacts. The fact that for more than twenty years I had been losing my vision hit me like a lead balloon. The change had been so subtle that I did not realize it until I no longer enjoyed reading and could no longer see my golf shots.

This same sort of subtle deterioration can happen to your

Nothing can be permitted into your life that could interfere with reaching your goals. Set your sights on your goals, and take off running.

goals if you are not prepared for the journey. You may start out all excited and ready to "knock 'em dead." You may have set your goals in place and have high expectations for reaching them. But don't forget the potential obstacles along the way that may interfere with your focus and try to cause you to fail to reach your goals.

The principle of focus is necessary to understand in order to conquer your goals in your fitness journey. You may start off with high expectations and calculate the course you plan to take. But you must also ignore all the doubters and skeptics who attempt to throw you off course. You must press on, refusing to allow anything to stop you. Nothing can be permitted into your life that could interfere with reaching your goals. Set your sights on your goals, and take off running.

Attitude

The right attitude will keep you right on course to reach your goals. Exercising the right attitude is the most important exercise you will ever do. I am certain you are *capable* of doing it, so I have all the confidence in the world that you *will* do it.

Because attitude is the single most important mental factor determining your success or failure, in order for attitude to have the greatest positive impact on the outcome of your plans it must remain positive. Whether your goals are to lose excess body fat, fill out your figure or improve your overall state of well-being, it will be your attitude that makes the difference in succeeding or failing.

The success and productivity of your life evolves around two basic principles: the principle of wasting your time, and the principle of investing your time. These principles can be applied to every aspect of body, soul and spirit.

If your life has been at a standstill, and you have not made any progress for quite some time, now would be the perfect time to make a change. It is time to stop wasting your time and start investing your time. By reevaluating your attitude and making any necessary attitude adjustments with respect to your time, the results will be an investment in your life.

The truth of the matter is this: If you are wasting your time then consequently you are wasting your life. Conversely, if you invest your time, then you are investing your life.

Regardless of whether you waste your time or invest your time, the results you experience are twofold—what you do with your time affects not only you, but it also affects the other people in your life. A man is not an island unto himself. Wasting time is never profitable. Wasting time has a negative connotation. People around such a person are turned off by the negative attitude that accompanies a wasted life. A person who is wasting time—and therefore life—is a negative person and, consequently, more of a detriment than a value to the people around.

On the other hand, if you invest your time, then great things happen. The results of investing are very positive. You accomplish more things in your life, you have the greatest potential for attaining your goals, and your life is fuller and worth living. Even your work becomes more enjoyable. The effect you have on people is very positive. People have a tendency to gravitate to people who have a positive attitude.

A positive attitude will carry you through dark times when doubt and discouragement arise in your soul. Others may jump ship when tough times come, running away as fast as they can. Consequently,

2-3

Checklist of Pitfalls

Setting goals too high to reach—The greater the expectations, the greater the discouragement. Set plenty of short-range goals. As you obtain each one, you will gain continual motivation and tenacity.

Plateau effect—Progress comes in leaps and bounds. Establish a monthly timeline for checking with your progress.

Negative feedback—Consider the source. Make yourself accountable to someone who is positive and encouraging. Review your goals, repeat your goals and mentally visualize them. Reject all negative words or comments.

Obsession—Stay balanced. Obsession is on the opposite end of neglect. Both are unhealthy. Keep focused, but enjoy the journey. Add humor to your lifestyle. Your balanced lifestyle is inspirational and appealing to others.

Negative thoughts—They come from the subconscious mind, which contains negative input. Choose to refute any and all such thoughts. Don't speak them, and remind yourself that you are an inspiration in transition.

their goals become nothing more than wishing and hoping. Don't do that. Let your positive attitude steer you to success.

Christopher Columbus faced continual resistance from the leaders of his country as he made plans to set out to discover a new land. His own peers and fellow seamen sneered at his wild ideas of discovering land on the other side of the ocean—that body of water so huge that it was frightening to imagine crossing it. He had never journeyed across the ocean—and neither had anyone else. There wasn't even any certainty that his belief that the earth was round was true. The possibility of falling off the earth threatened to intimidate his attitude.

There were rumors of sea monsters large enough to destroy a sea vessel, devouring him and his crew. Disease and plagues of deadly illnesses could possibly claim his life and those of his shipmates. Everybody and everything seemed to oppose his goals and plans. But they all misjudged one primary element that Columbus possessed—his positive attitude! His tenacity made all the difference—it brought success to him in his endeavor, and it will do the same for you and me.

Today we enjoy the freedom and lifestyles of living in America because Christopher Columbus set his mind in stone. He had his plans in place. He mapped the course, kept his focus on reaching America and did not allow anyone or anything to come against him or discourage him from reaching his goal.

What if Columbus had allowed the threat of possible negatives to affect his attitude? Where would we be today?

How about it? Are you ready for an attitude adjustment? Remember, people who invest their time are investing in their own lives as well as in the lives of others. They are in it for more than what they get for themselves. They are not takers but givers. They understand that they can be a positive influence on others who, like themselves, have struggled with differing issues but learned how to overcome.

Let me share a story with you that will illustrate the point I am making. A beggar lived in a run-down, dilapidated hut on the outskirts of a small village. Every day he journeyed into the village to beg for handouts from the village people.

After begging all day long, each evening he left the village and returned to his hut. There he emptied out his bag to see what he had received that day. He did this every day, month after month, year after year.

The village people were very proud of their village. They all worked hard to keep their village clean and neat. They made it a safe place for their children to play and for the old folks to walk at night. They were wonderful people who cared for one another, and they loved their king.

The king was a generous man. He adored the village people for their giving and caring spirits. Once a year the king visited the village, bringing gifts for everyone. This was the biggest event of the year for the people in the village. On the day the king was scheduled to arrive, the people made sure all the streets were spotless. Every limb on every tree was trimmed with colorful ribbons, and the whole village was prepared for the king's arrival. The streets were lined with the families and friends from the village as they anxiously awaited his entry.

This year was a big day for the beggar also. He actually managed to be the first in line this time. He stood with his bag outstretched, waiting for the king's carriage to stop so he could get a gift. As the carriage pulled up before the beggar, instead of giving the beggar a gift, the king spoke to the beggar, asking, "What do you have to give to the king?"

The beggar frantically searched through his bag to find something insignificant to give the king from the things he had received from the village people that day. Finally he pulled out a small token and handed it to the king. Then the king reached out his hand and placed something in the beggar's bag, moving on to the next person.

Needless to say, the beggar was so excited—he had received something from the *king!* His gift came from the king, not just the ordinary people of the village. Quickly he ran back to his hut to see what he had received from the king. He emptied his collections for the day, spreading the goods out on the bare floor in the room. Excitedly he examined everything he had received.

Nothing can stop the man with the right mental attitude from achieving his goal; nothing on the earth can help the man with the wrong mental attitude.

—Thomas Jefferson

Suddenly he saw a tiny, shiny speck of gold. The king had given him gold!

But suddenly he became very saddened. As he looked at that speck of gold, a terrifying thought came to his mind. *If this speck of gold is what I received from the king for giving him the least of my possessions, what would I have received if I gave my whole bag to the king?*

What if you gave your all to accomplishing your fitness goals? Your fitness journey will not end when you reach your own personal goals. You will go on to impact others. You will be an encouragement and inspiration to others who, like you, would like to feel healthier, have more energy and enjoy a strong, healthy body. They are watching you to see how you will do. Some will not make a move to begin their own fitness journey until you have succeeded at yours. So remember, you can pass the torch to others by pouring your best efforts into your life and by maintaining a positive attitude.

Bloodtypes
Bodytypes
YOU and

Section II

Instinctive Eating—
Eating According to
Your Blood Type

Chapter 3

How to Become an Instinctive Eater

Throughout the years, there have been too many different diet plans to even try to list them all. Each one promises to be your "knight in shining armor" . . . your "pot of gold at the end of the rainbow" . . . your "holy grail" to health. My goal in this book is not to help you pick a diet plan that will bring you success. We have been there, done that.

Neither do I intend to poke holes in the various diet plans, both popular and unpopular, that are available to you. Why not? The answer is simple: I am most interested in helping you to understand better the concept of instinctive eating. Then I will leave the rest up to you.

Instinctive eating is uniquely different from the typical diet plan. Instinctive eating requires that you grasp hold of your genetic or cellular profile, using that knowledge as the baseline or fundamental foundation for the way you eat.

You will understand the difference between diet plans and instinctive eating as you read the following pages. But more important than what you read—*you will experience the difference once you give it your best shot.* My intention here is to help you

If you are a dieter, have tried dieting to some degree or would like to take your first healthy step in the right direction, then get ready for some fascinating and life-changing information that you can try for yourself.

see what instinctive eating is and why it makes good sense to implement it as a part of your lifestyle. So if you are a dieter, have tried dieting to some degree or would like to take your first healthy step in the right direction, then get ready for some fascinating and life-changing information that you can try for yourself.

My experience throughout the years has taught me that the greatest majority of people who have searched for a diet plan wanted one that would help them to reach a goal of *permanent* weight loss. Yet seldom—if ever—have they found a plan that could succeed at that! For one reason or another, the plan they chose did not work—at least not at permanent weight loss. No doubt the main reason was that it was just too difficult to adapt to that diet plan as a lifestyle change.

Most people would love to find the answer to their fatigue, weight and health problems so they could feel better and enjoy their lives more. That's a normal human desire. But sometimes it takes a wake-up call to get a person's attention—something like a heart attack, stomach disorder or chronic illness that steals your money and, more importantly, your life.

The desire to better ourselves and to live longer lies within each of us. It's part of our natural, innate mechanism for survival. My main objectives are to get you on the path to instinctive eating and to keep you from the frustrating and unnecessary physical and emotional roller-coaster rides so often associated with diets.

In my book *Seven Pillars of Health*, I explain the perils of dieting by taking you on a cruise to Diet Island.[1] I think once you read it, you will absolutely identify with it.

If you have sought long-term results by following a diet plan that focuses strictly on end results, now would be a great time to take your first step by changing your thinking. Just the thought of going on a diet causes words to surface, words like *sacrifice, deprivation, going without* and *struggling to stay on a diet.*

Who said that making healthier food selections was a matter of pure sacrifice? Who said you could never deviate from the letter of the law? Certainly not me! That kind of a behavioral response has caused thousands of people like yourself to end up thinking that making healthy food selections is nothing more than a punishment/reward system of eating. Consequently, this mind-set will prohibit lifestyle adaptation.

The problem with this diet mentality is this: The focus is on the end results. It disregards the essentials—improving your health, becoming disease free and living a longer, healthier life with more energy. These essentials require a lifestyle adaptation.

You may have been victimized by the commercial slants placing all the emphasis on cosmetic results—not lifestyle. If you are wondering if marketing the "body beautiful" is a powerful tool, just ask any marketing genius from one of the huge weight-loss companies. I am sure they will tell you that it is much harder to sell good health than it is to sell the promise of beauty. Understand what I am saying here. While each one of us will have motivational influences that initially engage us to make dietary changes, in order to be successful over the long haul we must focus on the journey—not the destination.

Focus on the Journey

The road you travel, the path you choose to enjoy the journey of your life, needs to become your focus point, not merely the destination. When the focus is placed on the wrong thing, failure is inevitable. That's why the majority of the diet plans you have tried before never lasted.

As you analyze your dieting experiences in retrospect, you will probably agree that they were more of a "suck it up and give it all the will power you can muster for as long as you can" kind of experience—definitely not a journey.

Focusing on the journey offers many more rewards along the way than focusing only on the end results. The journey experience allows you

3-1

Benefits of the Journey Experience

- Continual awareness of your body's reactions to certain foods
- Realization of the positive or negative side effects from certain foods
- A constant increase in energy
- Better cholesterol readings
- Less need for medications
- Less down time caused by sickness and ill health

to enjoy the many benefits available by making adaptable dietary changes for a lifetime. These benefits come in many packages. (See Chart 3-1.)

Focusing on the journey will help you to enjoy life by spending more time with your family and friends and less time visiting hospitals and doctors. The path or road you decide to travel determines the lifestyle with which you will live.

Are you ready to make your choice? Are you ready to begin the journey?

Instinctive Eating

In this section of the book you will discover how to become an instinctive eater. Most people are not instinctive eaters. At one time neither was I. Instinctive eating is best understood by observing the creatures in the animal kingdom.

Let's look at the lion as one example. This cool cat has never taken a course in Nutrition 101 or purchased the latest weight-loss diet plan on the market. She was never influenced by medical and scientific documentation teaching her that all food is OK to eat as long as she ate it in moderation. This feline has never been formally educated.

But how fascinating it is to note that the lion possesses something far superior to what has—or has not been—scientifically proven. She has a dietary mechanism for survival, which is *instinctive eating*. When it comes to eating there are no guidelines for her to follow. There are no daily menus to follow. But when dinnertime rolls around, she absolutely knows what she should eat. The lion will always order meat for dinner. She would not be caught dead climbing a banana tree to eat bananas.

Her eating habits are not accidental. Nor are they coincidental. Animals eat instinctively because their inherent, natural, dietary mechanism for survival determines what they eat.

Consider the horse for a moment. A horse is a horse, of course. But when was the last time you saw a farmer strap a feed bag filled with chopped beef onto a horse? Try going to your local 4-H club to ask if chopped beef is OK for your horse. You would be laughed out of the barn. A horse's feed bag is always filled with oats.

Put a horse out to pasture, and it will naturally eat grass. Did you ever see a horse run through a pasture chasing squirrels or rabbits for a midafternoon snack?

You would be intrigued by what you can learn about animals. For example, did you know that most animals of the same species generally live to be the same age? Their dietary mechanism for survival allows them to live to the potential life span of that species. A very few may die of cancer or other rare diseases, or get killed by a predator, but most animals die of old age.

Not so for us humanoids; we are different. We generally die at a young age from a variety of different diseases, many of which are associated with our diets. Or we live out our last years in a less-than-desirable physical condition. I have always said that when it is my turn to go to heaven, I want to check out of Dodge City doing 180 miles per hour—not spending the last twenty years of life using a walker because I was negligent with my health.

The very thought of living to be one hundred years of age is, for most humans, quite a stretch. Up until now we did not have a clue about how to eat instinctively. Most people eat for reasons that fall far short of supplying our bodies with sound nutrition, good health and longevity. We all come from a huge dietary mixing bowl that swings like a pendulum. Some people or groups insist that everybody should be a vegetarian, while others refuse to give up their meats. Others will support the high-carbohydrate, zero-protein-and-fat diet while others support a high-protein, high-fat and no-carbohydrate diet. Throw in our taste buds, ethnic traditions, religious beliefs, social settings and the dilemma of the emotional, bulimic and anorexic eater, and it is easy to see why we have a lot to learn from the dietary instincts of our "inferior" animal counterparts.

Unless you have lived with gorillas for many years and learned all about instinctive eating as Anthony Hopkins did in the movie *Instinct*, how could you experience benefits from instinctive eating? How could you become an instinctive eater if at first you didn't have some guidelines or dietary strategies from which

Your first step in becoming an instinctive eater will be knowing your blood type. Are you a type A, B, AB or O?

to learn? Remember, we have never been enlightened to know how to eat instinctively. We must first learn.

The dietary guidelines in this book are based on your blood type. Your first step in becoming an instinctive eater will be knowing your blood type. Are you a type A, B, AB or O? (See page 55 to find out how to determine your blood type.)

I believe personally that I am communicating to you an approach to eating that is the most effective, individual and accurate method of making food selections that can become an adaptable lifestyle change. Because this method is genetically based, it will prove itself by the many ways your body responds to certain foods.

I do not expect you to take my word for it without some basic understanding and ultimately testing its validity for yourself. This is especially true when it comes to making dietary changes. The dietary changes must not impose restrictions so unrealistic that you find it impossible to reach your goals or so unattainable that the changes cannot become part of your lifestyle.

On the other hand, you must remember that anything worth doing is worth doing right. My desire is to help you live a healthy, more energetic and sickness-free life for as long as possible. What I am recommending is "doable." If it wasn't realistic enough to live with, we would both be wasting our time. I want you to become a "believer" like me, and like the people in this book who share their experiences and thousands of others who have put this dietary approach to the test.

Genetic Baseline

One of the primary reasons why different blood types respond differently to certain foods is due to the effect dietary lectins have on the host's body. Dietary lectins are protein molecules found in food. If a food is not compatible to your blood type, these lectins can create havoc in your body systems. These negative responses occur due to a chemical phenomenon referred to as *agglutination*. The lectins will bond themselves randomly to blood cells in an organ or bodily system and begin to interfere with the natural and normal function of that particular system or organ.

Typically, blood cells have a slippery surface and are unaffected by dietary lectins as long as the host consumes foods that are compatible. But dietary lectins present in foods that are incompatible with your blood type wreak havoc by attaching themselves to the blood cell.

Think for a moment about what would happen if you tried to roll a tennis ball over a strip of Velcro. The tennis ball would stick to that Velcro strip just like glue and be impossible to roll. This is what happens when you ingest foods that are not compatible to your blood type. Instead of the dietary lectins rolling over the blood cells in that system, they will stick like glue to the surface of the blood cells.

Let's take your digestive system for example. Suppose you consume some food that is not compatible to your blood type. The dietary lectins begin to attach themselves to the blood cells on the wall of your intestines. As this process continues, a clumping of blood cells takes place that begins to interfere with the normal function of that digestive system. Now your problems have just begun.

You may not be aware this is taking place, but your digestive system knows. It just took a hit, and it is beginning its downward spiral. Your body knows that it has just been poisoned, and it tries to let you know by sending you signals or warning signs. Sometimes these warnings or signals are subtle and less dangerous, giving you symptoms like gas, bloating or indigestion, things we normally just ignore.

But ignoring these symptoms is a dangerous thing to do. They often indicate a serious problem or disease that needs an immediate solution if we want to maintain good health.

If these symptoms persist, the next order of business is usually to medicate. Medicating a symptom is a behavioral reaction that most people do when they discover that part of their normal bodily function is malfunctioning. They respond this way because of their immediate need for satisfaction and relief. Often they are also unaware of good prevention and cure techniques.

Instead of addressing the root problem that is causing your body to send out these helpful warnings to you, you end up experiencing the possible loss of function of that system by medicating the symptoms. The time finally comes when these warnings can no longer be ignored or sufficiently medicated. You become nearly incapacitated by cramping, abdominal pain, continual fatigue and the lack of energy.

Instinctive eating can help you to pick up immediately on the signals your body is sending.

Soon you find yourself dealing with chronic digestive disorders like diverticulitis, irritable bowel syndrome (IBS), celiac sprue disease and possibly the eventuality of cancer of the colon. At this point your quality of life has taken a major dive.

How unfortunate it would be if your house were on fire and the firemen came and squirted water only on the smoke. With that kind of negligent approach it would not be very long before there was nothing left of your home. This is exactly what happens to your health and quality of life when you ignore the warning signs that your body is sending out.

Instinctive eating can help you to pick up immediately on the signals your body is sending. You will quickly become aware of the negative responses your body warns you about when you eat incompatible foods.

The things that I just described about your digestive system do not have to happen to your health. You can avoid them by learning to become an instinctive eater. You only have one body to carry you throughout life; why wouldn't you want to take care of it?

One day as I was mailing books at the local post office, one of the clerks asked me what the book was all about. After explaining the concept to her, I asked her why she had asked.

She told me that she had constant stomach pain and was taking medication for it. She was overweight and tired all the time. I gave her a book and told her to follow the dietary guidelines and menus for at least three weeks. I advised her to do her best to avoid the "Avoid" foods listed for her blood type.

As we talked, I asked her if she was a blood type B, which she said she was. I told her it would be imperative to avoid eating chicken. She was flabbergasted, because chicken was her staple. She ate it almost daily.

About three weeks later I went back to the post office, and

out from behind the counter this woman jumped. "What do you think?" she asked. (Keep in mind that I didn't know her.) Before I could say anything, she said that she had dropped sixteen pounds. She had no more stomach pain, was off her medications and felt great. Plus, she had tons of energy.

She confessed that one day her daughter brought over some fried chicken, but she ate only one piece. Twenty-four hours after she ate it, she had an upset stomach. The taste of the chicken had actually been totally unappealing to her. "I never would have believed it if I didn't try it," she said to me. "It was the easiest thing I ever did!"

Learning to be an instinctive eater may not be the easiest thing you will ever learn to do—but it will be one of the healthiest things you ever do for yourself. The next chapter will help you to get started by showing you how to complete a simple four-week test at instinctive eating. It's one test you will be glad you took.

Chapter 4

Your Four-Week Test Plan

Now that you have had this informal crash course, Instinctive Eating 101, you have a better understanding about the connection that exists between your specific blood type and the food you eat. By now you should be motivated to test this concept and prove it for yourself.

This four-week test period is what I refer to as *your window of opportunity*. If you will take this opportunity, believing that your good health is worth this investment of time, I believe you will discover for yourself that what I have told you will work for you.

This information can become your ticket to great health. By following the dietary and exercise guidelines in this book, you can turn your health around, control your weight, increase your energy, stabilize your blood sugar, lower your cholesterol and blood pressure and possibly get off prescription medications once and for all.

God did not make any mistakes when He made you and me. He created us to live long, healthy lives, and He placed on this earth all the necessary food sources for us to do just that. Just

Something as simple as adapting to a better dietary lifestyle by making behavior change(s) in advance of the onset of disease instead of after disease invades our body can increase our potential for living longer and healthier.

because we may not understand something new or unfamiliar does not mean we should discard it as useless to us.

The world of science is making continual biological advancements. Science is decoding and breaking down the understanding of DNA codes at a surprising rate. An entirely new world of health possibilities is right around the corner. Daily we are learning to better understand our bodies and how to keep them in optimal health.

Learning how to more accurately appropriate these new discoveries and biological findings may one day show us how to prevent diseases before they occur, simply by addressing the root issues. Something as simple as adapting to a better dietary lifestyle by making behavior change(s) in advance of the onset of disease instead of after disease invades our body can increase our potential for living longer and healthier.

This simple four-week test will give you the opportunity to experience for yourself, without any outside influences, that what I am telling you is real—and it works. It will answer many of your questions about whether there truly is a connection or link between your blood type and diet, health, disease, energy, weight loss, low blood sugar, sugar cravings and longevity. Keep in mind that individual results will vary because we are all different, even those of the same blood type. Each person is still uniquely made. Because none of us share the same physical conditions, medical history or body genetics, it is imperative for you to let your body be your only teacher. You can do that as you learn to become an instinctive eater.

Beginning Your Four-Week Test

Before you begin your four-week test, you will want to know your blood type. Chart 4-1 can help you to determine your specific blood type.

After you have determined your blood type, it is time to prepare for your four-week test. First, check with your physician before following these dietary guidelines. This four-week test is not to be misconstrued as a substitute for medical recommendations.

Determining Your Blood Type

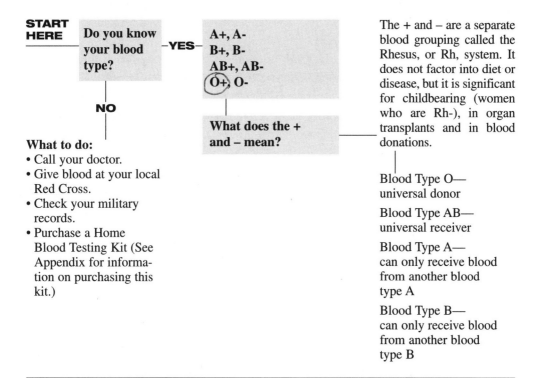

START HERE Do you know your blood type?

YES A+, A- B+, B- AB+, AB- O+, O-

What does the + and − mean?

NO

What to do:
• Call your doctor.
• Give blood at your local Red Cross.
• Check your military records.
• Purchase a Home Blood Testing Kit (See Appendix for information on purchasing this kit.)

The + and − are a separate blood grouping called the Rhesus, or Rh, system. It does not factor into diet or disease, but it is significant for childbearing (women who are Rh-), in organ transplants and in blood donations.

Blood Type O— universal donor

Blood Type AB— universal receiver

Blood Type A— can only receive blood from another blood type A

Blood Type B— can only receive blood from another blood type B

For the next four weeks, you will be monitoring the foods you eat. You will choose from the food groupings given in this book. However, the important thing to remember will be to choose from the appropriate food groupings for you. There are approximately sixteen food groups given for each blood type, which include all the various foods we eat as well as condiments, spices and juices. These food groups will give you a wonderful array of food to choose from, with many varieties in each group.

Each blood type has three categories for each food group— *beneficial foods*, *neutral foods* and *avoid foods*.

1. *Beneficial foods*—foods that your body, according to

your blood type, treats as medicine for healing systems and improving bodily function and performance

2. *Neutral foods*—foods that your body, according to your blood type, treats as compatible sources of energy

3. *Avoid foods*—foods that your body, according to your blood type, treats as poisons and toxins. (These are are not necessarily junk food. It may be your favorite food, one that all this time you thought was good for you.)

Window of Opportunity

The four-week test can be your window of opportunity. To get the most accurate results, follow the guidelines given below.

AVOID THE "AVOID" FOODS

During the next four weeks, do your best to avoid eating the Avoid Foods listed for your blood type. No one will be 100 percent successful at doing this, but give it your best attempt. Look for continued progress—not perfection. Avoid Foods are foods that are not compatible with your specific blood type; therefore, they should be avoided.

During this test period your body will undergo a detoxification process. Much of the detoxifying will take place within your digestive system, which is greatly influenced by the association of your blood type and dietary lectins from the food you eat. You will begin experiencing some wonderful changes. Some of the symptoms that you may have been experiencing prior to this test, such as gas, bloating, irritable bowel syndrome and gastroesophageal reflux disorder (GERD), have been known to disappear during this test period. In most cases these symptoms disappear in just a few days.

Within weeks, you may also experience a considerable drop in your elevated cholesterol and blood pressure levels—without the use of medications. If you struggle with hypoglycemia, or low blood sugar, your blood sugar levels will stabilize.

Within several days, you could discover that you have more

than enough energy to last all day long instead of feeling your energy drop off in the middle of the day, as I did while struggling with hypoglycemia for fifteen long unbearable years. (I haven't had low blood sugar problems in more than three and a half years.)

Along with the foods you avoid, avoid also the diet mentality that focuses on the end results only. Do not become trapped by thoughts of what you cannot eat. That's the old way of diet thinking. The avoidance of the Avoid Foods is not a form of punishment, nor is it a form of imprisonment. *You can eat anything you want!* But by adhering to these guidelines for this test period, you will have the opportunity to experience a cleansing and relief from some of the digestive disorders your body has been dealing with.

Keep in mind that the Avoid Foods play havoc with blood lipids and the proper function of your digestive system, immune system, liver and kidneys. The more you adhere to the guidelines for the test period, the greater the opportunity for your body to rid itself of damaging dietary lectins. Eliminating these dietary lectins found in the Avoid Foods will give you positive results now—and long term. You will accumulate the knowledge you need to truly become an instinctive eater.

Avoiding the Avoid Foods for your blood type will bring another benefit—weight loss! The toxins that have been stored up in the fat cells of your body as a result of eating the wrong foods will be eliminated, and the fat cells will begin to shrink as part of the detoxification process. Your digestive system and your metabolism will start to function properly and more efficiently as you eliminate dietary lectins, like wheat gluten, which slow down metabolism and digestive system functions. The results will be a healthy colon, a speedy metabolism and loss in body fat—all without going on a diet! I refer to the loss of body fat as a by-product of instinctive eating—not the by-product of dieting. I think you will agree.

CONCENTRATE ON THE BENEFICIAL FOODS

You may be wondering, *If I avoid the Avoid Foods, what can I find to eat?* You will have a delectable array of good nutritious foods from which to choose. Simply make all your

> **Along with the foods you avoid, avoid also the diet mentality that focuses on the end results only. Do not become trapped by thoughts of what you cannot eat.**

food selections from the twenty-eight-day menus or pick and choose your favorite food selections from the Beneficial Foods category for your blood type.

Once you complete the test period, your body has experienced a thorough cleansing and overhaul.

As you consider your food choices, you will discover that there are more food selections in the Beneficial Foods and Neutral Foods than you found on the Avoid Foods list, so don't despair. Do not even bother trying to count calories during the four-week test period—just eat. A good rule to follow is this: Eat when you are hungry, but stop when you are comfortably satisfied.

In some of the food groupings, you will see that there are no Beneficial Foods from which to choose. Your first choice should be to forego that particular food group, but if you must make a selection, do so from the Neutral Foods. Remember, the more correctly you eat for your blood type, the better the results, and your Beneficial Foods will promote the best results.

Once you complete the test period, your body has experienced a thorough cleansing and overhaul. You should have some wonderful experiences to share. Many people have called, e-mailed or written my office to share their positive experiences during their four-week test. I would love to hear from you, too. (See page 293 for contact information.)

MONITOR YOUR PROGRESS

It will be important to monitor your responses during this four-week period. Here are four important steps in the monitoring process:

1. If possible, have blood work done to know your current cholesterol readings before you start.
2. If possible, have your blood pressure taken before you start.
3. Record medication dosages, which medications and for what condition you are taking them.
4. Record your progress by comparing the changes from your current condition list to the test results list.

Use Chart 4-2 to monitor your progress.

Monitor Your Progress

Body Signpost	Current Condition	End of Four Weeks	Test Results
1. Cholesterol level	/	/	
2. Blood pressure	/	/	
3. Low blood sugar or hypoglycemia (yes/no)			
4. Body weight	Lbs.	Lbs.	Lost___Lbs.
5. Body fat percentage	%	%	
6. Energy level (high/low)			
7. Allergies: Hay fever, sinus, headaches, etc.			
8. Digestive symptoms: Gas, bloating, diarrhea, constipation, IBS, GERD, stomach pain, arthritic-like pain, etc.			
9. List any medications you are taking for the allergies or digestive symptoms described.			

Take the Acid Test

There is one final part to this test that is totally and completely contradictory to all that I have been telling you above. At the end of your four weeks, I want you to take one more test. This test will be the "proof of the pudding," the "topping on the cake." I want you to take the "acid test."

Here is what I want you to do. Immediately on the very next morning after you complete your four-week test of eating Beneficial Foods for your blood type, begin eating nothing but

Avoid Foods for two whole days! That's right—*eat all the Avoid Foods you want.*

Watch what happens. You will experience symptoms ranging from diarrhea or constipation to gastrointestinal abdominal pain. You will probably be bloated with gas, and you may experience low blood sugar, acid reflux and more. You will feel absolutely terrible!

You may ask, *Are you trying to inflict some sort of suicidal behavior on me?* Well, in a sense your actions could be suicidal—if you decided to live that way. But no doubt your mind will remind you that these symptoms are the very things you were experiencing over and over again before you started eating correctly for your blood type. The problem was, you had not yet learned to eat instinctively—so you knew no other way of living except in the pain and agony of such symptoms.

As you learn to eat correctly for your blood type, your body will function more properly, your metabolism will stay revved up and your digestive system will operate more efficiently. You will be able to control your weight without dieting and live longer with less to no incapacitating illnesses. More importantly, you will be able to enjoy your life to its fullest.

Eventually, your journey will allow you to be like the lioness that didn't need a menu to follow or a course in Nutrition 101 to eat instinctively. The lioness didn't need to be told that her way of eating was scientifically proven. She was an innate instinctive eater—and you will have learned to be an innate instinctive eater also.

Chapter 5

Diet and Nutrition

In this chapter I will discuss the benefits of eating for your blood type, the importance of whole, unprocessed foods and how to make this ideal a reality in your life. I have designed this section to help coach you along in your process. You *can* do it! You have already taken the first step just by reading this book!

The most important thing to remember when following any food plan is to make the food you eat interesting and delicious. If you are not enjoying what you put in your mouth, it really doesn't matter how healthy the food is. You won't eat it again. I know I wouldn't! An entire section has been created full of delicious recipes specific to each blood type. There is careful cross-referencing in the master index of the recipe section to insure those families with mixed blood types can peacefully coexist. Also, each recipe is marked with the blood types that it was meant for. You might actually find a variation of your favorite dish in there modified to suit your blood type. I promise you that you will not have to eat dull, bland or boring foods in order to implement this program in your life.

Eating healthily does not have to be boring. In fact, on your journey to good health you will no doubt find many new and interesting foods that you otherwise would never have experienced. The key to healthy eating is really to be a bit daring and try new things. The key word is to *try*. The basic guidelines for this program of eating are simple.

- Eat more protein than carbohydrates to keep your body in an anabolic state and your glycemic index as low as possible.
- Complex carbohydrates should be preferred over simple carbohydrates.
- All foods you choose should be compatible with your blood type.
- Decrease saturated fats. Use blood-type-appropriate monounsaturated and polyunsaturated fats instead.
- Drink plenty of water.
- Eat a minimum of one large serving of dark leafy vegetables (such as kale, chard, collard greens, mustard greens, dandelion greens or arugala) each day. The variety will depend upon your blood type requirements.
- Eat unprocessed foods whenever possible. Choose fresh foods.
- Eat organic foods whenever possible.

Protein, the Anabolic State and the Glycemic Index

Every time you eat protein the body produces glucagon and enters an anabolic state. This is the same state that happens when we abstain from excessive carbohydrates. Glucagon shifts the body into a burning mode. Proteins are converted to ketones, which are utilized for energy. Fat is released from the cells to be used as energy. The kidneys release excess water. Weight loss is the result.

Conversely, a catabolic state is when carbohydrates are converted to sugar in your body. The pancreas secretes insulin to keep the sugar levels in balance. The excess insulin places your body into a catabolic state. Catabolic state simply means that the insulin converts the protein into fats. These fats then are stored, resulting in excess weight. Another by-product of excess insulin production is the increase of cholesterol. The kidneys retain excess fluids, and glucose (sugar) is used as energy instead of fat. If our bodies are in a continual catabolic state, we subject ourselves to the risk of heart disease, high blood pressure, high cholesterol and many other health problems.

There is a definite difference in which types of carbohydrates cause a catabolic state. Simple carbohydrates such as white bread, wheat bread and rice cakes enter the blood stream at a rapid rate. Foods such as these have a high glycemic index rating. Other complex carbohydrates such as cherries, apples, peanuts, soybeans, peaches and rye bread enter the blood stream much more slowly, thus resulting in a lower glycemic index rating. The slower the introduction into the blood stream the better. Please refer to the glycemic

5-1

Glycemic Index of Common Foods

Cereals	100+
Puffed rice, rice cakes, puffed wheat	133
Maltose	110
Glucose	100
White bread, whole-wheat bread	100
Carrots	92
Oat bran, rolled oats	88
Honey	87
White rice, brown rice, corn, bananas	82
All Bran, kidney beans	72
Raisins, macaroni, beets	64
Pinto beans, sucrose	59
Peas, potato chips, yams	51
Orange juice, sweet potatoes, sponge cake	46
Oranges, navy beans, grapes, 100% rye bread	40
Nonfat yogurt	39
Tomato soup	38
Apples, chickpeas, ice cream, yogurt, milk	35
Lentils, peaches	29
Cherries, grapefruit, plums	25
Soybeans	15
Peanuts	12
Juice ratings:	
Peach, plum, cherry, grapefruit	Low
Pear, orange, apple, grape	Moderate
Banana	High

index chart to gain a better understanding of this principle.[1]

Bear in mind that when we talk about protein, we are referring to lean, good-quality animal protein, fish, tofu, tempeh and some legumes. Whenever possible it is advisable to consume "organic" or "free-range" animal products. These animal products are free from antibiotics, bovine growth hormones, steroids and other sundry chemical residues. While these products may cost slightly more, it is important to remember that the quality of the food you put into your body is just as important as the specific types. It is not my intention to endorse high-fat protein sources, which will cause untold troubles for all readers. Refer to your food lists for the specific protein sources of each blood type.

To purchase protein powder compatible with your blood type, or for more information on Body Genetics Protein Shake, the bloodtype-compatible protein drink mentioned throughout this book, see Appendix.

Blood Typing

Your blood type can tell a lot about you. It is a great place to begin when you are trying to choose what to eat. There are a lot of diets on the market. However, none are specifically tailored to an individual's needs. Most are very generic. How many times have you had a friend who could eat certain foods and have no ill effects, but when you ate the same foods, you experienced bloating, weight gain and other discomforts? We are not all alike. Knowing your blood type and the associated beneficial foods is one further step in being able to personalize a plan of eating.

The following food lists are intended to provide you with the benefits of prior research that indicates which foods tend to be best suited for each blood type. While these lists are not written in stone, they do provide the foundation for a blueprint of foods best suited for each blood type. However, because all individuals vary to some degree in body chemistry, your reaction to each food may vary. Only trial and error will tell you which foods are best for you.

It is important to take notice of adverse reactions to specific foods. Some ABs may not tolerate grape juice or sour cherries, which are very beneficial. Because of their body chemistry, these foods were too rich or were not tolerated well. Some may not tolerate tofu and wine at the same sitting. It may be necessary for some time to pass before they have a glass of wine.

Listen to your body. If what you are eating does not agree with you, *stop*. Your body has an instinctive mechanism and knows what its needs are and what it can tolerate. Remove any foods that you are having difficulty digesting immediately. There is no need to force your body to accept food that it instinctively rejects.

These food lists also do not account for the consumption of protein, fat and carbohydrates as they relate to the body's secretion of glucagon and insulin. For that reason the menus provided will help you with the balance to insure an anabolic state.

As you review the food lists, keep in mind that the beneficial foods tend to metabolize faster and easier because of blood enzymes. Conversely, avoid foods that do not digest or metabolize well, and thus disrupt normal metabolism. It is for this reason we suggest that when you start this regimen you eat as many foods from the beneficial foods as possible, slowly adding neutral foods as you gravitate to your specific goal.[2]

Also, since you may be eating more protein than you are used to, you need to drink plenty of water. Water is the universal solvent that aids in digestion and waste removal. As a rule of thumb, divide your body weight by 2, then convert the pounds into ounces of water. This will give you the amount of water you should be drinking each day. Example: 150 pounds $\div$ 2 = 75 ounces of water a day.[3]

> **Listen to your body. If what you are eating does not agree with you, *stop*.**

BLOOD TYPE A

The foods most harmful to As in the long run are meat and dairy. The elimination of these two food groups will allow type A individuals the greatest potential to avoid heart disease and cancer. Tofu, soy products, unsalted redskin peanuts, red wine and green tea are especially good for type As because they help fight cancer.[4] Type As typically have lost the ability to make pepsin, a protein-digesting enzyme. Therefore, a more vegetarian diet or one of less-dense protein products such as chicken, turkey and

Cornish hens is more easily digestible for As. Whole grains such as quinoa, millet, brown rice and wild rice are preferable over wheat products due to an oversensitivity to such products.[5]

BLOOD TYPE B

I encourage Type B individuals to eliminate all wheat, corn, tomatoes, peanuts and especially chicken from their diets. Chicken contains a dangerous lectin that may agglutinate the blood and can also lead to heart disease, cancer, diverticulitis, irritable bowel syndrome, spastic colon and intestinal tract illnesses.[6] Blood type Bs share the diet of both types A and O, which means they can eat and happily digest a wide range of foods. Type Bs can tolerate dairy products in moderation. Fermented dairy products like yogurt, kefir and cottage cheese would be the best for type Bs. Moderation is the key word for type Bs, who can handle a little bit of everything but should not go overboard on any single food.[7]

BLOOD TYPE AB

As the rarest blood type, AB is considered the modern blood type. ABs are very rare, making up less than 4 percent of the American population.[8] The single worst food for ABs is chicken. Chicken contains a dangerous lectin that may agglutinate (clot) the blood and may also lead to heart disease, cancer and/or a host of other digestive and intestinal tract illnesses. Tofu, soy products, salted redskin peanuts, red wine and green tea are especially good for type AB because they help fight cancer and heart disease.[9] Most dairy products can be tolerated in moderation.

BLOOD TYPE O

Type O appears to be the oldest blood type. Both dairy and grains should be eaten sparingly.[10] Many Os are lactose intolerant. Soy milk and soy cheeses are the easiest and most tasty ways of replacing those much-loved dairy products. Os have a greater predisposition to celiac/sprue disease, which is the inability to digest gluten. Therefore, try to stay away from the predominantly gluten-rich grains—wheat, rye, oats and barley.[11] I also recommend that they eliminate most dairy, nuts and grains, with the exceptions listed in the Beneficial and Neutral food list. Type Os that eliminate the "avoid" dairy and grain products and stick to lean protein tend to have very low cholesterol levels and stay quite healthy.[12]

The Fat Issue

Saturated fats are primarily derived from animal sources and rarely from plants. One characteristic of animal saturated fats is that when stored at room temperature they solidify. Examples would be meat, butter and cheeses. The common store-bought plant saturated fats you might recognize are coconut oil, peanut oil, cottonseed oil and palm kernel oil. There is a close association of cholesterol-related health issues with these types of fats, including potential obstruction of arteries, which could cause heart failure. Studies suggest that excessive saturated fat consumption is also linked to some forms of cancer.

Olive oil is the highest in monounsaturated fats available.

Monounsaturated and polyunsaturated oils do not promote the accumulation of cholesterol in the arteries as do the highly saturated fats. One of the best examples of these less destructive oils can be found in olive oil. Olive oil is the highest in monounsaturated fats available. In our "fat-crazed" society we tend to forget to differentiate saturated fats from monounsaturated and polyunsaturated fats. So enjoy that dressing you made with heart-friendly olive oil!

Green Leafy Vegetables

Dark leafy green vegetables such as kale, chard, collard greens, mustard greens, dandelion greens and arugala are especially important to mention. These vegetables have a host of benefits for everyone. They improve digestion of fats and proteins and improve circulation. Mustard greens in particular aid in dissolving stagnant or congealed blood. Dark leafy greens are considered the "blood cleaners" of the vegetable kingdom. They provide much-needed chlorophyll, which inhibits viruses and colds. Vitamin A, vitamin C and calcium are also part of the benefits. Some are rich in fiber as well. Women who are concerned about getting enough calcium should try eating an extra serving of these healthy greens.

Unprocessed, Fresh and Organic Foods

In my humble opinion, it's best to wipe the slate completely clean when it comes to processed foods.

Eating healthily can sometimes be daunting given the current advertising environment in this country. There are plenty of people touting that this product or that product is the best. But in the end, most fall short of being healthy or nutritious at all. We, as Americans, consume vast quantities of processed foods laden with sugar, fats and highly processed wheat. Items touted as "fat-free" should be a warning signal to each of us. In order for a product to be tasty, yet fat-free, the manufacturer will boost the sugar content. Sucrose, which is the standard white table sugar, contributes to diabetes, hypoglycemia and many other ailments. However, the point here is that there is nothing in these foods you really need. Products that are "fortified" or "enriched" are merely attempts to put back into the food that which has been processed out.

In my humble opinion, it's best to wipe the slate completely clean when it comes to processed foods. All the vitamins, minerals and nutrients you need can be found in the simplest, fresh produce. Again, the important factor is that you are making an investment in yourself. *You* are your most valuable asset. So the quality of what you put into your body is vitally important.

We have already covered organic and free-range animal products earlier. There are also organic vegetables, fruits and virtually every other kind of produce you can imagine. For something to be organic it has to be free of toxic chemical insecticides, fungicides, pesticides and herbicides. There is a tremendous difference in taste between an organic carrot and one harvested by traditional methods. Just try it! But more important than the taste is the basic principle of not putting anything laden with chemicals into your body.

If organic products are not available in your area or are undesirable to you, the next best thing would be to buy from local farmers. Most cities host some phenomenal fresh markets. If you are unsure of where to find a fresh market, contact your local Department of Agriculture. Farmers boast both traditional and organic produce. By buying from the farmers direct, you are insuring that you are getting the freshest produce possible, thereby giving you the maximum amount of vitamins and minerals. Also, you are avoiding the extra chemicals and waxing that is used to preserve the produce in transit to large grocery stores.

If you prefer the convenience of ordering online, you can visit the following sites. They can provide you with a variety of dried goods from grains, pastas and legumes to condiments.

- www.organicfruitsandnuts.com
- www.edenfoods.com
- www.kalustyans.com
- www.forspice.com

For chemical-free meat and grains, contact the following organizations: *Organic Meats*—Coleman Natural Products, Inc., 5140 Race Court, Denver, CO 80216, 800-442-8666; *Specialty Meat and Poultry*—D'Artagnan, 280 Wilson Ave., Newark, NJ 07605, 973-344-0565; *Spelt Flour and Pastas*—Purity Foods, 2871 W. Jolly Rd., Okemos, MI 48864, 517-351-9231.

The 80/20 Approach

A few hard-core disciplined individuals may be able to handle a night-and-day dietary change. But the majority of people will find chipping away at the mountain of dietary change a better option to go by. This group of people may make six steps forward, but two steps backward every so often. They will reach the goal, but it won't be a perfect journey. So before you decide to make a 180-degree turn, trying to make all your dietary changes at one time, you might want to consider my 80/20 approach. It will allow you to enjoy the journey more.

Making dietary changes can be very difficult. All of us have made emotional associations with our food choices. We may have established an elaborate reward-and-punishment system: *If I'm good for three days, I can reward myself with that.* Or, *If I cheat once, I can't have that for a whole month or more.* Or you may be an emotional eater—not necessarily eating out of hunger, but more as coping skill for handling your emotions.

Keep working until you can successfully choose and eat foods compatible to your blood type 80 percent of the time.

Physiological factors like sugar addiction may make it difficult for you. This is common and due to a constant over-response of insulin, which robs the blood of its sugar, causing low blood sugar and promoting a craving for sweets. Generally sugar addiction occurs from eating too many carbohydrates, particularly an overabundance of simple sugars that are not compatible to one's blood type.

Sometimes making dietary changes is difficult simply because of poor eating habits—like late-night eating, skipping breakfast or eating fast foods.

Whatever the reasons, there is a greater likelihood that you will be successful if you work your way up the path methodically. Keep working until you can successfully choose and eat foods compatible to your blood type 80 percent of the time. Choose the remaining 20 percent of your food selections for taste. Of course, I would prefer that all of us could make proper food choices 100 percent of the time, but we cannot do that—so relax.

Give yourself the benefit of the doubt. Don't place undue stress on yourself and potentially risk your long-term success. That is why I am suggesting my 80/20 approach to instinctive eating. It allows for a gradual adjustment and will feel more realistic. In this way you will make instinctive eating more adaptable to your permanent lifestyle. If you will follow this plan, before long you will find that the 20 percent has shrunk to 15 percent or less.

Putting It Into Action

We have gotten past all the "technical" information. So how do we put all this information to work? It's simple. I have tried to make this foolproof and easy. Just follow the steps below.

28-DAY PICK-A-MEAL PLANNER

Make copies of the 28-Day Pick-a-Meal Planner Chart located on page 81. The structure of your food plan is outlined below:

- Breakfast
- Snack
- Lunch

- Afternoon snack
- Dinner
- Evening snack
- Before bedtime—Body Genetics Protein Shake (See Appendix.)

This may seem like a lot of food. However, eating good, healthy food at several sittings during the day helps to keep your metabolism revving at its maximum. Conversely, if you ate six times a day, consuming sugary, high-carbohydrate foods, you would no doubt gain weight and feel extremely sluggish.

Give yourself the benefit of the doubt. Don't place undue stress on yourself and potentially risk your long-term success.

BLOOD TYPE

Identify your blood type. (See Determining Your Blood Type on page 55.) Then go to the chapter pertaining to that type. There you will find the following information:

- Beneficial Foods Grocery List
- Neutral Foods Grocery List
- Avoid Foods List
- Sample meal plans for twenty-eight days

Note: All the breakfasts are listed together, as are all the lunches, dinners and snacks.

BENEFICIAL AND NEUTRAL LISTS

Highlight all the foods you like or are familiar with from the beneficial and neutral lists. Seeing so many foods highlighted should give you the confidence that you can do this!

FILL IN PLANNER

Fill in your 28-Day Pick-a-Meal Planner with the meals that appeal to you in the menu section. You can mix and match the meals. The meals are not listed in any particular order. Breakfast #3 can peacefully coexist with Lunch #20. Or you can create your own meals.

Since I am blood type O I will show you an example of what my day's selection might look like. All meals are picked from the meal outline section.

Sample Pick-a-Meal Daily Plan #1   5-2

DAY	Breakfast	Lunch	Dinner	Daily Record
1	#18 Tex Mex Omelet	#12 Soup and Sandwich	#21 Cornish Hen	☑ Body Type Exercises ☑ Cardiovascular Training ☑ Nutritional Supplements ☑ Protein Drink
	Snack #4 Apple and Almond Butter	**Snack** #14 Pecan Sandies	**Snack** #28 Body Genetics Protein Shake	

Some meals are picked from the meal outline section and others are my own creation. You are not confined to the meals that we have suggested.

Sample Pick-a-Meal Daily Plan #2   5-3

DAY	Breakfast	Lunch	Dinner	Daily Record
12	2 eggs 1 pc. Ezekiel bread	#1 Chef's Salad	#8 Steak Onions and Mushrooms Steamed Kale	☑ Body Type Exercises ☑ Cardiovascular Training ☑ Nutritional Supplements ☑ Protein Drink
	Snack #4 1 apple with almond butter	**Snack** #18 Trail Mix	**Snack** #28 Body Genetics Protein Shake	

If you skim through the menu section for each specific blood type, you will find several menus that closely resemble menus for other blood types. Perhaps only the fruit or the cheese components have been revised. Also, there are several meals that can be consumed by several of the blood types without any changes. This will aid you in your process of planning for your family.

Tips for Making It Work

1. *Remove "avoid foods."* I suggest removing the foods you love that may be on the Avoid List from the household immediately. Donate them to charity or to a neighbor. They will be thankful for them.

2. *Plan ahead.* Try to fill in a week's worth of meal planning at first. From your meal plans you can create your shopping lists.

3. *Try something new.* Each week try to incorporate one or two new foods into your meal plans. For As, ABs or Os, if you have never tried tofu or tempeh, give it a whirl. Or try a new dish from our recipe section. You might discover that you really enjoy foods that previously you would not have tried.

4. *Cook your own meals.* This will cut down on the frustration of having your food prepared with spices, condiments or preservatives that may be undesirable for your blood type. Food you prepare yourself tastes better.

5. *Use healthy cooking methods.* Choose your preparation methods carefully to avoid excess saturated fats and undesirable ingredients. Desirable cooking methods include boiled, broiled, baked, steamed, sautéed (light on the oil), grilled or poached. Undesirable cooking methods include fried, pan-seared or BBQ (too much sauce).

6. *Rotate foods.* If you eat the same food every day you are bound to get bored. I would suggest giving yourself a three- to five-day rotation of foods. For example, if you eat Amaranth Flakes for breakfast on Monday, try not to eat these same flakes until Thursday. There are a variety of other cereals or menu possibilities for you to choose from in the interim. Your taste buds will be happy, and so will your metabolism. If you eat the same foods over and over, your metabolism is not challenged; therefore, it slows down. By giving your body many different varieties of fuel (food) it constantly remains challenged and working hard for you.

7. *Exercise.* Discover your body type and then follow the guidelines given in this book.

8. *Find a buddy.* Support is always helpful. You can coach each other through the program. You don't have to be the same blood type.

9. *Drink plenty of water.* Oftentimes we mistake our bodies' need for more water with hunger pains. Try drinking a small glass of water when you think you're hungry before you eat something.

10. *Chew . . . chew . . . chew.* Eat slowly and chew your food very well. This will aid the digestion process.

11. *Put your fork down.* Put your fork down between bites. This will slow down your meal consumption time and enable you to actually allow your body to feel full.

12. *Remember that this program is a "lifestyle change."* It is not a diet. Diets are temporary. Lifestyle changes are a lifelong practice.

13. *Take it easy.* Be patient with yourself. Any new regimen will take some getting used to.

14. *Take time for yourself.* Do something you enjoy at least ONCE a week. Doing something good for yourself helps you to remember that you are alive and worth the investment of having better health, a fuller life and a deeper commitment to yourself.

Dining Out Tips

1. *Have a game plan.* First and foremost know what the structure of your meal will look like *before* you go into a restaurant. We all have a tendency to glaze over when we see the glossy menus the

waiter hands to us. For example, the components of your dinner should look like this;

• Lean protein the size of your palm
• 1 serving dark leafy green vegetables
• 1 serving other vegetable
• 1 serving carbohydrate (optional)

    I usually will go to a restaurant that serves fish or steak. A meal out for me might consist of a tuna or beef steak, sautéed spinach, a side salad or a side order of O-appropriate vegetables and wild rice. Easy!

2. *Ask questions; special requests are OK.* Ask your waiter what is in the dish you are considering if you are unsure. Most waiters are happy to provide such information. If you would like a change to the dish, within reason, do not hesitate to ask. Most establishments are used to accommodating their customers' special dietary needs.

3. *Remove bread from the table.* There is no need to tempt yourself.

4. *Place a glass of water in front of you.* Instead of nibbling or drinking too much wine, you can satiate yourself with a little water.

5. *Choose desserts carefully.* If your dessert craving kicks in, try to pick a fruit-based dessert. It is usually the safest. Poached Pears or Peaches are delicious. Otherwise, forgo the dessert in the restaurant and have something you have prepared yourself when you get home. This may be a good time to use the 80/20 rule.

6. *Enjoy your dinner companions.* Focus on the people you are with rather than the food. After all, part of a good meal out is the company.

The Assault on Body Fat

The ratio between our body fat percentage and lean muscle weight matters most.

If one of your goals is to lose weight, then let me take this time to help you fully understand the difference between losing weight and losing body fat. When clients explain to me that one of their goals is to lose weight, I know exactly what they mean, or rather what they need. Since talking about losing body fat is sometimes too embarrassing or too revealing to most, it is easier just to say weight instead. If that makes you feel better, then fine, but don't miss what I am saying here. All of us, myself included, when talking about losing weight are actually referring to losing body fat, and that's a fact. So unless you or I have to weigh a certain weight on the scale, our weight means virtually nothing significant. It is the ratio between our body fat percentage and lean muscle weight that matters most. It always has been and always will be our body composition. So now that we have that hurdle behind us, let's move on.

Excess body fat has to go for all the health reasons associated with carrying too much fat as well as for cosmetic reasons. As you begin experiencing the benefits from eating food compatible to your blood type, you will experience how they affect your bodily functions, performance and health, plus influence your body composition. So rest assured that this approach to eating that is based on your blood type is accurate, individualized, balanced and healthy. Now what I want to do is give you some insights into losing body fat so you can reach your potential sooner.

Your furnace for burning body fat is muscle tissue, so you want to be very certain that you do not lose muscle. The less muscle tissue you carry as part of your body composition, or the more muscle tissue you lose from dieting, the more difficult it will be to lose body fat. In fact, less muscle tissue diminishes your body's ability to burn or utilize fat by severely slowing down your metabolism or your body's ability to burn fat calories. Since fat is burned inside your muscle and improper dieting can cause your body to lose muscle, then what you have done is sabotaged your fat-burning furnace by dieting. Your metabolism is key when it comes to burning calories, and yes, you must stimulate your metabolism so your body becomes a calorie burner, but let's look at a couple internal systems that must be considered or factored into the fat-burning formula also. The two systems I'm referring to that are necessary for consideration but are usually ignored are the endocrine (hormone) system and the digestive system.

For example, in the endocrine system the stimulation of IGF-1 (insulin growth factor), growth hormone and glucagon allows your body to burn body fat at an alarming rate. These hormones cause your body's metabolism to go into an "anabolic state," or fat-burning mode. They recruit dietary fats (fats you eat) along with stored body fat to go to your muscle tissue to be converted for energy. You might want to consider these hormones as fat-burning hormones. Of course, they serve the body in other ways, but for our purpose they are key for "releasing the grease." Furthermore, by stimulating these hormones your body will use fat for energy instead of its preferred source of fuel—carbohydrates. Without concerning yourself with every detail of how the endocrine system functions, let's concentrate on glucagon.

LEAN MUSCLE—YOUR BEST WEAPON

The way I suggest for you to wage war against that stubborn body fat is to create metabolic momentum. Metabolic momentum is simply getting your metabolism revved up and blazing like a fire in your fireplace. Your metabolism will become a blazing fire that will burn fat calories for energy, just as using wood as kindling in your fireplace causes the fire to blaze. Your body now becomes a calorie burner instead of a body that stores calories. To make this happen there are two primary factors you must include in your strategy.

First, to stimulate the fat-burning process and elevate your metabolic rate you must build muscle tissue—there's no getting around it. You have to exercise! Your program provided in this book is designed for your specific body type, and it will also provide the necessary stimulation for building lean muscle tissue. (Ladies, don't be afraid to gain muscle weight.) I'm not talking about bulging muscles but lean weight. Your program will promote an increase in your lean weight, which is where the furnace for burning body fat is located. When your body composition is such that you show an increase in muscle mass (see Chart 13-1, page 244), your body must utilize more calories. That means twenty-four hours a day. That means even when you are sleeping, sitting at your desk at work or just driving your car, because you have more muscle mass your body will burn more calories more efficiently and constantly while you are inactive. Of course, as you increase your activity level, you burn more calories as well, so building lean muscle will give you the best of both worlds.

Second, by making dietary changes or adjustments in which you increase your protein intake, you cause a glucagon (fat-burning hormone) response. This again is referred to as an *anabolic state*. By placing more emphasis on protein and reducing your carbohydrates or sugar intake, you reduce the sugar, or glycogen storage, which then allows your "fire to rage." This fire takes place in the mitochondria, or power plant in the muscle tissue. The mitochondria is the fat-burning furnace in your muscles and is where fat is converted to energy for your body to use. If your intake of carbohydrates exceeds your protein intake, then the body creates an insulin response that suppresses your metabolism over time, the very thing you are trying to stimulate. Increasing your protein intake always influences your body to naturally increase glucagon production. This increase in glucagon production also influences other fat-burning hormones that contribute to burning fat. Therefore, eating meals and snacks that have a greater percent of protein are considered anabolic meals or snacks, and they will contribute to a leaner, healthier body. If you are physically active, your body requires more protein to meet its demands. If your goal is to lose those extra fat calories that are stored up in your body, then I suggest you make it a point to eat more protein.

Add a Protein Shake

As you make your meal and snack selections for your blood type, you should consider adding a protein shake or protein powder to your meals and snacks, or substitute a meal or snack with a protein shake or smoothie.

Protein and Exercise 5-4

Your body needs up to 5% more protein when you start to exercise regularly.[13]

Recommended daily protein intake

Weight	Moderate exercise	Light exercise
110 lb.	60 grams	43 grams
135 lb.	72 grams	51 grams
154 lb.	84 grams	60 grams
176 lb.	96 grams	68 grams
198 lb.	108 grams	77 grams

Protein sources:
(Protein per 100 g serving)
- Roasted peanuts
  26 grams
- Tuna
  26 grams
- Beef (lean)
  24 grams

Muscles use proteins to grow and to repair damage

Smoothies are a great way to add variety and color to your meals. Add protein powder to your smoothies, and they can be used as part of your breakfast, a snack or dessert. The only real preparation for smoothies is to keep freezer bags full of your favorite fruits on hand.

It is very important to have enough protein in your diet. Protein helps promote muscle tissue repair and strength, strengthens your immune system and heart, keeps blood sugar level (combats low blood sugar and hypoglycemia), creates protein synthesis and stimulates a glucagon (fat-burning hormone) response, which you now know aids your body to burn fat calories more efficiently. Ultimately your diet with ample protein will contribute to a leaner, healthier, fat-burning body. (See Chart 5-4 for information about how much protein you need.)

Add Nutritional Supplements

Your body is your superstructure, and the better condition you keep it in the greater quality of life you will enjoy. When you eat correctly for blood type, your body will return to its naturally designed way of functioning. It will show improvements in performance and strengthen itself against disease and illness. By exercising regularly in concert with your diet, your body will undergo an increase in muscle and strength, improved circulation and improved body composition. But sometimes our

Your diet with ample protein will contribute to a leaner, healthier, fat-burning body.

best intentions are hindered by our schedules and everyday demands, not allowing us the proper time for eating and exercising though we should do our best to prioritize. This is why it is important to supplement your body with nutrients that will help safeguard your health whether you are in the gym or not. But supplementing your body with blood-type specific nutrition is key. By simply taking a daily nutritional supplement and your Body Genetics Protein Shake (see Appendix), you are ensuring your body of the nutritional base it needs. (See my book *Seven Pillars of Health* for important information about nutritional supplementation.)

Now you are ready to select your blood type options and begin. The next four chapters contain these specific eating plans.

28-Day Pick-a-Meal Planner

BLOOD TYPE: _____ **BODY TYPE:** _____

DAY	Breakfast	Lunch	Dinner	Daily
1				☐ Body Type Exercises ☐ Cardiovascular Training ☐ Nutritional Supplements
	Snack	Snack	Snack	☐ Protein Drink
2				☐ Body Type Exercises ☐ Cardiovascular Training ☐ Nutritional Supplements
	Snack	Snack	Snack	☐ Protein Drink
3				☐ Body Type Exercises ☐ Cardiovascular Training ☐ Nutritional Supplements
	Snack	Snack	Snack	☐ Protein Drink
4				☐ Body Type Exercises ☐ Cardiovascular Training ☐ Nutritional Supplements
	Snack	Snack	Snack	☐ Protein Drink
5				☐ Body Type Exercises ☐ Cardiovascular Training ☐ Nutritional Supplements
	Snack	Snack	Snack	☐ Protein Drink
6				☐ Body Type Exercises ☐ Cardiovascular Training ☐ Nutritional Supplements
	Snack	Snack	Snack	☐ Protein Drink
7				☐ Body Type Exercises ☐ Cardiovascular Training ☐ Nutritional Supplements
	Snack	Snack	Snack	☐ Protein Drink

NOTE: Add your chosen option number to the small boxes above for ready reference. Write the name of each option in the space provided.

Chapter 6
Blood Type A

Blood Type

Blood Type A
Grocery List of Beneficial Foods

Meats—
All Anabolic
☐ None

Seafood—
All Anabolic
☐ Carp
☐ Cod
☐ Grouper
☐ Mackerel
☐ Monkfish
☐ Ocean salmon
☐ Pickerel
☐ Rainbow trout
☐ Snapper
☐ Sardine
☐ Sea trout
☐ Silver perch
☐ Snail
☐ Whitefish
☐ Yellow perch

Beans/
Legumes
☐ Aduke
☐ Azuki
☐ Black
☐ Black-eyed peas
☐ Green
☐ Lentils,
    domestic,
    green, red
☐ Pinto
☐ Soy, black,
    brown, green
    Edamame *

Eggs/Dairy
☐ Soy cheese *
☐ Soy milk
☐ Body Genetics
    Protein Shake *

Nuts/Seeds
☐ Flaxseeds
☐ Organic peanut
    butter
☐ Pumpkin seeds
☐ Redskin peanuts,
    unsalted

Oils
☐ Linseed
    (Flaxseed)
☐ Olive

Cereals
☐ Amaranth
☐ Kasha

Breads
☐ Essene bread
☐ Ezekiel bread
☐ Flour, rice,
    oat, rye
☐ Rice cakes
☐ Sprouted wheat

Pastas/
Grains
☐ Artichoke pasta
☐ Kasha
☐ Oat flour
☐ Rice flour
☐ Rice pasta
☐ Soba noodles
☐ Spelt noodles

Vegetables
☐ Alfalfa sprouts
☐ Artichokes
☐ Beet leaves
☐ Broccoli
☐ Broccoli
    sprouts
☐ Carrots
☐ Chicory
☐ Collard greens

☐ Dandelion
    greens
☐ Escarole
☐ Garlic
☐ Horseradish
☐ Kohlrabi
☐ Leek
☐ Okra
☐ Onions, red,
    Spanish, yellow
☐ Parsley
☐ Parsnips
☐ Pumpkin
☐ Romaine
    lettuce
☐ Spinach
☐ Swiss chard
☐ Tempeh *
☐ Tofu *
☐ Turnips

Fruit
☐ Apricot
☐ Blackberries
☐ Blueberries
☐ Boysenberries
☐ Cherries
☐ Cranberries
☐ Figs, dried,
    fresh
☐ Grapefruit
☐ Lemons
☐ Pineapple
☐ Plum, dark
    green, red
☐ Prunes
☐ Raisins

Juice
☐ Apricot
☐ Black cherry
☐ Carrot
☐ Celery
☐ Grapefruit

☐ Pineapple
☐ Prune
☐ Water and
    lemon

Spices/
Condiments
☐ Barley malt
☐ Blackstrap
    molasses
☐ Garlic
☐ Ginger
☐ Miso
☐ Mustard
☐ Shoyu
☐ Soy sauce
☐ Tamari

Beverages
☐ Coffee, regular,
    decaf
☐ Green tea
☐ Red wine
☐ Water, distilled

Herbal Teas
☐ Alfalfa
☐ Aloe
☐ Burdock
☐ Chamomile
☐ Echinacea
☐ Fenugreek
☐ Ginger
☐ Ginseng
☐ Hawthorn
☐ Milk thistle
☐ Rose Hips
☐ Saint John's
    wort
☐ Slippery elm
☐ Strawberry leaf
☐ Valerian

* Anabolic (higher
   in protein than
   carbohydrates)

Blood Type A
Grocery List of Neutral Foods

Meats—
All Anabolic
- [ ] Chicken
- [ ] Cornish hens
- [ ] Turkey

Seafood—
All Anabolic
- [ ] Abalone
- [ ] Mahi-mahi
- [ ] Ocean perch
- [ ] Pike
- [ ] Porgy
- [ ] Sailfish
- [ ] Sea bass
- [ ] Shark
- [ ] Smelt
- [ ] Sturgeon
- [ ] Swordfish
- [ ] Tuna, albacore
- [ ] Weakfish
- [ ] White perch
- [ ] Yellowtail

Beans/
Legumes
- [ ] Broad
- [ ] Cannelloni
- [ ] Fava
- [ ] Jicama
- [ ] Peas, green, pod, snow
- [ ] Snap
- [ ] String
- [ ] White

Eggs/Dairy
- [ ] Eggs *
- [ ] Farmer's cheese *
- [ ] Feta cheese *
- [ ] Frozen yogurt, low fat
- [ ] Goat cheese *

- [ ] Mozzarella, low fat *
- [ ] Ricotta, low fat *
- [ ] String cheese *
- [ ] Goat milk
- [ ] Kefir
- [ ] Yogurt, low fat

Nuts/Seeds
- [ ] Almond butter *
- [ ] Chestnuts
- [ ] Filberts *
- [ ] Hickory *
- [ ] Litchi
- [ ] Pine (Pignoli)
- [ ] Poppy seeds
- [ ] Sesame seeds
- [ ] Sunflower butter
- [ ] Sunflower seeds
- [ ] Tahini (sesame butter)
- [ ] Walnuts *

Oils
- [ ] Canola
- [ ] Cod liver

Cereals
- [ ] Barley
- [ ] Buckwheat
- [ ] Corn Flakes
- [ ] Cream of Rice
- [ ] Kamut
- [ ] Oat Bran
- [ ] Oatmeal
- [ ] Puffed Millet
- [ ] Puffed Rice
- [ ] Rice Bran
- [ ] Spelt

Breads
- [ ] Brown rice
- [ ] Corn muffins
- [ ] Fin Crisp
- [ ] Gluten-free bread
- [ ] Hi-protein, no-wheat bread
- [ ] Ideal flat bread
- [ ] Oat-bran muffins
- [ ] Oatmeal
- [ ] Rye bread, 100 percent
- [ ] Rye Crisp
- [ ] Rye Vita
- [ ] Spelt bread
- [ ] Wasa
- [ ] Wheat bagels

Pastas/
Grains
- [ ] Corn meal
- [ ] Flour, barley, bulgur, wheat, graham, spelt, sprouted wheat
- [ ] Quinoa
- [ ] Rice, basmati, brown, white, wild
- [ ] Spelt pasta

Vegetables
- [ ] Arugala
- [ ] Asparagus
- [ ] Avocado, Florida
- [ ] Bamboo shoots
- [ ] Beets
- [ ] Bok choy
- [ ] Brussels sprouts
- [ ] Caraway

- [ ] Cauliflower
- [ ] Celery
- [ ] Chervil
- [ ] Coriander (cilantro)
- [ ] Corn, white, yellow
- [ ] Cucumber
- [ ] Daikon
- [ ] Endive
- [ ] Fennel
- [ ] Ferns
- [ ] Green olives
- [ ] Green onions
- [ ] Kale
- [ ] Lettuce, Bibb, iceberg, mesculen
- [ ] Mushrooms, abalone, enoki, portobella, tree oyster, shitaki
- [ ] Mustard greens
- [ ] Raddichio
- [ ] Radishes
- [ ] Rappini
- [ ] Rutabaga
- [ ] Scallion
- [ ] Seaweed
- [ ] Shallots
- [ ] Sprouts, mung, radish
- [ ] Squash, all types
- [ ] Water chestnut
- [ ] Watercress
- [ ] Zucchini

Juices
- [ ] Apple
- [ ] Apple cider
- [ ] Cabbage
- [ ] Cranberry
- [ ] Cucumber
- [ ] Grape
- [ ] Vegetable

Fruits
- [ ] Apples
- [ ] Black currants
- [ ] Dates
- [ ] Elderberries
- [ ] Gooseberries
- [ ] Grapes, black, concord, green, red
- [ ] Guava
- [ ] Kiwi
- [ ] Kumquat
- [ ] Limes
- [ ] Loganberries
- [ ] Melon, casaba, canang, Christmas, crenshaw, musk, Spanish
- [ ] Nectarines
- [ ] Peaches
- [ ] Pears
- [ ] Persimmons
- [ ] Pomegranates
- [ ] Prickly pears
- [ ] Raspberries
- [ ] Starfruit
- [ ] Strawberries
- [ ] Watermelon

Blood Type

A

Blood Type A
Grocery List of Neutral Foods (con't.)

Beverages
- [ ] Seltzer water
- [ ] White wine

Herbal Teas
- [ ] Chickweed
- [ ] Colts foot
- [ ] Dandelion
- [ ] Dong quai
- [ ] Elder
- [ ] Gentian
- [ ] Goldenseal
- [ ] Hops
- [ ] Horehound
- [ ] Licorice root
- [ ] Linden
- [ ] Mulberry
- [ ] Mullein
- [ ] Parsley
- [ ] Peppermint
- [ ] Raspberry
- [ ] Raspberry leaf
- [ ] Sage
- [ ] Sarsaparilla
- [ ] Senna
- [ ] Shepherd's purse
- [ ] Skullcap
- [ ] Spearmint
- [ ] Strawberry leaf
- [ ] Thyme
- [ ] Vervain
- [ ] White birch
- [ ] White oak bark
- [ ] Yarrow

Spices/ Condiments
- [ ] Agar
- [ ] Allspice
- [ ] Almond extract
- [ ] Anise
- [ ] Arrowroot
- [ ] Basil

- [ ] Bay leaf
- [ ] Bergamot
- [ ] Brown rice syrup
- [ ] Brown sugar
- [ ] Cardamom
- [ ] Carob
- [ ] Chervil
- [ ] Chives
- [ ] Chocolate
- [ ] Cinnamon
- [ ] Clove
- [ ] Coriander (cilantro)
- [ ] Corn Syrup
- [ ] Cornstarch
- [ ] Cream of tartar
- [ ] Cumin
- [ ] Curry
- [ ] Dill
- [ ] Dulse
- [ ] Honey
- [ ] Horseradish
- [ ] Jams/jelly, from appropriate fruit
- [ ] Kelp
- [ ] Maple syrup, pure
- [ ] Mint
- [ ] Mustard, dry
- [ ] Nutmeg
- [ ] Oregano
- [ ] Paprika
- [ ] Parsley
- [ ] Peppermint
- [ ] Pimiento
- [ ] Rice syrup
- [ ] Rosemary
- [ ] Saffron
- [ ] Sage
- [ ] Salt
- [ ] Savory

- [ ] Spearmint
- [ ] Stevia **
- [ ] Sucanat **
- [ ] Tamarind
- [ ] Tapioca
- [ ] Tarragon
- [ ] Thyme
- [ ] Turmeric
- [ ] Vanilla
- [ ] White sugar

* Anabolic (higher in protein than carbohydrate)
** Natural sweet- ener

Blood Type A
List of Foods to Avoid

Meats
- Beef
- Buffalo
- Duck
- Goose
- Heart
- Lamb
- Liver
- Mutton
- Partridge
- Pheasant
- Pork, all
- Rabbit
- Veal
- Venison
- Quail

Seafood
- Anchovy
- Barracuda
- Beluga
- Bluefish
- Bluegill bass, sea
- Catfish
- Caviar
- Clam
- Conch
- Crab
- Crayfish
- Eel
- Flounder
- Frog
- Gray sole
- Haddock
- Hake
- Halibut
- Herring, fresh, pickled
- Lobster
- Lox (smoked salmon)
- Mussels
- Octopus
- Oysters
- Scallop
- Shad
- Shrimp
- Sole
- Squid (calamari)
- Striped bass
- Tilefish
- Turtle

Beans/ Legumes
- Copper
- Garbanzo (chick peas)
- Kidney
- Lima
- Navy
- Red
- Tamarind

Eggs/Dairy
- American cheese
- Blue cheese
- Brie
- Buttermilk
- Camembert
- Casein
- Cheddar
- Colby
- Cottage cheese
- Cream cheese
- Edam
- Emmenthal
- Gouda
- Gruyere
- Ice cream
- Jarlsberg
- Milk, skim, 2 percent, whole
- Monterey Jack
- Muenster
- Neufchatel
- Parmesan
- Provolone
- Sherbet
- Sour cream, nonfat
- Swiss
- Whey

Nuts/Seeds
- Brazil
- Cashews
- Pistachio

Oils
- Corn
- Cottonseed
- Peanut
- Safflower
- Sesame

Vegetables
- Cabbage, red, white, Chinese
- Eggplant
- Mushrooms, domestic
- Olives, black, green, Spanish
- Peppers, red, yellow, green, jalapeno
- Potatoes, red, white, sweet
- Tomatoes
- Yams

Fruit
- Bananas
- Coconuts
- Mangoes
- Melons, cantaloupe, honeydew
- Oranges
- Papaya
- Plantains
- Rhubarb
- Tangerines

Cereals
- Cream of Wheat
- Familia
- Farina
- Granola
- Grape Nuts
- Wheat Germ
- Shredded Wheat
- Wheat Bran

Breads
- Seven Grain
- English muffins
- High-protein bread
- Pumpernickel
- Wheat bran muffins
- Wheat matzos
- Whole-wheat bread

Pastas/ Grains
- Semolina pasta
- Spinach pasta
- White flour
- Whole-wheat flour

Spices/ Condiments
- Capers
- Gelatin
- Ketchup
- Mayonnaise
- Pepper, black, peppercorn, white
- Pickles, all kinds
- Relish, all kinds
- Tabasco sauce
- Vinegar, apple cider, balsamic, red, white
- Wintergreen
- Worcestershire sauce

Juice
- Orange
- Papaya
- Tomato

Beverages
- Beer
- Liquor
- Seltzer water
- Sodas

Herbal Teas
- Black tea, regular, decaf

Blood Type

Blood Type A
28-Day Pick-a-Meal Breakfast Options

YOGURT   1

- 4 oz. grapefruit juice
- 6–8 oz. goat yogurt with honey
- ¼ cup muesli as a topping (see recipe)
- 1 pc. Ezekiel or Essene bread with whole-fruit jam
- 10–12 oz. coffee or green tea

YOGURT   2

- 4 oz. pineapple chunks
- 6–8 oz. plain yogurt or kefir with honey
- ground flaxseeds or sunflower seeds
- 1 pc. Ezekiel or Essene bread with whole-fruit jam
- 10–12 oz. coffee or chamomile tea

HOT CEREAL *   3

- 4 oz. vegetable juice
- medium bowl of oatmeal with soy milk
- ¼ chopped apple and raisins
- 4–5 chopped walnuts
- 1 pc. brown rice bread with whole-fruit jam
- 10–12 oz. coffee or strawberry leaf tea

HOT CEREAL *   4

- 3 oz. black cherry juice
- medium bowl of oatmeal made with soy milk
- blackberries, blueberries or raspberries
- 4–5 chopped filberts
- 1 pc. Ezekiel bread with whole-fruit jam
- 10–12 oz. coffee or strawberry leaf tea

HOT CEREAL *   5

- 3 oz. prune juice
- medium bowl of Kasha (hot) with soy milk
- 4–5 walnuts
- ½ chopped pear
- 1 pc. sprouted wheat bread with almond butter
- 10–12 oz. coffee or green tea

PANCAKES *   6

- 2 medium spelt and walnut pancakes
- blueberries, blackberries or strawberries
- pure maple syrup
- side of ricotta cheese
- 10–12 oz. coffee or green tea

DRY CEREAL *   7

- 4 oz. vegetable juice
- medium bowl of muesli with soy milk (see recipe)
- 1 pc. brown rice bread with soy cheese
- 10–12 oz. coffee or chamomile tea

DRY CEREAL *   8

- 4 oz. pineapple chunks
- medium bowl spelt flakes with soy milk
- 1 pc. 100 percent rye bread with almond butter
- 10–12 oz. coffee or strawberry leaf tea

DRY CEREAL *   9

- medium bowl of corn flakes with soy milk
- sliced kiwi and blackberries
- 1 pc. Ezekiel bread with organic peanut butter
- 10–12 oz. coffee or chamomile tea

* Anabolic (higher in protein than carbohydrates)

DRY CEREAL *   10

- 4 oz. prune juice
- medium bowl of Kamut Krisp with soy milk
- black currants and sunflower seeds
- 1 pc. Ezekiel bread with goat cheese
- 10–12 oz. coffee or chamomile tea

NUT BUTTER *   11

- ½ grapefruit or 4 oz. grapefruit juice
- 1 Ezekiel bagel
- organic peanut butter and whole-fruit jam
- 10–12 oz. coffee or green tea

NUT BUTTER   12

- 4 oz. vegetable juice
- 1 oat-bran muffin
- 1 apple with almond butter
- 10–12 oz. green tea or ginger tea

SMOOTHIE *   13

- Almond Bomb Smoothie (see recipe)
- 1 pc. Ezekiel or Essene bread with whole-fruit jam
- 2 plums
- 10–12 oz. green tea or peppermint tea

SMOOTHIE *   14

- Vanilla Cherry Smoothie (see recipe)
- 1 pc. 100 percent rye or Essene bread with whole-fruit jam
- 10–12 oz. coffee or green tea

SMOOTHIE *   15

- Peaches and Cream Smoothie (see recipe)
- 1 pc. 100 percent rye or Essene bread with whole-fruit jam
- 1 hard-boiled egg
- 10–12 oz. coffee or green tea

SMOOTHIE *   16

- Purple Passion Smoothie (see recipe)
- 1 pc. Essene bread with whole-fruit jam and almond butter
- 10–12 oz. coffee or peppermint tea

EGGS *   17

- 4 oz. vegetable juice
- 2 eggs, poached, boiled or scrambled
- 1–2 plums or 4–5 figs
- 1 pc. Ezekiel or Essene bread with whole-fruit jam
- 10–12 oz. coffee or chamomile tea

EGGS *   18

- ½ grapefruit
- 2 poached eggs
- steamed asparagus
- 1 pc. rye toast with whole-fruit jam
- 10–12 oz. coffee or green tea

EGGS *   19

- 4 oz. vegetable juice
- *Cheese Omelet*
    2 scrambled eggs with scallions
    soy cheese or goat cheese
- corn muffin with whole-fruit jam
- 10–12 oz. coffee or green tea

EGGS *   20

- *Salmon Scrambled Eggs*
    2 scrambled eggs
    crumpled salmon pieces
    alfalfa sprouts
- 2 sliced kiwis
- 1 pc. Ezekiel or Essene bread with whole-fruit jam
- 10–12 oz. green tea or chamomile tea

Blood Type

A

TOFU *   21

- *Spanish-Style Scrambled Tofu*
  2 squares firm tofu
  chopped onion and tomato
  pinch of cumin and oregano
- 1 slice soy cheese
- 1 pc. 100 percent rye bread with
  whole-fruit jam
- 10–12 oz. coffee or green tea

TOFU *   22

- *Tofu and Arame Scramble*
  2 squares firm tofu with turmeric
  shredded carrot and minced onions
  ¼ cup hydrated Arame (seaweed)
- 1 pc. Ezekiel or Essene bread with
  whole-fruit jam
- 10–12 oz. coffee or green tea

TOFU *   23

- tofu spread
- 4–5 walnuts
- Rye Crisps or Rye Vitas
- kiwi and pineapple
- 10–12 oz. green tea or coffee

TOFU *   24

- 4 oz. grapefruit juice
- 2 squares tofu, steamed
- steamed broccoli, zucchini and kale
- appropriate dressing
- 10–12 oz. coffee or green tea

CHEESE *   25

- 4 oz. apricot juice or 20–30 grapes
- raw carrots, celery, zucchini
- 4 oz. farmer's or feta cheese
- Rye Crisps or Rye Vitas
- 10–12 oz. coffee or rose hip tea

CHEESE *   26

- 4 oz. carrot juice
- 4 oz. assorted appropriate cheeses
- sliced tomato
- 20–30 grapes
- 1 pc. 100 percent rye toast
- 10–12 oz. coffee or green tea

CHEESE *   27

- 4 oz. vegetable juice
- 4 oz. ricotta or goat cheese
- 1 thin slice ocean salmon (raw or cooked)
- sliced onions and alfalfa sprouts
- 2 slices 100 percent rye toast
- 10–12 oz. coffee or rose hip tea

CHEESE   28

- 1 apple or pear
- *Grilled Cheese*
  2 pc. sprouted wheat bread
  4 oz. farmer's cheese
  sliced tomato
- 10–12 oz. peppermint tea or green tea

Blood Type A
28-Day Pick-a-Meal Lunch Options

TOFU *   1

- 2 squares tofu, steamed
- steamed broccoli, carrots, zucchini and
  Swiss chard
- Red Onion Dressing (see recipe)
- 10–12 oz. seltzer or bottled water

TOFU *   2

- scallion tofu spread
- redskin peanuts
- Rye Vitas or Rye Crisps
- small side salad with Green Goddess Dressing
  (see recipe)
- 10–12 oz. soda water or iced peppermint tea

TOFU *   3

- *Stir-Fry Tofu*
  1 square tofu
  broccoli, carrots, zucchini, asparagus and
  bamboo shoots
- shoyu, tamari or soy sauce
- 10–12 oz. iced peppermint tea or green tea

TOFU *   4

- miso soup
- 1 square grilled tofu
- asparagus and carrots
- side of brown rice
- 10–12 oz. ginger or green tea

TOFU *   5

- marinated grilled tofu in peanut sauce
- steamed broccoli, carrots and asparagus
- 1 apple
- 10–12 oz. spearmint or chamomile tea

* Anabolic (higher in protein than carbohydrates)

TEMPEH *   6

- sliced tempeh
- mixed green salad with bamboo shoots,
  watercress and water chestnuts
- Miso Dressing (see recipe)
- 10–12 oz. green tea or peppermint tea

TEMPEH *   7

- *Tempeh Open-Face Sandwich*
  grilled or baked tempeh
  1 slice soy cheese
  mushrooms and onions
  1 pc. Ezekiel bread
- 10–12 oz. green tea or iced ginger tea

TEMPEH *   8

- *Tempeh in Cheeseless Basil Pesto*
  grilled tempeh
  1 cup cooked spelt or artichoke pasta
  Cheeseless Basil Pesto (see recipe)
- small side salad
- 10–12 oz. iced peppermint tea or ginger tea

TEMPEH *   9

- marinated, grilled tempeh
- steamed broccoli, carrots and asparagus
- Herb Mock Vinaigrette Dressing (see recipe)
- 4–5 figs
- 10–12 oz. green tea or chamomile tea

TEMPEH *   10

- sliced tempeh with tahini sauce
- unsalted redskin peanuts
- watercress salad with alfalfa sprouts
- Lemon-Lime Cilantro Dressing (see recipe)
- 10–12 oz. iced peppermint
  or green tea

Blood Type

A

CHEESE *   11

- pumpkin soup
- *Grilled Cheese*
  soy cheese
  1 pc. Ezekiel or Essene bread
  sliced tomato and alfalfa sprouts
- 10–12 oz. distilled water or green tea

CHEESE *   12

- *Goat Cheese Salad*
  2 oz. goat cheese
  raw spinach and arugala
  tomatoes, walnuts and alfalfa sprouts
- Warm Cranberry Dressing (see recipe)
- 10–12 oz. distilled water or iced ginger tea

CHICKEN *   13

- 6–8 oz. broiled, roasted or grilled chicken
- 1 slice polenta or corn bread
- mesculen salad with tomatoes, beets, carrots, leeks
- Middle Eastern Dressing (see recipe)
- 10–12 oz. green tea or distilled water

CHICKEN *   14

- 4 oz. apple cider
- 6–8 oz. sliced chicken
- mesculen and raw spinach salad with tomatoes, beets, carrots, alfalfa sprouts, broccoli and soy beans
- Creamy Avocado Dressing (see recipe)
- 10–12 oz. green tea or distilled water

CHICKEN *   15

- 6–8 oz. roasted chicken
- roasted parsnips and pumpkin
- mixed greens with pimiento, tomato, cucumbers, scallions
- Herb Mock Vinaigrette Dressing (see recipe)
- 10–12 oz. soda water or green tea

SEAFOOD *   16

- 6–8 oz. snapper in lemon and dill
- spinach or collard greens
- side of parsnips
- 10–12 oz. green tea or Tazo "Refresh" Tea (peppermint, spearmint and tarragon blend)

SEAFOOD *   17

- *Sardine Salad*
  sardines
  1 hard-boiled egg
  appropriate lettuce and arugala
  tomato, Spanish onion and alfalfa sprouts
- Herb Mock Vinaigrette Dressing (see recipe)
- 10–12 oz. green tea or iced peppermint tea

SEAFOOD *   18

- tomato soup
- 6 oz. canned tuna or sockeye salmon
- raw spinach and arugala
- tomatoes, pumpkin seeds and alfalfa sprouts
- Creamy Avocado Dressing (see recipe)
- 10–12 oz. iced green tea or ginger tea

SEAFOOD *   19

- grilled grouper with lemon
- watercress, fennel salad with sliced peaches or nectarines
- Raspberry Mock Vinaigrette Dressing (see recipe)
- 10–12 oz. green tea or iced raspberry leaf tea

BEANS   20

- lentil dahl
- side of basmati rice
- blanched asparagus
- 10–12 oz. green tea or iced peppermint tea

BEANS *   21

- miso soup
- side of Edamame
- small side salad with daikon radish
- Miso Dressing (see recipe)
- 10–12 oz. green tea or distilled water

SOUP AND SANDWICH   22

- Minestrone Soup (see recipe)
- *Tuna Sandwich*
    6 oz albacore tuna, celery, minced onions
    (use Creamy Garlic Dressing as a
    mayonnaise substitute—see recipe)
    2 pc. Ezekiel bread
    lettuce and tomato
- 10–12 oz. green tea or spearmint tea

SOUP AND SANDWICH   23

- Turkish Red Lentil Soup (see recipe)
- *Salmon Sandwich*
    6 oz. sockeye salmon, celery, minced onions
    (use Creamy Garlic dressing as a
    mayonnaise substitute—see recipe)
    2 pc. Ezekiel bread
    lettuce and tomato
- 10–12 oz. bottled water or green tea

MIXED *   24

- *Chef's Salad*
    1 hard-boiled egg
    2 oz. turkey or chicken
    2 oz. soy cheese
    ¼ cup soy beans
    raw spinach and arugala
- Creamy Garlic Dressing (see recipe)
- 10–12 oz. green tea or iced peppermint tea

TURKEY *   25

- *Turkey Meatball Parmigian*
    2 turkey "meatballs" (100 percent turkey
    meat)
    1 slice mozzarella or soy cheese
- raw spinach and arugala
- tomatoes, cucumbers and alfalfa sprouts
- Herb Mock Vinaigrette Dressing (see recipe)
- 10–12 oz. bottled water or green tea

TURKEY *   26

- 6 oz. turkey burger
- slice mozzarella cheese
- sliced red onion and avocado
- small side salad
- Red Onion Dressing (see recipe)
- 10–12 oz. water or iced peppermint tea

TURKEY *   27

- *Mock Waldorf Salad*
    4 oz. sliced turkey
    4–5 chopped walnuts
    ½ chopped apple or pear
- mesculen salad
- Herb Mock Vinaigrette Dressing (see recipe)
- 10–12 oz. green tea or iced peppermint tea

TURKEY *   28

- *Thanksgiving Salad*
    6 oz. cubed turkey
    appropriate lettuce and dandelion greens
    tomato, red onion, cucumber and alfalfa
    sprouts
- Warm Cranberry Dressing (see recipe)
- 10–12 oz. distilled water or green tea

Blood Type

Blood Type A
28-Day Pick-a-Meal Dinner Options

TOFU *   1

- *Greek Polenta (serve hot or cold)*
  1 slice polenta
  1 square grilled tofu
  sautéed spinach and feta cheese
- 10–12 oz. green tea or raspberry tea

TOFU *   2

- *Italian Polenta (serve hot or cold)*
  1 slice polenta
  1 square grilled tofu
  1 slice mozzarella
  fresh tomato, basil and olive oil
- 10–12 oz. green tea or chamomile tea

TOFU *   3

- *Stir-Fry Tofu*
  2 squares tofu
  broccoli, asparagus and bamboo shoots
- shoyu, tamari or soy sauce
- 10–12 oz. ginger tea or green tea

TOFU *   4

- Herbed Tofu (see recipe)
- 2 oz. appropriate cheese
- redskin peanuts or macadamia nuts
- Rye Vitas or Rye Crisps
- small side salad with Miso Dressing (see recipe)
- 10–12 oz. ginger tea or iced peppermint tea

TOFU *   5

- Tofu in Cilantro Sauce (see recipe)
- sautéed collard greens, Swiss chard and kale
- side of brown rice
- 10–12 oz. green tea or distilled water

TOFU *   6

- 2 squares grilled tofu
- stir-fry baby bok choy, broccoli and onions
- side of brown rice
- 10–12 oz. green tea or distilled waterer

TEMPEH *   7

- grilled marinated tempeh
- sautéed collard greens, Swiss chard and kale
- side of brown rice or quinoa
- 10–12 oz. ginger tea or peppermint tea

TEMPEH *   8

- *Open-Face Tempeh Sandwich*
  grilled marinated tempeh
  avocados, alfalfa sprouts, onions and tomato
  1 pc. Ezekiel or Essene bread
- 1 apple or pear
- 10–12 oz. green tea or ginger tea

CHEESE *   9

- grilled portobella mushrooms, carrots and zucchini
- 2 oz. goat cheese
- Wasa bread
- unsalted redskin peanuts
- glass of red or white wine

CHEESE *   10

- 1 cup butternut, acorn or other appropriate squash
- 3–4 oz. cheddar cheese
- steamed broccoli
- 3–4 oz. turkey chunks
- small side salad with appropriate dressing
- 10–12 oz. green tea or seltzer water

* Anabolic (higher in protein than carbohydrates)

SEAFOOD * 11
- Fish With Herbs and Lime (see recipe)
- side of broccoli and cauliflower
- side of millet
- 10–12 oz. green tea or distilled water

SEAFOOD * 12
- 8 oz. grilled grouper with lemon
- steamed asparagus and carrots
- side of quinoa
- 10–12 oz. green tea or distilled water

SEAFOOD * 13
- cod or carp
- side of okra
- side or escarole or kale
- Lemon-Lime Cilantro Dressing (see recipe)
- 10–12 oz. green tea or iced ginseng tea

SEAFOOD * 14
- 6–8 oz. grilled marinated fresh tuna steak
- 1–2 artichokes, steamed
- small side salad with soy beans
- Miso Dressing (see recipe)
- 10–12 oz. green tea or glass of red wine

SEAFOOD * 15
- 6–8 oz. grilled swordfish marinated in red wine and appropriate herbs
- watercress salad with water chestnuts
- Green Goddess Dressing (see recipe)
- side of millet
- 10–12 oz. green tea or glass of red wine

SEAFOOD * 16
- broiled salmon with lemon, white wine and tarragon
- steamed broccoli
- side of beets
- 10–12 oz. green tea or glass of white wine

TURKEY * 17
- turkey burger
- 1 slice appropriate cheese
- sliced Spanish onion and avocado
- small side salad
- Garlic Yogurt Dressing (see recipe)
- 10–12 oz. distilled water or iced peppermint tea

TURKEY * 18
- roasted turkey
- roasted carrots, parsnips, onions and beets with rosemary
- side of cranberries
- chestnuts or pumpkin seeds
- 10–12 oz. green tea or distilled water

CORNISH HEN * 19
- 6–8 oz. roasted or grilled Cornish hen
- side of wild rice
- small side salad with beets, broccoli, tomato and fennel
- Red Onion Dressing (see recipe)
- 10–12 oz. distilled water or iced peppermint tea

CORNISH HEN * 20
- 6–8 oz. roasted or grilled Cornish hen
- sautéed fennel and onions (caramelize fennel and onions for extra flavor)
- Swiss chard
- chestnuts
- 10–12 oz. distilled water or glass of white wine

CHICKEN * 21
- 4–6 oz. stir-fry chicken
- stir -fry appropriate vegetables
- side of Edamame
- side of brown rice
- 10–12 oz. green tea or bottled water

Blood Type

A

CHICKEN *   22

- 6–8 oz. broiled chicken in lemon and white wine
- brown rice and wild rice (half and half blend suggested)
- steamed broccoli
- 10–12 oz. green tea or bottled water

CHICKEN *   23

- lemon-ginger glazed chicken
- basmati rice with almond slivers and currants
- side of Brussels sprouts
- 10–12 oz. green tea or ginger tea

CHICKEN *   24

- chicken cacciatore
- romaine lettuce and raddichio salad with tomatoes and fresh mozzarella cheese
- Herb Mock Vinaigrette Dressing (see recipe)
- 10–12 oz. green tea or distilled water

BEANS   25

- *Sautéed Swiss Chard and Cannelloni Beans*
  Swiss chard sautéed in vegetable stock and onions
  ¾ cup cannelloni beans
- 1 cup cooked artichoke pasta
- 10–12 oz. green tea or spearmint tea

BEANS   26

- Turkish Red Lentil Soup (see recipe)
- mesculen and mustard greens with grilled tofu, feta, cucumbers, tomatoes and alfalfa sprouts
- Herb Mock Vinaigrette Dressing (see recipe)
- 10–12 oz. green tea or glass of red wine

BEANS *   27

- miso soup
- side of Edamame
- side of Hiziki (seaweed)
- 4 oz. tuna or salmon, sashimi (raw fish) or cooked
- 10–12 oz. green tea or distilled water

BEANS *   28

- ½–¾ cup aduke or soy beans (cooked)
- side of pumpkin or butternut squash
- mixed green salad with tomato, cucumber and feta cheese
- Creamy Garlic Dressing (see recipe)
- 10–12 oz. green tea or glass of red wine

Blood Type A
28-Day Pick-a-Meal Snack Options

VEGGIES/BEANS *   1
- side of Edamame
- 10–12 oz. green tea

VEGGIES/BEANS *   2
- raw vegetables with Creamy Avocado Dressing (see recipe—make dressing into a thick dip-like consistency)
- 10–12 oz. green tea or spearmint tea

VEGGIES/BEANS *   3
- raw vegetables with Green Goddess Dressing (see recipe—make dressing into a thick dip-like consistency)
- 10–12 oz. green tea or spearmint tea

FRUIT   4
- large apple with almond butter
- 10–12 oz. green tea

FRUIT *   5
- 1 apple
- 4–6 whole walnuts
- 10–12 oz. green tea or peppermint tea

GRAINS/NUTS   6
- unsalted redskin peanuts
- 10–12 oz. ginger tea

GRAINS/NUTS *   7
- 1 pc. Ezekiel bread with almond butter and whole-fruit jam
- 10–12 oz. ginger tea or green tea

GRAINS/NUTS   8
- 2–3 Rye Vitas or Rye Crisps
- goat or farmer's cheese
- 10–12 oz. green tea

GRAINS/NUTS *   9
- 4-6 roasted chestnuts
- 4-5 figs, dried or fresh
- 10–12 oz. green tea or spearmint tea

GRAINS/NUTS *   10
- 4-6 walnuts
- 4-5 figs, dried or fresh
- 10–12 oz. green tea or peppermint tea

GRAINS/NUTS *   11
- oat-bran muffin
- 1 peach
- 10–12 oz. green tea or chamomile tea

GRAINS/NUTS   12
- 8 almonds
- 1 peach
- 10–12 oz. green tea or ginger tea

TRAIL MIX   13
- Basic Trail Mix # 1 (see recipe)
- 10–12 oz. green tea or peppermint tea

TRAIL MIX   14
- Apple "Pie" Trail Mix (see recipe)
- 10–12 oz. green tea or peppermint tea

TRAIL MIX   15
- Peanut Chocolate Trail Mix (see recipe)
- 10–12 oz. green tea or spearmint tea

DAIRY *   16
- 6 oz. low-fat yogurt
- 1 peach
- 10–12 oz. green tea or ginger tea

Blood Type

A

DAIRY *   17

- 6 oz. low-fat kefir
- 1 peach
- 10–12 oz. green tea or ginger tea

DAIRY *   18

- fresh strawberries with low-fat yogurt
- 10–12 oz. green tea or chamomile tea

DAIRY *   19

- fresh blueberries and raspberries with low-fat yogurt
- 10–12 oz. green tea or chamomile tea

SMOOTHIES *   20

- Almond Bomb Smoothie (see recipe)
  or
- Apricot Cream Smoothie (see recipe)

SMOOTHIES *   21

- Chocolate Raspberry Smoothie (see recipe)

SMOOTHIES *   22

- Cinnamon Vanilla Smoothie (see recipe)

SMOOTHIES *   23

- Cranberry Crush Smoothie (see recipe)

SMOOTHIES *   24

- Licorice Smoothie (see recipe)

SMOOTHIES *   25

- Peaches and Cream Smoothie (see recipe)

SMOOTHIES *   26

- Very Berry Smoothie (see recipe)

SMOOTHIES *   27

- Viennese Coffee Smoothie (see recipe)

SMOOTHIES *   28

- Body Genetics Protein Shake, vanilla or chocolate, mixed with water or soy milk

Blood Type A— Foods That Stimulate Weight Loss

- Vegetable oils—prevent water retention and aid digestion
- Soy foods—metabolize rapidly and aid digestion
- Vegetables—aid digestion and increase intestinal mobility
- Pineapple—increases calorie utilization and intestinal mobility

Blood Type A— Foods That Cause Weight Gain

- Meat—stores as fat, increases digestive toxins and digests poorly
- Dairy foods—inhibit nutrient metabolism
- Kidney beans, lima beans—slow metabolic rate and interfere with digestive enzymes
- Wheat—overabundance impairs calorie utilization

Note: Inhibited insulin production causes hypoglycemia, a lowering of blood sugar after meals, and leads to less efficient metabolism of foods.

* Anabolic (higher in protein than carbohydrates)

Chapter 7

Blood Type B

Blood Type B
Grocery List of Beneficial Foods

Meats—
All Anabolic
- [ ] Lamb
- [ ] Mutton
- [ ] Rabbit
- [ ] Venison

Seafood—
All Anabolic
- [ ] Caviar
   (sturgeon eggs)
- [ ] Cod
- [ ] Grouper
- [ ] Haddock
- [ ] Hake
- [ ] Halibut
- [ ] Mackerel
- [ ] Mahi-mahi
- [ ] Monkfish
- [ ] Ocean perch
- [ ] Pickerel
- [ ] Pike
- [ ] Porgy
- [ ] Salmon, ocean
- [ ] Sardine
- [ ] Scallops
- [ ] Sea trout
- [ ] Shad
- [ ] Sole
- [ ] Sturgeon

Beans/
Legumes
- [ ] Kidney
- [ ] Lima
- [ ] Navy
- [ ] Soy beans,
   black, brown,
   green
   Edamame *

Eggs/Dairy
- [ ] Cottage
   cheese *
- [ ] Farmer's
   cheese *
- [ ] Feta
   cheese *
- [ ] Frozen yogurt
- [ ] Goat cheese *
- [ ] Milk, skim or
   2 percent
- [ ] Mozzarella
   cheese, low fat *
- [ ] Ricotta cheese,
   low fat*
- [ ] Goat milk
- [ ] Kefir
- [ ] Body Genetics
   Protein Shake *
- [ ] Yogurt, low fat

Nuts/Seeds
- [ ] Macadamia

Oils
- [ ] Olive

Cereals
- [ ] Millet
- [ ] Oat Bran
- [ ] Oatmeal
- [ ] Puffed Millet
- [ ] Puffed Rice
- [ ] Rice Bran
- [ ] Spelt Flakes

Breads
- [ ] Brown rice
   bread
- [ ] Essene bread
- [ ] Ezekiel bread
- [ ] Oatmeal
- [ ] Millet
- [ ] Rice cakes

Pastas/
Grains
- [ ] Flour, oat, rice
- [ ] Rice pasta
- [ ] Spelt pasta

Vegetables
- [ ] Avocado,
   Florida
- [ ] Beet leaves
- [ ] Beets
- [ ] Broccoli
- [ ] Brussels
   sprouts
- [ ] Cabbage,
   Chinese, red,
   white
- [ ] Carrots
- [ ] Cauliflower
- [ ] Collard greens
- [ ] Eggplant
- [ ] Kale
- [ ] Mushrooms,
   shitaki
- [ ] Mustard greens
- [ ] Parsley
- [ ] Parsnips
- [ ] Peppers, green,
   red, yellow,
   jalepeño
- [ ] Sweet potatoes
- [ ] Yams, all kinds

Fruit
- [ ] Bananas
- [ ] Cranberries
- [ ] Figs, dried,
   fresh
- [ ] Grapes, black,
   concord, green,
   red
- [ ] Kiwi
- [ ] Papaya
- [ ] Pineapple
- [ ] Plum (dark
   green, red)

Juice
- [ ] Cabbage
- [ ] Cranberry
- [ ] Grape
- [ ] Papaya
- [ ] Pineapple

Spices/
Condiments
- [ ] Cayenne pepper
- [ ] Curry
- [ ] Ginger
- [ ] Horseradish
- [ ] Parsley

Beverages
- [ ] Green tea
- [ ] Water, distilled

Herbal Teas
- [ ] Ginger
- [ ] Ginseng
- [ ] Licorice root
- [ ] Parsley
- [ ] Peppermint
- [ ] Raspberry leaf
- [ ] Rose hips
- [ ] Sage

* Anabolic (higher
in protein than
carbohydrates)

Blood Type B
Grocery List of Neutral Foods

Meats—
All Anabolic
- [ ] Beef
- [ ] Ground beef
- [ ] Buffalo
- [ ] Liver
- [ ] Pheasant
- [ ] Turkey
- [ ] Veal

Seafood—
All Anabolic
- [ ] Abalone
- [ ] Bluefish
- [ ] Carp
- [ ] Catfish
- [ ] Herring
- [ ] Rainbow trout
- [ ] Red snapper
- [ ] Smelt
- [ ] Snapper
- [ ] Squid
- [ ] Swordfish
- [ ] Tilefish
- [ ] Tuna
- [ ] Whitefish
- [ ] White perch
- [ ] Yellow perch

Beans/
Legumes
- [ ] Broad
- [ ] Cannelloni
- [ ] Copper
- [ ] Fava
- [ ] Green
- [ ] Jicama
- [ ] Northern
- [ ] Peas, green, pod, snow
- [ ] Red
- [ ] Snap

- [ ] String
- [ ] Tamarind
- [ ] White

Eggs/Dairy
- [ ] Eggs *
- [ ] Butter
- [ ] Buttermilk
- [ ] Brie *
- [ ] Camembert *
- [ ] Casein *
- [ ] Cheddar *
- [ ] Colby *
- [ ] Cream cheese *
- [ ] Edam *
- [ ] Emmenthal *
- [ ] Gouda *
- [ ] Gruyere *
- [ ] Jarlsberg *
- [ ] Monterey Jack *
- [ ] Muenster *
- [ ] Neufchatel *
- [ ] Parmesan *
- [ ] Provolone *
- [ ] Soy cheese *
- [ ] Swiss *
- [ ] Sherbet
- [ ] Soy milk
- [ ] Whey *
- [ ] Whole milk

Nuts/Seeds
- [ ] Almond butter *
- [ ] Almonds *
- [ ] Brazil nuts *
- [ ] Chestnuts
- [ ] Hickory *
- [ ] Litchi
- [ ] Pine
- [ ] Pecans

Oils
- [ ] Cod liver
- [ ] Linseed (flaxseed)

Cereals
- [ ] Cream of Rice
- [ ] Familia
- [ ] Farina
- [ ] Granola
- [ ] Grape Nuts
- [ ] Oat Bran

Breads
- [ ] Gluten-free bread
- [ ] Hi-protein, no-wheat bread
- [ ] Oat-bran muffins
- [ ] Soy flour bread
- [ ] Spelt

Pastas/
Grains
- [ ] Flour, oat bran, graham, white
- [ ] Quinoa
- [ ] Rice, basmati, brown, white
- [ ] Semolina pasta
- [ ] Spinach pasta

Vegetables
- [ ] Alfalfa sprouts
- [ ] Arugala
- [ ] Asparagus
- [ ] Bok choy
- [ ] Celery
- [ ] Chicory
- [ ] Cucumber
- [ ] Dandelion greens
- [ ] Daikon radish

- [ ] Dill
- [ ] Endive
- [ ] Escarole
- [ ] Fennel
- [ ] Fiddlehead ferns
- [ ] Garlic
- [ ] Ginger
- [ ] Horseradish
- [ ] Kohlrabi
- [ ] Leek
- [ ] Lettuce, Bibb, Boston, iceberg, mesculen, romaine
- [ ] Mushrooms, abalone, domestic, enoki, portobella, tree oyster
- [ ] Okra
- [ ] Onions, green, red, Spanish, yellow
- [ ] Potatoes, red, white
- [ ] Radicchio
- [ ] Rappini
- [ ] Rutabaga
- [ ] Scallion
- [ ] Seaweed
- [ ] Shallots
- [ ] Spinach
- [ ] Squash, all types
- [ ] Turnips
- [ ] Water chestnut
- [ ] Watercress
- [ ] Zucchini

Juices
- [ ] Apple cider
- [ ] Apple

- [ ] Apricot
- [ ] Black cherry
- [ ] Carrot
- [ ] Celery
- [ ] Cucumber
- [ ] Grapefruit
- [ ] Orange
- [ ] Prune
- [ ] Vegetable
- [ ] Water and lemon

Fruits
- [ ] Apples
- [ ] Apricots
- [ ] Blackberries
- [ ] Blueberries
- [ ] Boysenberries
- [ ] Cherries
- [ ] Currants, red, black
- [ ] Dates
- [ ] Elderberries
- [ ] Gooseberries
- [ ] Grapefruit
- [ ] Guava
- [ ] Kumquat
- [ ] Lemons
- [ ] Limes
- [ ] Loganberries
- [ ] Mangoes
- [ ] Melon, all types
- [ ] Nectarines
- [ ] Oranges
- [ ] Peaches
- [ ] Prunes
- [ ] Raisins
- [ ] Raspberries

Blood Type

B

Blood Type B
Grocery List of Neutral Foods (con't.)

- ☐ Strawberries
- ☐ Tangerines

Beverages
- ☐ Black tea, regular, decaf
- ☐ Coffee, regular, decaf
- ☐ Red wine
- ☐ White wine

Herbal Teas
- ☐ Alfalfa
- ☐ Burdock
- ☐ Catnip
- ☐ Cayenne
- ☐ Chamomile
- ☐ Chickweed
- ☐ Dandelion
- ☐ Dong quai
- ☐ Echinacea
- ☐ Elder
- ☐ Hawthorn
- ☐ Horehound
- ☐ Mulberry
- ☐ Saint John's wort
- ☐ Sarsaparilla
- ☐ Slippery elm
- ☐ Spearmint
- ☐ Strawberry leaf
- ☐ Thyme
- ☐ Valerian
- ☐ Vervain
- ☐ White birch
- ☐ White oak bark
- ☐ Yarrow
- ☐ Yellow dock

Spices/ Condiments
- ☐ Agar
- ☐ Allspice
- ☐ Anise
- ☐ Apple butter
- ☐ Arrowroot
- ☐ Basil
- ☐ Bay leaf
- ☐ Bergamot
- ☐ Brown rice syrup
- ☐ Brown sugar
- ☐ Caraway
- ☐ Cardamom
- ☐ Carob
- ☐ Chervil
- ☐ Chives
- ☐ Chocolate
- ☐ Clove
- ☐ Coriander (cilantro)
- ☐ Cream of tartar
- ☐ Cumin
- ☐ Dill
- ☐ Dulse
- ☐ Honey
- ☐ Jam/jelly, from appropriate fruit
- ☐ Kelp
- ☐ Maple syrup, pure
- ☐ Mayonnaise
- ☐ Mint
- ☐ Molasses
- ☐ Mustard
- ☐ Mustard, dry
- ☐ Nutmeg
- ☐ Oregano
- ☐ Paprika
- ☐ Peppermint
- ☐ Pickles, dill,

kosher, sweet, sour
- ☐ Pimiento
- ☐ Relish
- ☐ Rice syrup
- ☐ Rosemary
- ☐ Saffron
- ☐ Sage
- ☐ Salad dressing
- ☐ Salt
- ☐ Savory
- ☐ Spearmint
- ☐ Stevia **
- ☐ Sucanat **
- ☐ Tabasco sauce
- ☐ Tamarind
- ☐ Tarragon
- ☐ Thyme
- ☐ Turmeric
- ☐ Vanilla
- ☐ Vinegar, apple cider, balsamic, red, white
- ☐ White sugar
- ☐ Wintergreen
- ☐ Worcestershire sauce

* Anabolic (higher in protein than carbohydrates)

** Natural sweetener

Blood Type B
List of Foods to Avoid

Meats
- Chicken
- Cornish hens
- Duck
- Goose
- Heart
- Partridge
- Pork, all kinds
- Quail

Seafood
- Anchovy
- Barracuda
- Beluga
- Bluegill bass, sea
- Clam
- Conch
- Crab
- Crayfish
- Eel
- Frog
- Lobster
- Lox (smoked salmon)
- Mussels
- Octopus
- Oysters
- Salmon, farm raised
- Sea bass
- Shrimp
- Snail
- Striped bass
- Turtle
- Yellowtail

Beans/ Legumes
- Aduke
- Azuki
- Black
- Black-eyed peas
- Garbanzo
- Lentils, domestic, green, red
- Pinto

Eggs/Dairy
- American cheese
- Blue cheese
- Ice cream
- String cheese

Nuts/Seeds
- Cashews
- Filberts
- Peanuts
- Peanut butter
- Pine (pignoli)
- Pistachio
- Poppy seeds
- Pumpkin seeds
- Sesame butter (tahini)
- Sesame seeds
- Sunflower butter
- Sunflower seeds

Oils
- Canola
- Corn
- Cottonseed
- Peanut
- Safflower
- Sesame
- Sunflower

Vegetables
- Artichokes, domestic, Jerusalem
- Avocados, California
- Corn, yellow, white
- Mung sprouts
- Olives, black,
  Greek, green,
  Spanish
- Pumpkin
- Radishes
- Tempeh
- Tofu
- Tomatoes

Fruit
- Coconut
- Persimmons
- Pomegranates
- Prickly pear
- Rhubarb
- Starfruit

Cereals
- Amaranth
- Barley
- Buckwheat
- Corn Flakes
- Cream of Wheat
- Kamut
- Rye
- Seven Grain
- Shredded Wheat
- Wheat Bran
- Wheat Germ

Breads
- Corn muffins
- Durum wheat bread
- Fin Crisp
- Gluten flour bread
- Ideal flat bread
- Multi-grain bread
- Pumpernickel bread
- Rye bread, 100 percent
- Rye Crisp
- Rye Vita
- Seven grain
- Wasa bread
- Wheat bagels
- Wheat-bran muffins
- Whole wheat

Spices/ Condiments
- Allspice
- Almond extract
- Barley malt
- Cinnamon
- Cornstarch
- Corn syrup
- Gelatin, plain
- Ketchup
- Pepper, black, white, ground
- Tapioca

Juice
- Tomato

Beverages
- Distilled liquor
- Sodas

Herbal Teas
- Aloe
- Coltsfoot
- Cornsilk
- Fenugreek
- Gentian
- Goldenseal
- Hops
- Linden
- Mullein
- Red clover
- Rhubarb
- Senns
- Shephard's purse
- Skullcap

Pastas/ Grains
- Artichoke pasta
- Barley flour
- Buckwheat
- Bulgur wheat
- Cornmeal
- Couscous
- Durum wheat
- Gluten flour
- Kasha
- Rye
- Whole-wheat flour
- Wild rice

Blood Type

B

Blood Type B
28-Day Pick-a-Meal Breakfast Options

SMOOTHIE *   **1**
- Blueberry Supreme Smoothie (see recipe)
- 1 pc. Ezekiel or Essene bread with apple butter and almond butter
- 10–12 oz. coffee or peppermint tea

SMOOTHIE *   **2**
- Cocoa Mochachino Smoothie (see recipe)
- 1 apple
- 1 pc. 100 percent rye or Essene bread with almond butter and whole-fruit jam
- 10–12 oz. distilled water or green tea

SMOOTHIE *   **3**
- Ginger Apple Smoothie (see recipe)
- 1 pc. 100 percent rye or Essene bread
- 1 slice Swiss or provolone cheese
- 10–12 oz. coffee or green tea

SMOOTHIE *   **4**
- Very Berry Smoothie (see recipe)
- 1 pc. 100 percent rye or Essene bread
- cream cheese and whole fruit jam
- 10–12 oz. coffee or peppermint tea

SMOOTHIE *   **5**
- Cinnamon Vanilla Smoothie (see recipe)
- 1 hard-boiled egg
- 1 pc. 100 percent rye or Essene bread
- almond butter
- 10–12 oz. coffee or green tea

SMOOTHIE *   **6**
- Tropical Smoothie (see recipe)
- 1 pc. 100 percent rye or Essene bread
- 6 Brazil nuts
- 10–12 oz. coffee or green tea

DRY CEREAL   **7**
- 4 oz. prune juice
- medium bowl of spelt flakes with skim milk
- sliced kiwi and strawberries
- 1 pc. spelt bread with almond butter and honey
- 10–12 oz. green tea or distilled water

DRY CEREAL *   **8**
- 4 oz. carrot juice
- medium bowl of puffed millet with soy milk
- 8–10 cherries
- 1 pc. Essene bread with whole-fruit jam
- 10–12 oz. green tea or distilled water

DRY CEREAL   **9**
- papaya wedge
- medium bowl of puffed rice with 2 percent milk
- 1 pc. spelt bread with almond butter
- 10–12 oz. green tea or spearmint tea

DRY CEREAL   **10**
- 4 oz. carrot juice
- medium bowl of granola
- blueberries and almond slivers
- 1 pc. Ezekiel bread with whole-fruit jam
- 10–12 oz. coffee or chamomile tea

HOT CEREAL   **11**
- 4 oz. prune juice
- medium bowl of oatmeal with appropriate milk
- 4–5 almonds
- 1 pc. Ezekiel bread with apple butter
- 10–12 oz. Tazo "Refresh" Tea (spearmint, peppermint and tarragon blend)

* Anabolic (higher in protein than carbohydrates)

HOT CEREAL   12

- 3 oz. grape juice
- medium bowl of oatmeal with appropriate milk
- cherries, blueberries or other appropriate fruit
- 4–5 chopped macadamia nuts
- 1 pc. Ezekiel bread with whole-fruit jam
- 10–12 oz. coffee or raspberry leaf tea

HOT CEREAL *   13

- 4 oz. cranberry juice
- medium bowl of oat bran with soy milk
- granola and crushed almonds as a topping
- 10–12 oz. coffee or green tea

HOT CEREAL *   14

- 4 oz. grape juice
- medium bowl of Cream of Rice with soy milk
- ½ Ezekiel bagel with whole-fruit jam and almond butter
- 10–12 oz. peppermint tea or green tea

NUT BUTTER *   15

- ½ grapefruit or 4 oz. grapefruit juice
- 1 Ezekiel bagel
- cream cheese and whole-fruit jam
- 10–12 oz. coffee or green tea

NUT BUTTER *   16

- 4 oz. carrot or tomato juice
- 2 pc. spelt bread
- almond butter and honey
- 20–30 grapes
- 10–12 oz. coffee or ginger tea

NUT BUTTER *   17

- 4 oz. carrot, celery, cucumber juice
- 1 pc. Ezekiel bread with pecan cream cheese and whole-fruit jam
- 2–3 plums
- 10–12 oz. coffee or distilled water

EGGS *   18

- 4 oz. tomato juice
- 2 eggs, poached, boiled or scrambled
- 2 kiwi
- 1 pc. Ezekiel or Essene bread with whole fruit jam
- 10–12 oz. coffee or chamomile tea

EGGS *   19

- 2 eggs, any style
- 2 slices turkey bacon (100 percent turkey)
- papaya wedge
- 1 pc. Ezekiel or Essene bread with whole fruit jam
- 10–12 oz. coffee or green tea

EGGS *   20

- *Salmon Scrambled Eggs*
    2 eggs, scrambled
    crumpled salmon pieces (ocean salmon)
- 2 kiwis
- 1 pc. Ezekiel or Essene bread with whole-fruit jam
- 10–12 oz. coffee or chamomile tea

EGGS *   21

- ½ grapefruit
- 2 poached eggs
- steamed spinach or collard greens
- 1 pc. brown rice bread with cream cheese
- 10–12 oz. coffee or green tea

EGGS *   22

- 4 oz. papaya juice
- *Scallion Shitaki Omelet*
    2 eggs, scrambled
    shitaki mushrooms and scallions
- 1 pc. Ezekiel or Essene bread with apple butter
- 10–12 oz. coffee or green tea

Blood Type

B

CHEESE *   23

- 4 oz. ricotta or cottage cheese
- kiwi, pineapple chunks, currants and almond slivers
- 1 pc. Ezekiel bread with whole-fruit jam
- 10–12 oz. Tazo "Refresh" Tea (spearmint, peppermint and tarragon blend)

CHEESE *   24

- 4 oz. carrot juice
- 4 oz. assorted appropriate cheeses
- alfalfa sprouts
- 20–30 grapes
- 1 pc. brown rice bread
- 10–12 oz. coffee or green tea

CHEESE *   25

- melon wedge
- cream cheese
- 1 thin slice ocean salmon, raw or cooked
- sliced onions and tomatoes
- 2 pc. Ezekiel bread
- 10–12 oz. coffee or rose hip tea

CHEESE *   26

- 4 oz. grapefruit juice or ½ grapefruit
- *Grilled Cheese*
    2 pc. spelt bread
    mozzarella cheese
- sliced tomato and Florida avocado
- 10–12 oz. Tazo "Refresh" Tea (spearmint, peppermint and tarragon blend)

YOGURT   27

- 6 oz. goat yogurt with honey
- 3–4 dates and granola as a topping
- 1 pc. spelt bread with almond butter
- 10–12 oz. coffee or green tea

YOGURT   28

- 4 oz. pineapple chunks
- 6 oz. plain yogurt or kefir with honey
- crushed Brazil nuts and walnuts
- 1 pc. Ezekiel or Essene bread with whole-fruit jam
- 10–12 oz. coffee or chamomile tea

Blood Type B
28-Day Pick-a-Meal Lunch Options

MIXED *   1

- *Chef's Salad #1*
  - 1 hard-boiled egg
  - 2 oz. roast beef
  - 2 oz. farmers cheese
  - ¼ cup white beans
  - sliced beets
  - mesculen salad
- Honey Mustard Dressing (see recipe)
- 10–12 oz. distilled water or iced peppermint tea

MIXED *   2

- *Chef's Salad #2*
  - 1 hard-boiled egg
  - 2 oz. turkey
  - 2 oz. soy cheese
  - 2 oz. roast beef
  - sliced fennel
  - raw spinach and arugala
- Miso Dressing (see recipe)
- 10–12 oz. distilled water or iced peppermint tea

MIXED *   3

- *Chef's Salad #3*
  - 3 oz. roast beef
  - 3 oz. lamb
  - appropriate lettuce
  - roasted red peppers and portobella mushrooms
- Oregano Feta Dressing (see recipe)
- 10–12 oz. distilled water or green tea

MIXED *   4

- *Chef's Salad #4*
  - 2 oz. mozzarella cheese
  - 3–4 oz. lamb or beef
  - grilled eggplant, zucchini and portobella mushrooms
  - mesculen salad
- Vinegarless Dressing (see recipe)
- 10–12 oz. ginger tea or iced peppermint tea

BEEF *   5

- 6 oz. sliced roast beef
- sautéed onions and mushrooms
- 1 slice mozzarella or cheddar cheese
- steamed asparagus, broccoli and carrots
- 10–12 oz. iced spearmint tea or green tea

BEEF *   6

- grilled beef/cheeseburger
- Honey Mustard Dressing (see recipe)
- mixed green salad
- artichoke hearts, jicama and carrots
- 10–12 oz. iced ginger tea or green tea

BEEF *   7

- 2 ground-beef stuffed peppers (no tomato sauce)
- mesculen salad with blanched asparagus, broccoli, radishes and Brazil nuts
- Herb Mock Vinaigrette Dressing (see recipe)
- 10–12 oz. green tea or ginseng tea

* Anabolic (higher in protein than carbohydrates)

Blood Type

B

SOUP AND SANDWICH   8

- medium bowl of Onion Soup (see recipe)
- meat loaf with 2 slices spelt bread
- 1 slice cheddar cheese, arugala and tomato
- 10–12 oz. distilled water or iced peppermint tea

SOUP AND SANDWICH   9

- Carrot Bisque (see recipe)
- *Grilled Cheese*
    2–3 oz. appropriate cheese
    2 pc. Ezekiel or Essene bread
- sliced avocado and alfalfa sprouts
- 10–12 oz. distilled water or iced peppermint tea

SOUP AND SANDWICH *   10

- White Bean and Escarole Soup (see recipe)
- broiled portobella mushroom with goat cheese
- arugala
- 2 pc. spelt bread
- 10–12 oz. bottled water or iced ginger tea

CHEESE *   11

- assorted appropriate cheese
- 2 rice cakes
- 1 kiwi and 20 grapes
- small side salad
- Raspberry Mock Vinaigrette Dressing
  (see recipe)
- 10–12 oz. iced ginger tea or green tea

CHEESE *   12

- *Goat Cheese Salad*
    2 oz. goat cheese
    raw spinach and arugala
    alfalfa sprouts, mushrooms, Brazil nuts and
    radishes
- Warm Cranberry Dressing (see recipe)
- 10–12 oz. distilled water or iced ginger tea

BEANS *   13

- miso soup
- side of Edamame
- small side salad with daikon radish
- Miso Dressing (see recipe)
- 10–12 oz. green tea or distilled water

BEANS   14

- 1 cup cooked artichoke pasta with fava beans,
  feta, artichoke hearts and onions tossed with
  olive oil, lemon and garlic
- blanched broccoli
- 10–12 oz. green tea or distilled water

BEANS *   15

- 4 oz. vegetable juice
- *Soy Beans and Pasta Salad*
    4 oz. soy beans
    1 cup cooked quinoa or spelt pasta
    (spirals or elbows)
    Spanish onions, carrots, broccoli and bell
    pepper
- Herb Mock Vinaigrette Dressing (see recipe)
- 10–12 oz. distilled water or iced peppermint tea

SEAFOOD *   16

- *Tuna and Spelt Pasta Salad*
    4 oz. canned tuna
    1 cup cooked spelt pasta (spirals or elbows)
    chopped broccoli, celery, scallions
    and carrots
- bed of mesculen salad
- Herb Mock Vinaigrette Dressing (see recipe)
- 10–12 oz. iced ginger tea or green tea

SEAFOOD *   17

- *Sardine Salad*
  sardines
  1 hard-boiled egg
  appropriate lettuce and arugala, fennel,
    onion, radish and roasted red peppers
- Herb Mock Vinaigrette Dressing (see recipe)
- 10–12 oz. club soda or iced peppermint tea

SEAFOOD *   18

- grilled mahi-mahi or grouper with lemon
- watercress, fennel salad with sliced peaches or
  nectarines
- Raspberry Mock Vinaigrette Dressing (see
  recipe)
- 10–12 oz. green tea or Tazo "Refresh" Tea
  (spearmint, peppermint and tarragon blend)

SEAFOOD *   19

- miso soup
- side of Edamame
- tuna or salmon teriyaki
- small side salad with daikon, radishes and
  carrot
- Miso Dressing (see recipe)
- 10–12 oz. green tea or bottled water

SEAFOOD *   20

- cucumber soup, cold
- 4 oz. sockeye salmon
- steamed or sautéed collard greens
- side of cottage cheese
- 10–12 oz. iced green tea or ginger tea

LAMB *   21

- grilled lamb chops with mint jelly
- side of Swiss chard
- side of brown rice with appropriate mushrooms
- 10–12 oz. soda water or glass of red wine

LAMB *   22

- *Lamb Salad*
  6 oz. lamb pieces
  side of white beans
  appropriate lettuce and dandelion greens
  cucumber, celery and avocado, Florida
- Honey Mustard Dressing (see recipe)
- 10–12 oz. club soda or glass of red wine

LIVER *   23

- *Liver Florentine*
  sautéed liver with spinach and onions
- side of broccoli, carrots or beets
- ½ cup appropriate beans
- 10–12 oz. green tea or glass of red wine

TURKEY *   24

- *Turkey Meatball Parmigiana*
  2 turkey "meatballs" (100 percent turkey
    meat)
  1 slice mozzarella or soy cheese
- raw spinach and arugala
- tomatoes, cucumbers and alfalfa sprouts
- Herb Mock Vinaigrette Dressing (see recipe)
- 10–12 oz. bottled water or green tea

TURKEY *   25

- *Turkey Salad*
  6 oz. cubed turkey
  appropriate lettuce and dandelion greens
  avocado, cucumber, beets
- Oregano Feta Dressing (see recipe)
- 10–12 oz. green tea or Tazo "Refresh" Tea
  (spearmint, peppermint and tarragon blend)

Blood Type

B

TURKEY *   26

- 6 oz. turkey burger
- 1 slice of non-fat mozzarella cheese
- sliced Spanish onion and avocado
- mixed green salad
- Honey Mustard Dressing (see recipe)
- 10–12 oz. water or iced peppermint tea

TURKEY *   27

- *Stuffed Baked Potato*
  baked sweet potato
  4 oz. turkey chunks
  cheddar cheese
- broccoli, steamed
- small side salad
- Honey Mustard Dressing (see recipe)
- 10–12 oz. green tea or seltzer

TURKEY *   28

- 4–6 oz. sliced turkey
- 5–6 chopped pecans
- pear slices
- mesculen salad
- Raspberry Mock Vinaigrette Dressing (see recipe)
- 10–12 oz. green tea or Tazo "Refresh" Tea (spearmint, peppermint and tarragon blend)

Blood Type B— Foods That Stimulate Weight Loss

- Green vegetables—aid metabolism
- Meat, liver—aid metabolism
- Eggs/low-fat dairy products—aid metabolism
- Licorice tea—counters hypoglycemia

Blood Type B— Foods That Cause Weight Gain

- Corn, lentils—hamper metabolic rate, inhibit insulin efficiency and cause hypoglycemia
- Peanuts—hamper metabolic efficiency, cause hypoglycemia and inhibit liver function
- Sesame seeds—hamper metabolic efficiency and cause hypoglycemia
- Buckwheat—inhibits digestion, causes hypoglycemia and hampers metabolic efficiency
- Wheat—slows digestive and metabolic processes, causes foods to store as fat and inhibits insulin efficiency

Note: Inhibited insulin production causes hypoglycemia, a lowering of blood sugar after meals, and leads to less efficient metabolism of foods.

Blood Type B
28-Day Pick-a-Meal Dinner Options

VEAL *   1

- veal chops in basil tarragon sauce
- side of peas and carrots
- mesculen salad with feta, peppers, onions, beets, blanched broccoli and cauliflower
- Herb Vinaigrette Dressing (see recipe)
- 10–12 oz. Tazo "Refresh" Tea (spearmint, peppermint and tarragon blend)

VEAL *   2

- sautéed veal cutlets in white wine, mushrooms, lemon and parsley
- steamed asparagus
- mixed green salad with fennel, cucumbers, beets and red onions
- Vinegarless Dressing (see recipe)
- 10–12 oz. green tea or glass of white wine

LIVER *   3

- liver and onions
- mesculen salad with cucumbers, tomatoes, celery, avocado, beets and ½ cup soy beans
- Raspberry Mock Vinaigrette Dressing (see recipe)
- 10–12 oz. distilled water or red wine

LIVER *   4

- *Liver Florentine*
    sautéed liver with spinach
- side of broccoli, carrots or beets
- ½ cup cannelloni beans
- 10–12 oz. red wine or green tea

BEEF *   5

- 6 oz. salisbury steak with own gravy
- sautéed onions and mushrooms
- side of quinoa or brown rice
- steamed peas and carrots
- small side salad
- Miso Dressing (see recipe)
- 10–12 oz. green tea or iced ginger tea

BEEF *   6

- 6–8 oz. flank steak or London broil
- sautéed onions and mushrooms
- steamed kale
- small sweet potato with side of cottage cheese
- 10–12 oz. green tea or distilled water

BEEF *   7

- miso soup (without tofu)
- 6 oz. beef teriyaki
- side of brown rice
- side of Hiziki (seaweed)
- salad with shredded daikon and carrots
- Miso Dressing (see recipe)
- 10–12 oz. green tea or iced ginger tea

BEEF *   8

- *Marinated Beef Kabobs*
    beef cubes, peppers and onion
- mixed greens with shredded cabbage, beets, mushrooms and okra
- side of quinoa
- 10–12 oz. Tazo "Refresh" Tea (spearmint, peppermint and tarragon blend)

* Anabolic (higher in protein than carbohydrates)

Blood Type

B

BEEF * 9
- 1 large slice meat loaf
- side of Brussels sprouts
- raw spinach and arugala salad with pine nuts, water chestnuts and beets
- Lemon-Lime Cilantro Dressing (see recipe)
- 10–12 oz. green tea or iced peppermint tea

BEEF * 10
- grilled beef cheeseburger (using appropriate cheese)
- mixed green salad
- Honey Mustard Dressing (see recipe)
- artichoke hearts, carrots and radish
- 10–12 oz. green tea or iced ginger tea

RABBIT * 11
- grilled rabbit
- roasted pumpkin or other squash
- zucchini
- side of appropriate beans with rosemary
- 10–12 oz. peppermint tea or glass of red wine

LAMB * 12
- lamb stew with red wine and appropriate vegetables
- small mixed green salad
- Oregano Feta Dressing (see recipe)
- side of millet
- 10–12 oz. ginger tea or glass of red wine

LAMB * 13
- lamb chops
- mesculen salad with mint leaves, steamed asparagus, cherry tomatoes
- Oregano Feta Dressing (see recipe)
- 10–12 oz. peppermint tea or glass of red wine

LAMB * 14
- 6 oz. roasted leg of lamb
- roasted carrots, parsnips, onions, sweet potato and beets with rosemary
- side of white beans
- 10–12 oz. peppermint tea or glass of red wine

TURKEY * 15
- 6 oz. roasted turkey
- roasted carrots, parsnips, onions, sweet potato and beets with rosemary
- side of cranberries
- chestnuts
- 10–12 oz. green tea or distilled water

TURKEY * 16
- turkey burger
- slice of appropriate cheese
- sliced Spanish onion and avocado
- small side salad
- Honey Mustard Dressing (see recipe)
- 10–12 oz. Tazo "Refresh" Tea (spearmint, peppermint and tarragon blend)

TURKEY * 17
- *Roasted Turkey and Quinoa Salad*
    6 oz. turkey chunks
    1 cup cooked quinoa
- Warm Cranberry Dressing (see recipe)
- 10–12 oz. green tea or ginger tea

TURKEY * 18
- 6-8 oz. turkey
- sautéed fennel and onions (caramelize fennel and onions for extra flavor)
- sautéed Swiss chard
- chestnuts
- 10–12 oz. ginger tea or glass of white wine

PHEASANT * 19

- 6–8 oz. roasted pheasant
- baked sweet potato
- side of cottage cheese
- broccoli and cauliflower
- 10–12 oz. distilled water or green tea

RABBIT * 20

- 6 oz. grilled rabbit
- roasted pumpkin or other squash
- zucchini
- side of fava beans with rosemary
- 10–12 oz. distilled water or red wine

SEAFOOD * 21

- Fish With Herbs and Lime (see recipe)
- side of broccoli and cauliflower
- side order of millet
- 10–12 oz. Tazo "Refresh" Tea (spearmint, peppermint and tarragon blend)

SEAFOOD * 22

- sautéed scallops in garlic, olive oil, fish stock or white wine and parsley
- steamed broccoli and carrots
- side of quinoa or brown rice
- 10–12 oz. green tea or lemon-lime water

SEAFOOD * 23

- 6–8 oz. salmon with lemon and dill
- side of asparagus with almond slivers
- side of basmati rice
- 10–12 oz. green tea or distilled water

SEAFOOD * 24

- 6 oz. grilled marinated fresh tuna steak
- sautéed bok choy and broccoli with soy sauce
- small sweet potato with butter
- 10–12 oz. green tea or strawberry leaf tea

SEAFOOD * 25

- 6–8 oz. halibut in Orange Ginger Sauce (see recipe)
- sautéed collard greens with currants
- small sweet potato with butter
- 10–12 oz. green tea or ginger tea

SEAFOOD * 26

- 6–8 oz. grilled swordfish marinated in red wine and appropriate herbs
- watercress salad with water chestnuts
- Herb Mock Vinaigrette Dressing (see recipe)
- side of basmati rice with currants and chestnuts
- 10–12 oz. distilled water or glass of red wine

VENISON * 27

- venison stew with red wine and appropriate vegetables
- side of quinoa
- small mixed green salad with chestnuts
- Herb Mock Vinaigrette Dressing (see recipe)
- 10–12 oz. green tea or glass of red wine

VENISON * 28

- 6–8 oz. venison steak
- carrots, rutabagas and sweet potato mixture, roasted or grilled
- small side salad
- Herb Mock Vinaigrette Dressing (see recipe)
- 10–12 oz. green tea

Blood Type

B

Blood Type B
28-Day Pick-a-Meal Snack Options

VEGGIES/BEANS *   1
- side of Edamame
- 10–12 oz. bottled water

VEGGIES/BEANS *   2
- raw vegetables with Creamy Cilantro Lime
  Dressing (see recipe—make dressing into a
  thick dip-like consistency)
- 10–12 oz. green tea or spearmint tea

VEGGIES/BEANS *   3
- raw vegetables
- 1 slice appropriate cheese
- 10–12 oz. green tea or spearmint tea

FRUIT   4
- 1 large apple with almond butter
- 10–12 oz. seltzer water

FRUIT *   5
- 1 sliced peach with almond slivers, currants
  and honey
- 10-12 oz. green tea

FRUIT   6
- 1 apple
- 4–6 whole walnuts
- 10–12 oz. green tea or peppermint tea

FRUIT *   7
- 1 peach
- 1 pc. Ezekiel bread with 1 slice farmer's cheese
- 10–12 oz. green tea or coffee

FRUIT *   8
- Poached Peaches (see recipe)
- 10–12 oz. green tea

FRUIT *   9
- small bowl of raspberries and strawberries
- glass of soy milk

GRAINS/NUTS *   10
- 8–10 almonds
- 10–12 oz. soda water

GRAINS/NUTS   11
- 1 pc. Ezekiel bread with almond butter and
  whole-fruit jam
- 10–12 oz. soda water

GRAINS/NUTS   12
- 2–3 Rye Vitas or Rye Crisps
- goat or farmer's cheese
- 10–12 oz. green tea

GRAINS/NUTS   13
- 4–6 roasted chestnuts
- 4–5 figs, dried or fresh
- 10-12 oz. green tea or coffee

GRAINS/NUTS   14
- 4–6 walnuts
- 4–6 almonds
- 10–12 oz. green tea or coffee

GRAINS/NUTS   15
- 2–3 Pecan Sandies (see recipe)
- glass of soy milk

GRAINS/NUTS   16
- 2–3 Almond Honey Cookies (see recipe)
- glass of soy milk

* Anabolic (higher in protein than carbohydrates)

TRAIL MIX *   17
- Basic Trail Mix # 3 (see recipe)
- 10–12 oz. green tea or peppermint tea

TRAIL MIX *   18
- Apple Walnut Trail Mix (see recipe)
- 10–12 oz. green tea or peppermint tea

DAIRY *   19
- 6 oz. low-fat fruit yogurt
- 1–2 Tbsp. granola or Grape Nuts
- 10-12 oz. green tea or ginger tea

DAIRY *   20
- 6 oz. low-fat yogurt
- 1 peach
- 10-12 oz. green tea or ginger tea

DAIRY *   21
- 6 oz. low-fat kefir
- 3–4 dates
- 10-12 oz. green tea or ginger tea

DAIRY *   22
- fresh strawberries with low-fat yogurt
- 10-12 oz. green tea or coffee

DAIRY *   23
- fresh blueberries and raspberries with low-fat yogurt
- 10–12 oz. green tea or coffee

SMOOTHIES *   24
- Banana Smoothie (see recipe)
  or
- Blueberry Supreme Smoothie (see recipe)

SMOOTHIES *   25
- Cinnamon Vanilla Smoothie (see recipe)
  or
- Cocoa Mochachino Smoothie (see recipe)

SMOOTHIES *   26
- Ginger Apple Smoothie (see recipe)
  or
- Purple Passion Smoothie (see recipe)

SMOOTHIES *   27
- Tropical Smoothie (see recipe)
  or
- Viennese Coffee Smoothie (see recipe)

SMOOTHIES *   28
- Body Genetics Protein Shake, vanilla or chocolate, mixed with appropriate milk or water

Blood Type

Chapter 8

Blood Type AB

Blood Type

AB

Blood Type AB
Grocery List of Beneficial Foods

**Meats—
All Anabolic**
- [ ] Lamb
- [ ] Mutton
- [ ] Rabbit
- [ ] Turkey

**Seafood—All
Anabolic**
- [ ] Cod
- [ ] Grouper
- [ ] Hake
- [ ] Mackerel
- [ ] Mahi-mahi
- [ ] Monkfish
- [ ] Ocean perch
- [ ] Pickerel
- [ ] Pike
- [ ] Porgy
- [ ] Rainbow trout
- [ ] Ocean salmon
- [ ] Sailfish
- [ ] Sardine
- [ ] Sea trout
- [ ] Shad
- [ ] Snail
- [ ] Snapper
- [ ] Sturgeon
- [ ] Tuna

**Beans/
Legumes**
- [ ] Lentils, green
- [ ] Navy
- [ ] Pinto
- [ ] Red
- [ ] Soy, brown, black, green Edamame*

Eggs/Dairy
- [ ] Cottage cheese, nonfat *
- [ ] Farmer's cheese *
- [ ] Feta cheese *
- [ ] Goat cheese *
- [ ] Mozzarella *
- [ ] Ricotta cheese *
- [ ] Sour cream, nonfat *
- [ ] Body Genetics Protein Shake *
- [ ] Yogurt

Nuts/Seeds
- [ ] Chestnuts
- [ ] Flaxseeds
- [ ] Peanut butter, organic
- [ ] Redskin peanuts, unsalted *
- [ ] Walnuts *

Oils
- [ ] Olive

Cereals
- [ ] Oat Bran
- [ ] Oatmeal
- [ ] Puffed Rice
- [ ] Puffed Millet
- [ ] Rice Bran
- [ ] Spelt

Breads
- [ ] Brown rice bread
- [ ] Essene bread
- [ ] Ezekiel bread
- [ ] Rye bread, 100 percent
- [ ] Rye Vita
- [ ] Rye Crisps
- [ ] Sprouted wheat
- [ ] Wasa bread

**Pastas/
Grains**
- [ ] Millet
- [ ] Oat flour
- [ ] Rice pasta
- [ ] Rye flour, 100 percent
- [ ] Soy flour
- [ ] Spelt pasta

Vegetables
- [ ] Alfalfa sprouts
- [ ] Avocado, Florida
- [ ] Beet leaves
- [ ] Beets
- [ ] Broccoli
- [ ] Broccoli sprouts
- [ ] Cauliflower
- [ ] Celery
- [ ] Collard greens
- [ ] Cucumber
- [ ] Dandelion

- [ ] Eggplant
- [ ] Kale
- [ ] Mushrooms, maitaki
- [ ] Mustard greens
- [ ] Parsley
- [ ] Parsnips
- [ ] Sweet potatoes
- [ ] Tempeh *
- [ ] Tofu *
- [ ] Yams, all kinds

Fruit
- [ ] Cherries
- [ ] Cranberries
- [ ] Figs, dried, fresh
- [ ] Gooseberries
- [ ] Grapefruit
- [ ] Grapes, black, concord, green, red
- [ ] Kiwi
- [ ] Lemon
- [ ] Loganberries
- [ ] Pineapple
- [ ] Plum, dark green, red

Juice
- [ ] Black cherry
- [ ] Cabbage
- [ ] Carrot
- [ ] Celery
- [ ] Cranberry
- [ ] Grape
- [ ] Papaya

**Spices/
Condiments**
- [ ] Curry
- [ ] Garlic
- [ ] Horseradish
- [ ] Miso
- [ ] Parsley

Beverages
- [ ] Coffee, regular, decaf
- [ ] Green tea
- [ ] Red wine
- [ ] Water, bottled, filtered

Herbal Teas
- [ ] Alfalfa
- [ ] Burdock
- [ ] Chamomile
- [ ] Echinacea
- [ ] Ginger
- [ ] Ginseng
- [ ] Hawthorn
- [ ] Licorice root
- [ ] Milk thistle
- [ ] Rose hips
- [ ] Strawberry leaf

* Anabolic (higher in protein than carbohydrates)

Blood Type AB
Grocery List of Neutral Foods

Meats—
All Anabolic
- [ ] Liver
- [ ] Pheasant

Seafood—
All Anabolic
- [ ] Abalone
- [ ] Bluefish
- [ ] Carp
- [ ] Catfish
- [ ] Caviar
- [ ] Herring, fresh
- [ ] Mussels
- [ ] Scallops
- [ ] Shark
- [ ] Silver perch
- [ ] Smelt
- [ ] Sole
- [ ] Squid
- [ ] Swordfish
- [ ] Tilefish
- [ ] Weakfish
- [ ] White perch
- [ ] Yellow perch

Beans/
Legumes
- [ ] Broad
- [ ] Cannelloni
- [ ] Copper
- [ ] Green
- [ ] Jicama
- [ ] Lentils, domestic, red
- [ ] Northern
- [ ] Peas, green, pod, snow
- [ ] Snap
- [ ] String
- [ ] Tamarind
- [ ] White

Eggs/Dairy
- [ ] Eggs *
- [ ] Casein cheese *
- [ ] Cheddar cheese *
- [ ] Colby cheese *
- [ ] Cream cheese *
- [ ] Edam *
- [ ] Emmenthal *
- [ ] Goat milk
- [ ] Gouda *
- [ ] Gruyere *
- [ ] Jarlsberg *
- [ ] Kefir
- [ ] Milk, skim, 2 percent
- [ ] Monterey Jack *
- [ ] Muenster *
- [ ] Neufchatel *
- [ ] Soy *
- [ ] String *
- [ ] Swiss *

Nuts/Seeds
- [ ] Almond butter *
- [ ] Almonds *
- [ ] Brazil nuts *
- [ ] Cashews
- [ ] Hickory *
- [ ] Litchi
- [ ] Macadamia
- [ ] Pine
- [ ] Pistachios

Oils
- [ ] Canola
- [ ] Cod liver

- [ ] Linseed (Flaxseed)
- [ ] Peanut

Cereals
- [ ] Amaranth
- [ ] Barley
- [ ] Cream of Rice
- [ ] Cream of Wheat
- [ ] Familia
- [ ] Farina
- [ ] Granola
- [ ] Grape Nuts
- [ ] Seven Grain
- [ ] Shredded Wheat
- [ ] Soy Flakes
- [ ] Wheat Bran
- [ ] Wheat Germ

Breads
- [ ] Durum wheat
- [ ] English muffin
- [ ] Gluten-free bread
- [ ] Hi-protein bread
- [ ] Ideal flat bread
- [ ] Multi-grain bread
- [ ] Oat-bran muffin
- [ ] Pumpernickel bread
- [ ] Seven grain
- [ ] Spelt
- [ ] Wheat bagel
- [ ] Wheat bran
- [ ] Wheat-bran muffins
- [ ] Wheat germ
- [ ] Wheat matzos
- [ ] Whole wheat

Pastas/
Grains
- [ ] Brown rice
- [ ] Couscous
- [ ] Flour, barley, bulgur wheat, durum wheat, gluten, graham, spelt, whole wheat
- [ ] Semolina pasta
- [ ] Spinach pasta
- [ ] Quinoa

Vegetables
- [ ] Arugala
- [ ] Asparagus
- [ ] Bamboo shoots
- [ ] Bok choy
- [ ] Brussels sprouts
- [ ] Cabbage, Chinese, red, white
- [ ] Carrots
- [ ] Chicory
- [ ] Daikon
- [ ] Endive
- [ ] Escarole
- [ ] Fennel
- [ ] Fiddlehead ferns
- [ ] Kohlrabi
- [ ] Leek
- [ ] Lettuce, Bibb, Boston, iceberg, mesculen, romaine

- [ ] Mushrooms, abalone, domestic, enoki, portobella, shitaki, tree oyster
- [ ] Okra
- [ ] Olives, Greek, green, Spanish
- [ ] Onions, green, red, Spanish, yellow
- [ ] Potatoes, red, white
- [ ] Raddichio
- [ ] Rappini
- [ ] Rutabaga
- [ ] Scallion
- [ ] Seaweed
- [ ] Shallots
- [ ] Spinach
- [ ] Squash, all types
- [ ] Swiss chard
- [ ] Tomato
- [ ] Turnips
- [ ] Water chestnuts
- [ ] Watercress
- [ ] Zucchini

Blood Type

AB

Blood Type AB
Grocery List of Neutral Foods (con't.)

Juices
- [ ] Apple cider
- [ ] Apple
- [ ] Apricot
- [ ] Cucumber
- [ ] Grapefruit
- [ ] Pineapple
- [ ] Prune
- [ ] Vegetable
- [ ] Water and lemon

Fruits
- [ ] Apples
- [ ] Apricots
- [ ] Blackberries
- [ ] Blueberries
- [ ] Boysenberries
- [ ] Currants, black, red
- [ ] Dates
- [ ] Elderberries
- [ ] Kumquat
- [ ] Limes
- [ ] Melon, all types
- [ ] Nectarines
- [ ] Papaya
- [ ] Peaches
- [ ] Pears
- [ ] Plantains
- [ ] Prunes
- [ ] Raisins
- [ ] Raspberries
- [ ] Strawberries
- [ ] Tangerines
- [ ] Watermelon

Beverages
- [ ] Club soda
- [ ] Seltzer water
- [ ] White wine

Herbal Teas
- [ ] Catnip
- [ ] Cayenne
- [ ] Chickweed
- [ ] Dandelion
- [ ] Dong quai
- [ ] Elder
- [ ] Goldenseal
- [ ] Horehound
- [ ] Mulberry
- [ ] Parsley
- [ ] Peppermint
- [ ] Raspberry leaf
- [ ] Sage
- [ ] Saint John's wort
- [ ] Sarsaparilla
- [ ] Slippery elm
- [ ] Spearmint
- [ ] Tarrow
- [ ] Thyme
- [ ] Valerian
- [ ] White birch
- [ ] White oak bark
- [ ] Yellow dock

Spices/Condiments
- [ ] Agar
- [ ] Arrowroot
- [ ] Basil
- [ ] Bay leaf
- [ ] Bergamot
- [ ] Brown rice syrup
- [ ] Brown sugar
- [ ] Caraway
- [ ] Cardamom
- [ ] Carob
- [ ] Chervil
- [ ] Chives
- [ ] Chocolate
- [ ] Cinnamon
- [ ] Clove
- [ ] Coriander (Cilantro)
- [ ] Cream of tartar
- [ ] Cumin
- [ ] Dill
- [ ] Dulse
- [ ] Ginger
- [ ] Honey
- [ ] Jam/jelly, from appropriate fruit
- [ ] Kelp
- [ ] Maple syrup
- [ ] Marjoram
- [ ] Mint
- [ ] Molasses
- [ ] Mustard, dry
- [ ] Nutmeg
- [ ] Paprika
- [ ] Peppermint
- [ ] Pimiento
- [ ] Rice syrup
- [ ] Rosemary
- [ ] Saffron
- [ ] Sage
- [ ] Salt
- [ ] Savory
- [ ] Shoyu
- [ ] Soy sauce
- [ ] Spearmint
- [ ] Stevia **
- [ ] Sucanat **
- [ ] Tamari
- [ ] Tamarind
- [ ] Tarragon
- [ ] Thyme
- [ ] Turmeric
- [ ] Vanilla
- [ ] Vinegar, apple cider, balsamic, red wine
- [ ] White sugar
- [ ] Wintergreen

* Anabolic (higher in protein than carbohydrates)
** Natural sweeteners

Blood Type AB
List of Foods to Avoid

Meats
- Bacon
- Beef
- Buffalo
- Chicken
- Cornish hens
- Duck
- Goose
- Heart
- Partridge
- Pork, all kinds
- Veal
- Venison
- Quail

Seafood
- Anchovy
- Barracuda
- Beluga
- Bluegill bass
- Clam
- Conch
- Crab
- Crayfish
- Eel
- Flounder
- Frog
- Gray sole
- Haddock
- Halibut
- Pickled herring
- Lobster
- Lox
- Octopus
- Oysters
- Salmon, farm–raised
- Sea Bass
- Shrimp
- Striped bass
- Turtle
- Yellow tail

Beans/ Legumes
- Aduke
- Azuki
- Black
- Black-eyed peas
- Fava
- Garbanzo
- Kidney
- Lima

Eggs/Dairy
- American cheese
- Blue cheese
- Brie
- Buttermilk
- Camembert
- Ice cream
- Milk, whole
- Parmesan
- Provolone
- Sherbet

Nuts/Seeds
- Filberts
- Poppy seeds
- Pumpkin seeds
- Sesame butter (tahini)
- Sesame seeds
- Sunflower seeds

Oils
- Corn
- Cottonseed
- Safflower
- Sesame
- Sunflower

Cereals
- Buckwheat
- Corn Flakes
- Kamut

Breads
- Corn muffins

Pastas/ Grains
- Artichoke pasta
- Barley flour
- Buckwheat
- Corn meal
- Soba noodles

Vegetables
- Artichokes, domestic, Jerusalem
- Avocados, California
- Corn, white, yellow
- Olives, black
- Peppers, red, green, yellow, jalepeno
- Radishes
- Radish sprouts
- Mung sprouts

Fruit
- Bananas
- Coconuts
- Guava
- Mangoes
- Oranges
- Persimmons
- Pomegranates
- Prickly pear
- Rhubarb
- Starfruit (carambola)

Juice
- Any of the fruits and vegetables listed above

Spices/ Condiments
- Allspice
- Almond extract
- Anise
- Barley malt
- Capers
- Cayenne
- Cornstarch
- Corn syrup
- Ketchup
- Pepper, black, cayenne, red flakes, pepper-corns, white
- Pickles, dill, kosher, sweet, sour
- Relish
- Tapioca
- Vinegar, white
- Worcestershire sauce

Beverages
- Black tea, regular, decaf
- Distilled liquor
- Sodas

Herbal Teas
- Aloe
- Coltsfoot
- Cornsilk
- Fenugreek
- Gentian
- Hops
- Linden
- Mullein
- Red clover
- Rhubarb
- Senna
- Shepards purse
- Skullcap

Blood Type
AB

Blood Type AB
28-Day Pick-a-Meal Breakfast Options

YOGURT   1

- 6 oz. plain yogurt
- 4 figs or dates and walnuts as a topping
- 1 pc. Ezekiel or Essene bread with whole-fruit jam
- 10–12 oz. green tea or ginger tea

YOGURT   2

- 4 oz. pineapple chunks
- 6 oz. plain yogurt or kefir
- ¼ cup granola as a topping
- 1 pc. Ezekiel or Essene bread with whole-fruit jam
- 10–12 oz. chamomile tea or sage tea

HOT CEREAL   3

- 4 oz. vegetable juice
- medium bowl of oatmeal
- ¼ chopped apple
- 4–5 chopped walnuts
- 1 pc. brown rice bread with whole-fruit jam
- 10–12 oz. coffee or strawberry leaf tea

HOT CEREAL   4

- 3 oz. grape juice
- medium bowl of oatmeal made with soy milk
- cherries, blueberries or other appropriate fruit
- 4–5 chopped macadamia nuts
- 1 pc. Ezekiel bread with whole-fruit jam
- 10–12 oz. coffee or strawberry leaf tea

HOT CEREAL *   5

- 4 oz. cranberry juice
- medium bowl of oatmeal made with soy milk
- granola and crushed walnuts as a topping
- 1–2 tsp. ground flaxseeds
- 10–12 oz. green tea or ginger tea

HOT CEREAL *   6

- 4 oz. apricot juice
- medium bowl of Cream of Wheat with soy milk
- ½ Ezekiel bagel with whole-fruit jam and organic peanut butter or almond butter
- 10–12 oz. peppermint tea or green tea

DRY CEREAL *   7

- lemon water (water with a squeeze of lemon)
- medium bowl of Shredded Wheat with soy milk
- sliced peaches
- 1 pc. Ezekiel bread with ricotta or goat cheese
- 10–12 oz. green tea or peppermint tea

PANCAKES   8

- ½ grapefruit
- 3 medium Oat Pancakes With Cranberries and Walnuts (see recipe)
- cranberries, blueberries or raspberries
- pure maple syrup or pure honey
- 10–12 oz. chamomile tea or green tea

DRY CEREAL *   9

- 4 oz. grapefruit juice
- medium bowl of Grape Nuts with soy milk
- 1 pc. 100 percent rye toast
- 1 slice soy cheese
- 10–12 oz. chamomile tea or green tea

DRY CEREAL   10

- 4 oz. vegetable juice
- medium bowl of puffed millet or rice
- 8–10 cherries
- 1 pc. brown rice bread with whole-fruit jam
- 10–12 oz. green tea or chamomile tea

* Anabolic (higher in protein than carbohydrates)

DRY CEREAL 11

- 4 oz. cranberry juice
- medium bowl of Fruit and Nut Granola (see recipe)
- ½ cup of raspberries and blueberries
- 1 pc. Ezekiel or Essene bread with whole-fruit jam
- 10–12 oz. coffee or chamomile tea

DRY CEREAL * 12

- 3 oz. carrot juice
- medium bowl of Soy Flakes or Grape Nuts
- 4–5 figs or dates
- 1 pc. 100 percent rye toast with whole-fruit jam
- 10–12 oz. strawberry leaf tea or coffee

NUT BUTTER * 13

- ½ grapefruit or 4 oz. grapefruit juice
- 1 Ezekiel bagel
- organic peanut butter and whole fruit jam
- 10–12 oz. coffee or green tea

NUT BUTTER * 14

- 4 oz. vegetable juice
- 2 pc. 100 percent rye or Ezekiel bread
- almond butter and honey
- 2 plums
- 10–12 oz. green tea or ginger tea

SCRAMBLED TOFU * 15

- 4 oz. grapefruit juice or ½ grapefruit
- *Curried Scrambled Tofu*
  4 oz. tofu with curry powder
- ribbons of beet, mustard or collard greens
- scallions or onions
- 1 pc. 100 percent rye bread with whole-fruit jam
- 10–12 oz. coffee or green tea

SCRAMBLED TOFU * 16

- *Scrambled "Egg" Tofu*
  4 oz. tofu with turmeric and minced onions
- 20–30 grapes
- 1 pc. brown rice bread with whole fruit jam
- 10–12 oz. coffee or chamomile tea

EGGS * 17

- 4 oz. vegetable juice
- 2 eggs, poached, boiled or scrambled
- 1–2 plums or 4–5 figs
- 1 pc. Ezekiel or Essene bread with whole-fruit jam
- 10–12 oz. coffee or chamomile tea

EGGS * 18

- *Tex-Mex Omelet*
  2 scrambled eggs filled with 2 Tbsp. pinto beans
  1 slice cheddar cheese, sliced tomato and cilantro
- melon wedge
- 1 pc. Ezekiel or Essene bread with whole-fruit jam
- 10–12 oz. coffee or green tea

EGGS * 19

- *Curried Scrambled Eggs*
  2 scrambled eggs with ½ tsp. curry powder
- slice of appropriate cheese
- melon wedge and strawberries
- 1 pc. Ezekiel or Essene bread with whole-fruit jam
- 10–12 oz. coffee or green tea

Blood Type

AB

EGGS *   20

- *Salmon Scrambled Eggs*
    2 scrambled eggs
    crumpled salmon pieces
- alfalfa sprouts
- 2 sliced kiwis
- 1 pc. Ezekiel or Essene bread with whole fruit jam
- 10–12 oz. green tea or chamomile tea

CHEESE *   21

- 4 oz. vegetable juice
- 4 oz. cup ricotta cheese
- 6–8 cherries and cranberries
- 1 sliced kiwi
- 1–2 tsp. ground flaxseeds
- 1 pc. brown rice bread with whole-fruit jam
- 10–12 oz. coffee or rose hip tea

CHEESE *   22

- 4 oz. carrot juice
- 4 oz. assorted appropriate cheeses
- alfalfa sprouts
- 20–30 grapes
- 1 pc. 100 percent rye toast
- 10–12 oz. coffee or green tea

CHEESE *   23

- 4 oz. vegetable juice
- 4 oz. ricotta or goat cheese
- 1 thin slice ocean salmon, raw or cooked
- sliced onions and alfalfa sprouts
- 2 slices 100 percent rye toast
- 10–12 oz. coffee or rose hip tea

CHEESE *   24

- 4 oz. grapefruit juice or ½ grapefruit
- *Grilled Cheese*
    2 pc. seven-grain bread
    4 oz. mozzarella cheese
- sliced tomato and alfalfa sprouts
- 10–12 oz. peppermint tea or green tea

SMOOTHIE *   25

- Chocolate Raspberry Smoothie (see recipe)
- 1 pc. Ezekiel or Essene bread with almond butter and whole-fruit jam
- 10–12 oz. green tea or peppermint tea

SMOOTHIE *   26

- Cranberry Crush Smoothie (see recipe)
- 1 pc. 100 percent rye or Essene bread with organic peanut butter and whole-fruit jam
- 10–12 oz. coffee or green tea

SMOOTHIE *   27

- Maple Magic Smoothie (see recipe)
- 1 peach
- 1 pc. 100 percent rye or Essene bread with organic peanut butter and whole-fruit jam
- 10–12 oz. coffee or green tea

SMOOTHIE *   28

- Viennese Coffee Smoothie (see recipe)
- ½ grapefruit
- 1 pc. Essene bread with whole-fruit jam and nonfat cream cheese
- 10–12 oz. peppermint tea or green tea

Blood Type AB
28-Day Pick-a-Meal Lunch Options

TURKEY *   1

- *Turkey Salad*
    6 oz. cubed turkey
    appropriate lettuce and mustard greens
    avocado, cucumber, beets and feta cheese
- Raspberry Mock Vinaigrette Dressing (see recipe)
- 10–12 oz. club soda or green tea

TURKEY *   2

- 6 oz. turkey burger
- 1 slice mozzarella cheese
- sliced Spanish onion and avocado
- small side salad
- Creamy Garlic Dressing (see recipe)
- 10–12 oz. water or iced peppermint tea

TURKEY *   3

- *Thanksgiving Salad*
    6 oz. cubed turkey
    appropriate lettuce and dandelion greens
    tomato, cucumber, alfalfa sprouts
- Warm Cranberry Dressing (see recipe)
- 10–12 oz. club soda or peppermint tea

TURKEY *   4

- 4 oz. cranberry juice
- 6 oz. sliced turkey
- small sweet potato
- small side salad
- Red Onion Dressing (see recipe)
- 10–12 oz. green tea or soda water

TURKEY *   5

- *Mock Waldorf Salad*
    4 oz. sliced turkey
    4–5 chopped walnuts
    ½ chopped apple or pear
- mesculen salad
- Herb Mock Vinaigrette Dressing (see recipe)
- 10–12 oz. green tea or peppermint tea

CHEESE *   6

- 4 oz. nonfat sour cream or nonfat cottage cheese
- kiwi, cherries, grapes and berries
- crushed almonds or walnuts
- 2 Tbsp. granola
- 10–12 oz. bottled water or strawberry leaf tea

CHEESE *   7

- *Antipasto*
    4 oz. sliced mozzarella cheese
    sliced tomato and fresh basil
- small side salad
- Red Onion Dressing (see recipe)
- 10–12 oz. seltzer or bottled water

CHEESE *   8

- assorted appropriate cheeses
- Rye Vitas or Rye Crisps
- 1 kiwi and 20 grapes
- small side salad
- Creamy Avocado Dressing (see recipe)
- 10–12 oz. seltzer or green tea

* Anabolic (higher in protein than carbohydrates)

Blood Type

AB

CHEESE *   9

- *Goat Cheese Salad*
  - 2 oz. goat cheese
  - raw spinach and arugala
  - tomatoes, walnuts and alfalfa sprouts
- Green Goddess Dressing (see recipe)
- 10–12 oz. bottled water or iced ginger tea

TEMPEH *   10

- marinated grilled tempeh
- steamed broccoli, carrots and asparagus
- Herb Mock Vinaigrette Dressing (see recipe)
- 4–5 figs
- 10–12 oz. seltzer or chamomile tea

TOFU *   11

- 1 square tofu, steamed
- steamed broccoli, carrots, zucchini and Swiss chard
- Miso Dressing (see recipe)
- 10–12 oz. seltzer or bottled water

TOFU *   12

- Herbed Tofu (see recipe)
- 2 oz. appropriate cheese
- redskin peanuts
- Rye Vitas or Rye Crisps
- small side salad
- Red Onion Dressing (see recipe)
- 10–12 oz. soda water or iced peppermint tea

TOFU *   13

- *Stir-Fry Tofu*
  - 1 square tofu
  - broccoli, carrots, zucchini, asparagus and bamboo shoots
- shoyu, tamari or soy sauce
- 10–12 oz. seltzer or green tea

TOFU *   14

- miso soup
- 1 square grilled tofu
- asparagus and carrots
- side of white or brown rice
- 10–12 oz. seltzer or green tea

SEAFOOD *   15

- 4 oz. canned tuna or sockeye salmon (use Creamy Garlic Dressing as mayonnaise substitute—see recipe)
- steamed or sautéed collard greens, kale and Swiss chard
- side of cottage cheese
- 10–12 oz. club soda or iced peppermint tea

SEAFOOD *   16

- *Tuna and Spelt Pasta Salad*
  - 4 oz. canned tuna
  - 1 cup cooked spelt pasta (spirals or elbows)
  - chopped broccoli, celery, scallions and carrots
- Herb Mock Vinaigrette Dressing (see recipe)
- bed of chopped spinach
- 10–12 oz. green tea or spearmint tea

SEAFOOD *   17

- *Sardine Salad*
  - sardines
  - 1 hard-boiled egg
  - appropriate lettuce and arugala
  - tomato, Spanish onion and alfalfa sprouts
- Herb Mock Vinaigrette Dressing (see recipe)
- 10–12 oz. club soda or iced peppermint tea

SEAFOOD *   18

- *Open-Face Sardine Sandwich*
  sardines
  Spanish onions, avocado, tomato and
  appropriate lettuce
  1 pc. Ezekiel or Essene bread
- 1 peach or pear
- 10–12 oz. club soda or chamomile tea

SEAFOOD *   19

- *Calamari (Squid) Salad*
  6 oz. unbreaded calamari sautéed in garlic
  and olive oil
  raw spinach and arugala
  tomato, celery, cucumber and carrots
- 10–12 oz. club soda or chamomile tea

SOUP AND SANDWICH   20

- Creamy Squash Bisque (see recipe)
- *Grilled Cheese*
  4 oz. appropriate cheese
  2 pc. Ezekiel or Essene bread
- sliced tomato and alfalfa sprouts
- 10–12 oz. club soda or green tea

SOUP AND SANDWICH   21

- Turkish Red Lentil Soup (see recipe)
- *Salmon Sandwich*
  6 oz sockeye salmon, celery, minced
  onions (use Creamy Garlic dressing as
  mayonnaise substitute—see recipe)
  2 pc. Ezekiel bread with lettuce and tomato
- 10–12 oz. bottled water or green tea

SOUP AND SANDWICH   22

- Minestrone Soup (see recipe)
- *Tuna Sandwich*
  6 oz albacore tuna, celery, minced onions
  (use Creamy Garlic Dressing as
  mayonnaise substitute—see recipe)
  2 pc. Ezekiel bread with lettuce and tomato
- 10–12 oz. green tea or spearmint tea

BEANS *   23

- miso soup
- side order of Edamame
- small side salad
- Miso Dressing (see recipe)
- 10–12 oz. bottled water or green tea

BEANS *   24

- 4 oz. vegetable juice
- *Pinto Bean and Pasta Salad*
  4 oz. pinto beans
  1 cup cooked rice pasta (spirals or elbows)
  Spanish onions, carrots, broccoli
- Mock Vinaigrette Dressing (see recipe)
- 10–12 oz. club soda or chamomile tea

MIXED *   25

- *Chef's Salad #1*
  1 hard-boiled egg
  2 oz. lamb
  2 oz. farmer's cheese
  4 cup pinto beans
  mesculen salad
- Miso Dressing (see recipe)
- 10–12 oz. club soda or iced peppermint tea

MIXED *   26

- *Chef's Salad #2*
  1 hard-boiled egg
  2 oz. turkey
  2 oz. soy cheese
  ¼ cup soy beans
  raw spinach and arugala
- Green Goddess Dressing (see recipe)
- 10–12 oz. club soda or iced peppermint tea

Blood Type

AB

LAMB *   27

• *Lamb Salad*
  6 oz. lamb
  side of white beans
  appropriate lettuce and arugala
  tomato, cucumber, celery and avocado
• Creamy Avocado Dressing (see recipe)
• 10–12 oz. club soda or green tea

LAMB *   28

• *Open-Face Lamb Sandwich*
  6 oz. lamb
  Spanish onions, avocado, tomato, mint
  leaves and appropriate lettuce
  1 pc. Ezekiel or Essene bread
• 4–5 figs
• 10–12 oz. club soda or chamomile tea

Blood Type AB— Foods That Stimulate Weight Loss

• Tofu—stimulates metabolic efficiency
• Seafood—promotes metabolic efficiency
• Dairy products—improve insulin productivity
• Green vegetables—improve metabolic efficiency

Blood Type AB— Foods That Cause Weight Gain

• Red meat—stores as fat, is poorly digested and creates toxicity in the intestinal tract
• Kidney beans, lima beans—cause hypoglycemia, slow metabolic rate and inhibit insulin efficiency
• Seeds—inhibit insulin efficiency
• Corn—causes hypoglycemia
• Buckwheat—decreases metabolism
• Wheat—decreases metabolism, is an inefficient use of calories, inhibits insulin efficiency

Note: Inhibited insulin production causes hypoglycemia, a lowering of blood sugar after meals, and leads to less efficient metabolism of foods.

Blood Type AB
28-Day Pick-a-Meal Dinner Options

SEAFOOD *   1
- Fish With Herbs and Lime (see recipe)
- side of broccoli and cauliflower
- side of millet
- 10–12 oz. green tea or soda water

SEAFOOD *   2
- 8 oz. grilled mahi-mahi or grouper
- steamed Brussels sprouts and carrots
- small baked sweet potato
- 10–12 oz. green tea or club soda

SEAFOOD *   3
- *Pan-Seared Salmon in Maple Glaze*
  8 oz. salmon
  ½ tsp. Garam Marsala spice
  1 Tbsp. pure maple syrup
- steamed or grilled asparagus
- 10–12 oz. green tea or bottled water

SEAFOOD *   4
- *Steamed Mussels and Scallops*
  mussels and scallops steamed in garlic,
  olive oil, fish stock and parsley
- broccoli
- side of quinoa or couscous
- 10–12 oz. green tea or lemon/lime water

SEAFOOD *   5
- *Steamed Mussels Over Pasta*
  mussels in garlic, olive oil, fish stock
  and parsley
  side of spelt or rice linguine
- side salad with ½ cup appropriate beans
- Herb Mock Vinaigrette Dressing (see recipe)
- 10–12 oz. green tea or lemon/lime water

SEAFOOD *   6
- 4–6 oz. canned tuna with celery and onions
  (use Creamy Garlic Dressing as mayonnaise
  substitute—see recipe)
- small side salad
- Oregano Feta Dressing (see recipe)
- side of couscous
- 10–12 oz. green tea or soda water

SEAFOOD *   7
- 6–8 oz. grilled marinated fresh tuna steak
- small sweet potato
- small side salad with ½ cup appropriate beans
- Raspberry Mock Vinaigrette Dressing
  (see recipe)
- 10–12 oz. green tea or strawberry leaf tea

SEAFOOD *   8
- 8 oz. catfish with lemon and dill
- sautéed Swiss chard or spinach
- parsnips or carrots
- 10–12 oz. green tea or lemon/lime water

PHEASANT *   9
- roasted pheasant
- baked sweet potato
- side of nonfat cottage cheese
- broccoli and cauliflower
- 10–12 oz. bottled water or green tea

RABBIT *   10
- grilled rabbit
- roasted pumpkin or other squash
- zucchini
- side of appropriate beans with rosemary
- 10–12 oz. bottled water or
  glass of red wine

Blood Type

AB

LIVER *   11
- liver and onions
- mesculen salad with cucumbers, tomatoes, celery, avocado, beets and ½ cup soy beans
- Miso Dressing (see recipe)
- 10–12 oz. club soda or glass of red wine

LIVER *   12
- *Liver Florentine*
  sautéed liver with spinach
- side of broccoli, carrots or beets
- ½ cup appropriate beans
- 10–12 oz. green tea or glass of red wine

LAMB *   13
- lamb chops
- mesculen salad with mint leaves, steamed asparagus, cherry tomatoes and feta cheese
- Middle Eastern Dressing (see recipe)
- 10–12 oz. peppermint tea or glass of red wine

LAMB *   14
- roasted leg of lamb
- roasted carrots, parsnips, onions, sweet potato and beets with rosemary
- side of nonfat cottage cheese
- 10–12 oz. peppermint tea or glass of red wine

TURKEY *   15
- 6 oz. roasted turkey
- roasted carrots, parsnips, onions, sweet potato and beets with rosemary
- side of cranberries
- chestnuts
- 10–12 oz. green tea or seltzer

TURKEY *   16
- *Roasted Turkey and Quinoa Salad*
  side of quinoa
  6 oz. sliced turkey
- Warm Cranberry Dressing (see recipe)
- 10–12 oz. green tea or soda water

TURKEY *   17
- turkey burger
- slice of appropriate cheese
- sliced Spanish onion and avocado
- small side salad
- Creamy Cilantro Lime Dressing (see recipe)
- 10–12 oz. water or iced peppermint tea

TURKEY *   18
- 4-6 oz. chopped turkey pieces with celery and onions (use Creamy Garlic Dressing as mayonnaise substitute—see recipe)
- Small side salad with ricotta cheese
- Red Onion Dressing (see recipe)
- 10–12 oz. green tea or soda water

CHEESE *   19
- *Stuffed Baked Potato*
  baked sweet potato
  steamed spinach or Swiss chard, chopped
  4 oz. cottage cheese or ricotta cheese
  3–4 oz. turkey, lamb or rabbit chunks
- small side salad
- Creamy Avocado Dressing (see recipe)
- 10–12 oz. bottled water or green tea

CHEESE *   20
- *Stuffed Baked Potato*
  broccoli, steamed
  baked sweet potato
  3–4 oz. cheddar cheese
  3–4 oz. turkey chunks
- small side salad
- Red Onion Dressing (see recipe)
- 10–12 oz. green tea or seltzer

BEANS   21

- *Sautéed Swiss Chard and White Beans*
    Swiss chard sautéed in vegetable stock
    and onions
    ¾ cup white beans
- 1 cup cooked rice or spelt pasta
- 10–12 oz. green tea or soda water

BEANS *   22

- lentil soup
- mesculen and mustard greens with grilled tofu,
  cucumbers, tomatoes and alfalfa sprouts
- Oregano Feta Dressing (see recipe)
- 10–12 oz. seltzer or glass of red wine

TOFU *   23

- Tofu in Cilantro Sauce (see recipe)
- sautéed collard greens, Swiss chard and kale
- side of brown rice
- 10–12 oz. green tea or seltzer

TOFU *   24

- 2 squares grilled tofu
- stir-fry baby bok choy, broccoli and onions
- side of brown rice
- 10–12 oz. green tea or soda water

TOFU *   25

- *Stir-Fry Tofu*
    2 squares tofu
    broccoli, asparagus and bamboo shoots
- shoyu, tamari or soy sauce
- 10–12 oz. seltzer or green tea

TOFU *   26

- Herbed Tofu (see recipe)
- 2 oz. appropriate cheese
- redskin peanuts or macadamia nuts
- Rye Vitas or Rye Crisps
- small side salad
- Creamy Garlic Dressing (see recipe)
- 10–12 oz. soda water or iced peppermint tea

TEMPEH *   27

- grilled marinated tempeh
- sautéed collard greens, Swiss chard and kale
- side of brown rice or quinoa
- 10–12 oz. green tea or soda water

TEMPEH *   28

- *Open-Face Tempeh Sandwich*
    grilled marinated tempeh
    avocados, alfalfa sprouts, onions and tomato
    1 pc. Ezekiel or Essene bread
- 1 apple or pear
- 10–12 oz. green tea or ginger tea

* Anabolic (higher in protein than carbohydrates)

Blood Type
AB

Blood Type AB
28-Day Pick-a-Meal Snack Options

VEGGIES/BEANS *   1
- side of Edamame
- 10–12 oz. bottled water

VEGGIES/BEANS *   2
- raw vegetables with Creamy Avocado Dressing (see recipe); make dressing into a thick dip-like consistency
- 10–12 oz. green tea or spearmint tea

VEGGIES/BEANS *   3
- raw vegetables with Green Goddess Dressing
- 10–12 oz. green tea or spearmint tea

FRUIT   4
- 1 large apple with organic peanut butter
- 10–12 oz. seltzer water

FRUIT *   5
- 10–12 cherries or berries
- 10–12 oz. green tea

FRUIT   6
- small bowl of raspberries and blueberries
- glass of soy milk

FRUIT *   7
- 1 apple
- 4–6 whole walnuts
- 10–12 oz. green tea or peppermint tea

FRUIT   8
- sliced pears and black currants
- 10–12 oz. green tea

FRUIT *   9
- Poached Peaches (see recipe)
- 10–12 oz. green tea

GRAINS/NUTS *   10
- unsalted redskin peanuts
- 10–12 oz. soda water

GRAINS/NUTS *   11
- 1 pc. Ezekiel bread with almond butter or organic peanut butter and whole-fruit jam
- 10–12 oz. soda water

GRAINS/NUTS   12
- 2–3 Rye Vitas or Rye Crisps
- goat or farmer's cheese
- 10–12 oz. green tea

GRAINS/NUTS   13
- 4–6 roasted chestnuts
- 4–5 figs, dried or fresh
- 10–12 oz. green tea or coffee

GRAINS/NUTS   14
- oat-bran muffin
- 1 peach
- 10–12 oz. green tea or coffee

GRAINS/NUTS   15
- 4–6 walnuts
- 4–5 figs, dried or fresh
- 10–12 oz. green tea or coffee

GRAINS/NUTS *   16
- 2–3 Almond Honey Cookies (see recipe)
- glass of soy milk

* Anabolic (higher in protein than carbohydrates)

GRAINS/NUTS *   17
- 2–3 Carob Almond Cookies (see recipe)
- glass of soy milk

TRAIL MIX *   18
- Basic Trail Mix #2 (see recipe)
- 10–12 oz. green tea or peppermint tea

TRAIL MIX *   19
- Peanut Chocolate Trail Mix (see recipe)
- 10–12 oz. green tea or spearmint tea

DAIRY   20
- 6 oz. low-fat yogurt
- 1 peach
- 10–12 oz. green tea or ginger tea

DAIRY   21
- 6 oz. low-fat kefir
- 1 peach
- 10–12 oz. green tea or ginger tea

DAIRY *   22
- ½ cup low-fat sour cream with fresh strawberries and honey
- 10–12 oz. green tea or coffee

DAIRY *   23
- ½ cup low-fat sour cream with fresh blueberries, raspberries and honey
- 10–12 oz. green tea or coffee

DAIRY *   24
- ½ cup riccota cheese with black currants
  and honey
- 10–12 oz. green tea

SMOOTHIES *   25
- Apricot Cream Smoothie (see recipe)
  or
- Chocolate Raspberry Smoothie (see recipe)
  or
- Cranberry Crush Smoothie (see recipe)

SMOOTHIES *   26
- Maple Magic Smoothie (see recipe)
  or
- Purple Passion Smoothie (see recipe)

SMOOTHIES *   27
- Vanilla Cherry Smoothie (see recipe)
  or
- Very Berry Smoothie (see recipe)
  or
- Viennese Coffee Smoothie (see recipe)

SMOOTHIES *   28
- Body Genetics Protein Shake, vanilla or
  chocolate, mixed with water or soy milk

Blood Type

AB

Chapter 9
Blood Type O

Blood Type O
Grocery List of Beneficial Foods

Meats—
All Anabolic
- [ ] Beef
- [ ] Ground beef
- [ ] Buffalo
- [ ] Heart
- [ ] Lamb
- [ ] Liver
- [ ] Mutton
- [ ] Veal
- [ ] Venison

Seafood—
All Anabolic
- [ ] Bluefish
- [ ] Cod
- [ ] Hake
- [ ] Halibut
- [ ] Fresh herring
- [ ] Mackerel
- [ ] Pike
- [ ] Rainbow trout
- [ ] Red snapper
- [ ] Salmon
- [ ] Sardines
- [ ] Shad
- [ ] Snapper
- [ ] Sole
- [ ] Swordfish
- [ ] Tilefish
- [ ] White perch
- [ ] Whitefish
- [ ] Yellow perch
- [ ] Yellowtail

Beans/
Legumes
- [ ] Aduke
- [ ] Azuki
- [ ] Black-eyed peas
- [ ] Pinto beans

Eggs/Dairy
- [ ] Mozzarella cheese, nonfat
- [ ] Sour cream, nonfat
- [ ] Body Genetics Protein Shake *

Nuts/Seeds
- [ ] Flaxseeds
- [ ] Macadamia nuts
- [ ] Pumpkin seeds
- [ ] Walnuts *

Oils
- [ ] Linseed (Flaxseed)
- [ ] Olive

Cereals
- [ ] None

Breads
- [ ] Essene bread
- [ ] Ezekiel bread

Pastas/
Grains
- [ ] None

Vegetables
- [ ] Artichokes, domestic and Jerusalem
- [ ] Avocado, Florida
- [ ] Beet leaves
- [ ] Broccoli
- [ ] Broccoli sprouts
- [ ] Chicory
- [ ] Collard greens
- [ ] Dandelion
- [ ] Escarole
- [ ] Kale
- [ ] Kohlrabi
- [ ] Leek
- [ ] Okra
- [ ] Onions, red, Spanish, yellow
- [ ] Parsnips
- [ ] Red peppers
- [ ] Romaine lettuce
- [ ] Sweet potatoes
- [ ] Pumpkin
- [ ] Seaweed
- [ ] Spinach
- [ ] Swiss chard
- [ ] Turnips

Fruit
- [ ] Figs, dried and fresh
- [ ] Plums, dark, green, red
- [ ] Prunes

Juice
- [ ] Black cherry
- [ ] Pineapple
- [ ] Prune

Spices/
Condiments
- [ ] Carob
- [ ] Cayenne pepper
- [ ] Curry
- [ ] Dulse
- [ ] Garlic
- [ ] Horseradish
- [ ] Kelp (bladderwrack)
- [ ] Parsley
- [ ] Tabasco
- [ ] Turmeric

Beverages
- [ ] Green tea
- [ ] Seltzer water
- [ ] Soda water
- [ ] Water, distilled

Herbal Teas
- [ ] Cayenne
- [ ] Chickweed
- [ ] Dandelion
- [ ] Fenugreek
- [ ] Ginger
- [ ] Hops
- [ ] Linden
- [ ] Milk thistle
- [ ] Mulberry
- [ ] Parsley
- [ ] Peppermint
- [ ] Rose hip
- [ ] Sarsaparilla
- [ ] Slippery elm

* Anabolic (higher in protein than carbohydrates)

Blood Type O
Grocery List of Neutral Foods

Meats—
All Anabolic
- [ ] Chicken
- [ ] Cornish hens
- [ ] Duck
- [ ] Partridge
- [ ] Pheasant
- [ ] Quail
- [ ] Rabbit
- [ ] Turkey

Seafood—All
Anabolic
- [ ] Abalone
- [ ] Anchovy
- [ ] Beluga
- [ ] Bluegill bass, sea bass
- [ ] Carp
- [ ] Clam
- [ ] Crab
- [ ] Crayfish
- [ ] Frog
- [ ] Flounder
- [ ] Gray sole
- [ ] Grouper
- [ ] Haddock
- [ ] Lobster
- [ ] Mahi-mahi
- [ ] Mussels
- [ ] Oysters
- [ ] Sea trout
- [ ] Tuna

Beans/
Legumes
- [ ] Black
- [ ] Broad
- [ ] Cannelloni
- [ ] Fava
- [ ] Garbanzo (chickpeas)
- [ ] Green
- [ ] Jicama
- [ ] Lima
- [ ] Northern
- [ ] Peas, green, snow, pod
- [ ] Red
- [ ] Soy, black, brown, green Edamame*
- [ ] Snap
- [ ] String
- [ ] White

Eggs/Dairy
- [ ] Eggs *
- [ ] Butter
- [ ] Farm cheese *
- [ ] Feta cheese *
- [ ] Goat cheese *
- [ ] Mozzarella *
- [ ] Soy cheese *
- [ ] Soy milk *

Nuts/Seeds
- [ ] Almonds
- [ ] Almond butter *
- [ ] Chestnuts
- [ ] Filberts *
- [ ] Hickory *
- [ ] Pecan
- [ ] Pine (pignoli)
- [ ] Sesame seeds
- [ ] Sunflower butter
- [ ] Sunflower seeds
- [ ] Tahini (sesame butter)

Oils
- [ ] Canola
- [ ] Cod liver
- [ ] Sesame

Cereals
- [ ] Amaranth
- [ ] Barley
- [ ] Buckwheat
- [ ] Cream of Rice
- [ ] Kamut
- [ ] Kasha
- [ ] Rice Bran
- [ ] Puffed Rice
- [ ] Puffed Millet
- [ ] Spelt Flakes

Breads
- [ ] Brown rice bread
- [ ] Buckwheat
- [ ] Fin Crisp
- [ ] Gluten-free bread
- [ ] Ideal flat bread
- [ ] Millet
- [ ] Rice cake
- [ ] Rye bread, 100 percent
- [ ] Rye Crisp
- [ ] Rye Vita
- [ ] Soy flour bread
- [ ] Spelt bread
- [ ] Wasa

Pastas/
Grains
- [ ] Artichoke pasta
- [ ] Barley
- [ ] Buckwheat
- [ ] Kamut
- [ ] Kasha
- [ ] Millet
- [ ] Rice, basmati, brown, white, wild
- [ ] Rye flour
- [ ] Millet
- [ ] Quinoa

Vegetables
- [ ] Arugala
- [ ] Asparagus
- [ ] Bamboo shoots
- [ ] Beets
- [ ] Bok choy
- [ ] Carrots
- [ ] Celery
- [ ] Cucumber
- [ ] Daikon
- [ ] Endive
- [ ] Fennel
- [ ] Fiddlehead ferns
- [ ] Lettuce, Bibb, Boston, iceberg, mesculen
- [ ] Mushrooms, enoki, portobella, tree oyster
- [ ] Green olives
- [ ] Green onions
- [ ] Peppers, green, jalepeño, yellow
- [ ] Raddichio
- [ ] Radishes
- [ ] Rappini
- [ ] Rutabaga
- [ ] Scallion
- [ ] Shallots
- [ ] Sprouts, mung, radish
- [ ] Squash, all types
- [ ] Tempeh *
- [ ] Tofu *
- [ ] Tomato
- [ ] Water chestnut
- [ ] Watercress
- [ ] Yams
- [ ] Zucchini

Juices
- [ ] Apricot
- [ ] Carrot
- [ ] Celery
- [ ] Cranberry
- [ ] Cucumber
- [ ] Grape
- [ ] Grapefruit
- [ ] Papaya
- [ ] Tomato
- [ ] Vegetable
- [ ] Water and lemon

Fruits
- [ ] Apples
- [ ] Apricots
- [ ] Bananas
- [ ] Blueberries
- [ ] Boysenberries
- [ ] Cherries
- [ ] Cranberries
- [ ] Currants, black, red
- [ ] Dates
- [ ] Elderberries
- [ ] Gooseberries
- [ ] Grapefruit
- [ ] Grapes, black, concord, green, red
- [ ] Guava
- [ ] Kiwi
- [ ] Kumquat
- [ ] Lemons
- [ ] Limes
- [ ] Loganberries
- [ ] Mangos

Blood Type

O

Blood Type O
Grocery List of Neutral Foods (con't.)

☐ Melons, casaba, Christmas, crenshaw, musk, Spanish
☐ Nectarines
☐ Papaya
☐ Peaches
☐ Pears
☐ Persimmons
☐ Pineapple
☐ Pomegranates
☐ Prickly pears
☐ Raisins
☐ Raspberries
☐ Starfruit
☐ Strawberries
☐ Watermelon

Beverages
☐ Green tea
☐ Red wine
☐ White wine

Herbal Teas
☐ Catnip
☐ Chamomile
☐ Dong quai
☐ Elder
☐ Ginseng
☐ Hawthorn
☐ Horehound
☐ Licorice
☐ Mullein
☐ Raspberry leaf
☐ Sage
☐ Skullcap
☐ Spearmint
☐ Thyme
☐ Valerian
☐ Vervain
☐ White birch
☐ White oak bark
☐ Yarrow

Spices/ Condiments
☐ Agar
☐ Allspice
☐ Almond extract
☐ Anise
☐ Apple butter
☐ Arrowroot
☐ Barley malt
☐ Basil
☐ Bay leaf
☐ Bergamot
☐ Brown rice syrup
☐ Brown sugar
☐ Caraway
☐ Cardamom
☐ Chervil
☐ Chives
☐ Chocolate
☐ Coriander (Cilantro)
☐ Cumin
☐ Dill
☐ Honey
☐ Jam/jelly from acceptable fruit
☐ Maple syrup, pure
☐ Marjoram
☐ Mayonnaise
☐ Mint
☐ Miso
☐ Molasses
☐ Mustard, dry
☐ Paprika
☐ Peppercorn
☐ Peppermint
☐ Pimiento
☐ Plain Gelatin
☐ Red pepper flakes
☐ Rice syrup

☐ Rosemary
☐ Saffron
☐ Sage
☐ Salt
☐ Savory
☐ Shoyu
☐ Soy sauce
☐ Spearmint
☐ Stevia **
☐ Sucanat **
☐ Tamari
☐ Tamarind
☐ Tapioca
☐ Tarragon
☐ Thyme
☐ Vanilla
☐ White sugar
☐ Wintergreen
☐ Worcestershire sauce

* Anabolic (higher in protein than carbohydrates)
** Natural sweetener

Blood Type O
List of Foods to Avoid

Meats
- Goose
- Pork, all

Seafood
- Barracuda
- Catfish
- Caviar
- Conch
- Pickled herring
- Lox, smoked salmon
- Octopus

Beans/ Legumes
- Copper
- Kidney
- Navy
- Tamarind
- Lentils, green domestic, red

Nuts/Seeds
- Brazil nuts
- Cashews
- Litchi
- Peanuts
- Peanut butter
- Pistachios
- Poppy seeds

Oils
- Corn
- Cottonseed
- Peanut
- Safflower

Cereals
- Corn Flakes
- Cream of Wheat
- Familia
- Farina
- Grape Nuts
- Oat Bran
- Oatmeal
- Shredded Wheat
- Wheat Bran
- Wheat Germ

Eggs/Dairy
- American cheese
- Blue cheese
- Brie
- Buttermilk
- Camembert
- Casein
- Cheddar
- Colby
- Cottage cheese
- Cream cheese
- Edam
- Emmenthal
- Goat milk
- Gouda
- Gruyere
- Ice cream
- Jarlsberg
- Kefir
- Milk, 2 percent, skim, whole
- Monterey Jack
- Muenster
- Parmesan
- Provolone
- Neufchatel
- Ricotta
- String cheese
- Swiss cheese
- Yogurt, all varieties
- Whey

Breads
- Corn muffins
- English muffins
- High-protein bread
- Multi-grain bread
- Oat-bran muffins
- Pumpernickel
- Seven-grain bread
- Wheat bagels
- Wheat-bran muffins
- Wheat matzos
- Whole-wheat bread

Vegetables
- Avocados, California
- Brussels sprouts
- Cabbage, Chinese, red, white
- Cauliflower
- Corn, white, yellow
- Eggplant
- Mushrooms, domestic, shitaki
- Mustard greens
- Olives, black, green, Spanish
- Potatoes, red, white
- Alfalfa sprouts

Fruit
- Blackberries
- Cantaloupe
- Coconut
- Honeydew melon
- Oranges
- Plantains
- Rhubarb
- Tangerine

Juice
- Apple
- Apple cider
- Cabbage
- Orange

Pastas/ Grains
- Bulgur wheat flour
- Cornmeal
- Couscous flour
- Durum wheat flour
- Gluten flour
- Graham flour
- Oat flour
- Oatmeal
- Semolina and spinach pasta
- Soba noodles
- White flour
- Whole-wheat flour

Spices/ Condiments
- Capers
- Cinnamon
- Cornstarch
- Corn syrup
- Nutmeg
- Pepper, black, white
- Vinegar, apple, red, white, balsamic
- Ketchup
- Pickles, dill, kosher, sweet, sour
- Relish

Beverages
- Coffee
- Distilled liquor
- Sodas

Herbal Teas
- Black tea, regular, decaf

Blood Type

Blood Type O
28-Day Pick-a-Meal Breakfast Options

SMOOTHIE *　　　　　　　　　　1
- Almond Bomb Smoothie (see recipe)
- 1 pc. Ezekiel or Essene bread with apple butter and tahini
- 10–12 oz. peppermint tea

SMOOTHIE *　　　　　　　　　　2
- Chocolate Raspberry Smoothie (see recipe)
- 1 pc. 100 percent rye or Essene bread with goat cheese
- 10–12 oz. green tea

SMOOTHIE *　　　　　　　　　　3
- Cranberry Crush Smoothie (see recipe)
- 1 pc. 100 percent rye or Essene bread
- 1 slice soy cheese
- 10–12 oz. green tea

SMOOTHIE *　　　　　　　　　　4
- Very Berry Smoothie (see recipe)
- 1 pc. 100 percent rye or Essene bread with almond butter and whole-fruit jam
- 10–12 oz. peppermint tea

SMOOTHIE *　　　　　　　　　　5
- Banana Smoothie (see recipe)
- 1 pc. 100 percent rye or Essene bread with almond butter and whole-fruit jam
- 10–12 oz. green tea

DRY CEREAL *　　　　　　　　　6
- medium bowl of Amaranth and Spelt Flakes (half and half mix is recommended) with soy milk
- ½ mango
- 1 pc. Ezekiel bread with almond butter
- 10–12 oz. chamomile tea

DRY CEREAL *　　　　　　　　　7
- 4 oz. grapefruit juice
- medium bowl of Kamut Krisps with soy milk
- 1 pc. Essene bread
- 1 slice soy cheese
- 10–12 oz. chamomile tea

DRY CEREAL　　　　　　　　　　8
- 4 oz. carrot juice
- medium bowl of Puffed Millet with soy milk
- 8–10 cherries
- 1 pc. Essene bread with whole-fruit jam
- 10–12 oz. green tea

DRY CEREAL　　　　　　　　　　9
- 4 oz. cranberry juice
- medium bowl of Amaranth Flakes with soy milk
- ½ cup raspberries, blueberries or loganberries
- 1 pc. Ezekiel or Essene bread with whole-fruit jam
- 10–12 oz. coffee or chamomile tea

DRY CEREAL　　　　　　　　　　10
- 3 oz. carrot juice
- medium bowl of soy flakes with soy milk
- sliced peaches or pears
- 1 pc. Ezekiel bread with whole-fruit jam
- 10–12 oz. strawberry leaf tea

* Anabolic (higher in protein than carbohydrates)

HOT CEREAL 11

- 4 oz. prune juice
- medium bowl of hot kasha with soy milk
- 4–5 walnuts
- 1 pc. Ezekiel bread with apple butter
- 10–12 oz. Tazo "Refresh" Tea (spearmint, peppermint and tarragon blend)

HOT CEREAL 12

- 4 oz. pineapple chunks
- medium bowl of hot Rice Bran with soy milk
- 1 pc. Ezekiel bread with farmer's cheese
- 10–12 oz. green tea

NUT BUTTER * 13

- ½ grapefruit or 4 oz. grapefruit juice
- 1 Ezekiel bagel
- almond butter and whole-fruit jam
- 10–12 oz. green tea

NUT BUTTER * 14

- 4 oz. carrot or tomato juice
- 2 pc. 100 percent rye or Ezekiel bread
- tahini and honey
- 2 plums
- 10–12 oz. ginger tea

SCRAMBLED TOFU * 15

- 4 oz. grapefruit juice or ½ grapefruit
- *Curried Scrambled Tofu*
  4 oz. tofu with curry powder
- ribbons of spinach, beet greens or collards
- scallions or onions
- 1 pc. Ezekiel bread with whole-fruit jam
- 10–12 oz. green tea

SCRAMBLED TOFU * 16

- *Scrambled "Egg" Tofu*
  4 oz. tofu with turmeric and minced onions
- 20–30 grapes
- 1 pc. brown rice bread with whole-fruit jam
- 10–12 oz. chamomile tea

EGGS * 17

- 4 oz. tomato juice
- 2 eggs, poached, boiled or scrambled
- 2 kiwi
- 1 pc. Ezekiel or Essene bread with whole-fruit jam
- 10–12 oz. chamomile tea

EGGS * 18

- *Tex-Mex Omelet*
  2 eggs, scrambled, filled with ¼ cup pinto beans
- ½ cup salsa
- melon wedge
- 1 pc. Ezekiel or Essene bread with whole-fruit jam
- 10–12 oz. green tea

EGGS * 19

- *Curried Scrambled Eggs*
  2 scrambled eggs with ½ tsp. curry powder
- 1 slice nonfat mozzarella cheese
- melon wedge and strawberries
- 1 pc. Ezekiel or Essene bread with whole-fruit jam
- 10–12 oz. green tea

Blood Type

O

EGGS *   20

- *Salmon Scrambled Eggs*
  2 scrambled eggs with crumpled salmon
  pieces
- 2 kiwis
- 1 pc. Ezekiel or Essene bread with whole-fruit
  jam
- 10–12 oz. chamomile tea

EGGS *   21

- 4 oz. apricot juice
- *Spanish Omelet*
  2 scrambled eggs with onions, mushrooms,
  red peppers
- 1 pc. Ezekiel bread with butter
- 10–12 oz. peppermint tea

EGGS   22

- 4 oz. grape juice
- *Spinach and Artichoke Omelet*
  2 scrambled eggs
  leeks, spinach,
  2–3 sliced artichoke hearts
- 1 pc. Ezekiel bread with whole-fruit jam

CHEESE *   23

- 4 oz. nonfat sour cream
- kiwi, pineapple chunks, raisins
- ground flaxseeds
- 4–5 crushed walnuts
- 1 pc. Ezekiel bread with whole-fruit jam
- 10–12 oz. Tazo "Refresh" Tea (spearmint, peppermint and tarragon blend)

CHEESE *   24

- 4 oz. carrot juice
- 4 oz. assorted appropriate cheeses
- radish sprouts
- 20–30 grapes
- 1 pc. 100 percent rye toast
- 10–12 oz. green tea

CHEESE *   25

- 3–4 apricots
- 4 oz. goat cheese
- 1 thin slice ocean salmon (raw or cooked)
- sliced onions and tomatoes
- 1 pc. Ezekiel bread
- 10–12 oz. rose hip tea

CHEESE *   26

- 4 oz. grapefruit juice or 2 grapefruit
- *Grilled Cheese*
  2 pc. spelt bread
  4 oz. mozzarella cheese
- sliced tomato and Florida avocado
- 10–12 oz. Tazo "Refresh" Tea (spearmint, peppermint and tarragon blend)

BEANS *   27

- melon wedge
- *Bean Hash*
  ½–¾ cup any appropriate bean (cooked)
  onions, red peppers, cayenne pepper
- nonfat mozzarella cheese
- 10–12 oz. green tea

BEANS *   28

- strawberries or blueberries
- *Bean Hash With Egg*
  ½–¾ cup any appropriate bean (cooked)
  onions, red peppers, cayenne pepper
  1 egg any style
- 10–12 oz. chamomile tea

Blood Type O
28-Day Pick-a-Meal Lunch Options

MIXED *   1

- *Chef's Salad #1*
  - 1 hard-boiled egg
  - 2 oz. roast beef
  - 2 oz. farmer's cheese
  - ¼ cup pinto beans
  - mesculen salad with sliced beets
- Red Onion Dressing (see recipe)
- 10–12 oz. club soda or iced peppermint tea

MIXED *   2

- *Chef's Salad #2*
  - 1 hard-boiled egg
  - 2 oz. turkey
  - 2 oz. soy cheese
  - 2 oz. roast beef
  - raw spinach and arugala with sliced fennel
- Green Goddess Dressing (see recipe)
- 10–12 oz. club soda or iced peppermint tea

MIXED *   3

- *Chef's Salad #3*
  - 3 oz. roast beef
  - 3 oz. lamb
  - feta cheese
  - appropriate lettuce
  - roasted red peppers and portobella mush-rooms
- Herb Mock Vinaigrette Dressing (see recipe)
- 10–12 oz. club soda or green tea

MIXED *   4

- *Chef's Salad #4*
  - 2 oz. roast beef
  - 2 oz. lamb
  - 2 oz. farmer's cheese
  - ¼ cup garbanzo beans (chickpeas)
  - mesculen salad with sliced beets
- Red Onion Dressing (see recipe)
- 10–12 oz. club soda or iced peppermint tea

BEEF   5

- medium bowl of beef chili (use pinto beans rather than kidney beans)
- mixed green salad
- tomato, cucumber, celery and onions
- 10–12-oz. iced green tea or soda water

BEEF *   6

- beef fajitas with onions and peppers (no tortillas)
- appropriate lettuce
- side of zucchini
- 10–12 oz. green tea or soda water

BEEF *   7

- *Antipasto*
  - 4 oz. sliced roast beef
  - 3 oz. sliced mozzarella cheese
  - sliced tomato, onions, fresh basil
  - roasted red peppers
  - bed of radicchio
- 10–12 oz. seltzer or bottled water

* Anabolic (higher in protein than carbohydrates)

Blood Type

BEEF *   8

- grilled beef cheeseburger (using appropriate cheese)
- mixed green salad
- Creamy Garlic Dressing (see recipe)
- artichoke hearts, tomato and radish
- 10–12 oz. iced ginger tea or green tea

BEEF *   9

- 6 oz. sliced roast beef
- sautéed onions and mushrooms
- 1 slice mozzarella
- steamed asparagus, broccoli and carrots
- 10–12 oz. iced spearmint tea or green tea

SOUP AND SANDWICH *   10

- medium bowl of Onion Soup (see recipe)
- 1 large slice meat loaf
- 2 pc. Ezekiel bread
- side order zucchini and carrots
- 10–12 oz. seltzer or bottled water

SOUP AND SANDWICH   11

- *Grilled Cheese*
    2–3 oz. appropriate cheese
    2 pc. Ezekiel or Essene bread
- medium bowl of Chicken Chili Soup (see recipe)
- sliced tomato and avocado
- 10–12 oz. club soda or green tea

SOUP AND SANDWICH   12

- medium bowl of Carrot Bisque (see recipe)
- broiled portobella mushroom with goat cheese
- arugala and tomato
- 2 pc. Ezekiel bread
- 10–12 oz. iced spearmint tea or green tea

TOFU *   13

- *Stir-Fry Tofu*
    1 square tofu
    broccoli, carrots, zucchini, asparagus, bamboo shoots
    shoyu, tamari or soy sauce
- 10–12 oz. seltzer or green tea

TOFU *   14

- Herbed Tofu (see recipe)
- 2 oz. appropriate cheese
- redskin peanuts
- Rye Vitas or Rye Crisps
- small side salad with Green Goddess Dressing (see recipe)
- 10–12 oz. soda water or iced peppermint tea

SEAFOOD *   15

- *Tuna and Artichoke Salad*
    1 hard-boiled egg
    6 oz. canned tuna or sockeye salmon
    artichoke hearts, tomato, onion, avocado
    mesculen salad and arugala
- Herb Mock Vinaigrette Dressing (see recipe)
- 10–12 oz. club soda or iced peppermint tea

SEAFOOD *   16

• *Tuna and Spelt Pasta Salad*
   4 oz. canned tuna
   1 cup cooked spelt pasta (spirals or elbows)
   chopped broccoli, celery, scallions and
   carrots
   bed of mesculen salad
• Herb Mock Vinaigrette Dressing (see recipe)
• 10–12 oz. green tea or spearmint tea

SEAFOOD *   17

• *Sardine Salad*
   sardines
   1 hard-boiled egg
   appropriate lettuce and arugala
   tomato, onion, radish, roasted red peppers
• Herb Mock Vinaigrette Dressing (see recipe)
• 10–12 oz. club soda or iced peppermint tea

SEAFOOD *   18

• *Open-Face Sardine Sandwich*
   sardines
   onions, avocado, tomato and
   appropriate lettuce
   1 pc. Ezekiel or Essene bread
• 1 peach or pear
• 10–12 oz. club soda or green tea

SEAFOOD *   19

• miso soup
• side order of Edamame
• tuna or salmon teriyaki
• small side salad with daikon, radishes and
  tomato
• Miso Dressing (see recipe)
• 10–12 oz. green tea or bottled water

CHEESE *   20

• *Goat Cheese Salad*
   4 oz. goat cheese
   raw spinach and arugala
   tomatoes, walnuts and radishes
• Warm Cranberry Dressing (see recipe)
• 10–12 oz. bottled water or iced ginger tea

LAMB *   21

• grilled lamb chops
• side of Swiss chard
• side of brown and wild rice (half and half mixture suggested) with appropriate mushrooms
• 10–12 oz. club soda or glass of red wine

LAMB *   22

• *Lamb Salad*
   6 oz. lamb pieces
   side of white beans
   appropriate lettuce and dandelion greens
   tomato, cucumber, celery, avocado
• Creamy Avocado Dressing (see recipe)
• 10–12 oz. club soda or glass of red wine

CHICKEN *   23

• 6–8 oz. roasted chicken
• roasted parsnips and pumpkin
• mixed greens with peppers, tomato, okra and
  scallions
• Creamy Garlic Dressing (see recipe)
• 10–12 oz. soda water or green tea

Blood Type

CHICKEN *   24

- *Pesto Pasta With Chicken*
  6–8 oz. grilled chicken slices or cubes
  1 cup cooked spelt pasta
  Cheeseless Basil Pesto (see recipe)
- side of broccoli
- 10–12 oz. green tea or glass of white wine

TURKEY *   25

- *Turkey Salad*
  6 oz. cubed turkey
  appropriate lettuce and dandelion greens
  avocado, cucumber, beets and feta cheese
- Warm Cranberry Dressing (see recipe)
- 10–12 oz. club soda or peppermint tea

TURKEY *   26

- 6 oz. turkey burger
- 1 slice nonfat mozzarella cheese
- sliced Spanish onion and avocado
- mixed greens salad
- Creamy Garlic Dressing (see recipe)
- 10–12 oz. water or iced peppermint tea

TURKEY *   27

- *Stuffed Baked Potato*
  baked sweet potato
  4 oz. turkey chunks
  ¼ cup nonfat sour cream
- broccoli, steamed
- small side salad
- Creamy Garlic Dressing (see recipe)
- 10–12 oz. green tea or seltzer

TURKEY *   28

- *Mock Waldorf Salad*
  4 oz. sliced turkey
  4–5 chopped walnuts
  ½ chopped apple or pear
  mesculen salad
- Raspberry Mock Vinaigrette Dressing (see recipe)
- 10–12 oz. green tea or raspberry leaf tea

Blood Type O— Foods That Stimulate Weight Loss

- Red meat—stimulates metabolism
- Broccoli, spinach and kale—stimulate metabolism
- Seafood, kelp—contain iodine and stimulate thyroid hormone production
- Iodized salt—contains iodine and stimulates thyroid hormone production
- Liver—stimulates metabolism

Blood Type O— Foods That Cause Weight Gain

- Corn—slows the metabolism
- Cabbage, cauliflower, Brussels sprouts—inhibit thyroid hormone
- Mustard greens—inhibits thyroid production
- Lentils—inhibit improper nutrient metabolism
- Navy beans, kidney beans—impair calorie utilization
- Wheat gluten—slows the metabolism

Note: Inhibited insulin production causes hypoglycemia, lowering of blood sugar after meals and leads to less efficient metabolism of foods.

Blood Type O
28-Day Pick-a-Meal Dinner Options

SEAFOOD *   1
- Fish With Herbs and Lime (see recipe)
- side of broccoli and cauliflower
- side of millet
- 10–12 oz. green tea or soda water

SEAFOOD *   2
- 8 oz. grilled mahi-mahi or grouper
- steamed broccoli sprouts and carrots
- small baked sweet potato
- 10–12 oz. green tea or club soda

SEAFOOD *   3
- *Pan-Seared Salmon in Maple Glaze*
  8 oz. salmon
  1 Tbsp. pure maple syrup
- side of asparagus
- 10–12 oz. green tea or bottled water

SEAFOOD *   4
- 6–8 oz. grilled marinated fresh tuna steak
- small sweet potato
- small side salad with appropriate bean
- 10–12 oz. green tea or strawberry leaf tea

SEAFOOD *   5
- 4–6 oz. canned tuna or sockeye salmon
- celery and onions (use Creamy Garlic Dressing as a mayonnaise substitute—see recipe)
- small side salad with feta cheese
- Red Onion Dressing (see recipe)
- side of quinoa
- 10–12 oz. green tea or soda water

SEAFOOD *   6
- 6–8 oz. grilled swordfish marinated in red wine and appropriate herbs
- watercress salad with water chestnuts
- Miso Dressing (see recipe)
- side of millet
- 10–12 oz. soda water or glass of red wine

BEEF *   7
- grilled beef cheeseburger (using appropriate cheese)
- mixed green salad
- Oregano Feta Cheese Dressing (see recipe)
- artichoke hearts, tomato and radish
- 10–12 oz. iced ginger tea

BEEF *   8
- 6–8 oz. steak
- sautéed onions and mushrooms
- steamed kale
- 10–12 oz. green tea or soda water

BEEF *   9
- miso soup
- 6–8 oz. beef teriyaki
- side of brown rice
- side of stir-fry with appropriate vegetables
- 10–12 oz. green tea or chamomile tea

BEEF *   10
- *Beef Kabobs*
  beef cubes, peppers and onion
- watercress salad with radish sprouts
- Miso Dressing (see recipe)
- side of millet
- 10–12 oz. green tea or iced ginger tea

* Anabolic (higher in protein than carbohydrates)

Blood Type
O

RABBIT *   11

- grilled rabbit
- roasted pumpkin or other squash
- zucchini
- side of appropriate beans with rosemary
- 10–12 oz. bottled water or glass of red wine

LAMB *   12

- lamb stew with red wine and appropriate
  vegetables
- small mixed greens salad
- Herb Mock Vinaigrette Dressing (see recipe)
- side of millet
- 10–12 oz. club soda or glass of red wine

LAMB *   13

- lamb chops
- mesculen salad with mint leaves, steamed
  asparagus, cherry tomatoes and feta cheese
- Red Onion Dressing (see recipe)
- 10–12 oz. peppermint tea or glass of red wine

LAMB *   14

- roasted leg of lamb
- roasted carrots, parsnips, onions, sweet potato
  and beets with rosemary
- side of white beans
- 10–12 oz. peppermint tea or glass of red wine

TURKEY *   15

- roasted turkey
- roasted carrots, parsnips, onions, sweet potato
  and beets with rosemary
- Warm Cranberry Dressing (see recipe)
- 10–12 oz. green tea or seltzer

TURKEY *   16

- turkey burger
- 1 slice appropriate cheese
- sliced Spanish onion and avocado
- small side salad with Creamy Garlic Dressing
  (see recipe)
- 10–12 oz. water or iced peppermint tea

CHICKEN *   17

- 6–8 oz. roasted chicken breast
- 2 steamed artichokes
- side of carrots and zucchini
- 10–12 oz. green tea or soda water

CHICKEN *   18

- 6–8 oz. cold chicken
- 1 cup cooked spelt or kamut pasta in Soy
  Cheese Sauce (see recipe)
- steamed Swiss chard or mustard greens
- 10–12 oz. green tea or club soda

CHICKEN *   19

- 4–6 oz. chicken teriyaki
- stir-fry with appropriate vegetables
- side of Edamame
- side of brown rice
- 10–12 oz. green tea or iced ginger tea

CHICKEN *   20

- grilled chicken in Mexican Spice Rub (see
  recipe)
- mixed green salad with tomato and cucumbers
- Creamy Avocado Dressing (see recipe)
- 10–12 oz. green tea or iced ginger tea

CORNISH HEN *   21

- 6–8 oz. roasted or grilled Cornish hen
- side of mashed parsnips and sweet potatoes (half and half mix is recommended)
- small side salad with Herb Mock Vinaigrette Dressing (see recipe)
- 10–12 oz. soda water or iced peppermint tea

PHEASANT *   22

- roasted pheasant
- baked sweet potato with nonfat sour cream
- broccoli and cauliflower
- 10–12 oz. bottled water or green tea

VENISON *   23

- venison stew with red wine and appropriate vegetables
- small mixed greens salad with chestnuts
- Herb Mock Vinaigrette Dressing (see recipe)
- side of millet
- 10–12 oz. green tea or spearmint tea

VENISON *   24

- 6–8 oz. venison steak
- carrots, rutabagas and yam mixture, roasted or grilled
- small side salad
- Herb Mock Vinaigrette Dressing (see recipe)
- 10–12 oz. soda water or green tea

TOFU *   25

- *Stir-Fry Tofu*
  2 squares tofu
  broccoli, asparagus and bamboo shoots
  shoyu, tamari or soy sauce
- 10–12 oz. seltzer or green tea

TOFU *   26

- 2 squares grilled tofu
- stir-fry baby bok choy, broccoli and onions
- side of brown rice
- 10–12 oz. green tea or soda water

LIVER *   27

- liver and onions
- mesculen salad with cucumbers, tomatoes, celery, avocado, beets and ½ cup of soy beans
- Herb Mock Vinaigrette Dressing (see recipe)
- 10–12 oz. club soda or glass of red wine

LIVER *   28

- *Liver Florentine*
  sautéed liver with spinach
- side of broccoli, carrots or beets
- ½ cup appropriate beans
- 10–12 oz. green tea or glass of red wine

Blood Type

Blood Type O
28-Day Pick-a-Meal Snack Options

VEGGIES/BEANS *   1
- side of Edamame
- 10–12 oz. bottled water

VEGGIES/BEANS *   2
- raw vegetables with Creamy Avocado Dressing
  (make dressing into a thick
  dip-like consistency)
- 10–12 oz. green tea or spearmint tea

VEGGIES/BEANS *   3
- raw vegetables with Green Goddess Dressing
  (make dressing into a thick
  dip-like consistency)
- 10–12 oz. green tea or spearmint tea

FRUIT   4
- 1 large apple with almond butter
- 10–12 oz. seltzer water

FRUIT *   5
- 10–12 cherries or berries
- 10–12 oz. green tea

FRUIT   6
- 1 apple
- 4–6 whole walnuts
- 10–12 oz. green tea or peppermint tea

GRAINS/NUTS *   7
- 8 almonds or walnuts
- 10–12 oz. soda water

GRAINS/NUTS *   8
- 1 pc. Ezekiel bread with almond butter
  and whole-fruit jam
- 10–12 oz. soda water

GRAINS/NUTS *   9
- 2–3 Rye Vitas or Rye Crisps
- goat or farmer's cheese
- 10–12 oz. green tea

GRAINS/NUTS *   10
- 4–6 roasted chestnuts
- 4–5 figs, dried or fresh
- 10–12 oz. green tea or ginger tea

GRAINS/NUTS *   11
- rice cake with almond butter and honey
- 1 peach
- 10–12 oz. green tea or raspberry leaf tea

GRAINS/NUTS *   12
- 4–6 walnuts
- 4–5 figs, dried or fresh
- 10–12 oz. green tea or iced peppermint tea

GRAINS/NUTS *   13
- 8 almonds
- 1 peach
- 10–12 oz. green tea or spearmint tea

GRAINS/NUTS   14
- 2–3 Pecan Sandies (see recipe)
- glass of soy milk

GRAINS/NUTS   15
- 2–3 Almond Honey Cookies (see recipe)
- glass of soy milk

GRAINS/NUTS *   16
- 2–3 Carob Almond Cookies (see recipe)
- glass of soy milk

TRAIL MIX * 17
- Basic Trail Mix #1 (see recipe)
- 10–12 oz. green tea or peppermint tea

TRAIL MIX * 18
- Basic Trail Mix #3 (see recipe)
- 10–12 oz. green tea or peppermint tea

TRAIL MIX * 19
- Apple Walnut Trail Mix (see recipe)
- 10–12 oz. green tea or ginger tea

TRAIL MIX * 20
- Apple Pie Trail Mix (see recipe)
- 10–12 oz. green tea or spearmint tea

DAIRY * 21
- ½ cup low-fat sour cream with fresh strawberries and honey
- 10–12 oz. green tea or ginger tea

DAIRY * 22
- ½ cup low-fat sour cream with fresh blueberries and raspberries and honey
- 10–12 oz. green tea or ginseng tea

SMOOTHIES * 23
- Almond Bomb Smoothie (see recipe)

SMOOTHIES * 24
- Banana Smoothie (see recipe)
  or
- Apricot Cream Smoothie (see recipe)

SMOOTHIES * 25
- Chocolate Raspberry Smoothie (see recipe)
  or
- Cranberry Crush Smoothie (see recipe)

SMOOTHIES *
- Maple Magic Smoothie (see recipe)
  or
- Purple Passion Smoothie (see recipe)

SMOOTHIES * 27
- Vanilla Cherry Smoothie (see recipe)
  or
- Very Berry Smoothie (see recipe)

SMOOTHIES * 28
- Body Genetics Protein Shake, chocolate or vanilla, mixed with water or soy milk

* Anabolic (higher in protein than carbohydrates)

Blood Type

Chapter 10

Family Meal Planning

Many people have asked how to make this program work for their families. Many families are a combination of blood types. Families with different blood types *can* make this work. To aid in the process I have created new grocery lists for a few of the possible combinations—A and O families, B and O families, AB and O families. I cross-referenced which foods would be mutually beneficial between the two blood types. Those foods have been asterisked. Then I listed all the other foods that they had in common on their beneficial and neutral lists. As you can see, the grocery lists are full of a variety of foods. I have also provided a seven-day family plan for each "family" combination to give you a head start.

Use the 28-Day Pick-a-Meal Planner and the steps outlined earlier to guide you in feeding your multi-blood type family. The basic principles are the same.

Family Planning AB and O
Grocery List

Meats— All Anabolic
☐ Lamb #
☐ Liver
☐ Mutton #
☐ Pheasant
☐ Rabbit
☐ Turkey

Seafood— All Anabolic
☐ Abalone
☐ Bluefish
☐ Carp
☐ Cod #
☐ Fresh herring
☐ Grouper
☐ Hake #
☐ Mackerel #
☐ Mahi-mahi
☐ Mussels
☐ Pike #
☐ Rainbow trout #
☐ Salmon, ocean #
☐ Sardines #
☐ Sea trout
☐ Shad #
☐ Snapper #
☐ Sole
☐ Swordfish
☐ Tilefish
☐ Tuna
☐ White perch
☐ Yellow perch

Beans/ Legumes
☐ Broad
☐ Cannelloni
☐ Green
☐ Jicama
☐ Northern
☐ Peas, green, pod, snow
☐ Pinto #
☐ Red
☐ Snap
☐ Soy, brown, black, green Edamame *
☐ String
☐ White

Eggs/Dairy
☐ Eggs *
☐ Soy cheese *
☐ Soy milk *
☐ Farmer's cheese *
☐ Feta cheese *
☐ Goat cheese *
☐ Mozzarella nonfat *
☐ Body Genetics Protein Shake *

Nuts/Seeds
☐ Almond butter *
☐ Almonds *
☐ Brazil nuts *
☐ Flaxseeds #
☐ Hickory *
☐ Macadamia nuts
☐ Pine (pignoli)
☐ Walnuts #

Oils
☐ Canola
☐ Cod liver
☐ Linseed (Flaxseed)

Cereals
☐ Amaranth
☐ Barley
☐ Puffed Millet
☐ Puffed Rice
☐ Rice Bran
☐ Spelt Flakes

Breads
☐ Brown rice bread
☐ Essene bread #
☐ Ezekiel bread #
☐ Gluten-free bread
☐ Ideal flat bread
☐ Rye bread, 100 percent
☐ Rye Crisps
☐ Rye Vita
☐ Spelt bread
☐ Wasa bread

Pastas/ Grains
☐ Millet
☐ Quinoa
☐ Spelt flour
☐ Spelt pasta

Vegetables
☐ Arugala
☐ Asparagus
☐ Avocado, Florida #
☐ Bamboo shoots
☐ Beet leaves #
☐ Beets #
☐ Bok Choy
☐ Broccoli #
☐ Broccoli sprouts #
☐ Carrots
☐ Celery
☐ Chicory
☐ Collard Greens #
☐ Cucumbers #
☐ Daikon
☐ Dandelion greens #
☐ Endive
☐ Escarole
☐ Fennel
☐ Fiddlehead ferns
☐ Kale #
☐ Kohlrabi
☐ Leek
☐ Lettuce, Bibb, Boston, iceberg, mesculen, romaine
☐ Mushrooms, enoki, porto-bella, tree oyster
☐ Okra
☐ Onions, green, red, Spanish, yellow
☐ Parsley #
☐ Parsnips #
☐ Raddichio
☐ Rappini
☐ Rutabaga
☐ Scallion
☐ Shallots
☐ Spinach
☐ Squash, all types
☐ Sweet potatoes #
☐ Swiss chard
☐ Tempeh
☐ Tofu
☐ Tomato
☐ Turnips
☐ Water chestnuts
☐ Watercress
☐ Yams, all kinds
☐ Zucchini

Juices
☐ Apricot
☐ Black cherry #
☐ Carrot
☐ Celery
☐ Cranberry
☐ Cucumber
☐ Grape
☐ Grapefruit
☐ Papaya
☐ Pineapple
☐ Prune
☐ Vegetable
☐ Water and lemon

Fruits
☐ Apples
☐ Apricots
☐ Blueberries
☐ Boysenberries
☐ Cherries
☐ Cranberries
☐ Currants, black, red
☐ Dates
☐ Elderberries
☐ Figs, dried or fresh #
☐ Gooseberries
☐ Grapefruit

- ☐ Grapes, black, concord, green, red
- ☐ Kiwi
- ☐ Kumquat
- ☐ Lemon
- ☐ Limes
- ☐ Loganberries
- ☐ Melon, all types
- ☐ Nectarines
- ☐ Papaya
- ☐ Peaches
- ☐ Pears
- ☐ Pineapple
- ☐ Plantains
- ☐ Plum, dark green, red
- ☐ Prunes
- ☐ Raspberries
- ☐ Strawberries
- ☐ Watermelon

Beverages
- ☐ Red wine
- ☐ Seltzer water
- ☐ White wine

Herbal Teas
- ☐ Catnip
- ☐ Cayenne
- ☐ Chickweed
- ☐ Dandelion
- ☐ Dong quai
- ☐ Elder
- ☐ Horehound
- ☐ Mulberry
- ☐ Parsley
- ☐ Peppermint
- ☐ Sage
- ☐ Sarsaparilla
- ☐ Slippery elm
- ☐ Spearmint
- ☐ Thyme
- ☐ Valerian

- ☐ White birch
- ☐ White oak bark

Spices/ Condiments
- ☐ Agar
- ☐ Arrowroot
- ☐ Basil
- ☐ Bay leaf
- ☐ Bergamot
- ☐ Brown rice syrup
- ☐ Brown sugar
- ☐ Caraway
- ☐ Carob
- ☐ Chervil
- ☐ Chives
- ☐ Chocolate
- ☐ Coriander (Cilantro)
- ☐ Cream of tartar
- ☐ Cumin
- ☐ Curry #
- ☐ Dill
- ☐ Dulse
- ☐ Garlic
- ☐ Ginger
- ☐ Honey
- ☐ Horseradish
- ☐ Jam/jelly, from appropriate fruit
- ☐ Kelp
- ☐ Maple syrup, pure
- ☐ Marjoram
- ☐ Mint
- ☐ Miso
- ☐ Molasses
- ☐ Paprika
- ☐ Parsley #
- ☐ Peppermint
- ☐ Pimento

- ☐ Rice syrup
- ☐ Rosemary
- ☐ Saffron
- ☐ Sage
- ☐ Salt
- ☐ Savory
- ☐ Shoyu
- ☐ Soy sauce
- ☐ Spearmint
- ☐ Stevia **
- ☐ Sucanat **
- ☐ Tamari
- ☐ Tamarind
- ☐ Tarragon
- ☐ Thyme
- ☐ Turmeric
- ☐ Vanilla
- ☐ White sugar

*   Anabolic (higher in protein than carbohydrates)
** Natural sweeteners
\#   Mutually beneficial foods

Blood Type
AB &O

Family Planning AB and O
7-Day Pick-a-Meal Menu Options

DAY 1

Breakfast:
• 4 oz. pineapple juice
• medium bowl of amaranth flakes with soy milk
• raspberries and crushed walnuts
• 1 pc. Ezekiel bread with whole-fruit jam
• 10–12 oz. green tea

Lunch:
• *Antipasto*
   3–4 oz. mozzarella cheese
   sliced tomato and fresh basil
   sliced red onions
• Herb Mock Vinaigrette Dressing (see recipe)
• 10–12 oz. green tea

Afternoon Snack:
• side order of Edamame
• 10–12 oz. green tea

Dinner:
• 6–8 oz. Rosemary Roasted Lamb With Roasted Vegetables (see recipe)
• side of millet
• small side salad with beets, broccoli, fennel and tomato
• Miso Dressing (see recipe)
• 10–12 oz. green tea

Evening Snack:
• 1 apple with almond butter
• 10–12 oz. green tea

Before Bedtime:
• 1 Body Genetics Protein Shake

DAY 2

Breakfast:
• 4 oz. carrot juice
• medium bowl of spelt flakes with soy milk
• blueberries and raspberries
• 1 pc. Essene bread with 1 slice soy cheese
• 10–12 oz. green tea

Lunch:
• *Goat Cheese Salad*
   2 oz. goat cheese
   lettuce, arugala, walnuts and radishes
• Raspberry Mock Vinaigrette Dressing (see recipe)
• 10–12 oz. green tea

Afternoon Snack:
• Very Berry Smoothie (see recipe)

Dinner:
• Trout stuffed with appropriate herbs
• side of broccoli or asparagus
• side of millet
• 10–12 oz. green tea

Evening Snack:
• 2–3 Almond Honey cookies (see recipe)
• glass of soy milk

Before Bedtime:
• 1 Body Genetics Protein Shake

DAY 3

Breakfast:
• *Salmon Scrambled Eggs*
   2 scrambled eggs and crumpled salmon
   pieces
• 2 kiwis
• 1 pc. spelt bread with whole-fruit jam
• 10–12 oz. green tea

Lunch:
• Onion Soup (see recipe)
• *Grilled Cheese Sandwich*
   2–3 oz. farmer's cheese
   2 slices 100 percent rye bread
• sliced Florida avocado and watercress
• Miso Dressing (see recipe)
• 10–12 oz. green tea

Afternoon Snack:
• Brazil nuts, almonds, walnuts (mixed)
• 10–12 oz. green tea

Dinner:
• 8 oz. grilled snapper
• steamed asparagus and carrots
• side of quinoa or millet
• 10–12 oz. green tea

Evening Snack:
• 1 pc. 100 percent rye bread with almond
   butter and honey
• 10–12 oz. green tea

Before Bedtime:
• 1 Body Genetics Protein Shake

DAY 4

Breakfast:
• 4 oz. grapefruit juice
• Spinach Mushroom Frittata (see recipe)
• 1 pc. 100 percent rye bread with goat
   cheese
• 10–12 oz. green tea

Lunch:
• Tomato Soup (see recipe)
• *Tuna Sandwich*
   6 oz. tuna with minced onions and celery
   lettuce and water chestnuts
   2 pcs. 100 percent rye bread
• 10–12 oz. green tea

Afternoon Snack:
• sliced pears and black currants
• 10–12 oz. green tea

Dinner:
• *Steamed Mussels Over Pasta*
   mussels in garlic, olive oil, fish stock
   and parsley
   side order of spelt pasta
• side salad with appropriate beans
• Herb Mock Vinaigrette Dressing (see
   recipe)
• 10–12 oz. green tea

Evening Snack:
• 2–3 Carob Almond cookies
• glass of soy milk

Before Bedtime:
• 1 Body Genetics Protein Shake

Blood Type
**AB
&O**

DAY 5

Breakfast:
• 4 oz. prune juice
• 2 soft-boiled eggs
• 1 pc. spelt bread with almond butter and whole-fruit jam
• 10–12 oz. green tea

Lunch:
• 6–8 oz. turkey cubes
• lettuce, dandelion greens and ¼ c. cannelloni beans
• Warm Cranberry Dressing (see recipe)
• 10–12 oz. green tea

Afternoon Snack:
• Vanilla Cherry Smoothie (see recipe)

Dinner:
• 6–8 oz. Grilled Marinated Tuna (see recipe)
• small sweet potato
• small side salad
• Lemon-Lime Cilantro Dressing (see recipe)
• 10–12 oz. green tea

Evening Snack:
• 1 pc. brown rice bread with 1 slice farmer's cheese
• 10–12 oz. green tea

Before Bedtime:
• 1 Body Genetics Protein Shake

DAY 6

Breakfast:
• 4 oz. vegetable juice
• 2 oz. goat cheese, 1 thin slice ocean salmon (cooked or raw—not lox), sliced onions
• 2 pcs. 100 percent rye bread
• 20 grapes
• 10–12 oz. green tea

Lunch:
• 6 oz. turkey burger
• 1 slice mozzarella cheese
• sliced red onions and avocado
• small side salad with Red Onion Dressing (see recipe)
• 10–12 oz. green tea

Afternoon Snack:
• 6 whole walnuts and 2–3 apricots
• 10–12 oz. green tea

Dinner:
• 6–8 oz. roasted turkey
• roasted carrots, beets and onions with rosemary and olive oil
• side of cranberries
• small side salad
• Miso Dressing (see recipe)
• 10–12 oz. green tea

Evening Snack:
• Poached Peaches (see recipe)
• 10–12 oz. green tea

Before Bedtime:
• 1 Body Genetics Protein Shake

DAY 7

Breakfast:
- Chocolate Raspberry Smoothie (see recipe)
- 1 pc. brown rice bread with almond butter and whole-fruit jam
- 10–12 oz. green tea

Lunch:
- Herbed Tofu (see recipe)
- Rye Vitas or Rye Crisps
- small side salad with Green Goddess Dressing (see recipe)
- wedge of cantaloupe
- 10–12 oz. green tea

Afternoon Snack:
- small bowl of fresh cranberries and almond slivers
- glass soy milk

Dinner:
- Tofu in Cilantro Sauce (see recipe)
- sautéed Swiss chard, collard greens and kale
- side of quinoa
- 10–12 oz. green tea

Evening Snack:
- walnuts, almonds and dates (mixed)
- 10–12 oz. green tea

Before Bedtime:
- 1 Body Genetics Protein Shake

Blood Type
**AB
&O**

Family Planning A and O
Grocery List

Meats—
All Anabolic
- [ ] Chicken
- [ ] Cornish hen
- [ ] Turkey

Seafood—
All Anabolic
- [ ] Abalone
- [ ] Carp
- [ ] Cod #
- [ ] Grouper
- [ ] Mackerel #
- [ ] Mahi-mahi
- [ ] Pike
- [ ] Rainbow trout #
- [ ] Sardines #
- [ ] Snapper #
- [ ] Swordfish
- [ ] Tuna, albacore
- [ ] White perch
- [ ] Whitefish #
- [ ] Yellowtail

Beans & Legumes
- [ ] Aduke #
- [ ] Azuki #
- [ ] Black
- [ ] Black-eyed peas
- [ ] Broad
- [ ] Cannelloni
- [ ] Fava
- [ ] Green
- [ ] Jicama
- [ ] Peas, green, pod, snow
- [ ] Pinto #
- [ ] Snap
- [ ] Soy, black, brown, green Edamame *
- [ ] String
- [ ] White

Eggs/Dairy
- [ ] Eggs *
- [ ] Farmer's cheese *
- [ ] Feta cheese *
- [ ] Goat cheese *
- [ ] Mozzarella, low fat *
- [ ] Soy cheese *
- [ ] Soy milk *
- [ ] Body Genetics Protein Shake *

Nuts/Seeds
- [ ] Almond butter *
- [ ] Chestnuts
- [ ] Filberts *
- [ ] Flaxseeds
- [ ] Hickory *
- [ ] Pine (pignoli)
- [ ] Pumpkin seeds
- [ ] Sesame seeds
- [ ] Sunflower butter
- [ ] Sunflower seeds
- [ ] Tahini (sesame butter)
- [ ] Walnuts *

Oils
- [ ] Canola
- [ ] Cod liver
- [ ] Linseed (Flaxseed)
- [ ] Olive

Cereals
- [ ] Amaranth
- [ ] Barley
- [ ] Buckwheat
- [ ] Cream of Rice
- [ ] Kamut
- [ ] Kasha

- [ ] Puffed Millet
- [ ] Puffed Rice
- [ ] Spelt Flakes

Breads
- [ ] Brown rice
- [ ] Essene bread
- [ ] Ezekiel bread
- [ ] Gluten-free bread
- [ ] Ideal flat bread
- [ ] Rice cakes
- [ ] Rye Crisp
- [ ] Rye bread, 100 percent
- [ ] Rye Vita
- [ ] Spelt bread
- [ ] Wasa bread

Pastas/ Grains
- [ ] Artichoke pasta
- [ ] Quinoa
- [ ] Rice, basmati, brown, white, wild
- [ ] Rice flour
- [ ] Rice pasta
- [ ] Rye flour
- [ ] Spelt flour
- [ ] Spelt pasta

Vegetables
- [ ] Artichokes #
- [ ] Arugala
- [ ] Asparagus
- [ ] Avocado, Florida
- [ ] Beet leaves #
- [ ] Beets
- [ ] Bok choy
- [ ] Broccoli #
- [ ] Broccoli sprouts #

- [ ] Carrots
- [ ] Cauliflower
- [ ] Celery
- [ ] Chicory #
- [ ] Collard greens #
- [ ] Cucumber
- [ ] Daikon
- [ ] Dandelion greens #
- [ ] Endive
- [ ] Escarole #
- [ ] Fennel
- [ ] Kale
- [ ] Kohlrabi #
- [ ] Leek #
- [ ] Lettuce, Bibb, iceberg, mes-culen, romaine
- [ ] Mushrooms, enoki, portobella, tree oyster
- [ ] Okra #
- [ ] Onions, red, Spanish, yellow
- [ ] Raddichio
- [ ] Radishes
- [ ] Rappini
- [ ] Rutabaga
- [ ] Scallion
- [ ] Seaweed
- [ ] Shallots
- [ ] Spinach #
- [ ] Sprouts, radish
- [ ] Squash, all types
- [ ] Swiss chard #
- [ ] Tempeh *
- [ ] Tofu *
- [ ] Water chestnuts
- [ ] Watercress
- [ ] Zucchini

Juices
- [ ] Apricot
- [ ] Black cherry #
- [ ] Carrot
- [ ] Celery
- [ ] Cranberry
- [ ] Cucumber
- [ ] Grape
- [ ] Grapefruit
- [ ] Pineapple #
- [ ] Prune #
- [ ] Vegetable
- [ ] Water and lemon

Fruits
- [ ] Apples
- [ ] Apricot
- [ ] Black currants
- [ ] Blueberries
- [ ] Boysenberries
- [ ] Cherries
- [ ] Cranberries
- [ ] Dates
- [ ] Elderberries
- [ ] Figs, dried and fresh #
- [ ] Gooseberries
- [ ] Grapefruit
- [ ] Grapes, black, concord, green, red
- [ ] Guava
- [ ] Kiwi
- [ ] Kumquat
- [ ] Lemons
- [ ] Limes
- [ ] Loganberries
- [ ] Melon, casaba, canang, Christmas, crenshaw, musk, Spanish

- ☐ Nectarines
- ☐ Peaches
- ☐ Pears
- ☐ Persimmons
- ☐ Pineapple
- ☐ Plums, dark green, red #
- ☐ Pomegranates
- ☐ Prickly pears
- ☐ Raisins
- ☐ Raspberries
- ☐ Starfruit
- ☐ Strawberries
- ☐ Watermelon

Beverages
- ☐ Green tea
- ☐ Red wine
- ☐ White wine

Herbal Teas
- ☐ Chamomile
- ☐ Chickweed
- ☐ Dandelion
- ☐ Dong quai
- ☐ Elder
- ☐ Fenugreek #
- ☐ Ginger #
- ☐ Ginseng
- ☐ Hawthorn
- ☐ Hops
- ☐ Licorice root
- ☐ Linden
- ☐ Milk thistle #
- ☐ Mulberry
- ☐ Mullein
- ☐ Parsley
- ☐ Peppermint
- ☐ Raspberry leaf
- ☐ Sage
- ☐ Sarsaparilla
- ☐ Skullcap
- ☐ Slippery elm #
- ☐ Spearmint

- ☐ Thyme
- ☐ Vervain
- ☐ White birch
- ☐ White oak bark
- ☐ Yarrow

Spices & Condiments
- ☐ Agar
- ☐ Allspice
- ☐ Almond extract
- ☐ Anise
- ☐ Barley malt
- ☐ Basil
- ☐ Bay leaf
- ☐ Bergamot
- ☐ Brown rice syrup
- ☐ Brown sugar
- ☐ Caraway
- ☐ Cardamom
- ☐ Carob
- ☐ Chervil
- ☐ Chives
- ☐ Chocolate
- ☐ Coriander (cilantro)
- ☐ Cumin
- ☐ Curry
- ☐ Dill
- ☐ Dulse
- ☐ Garlic #
- ☐ Ginger
- ☐ Honey
- ☐ Horseradish #
- ☐ Jams/jelly, from appropriate fruit
- ☐ Kelp
- ☐ Maple syrup, pure
- ☐ Mint
- ☐ Paprika

- ☐ Parsley #
- ☐ Peppermint
- ☐ Pimiento
- ☐ Rice syrup
- ☐ Rosemary
- ☐ Saffron
- ☐ Sage
- ☐ Salt
- ☐ Savory
- ☐ Shoyu
- ☐ Soy sauce
- ☐ Spearmint
- ☐ Stevia **
- ☐ Sucanat **
- ☐ Tamari
- ☐ Tamarind
- ☐ Tapioca
- ☐ Tarragon
- ☐ Thyme
- ☐ Turmeric
- ☐ Vanilla
- ☐ White sugar

* Anabolic (higher in protein than carbohydrates)

** Natural sweeteners

\# Mutually beneficial foods

Blood Type

A&
O

Family Planning A and O
7-Day Pick-a-Meal Menu Options

DAY 1

Breakfast:
- 4 oz. prune juice
- medium bowl of Kamut Krisp Flakes with soy milk
- black currants and sunflower seeds
- 1 pc. Ezekiel bread with almond butter
- 10–12 oz. green tea

Lunch:
- *Chef's Salad*
    1 hard-boiled egg
    3–4 oz. chicken
    1 oz. farmer's cheese
    sliced beets and Florida avocados
    lettuce and arugala
    Green Goddess Dressing (see recipe)
- 10–12 oz. green tea

Afternoon Snack:
- side of Edamame
- 10–12 oz. green tea

Dinner:
- 6–8 oz. Cornish hen in Greek Herb Crust (see recipe)
- side of wild rice with chopped portobella mushrooms
- small side salad with beets, broccoli and fennel
- Red Onion Dressing (see recipe)
- 10–12 oz. green tea

Evening Snack:
- Poached Peaches (see recipe)
- 10–12 oz. green tea

Before Bedtime:
- 1 Body Genetics Protein Shake

DAY 2

Breakfast:
- 4 oz. carrot juice
- medium bowl of Puffed Millet with soy milk
- 8–10 cherries
- 1 pc. Essene bread with 1 slice soy cheese
- 10–12 oz. green tea

Lunch:
- *Goat Cheese Salad*
    2 oz. goat cheese
    raw spinach, arugala, walnuts and radishes
- Raspberry Mock Vinaigrette Dressing (see recipe)
- 10–12 oz. green tea

Afternoon Snack:
- small bowl of blueberries and raspberries
- glass of soy milk

Dinner:
- Trout stuffed with appropriate herbs
- side of broccoli and cauliflower
- side of quinoa or basmati rice
- 10–12 oz. green tea

Evening Snack:
- sliced pears and black currants
- 10–12 oz. green tea

Before Bedtime:
- 1 Body Genetics Protein Shake

DAY 3

Breakfast:
- *Salmon Scrambled Eggs*
  2 scrambled eggs and crumpled salmon
  pieces
- 2 kiwis
- 1 pc. spelt bread with whole-fruit jam
- 10–12 oz. green tea

Lunch:
- Squash Bisque (see recipe)
- *Grilled Cheese Sandwich*
  2–3 oz. farmer's cheese
  2 slices 100 percent rye bread
- sliced Florida avocado and watercress
- 10–12 oz. green tea

Afternoon Snack:
- Apple "Pie" Trail Mix (see recipe)

Dinner:
- 6–8 oz. broiled ocean salmon in lemon,
  white wine and tarragon
- steamed broccoli and zucchini
- side of beets
- 10–12 oz. green tea

Evening Snack:
- Cherry Clafouti (see recipe)
- 10–12 oz. green tea

Before Bedtime:
- 1 Body Genetics Protein Shake

DAY 4

Breakfast:
- 4 oz. grapefruit juice
- *Cheese Omelet*
  2 scrambled eggs with soy or goat
  cheese and scallions
- 1 pc. brown rice bread with whole-fruit
  jam
- 10–12 oz. green tea

Lunch:
- Italian Minestrone Soup (see recipe)
- *Tuna Sandwich*
  6 oz. tuna with minced onions and celery
  lettuce and water chestnuts
  2 pcs. 100 percent rye bread
- 10–12 oz. green tea

Afternoon Snack:
- Basic Trail Mix #1 (see recipe)

Dinner:
- 8 oz. grilled mahi-mahi or grouper
- steamed asparagus and carrots
- side of quinoa
- 10–12 oz. green tea

Evening Snack:
- apple with almond butter
- 10–12 oz. green tea

Before Bedtime:
- 1 Body Genetics Protein Shake

Blood Type

DAY 5

Breakfast:
- 4 oz. pineapple juice
- Dandelion Greens and Leek Frittata (see recipe)
- 1 pc. spelt bread with almond butter and whole-fruit jam
- 10–12 oz. green tea

Lunch:
- 6–8 oz. roasted chicken
- mixed greens with pimiento, cucumbers, scallions and radish
- Creamy Avocado Dressing (see recipe)
- 10–12 oz. green tea

Afternoon Snack:
- Maple Magic Smoothie (see recipe)

Dinner:
- 6–8 oz. grilled swordfish marinated in red wine and appropriate herbs and spices
- watercress and water chestnut salad with Miso Dressing (see recipe)
- side of artichoke pasta
- 10–12 oz. green tea

Evening Snack:
- ½ cup riccota cheese with black currants and honey
- 10–12 oz. green tea

Before Bedtime:
- 1 Body Genetics Protein Shake

DAY 6

Breakfast:
- 4 oz. vegetable juice
- 2 oz. goat cheese, 1 thin slice ocean salmon (cooked or raw—not lox), sliced onions
- 2 pcs. 100 percent rye bread
- 20 grapes
- 10–12 oz. green tea

Lunch:
- 6 oz. turkey burger
- 1 slice mozzarella cheese
- sliced red onions and avocado
- small side salad with Red Onion Dressing (see recipe)
- 10–12 oz. green tea

Afternoon Snack:
- 6 whole walnuts and 4 dried figs
- 10–12 oz. green tea

Dinner:
- 6–8 oz. roasted turkey
- roasted carrots, beets and onions with rosemary and olive oil
- side of cranberries
- 4–6 roasted chestnuts
- 10–12 oz. green tea

Evening Snack:
- 2–3 Carob Almond cookies
- 10–12 oz. green tea

Before Bedtime:
- 1 Body Genetics Protein Shake

DAY 7

Breakfast:
• Almond Bomb Smoothie (see recipe)
• 1 pc. brown rice bread with almond butter
  and whole-fruit jam
• 10–12 oz. green tea

Lunch:
• *Stir-Fry Tofu*
    1 square tofu, broccoli, carrots, zucchini,
    asparagus and bamboo shoots
• shoyu, tamari or soy sauce
• 1 c. cooked brown rice
• 10–12 oz. green tea

Afternoon Snack:
• 1 slice spelt bread with almond butter and
  whole-fruit jam
• 10–12 oz. green tea

Dinner:
• 6–8 oz. cod or carp in lemon or lime and
  cilantro
• side of okra
• side of escarole or kale
• Lemon-Lime Cilantro Dressing (see
  recipe)
• 10–12 oz. green tea

Evening Snack:
• 2–3 plums and almonds
• 10–12 oz. green tea

Before Bedtime:
• 1 Body Genetics Protein Shake

Blood Type

A&
O

Family Planning B and O
Grocery List

Meats—
All Anabolic
- [ ] Beef
- [ ] Buffalo
- [ ] Ground beef
- [ ] Lamb #
- [ ] Liver
- [ ] Mutton #
- [ ] Pheasant
- [ ] Rabbit
- [ ] Turkey
- [ ] Veal
- [ ] Venison #

Seafood—
All Anabolic
- [ ] Abalone
- [ ] Bluefish
- [ ] Carp
- [ ] Cod #
- [ ] Grouper
- [ ] Haddock
- [ ] Hake #
- [ ] Halibut #
- [ ] Mackerel #
- [ ] Mahi-mahi
- [ ] Pike #
- [ ] Rainbow trout
- [ ] Salmon, ocean #
- [ ] Sardine #
- [ ] Sea trout
- [ ] Shad #
- [ ] Snapper
- [ ] Sole #
- [ ] Swordfish
- [ ] Tilefish
- [ ] Tuna
- [ ] White perch
- [ ] Whitefish
- [ ] Yellow perch

Beans/
Legumes
- [ ] Broad
- [ ] Cannelloni
- [ ] Fava
- [ ] Green
- [ ] Jicama
- [ ] Lima
- [ ] Northern
- [ ] Peas, green, pod, snow
- [ ] Red
- [ ] Snap
- [ ] Soy beans, black, brown, green Edamame *
- [ ] String
- [ ] White

Eggs/Dairy
- [ ] Eggs *
- [ ] Butter
- [ ] Soy cheese *
- [ ] Soy milk *
- [ ] Farmer's cheese *
- [ ] Feta cheese *
- [ ] Goat cheese *
- [ ] Mozzarella, low fat # *
- [ ] Body Genetics Protein Shake *

Nuts/Seeds
- [ ] Almond butter *
- [ ] Almonds *
- [ ] Chestnuts
- [ ] Hickory *
- [ ] Pine (pignoli)

Oils
- [ ] Cod liver
- [ ] Olive

Cereals
- [ ] Cream of Rice
- [ ] Puffed Millet
- [ ] Puffed Rice
- [ ] Rice Bran
- [ ] Spelt Flakes

Breads
- [ ] Brown rice bread
- [ ] Essene bread *
- [ ] Ezekiel bread *
- [ ] Gluten-free bread
- [ ] Millet
- [ ] Rice cakes
- [ ] Soy-flour bread
- [ ] Spelt bread

Pastas/
Grains
- [ ] Quinoa
- [ ] Rice, basmati, brown, white
- [ ] Spelt flour
- [ ] Spelt pasta

Vegetables
- [ ] Asparagus
- [ ] Beet leaves #
- [ ] Beets #
- [ ] Broccoli #
- [ ] Carrots
- [ ] Celery
- [ ] Chicory
- [ ] Collard greens #
- [ ] Cucumber
- [ ] Daikon radish
- [ ] Dandelion greens
- [ ] Endive
- [ ] Escarole
- [ ] Fennel
- [ ] Fiddlehead ferns
- [ ] Kale #
- [ ] Kohlrabi
- [ ] Leek
- [ ] Lettuce, Bibb, Boston, iceberg, mesculen, romaine
- [ ] Mushrooms, enoki, portobella, tree oyster
- [ ] Okra
- [ ] Onions, green, red, Spanish, yellow
- [ ] Parsnips #
- [ ] Pepper, green, red, yellow, jalepeño
- [ ] Radicchio
- [ ] Rappini
- [ ] Rutabaga
- [ ] Scallion
- [ ] Squash, all types
- [ ] Sweet potatoes #
- [ ] Turnips
- [ ] Water chestnuts
- [ ] Watercress
- [ ] Yams, all kinds
- [ ] Zucchini

Juices
- [ ] Black cherry
- [ ] Carrot
- [ ] Celery
- [ ] Cranberry
- [ ] Cucumber
- [ ] Grape
- [ ] Grapefruit
- [ ] Papaya

- [ ] Pineapple #
- [ ] Prune
- [ ] Vegetable
- [ ] Water and lemon

Fruits
- [ ] Apples
- [ ] Apricots
- [ ] Bananas
- [ ] Boysenberries
- [ ] Cherries
- [ ] Cranberries
- [ ] Currants, red, black
- [ ] Dates
- [ ] Elderberries
- [ ] Figs, dried or fresh #
- [ ] Gooseberries
- [ ] Grapefruit
- [ ] Grapes, black, concord, green, red
- [ ] Guava
- [ ] Kiwi
- [ ] Kumquat
- [ ] Lemons
- [ ] Limes
- [ ] Loganberries
- [ ] Mangoes
- [ ] Melon, all types
- [ ] Nectarines
- [ ] Papaya
- [ ] Peaches
- [ ] Pineapple
- [ ] Plum, dark green, red #
- [ ] Raisins
- [ ] Raspberries
- [ ] Strawberries

Beverages
- [ ] Green tea
- [ ] Red wine
- [ ] Water, distilled
- [ ] White wine

Herbal Teas
- [ ] Catnip
- [ ] Cayenne
- [ ] Chamomile
- [ ] Chickweed
- [ ] Dandelion
- [ ] Dong quai
- [ ] Elder
- [ ] Ginger #
- [ ] Ginseng
- [ ] Hawthorn
- [ ] Horehound
- [ ] Licorice root
- [ ] Mulberry
- [ ] Parsley #
- [ ] Peppermint #
- [ ] Raspberry leaf
- [ ] Rose hips
- [ ] Sage
- [ ] Sarsaparilla
- [ ] Slippery elm
- [ ] Spearmint
- [ ] Thyme
- [ ] Valerian
- [ ] Vervain
- [ ] White birch
- [ ] White oak bark
- [ ] Yarrow

Spices/ Condiments
- [ ] Agar
- [ ] Allspice
- [ ] Anise
- [ ] Apple butter
- [ ] Arrowroot
- [ ] Basil
- [ ] Bay leaf

- [ ] Bergamot
- [ ] Brown rice syrup
- [ ] Brown sugar
- [ ] Cardamom
- [ ] Carob
- [ ] Cayenne pepper #
- [ ] Chervil
- [ ] Chives
- [ ] Chocolate
- [ ] Coriander (cilantro)
- [ ] Cumin
- [ ] Curry #
- [ ] Dill
- [ ] Dulse
- [ ] Garlic
- [ ] Ginger
- [ ] Honey
- [ ] Horseradish
- [ ] Jam/jelly, from appropriate fruit
- [ ] Kelp
- [ ] Maple syrup, pure
- [ ] Mayonnaise
- [ ] Mint
- [ ] Molasses
- [ ] Paprika
- [ ] Parsley #
- [ ] Peppermint
- [ ] Pimiento
- [ ] Rice syrup
- [ ] Rosemary
- [ ] Saffron
- [ ] Sage
- [ ] Salt
- [ ] Savory
- [ ] Spearmint
- [ ] Stevia **
- [ ] Sucanat **

- [ ] Tabasco sauce
- [ ] Tamarind
- [ ] Tarragon
- [ ] Thyme
- [ ] Turmeric
- [ ] Vanilla
- [ ] White sugar
- [ ] Wintergreen
- [ ] Worcestershire sauce

* Anabolic (higher in protein than carbohydrates)

** Natural sweeteners

\# Mutually beneficial foods

Blood Type
**B&
O**

Family Planning B and O
7-Day Pick-a-Meal Menu Options

DAY 1

Breakfast:
- ½ grapefruit
- medium bowl of spelt flakes with soy milk and currants
- 1 pc. brown rice bread with 1 slice soy cheese
- 10–12 oz. green tea

Lunch:
- 6 oz. turkey burger
- 1 slice mozzarella or farmer's cheese
- sliced red onions
- small side salad with Herb Mock Vinaigrette Dressing (see recipe)
- 10–12 oz. green tea

Afternoon Snack:
- sliced peach with almond slivers, currants and honey
- 10–12 oz. green tea

Dinner:
- grilled lamb chops
- side of brown and wild rice with portobella mushrooms
- side of collard greens
- 10–12 oz. green tea

Evening Snack:
- 1 pc. spelt bread with almond butter and whole-fruit jam
- 10–12 oz. green tea

Before Bedtime:
- 1 Body Genetics Protein Shake

DAY 2

Breakfast:
- 4 oz. carrot juice
- medium bowl of Puffed Millet with soy milk
- 8–10 cherries
- 1 pc. Essene bread with goat cheese
- 10–12 oz. green tea

Lunch:
- *Mock Waldorf Salad*
    4 oz. sliced turkey
    4–5 chopped walnuts
    ½ chopped apple
- Raspberry Mock Vinaigrette Dressing (see recipe)
- 10–12 oz. green tea

Afternoon Snack:
- side of Edamame
- 10–12 oz. green tea

Dinner:
- Trout stuffed with appropriate herbs
- side of broccoli and carrots
- side of quinoa or basmati rice
- 10–12 oz. green tea

Evening Snack:
- apple with almond butter
- 10–12 oz. green tea

Before Bedtime:
- 1 Body Genetics Protein Shake

DAY 3

Breakfast:
• *Salmon Scrambled Eggs*
    2 scrambled eggs and crumpled salmon
    pieces
• 2 kiwi
• 1 pc. spelt bread with whole-fruit jam
• 10–12 oz. green tea

Lunch:
• Onion Soup (see recipe)
• *Meat Loaf Sandwich*
    1 slice meat loaf with lettuce
    2 slices brown rice bread
• side of zucchini
• 10–12 oz. green tea

Afternoon Snack:
• Apple Walnut Trail Mix (see recipe)

Dinner:
• *Pasta with Salmon*
    6 oz. broiled ocean salmon, broken into
    pieces
    side order of spelt pasta with
    Cheeseless Basil Pesto (see recipe)
• steamed broccoli florets and asparagus
• 10–12 oz. green tea

Evening Snack:
• small bowl of raspberries and strawberries
• glass of soy milk

Before Bedtime:
• 1 Body Genetics Protein Shake

DAY 4

Breakfast:
• 4 oz. grapefruit juice
• *Cheese Omelet*
    2 scrambled eggs with soy or goat
    cheese and scallions
• 1 pc. brown rice bread with whole-fruit
    jam
• 10–12 oz. green tea

Lunch:
• Italian Minestrone Soup (see recipe)
• *Tuna Sandwich*
    6 oz. tuna with minced onions and celery
    lettuce and water chestnuts
    2 pcs. 100 percent rye bread
• 10–12 oz. green tea

Afternoon Snack:
• Basic Trail Mix #3 (see recipe)

Dinner:
• veal chops in basil tarragon sauce
• side of peas and carrots
• mesculen salad with feta, peppers, red
    onions, beets and blanched broccoli
• Herb Mock Vinaigrette Dressing (see
    recipe)
• 10–12 oz. green tea

Evening Snack:
• banana with almond butter
• 10–12 oz. green tea

Before Bedtime:
• 1 Body Genetics Protein Shake

Blood Type

**B&
O**

DAY 5

Breakfast:
- 4 oz. carrot or vegetable juice
- 2 pc. spelt bread with almond butter and honey
- 2–3 plums or apricots
- 10–12 oz. green tea

Lunch:
- 6–8 oz. turkey cubes
- lettuce, dandelion greens and ¼ cup cannelloni beans
- Warm Cranberry Dressing (see recipe)
- 10–12 oz. green tea

Afternoon Snack:
- 2–3 Almond Honey cookies (see recipe)
- 10–12 oz. green tea

Dinner:
- sauteed veal cutlets in white wine, portobella mushrooms, lemon and parsley
- steamed asparagus
- mixed green salad with fennel, cucumbers, beets and red onions
- Herb Mock Vinaigrette Dressing (see recipe)
- 10–12 oz. green tea

Evening Snack:
- 1 pc. spelt bread with melted mozzarella cheese
- 10–12 oz. green tea

Before Bedtime:
- 1 Body Genetics Protein Shake

DAY 6

Breakfast:
- 4 oz. vegetable juice
- *Grilled Cheese*
    2 pc. spelt bread with 2–3 oz. mozzarella cheese
- 1 apple
- 10–12 oz. green tea

Lunch:
- *Feta Burger*
    6 oz. beef burger
    1–2 oz. feta cheese
- sliced red onions
- small side salad with Miso Dressing (see recipe)
- 10–12 oz. green tea

Afternoon Snack:
- Tropical Smoothie (see recipe)

Dinner:
- 6–8 oz. flank steak or London broil
- sauteed onions and portobella mushrooms
- mixed greens with beets
- Oregano Feta Dressing (see recipe)
- small sweet potato
- 10–12 oz. green tea

Evening Snack:
- 2–3 Pecan Sandies
- glass of soy milk

Before Bedtime:
- 1 Body Genetics Protein Shake

DAY 7

Breakfast:
- Blueberry Supreme Smoothie (see recipe)
- 1 pc. brown rice bread with almond butter
  and whole-fruit jam
- 10–12 oz. green tea

Lunch:
- *Lamb Salad*
     6 oz. lamb
     side of cannelloni beans
     appropriate lettuce, dandelion greens,
     cucumber, celery, fennel and red onions
- Herb Mock Vinaigrette Dressing (see
  recipe)
- 10–12 oz. green tea

Afternoon Snack:
- 1 slice spelt bread with almond butter and
  whole-fruit jam
- 10–12 oz. green tea

Dinner:
- 6–8 oz. cod or carp in lemon or lime and
  cilantro
- side of okra
- side of escarole or kale
- Lemon-Lime Cilantro Dressing (see
  recipe)
- 10–12 oz. green tea

Evening Snack:
- 6 whole walnuts and 4 dried figs
- 10–12 oz. green tea

Before Bedtime:
- 1 Body Genetics Protein Shake

Blood Type
**B&
O**

Chapter 11

28-Day Pick-a-Meal Recipes

:er Recipe Listing for Blood Type A

/5 recipes

- Almond Bomb Smoothie—A, O
- Almond Honey Cookies—ALL
- Apple "Pie" Trail Mix—A, O
- Apple Crisp—A, B, AB
- Applesauce Raisin Muffins—A
- Apricot Cream Smoothie—A, AB, O
- Basic Trail Mix #1—A, O
- Basmati Rice Pudding—A, B, O
- Broiled Portobella Mushrooms—ALL
- Carob Almond Cookies—ALL
- Carrot Bisque—ALL
- Cheeseless Basil Pesto—ALL
- Cherry Clafouti—ALL
- Chicken and Artichokes in Wine Sauce—A
- Chocolate Mousse—A
- Chocolate Raspberry Smoothie—A, AB, O
- Chocolate Riccota Cream—A, B, AB
- Cinnamon Vanilla Smoothie—A, B
- Collard Greens With Nuts—ALL
- Corn-Crusted Fish—A
- Cranberry Crush Smoothie—A, AB, O
- Creamy Avocado Dressing—A, AB, O
- Creamy Cilantro Lime Dressing—A, B, AB
- Creamy Garlic Dressing—A, B, AB
- Creamy Squash Bisque—A, B, AB
- Dandelion Greens and Leek Frittata—ALL
- Earthy Muesli—A
- Fish With Herbs and Lime—ALL
- French Herb Crust—ALL
- Greek Herb Crust—ALL
- Green Goddess Dressing—A, AB, O
- Herb Mock Vinaigrette Dressing—ALL
- Herbed Tofu—A, AB, O
- Honey Chicken With Lime—A
- Italian Herb Crust—ALL
- Italian Minestrone—ALL
- Jerusalem Artichoke Soup—A, O
- Lemon-Lime Cilantro Dressing—ALL

- Licorice Smoothie—ALL
- Maple Magic Smoothie—ALL
- Middle Eastern Dressing—A, B, AB
- Miso Dressing #1—ALL
- Miso Dressing #2—ALL
- Moroccan Spice Rub—A, B, AB
- Onion Soup—ALL
- Oregano Feta Dressing—ALL
- Peaches and Cream Smoothie—A, B, AB
- Peanut Butter Cookies—A, AB
- Peanut Chocolate Trail Mix—A, AB
- Poached Peaches—ALL
- Purple Passion Smoothie—ALL
- Raspberry Mock Vinaigrette Dressing—ALL
- Red Onion Dressing—A, AB, O
- Rosemary Chicken—A, O
- Sesame Chicken—A, O
- Sesame Turkey Fillets—A, O
- Soy Cheese Sauce—A, AB, O
- Spinach and Mushroom Frittata—A, B, AB
- Spinach Pesto—ALL
- Sunflower Pancakes—A
- Tofu Almondine—A, AB, O
- Tofu Burgers—A
- Tofu in Cilantro Sauce—A, AB, O
- Tofu Steak Teriyaki—A
- Traditional Herb Crust—ALL
- Turkish Red Lentil Soup—A, AB
- Vanilla Cherry Smoothie—ALL
- Very Berry Smoothie—ALL
- Viennese Coffee Smoothie—A, B, AB
- Vinegarless Dressing—ALL
- Warm Cranberry Dressing—ALL
- White Bean and Escarole Soup—ALL
- Yummy Rice Pudding—A, B, AB

Master Recipe Listing for Blood Type B

65 recipes

- Almond Honey Cookies—ALL
- Apple Crisp—A, B, AB
- Apple Walnut Trail Mix—B, O
- Banana Oat Muffins—B
- Banana Smoothie—B, O
- Basic Trail Mix #3—B, O
- Basmati Rice Pudding—A, B, O
- Beef and Garlic—B
- Blueberry Supreme Smoothie—B, O
- Broiled Portobella Mushrooms—ALL
- Carob Almond Cookies—ALL
- Carrot Bisque—ALL
- Cheeseless Basil Pesto—ALL
- Cherry Clafouti—ALL
- Chocolate Riccota Cream—A, B, AB
- Cinnamon Vanilla Smoothie—A, B
- Cocoa Mochachino Smoothie—B
- Collard Greens With Nuts—ALL
- Creamy Cilantro Lime Dressing—A, B, AB
- Creamy Garlic Dressing—A, B, AB
- Creamy Squash Bisque—A, B, AB
- Crockpot Greek Lamb Salad—B, AB, O
- Dandelion Greens and Leek Frittata—ALL
- Eggplant Casserole—B
- Fish With Herbs and Lime—ALL
- French Herb Crust—ALL
- Ginger Apple Smoothie—B, O
- Greek Herb Crust—ALL
- Hearty Beef Stew—B
- Herb Mock Vinaigrette Dressing—ALL
- Honey Mustard Dressing—B
- Italian Herb Crust—ALL
- Italian Minestrone—ALL
- Lemon-Lime Cilantro Dressing—ALL
- Licorice Smoothie—ALL
- Maple Magic Smoothie—ALL
- Middle Eastern Dressing—A, B, AB
- Miso Dressing #1—ALL
- Miso Dressing #2—ALL
- Moroccan Spice Rub—A, B, AB
- Nutty Granola—B
- Onion Soup—ALL
- Orange Ginger Fish—B
- Orange Marinated Salmon—B
- Oregano Feta Dressing—ALL
- Peaches and Cream Smoothie—A, B, AB
- Pecan Pancakes—B
- Pecan Sandies—B, O
- Pizza Sauce—B, O
- Poached Peaches—ALL
- Purple Passion Smoothie—ALL
- Raspberry Mock Vinaigrette Dressing—ALL
- Rosemary Roasted Lamb With Roasted Vegetables—B, AB, O
- Spicy Fries—B, AB, O
- Spinach and Mushroom Frittata—A, B, AB
- Spinach Pesto—ALL
- Traditional Herb Crust—ALL
- Tropical Smoothie—B, O
- Vanilla Cherry Smoothie—ALL
- Very Berry Smoothie—ALL
- Viennese Coffee Smoothie—A, B, AB
- Vinegarless Dressing—ALL
- Warm Cranberry Dressing—ALL
- White Bean and Escarole Soup—ALL
- Yummy Rice Pudding—A, B, AB

Master Recipe Listing for Blood Type AB

69 recipes

- Almond Honey Cookies—ALL
- Apple Crisp—A, B, AB
- Apple Muesli—AB
- Apricot Cream Smoothie—A, AB, O
- Basic Trail Mix #2—AB
- Bran Muffins—AB
- Broiled Portobella Mushrooms—ALL
- Carob Almond Cookies—ALL
- Carrot Bisque—ALL
- Cheeseless Basil Pesto—ALL
- Cherry Clafouti—ALL
- Chocolate Raspberry Smoothie—A, AB, O
- Chocolate Riccota Cream—A, B, AB
- Collard Greens With Nuts—ALL
- Cranberry Crush Smoothie—A, AB, O
- Creamy Avocado Dressing—A, AB, O
- Creamy Cilantro Lime Dressing—A, B, AB
- Creamy Garlic Dressing—A, B, AB
- Creamy Squash Bisque—A, B, AB
- Crockpot Greek Lamb Salad—B, AB, O
- Curried Scallops and Vegetables—AB
- Dandelion Greens and Leek Frittata—ALL
- Fish With Herbs and Lime—ALL
- French Herb Crust—ALL
- Fruit and Nut Granola—AB
- Greek Herb Crust—ALL
- Green Goddess Dressing—A, AB, O
- Herb Mock Vinaigrette Dressing—ALL
- Herbed Tofu—A, AB, O
- Italian Herb Crust—ALL
- Italian Minestrone—ALL
- Lemon-Lime Cilantro Dressing—ALL
- Licorice Smoothie—ALL
- Maple Magic Smoothie—ALL
- Middle Eastern Dressing—A, B, AB
- Miso Dressing #1—ALL
- Miso Dressing #2—ALL
- Moroccan Spice Rub—A, B, AB
- Oat Pancakes With Cranberries and Walnuts—AB
- Onion Soup—ALL
- Oregano Feta Dressing—ALL
- Peaches and Cream Smoothie—A, B, AB
- Peanut Butter Cookies—A, AB
- Peanut Chocolate Trail Mix—A, AB
- Poached Peaches—ALL
- Purple Passion Smoothie—ALL
- Raspberry Mock Vinaigrette Dressing—ALL
- Red Onion Dressing—A, AB, O
- Rice and Salmon—AB
- Rosemary Roasted Lamb With Roasted Vegetables—B, AB, O
- Scallops in Garlic Sauce—AB
- Soy Cheese Sauce—A, AB, O
- Spicy Fries—B, AB, O
- Spinach and Mushroom Frittata—A, B, AB
- Spinach Pesto—ALL
- Swiss Chard and Feta Frittata—AB, O
- Tofu Almondine—A, AB, O
- Tofu in Cilantro Sauce—A, AB, O
- Tomato Italiano Sauce With Tuna—AB, O
- Tomato Soup—AB, O
- Traditional Herb Crust—ALL
- Turkish Red Lentil Soup—A, AB
- Vanilla Cherry Smoothie—ALL
- Very Berry Smoothie—ALL
- Viennese Coffee Smoothie—A, B, AB
- Vinegarless Dressing—ALL
- Warm Cranberry Dressing—ALL
- White Bean and Escarole Soup—ALL
- Yummy Rice Pudding—A, B, AB

Bloodtypes
Bodytypes
and YOU

Section III

Body Genetics—
Reaching Your
Genetic Potential

Chapter 12

Body Genetics

Before we start, congratulations on the wise decision you have made to move forward with your health and physical condition, not allowing the status quo to be an acceptable part of your lifestyle.

It is very good that you are interested, motivated and willing to begin an exercise workout program. From experience I know that most people find exercise an aspect of good health that is difficult to incorporate into their lifestyles. For some, just the thought of exercise is distressing—because they have never tried it or experienced it. Others have tried—but they weren't given the proper tools and guidelines necessary to succeed.

I find it interesting that those who hate to exercise can come up with all kinds of excuses why they hate it. Yet those who exercise regularly sing the praises of how wonderful they feel since they started exercising.

In my book *Seven Pillars of Health*, I share how exercise, in and of itself, might not be as enjoyable to some as to others because their focus is on the wrong area. If you focus on the right area—such as the exercise experience itself, rather than just the results—then you are more likely to stick with your exercise plan long enough to benefit from the results. Otherwise you will lose out on the benefits by refusing to give exercise a try.

In the minds of many, the concept of exercise is just plain old work. And who needs more work than what they already have in their life? But if you will hang in with me long enough, I assure you that you will develop an appreciation for exercise—not only for the results, but for how it makes you feel about yourself.

The biggest hurdle can be the decision-making process.

Mentally processing all that is involved with exercise can be somewhat paradoxical in nature. What do I mean? There is more to beginning an exercise program than just reading success stories or being personally motivated by a friend who has done well and is encouraging you to begin. Before you even think of starting, you must understand what is involved in the decision-making process.

The biggest hurdle can be the decision-making process. There are seemingly contradictory factors—things that can seem like polar opposites. Let me put it this way: Perhaps you are tired all the time. You have very little, if any, energy—which keeps you from exercising. In fact, you can't imagine exercising, even if you wanted to. You need energy to exercise. But here's the contradiction—you need to exercise to induce energy!

To have a constant supply of increased energy, you must exercise regularly—for as long as you want the increased energy. Thus enters another paradox—exercising causes muscle fatigue, which makes you feel tired, and the only way to get over being tired is to exercise more! As your body adjusts to exercising regularly, it greatly improves its ability to recover from the new workload. Even though exercise makes you tired for a short time, ultimately it increases your recovery rate, which increases your energy supply quickly throughout each day.

With this increase of energy, you are able to enjoy participating in more physical activities, thus making your lifestyle more energetic. Because your body is now functioning at a greater level of efficiency and performance, it becomes much easier to make exercise a regular part of your life.

Exercise is also paradoxical because it is not merely a

physical issue. Many are unwilling to exercise because they do not have the mental energy to exert. A person who leads a sedentary, de-energized lifestyle may be too tired mentally to participate. Thus, for them, the issue of exercising—or not exercising—is a mental issue.

If you are like most people, I am sure you would like to feel good all of the time, with energy to spare. Since most people procrastinate when it comes to exercise, consequently only a few will step out and make it happen. It seems obvious to me that it will take a combination of mental and physical exertion to get started—both factors an important part of the decision-making process.

Let me assure you of this one thing: If you are mentally willing to do what is healthy and sound for your immediate and future health, the rest will follow. The most strenuous exercise in your entire program is getting up from the couch and stepping out to exercise. That decision takes both great mental and physical exertion.

Achieving a balance between the mental and physical aspects of exercising, allowing them to work together in concert, will be more difficult than the actual exercises in your entire fitness program. Once you become more familiar with regular exercise, this balance will be easier to maintain. Exercise

Exercise Paradox

12-1

- No exercise = no energy
  No energy = no exercise
- Mental laziness = procrastination
  Procrastination = no action
- Mental effort = mental energy
  Physical effort = physical energy
- Mental/physical energy = mental/physical fitness

will begin to play a key role in your journey for living a healthier and more active life as it becomes a regular part of your daily life. We will work together as a team to accomplish your specific goals. So if you are ready, so am I.

Throughout the many years I have been involved in the world of health and fitness, I have observed thousands of men and women who were training in health clubs, YMCAs and other fitness facilities. All of them seemed to be working so very hard and diligently. Yet although many of them wanted desperately to

The most strenuous exercise in your entire program is getting up from the couch and stepping out to exercise. That decision takes both great mental and physical exertion.

reach their fitness goals, even after weeks—and sometimes months—of relentless effort, they failed to get the results, or failed to see results fast enough.

Maybe you are one of them. Maybe right now you are saying, "Been there, done that." Maybe you became so discouraged and frustrated with the whole fitness thing that you quit and allowed your fitness goals to elude you. Don't feel alone. That is a common pitfall for many. Over the years, it is those very people—who feel discouraged, isolated and failing—who have motivated me to encourage them and you to get back on track, to believe in yourself and to know that you can reach your fitness goals.

I try to stay on the cutting edge in the world of health and fitness. I like to "push the envelope" by providing advanced exercise techniques and ground-breaking dietary and nutritional programs that are tailored and customized specifically for each individual. My philosophy is to provide the most effective and accurate applications of exercise methodologies, yet making them as simple as possible while being totally productive. Far too many people for far too long have believed that if they did not kill themselves in the gyms, they would not get the results they wanted.

The truth of the matter is that it does take physical and mental effort. But when done properly and progressively, it is easy to adapt exercise into your lifestyle. I want to provide you with the tools and mechanisms to get you to your goals while enabling you to keep advancing your level of health and vitality for years and years to come.

I know that even today there are hundreds of people who desire to improve their physical conditions but have lost their willingness to hang in there or start up again because of some unfortunate experience at a health club. Perhaps you are one of these individuals. This book will give you a new and fresh attitude about taking control of your life.

In this section of the book, I have provided you with mechanisms for determining your body type, for choosing the strategies that will work best for your body and for selecting the exercise programs that best suit your body's genetics. I will guide you on your fitness journey so that you will never repeat and experience the negative results you experienced in your past. Your results will come quickly, because I am taking you on the fastest route to success by tapping into your genetics.

If getting your body in shape and taking on a healthy lifestyle is a brand-new adventure for you, then I can help you avoid the pitfalls that would interfere and keep you from reaching your goals.

But before I take you to your fitness program, let me share with you a couple of traps that are common when planning a fitness journey. If you don't do your homework, these traps will set you up for failure every time.

The Perils of Getting in Shape

It is absolutely imperative that you understand the preparations you must make before you start your program.

You may believe you are already motivated to begin exercising. Maybe you have been asked to be a part of a wedding party in the near future—or maybe you are getting married yourself. Or that twenty-year reunion may be just around the corner. Perhaps while you were munching on that incredibly rich dessert, you heard a comment from someone else about those extra pounds you are carrying. Whatever the reasons, they got your attention, and you are motivated to get started.

"WHAT PROGRAM WILL I FOLLOW?"

Your first decision will be to decide what program to follow. Sure, there is an endless supply of videotape programs, but are they really designed to meet your specific genetic requirements? Or are they just total body workout programs that lack the key genetic components for your body type?

You may have a pair or two of dumbbells and a workout bench at home, but can you design a specific program for yourself that will work in concert with your genetics? Better yet, do you know what your genetics are? If you don't, then you certainly don't want to start on your fitness journey yet. Wasting your time on a program that may not work is very expensive—both financially and emotionally.

The truth of the matter is that it does take physical and mental effort. But when done properly and progressively, it is easy to adapt exercise into your lifestyle.

"WHAT ABOUT THE BUDDY SYSTEM?"

Your next decision is to decide whether you will train alone, hire a personal trainer or do the buddy system and get your best friend to go with you. Perhaps you choose to try out the buddy system. You know what I mean—dragging one of your friends into your dream world with hopes that both of you will hang in there long enough for you to get the results you want for yourself. My concern with the buddy approach is this: Is the program that will work best for you a program that will work best for your buddy also? Do you know enough about your genetics—and your training buddy's genetics—to design specific programs for each of your body types? Having a training partner is very profitable, but only if both know what they are doing.

"SHOULD I HIRE A PERSONAL TRAINER?"

Hiring a personal trainer is your next option. There are many benefits to a personal trainer. It is a very good direction to take—if you can afford one. But there is a downside to hiring a personal trainer. That person must be qualified to design a program specific enough to meet your body's genetic requirements. Your trainer must be capable of designing a nutritional dietary program that is compatible to your blood type. He or she must also have the experience to work with you in harmony with your specific exercise program.

Can your trainer deliver a complete fitness package with genetic continuity in all areas of your fitness program? Remember, you are paying big bucks for the results you want, so every dollar you spend will be either an investment in yourself or a loss. Many of the people I have seen working diligently in gyms have had personal trainers—and they still failed to reach their goals and became frustrated when they did not see the results they had anticipated.

"WHERE WILL I WORK OUT?"

Your next decision will be whether you will work out at a gym, health club, apartment complex or in the privacy of your own home. You may have decided to hire a personal trainer and arranged to meet him or her at a commercial fitness facility.

Most personal trainers charge by the hour, so you have committed one hour of your time for exercise. Yet by the time you spend
a minimum of twenty to thirty minutes traveling to the facility,
then doubled that time for the return trip home, you have added
another forty minutes to that first hour. To see any results at all,
you should plan on at least a minimum of three workouts per
week. Already you are spending nearly two hours a day, three
days a week, or a total of six hours a week, in your exercise program—three hours of which are spent traveling.

Prioritizing your time can almost be an impossibility. You must be motivated to do it.

Now factor in your payment of anything from $250 to $1500
a month for personal training fees. These fees will depend on
where you live in the country. And you still haven't started your
workout yet.

"HOW WILL I FIND THE TIME?"

How will you squeeze in some precious spare time from
your busy schedule to go to the gym and train? Prioritizing your
time can almost be an impossibility. You must be motivated to do
it. I am a firm believer that you, like anybody else, can do anything you want to do—*if you really want to do it.*

Before you hire that trainer and get started, be sure that you
have weighed in all the factors and have taken first things first.
Know your body genetics before you begin. I am not opposed
to having a personal trainer—indeed, I am one. A good trainer
will help you tremendously. But if you have not taken the time
to understand your body's genetic makeup, then you have not
adequately prepared for success. I want you to be as prepared as
possible before you start training your body.

Getting the Picture

The path that will eventually lead you to reaching your genetic
potential must be paved with a basic understanding of some key
body genetic components, along with the proper exercises and
methodology of exercises that are compatible with your genetics. This is necessary for success. The one major genetic component that will solidify the pavement on which you walk, and
which is absolutely crucial for optimum results, is knowing

Your body type—or body genetics—is the foundation of the "house" that is you.

what you are before you begin the journey. No, I don't mean knowing whether you are male or female, white or black, tall or short. You need to know your body genetics . . . simply put, you need to know what body type you are.

Your Genes—the Clay

It is estimated that approximately 75 percent of our body typing comes from our genes. As a matter of fact, all that comprises your genetic baseline was already determined by the time you were born. You didn't put in an order for how you wanted to look, what color you wanted your hair to be or how tall you wanted to be. Your gene pool had determined what your body type was going to be generations before you even got here.

Your body type—or body genetics—is the foundation of the "house" that is you. But custom-building your house to your satisfaction requires that you understand what strategies or building plans will work the best.

How many times have you heard someone say, "She has her mother's figure"? Our genetics play a key role in our overall makeup, but most people do not consider genetics when it comes to determining what exercise program is best for them. Your basic genetics can be enhanced and redesigned by using the proper methodology of exercise and diet.

I have four wonderful sisters-in-law who favor their father's genetics more than their mother's. Their musculoskeletal systems—or body structures—are dominantly inherited from their father's genes. My wife, Lori, has the same basic genetics as her sisters, but because she exercises regularly she has taken her genetics to another level of aesthetics.

I have three daughters, two of whom are twins. All three daughters have great genetics for building symmetrical bodies through exercise. In fact, some years ago at the age of seventeen, my daughter Jenifer competed in the Miss Buffalo Bodybuilding Championships and won the title from women who were as much as ten years older than she was. She has the proper genetics to work with to become a competitive bodybuilder.

Not everyone has inherited the genetics to be a competitive

bodybuilder, but not everyone wants to be one, either. But everyone has a genetic baseline from which to start customizing his or her body. The key to success is found in understanding your body genetics. Then you can maximize your results.

Most of our genetics were determined by our parents—and their parents. But heredity is not completely responsible for your shape. There are things that can be done to redesign and improve the aesthetics and symmetry of your body—regardless of the gene pool from which you came.

Know Your Genetic Limitations

As a personal trainer, before I design an exercise program for a student, I do a simple body genetic analysis. In many cases I have never met my students. Therefore I conduct my body genetic analysis for many students by long distance—by simply requesting that each person send me a photo for review. I ask the student to wear a swimsuit or a pair of shorts and a top so that I can see the body shape. Then I am able to make a valid determination of that person's basic body type. By reviewing each person's photo I can also determine that person's present condition *and* the specialized work his or her body will need. After the body analysis, I design the personalized program a student will need to follow in order to balance her body's genetics.

When a student visits me for a one-on-one evaluation, the first thing I do is ask that person to stand in front of me so I can make a determination as to his body type. It's interesting that after all these years of doing body genetic analyses, I can actually make an immediate determination of a person's body type the minute they walk into a room. But before I can prescribe the exercise program and strategy, I also need to determine each person's current condition. The four primary body sites I choose to be factored into the formula include:

1. The shoulders
2. The chest/bust
3. The waistline
4. The hips/thighs

Using these key sites representing the person's genetic foundation, I can determine the body type and present physical condition. This genetic information will enable me to determine into which body makeover category the person fits based on body type and physical condition. Then I can design their specialized program.

Three Body Makeover Categories

Your genetics and current condition are not identical to that of any other person.

Your genetics and current condition are not identical to that of any other person. To maximize your genetic potential, you will need to focus on one of the three body makeover categories of fine-tuning, minor makeover or complete makeover.

CATEGORY 1—FINE-TUNING

If a person's body analysis reveals that all four key sites are balanced or symmetrical, that person will require a fine-tuning program. This program helps the individual to enhance natural symmetry by training correctly for her body type. The exercise strategy for this category is probably the easiest of the three categories for two basic reasons. People in this category are blessed with pleasingly balanced body genetics, and they maintain their bodies in good condition rather easily. There may even be a very few people who seem to do very little and get maximum results anyway.

The second reason this category may be easier is because many of the individuals who fit in this category have worked diligently in the past to develop their physique. They balanced and toned their body parts and acquired that symmetrical—or hourglass—body shape through hard work.

If the body analysis for an individual reveals an imbalance or poor symmetry of these key body sites, it will be more difficult to apply the next two body makeover programs. When symmetry—or that hourglass shape—is lacking, a more tailored and specific prescription of exercise will be necessary.

CATEGORY 2—MINOR MAKEOVER

Some people have worked to achieve a level of balance or symmetry between their upper and lower bodies—but are not quite there. These individuals would need to be a part of this second category, focusing on a minor makeover. Some people in this category exercise and have made progress, but they may have hit a plateau. Or they may have naturally pleasing genetics, but need to do more work to reach their potential. Their prescription of exercise will differ from the one who requires fine-tuning. It will align more closely to the third category, which is for those needing a major body makeover.

The people in this second category have already begun improving on their body genetics and are in the transformation process or in transition. Their program would be designed to take their advancing condition up another level or two to obtain a totally balanced symmetrical look.

CATEGORY 3—MAJOR BODY MAKEOVER

This category is for people whose condition is usually recognized as being *de-conditioned*—or just plain out of shape. Typically they are people who do not exercise, have a high level of body fat and are in poor shape. For this reason their bodies have very little or no balance or symmetry of the key body parts. Possibly some do exercise, but they have not been shown how to apply the proper exercise methodology for their body type.

Whatever the case, people in this category need a major body makeover—head to toe. Their exercise prescription will differ from the other two examples, because the requirements are obviously different.

Unfortunately, the majority of people's bodies fall into this category. But don't be embarrassed or worry if this is you, because many bodies who have turned out beautifully once needed a major body makeover.

A Solution for Everyone

Sometimes I look at my profession as being an artist or sculptor. For me it is like being given a piece of clay and then working to redesign it into an aesthetic piece of fine art. Taking a body and redesigning it so it can take on an entirely new transformed shape is truly a reward in itself. By applying the correct strategy of exercise and diet to match individual genetics, a body that is

By applying the correct strategy of exercise and diet to match individual genetics, a body that is out of balance can develop pleasing body contour.

out of balance can develop pleasing body contour. When the main body parts are in balance, or symmetrical, your entire body image takes on a whole new, pleasing look.

I believe this is what almost everyone is looking for when they pursue an exercise program—not the *perfect* body, but a *balanced* body. During the initial interview with my students, I ask them to fill out a questionnaire asking what changes they want to see in their bodies. After years of observing hundreds of students, I have found that an overwhelming number reply that they want a balanced shape.

A balanced shape is what I refer to as *the hourglass or V-shape*. Of course, *wanting* a balanced figure is one thing— *obtaining* a balanced shape is a totally different story. Most people are not aware of what it takes to obtain that goal. There is a science to body redesigning, but being able to reach that goal requires knowing the methodology of how to get to the goal. And it requires applying that knowledge to your lifestyle—*doing* it, not just *knowing* it!

Facing Genetic Limitations

Body genetics is the baseline from which I build for every exercise prescription I prescribe. Even though I have been able to accurately prescribe the right program for a specific body type, each person will have genetic limitations with which he or she will need to contend.

There are genetic limitations that will have to be addressed as your program is designed. Such genetic limitations are found in your musculoskeletal system, the God-given genetic structure that is impossible to redesign. These limitations deal with your bone structure, length and size, and they are unchangeable. For example, let's say that your pelvic bones or hip structure measures thirty-six inches. There is nothing you and I can do to reduce that measurement, unless we could shave off some of your bone. But if your hips measure forty-two and a half inches on a thirty-six-inch pelvic bone measurement, then I can show you how to reduce those forty-two inches down closer to the thirty-six-inch bone measurement.

The same is true for your shoulder width. If your genetic limitations include clavicles that are short, then your narrow shoulder width must be factored into your program design. I can't do anything to make the clavicles longer. But I can show you how to broaden your overall shoulder girth by selecting specific exercises that are compatible to your particular genetic limitations.

These limitations apply to the size and length of your ribs, muscle insertion and origin and the length and size of your bones. You cannot outsmart your genes, but you can use exercise strategies that are compatible to them. For that reason, identifying your body type—including your genetic limitations—is the first order of business. A further look at your genes will help you to predetermine your outcome, or at least an understanding of what you can expect from your exercise program.

There is a difference between getting the normal results from increased physical activity and obtaining the specific results you want.

Spinning Your Wheels

There is a difference between getting the normal results from increased physical activity and obtaining the specific results you want. Even a person with a physically sedentary lifestyle, doing no more in the way of exercise than taking the garbage out to the curb once a week, will see results if that person starts exercising regularly. Our bodies were made for physical activity, and they respond accordingly.

But obtaining specific body redesigning results depends on following a specific exercise methodology. The focus of body redesigning must be getting the specific results for which you are looking. You should settle for nothing less.

Let me state this clearly: *You should train specifically with exercises designed for your body type.* On page 251 you will find a chart designed to help you determine your specific body type. If you have a pear-shaped body, then you should perform exercises designed for the pear shape. This will save you a lot of wasted time and energy, and will give you a shapelier hourglass figure. You won't simply become a smaller pear. Regardless of whether your body type is a pear, an apple or a banana, understanding the points I have been making will make your efforts so much easier. Applying these principles will give you the ability to stay focused while on your journey.

By following the mapping charts in this book that will help you determine your body type, you will be ready to select your specific exercise program. The exercise programs for each specific body type are located in Section V. I have already factored in the specifications necessary for meeting your body's needs. The workout programs are designed according to basic body genetics or body types and on your predisposed limitations and present physical condition. The programs contain the proper selection of exercises, including the exact sets, repetitions and days per week to follow. I have also included additional tips to provide you with maximum results.

My ultimate goal for your exercise program is to help you reach your genetic potential.

Let me state this clearly: *You should train specifically with exercises designed for your body type.*

Chapter 13

A Survival Kit for Your Journey

I am sure you have heard of the survival of the fittest, or of the law of the jungle, which says that only the strong survive. You have also heard of the battle between the sexes. Well, your fitness journey to reach your genetic potential is not a matter of competing against anyone. As a matter of fact, the beauty of your fitness journey is that it is personal—it is yours alone.

Don't concern yourself with the progress other people are—or are not—making. You may have friends or family members who have decided to get in shape. That's all well and good, but don't get sidetracked by their progress, even though a little friendly competition goes a long way.

I can't tell you how often I have heard about a wife who gets frustrated to the point of wanting to quit her program because her husband is making faster progress than she is. If you are a woman, my suggestion is to forget that kind of thinking! Men generally make faster progress than women because of their genetics.

Forget about how everybody else is doing. Focus on yourself. I know everyone has a tendency to compare themselves with others, but that will set you up for discouragement and failure if you don't keep things in perspective. Remember, you do not have to measure up to anyone else. The only person with whom you are competing is yourself! This is *your* fitness journey. It's all about you competing against yourself.

As you journey down the path of reaching your genetic potential, you will encounter potential obstacles. Some of these obstacles will be mental, and some will be physical.

As you journey down the path of reaching your genetic potential, you will encounter potential obstacles. Some of these obstacles will be mental, and some will be physical. They can creep into your plans without warning. If you are not prepared for them, they can wreak havoc on your progress.

In order to make it through your journey, you need to be a survivor. You will need to know how to deal with the mental and physical obstacles as they pop up. I won't be so cruel as to send you to an island empty-handed to see how long you can survive. We'll leave that up to TV programming. But since I am your personal trainer, I want to provide you with a survival kit to take along with you.

Your survival kit contains several components that will give you answers to common questions that will arise while you are on the path. These pertinent tips will help you avoid some "potholes" that could slow you down. They will also provide you with specific principles in this book to reinforce your decision-making process, stimulate your thinking and redirect your focus should you lose your direction. They will serve as key reminders to help you stay on track.

Every physically fit person you have seen has learned how to win these battles that are common with a fitness journey. Without this foundation from which to work and a reference point to turn to when the battles rage, you could be defeated easily and never see your goals come true.

The Survival Kit

There are three basic components found in your survival kit: mental, physical and dietary. Each unique component covers a variety of issues. They will be very useful to you *if you use them*—so be certain to use them! Start your journey by reading through each section describing these components. Be sure you are on the right track from the beginning. Refer to them whenever you sense your-self losing control or starting to backslide. Use them as often as you need for extra confirmation and reinforcement.

YOUR MENTAL COMPONENT

From the moment you made your initial decision to begin your fitness journey, I'm certain you realized it would involve a massive amount of mental strength along with a positive atti-tude. Getting in shape physically is not a matter of physical work only—it demands a heavy dependence on your mental strength also. Being successful at making your physical fitness program a part of your lifestyle will hinge on your psychological adapta-tion more than on your physiological adaptation to the program.

Read the questions and answers below carefully. Internalize the answers *before* you are faced with similar questions. Prepare for the journey by preparing your mind for the task ahead. Mental preparation is as important as physical preparation.

Q/1: *What should you do should you start finding yourself losing the fire and drive you once had?*

A/1: Regenerating the fire and drive back into your journey is going to require a renewing of your mind!

We all need to go back to the basics mentally at certain times along the journey. Doing so will help you regain your enthusiasm and put things in proper perspective. Every cham-pion, every winner has confronted the issue of losing the fire. I heard Arnold Schwarzenegger comment once, "I have to stay hungry in order to keep the fire and drive alive."

Begin by reviewing the section on Time for a Change from chapter 2 (page 29). Remind yourself of all the reasons you chose to start your exercise program. What prompted you to make these changes in the first place? Reevaluate why you ini-tially wanted to go from your present condition and lifestyle to a healthier and more energetic and productive lifestyle. Review the reasons you wrote down when you started your journey. Keep those initial reasons posted somewhere so you can look at them often. They will be a constant reminder to you of why you are working so hard to make the changes.

Getting in shape physically is not a matter of physical work only—it demands a heavy dependence on your mental strength also.

Q/2: *How do you overcome your impatience when your results do not come as fast as you'd like?*

A/2: Patience is a virtue. Your fitness journey will definitely challenge your patience. Go back to chapter 2 and review the section on Goal Setting (page 32). At times you will need to reevaluate the goals you have set for yourself. Make sure they are obtainable and realistic. Double-check to see the value you originally placed on them.

As you travel on your journey, your goals may change. As you see progress in your body, there is a tendency to shift your focus to a different area or goal. For example, people who were once overweight have an initial goal of losing weight. As they lose a significant amount of weight and get closer to their potential, they shift their focus from just losing weight to becoming more firmed and toned.

The original goal(s) can change as you move forward. Write down your new goals, put a price tag on them and repeat them to yourself daily as often as you need to do so. Pin them up where you can visibly see them as a regular reminder. To help you with patience, remember over and over that "your body is in a state of transition." As you stay committed to your program, your body will continually keep changing also, so adjustments in your goals are inevitable. *One day you will get there.*

Q/3: *How can I prevent slipping back and returning to some of the old dietary ways of eating that I had, or slipping in laziness toward training?*

A/3: Backsliding is a real challenge—be aware of it. You and I are creatures of habit. There will be a tendency to go back to the former ways that were once familiar. That is why it is so important to remind yourself regularly of where you want to go.

If you shoot for nothing you will always hit it! Remember that you are making lifestyle changes, and they don't always come easily. That's why you have the survival kit to help you through these times.

The key is not to look to the right or the left—look straight ahead. A runner must always look toward the finish line, never back, if he expects to complete the course. Go back and read Staying Focused from chapter 2 (page 34). Don't feel badly about struggling with backsliding—everyone has moments when they lose focus. In many instances even the greatest of champions find themselves drifting off the path.

The way to stay on the path—or return to the path—is to refocus. Evaluate your current mental attitude in comparison to what it was when you started. See if you can determine what caused you to drift from your focus. As you identify the cause(s), eliminate it from your path. Readjust your sight, placing it on your goals. Check out your emotions and compare them to earlier. Raise your excitement and enthusiasm levels.

The way to stay on the path— or return to the path—is to refocus.

It is impossible to ride high emotionally every day of the week. From time to time it will be necessary to rev it back up again. Most of the time, slipping backward is due to your mental attitude. Surround yourself with positive, successful, goal-oriented people.

All the tips and directions in this section of your survival kit represent the mental attitude side of your journey, which will be the most demanding. Simply go through the mental exercises, thinking carefully and specifically. Evaluating your current mental attitude will help you to more accurately make the attitude adjustments necessary for the present. Reread the section on Attitude in chapter 2 (page 36).

Remember, roads were not built for destinations—roads were built for the journey. Your journey is a part of your life. Cherish it.

YOUR PHYSICAL COMPONENT

Moving from a sedentary lifestyle to a physically active way of life is not an overnight accomplishment. Your body will need to be stimulated regularly by physical exercise and activities. Your body redesigning training program is a genetically designed approach for meeting the requirements of your unique body type. The specific exercises work in concert with your body type. While they are unequivocally necessary, your exercises are only the means to an end—not the end itself. Additional physical activities should be incorporated into your life to counterbalance the potential boredom and staleness of the exercise portion of the journey. The variety of physical activities you add to your program will bring more excitement and staying power into your whole being.

Q/1: *Why does it take so long to redesign my body?*

A/1: A person who wants to lose weight will be successful when they have developed a mind-set that allows them to feel satisfaction and acceptance of losing the first pound—and every pound thereafter—or that person will never reach the goal. Accept that first pound, that first inch, as a victory, or you will never get to enjoy that new outfit you were going to reward yourself with at the end of the journey.

Review the Determining Your Body Type chart on page 251. It is imperative that you know your body type before starting your program. Then go to the Troubleshooting charts on pages 252–254 so you can identify the problem areas common to your body type.

Make sure you are performing the exercises correctly for your body type. Technique is very important! Turn to the Body Type Workout Programs in Section V, and follow the directions for each *start/finish* and *midpoint* position using the photos to guide you. Your technique will make all the difference to the success you have in redesigning and reshaping your body.

Don't spin your wheels, going nowhere. Be certain of the proper technique for performing each exercise, or you will not receive 100 percent results from your efforts. If you are committing yourself to nearly an hour of training, you want to get an hour's worth of results!

Another area of your training that you should check is your cardiovascular workouts. Follow the directions given for your "off-day" workouts. Your cardiovascular workouts will supplement your primary training by speeding up the fat-burning process and improving your stamina and endurance. They will also improve your circulatory system by strengthening your heart and lungs.

Remember that your program is designed to get you where

you want to go just as fast as possible. But it will take some time to turn around your physical condition. After all, in most cases it took years to get your body out of shape.

Q/2: *What do I do when I find myself getting bored with my workout program and losing the drive I had in the beginning?*

A/2: Please don't allow yourself to get frustrated! We all go through those moments of getting bored with doing the same old thing over and over. This is not the time to let frustration set in. Get creative. Revitalize your program by simply reversing the order of the exercises. After a while, being familiar with the same exercise routine can be somewhat boring, so a change is great for keeping a positive attitude.

Changing the order of exercises is also good for muscle response. Select a body part or muscle group you favor more than others, and exercise that part first. Follow with the remaining muscle groups.

It could be you are experiencing a plateau or a sticking point in your progress, and you need to make some adjustments to keep your momentum. Perhaps the lagging area you want to target is the lower body. Perform the exercises designed for the lower body according to your body type. Then increase the intensity by increasing to a five-day exercise program. Jump-start your lower body that way for a two- to three-week period.

By intensifying and shocking the muscle groups you are sure to get past those sticking points and plateaus and experience more results almost immediately. This will do wonders for your body—and for your mind. Consider this specialization or targeting of your muscles every couple of months whether you plateau or not. You can use this periodic shocking system for any body part at anytime. This is a great way to give each body part priority. After you have intensified your program for those few weeks, return to your normal workout program again.

You may want to add some competitive sports or recreational sports to your routine also. Maybe you want to add some tennis, basketball or any physical activity you enjoy. Always choose an activity you enjoy—the more you enjoy it the longer

> By intensifying and shocking the muscle groups you are sure to get past those sticking points and plateaus and experience more results almost immediately.

you will stay with it. Be creative with your routine and with your outside activities, and stay physical! It will add a pinch of healthy spice to your lifestyle.

YOUR DIETARY COMPONENT

Even though your total fitness journey produces results and enhances your entire life by involving the constant application of the mental and physical aspects, your results would be incomplete without the dietary component. You eat more times per day . . . week . . . month . . . than you exercise. It only stands to reason that watching your diet is very important.

But notice, I did not say, "Go on a diet." I said, "Watch your diet." In structuring the diet plan you should use to accompany your exercise program, I created your dietary program based on your blood type. From research and from my own personal and professional experiences and the testimonials of others, I believe eating foods compatible to your blood type produces tremendous results and is most accurate!

Q/1: *How do I stop eating my favorite foods when they are categorized as "Avoid" foods?*

A/1: Generally speaking, making dietary changes seems to be a more difficult behavioral change than beginning an exercise program for the first time. We all have a tendency to eat for taste before health. Fortunately we are wired in such a way that we can abuse our bodies for years before we experience serious consequences to our health. But violating physical laws for our health and continuing to eat foods not compatible to our blood type contribute to poor health. It is only a matter of time until our health starts to break down. For some that happens during their twenties and thirties. Yet others don't seem to have health problems until their forties, fifties or even sixties. But whenever that ugly face of ill health pops up and says "You're mine," everything you have going on in your life comes to a screeching halt.

To help you make the adjustments to better eating, I recommend you try the 80/20 approach (page 69). Work your way up to making 80 percent of your food selections from foods compatible for your blood type. Leave the remaining 20 percent for taste alone. This will be more realistic and easier to stay with, and it will allow you the dietary freedom that going on a diet doesn't allow.

Dietary changes are difficult to make. Not everyone can make a 180-degree turnaround. Try simply removing one or two Avoid foods from your diet every week or so. This will allow your body the time to adjust to compatible foods and will allow a natural detoxification. You will discover that you can eat anything you want, but your body will dictate which foods are best for you by the quality of life you enjoy. You'll become an instinctive eater and not a dieter.

Q/2: *What should I do if I am not seeing results from dietary changes as fast as I would like?*

A/2: Many times I have done a dietary analysis for students who thought they were eating correctly for their blood type, only to discover room to tighten up the food selections. These students often were consuming many Avoid foods, but then forgot about eating these foods.

To check your own diet, use the Dietary Analysis chart (page 250). You will be amazed how easily you forget or fail to count certain meals or snacks that were not compatible for your blood type.

This approach to eating is not a matter of being *good* when you eat compatible foods and *bad* when you eat incompatible foods. Learning to eat correctly according to your blood type for optimum bodily function and performance is very important.

Another key point you will want to remember is to make your food selections from the Beneficial Foods category for best and fastest results. The beneficial foods for your particular blood type act as medicines for healing, normalizing and improving your bodily and systemic functions. For example, if your digestive system does not function properly, you cannot digest and assimilate food properly. Or, if you eat foods that interfere with your body's ability to metabolize foods normally, it will be difficult to lose weight (body fat).

The purpose for eating is not to meet our emotional needs.

Work your way up to making 80 percent of your food selections from foods compatible for your blood type. Leave the remaining 20 percent for taste alone.

Eating is the way we supply our body with the proper nutrition to meet its demands. By eating correctly for your blood type, your body will become a finely tuned fat-burning machine.

Monitoring Your Progress

It is imperative for you to use some form of tracking device that will assist you to better evaluate your progress. I have included the following to help monitor your progress.

1. Initial Measurement Sheet
2. 90-Day Master Measurement Recording Sheet
3. Progress Report Card
4. Body Fat Test
5. Dietary Analysis

Before you use these charts, read the sections that follow, describing each of these charts and telling you how to use them.

INITIAL MEASUREMENT SHEET

I have prepared an initial measurement recording sheet for you to use. (See page 247.) It will establish your original measurements before you begin your program, along with directions for taking your own "before" photographs. Recording your initial statistics gives you something with which to compare your progress during your program. Your "before" photo will be followed with an "after" photo, but not until your ninety-day program is completed.

90-DAY MASTER MEASUREMENT RECORDING SHEET

Once you have started your program and have your initial measurements recorded, you will need another measurement recording sheet that will allow you to keep a record as you progress from month to month through your entire ninety-day program. (See page 248.) On the thirtieth, sixtieth and ninetieth days from the date of your original measurements, remeasure and record your new measurements. By comparing your new measurements to your original measurements monthly, you will begin to see the results on paper as well as in the mirror. Your measurement results will track the progress you are making and show you how your exercise program is working. It will show you the body parts that need more attention and help you to determine what changes you should make in your exercise program.

It will also serve as a motivational tool to keep you pumped up. The 90-Day Master Measurement Recording Sheet will allow you to record the total amount of inches, pounds and body fat lost. There is an area on this recording sheet to record your comments in each major component of your program. Write down how you feel about your progress—and about yourself.

PROGRESS REPORT CARD

After you have recorded your results for the first month on the 90-Day Master Measurement Recording Sheet, you will want to record the same information in the Progress Report Card. (See page 249.) You will repeat this process at the end of second month and at the end of the third month. (Duplicate the chart in the book so that you have several copies for your recording purposes.) The Progress Report Card will ask you a few pertinent questions that apply to your overall program. It is more in depth than the ninety-day sheet and is designed to help you stay focused and accountable. Just by taking the time to record your results and answer the questions on the sheet, you will stimulate your thinking for making sure you are doing everything you should be. Remember, these are the things I would be asking of you if I were there with you as your personal trainer. Stay accountable—and stay focused.

BODY FAT TEST

Just in case you weren't clear about the kind of personal trainer I am, let me remind you. I have learned throughout all my professional years of involvement in the personal training field that there are no questions too personal to ask. There are no areas or issues that can be hidden away and not dealt with. That's why I ask all my students if they know their percentage of body fat.

I know it's somewhat intimidating, but there are good reasons for asking. One major reason is because knowing your percentage

dy Fat Test

You can make a reasonable estimate of your fat-to-muscle ratio by using the following charts. Women, measure your hip girth and height, and draw a line from your hip girth to your height. Men, draw a line from your weight to your waist girth. This will give you an approximate measure of your body fat. Subtract that from 100 percent, and you know your muscle rating.

MEN

170-pound man

34" Waist = 18% body fat

WOMEN

5'4" woman

39" hips = 30% body fat

of body fat could be a matter of life and death. If you are carrying more body fat than you should carry, you are potentially setting yourself up for some serious health-related problems.

In addition, my philosophy of health and fitness causes me to be much more interested in your percentage of body fat than I am in what you weigh. In my book *Seven Pillars of Health* I go into great detail to explain why everyone should be more concerned about their percentage of body fat than they are about the amount of weight they are carrying. It is all a matter of body composition—not of weight.

The reason I have included the body fat test is to help you

understand the importance of the quality of your weight vs. the weight itself. The most important reason for getting in shape should be to obtain a better quality of life. That will happen as you reduce your percentage of body fat. The less body fat, the less the likelihood of poor health.

You will need to know your body fat percentage in order to plan the correct strategies for redesigning your physique or figure. Emphasis must be placed on lowering your body fat percentage while increasing your muscle weight, or your results will not be complete. If you plan to measure your progress by weighing yourself on your bathroom scale, then forget it! Your scale is a liar and not your friend. It never tells you the truth about what it's weighing; it only tells you how much. Consequently, your scale can weigh a pile of bricks, a human body or a bag of beans.

Remember, it is not your weight that measures your success. By measuring your body fat you will know exactly how much muscle you are building and how much body fat you are losing. Your success is best measured by the percentage of body fat you carry.

By following the simple directions on the body fat test formula on page 244, you will see how your results are influenced by the amount of body fat you have.

DIETARY ANALYSIS

Recording your consumption of food can be very helpful. Most of us don't realize the amount of little tastes or little bites of food we have consumed throughout each day. As you track your eating, you will be amazed at how far off the mark of optimal eating you have been—and yet you never saw it happening.

This tracking device on page 250 is best to use before you start out on your journey. That way you get a realistic look at your present eating habits. As you proceed through your exercise journey, repeat the dietary analysis as often as you feel the need to double-check yourself. Each time continue the tracking for three consecutive days.

For three days, simply record everything you eat and drink. Record the time you eat each meal or snack. Record the number of cups of coffee and/or cans of soda. If you eat a cookie or have a bowl of ice cream, write down an accurate record of what you ate.

Your dietary analysis will give you an accurate account of whether you are consuming foods that are compatible for your blood type. It will also help you to stay on track.

If I were your personal trainer, I would be asking you dietary questions all the time. Tracking your diet will make a big difference in your success or failure—especially when you hit a plateau.

The following information in the Rule of Thumb for Healthy Eating chart will help you to eat correctly while on your exercise program. Food can work for you or against you. It can stimulate weight loss, or it can cause weight gain. See the weight loss/gain lists for each blood type, and discover which foods are compatible for weight loss and which are Avoid foods, causing weight gain. (Blood type A, see page 98. Blood type B, see page 110. Blood type AB, see page 128. Blood type O, see page 146.)

Rule of Thumb for Healthy Eating[1]

13-2

1. Eat when you are hungry.

2. Eat until you are satisfied (not stuffed).

3. Put the brakes on, and stop eating if you are full.

Now take the time to look over each of the charts on the following pages and to fill them in with your specific information. When you are finished, you are ready to determine your body type and move on to start your exercise program.

Initial Measurement Sheet

GENERAL INSTRUCTIONS FOR TAKING YOUR MEASUREMENTS

Always measure and remeasure from the same points for accuracy. Keep the tape measure level.

Body parts	Where to measure	Measurements
1. Shoulders	around the largest point	_____
2. Chest/Bust	midpoint of chest/bust and upper back	_____
3. Arms	largest point while arm is hanging	R_____ L _____
4. Waist	smallest point above navel	_____
5. Hips (female)	midpoint between navel/crotch	_____
6. Thighs	largest upper point	R_____ L _____
7. Calves	largest point	R_____ L _____
8. Wrists	at the bend	R_____ L _____
9. Ankles	at the bend	R_____ L _____
10. Height/Weight	shoes off.	H_____ W _____

GENERAL INSTRUCTIONS FOR YOUR "BEFORE" PHOTOGRAPHS

You will need to take "before" photographs to help you determine your body type and your specific exercise program as outlined in this book. Use the following guidelines:

- **Clothing**—Wear something that will allow your physique or figure to be seen clearly (leotards, swimsuit or shorts and tank top).
- **Photos**—Take three photographs: front, side and back.
- **Poses**—Stand relaxed with heels together and look straight ahead in each photo.
- **Camera Tips**—Be sure to use a solid-color backdrop, and be sure your figure fills the camera frame from head to toe.

13-4

90-Day Master Measurement Recording Sheet

Name _____   Start Date ___/___/____

Body Part	Initial	1ST Month	2ND Month	3RD Month
Shoulders	_____	_____	_____	_____
Chest/Bust	_____	_____	_____	_____
Right Arm	_____	_____	_____	_____
Left Arm	_____	_____	_____	_____
Waist	_____	_____	_____	_____
Hips	_____	_____	_____	_____
Right Thigh	_____	_____	_____	_____
Left Thigh	_____	_____	_____	_____
Calves	_____	_____	_____	_____
Ankles	_____	_____	_____	_____
Height	_____	_____	_____	_____
Weight	_____	_____	_____	_____
Body Fat Percent	_____	_____	_____	_____
Total Inches Lost		_____	_____	_____
Total Weight Lost		_____	_____	_____
Total Body Fat Percent Lost		_____	_____	_____

Comments

Dietary: _____
_____
_____
_____

Exercise: _____
_____
_____
_____

Supplements: _____
_____
_____
_____

Progress Report Card

Name_____ Date ___/___/___

GENERAL INSTRUCTIONS

Always measure and remeasure from the same points for accuracy. Keep tape level when measuring.

Body parts	Where to measure	Measurements
1. Shoulders	around the largest point	_____
2. Chest/Bust	midpoint of chest/bust and upper back	_____
3. Arms	largest point while arm is hanging	R_____ L _____
4. Waist	smallest point above navel	_____
5. Hips (female)	midpoint between navel/crotch	_____
6. Thighs	largest upper point	R_____ L _____
7. Calves	largest point	R_____ L _____
8. Wrists	at the bend	R_____ L _____
9. Ankles	at the bend	R_____ L _____
10. Height/Weight	shoes off	H_____ W _____

PLEASE ANSWER THE FOLLOWING QUESTIONS

(circle correct answer):

How many times do you train weekly:	1	2	3	4
What is your percentage of healthy eating?	60%	70%	80%	90%
Are you keeping a positive attitude?	Often	Sometimes	Never	
In what areas are you having the most difficulty?	Eating	Training		

Explain: _____

_____

_____

What changes have you noticed about yourself since you started the program?
When do you see yourself reaching your goals: Months _____
Are you able to complete ALL the sets and reps per exercise
by the end of this month's program?   Yes   No
Explain: _____

_____

_____

Remember: Commitment is a positive attitude in constant motion.

Dietary Analysis

13-6

Please list ALL the foods and liquids that you consume for three days—*including the amounts.*

DAY 1:

Breakfast _____

Midmorning _____

Noon _____

Midafternoon _____

Dinner _____

After dinner _____

DAY 2:

Breakfast _____

Midmorning _____

Noon _____

Midafternoon _____

Dinner _____

After dinner _____

DAY 3:

Breakfast _____

Midmorning _____

Noon _____

Midafternoon _____

Dinner _____

After dinner _____

Important: Remember to include ALL the Oreos, slices of pizza, cans of soda, etc.

If you take nutritional supplements, PLEASE LIST THEM:

_____

_____

_____

Determining Your Body Type

Identifying your body type and your inherited genetic problem areas is very important and *is a must-know.* To determine your body type simply ask this question:

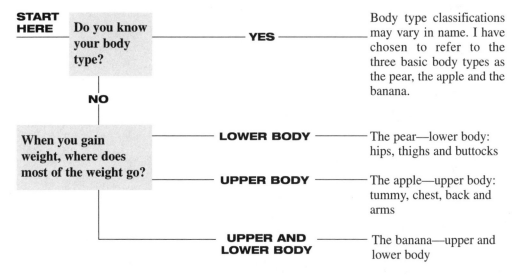

As you understand your body genetics and problem areas, you are paving the path to success. Now that you have identified your body type, go to pages 252–254 and study your body type further.

Troubleshooting Your Body Type

Now that you have worked through the five charts included earlier in this chapter and completed the Determining Your Body Type chart on this page, it is time to begin your workouts. To better understand the work that is ahead of you, look over the appropriate troubleshooting chart for your body type on pages 252–254.

Troubleshooting the Pear Body Type

TROUBLE AREAS
Weight Distribution Problems
When the pear gains weight, the weight mostly goes to the hips, thighs and buttocks.

Lower Body
- Most body fat accumulates in the hips, thighs and buttocks
- Considered bottom heavy

Upper Body
- Generally slender
- Shallow bustline
- Narrow shoulders
- Straight waist

Inherited Genetic Problems
The following are the primary inherent genetic factors:
- Narrow shoulders due to short clavicles
- Shallow and small bustline due to less upper body fat
- Wide pelvic and hip structure
- Excessive adipose fat tissue (cells) on the hips, thighs and buttocks
- Straight waistline due to narrow or small ribs

BODY REDESIGNING STRATEGIES
Perform exercises designed to:
Upper Body
- Fill out the chest/bust
- Broaden back and add width to the shoulders
- Firm and tone the arms (biceps and triceps)
- Firm the abdominal muscles

Lower Body
- Isolate hips, thighs and buttocks
- Elongate, firm and tone
- Reduce lower body major muscles

Avoid any exercises or physical activities that would tend to stimulate the lower body to grow. Concentrate on building muscle mass for the upper body while reducing the lower body.

Note: See the Pear Shape Workout Program on page 297–307.

Troubleshooting the Apple Body Type

TROUBLE AREAS
Weight Distribution Problems
When the apple gains weight, the weight mostly goes to the upper body. The apple lacks upper body/lower body symmetry or balance.

Lower Body
- Generally leaner but lagging in size in comparison to the upper body

Upper Body
- Most body fat stored around the waist, upper back and arms

Inherited Genetic Problems
The following are the primary inherent genetic factors:
- Excessive adipose tissue (cells) on the upper body, usually in the abdominal region, the chest/bust, back and arms
- Abdominal muscles usually protrude forward or bulge outward
- Generally longer upper torso and shorter lower torso
- Thin legs and buttocks, in some instances too thin or undersized from a symmetrical viewpoint

BODY REDESIGNING STRATEGIES
Perform exercises that:
Upper Body
- Shape and tone only
- Isolate abdominal muscles

Lower Body
- Build the upper and lower leg muscles
- Build, firm and tone the buttocks

Avoid exercises that tend to build mass on the upper body. Exercises for the upper body should be done for the sole purpose of firming and toning each muscle group. Concentrate on the abdominal muscles for strengthening and flattening. Incorporate exercises that will stimulate lower body muscles. Using dumbbells will help develop a symmetrical hourglass shape.

Note: See the Apple Shape Workout Program on page 308–316.

Troubleshooting the Banana Body Type

TROUBLE AREAS
Weight Distribution Problems
When the banana gains weight, the weight goes equally to the upper and lower body.
- Mainly lacks curves or shapeliness
- Tends to have a straight-line figure or physique

Inherited Genetic Problems
The following are the primary inherent genetic factors:
- The musculoskeletal system is such that the pelvic bone, ribs and shoulder width are similar.
- Wide waistline due to above
- Adipose fat tissue (cells) evenly dispersed on the upper and lower body

BODY REDESIGNING STRATEGIES
Perform exercises that:
Upper Body: Firm, tone and build muscles; strengthen and tone the abdominal muscles.
Lower Body: Elongate the thighs; firm and tone the buttocks.

The banana shape may be somewhat confusing to identify. The idea of having a banana shape makes you think the body would be thin. In most cases this is true, until the banana gains weight. Then the thin banana becomes a full banana, and the weight is dispersed equally in the upper and lower body. Therefore both banana types must incorporate exercises that will even out their shape and add curves and lines. Because the upper and lower relatively balanced, or symmetrical, the fuller banana will want to add additional cardiovascular workouts to their Body Redesigning program.

Note: See The Banana Shape Workout Program on page 317–328.

Get on Your Mark; Get Set; GO!

Are you ready? No more analyzing to do . . . no more charts to fill out . . . no more delays! It's time to begin your workouts. Section V outlines the specific workout program for each body type. Go to the specific program for your body type—and get moving. Come on, you can do it!

Chapter 14

Body Redesigning 90-Day Workout Programs

Once you have determined your body type you can proceed to the appropriate Body Redesigning program. Your program is progressive in nature and based on a ninety-day period. The exercises and prescribed amount of sets and repetitions listed in your program are designed to target each muscle group to meet your genetic requirements in a progressive manner. The workout charts are designed for thirty-day increments, allowing you to progress monthly at your individual fitness condition.

The Body Redesigning 90-Day Workout Program will help the beginner advance to the intermediate, then to the advanced level. If you are a beginner, you should start with the workout chart marked Month 1. From there you will progress to Month 2 and then Month 3, thus completing your ninety-day program.

If your fitness condition is more advanced than a beginner level, then you should use workout chart Month 2 and forego Month 1. Then simply progress to Month 3 and stay there for the next thirty days. The strategy of your program is to make progress over ninety days. Eventually you will reach the level of the third month.

By the end of the first thirty days, your metabolism will burn fat calories at a higher rate of efficiency, no longer allowing your body to store calories.

Your fitness condition will improve as you progress through the program, but you should dictate just how long that will take. As you get familiar with your program and with its tempo, you can estimate the time it will take to complete each workout. The time will vary because of your present condition and physical limitations.

Listed below are approximate times the program should take:

1. Month 1 Workout Chart—Beginner level
    Approximately twenty minutes (after warm-up)
2. Month 2 Workout Chart—Intermediate level
    Approximately thirty minutes (after warm-up)
3. Month 3 Workout Chart—Advanced level
    Approximately forty-five minutes (after warm-up)

Your program gives you the best of three worlds. In one workout you will benefit from shaping and toning each muscle group and improving your cardiovascular condition while burning fat calories for the energy to perform the workout. The exercises are targeted to correct the problem areas so your total body symmetry will be more balanced. The first thirty days of training will strengthen your muscles and joints and speed up the recovery factor from exercise. This is the beginning of the strength and toning process, and in a very short time your cardiovascular condition will improve and promote increased endurance and stamina as you are able to progressively pick up the tempo.

By the end of the first thirty days, your metabolism will burn fat calories at a higher rate of efficiency, no longer allowing your body to store calories. Since your metabolism will have been stimulated regularly by following your program, you should start experiencing changes in the way your clothes fit and the way you look in the mirror. I call this process metabolic momentum.

It is not important to me how much weight you lose, and it shouldn't matter to you either. I realize that losing weight is the common monitoring mechanism everybody has used for decades, but you and I have agreed to make changes both physically and mentally. Therefore keep tabs on how your clothes fit and what the mirror says. The key is your body composition—body fat vs. lean weight.

At the end of every thirty days you should document your progress so you can make comparisons to where you started. Be sure to fill out your monthly Progress Report Card, entering the information on your 90-Day Master Recording Sheet.

The Pretest Workout

This workout is different from all the other workouts. This workout gets you acquainted with the exercises in your program and helps you to select the most suitable weight for each exercise.

STUDY THE WORKOUT CHART AND THE GLOSSARY OF EXERCISES

The workout chart for each body type lists the names of all the exercises and the number of sets and repetitions that have been prescribed for that body type program. There are appropriate spaces for penciling in the amount of weight you choose and the number of sets and reps you do for each workout. At the top of the workout chart are the spaces to record each day, date and workout number you'll be doing.

The workout charts can be found in the four-color, perforated section in the back of the book. Following the color-coded workout charts for each body type, you will find the specific exercises for that body type.

Pull out the color-coded section for your body type, put it in an easy-to-refer-to binder, and take it with you when you go to the gym. Be sure to mark your workout chart each time you exercise.

The Glossary of Exercises for each body type in Section V will show you the start/finish position and midpoint of each exercise. Beside each exercise is an explanation of how to position yourself and perform the exercise properly. Once you have become familiar with the technique of each exercise, it is time to select the proper amount of weight for each exercise and record it on your workout chart.

SELECTING HOW MUCH WEIGHT TO USE

Experience has allowed me to set a predetermined amount

of weight per exercise that you can try in your pretest workout. These selections are based on the *average* amount of weight used by all the students whom I have personally trained and pretested. These selections will minimize your task and time of determining how much weight you can use.

Selecting How Much Weight to Use

EXERCISE	WOMEN	MEN
Chest:		
Bench press	5–8 lb. dumbbells	12–15 lb. dumbbells
Flies	3–5 lb. dumbbells	8–12 lb. dumbbells
Back:		
1-arm rowing	5–10 lb. dumbbells	15–25 lb. dumbbells
Pullovers	5–8 lb. dumbbells	12–15 lb. dumbbells
Shoulders:		
S. laterals	3–8 lb. dumbbells	10–15 lb. dumbbells
S.F. laterals	3–8 lb. dumbbells	10–12 lb. dumbbells
Arms/Biceps:		
S. curls	5–8 lb. dumbbells	10–15 lb. dumbbells
Standing curls	5–8 lb. dumbbells	10–15 lb. dumbbells
Arms/Triceps:		
Lying tricep extension	5–8 lb. dumbbells	10–12 lb. dumbbells
2-arm extension	5 lb. dumbbells	10–12 lb. dumbbells

Before You Begin

You will find your body-type-specific workout program in the color-coded, perforated insert at the back of the book. But there are a few very important considerations before you start:

1. **Consult your physician** before you begin this or any other exercise program.
2. **Before you begin each workout,** do the following: Warm up for five to ten minutes using a stationary bike, treadmill, stepping in place or by walking. Your 90-day exercise program is designed for up to

three 45-minute workouts per week. This includes
your warm-ups and stretching.

3. **After each workout,** cool down for five to ten min-
    utes, using the stretching exercises on page 264.

4. **Aerobic training**—Three 30- to 45-minute aerobic
    workouts per week in addition to your regular
    workouts are recommended. These can be done on
    your "off" days. This will assure you of good car-
    diovascular conditioning and extra fat burning.
    Suggested aerobic exercises include stationary bike
    riding, treadmill, power walks and stair climbers.
    Remember these important tips: Calculate your
    Training Heart Rate (THR) using the chart below.
    (Example: The THR for a 40-year-old should be
    between 132 beats per minute, or 22 beats per ten
    seconds at 70 percent maximum heart rate, and 156
    beats per minute, or 26 beats per ten seconds at 85
    percent maximum heart rate.) Monitor your THR
    by taking your pulse every ten minutes. Maintain a
    constant THR throughout each workout.

5. **Discontinue exercise** if you feel faint, nauseous,
    experience chest pains or have difficulty breathing.
    If symptoms persist, contact your physician.

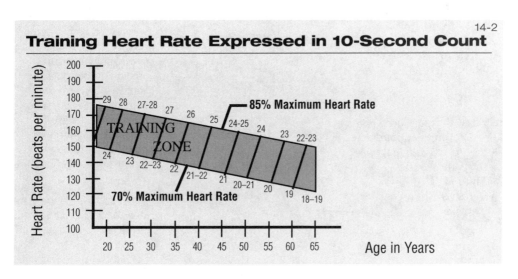

14-2

Training Heart Rate Expressed in 10-Second Count

Regulating Your Body Weight

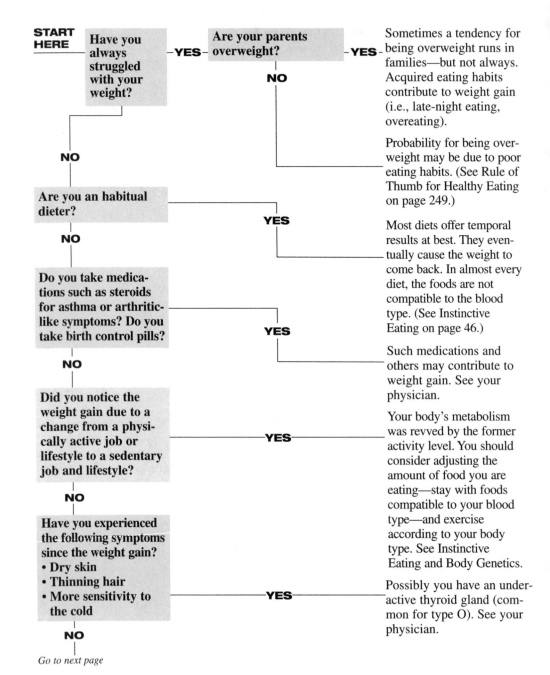

START HERE Have you always struggled with your weight? —**YES**— Are your parents overweight? —**YES**— Sometimes a tendency for being overweight runs in families—but not always. Acquired eating habits contribute to weight gain (i.e., late-night eating, overeating).

NO (parents overweight)

Probability for being overweight may be due to poor eating habits. (See Rule of Thumb for Healthy Eating on page 249.)

NO

Are you an habitual dieter? —————**YES**—— Most diets offer temporal results at best. They eventually cause the weight to come back. In almost every diet, the foods are not compatible to the blood type. (See Instinctive Eating on page 46.)

NO

Do you take medications such as steroids for asthma or arthritic-like symptoms? Do you take birth control pills? —————**YES**—— Such medications and others may contribute to weight gain. See your physician.

NO

Did you notice the weight gain due to a change from a physically active job or lifestyle to a sedentary job and lifestyle? —————**YES**————— Your body's metabolism was revved by the former activity level. You should consider adjusting the amount of food you are eating—stay with foods compatible to your blood type—and exercise according to your body type. See Instinctive Eating and Body Genetics.

NO

Have you experienced the following symptoms since the weight gain?
• **Dry skin**
• **Thinning hair**
• **More sensitivity to the cold** —————**YES**————— Possibly you have an underactive thyroid gland (common for type O). See your physician.

NO

Go to next page

Continued from previous page

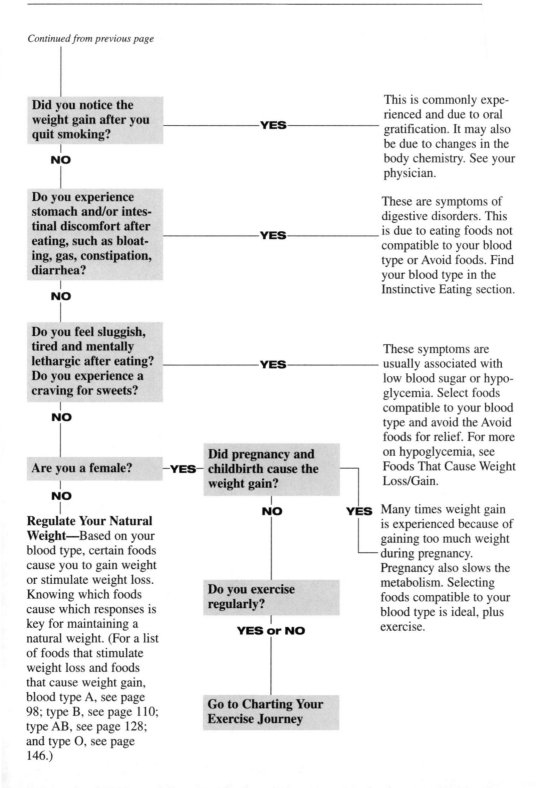

Did you notice the weight gain after you quit smoking?

————YES————

This is commonly experienced and due to oral gratification. It may also be due to changes in the body chemistry. See your physician.

NO

Do you experience stomach and/or intestinal discomfort after eating, such as bloating, gas, constipation, diarrhea?

————YES————

These are symptoms of digestive disorders. This is due to eating foods not compatible to your blood type or Avoid foods. Find your blood type in the Instinctive Eating section.

NO

Do you feel sluggish, tired and mentally lethargic after eating? Do you experience a craving for sweets?

————YES————

These symptoms are usually associated with low blood sugar or hypoglycemia. Select foods compatible to your blood type and avoid the Avoid foods for relief. For more on hypoglycemia, see Foods That Cause Weight Loss/Gain.

NO

Are you a female? —YES— **Did pregnancy and childbirth cause the weight gain?**

NO

Regulate Your Natural Weight—Based on your blood type, certain foods cause you to gain weight or stimulate weight loss. Knowing which foods cause which responses is key for maintaining a natural weight. (For a list of foods that stimulate weight loss and foods that cause weight gain, blood type A, see page 98; type B, see page 110; type AB, see page 128; and type O, see page 146.)

NO

YES Many times weight gain is experienced because of gaining too much weight during pregnancy. Pregnancy also slows the metabolism. Selecting foods compatible to your blood type is ideal, plus exercise.

Do you exercise regularly?

YES or NO

Go to Charting Your Exercise Journey

Charting Your Exercise Journey

START HERE

Do you have medical or physical limitations (i.e., low back problems, high blood pressure, arthritis, heart disease, elevated cholesterol, diabetes) that you feel prevents you from exercising? ——————YES——————

Exercise has been proven to strengthen the heart, improve circulation, regulate insulin, lower risk for heart disease, diabetes, and blood pressure. Exercise stimulates the immune system; slows down the aging process. Exercise strengthens muscle tissue, improves joint movement, lubricates joints and contributes to functional age (get a green light from your physician and go for it).

NO

Would you be willing to start an exercise program if you were instructed and shown how to go about it? ——————YES——————

Since you are willing to get started or if you already exercise and want to make advances in your progress, there are several things to know and do before you get started. (Go to Body Genetics on page 219.)

NO

Does your doctor know you are ready to start an exercise program? ——————YES——————

This preliminary step is a safeguard to establish an individual medical baseline. It also relieves the mind, knowing you did the right thing.

NO

It's best to have a medical checkup before you begin. If you are a male 35 or older or a female 40 or older, it is a wise step to take before going further (see your physician).

Go to next page

Continued from previous page

SETTING YOUR GOALS

Have you established your goals? —————————**YES**—————————

Obviously that was an important part of your exercise journey. But sometimes a quick go-over will help re-assess your goals (see Goal Setting on page 32).

|
NO
|

Without goals it will be impossible to succeed. If you don't have a target to aim at, you'll hit it every time! To help you with this very important step, see Goal Setting on page 32.

WORKING WITH YOUR GENETICS

Are you aware of your body genetics—your inherited genetic problem areas? —————————**YES**—————————

Since you are aware of your body genetics and problem areas, then now is as good of a time as any to start your Body Redesigning 90-Day Program. Go to appropriate workout program for your body type.

|
NO
|

It is imperative to know what you are working with to succeed (see Determining Your Body Type on page 254). Also, each body type has its genetic problem areas. To identify best with your body type, go to Troubleshooting Your Body Type on pages 255–257.

Stretching Exercises

To make your exercise program complete, it is vitally important to add some stretching exercises. Stretching helps to elongate the muscles, assist in relieving muscle tightness and soreness and improve the mobility and range of motion (ROM) of your joints. It is best to stretch *after* your exercise workout.

Use the following static stretching exercises. Static stretching gently pulls or stretches the intended muscle group. It avoids any form of bouncing or erratic motion. Do not overstretch a muscle group to the point of discomfort. The key is to relax, breathe freely, stretch, hold for 15–25 seconds and release.

CAT/COW STRETCH
(LOWER, MID AND UPPER BACK)

Position 1—Get down on all fours. Sag your back while lifting your head upward.

Position 2—Arch your back and lower your head. Hold the stretch for 15–25 seconds.

Position 3—Lean back onto your heels. Hold the stretch for 15–25 seconds.

Repeat three to four times.

KNEE/QUAD STRETCH (QUADRICEPS)

Position—Lie face down. Reach back with your left hand and grasp your left ankle. Pull and hold the stretch for 15–25 seconds. Repeat same on opposite leg.

Repeat three to four times.

DOUBLE LEG STRETCH (LOWER BACK)

Position—Lie on your back with your knees slightly bent. Grasp both legs and gently pull them to your chest, lifting your tail bone off the floor. Hold the stretch for 15–25 seconds. Relax, and then repeat three to four times.

Section IV

Real People, Real Results

"Getting Up in the Morning Is a Joy"—Joe Christiano

Before and after photos really say a lot about a person. As I stood in an "all you can eat" line for a Hawaiian buffet, I had my unexpected "Kodak" moment. What I really looked like had never occurred to me prior to that moment. I'm not certain if that moment was defined by the bushel-basket face I had developed, the 305 pounds to which I had zoomed or the fact that the producers at Sea World were looking for a human Shamu and thought I was a candidate. But my before photo did get my attention.

Two questions loomed before me, immediately demanding answers—How did I get here? How was I going to turn this around?

Whether the picture motivated me or the realization that I was out of control, I made a vow to myself that I would no longer walk around the face of this earth looking like that photo. I decided to make the necessary changes—in my eating, in my exercise program and, more importantly, in my mental attitude.

That before picture was taken in April 1981 when I weighed 305 pounds. By December 1981 I had gone down to 220 pounds. I was serious! I've been serious for the nineteen years since then—and I've kept the weight off during that time. I might gain a pound or two here or there, but I am careful to never allow myself to go beyond a certain point.

I had been healthy for most of my life. I had the usual health challenges growing up, but nothing out of the ordinary. I did have rheumatic fever as a child, which is interesting considering the fact that I am blood type O (more susceptible to blood disorders), but I did not incur any heart damage. I also managed to get a stomach ulcer at the age of eleven, which is common for blood type O.

I live an active life, and I have been exercising since I was thirteen years of age. Other than a few broken bones and injuries from competitive sports, I've been a pretty healthy camper. But as time passed, I began to deal with one recurring health issue—hypoglycemia. I struggled with it for fifteen years. Anyone who has experienced hypoglycemia, or low blood sugar, knows that it can be a nightmare. It was for me.

My condition became so severe that I could not go for more than one hour without eating. If more time passed, I would "crash." It happened like clockwork—at ten in the morning and three in the afternoon. I would feel lethargic, lightheaded and nauseous at times, irritable and tired. I battled bouts of depression for no known reason. After researching every diet concept, seeking medical advice and attempting to mix and match the foods I ate, eventually I began testing the concept of eating foods compatible to my blood type. In my research I learned about the link that exists between blood types and food, and I thought I would give it a try.

As blood type O, I discovered that foods like pasta, bread

Before—305 lbs.
April 1981

After—220 lbs.
December 1981

(wheat) and dairy foods should be avoided. Interestingly, some of these foods were the very foods the doctor had told me I should eat for my low-sugar problem. The big hurdle for me to get over as an Italian was the fact that I could no longer eat pasta five times a week. Pasta was my staple—it seemed an impossibility to do without it.

But I figured that if I was going to whip this low-blood-sugar thing, I'd have to give it 100 percent.

As a blood type O, I began adding red meat as a protein source, which is beneficial to my diet. The protein contributed most to the stabilizing of my blood sugar. I eventually started drinking protein drinks as a meal or snack replacement. This further helped to stabilize my blood sugar. Amazingly, I immediately started experiencing gastrointestinal relief—no more gas! I started losing weight (body fat). Most gratifying, I was no longer "crashing."

After eating foods compatible to my blood type for approximately five to ten days, and avoiding foods that were incompatible, not only did I feel better, but I also had constant energy due to the stabilization of my blood sugar. Now my blood sugar has been stabilized for more than three and a half years.

My before and after photos are just a reminder to me of what can happen if I should let things get out of control. When I am consistent at eating food compatible for my blood type, taking my nutritional supplements and including regular daily exercise and physical activities, I am constantly reminded of the improvement in my appearance, mental outlook and feelings of accomplishment.

As I make regular exercise and instinctive eating a major part of my life, I am able to enjoy my life to its fullest. I have the energy to work and play. I have no medical bills to pay. Getting up in the morning is a joy. Most importantly, staying healthy makes me more appreciative and grateful to God for uniquely creating the human body to respond naturally and positively to the proper preventative lifestyle.

"I Feel Better Than I Have in Years"—Patty

My story is a typical one—I'm the thirty-nine-year-old mother of two teenage children, and I've tried anything and everything to lose weight. All my life I have struggled with this battle. As a teenager I tried crash and fad diets, which always became a vicious cycle. In my early twenties I tried pills and liquid diets after packing on the pounds after the births of my two children. In my late twenties I tried Weight Watchers and was able to lose weight, but when my lifestyle changed with a return to school and a career advancement, the weight came right back. My thirties brought Jenny Craig, on which I did well until I discontinued eating the food.

My sister got my attention when she told me about the lifestyle changes she was making and the weight loss results she had experienced. She said the plan she used worked by eating according to your blood type. As a nurse, I was very skeptical—how in the world could your weight have anything to do with your blood type?

I was willing to try this "one last miracle diet" to shed the weight I've tried to lose for years. I was tipping the scales at 250 pounds, even though at five foot seven inches I thought I was able to carry the weight without looking like I weighed that much. But I could feel what that weight was doing to my body and to my self-esteem.

Six months ago I made a lifestyle change by beginning to eat according to my blood type. I am on my way to becoming healthy. Currently I'm down to 192 pounds, and I feel like a new person! I still have thirty pounds to lose, but I know I'll reach my goal. Going from a size 3X to an XL has been an accomplishment for me.

I feel better than I have in years. The most satisfying part about this lifestyle change is the fact I can still sit down with my family and eat regular food. I am more aware of reading labels on foods than I've ever been. The best way to describe my feelings is to say that I no longer experience the highs and lows I used to

> **I was tipping the scales at 250 pounds. Six months ago I made a lifestyle change by beginning to eat according to my blood type. I am on my way to becoming healthy. Currently I'm down to 192 pounds, and I feel like a new person!**

have. The gastrointestinal problems I used to have are nonexistent since I made these changes in my diet.

Being overweight for the majority of my life had made me depressed—even not caring—especially about the cookie no one else saw me eat. Now I have my self-esteem back, and I'm feeling good about myself. I am able to be in control of the foods I choose to eat. I avoid the foods I should not eat, and I consistently lose more weight.

Next summer I'll be forty, and my goal is to be healthy and fit by then. I am very confident that I will be able to shed the rest of the weight and be a much healthier and happier person for the rest of my life.

"It's a Lifestyle Now"—Stacy

We weren't looking for another diet and exercise program. We've done them all! What we were looking for was a baby. Rod and I have struggled with infertility since 1998 when I was diagnosed with a tumor on my pituitary gland. It wreaked havoc on my hormonal system and caused my progesterone level to be quite low. Conception was very difficult. It also caused weight gain, which added to my depression.

Then in August of 1999 my mother passed away from cancer of the brain. My anxiety, stress and weight were at an all-time high. I needed hope again. And I found it by changing my lifestyle.

Rod and I were both increasingly disgusted with our bodies because of poor eating habits and little or no physical activity. We had low energy and little will power to resist the foods that were causing our "growing" problem. It seemed overwhelming at times.

When we were introduced to the concept of eating according to our blood type, we were both a bit skeptical. We made the mistake of looking first at the Avoid lists and began to protest.

But after about a week of eating mostly beneficial and some neutral foods for my blood type, I stopped craving the nachos *I had to have!* Our energy levels increased incredibly, and combined with the exercises Joe showed us, we had amazing results.

In twelve weeks of eating according to our blood types and exercising, we lost fat and inches, gained muscle and improved our health. Rod lost forty-two pounds of fat and normalized his cholesterol (which was high prior to this) and his blood pressure. I lost thirty pounds of fat, gained five pounds of muscle, went down three dress sizes and lost forty-seven total inches of body size. When we checked my progesterone level, it was absolutely normal!

We like having the three-month goal as a motivation, and when we finish three months, we just start three more. It really is a lifestyle for us now.

"Energy Is Not a Problem Anymore"—Rod

I went to college with under 9 percent body fat. Stacy and I met Joe Christiano through a friend of ours who went to one of his Body Redesigning classes. At that time I thought I was doing all right; I believed I was in pretty good shape and feeling strong. So we didn't do anything then. It really started when my wife's mom found out that she had cancer. She wanted to do something natural to combat the disease—not just try all the medical remedies.

Joe and his wife came over to our home—along with fifteen other guests—one evening, and we drilled him with questions about his book *The Answer is in Your Bloodtype.* Joe told us that this plan would help us lose weight, but said that the primary focus was getting healthy and feeling good. One thing he said really made me think: "If you think you feel good now," he told me, "just wait until you eat right for just two weeks. Then you will really know what it is to feel good!"

We decided to take some "Before" shots to help motivate us in our quest to feel good. I hardly recognized the big, fat, kind

 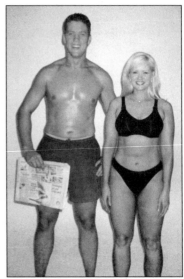

Rod and Stacy Before   Rod and Stacy After

of goofy-looking guy in some of the photos. It was me! I said to my wife, "Honey, I've been kidding myself. I am FAT!"

Overnight I woke up out of shape and with over 23 percent body fat. It shocked me. So then I really wanted to do something about it. We embarked on a journey that day that would change our lives forever. We started getting healthy again. All we did was eat what we are—that is, according to our blood types. We worked out one hour per day, three days a week, and did twenty minutes of intense cardiovascular work another three days a week.

In just twelve weeks I went from 23 percent body fat to under 10 percent, lost forty-two pounds of fat and went from a tight size forty pants to a very comfortable thirty-six. I am six foot four inches tall and weigh 225 pounds, so a thirty-six is pretty good!

All the fat loss was great, awesome and all of that, but the real story is our energy levels and our health. Not only did our energy levels stabilize, but they went through the roof. I am a full-time youth pastor, a part-time Terminator at University Studios in Florida and a full-time husband. My lifestyle demands a lot from me. My wife is a full-time singer/entertainer and a wonderful wife, so hers is equally demanding. Let's just say that energy is not a problem anymore!

We really feel good. We look better, so we feel better about ourselves. All areas of our lives have improved. We are both more confident and less inhibited to try new things. Now that we have done this whole body redesign, we have found that if we can discipline ourselves in one area of our lives, we can do it in any area. Not only are our bodies in better shape—our lives are in better shape. We can do anything we put our minds to! We are so proud of each other, and we have a greater respect for each other. Every part of our relationship has improved. We are so glad we met Joe. He has been a very big help to us!

"I Feel Great"
—Sue Ann

What a difference I have seen in my health since applying the principles of eating the foods compatible to my blood type.

For three years I experienced severe bouts of fatigue, moments of lightheadedness, headaches and feelings of anxiety. I tried to eat healthy foods, took several supplements and had all my mercury fillings removed. I went to general practitioners, holistic physicians, chiropractors and tried homeopathic remedies, but still I felt these symptoms. It was very frustrating. I went to great lengths to feel normal again.

When I heard you tell your own story on television, it sounded so familiar to me. The whole concept of eating foods compatible to your blood type made so much sense to me that I decided to give it a try.

Being blood type O, I immediately eliminated wheat and dairy from my diet. Then I began to eliminate the other foods on my Avoid list. I have found that I really enjoy Ezekiel bread, soy milk and some fruits and vegetables I had never tried before. Most of all, I would not be without my personal protein powder!

My energy has returned, my headaches are gone and my anxiety has subsided. I feel great! I have introduced these principles to my loved ones and friends. My husband, Mike, who is blood type A, also eats according to his blood type, and he has felt the difference—especially when he cheats. Our three sons, Matt, Justin and Joey, are aware of what foods they should eat, which is a step in the right direction. Our son Joey actually requests soy protein shakes. When he drinks them, he's happy, and I'm happy knowing that he's drinking something so healthy for him.

When I go to the grocery store, I always take my Avoid food list. I usually buy fish since it is compatible to both my husband and myself. I have found many foods we both can eat.

I am happy to share my story, and it is my hope that your book reaches many more people just like me.

> **For three years I experienced severe bouts of fatigue, moments of lightheadedness, headaches and feelings of anxiety. My energy has returned, my headaches are gone and my anxiety has subsided. I feel great! I have introduced these principles to my loved ones and friends.**

"What a Difference I Felt"
—Vicky

I am a forty-year-old wife and mother of two boys aged twenty and seventeen. I have lost thirty pounds in the last eight months eating foods compatible for my blood type O. My dress size has gone from XXL to 18. I am currently working on my next thirty pounds, and plan to have it off by Christmas.

I carry the royal title "Queen of Diets"! I have lost thirty pounds in the last eight months eating foods compatible for my blood type O. My dress size has gone from XXL to 18.

I carry the royal title "Queen of Diets"! I have tried most of them. I could lose the weight, but never reached my goal before I stopped eating the diet foods and gained back the weight in a short period of time—plus more.

My boss started to eat according to her blood type, which is also blood type O, so I was able to see the kinds of food she ate. She ate a lot of red meat, which I love. I remember thinking, *This wouldn't be so bad.* I was so tired of worrying about my weight that I had just given up. As the days passed, I saw the weight melt off her, and I decided to give eating by my blood type a try.

She gave me your book, and I took it home to my husband, who is a type B. We compared the foods, and decided we would both give it a try. Because coffee, which I love, is on my Avoid list, I gave it up cold turkey. My body wanted coffee, and I didn't feel the greatest, but I made it through that first week. What a difference I felt from that point on. I felt so much better. No more bloating.

As long as I eat from the Beneficial list, I feel great. When I eat something from the Avoid list, I sure can feel the difference. The weight is coming off slowly, but I am happy with it. In the past, whenever I lost weight quickly, I ended up gaining it back. Your book has made it so much easier to follow my new lifestyle.

"My Energy Level Has Skyrocketed"—Tom

On April 14 I went to the doctor for a checkup. He was astounded at the way I looked. I had lost forty-seven pounds (down from 238 pounds to 191 pounds).

One day in November 1999, my wife came home with a new book—*The Answer is in Your Bloodtype*. She told me how her boss lost forty-two pounds by using the method described in the book. She said she was going to give it a try, and asked if I would also.

I skimmed the book and decided that this was just another fad. At first I was not going to try it, but I decided it would be easier for her if I was doing it also, so I told her I would try it with her.

I am so glad I did. I soon learned it was not just a fad, but that it worked. I began eating by my blood type on January 3, 2000. Prior to starting, I had blood work done to check my cholesterol levels. On April 14 I went to the doctor for a checkup. He was astounded at the way I looked. I had lost forty-seven pounds (down from 238 pounds to 191 pounds). I went from size 43 pants to a size 38. My shirt size went from 17½ to 16½. In three months, my cholesterol dropped from 254 to 200.

The doctor wanted to know what I had done, and I gladly told him. In fact I gave him a copy of the book and asked him to read it.

My energy level has skyrocketed. I had been diagnosed with esophageal reflux disease and was taking Prilosec. I stopped taking it on January 3 and haven't had a problem.

I have given up some things—pork, chicken and sodas, to name a few—but now that I am eating for my blood type, my body uses the right food properly, and I don't miss what I gave up. People who haven't seen me since January are astounded.

This program is not a diet—it is an eating lifestyle I expect to continue. Over the past forty years I have tried many diets to control my weight, but eating for my blood type has worked the best for me to lose and maintain my weight. Thank you for doing the research and writing the book. It has made a difference in my life.

"I Will Never Go Back"
—Earlyne

I am married, the mother of four grown children, twelve grand-children and one great-grandson. In 1981 I was diagnosed with cancer, and now I am completely healed and enjoying good health. Going through this experience made me appreciate my health and quality of life. My husband and I began trying to eat healthy and learn all we could about nutrition.

It has been six months since I purchased your first book, and my life has changed for the better. Immediately I realized that this was the answer to all my questions about eating properly. I determined in my heart that I would eat the Beneficial foods and eliminate the Avoid foods. Within three days I experienced the results. I had previously experienced a lot of stomach disorders, was hospitalized on several occasions and discharged because the doctors could not determine the cause. Now they are all gone, and my energy level is great. I realize now that I was allergic to some of the food I was eating.

In addition I have lost weight and two dress sizes. To me this is not a diet—but a way of life. I will never go back to my old style of eating again. Another benefit is that we have eliminated sickness from our lives by eating according to our blood types and exercising, along with other modifications to our lifestyle. My husband, George, is a diabetic, and since eating according to his blood type he has decreased his insulin requirement by half and has noticed a remarkable improvement in his well-being. In fact, he went out and purchased a bike. This truly is a blessing to both of us.

I am blood type O and Gordon is A, but we have no difficulty eating what is beneficial for both of us. I intend to keep telling others about this new way of eating to live, and I look forward to learning more, as Joseph Christiano's new books become available.

A Way of Life

"The Proof Is in the Pudding"
—Spero and Dallas

We have been eating according to our blood types since the end of January 2000. We have seen a very big difference in how we feel and in our energy level. I am type O and my husband is type A. I have had to change the way I cook because of differences in our blood types, but that is a small price to pay for feeling better. Two of our four children live in the same town as we do, and they have seen a difference in how we feel and are very interested in joining us in our quest for good health.

My oldest son asked me to run off a copy of the Avoid foods for him (he and his brother are type O), and both of them are now eating according to their blood type.

There is a fully equipped kitchen where my husband works because the men who work there love to cook. One day one of the men decided to make a dish loaded with hot peppers. My husband, who loves hot peppers, ate a big helping. The next day he was taken to the hospital with chest pains. The doctor told him it was only gas. Needless to say, he learned a big lesson that day. He will not stray from his approved foods again.

We have both learned that eating the Avoid foods is like taking poison into our systems. I would say we have learned to follow the eating regimen that is laid out in the book 85–90 percent of the time.

I no longer have acid reflux or irritable bowel syndrome, and I no longer have a bloated stomach. My husband no longer has to take high blood pressure medicine. My husband and I sleep better, we feel better and we look better. My husband has even lost a little weight by eating the proper foods. This concept makes more sense than anything else we have tried.

You know the old cliché, "The proof is in the pudding." Well, here is your pudding—start eating.

> We have seen a very big difference in how we feel and in our energy level. I no longer have acid reflux or irritable bowel syndrome, and I no longer have a bloated stomach. My husband no longer has to take high blood pressure medicine. My husband and I sleep better, we feel better and we look better.

"Others Notice Something Is Different"—Debbie

One year ago I began a Fitness and Fellowship class with Joe and Lori Christiano. At the time I was extremely overweight and had no energy. My lifestyle consisted of consuming eight to twelve cans of Diet Pepsi a day and eating a lot of food packed with fat, sugars and no nutrients.

I began following Joe's program of eating according to my blood type and exercising on a regular basis. I noticed immediate results. Within three weeks, I had blood work done, and my cholesterol had dropped over sixty points. When I went to the doctor's office for the lab results, she burst into the room saying, "I am thrilled at the results of your blood work. Whatever you are doing, keep it up."

Prior to embracing this lifestyle, I had a thyroidectomy. My doctor has consistently lowered my medication since I began the program because my body is more in line with the way it should be. Another benefit was the immediate increased energy I felt. I no longer dreaded getting out of bed and dragging myself through the day. The exercise became a part of my daily routine, and very soon I felt something was missing on the days I could not exercise.

I do not have a scale, and really don't know how much weight I've lost; however I have lost six dress sizes. Even during Thanksgiving and Christmas holidays I continued to lose sizes. We went to more Christmas parties than we had ever attended, and I ate a lot of food. But I just ate food appropriate for blood type O as much as possible.

Since I have lost so many sizes it is not difficult for others to notice that something is different. I enjoy sharing with them the secrets to my success—eating right and regular exercise. Several people I know have begun eating according to their blood type and have had great results.

Within three weeks, I had blood work done, and my cholesterol had dropped over sixty points. Even during Thanksgiving and Christmas holidays I continued to lose sizes.

"It Doesn't Interfere With My Lifestyle"—Joanne and Desiree

I want to take a moment to tell you how much your first book has changed my life—as well as that of my daughter, Desiree.

I saw you on television explaining how certain blood types react differently to certain foods, and suddenly the success and failure of different diets I have tried over the years made sense. I immediately ordered a book. My then nineteen-year-old daughter has watched me struggle with weight all my life, and she was beginning to make the same mistakes I had made at her age. She was using an over-the-counter diet aid that guaranteed to burn fat as you ate. Along with that she was skipping meals and showing definite signs of anorexia.

After I read the book, I asked her to read it and give the diet a chance. Because your explanations and examples were so easy to follow, she read it and agreed to stop her diet pills and give the diet a chance. As we both have blood type O, it was easy to build our meals around the Beneficial and Neutral food lists.

We were shocked to find that some of the foods we thought were good for us were in the Neutral or Avoid lists (example, lentils). We had just about given up on red meat, going along with the common theory that chicken and turkey were better.

My daughter, Desiree, has lost over thirty pounds in less than six months. It is amazing, because she is eating regular meals and more food than she has in the past year. Her goal is to stay completely away from the Avoid foods and stay 80 percent of the time with the beneficial foods. Foods from the Neutral list make up the other 20 percent of her diet.

What she likes most about this way of eating is that it doesn't interfere with her lifestyle. She no longer feels bloated after eating. She can go out to dinner with friends and order off the menu without straying from the diet. She looks and feels so much better, and I am no longer worried about her health and the negative effects of the diet aids she was using. She considers her protein shake mix the most important food item in the house, and takes her powder with her wherever she goes. She is working toward a career as a model or in television, and she loves the fact that everyone tells her how good and healthy she looks. Even her hairdresser says that her hair is thicker and healthier now that she is eating right.

As for me, I struggled with hypoglycemia and chronic fatigue syndrome for years. After a hysterectomy, the symptoms intensified. My short-term memory was affected, and I wasn't sure how long I could keep working in my chosen career. I have a very demanding sales job, and I would find myself exhausted by 4 P.M. in the afternoon.

Since beginning your plan I no longer have those sugar highs and lows. My energy and my mental acuity have increased significantly. I feel better than I have in years. I have a shake for breakfast and don't even know it's lunchtime until I look at the clock. I no longer struggle with food cravings, and when I drink a shake before bed, I sleep better and wake up energized.

In the past year we have started many friends and family members on your plan and shakes. Everyone who has tried it has agreed that it is better than anything they have tried before.

Before   After

"What a Difference It Made"
—Lyn

It is amazing how one person can change your life forever, give you a positive outlook and help you achieve your goals.

As a child growing up, I never had to worry about my weight. That is, until I became a teenager, when my hormones were racing and my body was going through many changes. I put on forty to fifty pounds within a few months. Everyone knows that being a teenager is not easy, and for me, being overweight made it even harder. I wore baggy clothes, trying to cover up the weight so that people wouldn't notice. Sometimes when people looked at me, I thought they were looking at my weight—not at me as a person. Because of that I lost a lot of self-confidence.

Throughout high school and college I was very active, playing softball, cheerleading and dancing, but something was still missing. I tried so many different diet plans, pills and programs, but nothing helped—it only got worse. I would lose a little weight and then put it right back on. I couldn't find a program that catered to my needs, body and schedule. I felt overwhelmed and lost.

I had a lot of friends and enjoyed going out and being with people, but deep down inside, I came to realize that I wasn't happy with myself. I knew that one of the most important parts of life was to love me for who I was.

I have many goals in life, and one of them was to compete in the Miss New York USA Pageant. I've been involved in pageants since I was thirteen, but I would not compete in a pageant if there was a swimsuit competition. I am very independent and goal-oriented, but how could I compete in the pageant when I was overweight?

As a subscriber to *Pageantry Magazine*, I had seen Joe Christiano and the Back to Basics Program in several editions, and the work he had done with pageant contestants. The pictures accompanying the articles were amazing. With some of the women, the transition from before to after was unbelievable. I thought that if I was going to achieve my goals, a good place to start would be by giving Joe a call. That call changed my life.

I talked extensively with Joe over the phone, and within a few weeks, I was on a regular workout schedule and diet program. It wasn't really like a diet—it was more like an eating regimen. There were several factors that attracted me to the program. First, it was one-on-one counseling. Second, I could work out in the privacy of my own home.

Joe and I corresponded by mail and talked at least once a week for the first month, and then once or twice a month thereafter. At any given time, though, if I felt discouraged or needed encouragement, he was always there to help. In order for him to see my progress and make changes to my program, I took my measurements and mailed them to him on a weekly basis. He was very encouraging, supportive and motivating. Whenever I needed him, he was always there—even when I wanted to quit.

Within the first nine months, I had lost thirty pounds and a total of seventeen and a half inches from my shoulders to my ankles. I could not believe it. I saw results in the first month. Nine months later I was walking down the runway at the Miss New York USA Pageant. Even though I didn't place that first year, my self-esteem and confidence just in taking that walk were amazing.

I continued to work with Joe, and we began to fine-tune my body and program in preparation for the next pageant. That's when he introduced me to eating according to my blood type. I was at a standstill; I wasn't losing any more, and I had reached a plateau. The blood type program was genetically designed to target my specific blood type. My eating habits changed once again. Foods that before I thought were good for me now actually had a negative effect on my body. This meant that they were not being properly digested.

There was a list of beneficial and neutral foods that were designed for my blood type, and that helped me to increase my metabolism and protein intake. At the same time, Joe redesigned my workout program to target specific areas of my body that needed to be reshaped. He increased the sets and repetitions for my legs, thighs and abdomen exercises. I worked out my upper body on a regular basis too, but at that point, the emphasis needed to be on my lower body. What a difference it made. I was losing body fat, not muscle fat. My muscles were more defined and lean. I felt great.

Through all of this there were many times when I wanted to give up. I started on this program on my own—without assistance from anyone. I was determined to succeed, but I would be amiss if I didn't say what a struggle it was without the support of a partner, friend or family member working right along with me. Although my family was very supportive, I had to do this on my own. When I wanted to give up, the continual support provided by Joe was the one facet of this program that worked for me. He lent himself to me as a mentor, friend and personal trainer. He never let me become disillusioned with myself. There were pep talks to bolster my self-image and positive encouragement to help me build my self-confidence and continue with my determination to reach my goals. He possessed the very important skill of being a great listener.

Before   After

My attitude and personality changed dramatically. While working with Joe, I learned proper eating habits and ways to work out and challenge my body. I will be able to incorporate everything I learned into the rest of my life, even if I do gain a few pounds now and then.

In my life, it is important for me to keep a nutritionally sound, well-balanced diet and to exercise on a regular basis. With a family history of severe health problems that will affect me, staying focused on this regimen is one way of maintaining a healthy life and hopefully avoiding, or at least preventing, some of these problems.

To date, I continue to model my life around the techniques I've learned, and I realize that even if I gain a few pounds for one reason or another, I have built a solid foundation to support me.

"A Real Winner Would Take the Stairs!"—Cindy

I was naïve and inexperienced when I entered my first couple of pageant competitions in 1987—but I was having fun. I won at the mall among only a handful of contestants, which propelled me into my first state competition. Much to my surprise, I placed second runner-up in the Mrs. Florida Pageant, competing with forty-six other contestants. Having no real expectations of major success, I was thrilled. The next year I was able to move up one spot to finish as first runner-up.

In 1989 I decided to try again. I was devastated when my placement stalled at first runner-up again. This was the year I had set my sights on winning. As the weeks and months went by, my devastation turned to sheer determination. I realized that to win at the level of competition in which I found myself (seventy-plus women competing for one prize), relying on my natural physical conditioning was not good enough.

I had heard about Joe Christiano from friends in the pageant arena, and I decided to consult with him. We met, came up with an initial plan of attack and proceeded. Not only was Joe able to push me to—and past—my limits while at his gym, but he motivated me to continue pushing myself while training on my own.

Amazingly enough, Joe could tell me all the things I needed to change or improve (diet, exercise, etc.), and I would accept it. Although I did not relish changing my habits (especially giving up candy bars and diet sodas) or pushing myself as hard as he said I should, he commanded a certain respect for what he did. He never asked me to do anything he had not already done himself a thousand times over.

One day Joe decided it was "leg day," which meant *giant sets* of leg extensions, hyperextensions and lunges—everyone's favorite, right? By the time the training session ended, my legs could barely support me as I walked out the door with my family and toward the elevator. "What do you think you're doing?" Joe asked. I was taken aback for a moment, wondering what he was talking about. "Why are you using the elevator?" he asked me. "A real winner would take the stairs!"

Given the way I felt at that moment, if anyone else had said that to me I would have told him or her to go play in traffic! But no one said that to Joe. He pushed me to the breaking point, but I was better for it. I went into the next competition knowing I was better prepared physically than I ever dreamed I could be.

Joe's personal faith in God and his undying support and friendship toward us were very important. His knowledge, experience and confidence exuded to a point that I just knew I could do it. With my husband and two-year-old son looking on, and our nine-month-old baby in the hotel room with the babysitter, I finally achieved the title that had eluded me for four years—Mrs. Florida 1991.

Joe immediately began preparing me for the Mrs. America pageant. The fairy-tale ending we had hoped for did not occur. However, I placed a very pleasing third runner-up to the newly crowned Mrs. America, and was told that I had the highest score of the swimsuit competition. I was truly honored just to be a part of the national competition, and I readily accepted the choice of the judges—a truly spectacular woman from Indiana.

Having worked with Joe for a period of almost three years at that time, I came to realize that not only was his knowledge of training and nutrition invaluable and always "right-on," but his ability to provide me with the mental edge I needed was equally important. I could be assured that Joe would be always be honest with me—sometimes brutally honest—about what I needed to accomplish my goals. To this day I still follow many of Joe's training and nutritional tips, as they have become an integral part of my life. My "title" dreams now exist in the form of goals in the business world, and the confidence and training values instilled in me by Joe still do, and will always, play an important role in whatever future success I achieve.

Mrs. Florida 1991

Epilogue

My purpose for writing this book has been to provide you with a vehicle that functions as the next best thing to having your own personal trainer and nutritional guide. Throughout the book everything necessary for you and me to establish an interactive one-on-one relationship has been provided. Now the rest of your journey is up to you.

Having familiarized yourself with the materials in my book, I hope your thinking has been stimulated, your attitude challenged and your new goals set. Additionally, I hope you have already started your fitness journey—and are experiencing the blessings of a healthier lifestyle firsthand.

Discovering the connection between your genetics and how your body functions should overwhelm you with the knowledge that you have been wonderfully and incredibly made. You are not just another body on this planet. You possess a uniqueness that makes you different from anyone else—and worthy of your best effort. Your genetic potential is just waiting to be tapped, and it is yours and yours alone.

You have all the tools at your disposal for making continual progress toward redesigning and improving the condition of your body. The 28-Day Pick-a-Meal plan, the sample family planning menus and the delicious, blood-type-compatible recipes are yours to use. With their help you will develop your innate survival mechanism—*instinctive eating.* Instinctive eating is far superior to any diet concept. It is controlled purely by the way your body responds based on your blood type. It satisfies your desire to lose weight, it eases painful digestive discomfort, *and* it enhances your energy level, promotes vitality and greatly contributes to longer, disease-free living.

Your 90-Day Body Redesigning Workout program has been designed according to your body genetics. It is filled with how-to photos, tear-out monthly workout charts, the survival kit and other charts and aids to ensure that you reach your fitness goals.

It is the synergy of the "fitness twins"—instinctive eating and regular exercise—that creates a lifestyle high on performance and low on maintenance.

Your fitness journey is something dynamic and powerful. It affects every area of your life. It will give you a wonderful sense of accomplishment plus a new appreciation for your entire life. Equally important, you will be a shining star to someone else in your life who needs to hear this message and see your results. Your redesigned body and energetic lifestyle will be an inspiring billboard to everyone who sees you.

I designed this interactive journey to help you reach your genetic potential. Continue on the journey—stay focused, remain positive and always remember that you are *an inspiration in transition.*

May God bless you with the best of health.

—JOSEPH CHRISTIANO

Notes

Introduction

1. Source obtained from the Internet: "Statistics Related to Overweight and Obesity," National Institute of Diabetes and Digestive and Kidney Diseases (NIDDK), www.niddk.nih/gov/health/nutrit/pubs/statobes.
2. Rob Wilkins and Mike O'Hearn, "Obesity! Public Enemy Number One," *Natural Muscle Magazine* (January 2000): 28.
3. Brad Darrach, "The War on Aging," *Life* (October 1992): 36.

Chapter 1: Genetics—Your Foundation for Success

1. Jesper L. Anderson, Peter Schjerling and Bengt Saltin, "Muscle, Genes and Athletic Performance," *Scientific American* (September 2000): 49–55.
2. Ibid.
3. "Diabetes risk written on a gene," *USA Today* (August 28, 2000): 6D.
4. "Discovery opens door to treat obesity, diabetes," *Orlando Sentinel* (September 20, 2000): A3.
5. Nancy McVicar, "Genome work spurs grant for Miami school," *Orlando Sentinel* (August 30, 2000), D5.
6. Source obtained from the Internet: Jonathan Safarti, "Blood Types and Their Origins (Answering the Critics)," first published in *Creation Ex Nihilo Technical Journal* 11(1):31–32 (1997), www.answersingenesis.org/docs/ 490.asp.
7. Source obtained from the Internet: Michael Denton, *Evolution: A Theory in Crisis* (Bethesda, MD: Adler and Adler, 1985), 16, as quoted in a dissertation by Dr. Carl E. Baugh, "Conventional Explanation for Human Antiquities in Question," www.creationevidence.org/HomePage/Degree_Dissertation/disv1fr/diss1/ diss1.htm.
8. Steven M. Weissberg and Joseph Christiano, *The Answer is in Your Bloodtype* (Lake Mary, FL: Personal Nutrition USA, 1999).
9. Ibid., 28–36.
10. Ibid., 37–43.
11. Ibid., 44–47.
12. Ibid., 48–53.

Chapter 2: Bridging the Gap

1. Source obtained from the Internet: Psychology Commencement Address, Marc S. Lewis, Ph.D., 19 May 2000, http://homepage.psy.utexas.edu/homepage/admin/ Grad/lewis.
2. No source available for this story.

Chapter 3: How to Become an Instinctive Eater

1. Joseph Christiano, *Seven Pillars of Health* (Lake Mary, FL: Creation House, 2000), 43–47.

Chapter 5: Diet and Nutrition

1. Weissberg and Christiano, *The Answer is in Your Bloodtype,* 119; further expanded with information from Bio-Foods, Inc., Santa Barbara, California.
2. Weissberg and Christiano, *The Answer is in Your Bloodtype,* 125–127.
3. Ibid., 127.
4. Ibid., 154.
5. Ann Louise Gittleman, M.S., with James Templeton and Candace Versace, *Your Body Knows Best* (New York: Pocket Books, a div. of Simon and Schuster, Inc., 1996), 126–127.
6. Weissberg and Christiano, *The Answer is in Your Bloodtype,* 155.
7. Gittleman, *Your Body Knows Best,* 127.
8. Ibid., 128.
9. Ibid., 127.
10. Ibid., 124.
11. Ibid.
12. Weissberg and Christiano, *The Answer is in Your Bloodtype,* 155.
13. "On Health: Protein and Exercise," *Orlando Sentinel.*

Chapter 11: 28-Day Pick-a-Meal Recipes

1. Molly O'Neill, *New York Cookbook* (n.p., n.d.), 326–327.
2. The Moosewood Collective, *Moosewood Restaurant Low-Fat Favorites* (n.p., 1996), 289.
3. Adapted with slight changes from *Prevention's the Healthy Cook* by the editors of *Prevention Magazine* Health Books (Emmaus, PA: Rodale Press, Inc., 1997), 255.
4. Adapted with slight changes from *The Kripalu Cookbook* by Atma Joanne Levitt (Lee, MA: Berkshire House Publishers, 1995), 30.
5. Adapted with slight changes from *Vegetarian Times Complete Cookbook* by Vegetarian Times, Inc. (New York: Macmillan, 1995), 403.
6. Adapted with slight changes from *The Kripalu Cookbook,* 291.
7. Adapted with slight changes from *The Self-Healing Cookbook,* 7th edition, by Kristina Turner (Vashon Island, WA: Earthtones Press, 1998), 113.

Chapter 13: A Survival Kit for Your Journey

1. Christiano, *Seven Pillars of Health,* 37.

BODY GENETICS PROTEIN SHAKES® are an excellent source of soy protein. Each protein shake is of the highest quality of soy protein. They are compatible to all four blood types: A, B, AB and O. Research has indicated that soy protein contributes to a healthy heart. Each shake is formulated with the proper digestive enzymes for making digestion and assimilation natural and easy. Body Genetics Protein Shakes® are fat free, lactose free, sugar free, aspartame free and come in delicious chocolate and vanilla flavors.

Suggested Use: Drink one or two shakes per day as a snack or meal replacement. Mix ½–1 scoop with water, compatible juice or soy milk. Add to smoothies to boost the fat-burning/anabolic benefit.

BODY GENETICS A.M./P.M.® are nutritional supplements formulated for individual blood types. Each formula contains nutrients, vitamins, minerals and herbs that are blood type specific.

Suggested Use: Take one capsule after breakfast, and one capsule after dinner.

HOME BLOOD TYPE TESTING KIT is a simple fingerprick test that takes approximately eight to ten minutes to determine your blood type. The kit comes with easy-to-follow directions that make blood typing easy to do, convenient and inexpensive. Its usage is intended for one person only.

BODY TYPE WORKOUT VIDEOS—Each 20-minute video is with Joseph Christiano as your personal trainer. All you need are a couple of pairs of dumbbells and a bench or chair. Each body-type video is specifically designed with exercises to redesign your body type. The three body type workout videos from which to choose are The Pear, The Apple and The Banana.

Each body-type workout video comes with a "slim belt" that is designed to be worn during each workout, creating additional perspiration around the waist area.

Included for women is an additional video called *Dress Up, Slim Down.* This video teaches women how to dress according to their body types to look taller and slimmer immediately.

For further information on how to order these and other products, contact us at:

BODY REDESIGNING BY JOSEPH CHRISTIANO®

P. O. Box 951479

Lake Mary, Florida 32795

Phone: 1-800-259-BODY (2639)

Website: www.bodyredesigning.com

E-mail: jac10@aol.com

Bloodtypes Bodytypes and YOU

Section V

Body Type
Workout Programs